THE PAPERS OF ULYSSES S. GRANT

THE PAPERS OF

ULYSSES S. GRANT

Volume 31:

January 1, 1883–July 23, 1885

Edited by John Y. Simon

ASSOCIATE EDITOR

Aaron M. Lisec

TEXTUAL EDITOR

Cheryl R. Ragar

——

SOUTHERN ILLINOIS UNIVERSITY PRESS

CARBONDALE

Library of Congress Cataloging in Publication Data (Revised)

Grant, Ulysses Simpson, Pres. U.S., 1822–1885.
  The papers of Ulysses S. Grant.

  Prepared under the auspices of the Ulysses S. Grant Association.
  Bibliographical footnotes.
  CONTENTS: v. 1. 1837–1861.—v. 2. April–September 1861.—
v. 3. October 1, 1861–January 7, 1862.—v. 4. January 8–March 31,
1862.—v. 5. April 1–August 31, 1862.—v. 6. September 1–December 8,
1862.—v. 7. December 9, 1862–March 31, 1863.—v. 8. April 1–July 6,
1863.—v. 9. July 7–December 31, 1863.—v. 10. January 1–May 31,
1864.—v. 11. June 1–August 15, 1864.—v. 12. August 16–November 15,
1864.—v. 13. November 16, 1864–February 20, 1865.—v. 14. February 21–April 30, 1865.—v. 15. May 1–December 31, 1865.—
v. 16. 1866.—v. 17. January 1–September 30, 1867.—v. 18. October 1,
1867–June 30, 1868.—v. 19. July 1, 1868–October 31, 1869.—v. 20. November 1, 1869–October 31, 1870.—v. 21. November 1, 1870–May 31,
1871.—v. 22. June 1, 1871–January 31, 1872.—v. 23. February 1–
December 31, 1872.—v. 24. 1873.—v. 25. 1874.—v. 26. 1875—v. 27.
January 1–October 31, 1876.—v. 28. November 1, 1876–September 30,
1878.—v. 29. October 1, 1878–September 30, 1880.—v. 30. October 1,
1880–December 31, 1882.—v. 31. January 1, 1883–July 23, 1885.
  1. Grant, Ulysses Simpson, Pres. U.S., 1822–1885. 2. United
States—History—Civil War, 1861–1865—Campaigns and battles—
Sources. 3. United States—Politics and government—1869–1877—
Sources. 4. Presidents—United States—Biography. 5. Generals—
United States—Biography. I. Simon, John Y., ed. II. Ulysses S. Grant
Association.
E660.G756   1967   973.89'2'90924   67-10725
ISBN-13: 978-0-8093-2879-6 (v. 31)
ISBN-10: 0-8093-2879-8 (v. 31)

The paper used in this publication meets the minimum requirements of
American National Standard for Information Sciences—Permanence
of Paper for Printed Library Materials, ANSI Z39.48–1992. ♾

Published with the assistance of a grant from the National Historical
Publications and Records Commission.

Contents

———

Dedication

Professor John Y. Simon
June 25, 1933–July 8, 2008

T‌HIS, THE THIRTY-FIRST volume of *The Papers of Ulysses S. Grant*, represents the final achievement of one man above all, Professor John Y. Simon, until his death the executive director and managing editor of *The Papers*, titles he had held since 1962. That year, the newly established Ulysses S. Grant Association laid before Professor Simon a task that was nothing short of herculean: to collect, edit, and organize tens of thousands of documents by and about Ulysses S. Grant into a unified multivolume collection. He excelled at the task.

Professor Simon tirelessly devoted forty-six of his best years to compiling the thirty-one volumes of *The Papers*, and in so doing he rose to become one of the foremost documentary historians in the world. Richard Gilder and Lewis Lehrman, who endow the prestigious Lincoln Prize, described Professor Simon as the "dean of documentary editors" when he received that prize in 2002.

Not content simply to tread where others had gone before, Professor Simon was a pioneer. He matched incoming correspondence with outgoing correspondence so that researchers would have a complete exchange. He included editorial commentary that is more insightful and more substantial than traditional footnotes—actually a comprehensive biography of the man called Grant. He wrote introductions to each volume that give researchers and enthusiasts a deeper understanding of the documentary process and the context of Grant's papers and writings. It is no exaggeration to say that John Y. Simon set the bar for future documentary projects, and it is a high bar indeed. The distinguished historian James McPherson has called John Y. Simon "the leading Grant Scholar."

But Professor Simon was more than a scholar, more than a beloved teacher, more even than a great man; he was a great friend. I hope and expect that as you look through these pages, or any volume of *The Papers of Ulysses S. Grant*, you will appreciate some of the brilliance and wit of its editor. While a supplemental volume of *The Papers* and an annotated edition of *The Memoirs of Ulysses S. Grant* remain, it is a fitting irony that John Y. Simon died having completed work on the volume covering the end of Grant's life.

He is truly missed.

FRANK J. WILLIAMS
PRESIDENT
ULYSSES S. GRANT ASSOCIATION

Foreword

BY THE NEW MANAGING EDITOR

WHEN JOHN Y. SIMON died in July 2008, the scholarly world lost one of its shining lights. Soon after, the Ulysses S. Grant Association's board of directors asked me to become only its second executive director and managing editor in the forty-six-year history of the organization. During these years, the officers and the board have provided inspiration and steady leadership, without which the *Papers* project could not have succeeded.

John Y. Simon spent all but two years of his documentary career at Southern Illinois University. It was there in the Morris Library that he gathered, analyzed, and published the Grant Papers. The Southern Illinois University Press has published all thirty-one volumes of the Papers in a quality manner, and it is anticipated that it will continue publication of all future volumes.

In December, 2008, the Ulysses S. Grant Association relocated the Grant Papers to the Mitchell Memorial Library, Mississippi State University. Here, a new editorial team will complete the great work achieved by John Y. Simon and his many assistant editors at Southern Illinois University. A supplementary volume will include those papers not available when the first thirty-one volumes were published. The new editors will produce a scholarly edition of the *Memoirs* and a digitized edition of the entire series of published volumes. They will also prepare a cumulative index. Over time, the prodigious collection will be opened to qualified researchers.

The proofreading of volume 31 and the preparation of the index for the volume were conducted by assistant textual editor David Slay under my direction. Jeanne A. Marszalek played an important role in preparing the final copy for publication. Harriet F. Simon, who for so many years was John Y's love and support, provided advice and encouragement for the new editor, which has meant more than she can imagine. In the end, this project will always be John Y. Simon's, and it is only fitting and proper that his widow continue to play her important role in completing it.

JOHN F. MARSZALEK

EXECUTIVE DIRECTOR AND MANAGING EDITOR

THE ULYSSES S. GRANT ASSOCIATION

March 15, 2009

Introduction

═══

In May, 1883, Ulysses S. Grant expressed an optimistic vision of close future ties with Mexico. "I feel that the way is opened for all good work in Mexico on the part of the United States. We want nothing but a commercial and social conquest. The time may come when all this continent will be bound together in such a political sense that if you touch one part you touch all; but for the present we want to attend to our own business, make peace, and go straight ahead." Grant's commitment to improving trade and development and his personal interest in building the Mexican Southern Railroad made him an obvious choice the previous August when President Chester A. Arthur chose United States commissioners to negotiate a commercial treaty. In January, Grant spent weeks in Washington, D.C., renewing old contacts, enjoying capital society, and successfully concluding a treaty with the help of his Mexican counterpart and friend, Matías Romero. The Senate ultimately killed the treaty, thanks to powerful sugar interests, although Grant also faced allegations that he had provided for his own gain through the treaty. In his Mexican Southern charter, negotiated in 1881, Grant had declined to accept a subsidy from Mexico, preferring the independence and greater return of raising the capital himself. This proved more difficult than Grant had anticipated. After an initial flurry of activity, the project languished, and construction never began.

Grant's apparent success in other investments offset his disappointment over the Mexican Southern. He was a full partner in the brokerage firm of Grant & Ward, founded by Ulysses S. Grant, Jr., and Ferdinand Ward, and the Grant family watched earnings grow on paper while leaving actual investment decisions to Ward. By early 1884, Grant & Ward had absorbed all of Grant's assets except for the farm near St. Louis that could not be sold on favorable terms and other scattered property. While paper profits rose, proceeds from a trust fund assembled by friends and admirers provided Grant with sufficient income to live comfortably. Grant began to think and act like a wealthy man. In their fashionable Manhattan brownstone, steps from Central Park and Fifth Avenue, furnished with treasures from their trip around the world, the Grants felt at home for the first time since their White House days. It was difficult to imagine leaving, even when they had booked passage to visit daughter Nellie in England. "But as the time approached I got to thinking what in the world did I want to leave my pleasant home for to live in hotels and in trunks so gave up my rooms and all idea of visiting Europe again, at least for the present."

After his initial enthusiasm for Arthur soured, Grant gradually withdrew from politics and patronage struggles. He retained a keen interest in foreign affairs, especially in the Far East, where he encouraged commerce and diplomacy with China and Japan. Although he succeeded in winning the appointment of his friend and travel biographer, John Russell Young, as minister to China, Grant's efforts to bolster America's role in the region had little effect. His influence in domestic and foreign policies waned, but he retained the adulation of a constituency whose collective power continued to grow. Veterans eagerly sought Grant's presence at their reunions. Grant politely declined most of these invitations for purely logistical reasons, but those he attended invariably proved enjoyable. Ever magnanimous, Grant always acknowledged the contributions of the volunteers, and he expressed "hearty sympathy" with moves toward reconciliation between Union and Confederate soldiers. "The men who faced each other in deadly conflict can well afford to be the best of friends now, and only strive for rivalry in seeing which can be the best citizens of the grandest country on earth." Believing that the results of the Civil War had ensured "perpetual peace at home" and a "national strength" that minimized threats from other countries, Grant steadfastly asserted "that the war was worth all it cost us, fearful as that was."

Grant's standing as the nation's preeminent veteran attracted constant appeals from officers seeking promotion and former soldiers, or their dependents, seeking pension benefits or public positions. Grant extended assistance in many cases at the risk of disappointing rival claimants or showing the limits of his political influence. Further awkwardness arose from the fact that friendly legislators regularly proposed bills to restore him to the army at his former rank of general but were unable to secure passage over determined and vocal opponents. Grant did not help his own cause by his determined and controversial support of Fitz John Porter, who sought reversal of a wartime court-martial. When Arthur vetoed remedial legislation, a disappointed Grant tried to encourage a dispirited Porter. "Be of good cheer and pray that justice may yet be done you and yours."

It was easiest for Grant to be light-hearted when among his children and grandchildren. He felt immense satisfaction as his sons established themselves in business, purchased homes, and raised their families. He wished that Nellie's family did not live overseas and eagerly looked forward to her visits with her children. "The fact is your Ma & I are very proud of our grand children," Grant observed in one of his letters to his daughter. Grant showed his regard for his granddaughters by giving each of the four $2,500 bonds as Christmas gifts in 1883. As that year drew to a close, Grant sketched a pleasant picture for Nellie. "We are all well. Your brothers are all doing well and are happy. As a family we are much better off than ever we were before. The necessity for strict economy does not exist, or is not so pressing, as it has heretofore been."

Everything changed after Grant slipped on ice outside the doorway to his New York City home on Christmas Eve, 1883, and severely injured his upper leg. Grant later informed a friend how matters quickly worsened. "Although I am not aware of ever having had a twinge of rheumatism in my life before, some two weeks after the accident occurred the rheumatism attacked me, first in the well leg, but soon transferred itself to the injured part of the other leg." In excruciating pain, unable to walk without aid or even to dress himself, Grant spent a difficult winter simply trying to regain mobility. On the Virginia coast, where he had gone in search of warmer weather, he finally found some relief through physical therapy. By spring, he remained largely disabled but at least could move about on crutches.

A more devastating blow hit Grant on May 6, 1884, when Grant & Ward collapsed and instantly plunged his entire family into financial ruin. Writing to his sister soon after "the great disaster," Grant adopted a hopeful view. "We are all well, and are trying to be happy. Do not be the slightest uneasy." He soon learned, however, that any hope of recovering assets from Grant & Ward was illusory. Ferdinand Ward had duped his partners and gullible investors through systematic and stupendous frauds. "The events of the last few days are much more disastrous than I supposed when the failure first occurred." Grant's most pressing needs included paying a $150,000 personal loan given him by William H. Vanderbilt, immediately lost in the Grant & Ward collapse, and finding cash to meet household expenses. Grant mortgaged his memorabilia and St. Louis County farm to Vanderbilt to cover the loan and kept his household operating with modest monetary gifts that arrived unsolicited, including one from Charles Wood, a brush manufacturer in Lansingburgh, New York. Despite Grant's protest, Vanderbilt later erased the debt through legal action and restored the memorabilia to Julia Dent Grant, who then donated the collection to the national government.

The financial catastrophe renewed interest in legislation to place Grant back on the army rolls to provide him with a salary. "I need it very much and would feel grateful for it," Grant told a friend. Legislative delays, however, forced Grant to seek other income. For many years he had declined invitations from publishers to write about his military career, and the prospect still dismayed him. "I do not feel equal to the task of collecting all the data necessary to write a book upon the War, or of my travels." Nevertheless, he agreed to prepare four articles for *Century Magazine* to appear in a new series on the Civil War. Each article would pay $1,000, a sum Grant then deemed substantial as he scrambled to raise funds through sales of small stock holdings and his wife's rental properties in Washington, D.C. "Even the small sum of $150 00 is a matter of great importance to me just now when every thing has been swept from me." To his surprise, Grant found that he enjoyed writing, and with the assistance of his son Frederick and Adam Badeau, he completed articles on Shiloh, Vicksburg, Chattanooga, and the Virginia campaign by the end of the summer. In these articles, which he knew would attract criticism, Grant strove for fairness and what he described to a reader of his Shiloh piece as "the exact truth as I saw it." About this time, Grant also decided to write his memoirs, a project that promised to earn considerably more money.

While writing at Long Branch during the summer, Grant suffered increasingly sharp pains in his throat. Busy with his work, Grant postponed a thorough examination until autumn and then learned that he suffered from cancer. The malignancy heightened the urgency of his writing. Grant pushed ahead on his manuscript through the fall and winter as his health deteriorated and legal proceedings related to the Grant & Ward failure harassed him. After reviewing proposals from several firms, Grant signed a contract with Charles L. Webster & Company to publish the *Personal Memoirs of U. S. Grant* for subscription sale. Samuel L. Clemens, who possessed unbounded enthusiasm for the book, headed this company and extended generous financial terms to Grant, who took steps to see that the large anticipated earnings went to his family and not to Grant & Ward creditors.

As winter turned to spring in 1885, it became sadly apparent that Grant's health might not enable him to complete his manuscript. "It is very difficult for me to swallow enough to maintain my strength, and nothing gives me so much pain as swallowing water," he revealed to a friend. Passage of the bill to restore him to the army in early March and an unexpected physical rally in

April revived hope that Grant might live several more months. He continued to produce and revise manuscript with the assistance of his sons, Badeau, and stenographers who took dictation when his throat permitted him to speak more rapidly than he could write. Badeau's assistance ended abruptly in early May after he proposed an agreement for increased compensation that infuriated Grant, as well as his family, by suggesting that Badeau, rather than Grant, had written much of the manuscript. Grant scathingly replied to Badeau's lament of lost literary fame once the memoirs eclipsed his own military history of Grant. "Allow me to say, this is all bosh, and is evidently the work of a distempered mind that has evidently been growing moody by too much reflection upon these matters." Grant firmly, and properly, insisted that he composed his memoirs. The break with Badeau later involved Grant's family in lengthy and acrimonious litigation.

Oppressive heat in New York City that added to Grant's discomfort led to his move to the cottage of a friend, Joseph W. Drexel, at Mount McGregor, New York, not far from Saratoga. A carefully planned train ride took Grant and his family from New York City to Mount McGregor on June 16. Grant modified his memoirs when his strength allowed and oversaw the correction of proof. "There is much more that I could do if I was a well man," he apologized to Clemens. "I do not write quite as clearly as I could if well." To his profound relief, Grant lived long enough to consider his memoirs complete.

Grant kept up his spirits for his family's sake, as he had throughout his painful illness, but he knew that his hold on life was tenuous. "I should prefer going now to enduring my present suffering for a single day without hope of recovery." The many notes that he wrote his doctors after losing his voice document in excruciating detail the final course of the cancer and the stoic bearing of the patient. Throughout the ordeal, his affection for his wife Julia, and her affection for him, never wavered. "Your loving and affectionate husband," concluded a final letter on July 8. A sharp downturn in his condition two weeks later signaled Grant's imminent death, and he died on July 23, surrounded by his wife and children, his minister, and devoted medical attendants.

We are indebted to J. Dane Hartgrove and Howard H. Wehmann for assistance in searching the National Archives; to Harriet F. Simon for proofreading; and to Anastasia Saverino, Molly White, and Abigail Wheetley, graduate students at Southern Illinois University, for research assistance.

Financial support for the period during which this volume was prepared came from Southern Illinois University, the National Endowment for the Humanities, and the National Historical Publications and Records Commission.

JOHN Y. SIMON

August 16, 2006

Editorial Procedure

1. Editorial Insertions

A.   Words or letters in roman type within brackets represent editorial reconstruction of parts of manuscripts torn, mutilated, or illegible.

B.   [. . .] or [— — —] within brackets represent lost material which cannot be reconstructed. The number of dots represents the approximate number of lost letters; dashes represent lost words.

C.   Words in *italic* type within brackets represent material such as dates which were not part of the original manuscript.

D.   Other material crossed out is indicated by ~~cancelled type~~.

E.   Material raised in manuscript, as "4th," has been brought in line, as "4th."

2. Symbols Used to Describe Manuscripts

AD	Autograph Document
ADS	Autograph Document Signed
ADf	Autograph Draft
ADfS	Autograph Draft Signed
AES	Autograph Endorsement Signed
AL	Autograph Letter
ALS	Autograph Letter Signed

ANS	Autograph Note Signed
D	Document
DS	Document Signed
Df	Draft
DfS	Draft Signed
ES	Endorsement Signed
LS	Letter Signed

3. Military Terms and Abbreviations

Act.	Acting
Adjt.	Adjutant
AG	Adjutant General
AGO	Adjutant General's Office
Art.	Artillery
Asst.	Assistant
Bvt.	Brevet
Brig.	Brigadier
Capt.	Captain
Cav.	Cavalry
Col.	Colonel
Co.	Company
C.S.A.	Confederate States of America
Dept.	Department
Div.	Division
Gen.	General
Hd. Qrs.	Headquarters
Inf.	Infantry
Lt.	Lieutenant
Maj.	Major
Q. M.	Quartermaster
Regt.	Regiment or regimental
Sgt.	Sergeant
USMA	United States Military Academy, West Point, N.Y.
Vols.	Volunteers

4. Short Titles and Abbreviations

ABPC	*American Book Prices Current* (New York, 1895–)
Badeau	Adam Badeau, *Grant in Peace. From Appomattox to Mount McGregor* (Hartford, Conn., 1887)
CG	*Congressional Globe.* Numbers following represent the Congress, session, and page.
J. G. Cramer	Jesse Grant Cramer, ed., *Letters of Ulysses S. Grant to his Father and his Youngest Sister, 1857–78* (New York and London, 1912)
DAB	*Dictionary of American Biography* (New York, 1928–36)
Foreign Relations	*Papers Relating to the Foreign Relations of the United States* (Washington, 1869–)
Garland	Hamlin Garland, *Ulysses S. Grant: His Life and Character* (New York, 1898)
Julia Grant	John Y. Simon, ed., *The Personal Memoirs of Julia Dent Grant* (New York, 1975)
HED	*House Executive Documents*
HMD	*House Miscellaneous Documents*
HRC	*House Reports of Committees.* Numbers following *HED, HMD,* or *HRC* represent the number of the Congress, the session, and the document.
Ill. AG Report	J. N. Reece, ed., *Report of the Adjutant General of the State of Illinois* (Springfield, 1900)
Johnson, Papers	LeRoy P. Graf and Ralph W. Haskins, eds., *The Papers of Andrew Johnson* (Knoxville, 1967–2000)
Lewis	Lloyd Lewis, *Captain Sam Grant* (Boston, 1950)
Lincoln, Works	Roy P. Basler, Marion Dolores Pratt, and Lloyd A. Dunlap, eds., *The Collected Works of Abraham Lincoln* (New Brunswick, 1953–55)
Memoirs	*Personal Memoirs of U. S. Grant* (New York, 1885–86)
Nevins, Fish	Allan Nevins, *Hamilton Fish: The Inner History of the Grant Administration* (New York, 1936)

O.R.	*The War of the Rebellion: A Compilation of the Official Records of the Union and Confederate Armies* (Washington, 1880–1901)
O.R. (Navy)	*Official Records of the Union and Confederate Navies in the War of the Rebellion* (Washington, 1894–1927). Roman numerals following *O.R.* or *O.R.* (Navy) represent the series and the volume.
PUSG	John Y. Simon, ed., *The Papers of Ulysses S. Grant* (Carbondale and Edwardsville, 1967–)
Richardson	Albert D. Richardson, *A Personal History of Ulysses S. Grant* (Hartford, Conn., 1868)
SED	*Senate Executive Documents*
SMD	*Senate Miscellaneous Documents*
SRC	*Senate Reports of Committees.* Numbers following *SED, SMD,* or *SRC* represent the number of the Congress, the session, and the document.
USGA Newsletter	*Ulysses S. Grant Association Newsletter*
Young	John Russell Young, *Around the World with General Grant* (New York, 1879)

5. Location Symbols

CLU	University of California at Los Angeles, Los Angeles, Calif.
CoHi	Colorado State Historical Society, Denver, Colo.
CSmH	Henry E. Huntington Library, San Marino, Calif.
CSt	Stanford University, Stanford, Calif.
CtY	Yale University, New Haven, Conn.
CU-B	Bancroft Library, University of California, Berkeley, Calif.
DLC	Library of Congress, Washington, D.C. Numbers following DLC-USG represent the series and volume of military records in the USG papers.

DNA	National Archives, Washington, D.C. Additional numbers identify record groups.
IaHA	Iowa Historical Society, Des Moines, Iowa.
I-ar	Illinois State Archives, Springfield, Ill.
IC	Chicago Public Library, Chicago, Ill.
ICarbS	Southern Illinois University, Carbondale, Ill.
ICHi	Chicago Historical Society, Chicago, Ill.
ICN	Newberry Library, Chicago, Ill.
ICU	University of Chicago, Chicago, Ill.
IHi	Illinois State Historical Library, Springfield, Ill.
In	Indiana State Library, Indianapolis, Ind.
InFtwL	Lincoln National Life Foundation, Fort Wayne, Ind.
InHi	Indiana Historical Society, Indianapolis, Ind.
InNd	University of Notre Dame, Notre Dame, Ind.
InU	Indiana University, Bloomington, Ind.
KHi	Kansas State Historical Society, Topeka, Kan.
MdAN	United States Naval Academy Museum, Annapolis, Md.
MeB	Bowdoin College, Brunswick, Me.
MH	Harvard University, Cambridge, Mass.
MHi	Massachusetts Historical Society, Boston, Mass.
MiD	Detroit Public Library, Detroit, Mich.
MiU-C	William L. Clements Library, University of Michigan, Ann Arbor, Mich.
MoSHi	Missouri Historical Society, St. Louis, Mo.
NHi	New-York Historical Society, New York, N.Y.
NIC	Cornell University, Ithaca, N.Y.
NjP	Princeton University, Princeton, N.J.
NjR	Rutgers University, New Brunswick, N.J.
NN	New York Public Library, New York, N.Y.
NNP	Pierpont Morgan Library, New York, N.Y.
NRU	University of Rochester, Rochester, N.Y.
OClWHi	Western Reserve Historical Society, Cleveland, Ohio.
OFH	Rutherford B. Hayes Library, Fremont, Ohio.

OHi	Ohio Historical Society, Columbus, Ohio.
OrHi	Oregon Historical Society, Portland, Ore.
PCarlA	U.S. Army Heritage Center, Carlisle Barracks, Pa.
PHi	Historical Society of Pennsylvania, Philadelphia, Pa.
PPRF	Rosenbach Foundation, Philadelphia, Pa.
RPB	Brown University, Providence, R.I.
TxHR	Rice University, Houston, Tex.
USG 3	Maj. Gen. Ulysses S. Grant 3rd, Clinton, N.Y.
USMA	United States Military Academy Library, West Point, N.Y.
ViHi	Virginia Historical Society, Richmond, Va.
ViU	University of Virginia, Charlottesville, Va.
WHi	State Historical Society of Wisconsin, Madison, Wis.
Wy-Ar	Wyoming State Archives and Historical Department, Cheyenne, Wyo.
WyU	University of Wyoming, Laramie, Wyo.

Chronology

January 1, 1883–July 23, 1885

━━━

1883, JAN. 2–24. In Washington, D.C., USG negotiated the Mexican treaty, concluded on Jan. 20.

FEB. 13. USG testified about the Mexican treaty before a Senate committee.

FEB. 16. USG served as pallbearer at Edwin D. Morgan's funeral.

APRIL 3. USG was elected president of the National Rifle Association.

APRIL 4. USG hosted a dinner for Porfirio Díaz at the Union League Club.

MAY 1. USG attended a baseball game at the Polo Grounds, where New York defeated Boston 7–5.

MAY 11. Hannah Simpson Grant died at Elizabeth, N.J.

MAY 14. USG buried his mother beside his father in Cincinnati.

MAY 24–JUNE 2. USG and Julia Grant visited Chicago, Galena, and St. Louis.

JUNE 3. At Louisville, USG said: "I have washed my hands of politics."

JUNE 4–6. Illness to Julia Grant between Louisville and New York City forced a stop at Washington, D.C.

JUNE 9–12. USG visited West Point.

JUNE 21. At Jersey City, USG presented diplomas to graduates of Hasbrouck Institute, including his niece, Clara V. Cramer.

AUG. 1–3. The Grants journeyed to the Catskill Mountains.

AUG. 4. USG attended a clam bake at Monmouth, N.J.

AUG. 17. From Deer Park, Md., USG and Edward F. Beale visited the Elk Garden mines in West Va.

AUG. 18. USG returned to Long Branch.

AUG. 30–SEPT. 21. USG accompanied an excursion to celebrate the completion of the Northern Pacific Railroad in Montana Territory. Stops included Chicago, Minneapolis, and Portland, Ore.

SEPT. 28. Chaffee Grant, son of Ulysses, Jr., was born.

SEPT. 29–OCT. 1. USG and Julia Grant visited Frederick Dent Grant at Morristown, N.J.

NOV. 15–18. En route to Buffalo and Rochester, N.Y., USG toured the Pa. oil region and inspected the Kinzua railroad viaduct near Bradford, Pa.

NOV. 26. USG participated in ceremonies marking the centennial of the British evacuation of New York City.

NOV. 27. USG and Julia Grant attended the wedding of Mae E. Drexel in Philadelphia.

DEC. 24. When USG slipped on ice in front of his home he injured his left leg.

1884, JAN. 18. The Senate rejected the Mexican treaty.

JAN. 21. USG reported himself "still a great sufferer, confined to my room."

MAR. 6. USG and Julia Grant left for Old Point Comfort, Va., where USG received physical therapy.

MAR. 8. Fort Monroe fired a salute on USG's arrival.

MAR. 17–APRIL 11. At Washington, D.C., USG met Arthur and attended several veterans' gatherings.

APRIL 12. The Grants returned to New York City.

MAY 4. Hoping to prevent the failure of Grant & Ward, USG borrowed $150,000 from William H. Vanderbilt.

MAY 6. Grant & Ward and the associated Marine National Bank both failed.

MAY 7. USG told Vanderbilt that he would liquidate his and Julia Grant's assets to pay back the $150,000. Ward admitted to Grant, Jr., "that he had been a wicked thief and a great rascal." Senator George F. Edmunds of Vt. introduced a bill to retire USG as gen. on full pay.

MAY 8. Grant & Ward's assets were assigned to creditors.

MAY 9. Grant, Jr., told a reporter: "The Grant family has lost its entire fortune; the ruin is complete."

MAY 21. Ward was arrested.

MAY 26. James D. Fish, Marine Bank president, was arrested.

MAY 30. USG observed Memorial Day in Brooklyn.

JUNE 6.   In Chicago, Republicans nominated James G. Blaine and John A. Logan to head the fall ticket.

JUNE 11.   USG addressed an Army of the Potomac reunion in Brooklyn.

JUNE 23.   From Long Branch, USG thanked Matías Romero for financial assistance.

JUNE 30.   USG submitted an article on Shiloh to the *Century Magazine* and received $500. By Sept. 10, USG had written similar articles on Vicksburg, Chattanooga, and the Wilderness campaign.

JULY 2.   Arthur vetoed a bill to reinstate Fitz John Porter.

JULY 19.   USG declined to attend the Army of the Tennessee reunion, writing that he was still on crutches.

AUG. 2.   At Ocean Grove, N.J., USG addressed a reunion of Christian and Sanitary Commission workers and army chaplains.

AUG. 8.   Busy with the *Century* articles, USG wrote that he had decided to compile his *Memoirs*.

SEPT. 5.   USG's will was witnessed at Long Branch.

SEPT. 17.   The Grants returned to New York City.

SEPT. 19.   USG met Blaine.

OCT. 9.   USG testified about trade and consular reform to a visiting commission.

NOV. 4.   Grover Cleveland defeated Blaine.

NOV. 18.   USG wrote of having "a sore throat" for four months.

DEC. 4.   U.S. Senator John I. Mitchell of Pa. introduced a bill to grant USG a pension. On Dec. 5, USG wrote to Mitchell that he would not accept it. On Dec. 8, Mitchell withdrew the bill.

DEC. 16.   USG wrote: "It is nearly impossible for me to swallow enough to sustain life, and what I do swallow is attended with great pain."

1885, JAN. 3.   USG asked Vanderbilt to "have the property upon which you hold a mortgage sold for what it will bring, and have the amount credited to what I owe you."

JAN. 10.   Vanderbilt arranged to present USG's mementoes to the U.S. government.

JAN. 12.   Phineas T. Barnum offered USG $100,000 to display the mementoes.

JAN. 13.   Schuyler Colfax died in Minn.

JAN. 14.   The Senate passed a bill to retire USG on full pay as gen.

FEB. 19.   Doctors diagnosed USG with throat cancer.

FEB. 27.   USG contracted with Charles L. Webster & Co., controlled by Clemens, to publish his *Memoirs.*

MAR. 3–4.   The House of Representatives passed the retirement bill. Arthur then nominated and the Senate confirmed USG as gen., retired.

MAR. 26.   USG was deposed in Fish's trial.

MAR. 29.   USG nearly died in a choking fit.

APRIL 3.   USG wrote to a future president asking the appointment of his grandson, Ulysses S. Grant 3rd, as military academy cadet. On March 30, 1898, President William McKinley approved the request.

APRIL 6.   USG told his doctors: "My chances, I think, of pulling through this are one in a hundred."

APRIL 7.   USG had another near fatal episode.

APRIL 12.   Fish was convicted of bank fraud and sentenced to ten years in prison. On Oct. 29, Ward was convicted of grand larceny and sentenced to ten years at hard labor.

APRIL 15.   Julia Dent Grant, daughter of Ulysses, Jr., was born.

APRIL 27.   USG thanked all who had sent birthday greetings.

MAY 2.   USG publicly denied claims that Adam Badeau was the true author of his *Memoirs.* Privately, USG dismissed Badeau from further work on the project.

MAY 16.   In Central Park, USG greeted children from a nearby school.

MAY 23.   USG dedicated his *Memoirs* "to the American soldier and sailor."

MAY 29.   USG planned the disposition of *Memoirs* proceeds.

MAY 30.   From his window, USG reviewed a Memorial Day parade.

JUNE 16.   USG and family moved to Mount McGregor, N.Y., to escape New York City heat.

JUNE 18.   USG and his family were photographed at Mount McGregor.

JUNE 26.   USG made a brief excursion in a bath chair.

JUNE 29.   In a farewell letter to Julia Grant, USG asked her to choose his gravesite.

JUNE 29–JULY 1.   Clemens visited USG.

JULY 2.   USG expressed gratitude that he had been given time to write his *Memoirs.*

JULY 8.   A delegation of Mexican journalists visited USG.

JULY 10.   Simon B. Buckner visited USG.

JULY 16.   USG wrote of his *Memoirs*: "There is nothing more I should do to it now."

JULY 20.   USG wrote his doctor: "What do you think of my taking the bath wagon and going down to overlook the south view?"

JULY 23, 8:00 A.M.   USG died at Mount McGregor.

The Papers of Ulysses S. Grant
January 1, 1883–July 23, 1885

Interview

———

[*Washington, D. C., Jan. 5, 1883*]

I regard Gambetta as the foremost man of his time in France. I found him to be a very different sort of man from the Gambetta of whom I had read in the papers. I had made up my mind that he was one whose basis of belief was "whatever is is wrong," without having any plan to replace the wrong. But I found that he always knew exactly what he wanted, and as an editor worked toward his ideal, knowing that he could not get all he wanted. His strength with the people lay in the fact that they had the utmost confidence in him, and had never any reason to doubt him. When I was in Paris, and there formed the acquaintance of Gambetta, McMahon was president of the republic. McMahon was never a republican, and he honestly believed that the people of France preferred a monarchy. There are in France people who can raise a great cry without being strong in numbers. They remind me, when I recall that clamor, of the wolves I used to hear when riding across northern Texas. From the howling and howling and howling that they would set up I would think that there were more wolves than could be put in Lafayette square, but when I rode to where the noise came from there was never more than one or two wolves, and they would be sitting on their haunches and giving their whole attention to howling. Unfortunately for McMahon, he believed the clamor against a republican form of government came from the greater part of the people, and he made the change of officers all over France, turning out the prefects and postmasters, in the belief that he was giving the people what they wanted sooner than they could get it by waiting for an expression at the polls. The power to order an election was in his hands as president, and so the people were chafing under the removal of the men who really represented them. At this juncture, when a popular protest was imminent, Gambetta showed his leadership. He told the people to be quiet and patient—to wait—and when it came time to go to the polls to go there and express themselves. You will remember that they had everywhere overwhelming majorities. In this, I say, Gambetta showed his greatness, and to him more than to any one else in France—to him alone, I will say—is due the preservation of the republican idea, strong in the hearts of Frenchmen, but menaced by McMahon's misunderstanding of their temper.[1]

The republican idea has grown into everything in France. The French are naturally republicans, and never will be anything else. Gambetta knew this, and led them to the kind of government they wanted. He lived to see it firmly established, and his death will not shake it. Had he died five years ago there might have been trouble and there certainly would have been danger.

There are always many who might be leaders, but when the time of greatest danger comes those who are capable to lead are averse to swapping horses at that time, as Lincoln said. The danger is over in France and there are many capable men there who thought and worked with Gambetta. Yes, there are always men enough who may be leaders. The difference in them is that one who has had experience before the time of greatest danger comes is generally best fitted to lead, and the ablest of his contemporaries are content to have him, as has always been the case in this country.

[*Gambetta*] was a very inactive man in every way excepting mentally. He understood the English language perfectly, whether he read it or heard it spoken. I often found him reading the English papers; but when it came to talking he would always use the French language, and an interpreter was necessary to my understanding of it. What I said to him he understood as readily as you can understand me now. He needed no interpreter. I always thought he might have spoken in English had he wanted to, but perhaps it would have troubled him to pronounce. He had a wonderfully quick understanding.

Washington National Republican, Jan. 6, 1883. French statesman Léon Gambetta died Dec. 31, 1882.

In late May, 1883, in Chicago, USG met Joseph Cook, a Boston minister and prominent lecturer. Cook reminded USG "that you said the four greatest men you met while abroad were Gambetta, Bismarck, Gladstone, and Li Hung Chang, of China." USG replied. "Yes, I said that, and I still adhere to it . . . . I think Bismarck is the greatest man in Europe and Gambetta was the greatest man in France at the time I was there. I had formed quite a different opinion of him. I supposed he was one of those men who wanted a change without knowing why; that kind which leave their country for their country's good, and come here and undertake to overturn things without knowing what they want. But, in my judgment, there was no man in France who saw so clearly just what was needed in the crisis which followed the Franco-Prussian war as did Gambetta. It is true, he assumed the position almost of a dictator. He took the reins in his own hands. He overthrew all the city government, put down all other authority, and removed all the police officers, and after he had prepared everything, he then ordered the election to be quiet and orderly. The people were told (and they knew the army was back of him) that they could go to the polls and vote for whomsoever they chose. Now, all this looked like royalty and a monarchy, but it wasn't. That was a dangerous period in the history of France, and Gambetta knew it. The people, when they had a chance, voted and elected Republicans almost every time, and so France was saved as a Republic. Gambetta was a level-headed, far-sighted man. . . . I call that true greatness, a man who knows the hour and understands the situation. I think you will find that France can never be anything else now but a republic. Whatever changes take place the republic will come up every time. Mr. Gladstone is the greatest living Englishman to-day, I think. I became greatly attached to him during my visit abroad. The people of Japan are a wonderful people. I cannot begin to tell you how much they interested me." Cook said: "General Grant, one of the best things you ever did, in my judgment, was when you refused to receive the card of Dennis Kearney." "Yes, I am glad I did it, and from about that time that whole movement collapsed." *Chicago Inter-Ocean* (reprinted from *Chicago Advance*), June 2, 1883. In a second meeting with Cook, USG spoke at length about Mexico. "In my judgment Congress has made a great mistake in not consummating a treaty with that country which shall insure us the commercial advantages which are properly ours. It ought not to be true that the wealth of Mexico should be poured into the lap of of Europe instead of the United States, where it properly belongs. I was in the Mexican war, though I believed at the time it was a most unrighteous thing. I tried to do my duty as a soldier, and you all know what the result was. A few years ago, when I met General Diaz in Mexico, we talked it all over . . . . I told him squarely that we did not want Mexico; that we wouldn't have it as a gift; . . . I then told him that nations were very much like individuals: if one did a thing that was looked upon by others as wrong, they were apt to quarrel, and a quarrel meant a fight, and in a fight he must know that the stronger nation would conquer; but if anything of that kind should occur we might be perfectly willing to take as an indemnity what we would not have as a gift . . . . And now I feel that the way is opened for all good work in Mexico on the part of the United States. We want nothing but a commercial and social conquest. The time may come when all this continent will be bound together in such a political sense that if you touch one part you touch all; but for the present we want to attend to our own business, make peace, and go straight ahead." *Ibid.* In Oct., 1879, John Russell Young had written that USG "regarded Bismarck, Gambetta and Beaconsfield as the three greatest men he had met in Europe." *Philadelphia Times*, Oct. 20, 1879. See *PUSG*, 29, 231. For Denis Kearney, see *ibid.*, p. 280.

1. See *ibid.*, 28, 311.

To Vannoy H. Manning

———

Washington D. C.
Jan.y 8th 1883

Hon. V. H. Manning M. C.
Dear Sir:

This will present Mr. Theo. Smith, a relative of a former Commissioner of Indian Affairs, now deceased.[1]

Mr. Smith wishes to call your attention to a bill which is now in the House—having passed the Senate—which he is interested in as a relative of the deceased commissioner.

May I ask an interview for Mr Smith?

Very respectfully
U. S. Grant

ALS (facsimile), North Shore Manuscript Co., Inc., Aug. 2000. Former col., 3rd Ark. (C.S.A.), Vannoy H. Manning practiced law in Holly Springs, Miss., before entering Congress in 1877.

1. A Yale graduate and former minister, Edward P. Smith (1827–1876) was an agent of the U.S. Christian Commission and American Missionary Association before serving in the Bureau of Indian Affairs under USG. On Feb. 15, 1883, Manning, Judiciary Committee chairman, shepherded passage of a bill to settle Smith's accounts as Chippewa agent. See *CR*, 47-2, 2749–50; *PUSG*, 9, 637–38; *ibid.*, 13, 536; *ibid.*, 23, 316; *ibid.*, 25, 347; *ibid.*, 26, 365–66.

To James Tanner

———

[*Washington, D. C., Jan. 8, 1883*]

To-morrow at 10 I have a meeting with treaty commissioners. How long we will set I do not know. Will see you probably about 1 p m. If not in at that hour then more certainly about 5 p m.—I spoke to the President in your behalf.—Your note was very plain; but the signature I could not make out.

yours
U. S. Grant

ANS, Tom Wheeler, Columbus, Ohio. Written on a letter of Jan. 8, 1883, from James Tanner, Washington, D. C., to USG. "I am afraid from my messengers story that my wild penmanship left you in doubt as to who was addressing you. Whenever you can figure out a few moments for me I shall be pleased to wait on you" ALS (on Ebbitt House stationery), *ibid.* Known as "Corporal" for his wartime rank in the 87th N. Y., Tanner was active in Brooklyn politics and in the Grand Army of the Republic. On Jan. 11, 1883, a correspondent reported from Washington, D. C. "I hear it stated that Grant is supporting Collector Tanner for the surveyorship of the port. If this is the case, the support of the General cannot have carried much weight, for it seems to be decided that the place is to go to Lydecker, of New York." *Brooklyn Eagle,* Jan. 11, 1883. On March 1, President Chester A. Arthur nominated James L. Benedict as surveyor of customs, New York City.

On April 19, 1869, Tanner, Washington, D. C., had written to USG. "I enclose herewith the endorsements of my application for Associate Justice of one of the Territories—After *four weeks* consideration and once nominating me to you I am sorry to learn the Atty Gen'l has finally concluded that I am to inexperienced in the law to fill the position—I understand from the Atty Gen'l that you have expressed a disposition to accord me some position under the Gov't. With this understanding I have the honor to renew my application, made to you personally the other day for the position of Consul at Leith, Scotland, Basle, Switzerland or some other equally desirable location. The one at Leith has been held by the present app incumbent for many years & the salary is the fees which I understand am't to about $2300—For Basle a person by the name of Henry Erni has lately been nominated but I am informed he was dismissed from his present position of Clerk in the Patent Office soon after the close of the war for disloyal utterances and was reinstated by order of Andrew Johnson—I presume his name will be withdrawn. The salary at Basle is $2000—I hope one of these positions may be accorded me—I make my application direct to you because the time is so short—If you consider that I had both of my legs shot off while opposing Gen Longstreet at the 2nd Bull Run you will readily see that it will be under peculiarly aggravating circumstances that I shall return to my family if beaten—With the hope and belief that the President desires and intends to do justice to those who helped him save the country I submit the foregoing—" ALS, DNA, RG 59, Letters of Application and Recommendation. Related papers are *ibid.* On March 18, 1870, Orville E. Babcock wrote to Moses H. Grinnell, collector of customs, New York City. "The bearer of this is known by the President. He is a lawyer who lost both legs during the war. The President will be pleased to have you see him and to have you give him such a place as his education and ability may fit him for and as he, in his crippled condition, can fill." Copy, DLC-USG, II, 1. Appointed chief clerk, Tanner rose to deputy collector. See *New York Times,* Feb. 11, 1894, Oct. 3, 1927.

To Gen. William T. Sherman

Washington, D. C.
Jan.y 22d 1883

DEAR GENERAL:

Mrs. Grant & I would be very glad to accept the kind invitation of Mrs. Sherman and yourself to dine with you on the 28th instant if it was possible for us to remain here until that time. I have however been longer in the city than I expected, and my work being finished all but the presentation to the Sec. of State—that will be done to-morrow—I must go back to New York on Wednesday.[1] Then too the Chinese Minister invited me last week to a similar entertainment to that given by the Japanese, for saturday the 27th which I declined because I could not remain in the city so long.

Very Truly your Friend

U. S. GRANT

ALS, DLC-William T. Sherman. Written on letterhead of Willard's Hotel.

In Washington, D. C., for more than three weeks to negotiate the Mexican reciprocity treaty, USG attended receptions and dinners given in his honor by Edward F. Beale (Jan. 2, 1883), Secretary of State Frederick Frelinghuysen (Jan. 9), President Chester A. Arthur (Jan. 10), and Japanese minister Terashima Munenori (Jan. 19), as well as the wedding of Virginia R. Cameron, daughter of U.S. Senator James D. Cameron of Pa., to Lt. Alexander Rodgers (Jan. 11).

On Jan. 12, during a visit to the Post Office Dept., USG responded to a comment about visiting Washington, D. C. "Yes, I always like to come here. It gives me an opportunity, you know, to make suggestions in regard to filling the places in all the departments. I could fill them all you know." *Washington Evening Star,* Jan. 12, 1883.

1. USG returned to New York City on Wednesday, Jan. 24.

Interview

———

[*Washington, D. C., Jan. 22, 1883*]

Railway communications with Mexico, already projected under concessions by her, will, within the next fifteen months, place the City of Mexico within all rail communication with the railroad systems of the United States by their different routes.[1] In exchange for all these advantages, the United States would, if the treaty is ratified, admit free of duty twenty-eight articles of Mexican production. Of these twenty are already on the free list under the existing tariff law, six are articles not produced in the United States, and the other two are crude sugar and leaf tobacco.[2] As to the leaf tobacco, it would not come in competition with the tobacco of which our conestogas, which sell for a cent apiece, are made, but would rather introduce a new industry in the manufacturing, both for consumption and exportation, of fine segars, such as we now depend on Havana for.

It was at City Point during the war that I first met Senor Romero.[3] He was then the minister from the Mexican republic, under President Juarez. I made known to him the strong interest I felt in Mexico, and that I regarded her invasion by the French as very much like a declaration of war against the United States. I had a conviction that but for our own condition no such thing would have happened, and felt that the situation was to be permitted by our government only so long as we were engaged in suppressing a rebellion against our own authority. These views I communicated to President Lincoln, who never said anything which led me to doubt that he was of my opinion. Immediately upon the surrender of Lee I sent a corps of the army to the Rio Grande, with a view to the security of the transmississippi region. I put it under the command of Gen. Sheridan, a very good man for a command of that sort. He spread the troops all up and down the Rio Grande, and the French retired from the border. The French minister at Washington called upon Mr. Lincoln, and besought him, saying, "Don't kick us out; we will go as soon as we can." It was not long after this that the French evacuated, and the Mexican adherents of the empire were soon subdued, and the republic restored.[4]

It had been my desire for years to visit Mexico, where I had been as a young second lieutenant during the Mexican war. Upon my return from Europe in 1879 I went, and was received as the guest of the nation. I found that my attitude toward that country during the war was well understood, and I was welcomed in the heartiest manner by all with whom I came in contact. A commodious residence was placed at my disposal, and everything was done for my comfort. President Diaz was most cordial, and with him I held many conferences. I found that jealousy of this country and suspicions as to its purposes toward Mexico were prevalent. I frankly told him that I could not wonder at that, for our country had dealt harshly with his in years past, and that, although I had been in the military service at that time, I had always felt that the war was unjust. I said to him that there then existed in this country an institution which could not sustain itself unless it could maintain political supremacy. To enable it to dominate the government it must have new states, and these it could only hope for at the south; that at a cost of many lives and much money we had disposed of that institution, and that now there was no motive for desiring any extension of territory; that we had already indeed more territory than we could well manage. I found many seekers there for government concessions for railway building, but their petitions were not regarded with favor. President Diaz I found to be an enlightened and progressive man. He said his country could not afford to remain behind the age, and must encourage railway building. He said, however, that a large and influential class was opposed to allowing railway commu[n]ication with the United States. They favored a system which should radiate from the city of Mexico to points in the interior, distant twenty leagues from the United States' border. That is to say, they were to lead no-where, but were to be merely local, supplying the interior from the seaboard, drawing therefore from Europe, from whence the capital was to be derived for the construction of the roads. This policy was urged on the ground that if the states on the border were in com-munication by rail with the outside world, there would be nothing to draw them to the center, and they would gradually slough off and become annexed to the United States.

I told him that if there was any danger to the integrity of Mex-ico this scheme would be the very way to increase it. I assured him, however, that not five of our citizens in a hundred had any sympathy with the expressions sometimes indulged in by thought-less and irresponsible people in favor of the acquisition of Mexican territory. I told him that for Mexico to refuse intercourse with a neighbor, and to deal with European countries instead, would have an appeara[n]ce of hostility which would be much more likely to lead to trouble than would free railroad communication with us. I reminded him that experience had always shown that when two men begin to quarrel it usually ends in a fight where one was much the more powerful, and that in this respect nations were like men.

Washington National Republican, Jan. 23, 1883. Interviewed "in his parlor at Willard's," USG "said the work upon which he had engaged with Senor Romero, of arranging for submission to the government a reciprocity treaty with Mexico, was fully completed and had been submitted to the State department. He explained its provisions at considerable length. It proposes free entry into Mexico of articles under seventy-three different heads, some of these embracing many different articles. He laid special stress on the articles of machinery, agricultural implements, railway materials, and vehicles, the manufacture of which in this country for use in Mexico would give employment to thousands of people, and open up to enterprising Americans these mines of untold wealth and plantations of vast extent . . . . The General expects to remain until the State department shall have considered the terms of the proposed treaty, which may be several days." *Ibid.*

On Jan. 11, 1883, a correspondent reported from Washington, D. C. "Gen. Grant and Minister Romero were at the Capitol today to explain to the foreign relations committee the provisions of the draft of the commercial treaty between the United States and Mexico. There was not a majority of the committee present, and there was, therefore, an informal talk. Gen. Grant explained the provisions of the treaty and stated what articles were to be admitted free by Mexico and what articles were to be admitted free by the United States. Mr. R[o]mero, it is understood, stated the occasion of his trip to Mexico last December with a draft of the treaty, his action there, and the result of his trip. Mr. Romero then took his departure, and Gen. Grant remained with the members of the committee, and explained that he desired an expression of the committee with regard to the terms of the treaty, for two reasons: First, because if the treaty were satisfactory to the committee, it would probably be satisfactory to Congress, and if any immaterial modifications were thought advisable, modifications could be made before the commissioners appointed to negotiate the treaty assembled, so that there would be nothing for them to do but sign the instrument. The second reason that Grant gave was that he had not formally accepted the position of commissioner; he had acted in conjunction with Mr. Romero in framing the instrument which was in possession of the State Department. He had done this before the Mexican commissioners were appointed because, in his opinion and in the opinion of Mr. Romero, a draft of the proposed treaty was necessary to show the Mexican authorities, in order to prove to them that the treaty would not be injurious to their interests. Without this proof Mexico would not have appointed commissioners, and the treaty scheme would have been a failure. Gen. Grant said he had exercised his best judgment in the matter, and if the treaty was not likely to prove satisfactory, he wanted to know it. In that event, he probably would not accept the position of commissioner; some other person had better be appointed in his place. The members of the committee said they could give no intimation how they would regard the treaty until they had considered it in full committee. As the treaty affects the revenue, it will require the action of both houses. The sugar interests which are asking for the abrogation of the Hawaiian treaty, will oppose this Mexican treaty." *New Orleans Times-Democrat*, Jan. 12, 1883.

On Jan. 20, USG, William H. Trescot, Matías Romero, and Estanislao Cañedo concluded a commercial treaty between the U.S. and Mexico. Copy, USG 3. *SED*, 47-2-75, 48-2-47, 714–20; *HRC*, 49-1-2615, 11–14. On the same day, a reporter called USG's attention "to the statements in a New York paper to the effect that his object in negotiating the Mexican commercial treaty was to so reduce the revenues of the Mexican government as to make it impossible for that government to pay the subsidies pledged to the railways now being constructed in that country, and thereby place them on an equality with the Gould unsubsidized projected line. The General says the statements are entirely incorrect; that he never spoke to Mr. Gould upon the subject, and that his belief is that should the treaty be carried into operation the effect would be rather to increase than to diminish the Mexican revenues by the increased trade it would develop. The Gould road is one of the subsidized lines, and would be as much affected by the reduction of the Mexican revenues as any other of the subsidized lines. Gen. Grant says he has acted in this matter in the interest and as the representative of the American people, and he expects that the results of the treaty will be highly advantageous to the commercial interests of both countries. There is no probability that it will interfere with the sugar-producing interests of the United States, as Mexico does not produce enough sugar for her own consumption and will not for years to come be able to raise a surplus for exportation. He is fully satisfied that if ratified the treaty will give our country a decided advantage over Germany, France, and England in the competition for the Mexican trade." *Washington National Republican*, Jan. 22, 1883.

On Jan. 23, William J. Palmer, Mexican National Railway Co., New York City, wrote to USG. "I have watched with great interest your efforts to bring about an advantageous reciprocity treaty between the United States and Mexico.—This is a most important movement affecting the welfare of both countries, and as I have observed published statements that the influence of our enterprize—the Mexican National Railway—was enlisted against such treaty, I beg to assure you that I appreciate most fully its value to American interests and especially to the railways that Americans are constructing in that Republic.—In case it happens that the influence or efforts of my associates or myself can be made of service in furthering the adoption of the proposed treaty, I will be glad to have any suggestions from you to that end.—in order that we may help to the Extent it may be possible" LS, USG 3. On the same day, Palmer wrote to Romero on the same subject. LS, DLC-Matías Romero.

On [Jan. 23], Tuesday, William Henry Hurlbert, *New York World*, wrote to Romero. "Thanks for your note just received. I am sorry to say that Mr Trescott's denial is not Equivalent to evidence in the matter of his reletions with Mr Blaine. In looking over the letter of my Washington Correspondent I see that it is not written in a friendly spirit to Mr Trescott—but I am sorry to say that Mr Trescotts connexion with the Mexican Treaty is more likely to hurt than to help it both in & out of Congress. I know no person of character in Either party who has any confidence in him, and as I think I told you some time ago it was an act by no means friendly to General Grant to handicap him in such a negotiation with such an associate. You are quite at liberty to shew this letter if you should think fit to Mr Canedo, General Grant and Mr Trescott himself. The attacks on the Hawaiian treaty need to be met I think as the true attack on the Mexican Treaty. Both are outposts in the real battle coming on now." ALS, *ibid.*

On Jan. 25, Thursday, a reporter visited USG in New York City to ask "whether it was true as reported, that the Mexican reciprocity treaty had been signed on Tuesday, or if, as is stated in contradiction of the former report, negotiations have not yet been completed. The general was feeling unwell and could not be seen. In answer to a written inquiry he replied that all he could say in reference to the matter was that it is entirely under the control of the state department. He declined giving any further information on the subject." *Washington National Republican*, Jan. 26, 1883. See *PUSG*, 30, 465–66; Speech, [Feb. 8, 1883].

1. The reporter here interjected. "In view of these greatly-increased facilities of communication, the trade between the two nations will naturally be greatly accelerated." *Washington National Republican*, Jan. *23*, 1883.

2. The reporter here summarized. "He expressed the opinion that the Mexicans would raise very little sugar for exportation during the six years the treaty would run, and that their desire to have it included was rather in the hope of encouraging and stimulating its production for benefits to come later." *Ibid.*

3. See *PUSG*, 12, 461.

4. The impossible sequence of events in this passage presumably reflects reporter error.

To Adam Badeau

New York City,
Feb.y 4th 1883.

DEAR BADEAU:

I have had three or four letters from you since my last. The last one was through the state Department. I had heard before that the English had sent their Vice Consul to Cuba to Mexico, ostensibly to reniew intercourse with that government, but more particularly to cooperate with the Germans and French to defeat a Commercial treaty with the United States. I sent your letter, with one from myself, to the Sec. of state.—You should by all means write to the Sec. of state saying to him substantially what you say to me in your letter of the 3d of January. Of course I can not send that letter. We were successful in negociating a Commercial treaty, which is practically ratified so far as the Mexican Govt. is concerned. We will see what our senate will do with it, if the President sends it in. It was delivered to the Sec. of state two weeks ago, with report; but so far it has not seen the light.

yours Truly
U. S. GRANT

ALS, Munson-Williams-Proctor Institute, Utica, N. Y. On Feb. 5, 1883, President Chester A. Arthur sent the Mexican reciprocity treaty to the Senate. See Speech, [*Feb. 8, 1883*].

To Edward F. Beale

———

Feb.y 6th 1883.

MY DEAR GENERAL BEALE:

Mrs. Grant is very sorry Mrs. Beale could not be here to-day—
her last reception—and hopes yet you and she can come this week.
As I have just telegraphed you Buck will probably be here by the
18th inst.[1] and we expect him and his wife to stay with us until
they get rested before going to Michigan for their little girl. They
sail on Saturday of this week. Pack your valises—like Mrs. Grant
takes to your house—and come on.

Very Truly yours
U. S. GRANT

ALS, DLC-Decatur House Papers. On Feb. 5 (Monday), 6, and 7, [*1883*], USG telegraphed to Edward F. Beale, Washington, D. C. "WHAT DAY THIS WEEK MAY
WE LOOK FOR YOU AND MRS. BEALE." "Tuesday will do but wish you would
come this week we want a long visit from you Bude [*Buck*] will arrive about the Eighteenth & will spend some time with us" "WILL MEET YOU AT STATION MON-
DAY MRS. GR[*AN*]T HAS INVITED COMPANY TO MEET YOU AT DINNER
WEDNESDAY." Telegrams received (at 2:50, 4:00, and 6:30 P.M.), *ibid.*

On Feb. 4, USG had written to Hamilton and Julia K. Fish accepting a dinner invitation. *The Collector,* No. 2, 1958. On Feb. 10, USG wrote to Julia Fish to cancel these
plans, explaining that he had "received a letter from the Secretary of State requesting
my presence in Washington the first of the coming week in connection with the commercial treaty between the United States and Mexico." *The Flying Quill,* April, 1977,
no. 32. USG testified before a Senate committee on Feb. 13 and was back in New York
City on Feb. 16 to serve as pallbearer for Edwin D. Morgan, who died Feb. 14.

1. Ulysses S. Grant, Jr., and Fannie C. Grant arrived aboard the *Servia* from Liv-
erpool on Feb. 21.

Speech

———

[*Feb. 8, 1883*]

Every reader of history is aware of the republican patriotism of
Mexico. The inhabitants live in a country where great effort is
not necessary to secure a livelihood. Clothing is not a necessity.
The country is mountainous. To construct ordinary wagon roads

requires concerted action. The people have not the incentives to work which we have. We have to make hay while the sun shines, which makes it possible for us to develop industries on the Pacific coast. Mexico has not the incentives we have. But as we developed resources reached by wagons we had to develop resources which brought railways, even with those already developed. It has now become necessary for Mexico to make a similar development. Mexico believes that her neighboring republics ought to be first, fast, and the best of friends. We are on the high road to establish relations between our sister republic, Mexico, and the United States. We have railways in northern Mexico. Within twenty-five months—fifteen months at the least—it will be possible to go to Mexico from any point in the United States. The thermometer there reaches 85° at any time of the year, and there exists a perpetual spring. The new treaty proposed will go far to cement union between the two republics. It will open a market for many manufactures which Mexico does not produce, and which we do, and it will be a most advantageous thing for both countries.

Washington National Republican, Feb. 9, 1883. USG spoke at a dinner honoring Salvador Malo, a Mexican financier, attended by Matías Romero, Estanislao Cañedo, James H. Work, and others. See Interview, [*Jan. 22, 1883*].

On Feb. 3, 1883, Saturday, Work, New York City, wrote twice to Romero. "I have your letter of yesterday and in reply will say that it will be in ample time if you are in New York and can give me the opinions which I asked you to let me have, when you are here. I have been waited on lately by some of the people of this City who are interested in land operations in Mexico, and who are about to give a dinner to Senor Malo— (Salvador Malo I think his name is) of Mexico City, who is now here. The dinner is to be given next Wednesday or Thursday, and they have been in to see me to ask if they might send invitations to you and to Gen Cañedo—whose name I suggested to them. They have asked Gen Grant to be present, and he has expressed his willingness to accept, and has told me personally that he desired to meet Senor Malo, who was, he says, very kind to him when in Mexico, and showed him attention when there, and he has or will call upon Sr. Malo or leave his card for him at his hotel. I thought I would advise you of this without waiting for the formal invitation, (although I suppose that will be going to you within a day or so) and to ask you in case you thought well of the dinner, to be sure to be present on the occasion." "Parties here have been asking us for some statistics showing the financial condition of Mexico, and the changes that have occurred in it within the last five years; the amount of imports, and duties collected, and exports, and the kind and value and the relative increase of trade in both directions, and of the revenues during this period of time. Can you without too much trouble direct us to the source from which this information can be obtained?" LS, DLC-Matías Romero. On Feb. 5, Work wrote to Romero transmitting invitations. LS, *ibid.*

On Feb. 11, USG granted a lengthy interview concerning the Mexican reciprocity treaty. "I see by despatches from Washington City that while the commercial treaty with Mexico is likely to be reported favorably by the committee having it in charge, it may meet with opposition in the Senate from the fact that it seems to leave it possible to ship sugar from Havana to Mexico and reship it to this country as if it were the product of Mexican soil. It may be possible that such shipments will be made from time to time, but at great risk to the persons who engage in that business, precisely in the same way as goods are now smuggled in from Cuba and from Europe. Sooner or later, however, they are detected and the parties engaged in the business are punished by forfeiture and fine, and it is not probable that this business will be carried on successfully to any great extent, any more than smuggling is now. In other words, it is a question which concerns not the treaty-making power, but the administration of the Treasury . . . . The development of our railroads running into Mexico and the development in Mexico consequent upon the building of those roads and the increase of general business and industry in Mexico must inevitably make Mexico a large commercial country, increasing in importance from year to year in a very rapid ratio; and if we fail now to use this first opportunity that we have had of cultivating closer relations it is not only possible but it is very probable that it will be many years before we can expect another opportunity of negotiating such a treaty. With this ratified by both governments, it may be assumed that it will be possible to make another treaty subsequently which shall remedy any defects which may be found in the working of this. Another very good reason for its ratification is the fact that it has been and is now violently opposed by all the European merchants and agents residing in Mexico. The foreign merchants there are an influential class, because they import pretty nearly all of the goods that are imported into the country, and consequently pay into the Mexican treasury a large percentage of all the present revenues of that country. Their influence is increased by the fact that the small retailers are generally natives of the country, who purchase their goods from these importers on long credits, paying for them out of the sales of the goods. Consequently, as you see, these foreign merchants have great influence, both with the governing officials and with the enterprising Mexican dealers. They are upon the spot to work against this treaty, while we have no corresponding class of American citizens at present in that country to represent our side of the question. The President of the republic, however, and his Cabinet, have had the independence and, as I think, the good sense to accept this treaty as it is now presented to our Senate, and they accepted this, though they had begun by being very strongly prejudiced against making any commercial treaty with the United States. I know an objection has been or may be raised to this treaty from the fact that there is nothing in it which prohibits Mexico from making similar treaties with other countries. It would have been hardly fair for us to have asked Mexico to have restricted her own powers without our restricting ourselves in the same way, and it is not probable any treaty could have been ratified by the Senate of the United States which contained a clause prohibiting the United States from making a treaty like this or any other treaty with other countries whenever it should seem proper and advantageous to do so. But it is not likely that Mexico will consider a similar treaty with any European country, because there is no European country that can give Mexico the market for her surplus products that we can, and they are furthermore remote from Mexico and not neighbors as we are. This treaty if it goes into effect will naturally bring the peoples of two adjoining republics closer together. But it gives material advantages in another [way] to both of us. We receive from Mexico all [the products which she is capable of producing—]unmanufactured articles—that is, twenty-eight in number. Of these articles twenty are at present on our free list and six are articles which enter to a greater or less extent into our manufactures and which we do not produce. There are but two articles produced by us which are admitted free from Mexico under the treaty. One is crude sugar and the other is leaf tobacco. Taking the latter into consideration first, I conceive that the treaty would be very advantageous to us and certainly very advantageous to Mexico, because under it we are only to receive tobacco free from duty in its unmanufactured state, and the tobacco which they raise does not correspond at all to the article raised by us, but is similar and equal in quality to the tobacco raised in Cuba. It is to be presumed that when Mexico raises enough of this tobacco to supply the market the manufacture of our own Havana cigars will take place in our own country, and tobacco of Mexico being free from an export duty in Mexico, we shall be largely able to compete with Havana in the outside markets of the world in the two articles of manufactured tobacco and cigars. In regard to her sugar, Mexico at the present time does not raise perhaps a quarter of what her own consumption is or will be with railroads to distribute it . . . . The advantages to us consist in the large number of our manufactured articles which Mexico will receive free, not only from port duties but from internal taxation while in transit to the place of consumption—articles which Mexicans very much require in the development of their country and on which the present duties are so high that they produce little or no revenue to the Mexican government. The duties are prohibitory. The articles to be so admitted are under seventy-three heads. Under some of these heads you might enumerate a great many, I might say hundreds, of special articles. I will give you a few of them. Under one head they admit machinery of all sorts, classes and descriptions, for mining, agricultural and other purposes; under another heading they admit agricultural implements; under another, wagons, coaches and all sorts of vehicles that are pulled by animals; and under the head of tools for mechanical, scientific and all other purposes, they admit tools that are composed of brass, iron, steel or wood, or any combination of these materials. Under another head they admit free all classes of rolling stock, from the passenger car to the steam-engine, that are used upon railroads. Then there are many other articles which are admitted under heads which do not admit of such minute specification as to the articles themselves, but among them are petroleum, crude and refined; barbed wire for fencing, with all its fixtures; houses of wood or iron, built ready to put up in that country; pumps for mines, irrigating and all other purposes for which pumps can be used; clocks and many other articles extensively manufactured in this country are put under the seventy-three heads. It is believed that these articles being received free from all duty will find a very large market in Mexico, and Mexico will find a corresponding benefit in the rapid development of her resources and to some extent by finding a market in our country for her products, protected as it is by a tariff upon similar articles that are brought here from other countries than Mexico . . . . I was very anxious to have embodied in this treaty a clause which would require all goods transported by water between the two countries to be transported in ships built in the United States or in Mexico, and owned in one or the other of the two countries and run under the laws of the country to which the ships belong, to have the benefit of the free trade established by this treaty. But it was a matter which did not suggest itself to my mind until the treaty had been submitted to the Mexican President and Cabinet; and when it did occur to me I communicated my desire in this matter to the Minister for that country, who communicated it at once to his own Government. There has been no reply as yet to the request to have that inserted in the treaty as an article, but I have sincere hopes that if this treaty is ratified a supplementary treaty embracing that provision, which would be so advantageous to both countries, might be made . . . . While the benefits of this treaty will be felt in all parts of our country there is probably no part of it which will feel it so much as just that portion which does produce the little sugar that we make. New Orleans and Galveston, and probably Mobile, will become large shipping points between the two countries in the exchange of their commodities." *New York World* and *Washington National Republican*, Feb. 12, 1883.

Also on Feb. 11, Sunday, a correspondent reported from Washington, D. C. "After the Mexican reciprocity treaty had been signed and sent to the Senate the American Commissioners desired to amend it by adding a number of articles to the free list, and proposed to the Mexican Commissioners to have the treaty recalled and the articles inserted. The Mexican Commissioners did not have the necessary authority to make the desired change without communicating with their Government. The treaty was therefore withdrawn from the Senate and held under advisement until Señor Romero and Gen. Canedo had obtained further instructions. It was then amended in the manner proposed by the American Commissioners and returned to the Senate. It is now in the hands of the Senate Committee on Foreign Relations, and that committee has invited Gen. Grant and Mr. Trescot, the American Commissioners who negotiated the treaty, to appear before them on Tuesday next, when its provisions will be considered and discussed." New York Times, Feb. 12, 1883. USG drafted an amendment to the treaty. "Amend by requiring all free goods entering either country to be transported either by the rail roads connecting them or on vessels built, ~~owned and manned by and sailed by by with Men~~ in one of the treaty making parties & owned ~~and~~ manned and sailed under the flag of one of them." ADf (undated), George Washington University, Washington, D. C. On Feb. 15, Matías Romero, Washington, D. C., wrote to USG. "I could not ~~returned~~ to Washington, until yesterday morning, and I therefore lost the opportunity of meeting you here; but I have heard both from Mr. Frelinghuysen and from Mr. Trescot, that your meeting with the Senate Committee was a very pleasant one and that they all were very favorably impressed with your views and the treaty. Mr Frelinghuysen expects a unanimous report. Until yesterday I could [not] communicate to President Gonzales, the contents of your letter to me of Dec. 6th 1882 so far as the debt question is concerned. You sent that letter to me to Mexico, and I received it here a few days ago. As soon as I have an answer from President Gonzales, I will communicate to you. I have just received an oficial letter from the State Department of Mexico in answer to mine transmitting your addition to the treaty to the effect that articles free of duties should only be transported by railroads or ships built in either country. Mr Mariscal tells me that after studying this question at the State and Treasury Departments, your addition is noft found acceptable. I suppose by modifying it somewhat it might be acceptable. To-morrow's Herald will publish a good article from here about the commercial treaty" ALS, USG 3. On Feb. 19, USG wrote to Romero concerning Mexico's debt. Typed copy (in Spanish), DLC-Matías Romero. See letter to Editor, *Washington Evening Star*, Jan. 22, 1884; David M. Pletcher, *Rails, Mines, and Progress: Seven American Promoters in Mexico, 1867–1911* (Ithaca, N. Y., 1958), pp. 171–77.

On Feb. 27, Secretary of War Robert T. Lincoln wrote to USG. "Will ex-President Diaz land from ship at New Orleans? If so, a salute from field pieces can be given at Jackson Barracks. Nothing else in order in that neighborhood. The two ports below the city have no garrisons. Would be glad to know name of vessel and probable date of arrival." Copy, DNA, RG 107, Letters Sent, Military Affairs. On March 4, Porfirio Díaz, New Orleans, wrote to USG. "I received by the hands of Mr. Mensac [*Masač*], your letter of the 26th of last month, in which you congratulate me with my arrival in this city—I am very grateful for this attention and for the many other kindnesses, which you and M' Gould show me and I send you the expressions of my warm gratitude,—asking you to communicate them in my name to Mr Gould, till I can do this personally and take him by the hand." LS (in Spanish) and translation, James S. Copley Library, La Jolla, Calif.

On April 4, USG hosted a dinner for Díaz at the Union League Club. "About 11 o'clock Gen. Grant arose and proposed the health of Gen. Diaz. He said that it was unnecessary to introduce the distinguished Mexican, or to tell what he had been, what he was, or what he would be. Gen. Diaz had figured very largely in the history of the Mexican Republic. He made himself the head of the army, and fought for the preservation of the republic. He subsequently, in the natural course of events, became the executive head of the new republic, and the progress that has been developed so rapidly there during the past three years was started by him. That development Gen. Grant believed was destined to make of Mexico a sister republic of which the United States might feel proud. Mexico possesses natural advantages and resources equaled by few countries, and with the development that intelligence and capital can give there is no telling what the future of that country may be. Gen. Grant said that the people of this country were watching with deep interest the progress of events made across the Mexican borders, and it seemed that the interests of the two republics were bound to become common interests. He hoped that the relations between the two peoples might always be close and friendly." Díaz, translated by Salvador Malo, responded "that he was glad that the great American soldier appreciated the condition and advantages of Mexico sufficiently to engage in business enterprises there. He thought there should be free and friendly commercial intercourse between the two countries." *New York Times*, April 5, 1883. An invitation to this event is in DLC-William T. Sherman. On March 13, Lt. Gen. Philip H. Sheridan, Chicago, had written to USG. "It was too late last night to reply to your telegram. I regret exceedingly I cannot attend the dinner to President Diaz. I leave for Texas and New Mexico on Fifteenth, and will be gone three weeks." Copy, DLC-Philip H. Sheridan.

On April 5, USG wrote to Frederick O. Prince, Nathan Appleton, and John W. Wolcott, Boston. "Your letter of the 3rd inst. kindly inviting me to visit Boston at the same time with Gen Diaz & party, and to be the guest of the Foreign Exhibition Assn, is received, and in reply I regret that I will not be able to accept your kind invitation. I have been so continuously on the go recently that I feel that I must have some rest, and I also have other invitations which I have partially accepted that will come within the time Gen Diaz & party will be in Boston." LS, Boston University, Boston, Mass.

On April 13, USG attended another dinner to Díaz, given by James B. Houston, Pacific Mail Steamship Co., at Delmonico's. "Gen. Grant said he felt very much embarrassed by what had been said as to the part he had played in making the different parts of this country one Nation. He was very happy that they were one Nation, which he considered the greatest Nation on earth, and he was very happy to have all sections contribute to that greatness. One other desire he had was to see all the other republics of this continent join us in the order of their contiguity, with their capital and their good will, in developing the resources and strengthening the influence of America. Mexico, standing next to us in position, naturally deserves the first consideration. When he first went there, something more than three years ago, he detected some suspicions of the motives of the United States toward that country, and he took pains to assure the people that no ideas of annexation were entertained by or were likely to find favor with us unless agreeable to the Mexicans also. In conclusion, he spoke of the awakening in Mexico of progressive ideas and predicted a bright future for that country." *New York Times*, April 14, 1883.

To Fitz John Porter

———

New York City
Feb.y 21st 1883,

DEAR GENERAL:

I have your letter of this am. I beg you to give yourself no concern about the bill for my retirement. I care nothing about it, in fact should be governed in my acceptance or declination of its benefits,—if it were to pass and receive the signature of the President—by the discussion in Congress and comments by the public. Of course I should esteem it a great compliment if Congress, with great unanimity, should pass the bill before the house and it should be received with favor by the public. Otherwise I would not accept. But even if I was anxious for the passage of the bill retiring me I would not have it at the expense of one so deeply wronged as I now know you have been

Yours Truly
U. S. GRANT

GN. F. J. PORTER

ALS, Porter Collection, USMA. See *PUSG*, 30, 463–64.

To George W. Childs

———

New York City
Feb.y 23d 1883,

MY DEAR MR. CHILDS:

If you have not rented my Long Branch house you need not do so. Mrs. Grant & I have come to the conclusion that we will not go to Europe this summer. If the house is not rented therefore we will occupy it ourselves and keep you company.

With kind regards to Mrs. Childs,

Very Truly yours
U. S. GRANT

ALS, Arizona State University, Tempe, Ariz.

To Gen. William T. Sherman

New York City
Feb.y 23d 1883.

DEAR GENERAL:

I take pleasure in presenting to you and Mrs. Sherman Mr. McNamee and wife. Mr. McNamee is a lawyer of the firm of Davis, Work & Co.¹ and his wife is the daughter of Capt. Vanderbilt.² The visit Washington for a little holiday and express a desire to make your acquaintance, and will no doubt esteem it a favor to be presented to some of the officials of the Capitol.

Very Truly yours
U. S. GRANT

GN. W. T. SHERMAN

ALS, DLC-William T. Sherman. On Feb. 27, 1883, James H. Work, New York City, wrote to Matías Romero, Washington, D. C. "I write this note to introduce to you, or rather to bring again to your recollection my partner Mr James McNamee, whom you have I think met on several occasions in our office in New York. He is visiting Washington, for a little rest and recreation, with his wife, who is, by the way a daughter of Capt. Jacob Vanderbilt, a brother of the late Commodore Vanderbilt. Mr McNamee simply desired to call upon you when he was in Washington and to have you recollect who he was. It is quite unnecessary for me to say that if there is anything you can do for him in any way we will all appreciate it." LS, DLC-Matías Romero.

1. Davies, Work & McNamee served as counsel for Grant & Ward. See *New York Times*, June 18, 1884, July 1, 1885.
2. Born in 1807 on Staten Island, N. Y., Jacob H. Vanderbilt captained steamboats on the Hudson River and served as president of the Staten Island East Shore Railroad. His daughter Clara married James McNamee in 1869. See *ibid.*, March 20, 1893, Jan. 30, 1896, July 10, 1903.

To Adam Badeau

New York City
Feb.y 28th 1883.

MY DEAR GENERAL BADEAU;

I was much pleased to receive your letter of the 22d inst. I was tempted to give what you say about the use of Mexican tobacco;¹

its use in Cuba; the feelings of Cubans in regard to the effect of the treaty &c. to the press. Of course I should only have given it as from a friend of mine writing from Havana. But on reflection I concluded that the public would know who my friend in Cuba was so concluded not to. I wish however you would write the same thing to the state Debt. You will learn by the mail that carries this that consideration of the treaty has been deferred until December next. This I fear will defeat the treaty in Mexico where there will be untiring efforts by foreign merchants and Diplomats to prejudice the government against it.

You will see—or have seen—that J. W. Foster has been appointed to Spain.[2] Foster did not want the place but has accepted it temporarily, as I understand, to transact a special and important mission which will probably occupy but a few months. In some way that I am not quite well enough informed to write about a question has arisen in regard to what constitutes a naturalization of a Spanish subject, to make him a citizen of the United States. The present Sec. is not willing that Spain should interpret our laws on the subject.—Confidentially I do not doubt but that Arthur would be very glad to have you around Foster. But he seems more afraid of his enemies and through this fear, more influenced by them than guided either by his judgement, personal feelings or friendly influences. I hope he will prove me wrong in this judgement.

I saw Gould a few weeks ago about your apt. as superintendent of American telegraph interest in Cuba, and he seemed interested. He asked me to write the President of the Co. on the subject and he would speak to him personally & did so.[3]

Mrs. Grant tells me to say that she is just reading your history and thinks more of you than ever. She is now in the second volume.

Yours Truly
U. S. GRANT

ALS, Munson-Williams-Proctor Institute, Utica, N. Y.

1. See Speech, [*Feb. 8, 1883*]; *New York Times*, Feb. 19, 1883.
2. See *ibid.*, Feb. 26, 1883.
3. See *PUSG*, 30, 459–60.

To Ellen Grant Sartoris

———

New York City
March 22d 1883.

Dear Daughter:

I found this morning that none of the family had written to you for several weeks so I write myself.

The only piece of news I have to give you will not be pleasant. I had secured rooms on the City of Berlin, for the 10th of May. But as the time approached I got to thinking what in the world did I want to leave my pleasant home for to live in hotels and in trunks so gave up my rooms and all idea of visiting Europe again, at least for the present. Buck & Fanny had a fearful passage over and have made up their minds never to cross the ocean again. They will probably keep this resolution for a year or two. All the family are very well and talk often about you. I would like to see you, Algie and the children here very much.

All send love to you Algie and the children.

Yours Affectionately
U. S. Grant

ALS, ICHi.

To Ira N. Burritt

———

New York, Apl 5 *1883*

J. N. Burrett Esq
Secy— &c. Ebbitt House
Washington D. C.
Dear Sir,

Your favor of March 31st inviting me to be present at the Annual Reunion of the Society of the Army of the Potomac, on March 16 & 17th[1] is received and in reply, I accept with pleasure the kind invitation to be present on that occasion, if I should be

here, or where it would be possible for me to attend. But I have to
ask to be excused from being allotted to respond to any toast whatever because of the uncertainty of my attending the Reunion.

Truly Yours,

U. S. GRANT

LS (facsimile), Liberty Historic Manuscripts, Inc., Nov. 21, 1995, no. 146. Former
capt., 56th Pa., Ira N. Bullitt edited the *Sunday Herald,* an army and navy weekly in
Washington, D. C.

1. The Society of the Army of the Potomac held its reunion May 16–17, 1883, in
Washington, D. C. USG did not attend, but was nominated to serve as the society's
next president. Col. John Newton, USMA 1842, defeated USG 155-117 in the ensuing
election. See *New York Times,* May 17, 1883; *PUSG,* 30, 392; Speech, [*June 11, 1884*].

To King Chulalongkorn

New York City,
April 10th, 1883.

HIS MAJESTY,
SOMDETCH PHRA PARAMINDR MAHA CHULALONKORN,
KING OF SIAM.
MY GOOD FRIEND:—

It is long since I have written to you, although I often think of
you and your kind hospitality to me and mine during our visit to
your country and Capital. I also hear from Siam through Colonel
Sickels, who, since his official residence in your country, takes the
deepest interest in all that concerns Siam. He is a great admirer of
Your Majesty and always speaks of you when we meet. Should you
ever want to be represented in this country by an American citizen,
or any foreigner, I am sure you could find no one who would have
your interests and the interests of your country more at heart than
General Sickels.

A year or two ago we were led to believe that the United States
was to be honored by a visit from you. I hope the visit is only postponed, not abandoned. You would receive a most hearty welcome
here from both Government and the People. I and my family retain the liveliest recollection of our visit to Siam and of your kind

hospitality and would enjoy much a second visit. But at my time of life, I can hardly expect ever again to take so long a journey.

With assurances of my sincere friendship and well wishes for Your Majesty and the people over whom you rule, I am,

Your Obedient Servant,
U. S. GRANT.

Typed copy, DNA, RG 59, Applications and Recommendations, Hayes-Arthur. On April 12, 1883, Thomas W. Knox, New York City, wrote to King Chulalongkorn recommending David B. Sickels to represent Siam as consul gen., New York City. Typed copy, *ibid.* Related papers are *ibid.* For Sickels, see *PUSG*, 25, 322; *New York Times*, July 20, 1918. For Chulalongkorn's rumored visit, see *ibid.*, March 30, 1880.

To Charles H. Gray

New York City
Apl. 13th 1883—

DEAR SIR:

I have your letter of yesterday requesting a letter from me to the President endorsing Col. Conger[1] for the position of Inspector Government in the N. Pacific Rail-road—If I was giving such letters—I would gladly do so for Col. Conger—and sincerely hope he ~~will~~ may receive the appointment. But I have written so many letters to the President on the subject of appointments—and am requested to do so, so often, daily, that a short time since I resolved not to do so again—

Trusting that this will be satisfactory to Col. Conger and with the additional statement that he is at liberty to say to Gen. Logan. Sen. Cameron and any other of my friends he may meet that his appointment would gratify me, and would have my support—if I was in a position where I could aid him—I am

Very Truly Yours
U. S. GRANT

Copy, OFH. Charles H. Gray was a journalist active in Ohio Republican politics. See Gray to William McKinley, June 26, 1901, DLC-William McKinley.

1. Akron manufacturer Arthur L. Conger, former 1st lt., 115th Ohio, chaired the Republican state central committee. On June 8, 1883, President Chester A. Arthur appointed Conger director, Union Pacific Railroad.

To Ellen Grant Sartoris

New York City,
Apl. 18th 1883.

DEAR DAUGHTER:

On the 19th of May Senator Cameron sails for Europe with all his family. This is their first visit abroad so they will feel quite like strangers. I hope you and Algie will call on them as soon as they arrive; and if Algie will shew the Senator around I know he will appreciate it highly. You know Cameron is now a member of the United States Senate in his second term. He was Secretary of War with me. His father was elected to the Senate either three or four times—four I think—represented this Government at St. Petersburg, and filled a Cabinet position under Mr Lincoln. He has been one of the most prominent men in the politics—is yet—of Pensylvania for more than fifty years.

If Algie could shew the Senator around, and introduce him to some prominent gentlemen, and you could do the same for Mrs. Cameron I know they would appreciate it highly. If Algie knows Mr Hopping,[1] our Secretary of Legation, I wish he would tell him, for me, that the Senator and family are going and that I would appreciate any courtisy he might shew them.—We are all well and your Ma is anxiously awaiting a letter from you, which she hopes still may announce that you, Algie & the children will yet come over.

Love and kisses to all the children,

Affectionately
U. S. GRANT

ALS, ICHi. On May 4, 1883, USG wrote to the Duke of Argyll, introducing "the Hon J. D. Cameron, who was Sec. of War while I was President and who is now a United States Senator. The Senator with his family expect to make an extended sojourn in Europe ... His father represented his state—Pennsylvania—some four times in the Senate, ... " Charles Hamilton Auction No. 43, July 23, 1970, no. 184. See *New York Times*, Sept. 5, 1883, Feb. 19, May 21, 1884.

1. For William J. Hoppin, see *PUSG*, 29, 101.

To Marye Dabney

———

New York, Apl 23 *1883*

M. DABNEY ESQ
EDWARDS, MISS.
DEAR SIR:

Your letter of the 29th Jany was no doubt duly received, but has been overlooked, and just come to light. I have, however, no recollection of the circumstances related in the letter. I do not remember even any of the servants that were about the house of Mrs Lum while I was there.

Truly Yours

U. S. GRANT

LS, Gallery of History, Las Vegas, Nev. Born in 1846, former private, 3rd Miss., Marye Dabney practiced law in Edwards. Ann Lum died in 1870. See *PUSG*, 15, 612–13; *SD*, 58-2-63.

To Frank A. Flower

———

New York, Apl 23 *1883*

MR FRANK A. FLOWER
"EVENING WISCONSIN"
MILWAUKEE WIS.
DEAR SIR:

Your letter of the 14th of December was no doubt received in due time, but at this late date I find it open, among an accumulation of unanswered letters, and have to ask your pardon for not replying to it earlier. If not too late I will now say that I remember the visit of the late Sen. Carpenter to Long Branch at the time the New York Tribune—(if my memory serves me correctly) made such a terrible charge against him.[1] The Senator called at my house, either on business or socially—I do not remember which. I know nothing, however, of the lady who accompanied him to the Branch.

The Senator entered West Point after I graduated so that I know nothing about his West Point career except that I have always understood that his standing in his class was very high and that after two years, when in the second class and on vacation, he concluded not to return to the Military Academy, but to go into the study of the law, and therefore sent in his resignation as a cadet. His standing must have been good because at the time of his resignation he had been made a sergeant of his Company, showing that his military record was good.

I cannot answer what Senator Carpenters particular duties were as a member of the West Point Board of Visitors in 1871. The duties of Boards of Visitors, however, are to witness the Examinations, the mode of instruction, the drill and discipline of the cadets, and to report to the government their impressions of the institution, and suggest any changes if they think any should be made.

Truly Yours
U. S. GRANT

LS, WHi. Born in 1854 in N. Y., Frank A. Flower settled in Wis., where he entered journalism and served as labor commissioner. On Sept. 25, 1883, USG wrote to [Flower] concerning an 1869 cabinet decision. "... I had, at that time, contemplated making Mr. Carpenter my attorney-general; but finally abstained from doing so because the opinion prevailed—in which I concurred—that it would not be well to take him from the United States senate." Frank A. Flower, *Life of Matthew Hale Carpenter* (Madison, 1883), p. 566.

1. See *PUSG*, 24, 230–31.

To Collis P. Huntington

New York City,
Apl. 23d 1883.

C. P. HUNTINGTON ESQ.

DEAR SIR:

On my return from Long Branch this am I find your invitation to dine at Union League Club on Saturday, Apl. 21st. I regret that I was not here to accept your invitation, or to acknowledge it.

Saturday last I was not down town at all, and the day before but for a few minuets, having an engagement to accompany Gen. Diaz on a visit to the Normal College[1] on 68th st. hence did not see your invitation until this moment.

Very Truly yours
U. S. Grant

ALS, CSmH. USG was mistakenly listed among guests at Collis P. Huntington's dinner for Porfirio Díaz. *New York Times*, April 22, 1883.

    1. See *ibid.*, April 21, 1883.

To Henry Villard

New York City
Apl. 24th 1883.

H. Villard,
President N. P. R. R.
Dear Sir:

I give this letter to present Maj. A. V. Richards, formerly of Galena, Ill. but now of Freeport, same state. Major Richards is a man of about Forty years of age, of good constitution, good habits and of character and capacity. He has had a large experience i[n] the survey of public lands in the West and I think his record in the Interior Dept. Washington, will shew his work as satisfactory as that of any surveyor. For the last six or seven years he has been engaged in editing and conducting a paper, a duty which he has proven well qualified for. He has now sold his paper and is desirous of getting into the service of the N P R. R. I can endorse him as man well worthy of your consideration and one who would prove highly serviceable in any position the duties of which he would accept. I leave Major Richards to make application for the particular line of service where he thinks he could render the greatest service.

Very Truly yours
U. S. Grant

ALS, WHi. A German immigrant, Henry Villard covered the Lincoln-Douglas debates and the Civil War as a reporter, and in the 1870s turned to railroad finance and promotion, taking control of the Northern Pacific in 1881.

On April 7, 1883, USG wrote to Alonzo V. Richards, Freeport, Ill. "Your letter of Mch. 14th has been received, and in reply, I do not feel inclined to ask anything from the Administration—I have not been very successful in what I have asked for, and it is discouraging trying for them." LS, *ibid.* See *PUSG*, 30, 277–78; letter to Alonzo V. Richards, Sept. 30, 1884.

To Cavender & Rowse

New York City,
Apl. 27th 1883.

Messrs Cavender & Rowse,
Dear Sirs:

I have your letter inclosing the proposition of E. D. Taylor[1] to lease my St. Louis Co farm. I could not hear to such a proposition for a moment. From the account of Mr Taylor I would be very glad to have him for a tenant. But I would not be willing to have the fencing timber cut. I would not be willing to fix a price now at which the tenant should have the option to purchase the whole or any part of the land within five or ten years. I would sell now, if I could get it for the 646 acres, at $100 00 pr acre, a reasonable cash payment with real estate notes that I might convert into cash without much discount. I would let Mr. Taylor occupy the place if he will make the necessary repairs to the house, barns & fences, and pay the taxes up to March /85, and for ~~three~~ four years after that time, if the place should not be sold, on about the terms he proposes. I expect to be in St. Louis however within three weeks of now when I can confer with you more particularly.

yours

U. S. Grant

ALS, ICarbS. See *PUSG*, 30, 266–67; letter to Cavender & Rowse, May 21, 1884.

1. Edward D. Taylor, deputy collector of Internal Revenue, St. Louis, lived in nearby Carondelet.

To Adam Badeau

———

New York City
Apl. 30th 1883.

DEAR BADEAU:

I beg your pardon for not answering your letter requesting my views about the capabilities of the defences of the harbor of Havana to resist any Navy. I supposed I had answered it, but your last letter reminds me that I have not. On my visit to Havana three years ago I had the opportunity of seeing the forts and armament.[1] Both are formidable, and with additions that could easily be made before any country could attack them, impregnible from direct attack. But I should not regard Havana as a difficult place to capture with a combined Army & Navy. It would have to be done however by effecting a landing elsewhere and cutting off land communication with Army while the Navy would perform the same service on the water. The hostility of the native population to the Spanish Authority would make this a comparitively easy task for any first class power, and especially easy for the United States in case of a war with Spain. I have no special news to write you. Buck & Jesse have returned from abroad all well.

Yours Truly
U. S. GRANT

ALS, British Museum. Facsimile printed in *Leslie's Weekly*, March 31, 1898, from the original then owned by James Grant Wilson.

1. See *PUSG*, 29, 359.

Concerning Thomas Nast

———

New York City,
May 2d 1883.

This will present my friend, Thos Nast, Artist, to my friends and his countrymen in Europe ~~which~~ where he visits this Summer.

To Americans it is not necessary to say who Mr Nast is his work in this city for so many years past being familiar to all of them. To others I can say that Mr. Nast is a genial gentleman, and is professionally distinguished, and will appreciate, as I will also any attention he may receive.

U. S. GRANT

ADS, ICarbS.

To Michael J. Cramer

———

NEW YORK CITY, May 4, 1883.

MY DEAR MR. CRAMER: This letter will present the Hon. Charles H. A. and family, friends of mine and neighbors in this city. Mr. A. goes abroad to see the Old World, and will probably remain there for a year or more. No doubt his summer travel will carry him into Switzerland, where I hope you may meet him.

Mr. A. has been a personal as well as political friend of mine, and I hope you will be able to make his and his family's visit to the Swiss capital pleasant.

Very truly yours,
U. S. GRANT.

M. J. Cramer, *Ulysses S. Grant: Conversations and Unpublished Letters* (New York, 1897), pp. 171–72.

On May 4, 1883, USG wrote to John Russell Young, U.S. minister, Peking. "I take pleasure in introducing to you Hon Charles Aldrich, an American gentleman, and a citizen of Iowa, who visits Europe, and makes a trip around the world for pleasure, and is Entitled to the friendly consideration of our representatives abroad." LS, MH. On the same day, USG wrote to William Waldorf Astor, U.S. minister, Rome, introducing Charles Aldrich. LS, IaHA. See *New York Times*, Feb. 17, 1882, Dec. 18, 1885; Ruthven Deane, "In Memoriam: Charles Aldrich," *The Auk: A Quarterly Journal of Ornithology*, XXVII, 2 (April, 1910), 119–24.

To Frederick T. Frelinghuysen

New York City,
May 5th 1883.

HON. F. T. FRELINGHUYSEN
SEC. OF STATE:
DEAR SIR:

Col. Chas W. Woolsey proposes to make an application for a foreign Mission. I am asked to favor his application. I can only say from my limited acquaintance with the Colonel that I think he has all the qualifications of education, ability and social standing to qualify him for such a position. The Colonel served on the Staff of General Seth Williams with the Army of the Potomac. During the last campaign from Petersburgh to Appomattox, and for a short time preceding, General Williams—with the Col. as a Staff officer—served directly with me where I had an opportunity of knowing more of Col. Woolsey than I did before.

Very Truly yours
U. S. GRANT

ALS, DNA, RG 59, Applications and Recommendations, Hayes-Arthur. Related papers are *ibid.* No appointment followed for Charles W. Woolsey, a New York City philanthropist.

Speech

[*May 8, 1883*]

The first part of this toast would be a voluminous one to respond to on a single occasion. Bancroft began publishing his notes of the 'History of the United States,' starting even before President Lane[1] established this Chamber. But instead of bringing those volumes of Bancroft here and reading them to you I will give the reporters an opportunity to publish them as a prelude to what I am going to say. In speaking of the United States, we who are native born have a country of which we may well be proud. Those of us who have been abroad are better able, perhaps, to make comparison of our enjoyments and our comforts than those who have always stayed at home. It has been the fortune, I presume, of the majority of those present to compare the life and the circumstances of the average people abroad with ours here. We have here a country that affords room for all and room for every enterprise. We have industries which encourage every man who has industry and ability to rise from a position in which he may find himself to any position in the land.[2] We offer an as[y]lum to every man of foreign birth who chooses to come here and settle upon our soil. We make him, after a few years' residence, a citizen endowed with all the rights that any of us have, except, perhaps, the single one of being elected President of the United States. There is no other privilege that the native, no matter what he has done for the country, has that the adopted citizen of five years' standing has not got. I contend that that places upon them an obligation which I am sorry to say a few of them seemingly do not appreciate. We have witnessed on many occasions the adopted citizen claiming rights and privileges because he was an adopted citizen. That is all wrong. Let him come here and enjoy all the privileges that we enjoy, but let him perform all the obligations that we expect him to perform. I am happy to say that a great majority of them do it, but some of them who mingle in politics seem to bank largely upon the fact that they are adopted citizens, and that class I am opposed to.

New York Herald, May 9, 1883. USG spoke at the annual dinner of the New York City Chamber of Commerce.

On May 17, 1883, Edwin Cornell, sachem, and James A. Lucas, "Washington Chapter No 2 Order of United Americans," New York City, wrote to USG. " . . . Resolved, That in the patriotic expressions contained in the response of General Grant we recognize the the essence of the fundamental principles on which our beloved organization are based. Viz. The cultivation of the principles of patriotism and love of Country. Resolved, That it is the Sense of this Chapter that in giving expression to the patriotic Sentiments contained in this response General Grant has added another, to the many grand and glorious deeds which command the admiration and gratitude of all patriotic and liberty loving men throughout this Country . . . ." DS, USG 3. "Thirty-five years ago, when the roost was ruled exclusively by Americans, the United Order of Americans held the balance of power in New-York City, and whomsoever they willed was elected to the State and Municipal offices . . . ." *New York Times,* Feb. 23, 1881.

1. Prominent tea merchant George W. Lane was elected chamber president in May, 1882. See *ibid.*, Dec. 31, 1883.

2. In another version, USG here remarked. "There is one portion of this sentiment about which I wish to say a few words, because I think they will be timely. The toast says, 'May those who seek the blessings of its free institutions and the protection of its flag, remember the obligation they impose.' I think that here is a text upon which my brother Beecher and my brother Newman might well preach a long sermon." *Ibid.*, May 9, 1883.

To John Russell Young

———

[New York City, May 18, 1883]

MY DEAR COMMODORE:

Your letter of the 8th of March is received. I really feel ashamed that I have not answered your letters more promptly. All you have written me up to the above date have been received and read with great interest.

You have unquestionably conducted your duties with great skill and ability, and as I had occasion to remark within the last few days, have accomplished more than all our Ministers to China combined since I have been acquainted with our relations with that country.

Your former acquaintance with Li has no doubt been of great benefit. If you can keep these two countries, China and Japan, from laying hands on each other[,] you will have rendered a service worthy of any mission. Such a conflict could only end in disaster to both because, no matter which power proved the stronger, it would end not only in exhaustion of both[,] but in European powers intervening and compelling a peace humiliating and degrading to both.

Some rainy day I will try to take up your letters and write you a complete answer to them, using a stenographer because of my growing—but always with me—indolence.

The papers keep you advised pretty well of the situation in this country. You can hardly fail to see that the cry against [Bossism] has grown to such magnitude that the Republican party is

governed—what there is left of it—by unrelenting [bosses ~~bosses~~]
~~who are not.~~

There is no possible hope for the Republican party in 1884[,]
except in the folly of the democrats in the State and National Legislatures between now and then, together with the position they
are being pushed into on the tariff.

I was very sorry to hear that Mrs. Young had to leave you on
account of her health.[1]

My mother died last Friday[2] at the advanced age of near 85.
She has a brother and sister, both older, mourning [~~surviving~~ sur-
viving].[3] She died without sickness and without pain, possessing
her hearing, eyesight and interest in affairs around her to the last.

The morning of her death she dressed herself, ate her breakfast
and read the morning papers. She died as she often expressed a
wish to die, without becoming a burden to herself or friends. The
first time in her mature life that she had to be assisted to bed was
two hours before she breathed her last.

Present my kindest regards to Prince Kung and Li Hung
Chang, and assure them that I feel a deep interest in all that concerns them and the East generally.

Very truly yours,
U. S. GRANT.

Typescript, DLC-John Russell Young; John Russell Young, *Men and Memories* (New
York, 1901), pp. 301–2. On March 8, 1883, John Russell Young, U.S. minister, Peking,
wrote to USG. "In order to give you some idea of the inside condition of affairs, I send
you a correspondence I have had with Inouye and a letter from Li.—Please destroy
them when read, as I intend them only for the colonel and yourself.—The Japanese
you will see, seem more disposed to confer with me than with Mr Bingham. I have
succeeded in doing away with the ill feeling created by the manner in which we made
our Shufeldt convention, and Mr. Inouye you will see is not willing to take the best
view of that treaty.—I am very much in hopes that we can bring Japan and China
to an understanding.—I hope you will approve of my advice to Inouye.—I am going
down to Tientsin in a few days to have a talk with Li on this business. That will be my
real errand, although I shall nominally go on personal affairs. Li has paid the Ward
claims,—about 60000, and promises after a time to pay Hill.—We came down from 10
to 9 per cent. Hill is very angry, not with me, but with Holcombe. As China could borrow a hundred millions at 6.—and only pays 8 for loans now selling at 11% I do not see
that we have lost much in taking 9. But when a man is on the money scent he is never
reasonable.—I am sure, if you were President, you would commend my success in the
Ward matter. Li pays the sum very handsomely, and in talking with Holcombe, said I
was the only minister in Peking he cared about. Of course, I owe this and my stand-

ing with Japan to you & I have faithfully tried to do out here, what I know would meet with your approval.—I feel a sense of great responsibility, standing as it were between those two statesman, having the confidence of each, and trying to make them see the value of peace.—All this will be more clear to you than to the Department, as you know the situation.—I have received from the government at home, the best and most encouraging support,—which I value.—So far away at home, I must act largely on my own observation. Mrs. Young has had a good winter. The doctors wish her to have a radical change, however, and I will send her to France as soon as navigation opens. So I shall be alone.—You may have an idea of how busy I have been when I say that I have written nearly 400 despatches official and over 400 letters unofficial—But I have never enjoyed any work more and take the deepest interest in it all Mrs. Y. sends her love to Mrs. Grant & the ladies. Give my best regards to all the family, . . . I hope the Badeau books were all delivered and acknowledged" ALS, USG 3.

On Jan. 31 and Feb. 3, Young had written to USG. "I have been thinking whether there is not some way of opening relations between China and Mexico. I had a short conversation with Mr. Romero, but it was only in the railway train.—The position is this.—California and Oregon have closed their fields and shops to Chinese labor.—British America and ~~Calif~~ Mexico remain.—There must be an outlet for this population, and the disposition to emigrate is not easily checked. The English who have recently annexed North Borneo, an island almost continental in its dimensions, are making all their arrangements for colonizing upon the basis of Chinese labor.—The emigration of Chinese to Peru and Cuba never was to be encouraged because it degenerated into a form of slavery, or peonage.—But there is no reason why it should be so in Mexico,—no reason why the undeveloped resources of Mexico should not have the advantage which Californians have thrown away. It will occur to you, of course, as knowing a thousand times more than I do about these matters, how I can serve Mexican interests in this or in any other way.—I should only be too glad to do so.—The State Department would no doubt direct me to do anything Mexico wanted, in the way for instance of making a commercial treaty between the two countries.—If you have the opportunity and think it worth while, you might say to the Mexican minister, that if there is any way in which I can advance ~~American~~ Mexican interests I shall be glad to do so.—This is the Chinese holiday season, their New Year, and everybody is having a good time. Prince Kung continues ill, and there are all kind of rumors about the palace.—My Shanghae problem still hangs,—and I hope will blow over.—The Viceroy writes a pathetic letter and says if he allows foreign machinery in China, his people will lose all their industry & must either rob or starve. The Viceroy is simply a high protectionist and talks like an old-time Whig. But machinery will come all the same.—I suppose this will find you in Mexico,—with Mr. Trescott. Remember me to that gentleman,—and if Mrs. Grant is with you, give her my best regards, in which Mrs. Young joins with all sincerity." "I sent your message to Li, and now enclose you a copy of his answer.—The 'negotiations,' to which he refers, mean, Hill's claim which has been referred to him for settlement.—Holcombe is now in Tientsin trying to worry the money out of him,—with Hill looking on in a state of agony & despair,—and writing me daily letters about Holcombe was trying to sell him out, because he wanted Denny minister, and feeling, I am afraid, that nothing but my own weakness and vacillation keeps me from going down with a club and ending the business.—I have done all I can for Mr. Hill, but I am not authorized to deliver an ultimatum to the Viceroy and declare war. So, I presume, however, it may end I shall be blamed for the result—I wish the business were well settled and out of the way. The Chinese have sent us a stiff and firm note on the manufacturing question, one that would do honor to Kelley of Penna.

I have referred the whole question home and do not mean to move any more until the government decides—I question if we are very much concerned in the business." ALS, *ibid.* On Jan. 26, Li Hung-chang, Tientsin, had written to Young. "I have the pleasure to acknowledge the receipt of your kind letter of the 24th instant conveying a message from our illustrious friend Ex President Grant. I shall be greatly obliged if you will, when you write to the Ex President, remember me to him, thank him for the message and inform him that I fully appreciate his views on the amicable and peaceful relations between the two asiatic Powers. I will answer your two last letters seperately. I regret exceedingly much that there is little prospect of arriving at a very satisfactory result of the negotiations of the question you wrote me. I avail myself of this opportunity to assure you of my highest consideration" L, *ibid.* For Charles E. Hill, see letter to John Russell Young, Aug. 25, 1883.

1. USG had attended the wedding of Young and Julia E. Coleman, niece of Marshall Jewell, in Hartford, April 25, 1882. Julia Young died Oct. 22, 1883, in Paris.

2. May 11. On May 12, USG attended services in Jersey City, then left for Cincinnati, where Hannah Simpson Grant was buried on May 14. See *New York Times*, May 12, 13, 15, 1883.

3. Mary Simpson Griffith, born 1794, and Samuel Simpson, born 1796, both lived in Clermont County, Ohio.

To Robert T. Lincoln

New York City May 19 1883

HON ROBT LINCOLN
SEC OF WAR

DEAR SIR—Knowing that Capt Eads has resigned from the Mississippi River Commission, I take the liberty of suggesting for your consideration the name of General E P Alexander of Ga. to take his place. General Alexander is a graduate of West Point & was in the Engineer Corps having graduated third in his class. He has been engaged as a Civil Engineer most of the time since the close of the war—He can however give the best of testimonials as to his professional qualifications—I fully endorse General Alexander in all other respects.

He is a Southern Man & it would look to me as specially appropriate to have a Southern man on such a Commission when the work to be done is in the South.

Very truly yours
U. S. GRANT

Copy, University of North Carolina, Chapel Hill, N. C. On May 25, 1883, Gen. William T. Sherman, act. secretary of war, wrote to Edward Porter Alexander, care of George G. Hull, New York City. "In accordance with your request of the 22nd instant, I return herewith a letter dated the 19th instant, from General U. S. Grant, recommending you for appointment as a member of the Mississippi River Commission, in place of Captain James B. Eads, who recently resigned." Copy, DNA, RG 107, Letters Sent, Military Affairs. Alexander, USMA 1857, had served in the C.S. Army. For James B. Eads's resignation, see *New York Times*, March 22, 1883. Samuel W. Ferguson replaced Eads.

To Logan C. Murray

Chicago, May 24th *1883*

MY DEAR MR. MURRAY:

I am here on my way to Galena and St. Louis. Will remain here until Saturday[1] and at Galena until Monday next when I will leave for St Louis to remain until about Saturday of next week. I think something of taking your track—backwards—for home, going to Louisville about Saturday week. The object of this letter is to ask you who I shall apply to to get a car from Louisville through Ky. & W. Va east. I would like also the privilege of having the car cut off for one train at Charleston W. Va and also at the White Sulphur Springs. If Mr. C. P. Huntington controlls the road—as I believe he used to—I would apply to him. If you could answer this to the Lindell Hotel, St. Louis I would get your letter in time to make my arrangements.

Very Truly yours
U. S. GRANT

ALS, NjP. Written on stationery of the Palmer House. Born in 1845 in Ky., Logan C. Murray graduated Princeton (1866), was a founder of the American Bankers Association (1874), and served as director of the Louisville and Nashville Railroad. See *New York Times*, June 2, 1924.

On June 10, 1884, USG wrote to Murray, president, United States National Bank, New York City. "I have heard from Chicago scarcity of money is the reply as a reason for not purchasing the stock which you sold as collateral on my loan. You may let Mr. Pullman have it therefore, if he does not pay accured interest I will do so." Typed copy, USGA. See *PUSG*, 30, 474.

USG wrote an undated note to Murray. "I will try to remember the matter mentioned in your note, and speak to the Sec. of the Treasury about it." ANS, NjP.

1. May 26, 1883. On May 24, USG spoke to a reporter at the Palmer House. "Yes, I have grown considerably since the war. I am little ahead of two hundred pounds now . . . . I am going to Galena and then to St. Louis, and thence back home to New York." Concerning Brig. Gen. George Crook's raid against Apaches in Mexico, USG said: "I have no knowledge of it except what I read in the newspapers . . . . Gen. Crook is an able officer. As an Indian-fighter I have every confidence in him. He has not entered into this engagement with the Apaches without considering the obstacles that were sure to spring up before him. His progress must necessarily be slow, and in the mountainous regions of Mexico the Indians, accustomed to the country, may temporarily intrench themselves, but that was to be expected. That Gen. Crook will dislodge and capture them, there is no good reason to doubt . . . . My knowledge of Gen. Crook, the character of his support, bearing in mind that he has Indian scouts of great experience and some cavalry at his hand, forbids me entertaining the thought that Gen. Crook has met with disaster. At any rate, it will take official information to convince me that he is not gaining advantage of these hostile Apaches and that he will drive them to the wall." USG discussed Mexico and Porfirio Díaz's prospects to regain the Mexican presidency. "American capital has flowed into Mexico to a pretty considerable amount, and our people are taking up their residence there and going into business . . . . I saw a great deal of him when he was in New York . . . . There is no doubt of that. In fact there will be no opposition to him. This is the way I understand it from both Gen. Diaz and his friends . . . . I put some money into a railroad that is being built through the southern part of Mexico, and whether I will ever get my money back out of the investment I do not know. I am interested in the welfare of Mexico. Her interests are closely allied to those of the United States, and commerce is springing up between the two countries, and this will be greatly enhanced if the present treaty pending in the United States senate is ratified. The question is, Will the United States government take advantage of the friendly feeling that Mexico manifests toward us? She is our neighbor; her lands are rich with wealth; the country is opening up to settlement, and even in spite of the fact that our government hesitates to assume supremacy and prevent other nations from securing what by right belongs to us, our people are mixing up with Mexicans and making money . . . . The hesitancy of the United States to ratify this treaty between us has led Germany to get one up, and it is now before her congress, but the United States will never permit another nation to possess advantages over us on our own territory. Germany has, however, gained slight advantages over us, and been allowed to secure a foothold in a way that is not explainable and demands the intervention of our government. Her commercial standing with Mexico is dangerous to the United States' interests." USG was asked about his recent nomination for president of the Society of the Army of the Potomac. "The bringing of my name before that gathering was entirely out of place. I would not have accepted of any office had it been tendered me. I have no right to expect anything of that character from the Army of the Potomac. During the war I did not have much to do with the army of the Potomac. I was at one time in command of the Army of the Tennessee, a division of it, but the homage given at the gathering to Gen. Newton and Gen. McClellan was due and, I think, appropriate." As for the 1884 presidential campaign, USG said: "I have met a great many politicians in New York from all over the country, but as to their opinions about the success of the republican party or the democratic party in the future they are held in abeyance. In fact there appears to be nothing stirring of a political character to talk about, and so far as I am personally concerned I have nothing but an ordinary interest in political affairs, and am certainly not taking part in any political movement,

and if politics is not broached until I bring it up, political news will be dull." *Chicago Times*, May 25, 1883. USG discussed Crook's raid in another interview. "Gen. Crook is one of the most experienced and sagacious Indian-fighters in this country, and probably has a more thorough knowledge of the characteristics of the Indian than any other man in the army. I have never yet felt alarmed, and will not until disastrous news is received. He understands Indian-fighting so well that if he is not able to defeat the enemy in a fight he will have left an avenue for a safe retreat. Of course, there is possibility of Crook being betrayed by his Indian scouts, but it is only a slight one, as the General doubtless knows as much about his little army as the average parent does of his family. I remember well when the country was alarmed about the safety of Gen. Sherman on his Atlanta expedition. President Lincoln telegraphed me what the opinion was and asked my advice. I replied that he need have no fears, for Gen. Sherman, with 65,000 trained men could not be caught. Notwithstanding the fact that all information as to his position came through rebel sources, I felt then just as I now do about Gen. Crook." *New York Times*, May 28, 1883. See *ibid.*, June 13, 1883.

To Roswell M. Grant

———

New York
June 3d 1883

DEAR UNCLE:

Enclosed please find my check for One Hundred dollars. I should have stopped over a day at Charleston on my late trip only that I learned at Louisville or Lexington that the wedding of the youngest daughter of my Secretary of State was to be married on the Six of June and Mrs. Grant and I were expected to be there. We had to continue our journey without stopping to reach this city about midnight of the fifth. The morning after we passed Charleston Mrs. Grant was taken so sick however as to confine her to her bed all the next—that—day. Fortunately we had a special car so that we were able to keep on as far as Washington where we were obliged to give it up and stop over. We missed the wedding by this after all. I was sorry then that we had not stopped off at Charleston not only for the night but for a couple of days as I could have done as well as not but for the reason stated above. My kind regards to all your family, to Col. Swann and his family.

yours Very Truly
U. S. GRANT

ALS (misdated), ICarbS. USG did not return to New York City until late on June 6, 1883. See letter to Roswell M. Grant, June 7, 1883.

On June 9, 1882, USG had written to "Dear Cousin," probably America Marton Grant Baldwin. "In answer to your letter of the 7th inst. I have to state that I have no recollection of ever hearing that Uncle Roswell was a drummer in the war of 1812. If the records in Washington, or at the State Capitol of the State from which he volunteered, were kept then as they are now I suppose they would shew the facts." ALS, ICarbS. USG had appointed Baldwin postmaster, St. Albans, West Va., a post she still held. Her father, Roswell M. Grant, a younger brother of Jesse Root Grant, lived with his daughter. Born 1802 in Ohio, he was a "drummer-boy in Col. Todd's Regiment, War of 1812." Arthur Hastings Grant, *The Grant Family* (Poughkeepsie, N. Y., 1898), p. 66. See *New York Times*, Jan. 25, 1885, July 24, 1929.

Interview

[*Louisville, June 3, 1883*]

Mexico is a great country, and it is destined to be a still greater country. The history of California will be repeated. It is a country of boundless possibilities. Railroads are springing up in every direction and capital is pouring in.

Yes, American capital and American enterprise are doing much to build up the country. The railroads are mainly built by Mexican laborers. There used to be some animosity between the Mexicans and the Americans, but it is fast dying out. The effect of all this American push and enterprise will be to make Mexico a magnificent country. The failure to ratify that commercial treaty last spring was a grievous blunder.[1]

I think the effect [*of American investment*] will be just the opposite [*of annexation*]. We have all the territory we want. What do we want Mexico for? No, sir; I think the only effect of this new emigration will be to make Mexico a strong, firm, prosperous Government.

I have washed my hands of politics.

What are the prospects of the Republicans for continuing their hold of the Government?

Ah, that wouldn't do to tell a Democrat. Anyhow it is too far off yet. We will depend in a great measure on the blunders the

Democrats are sure to make. At present the prospects are not very flattering.

There is no man who towers above the rest very conspicuously. I think the two most prominent candidates are Blaine and Logan. Either one of them, in my judgment, will be the nominee. But there are so many things that may occur to bring out other leaders that it is guesswork to name the strongest man now. But I think Blaine and Logan will go into the convention with the most strength.[2]

I am not in politics now.

I do not know what [*Roscoe Conkling's*] future intentions are. I know that he now intends to devote his time to his profession. He has no intention, I think, to become a public man. Why, he don't even notice the attacks that are made on him.

It is too far off yet to tell, but I think [*the tariff question*] will play a most important part. The Republicans will doubtless stand by home industries, and the Democrats will come out for a tariff for revenue only. The next campaign will be a most exciting one.

I am in favor of wiping out the internal revenue system and making the burden of taxation fall upon the imported articles. The States themselves should have charge of the liquor and tobacco tax and do what they please with it.

Louisville Courier-Journal, June 4, 1883. USG spoke at the Galt House before he left for New York City. On June 7, 1883, USG addressed a dinner at Delmonico's for promoters of a Louisville exposition planned for Aug. "I agree with the gentlemen who have already spoken that what we want more than any other one thing is that the people of the two sections north and south of that line which I had thought was obliterated should be brought together. This exposition will furnish the occasion when we can meet together, for great numbers of people from the North and South will there congregate. They will then find that after all there is very little difference between them. The institution that was wiped out by the rebellion has made us one people. We should no longer know any North or South or East or West. I am sure there is great ignorance on both sides of the line of how those in the two sections think and act. It has been my fortune to have visited every State where slavery existed before the rebellion. I have been treated by their residents with the greatest hospitality. I remember meeting in Saratoga the Speaker of the Louisiana Legislature, who had during my visit to that State presented me to his associates in a speech so hospitable that I was embarrassed for language to reply to it. He was having a high time at Saratoga. He admitted to me that he had thought that the people of the North were poor and that the grass was growing in our streets. He had been to Lake George, he said, and all over. He was amazed at what he saw. He had never seen anything like it. The best thing that Congress could do, he said, was to make an appropriation to send people from the North to the South, and particularly from the South to the North, in order that they might get better acquainted with one another. I suppose it will be a long time before Congress will consent to do that, but the next best thing that can be done is the holding of just such an exposition as this right on the border. I for one will go down there to shake hands with those who meet there." *New York Times*, June 8, 1883.

1. See Speech, [*Feb. 8, 1883*]. On May 5, USG addressed a Saturday Night Club dinner at the Hotel Brunswick. "I hope, gentlemen, and hope earnestly, that in the years to come, be he a Republican or a Democrat who guides our ship of state, it will be his object to preserve the most intimate relations between the great and little republics of this continent. We must take our neighbor under our wing. We must help her to cultivate her own great resources. We must teach her that it is for her interest to maintain a close alliance with us. This must be our object, and statesmen should think of this and think deeply on it. Mexico possesses all the essential elements of unlimited prosperity. Her mines are rich. Railways are now developing her commercial resources, and educational facilities are making shrewd statesmen, gentlemen, in that little republic south of us. Let the two countries be united in friendly alliance, and if this were done and war should follow the two countries combined could shut themselves up in their shell and sustain themselves longer than the attacking parties could do without the products of the two republics of this continent." *The Two Republics*, May 24, 1883.

2. On April 10, USG had responded to the toast, "The President," at a dinner for Charles de Lesseps, vice president, Panama Canal Co. "... Our Nation has 50,000,000 of busy, thinking, reading, enterprising, intelligent people. When they select a ruler for four years it is the greatest honor that can be conferred upon man on earth. Persons who reign by the accident of birth may not be a credit to their country. Their fitness has had nothing to do with their selection. But when a man gets to the head of a Nation like ours it means much. It implies something in the man himself. We have a man in the office who has filled it for a part of a term. We hope for the best results from his experience. When his term expires he must necessarily go out and the choice of 50,000,000 of people will go in. We can well afford to rest content with that choice, whatever party he may belong to. If he don't do well he is sure to go out anyhow." *New York Times*, April 11, 1883.

To Hamilton and Julia K. Fish

New York City,
June 7th 1883.

MY DEAR GOVERNOR AND MRS. FISH:

Allow me, after my congratulations, to express my regret at not being present yesterday to witness the ceremony of the marriage of your daughter to Mr. Northcote.[1] My trip to the West was delayed for some time on account of the death of my mother.[2] It was necessary because the lease of my land there had expired and it was necessary to make some arrangement for its care. Mrs. Grant & I knew that Miss Edith's wedding was to take place early in June, but did not know the exact day until we read it in the papers, in Lexington, Ky. that it was to be the sixth. Knowing that we would have an invitation we started from Lexington Monday afternoon,[3] in time to reach New York Tuesday night. But the extremely hot weather, and possibly something Mrs. Grant eat, made her very sick all day Tuesday so that we were obliged to stop over in Washington until yesterday, making it too late to attend the wedding. Mrs. Grant & I regret very much our absence and unite in our congratulation, and best wishes for the happiness of the young couple.

Very Truly yours
U. S. GRANT

ALS, DLC-Hamilton Fish.

    1. On June 6, 1883, Edith L. Fish married Hugh O. Northcote near New York City.

    2. Hannah Simpson Grant had died on May 11.

    3. June 4.

To Roswell M. Grant

New York, June 7th 1883

DEAR UNCLE:

Enclosed find my check for fifty dollars. When in St. Louis I hoped to be able to stop over one train at Charleston so as to see you; but I found that all the trains from Louisville passed in the night. Also I was in a hurry expecting to get here in time to attend the wedding of the daughter of my Secretary of State—Governor Fish—which took place yesterday. But Mrs. Grant was so sick between Charleston and Washington that I was compelled to stop over there and missed the wedding after all. If I could have fore-

seen that I would have stopped over for a day anyhow. Mrs. Grant
is now well. Her attack was Cholera Morbus.

Yours Very Truly
U. S. GRANT

ALS, ICarbS. Written on letterhead of Grant & Ward. See letter to Roswell M. Grant,
June 3, 1883.

To Henry Whitney Cleveland

———

New York City,
June 14th 1883.

DEAR SIR:

Your letter of the 13th of May, enclosed to me by General
Longstreet, in which you ask a few words from me in regard to my
estimate of the late Honorable Alexander A. Stevens, reached my
office during my absence in the West. Since that time I have I have
been in my office but three or four days, and finding an accumulation of letters I am not yet through with the disposal of them. This
is my apology for not answering your letter earlyer.

I never had the pleasure of a personal acquaintance with
Mr. Stevens until he, with Mr. Hunter and Judge Campbell visited
my Head Quarters, at City Point, Va during the last year of the
rebellion. I had however known him well by reputation for many
years before, and placed a [hig]h estimate upon his character and
ability, and, I might [s]ay, [stat]esmanship My personal acquaintance, though we differed so widely on matters largely effecting
our common country, only increased my admiration for the man.
As I understand, without being a man of large means, he devoted
largely from what he could earn to the greatest good of of the
greatest number. Through him many a deserving young man has
found the means of acquiring a fair education to give him a start
in the world, and in most cases, if I am correctly informed, he has
been compensated by seeing those who had these favors conferred
upon them do honor to their benefactor.

In all his public utterances Mr. Stephens impressed me as a

man who was not afraid to speak his honest convictions without regard to whether they would be popularly received or not. To the day of his death I retained the high estimate of his life and character that I had formed before I knew him, increased by a personal acquaintance.

Very Truly yours

U. S. Grant

Rev. H. W. Cleveland Atlanta Ga

ALS, Presbyterian Historical Society, Philadelphia, Pa. Alexander H. Stephens died March 4, 1883. Henry Whitney Cleveland, journalist and Stephens biographer, eulogized him in "A Southern Statesman," *The Continent*, III, 19 (May 9, 1883), 577–85. Cleveland later published a facsimile of USG's letter in "General Grant's Military Abilities: By a Confederate Officer," *Magazine of American History*, XIV (Oct., 1885), 341–50. This facsimile, apparently forged from the original, closely resembles that held by Morristown National Historical Park, Morristown, N. J. A slightly different version, also forged, is held by the University of Georgia, Athens, Ga. A letter from USG to James Longstreet, Atlanta, also dated June 14, 1883, is another probable Cleveland forgery. "Your letter of the 14th of May, enclosed to me, in which you ask a few words from me expressing my estimate of the late Honorable Alexander H Stephens—reached my office during my absence—In all his public utterances Mr Stephens impressed me as a man who was never afraid to speak his honest convictions without regard to whether they would be popularly received or not To the day of his death I retained the high estimate of his life and character formed before I knew him—increased by a personal acquaintance" Facsimile, *Confederate Veteran*, VIII (Aug., 1900), 358. Cleveland may have also forged letters from Abraham Lincoln to Stephens. See "Forged Lincoln Letters," *Proceedings of the Massachusetts Historical Society*, LXI (May, 1928), 183–95; "Four Spurious Lincoln Letters," *Bulletin of the Abraham Lincoln Association*, 21 (Dec., 1930), 8–9; Charles Hamilton, *Great Forgers and Famous Fakes* ... (New York, 1980), pp. 216–17.

On June 30, 1873, Cleveland, Ramsgate, England, had written to USG. "I am a Southern Officer, in great need of kindness, and with no claim either upon the distinguished gentleman to whom I write, nor on the American people. Still I can tell of some few things, which still entitle me to the same hearing, as you would give to a good citizen. In the year 1860, I was Chief Editor of the *Constitutionalist*, Augusta Ga, and Delegate to the Charleston and Baltimore Conventions. For supporting the Union, so long as there was any hope, and for so voting, until General Butler and Mr Cushing, *then* good Rebels! put me, with nine others, out of the Convention; I was burned in effigy an[d] play-carded as a 'Traitor,' in my state. I did afterwards advocate Secession but only,—as I then stated,—to make a strong show and avoid war. I wa[s] the friend and correspondent of Judge Douglas. During the war, I was a Lieutena[nt,] my commission, May, 1861, being from Gov Joseph E. Brown, and one of the first in the South. After I was your prisoner, and saved from starvation [by] your excellent *rations* in Vicksburg, I left service, and did all I could through the press, to prevent the breach of parole when Mr Davis ordered us [to] arms again. I may say that it w[as] the fruit of my publications with the Stephenson Division, that gave you [the] battle of Missionary Ridge. The Vicksburg troops simply *did not fight*, as we swore not to, and were *not* exchange[d.] I was afterwards protected by a commission as Colonel,

on the staff o[f] Governor Joseph. E. Brown, and had some 68.000. lbs of powder of old U. S. make, which I delivered to General Upton, and which he let get stolen from the Greensboro school-house. From 1863 to 1865, I wrote reconstruction Editorials, and it was my pen that wrote the leaders in the *Constitutionalist*, 1865, for which I was discharged from its pay the *second* time, and for which John L. Stockton got U. S. Government patronage. I also wrote the leaders for the Chronicle & Sentinel,—two thirds of them,—for which Judge Hilliard and Nathan S. Morse claimed Government recompense. I was the Vice President (I think) and I know I was secretary, of the first Union Meetings held in the South, after the war really ended. Of one held in Augusta Ga, early in 1865, Rev Dr Scott and my self were the originators, and I have the printed proceedings. I have never voted for you, as I was never at home in a Presidential contest since Johnson & Prest. Lincoln, but I never voted against you, and I did vote for Henry Stephens, a negro, in Ga, against Capt Frank, Holden, a Confederat[e] officer. I have been as good a Union man, as Amos T. Akerman, who was Lieut. Col. in Toombs Brigade, Savanna[h,] and I have *written* more, *spoken* more, *risked* more, and *suffered* more, than nine tenths of the Southern men whom you have helped. This I can PROVE I had a plantation in Ga, and Tom Lyne, a wealthy Ku-Klux leader offered me $1000, for what cost, with stock, Etc, $6000, and came to my house to threaten me with the gang, if [I] stayed in the County. I have had m[y] private letters broken open, and endorsed 'opened by the K. K. K.' I was the first man in Georgia to let negroes ha[ve] land, (so far as I know,) and I pai[d] 100 Acres, of as good as I had, for a Ditch, and The Springfield Church now stands on it, with the Church helped-in by [me.] The interferance with my labor, and [*the*] constant armed watch I had to keep, force[d] me to sell out, and at so great a sacrifice, that, with the failure of the Publisher from whom I had promises in England, I am very poor. *But I do not ask any office*, for I do not feel that I deserve any. I have a new patent,—new so far as I know,—for field and ship guns, and also for a new paper, that will prevent counterfeits to currency paper. I am a good Editor, and I am probably a warmer advocate of your *third* Election, and *several more*, than you are. I seek your *personal* friendship, and I will do anything, from grooming your horses, to dividing Patent profits with you, or Editing for you; so I can only get back to America. If you reply, please direct *care of* Mr Edward Hodges, U. S. Consul, here, as I may manage to get a passage sooner. I am smart and grateful—try me."
ALS, DNA, RG 59, Miscellaneous Letters.

To William T. Smith

New York, June 14 *1883*

WM T. SMITH ESQ.
OSKALOOSA IOWA
DEAR SIR:

Your letter of June 4th inviting me to attend the next State Fair, is at hand, and in reply I will say that it would afford me very great pleasure to accept but the time for holding your fair is somewhat distant,[1] and I have had it in contemplation to visit the Pacific

Coast over the Northern Pacific when it is finished,[2] and if I Should do so it would probably prevent my accepting your invitation. At a later date however I may be able to give you a different answer, and I can assure you that if possible, it would give me very great pleasure to accept Your very kind invitation.

Truly Yours

U. S. GRANT

LS, IaHA. Lawyer, banker, and civic promoter, William T. Smith was president of the Iowa State Agricultural Society. On Aug. 6, 1883, Smith, Oskaloosa, wrote to USG. "You will pardon me for again, at this time, recalling your attention to to my letter to you, under date of June 4th and the letters of Gov Sherman Senator Jas F. Wilson, Hon Jno A. Kasson & Judge Cole inviting & *urging* you to attend our coming fair, and I do so, by reason of your statement in your letter of 14th of June, that 'At a later date however, I may be able to give you a different answer'. If it is now possible for you to so arrange your travel & time, so as to comply with our *urgent* and *anxious* solicitation, I can assure you we will give you a hearty reception." ALS, *ibid.* On Aug. 10, USG wrote to Smith. "Your letter of 6th inst calling my attention to a previous letter from you inviting me to be present the fi[r]st part of September at the Fair of the Iowa State Agricultural Society, is received, and in answer I regret that I will not be able to be present. About the 1st of September I start for the Northern Pacific R. R. and will not probably be back until after your Fair I should enjoy a visit to Iowa on such an occasion very much, but can only regret that circumstances are such that I will not be able to go." LS, *ibid.*

    1. Sept. 3–7.
    2. Henry Villard, president, Northern Pacific Railroad, arranged a tour to mark the railroad's completion. See *New York Times*, July 14, Aug. 2, 1883; Henry J. Winser, *The Great Northwest: A Guide-Book and Itinerary for the Use of Tourists and Travellers Over the Lines of the Northern Pacific Railroad* . . . (New York, 1883); Eugene V. Smalley, *History of the Northern Pacific Railroad* (New York, 1883); *Memoirs of Henry Villard: Journalist and Financier 1835–1900* (Boston, 1904), II, 295–312; Robin W. Winks, *Frederick Billings: A Life* (New York, 1991), pp. 238–64.

To Louis Garesché

———

New York, June 15 *1883*

MR LOUIS GARESCHE
911 NEW YORK AVE
WASHINGTON D C
DEAR SIR:

    Your letter of the 13th inst is at hand. I would not be able to write of my own personal knowledge anything that would be of advantage in the biographical sketch of Col. Garesche that you ask. The accidents of service have not brought us together that I remember of since his graduation at West Point in 1841. I being two years after him at the Military Academy, our personal acquaintance was very limited. It would be impossible, therefore, for me to say anything from personal knowledge, but I know that he enjoyed the best of reputation at the Military Academy and also as an officer of the Army.

Truly Yours

U. S. GRANT

LS, Herbert E. Klingelhofer, Bethesda, Md.

On March 8, 1874, Louis Garesché, St. Louis, wrote to USG. "I respectfully appeal to you for an appointment as Naval Cadet. Representing to your Excellency most truthfully that I am an entire orphan, the son of Lieut. Colonel Julius P. Garesché who, while he was Aid of General Rosecrans, was killed in the late war at the battle of Stone River. My age was 17 years on the 30th day of June last." ALS, Benjamin Kohn, Silver Spring, Md. On March 12, Gen. William T. Sherman endorsed this letter. "Respectfully submitted to the President—Recommended, as a graceful act of recognition of the merits of the Father, a noble Soldier & Gentleman. Killed in Battle." AES, *ibid.* On July 2, USG issued an order. "The Acting Secretary of the Navy may authorize Louis Garesché to appear for examination at the Naval Academy if there be a vacancy to justify it. The first vacancy occurring may be reserved for the purpose of appointing this applicant" Copy, *ibid.* On July 24, Garesché wrote to USG. "Knowing the respect with which you venerate the memory of my deceased father, Lieut. Colonel Julius P. Garesché, I feel no hesitation in applying to you for a favour. It is my great desire now to obtain an appointment to West Point for the year 1875, and I sincerely hope that you will use your interest in obtaining it for me. My age at present is 18 years." ALS, DNA, RG 94, Correspondence, USMA. Related papers are *ibid.* Admitted to USMA in 1875, Garesché did not graduate, but enlisted and later clerked in the AG Dept. See his *Biography of Lieut. Col. Julius P. Garesché, Assistant Adjutant-General, U. S. Army* (Philadelphia, 1887), p. 495.

To Adam Badeau

———

New York City,

June 21st 1883

DEAR GENERAL:

I am just in receipt of your letter of the 16th inst. I have been absent from the city most of the time for six or seven weeks, returning for a couple of days twice during the time. General Sicles wrote me a letter on the subject referred to in yours during these absences. Mails accumulated so that I did not get to his letter until some time after it was written. I then found a second letter from him, on a different subject, and answered both in one letter. I have not heard from him since, but hope my letter was satisfactory.

When you come North, and visit Long Branch, come directly to my house. whether I have company or not there will always be a room for you. Of course I mean this as an invitation to you to come to Long Branch notwithstanding the ambiguity of the preceding sentence.

yours Truly
U. S. GRANT

ALS, Munson-Proctor-Williams Institute, Utica, N. Y. "This refers to the suit brought by me in the Court of Claims to defend my right to a position in the army. The War Department uniformly held that this right was undoubted, but one of the auditors of the Treasury took a different view, . . . General Sickles, as well as myself, had been retired by President Grant in order to enable him to accept diplomatic rank, and he had written to General Grant to obtain some information in regard to the General's action as President. The letter was not answered promptly, and General Sickles inquired of me if it had been received." *Badeau*, p. 550. See *New York Times*, May 25, 1883.

On Jan. 14, 1885, Secretary of War Robert T. Lincoln wrote to USG. "In reply to your telegram, I made up my mind yesterday to issue the order for Badeau's pay from the time he ceased to be consul general, and the order has been issued today." Copy, DNA, RG 107, Letters Sent. See letter to Adam Badeau, July 12, 1885, note 3.

Concerning Henry I. Raymond

New York City,
June 21st 1883.

This will present to my friends in Mexico Dr. H. I. Raymond, of the United States Army, who contemplates resigning for the purpose of settling in Mexico for ~~the~~ to practice his profession there. To enter the U. S. Army as an Assistant Surgeon requires an examination which is itself the best guarantee of the professional qualifications of the person holding such a commission he could have. I therefore commend Dr Raymond to the community in which he may locate.

U. S. GRANT

ADS, ICarbS. Born in 1857 in Ind., Henry I. Raymond graduated Bellevue Hospital
Medical College (1880), resigned as asst. surgeon as of Sept., 1883, and was appointed
1st lt., asst. surgeon, as of Jan., 1885.

To Roland Worthington

Long Branch, N. J.
July 3d 1883.

MY DEAR MR. WORTHINGTON;

May I request you, as I did last year, to employ R. H. Terrell
during the vacation in the Boston Custom House. As you are aware
Terrell is a colored man now in the Senior class at Harvard and has
to earn his own living while prosecuting his studies. My special
interest in him is from the fact that his father—a most estimable
man—is my butler, beside I should feel an interest in any young man,
white or colored, who had the courage and ability to graduate himself at Harvard without other pecuniary aid than what he could earn.

Very Truly yours
U. S. GRANT

ALS, deCoppet Collection, NjP. See *PUSG*, 30, 382.

To John A. J. Creswell

[Long Branch, July 11, 1883]
While in the city yesterday I found your letter giving the reason why you could not accept Mrs. Grant's and my invitation for
the time named. We do not propose to give it up just so. On the
6th of August W. McLean and wife of Cincinnati are coming to
spend a week with us. I leave it to Mrs. Crewell to name any time
in August after their visit . . . trusting that you will accompany
her, just for company and to look after the baggage.

Kenneth W. Rendell, Inc., Catalogue 84 [n. d.], no. 98. On July 27, 1883, USG wrote to
Hannah J. Creswell presumably concerning the Creswells' visit. Edward Eberstadt &

Sons, No. 129, 1951, no. 97. On June 28, USG had written to John A. J. Creswell. John Heise, Catalog No. 2453 [n. d.], no. 53.

To Fannie E. Musgrave

———

Long Branch, N. J.
July 11th 1883.

MY DEAR MRS. MUSGRAVE:

Mrs. Grant has just handed me your kind letter of the 8th inst. inviting us to visit you for ten days, commencing on the 8th of August, at Bar Harbor, Me. and requests me to answer it. Both of us would enjoy the visit very much, and are under obligations to you and your husband for the invitation: but we have visitors coming to us on the Sixth of August to be succeeded by others until about the first of September. In the mean time we have company with the exception of a week reserved for a little trip to the Catskills.

Thanking you and Mr Musg for your kind invitation, and with the best regards of Mrs. Grant and myself,

Very Truly yours
U. S. GRANT

ALS (facsimile), Alexander Autographs, Inc., June 16, 2007, no. 194. Fannie E. Musgrave and her husband, a Wall Street stockbroker, entertained frequently at their Fifth Avenue home. See letter to Adam Badeau, Jan. 25, 1884; *New York Times*, March 30, 1881, Sept. 4, 1889.

To William W. Smith

———

New York City,
July 24th 1883.

DEAR SMITH:

I forgot to answer your letter promptly as I intended. When it was received I was going out and forgot the matter until now. The prescription I used with such good effect when the Epozootic was raging a few years ago[1] was a heaping teaspoon full of clorate of potash dissolved in a bucket of water and this given to four horses, three times a day.

We will start to go over the N. Pacific road[2] about the first of September. Time is not yet definitely fixed. Hold yourself in readiness and I will telegraph you when to join us.

Very Truly yours
U. S. GRANT

ALS, Washington County Historical Society, Washington, Pa.

1. Horse influenza spread across the U.S. in 1872–73.
2. See letter to William T. Smith, June 14, 1883, note 1.

To Edward F. Beale

———

Long Branch, N. J.
July 25th 1883

MY DEAR GENERAL BEALE:

Mrs. Grant & I more than half promised, when Elkins and his wife were here, to go to Deer Park for a few days after the 13th of August. We now find that we cannot go. We have company coming continuously until the first of September excepting the first five days of August which Mrs. Grant and I propose to spend in making a little trip through the Catskills. About the 1st of September I go with a large party over the North Pacific rail-road to drive the last spike. I will be gone probably three weeks and I presume Mrs. Grant and Miss Sharp will go to the city as soon after I start as the weather will permit. We are sorry we cannot have a visit from Mrs. Beale and Emily. Why can you not run down and spend a few days? You can come any time, except while we are in the mountains, without regard to other company. We have you know a bachilor room on the first floor where I put my company without regard to who Mrs. Grant has.

With kind regards to Mrs. Beale and Miss Emily,

Very Truly yours
U. S. GRANT

ALS, DLC-Decatur House Papers.

To Ellen Grant Sartoris

———

Long Branch, N. J.
July 25th /83

DEAR DAUGHTER:

We have now been at L. B. a month. Our family is your Ma, Bessie Sharpe and myself. But we have scarsely been a day without other company. At this time your Uncle Casey, Aunt Emma and the three youngest children are with us. They leave on Saturday[1] when your Aunt Anna and Betty[2] are to come. When they leave— on Wednesday of next week—your Ma and I go to the Catskill Mountains for a few days. On our return we are to have other company continuously until the first of September when I go over the North Pacific road to Oregon and back. The boys, with their families, have all visited us for a few days each. Fred has taken a house in Morristown, N. J. Jesse one at East Lyme, Conn. and Buck you know is at his farm. He has lost none of his interest in farming. Jesse has a yacht[3] and enjoys it and fishing very much. All the children are well and grow in interest every day. The fact is your Ma & I are very proud of our grand children. We hope to have you with your children with us the coming Winter.

Long Branch and vicinity has grown very much since you were here. We see no greatdeal of the people here however except in their carriages on the Avenue. We never go to the hotels.

With kind regards to Mr Sartoris, and love and kisses to you and the children, Affectionately yours,

U. S. GRANT

ALS, ICHi.
    In late June, 1883, reports linked Algernon Sartoris, then visiting family property in Wis., to a Mrs. H. B. Bush. See *New York Times*, June 28, July 2, 8, 1883.

    1. July 28.
    2. Betty Dent, daughter of Lewis and Anna E. Dent, was born in 1869.
    3. Jesse Root Grant, Jr., was an incorporator of the American Yacht Club, recently founded by Jay Gould. See *New York Times*, May 18, June 6, 1883.

To John P. Tracey

NEW YORK, July 27, 1883.

To Col. J. P. TRACEY, Springfield, Mo.:

DEAR COLONEL—I have your letter of the 23d inst., inviting me to be present at the reunion of the survivors of the soldiers engaged at Wilson's creek, to be held in Springfield on the 10th prox., the 23d anniversary of that battle. It would afford me very great pleasure to meet the veterans of the two armies engaged in that battle on such an occasion, but it would be impossible for me to leave home at that time as I have guests invited to be at my country home at the same time of your reunion. I hope you will find the occasion a very enjoyable one and that the soldiers who were arrayed against each other twenty-two years ago will be no less friends than if they had been engaged in the same cause and the only rivalry that may exist between them hereafter will be to see who can prove the best citizen of a common and great country.

Very truly yours,
U. S. GRANT.

Missouri Republican, Aug. 10, 1883. Former 1st lt., 8th Mo. Militia Cav., John P. Tracey was a lawyer and journalist.

To Jesse Root Grant, Jr.

Kaaterskill (P. O.) N. Y. Aug 2d *1883*

DEAR JESSE:

I telegraphed you from Kingston yesterday inviting you and family and Mrs. Chapman[1] to go to us at Long Branch on Saturday[2] or Monday next to remain until the close of the season, and for you and Lizzie to stay with us in the city afterwards. I hope you will do this. About the 1st of September we would start for the Pacific, over the N. P road, and the ladies would stay at Long Branch either until we returned or would be moved into the city to meet us when we get back.

Your Ma is very anxious to have you and Lizzie—and little Tott[3]—with us.—We will be back to Long Branch on Saturday afternoon. We will have no company that will interfere with your three rooms.

Yours &c.

U. S. GRANT

ALS, Chapman Grant, Escondido, Calif. Written on stationery of the Hotel Kaater-skill, opened in 1881. See *New York Times*, Aug. 1, 1881.

1. Sarah A. Chapman, mother-in-law of Jesse Root Grant, Jr.
2. Aug. 4, 1883.
3. Nellie Grant, born Aug. 5, 1881, at Long Branch.

To Henry Coppée

New York City

Aug. 21st 18[8]3

My Dear Prof. Coppeé:

I have your letter informing me that Gen. Hancock will not be at the Astec dinner &c. Will it not be proper for him—or me—to authorize you to act as President in the absence of both the President & Vice President? If so I authorize you to act so far as my authority goes. It is bearly possible that I may be back in time for the dinner. The party that I go with start four or five days earlyer than was expected when I wrote you before. A portion of the party will go no further than where the two ends of the North Pacific are to be united. If I return from that point I shall expect to be back by the Fourteenth of September. You may put me down therefore to be present so far as the preparation of the dinner is concerned.

Very Truly yours

U. S. GRANT

ALS, Goodspeed's Book Shop, Inc., Boston, Mass. See letter to Henry Coppée, Sept. 26, 1883.

To Col. Frederick T. Dent

New York City

August 23d 1883.

Dear Dent:

Thank the proprietor of Orkney springs for me for his kind invitation to Mrs. Grant and I to visit the Springs as his guests. I supposed that I had put the Drs letter in my pocket to answer from my office this morning. But I find I did not and cannot recall the name. Otherwise I should have written directly to him thanking him for his courtisy. We will not be able to accept however. On Thursday next[1] I start for the Pacific coast, over the North Pacific road and will not return until to late to visit any Summer resort.

We are all well and hope that you an Hellen are also.

Very Truly yours

U. S. Grant

ALS (facsimile), Manuscript Society Sale, May, 1990, no. 8167. M. and H. C. Maddox operated a resort at Orkney Springs, Va. See *New York Times*, Aug. 31, 1883.

1. Aug. 30, 1883.

To John W. Powell

New York City,

August 23d 1883

Maj. Jno. W. Powell:

Director of Geological Surveys &c.

Dear Maj.

I write this to interest you if I can in behalf of Mrs. Sophie Maconochie, and to induce you to give her a place where she may be able to support herself and two little children. Mrs. M. is the daughter of Major Ringgold,[1] late a Paymaster in the Army, who spent the most of his mature years in the service of his country,—

died in it,—and leaves this daughter, with two children and no means of support except such as she can make for herself. I hope you can give her a place.

Very Truly yours
U. S. GRANT

ALS, National Anthropological Archives, Smithsonian Institution.

1. Born in 1814 in Md., USMA 1833, George H. Ringgold rose to lt. col., deputy paymaster gen., and died in 1864. See *PUSG*, 26, 474.

To John Russell Young

Long Branch, N. J.
Aug. 25th 1883.

MY DEAR COMMODORE;

I inclose you a letter I received from Mr. Hill yesterday. I cannot do what he requests, i e procure him an interview with Li, suggesting a settlement preliminary to urging the settlement of the claim of China against this government. But I think there is no doubt but Hill's claim should be settled by China entirely irrespective of any claim China has, or supposes she has, against the United States. Mr. Hill is a citizen of the United States whos property was taken for use by the Chinese Governmen[t] and destroyed. The claim o[f] China is simply for the return of a sum of money overpaid by her to the United States.

I believe with Mr. Hill that no claim represented by Holcombe can be settled so long as Li Hung Chang represents the Chinese Government in the settlement.

I do not know what your instructions may be in this matter, but if they authorize it could you not negociate directly with Li in the matter.—I would suggest that if this matter should be get out of the way that Trescott[1] would be as serviceable an agent as China could select to act as their Agent in Washington. He is thoroughly conversant with the ways of the of the State Department and Con-

gress on all diplomatic questions, and with precedents bearing
upon the case in point.

Very Truly yours,

U. S. GRANT

P. S. Present my kindest regards to Prince Kung and to Li
Hung Chang, and say that if I can at any time be of service to them
to command me.[2]

U. S. G.

ALS, DLC-John Russell Young. American merchant Charles E. Hill pursued a claim
against China for the loss of a steamer in an 1863 rebellion. See letter to John Russell
Young, May 18, 1883; *SED*, 45-2-48; *New York Times*, June 2, 1881, March 17, 1885.

    1. Veteran diplomat and lobbyist, William H. Trescot had recently served as com-
missioner to negotiate treaties with China and Mexico, the latter with USG.
    2. On Nov. 16, 1883, Prince Kung wrote to John Russell Young, U.S. minister,
Peking, acknowledging USG's greeting. " . . . Since the conversations had with General Grant when in Peking I have retained the deepest admiration for his character,
and, since his departure, when I have heard from time to time that he retained so deep
an interest in all that seriously concerned China, the fact has filled me with the most
profound gratitude. As I reckon it up, I find it to be a number of years since he was
here, and yet his interest in our affairs remains. The deep and abiding friendship between our two nations is proof of the earnest care of the former President for which I
must beg you to give him my most grateful thanks." Copy, DNA, RG 59, Diplomatic
Despatches, China.

To Adam Badeau

————

~~New York City~~, Long Branch, N. J
Aug. 27th /83

DEAR BADEAU;

    I am just now in receipt of your letter of the 24th inst. It is the
first I had heard of your arrival though I supposed you were some
place in the Catskills. Jesse and family expect to go to the Kaater-
skill house to-morrow, his family to remain until he and I return
from our trip over the North Pacific rail-road. We start on that
trip on Thursday next.[1] It is probable that we will go no further
than where the two ends are to be united—the last spike driven. In

that case we will be back from the 12th to 14th of Sept. I am sorry that I cannot see you before starting; but I presume I will be back before you will want to go to Washingt[on.] I would suggest that you write the Sec. of State a note saying that from your condition owing to your long delay in Havana that you will not go to Washington until after the first frost.

Very Truly yours

U. S. GRANT

ALS, Munson-Williams-Proctor Institute, Utica, N. Y.

    1. Aug. 30, 1883.

To Julia Dent Grant

Chicago, Sept. 1st *1883*

DEAR JULIA;

    Jesse & I arrived here an hour or two ago; have had time to take our baths and change underclothes and will be off for St Paul as soon as we get some lunch. The trip was pleasant and the company pleasant though we were several hours late reaching here on account of our long heavy train. Will Smith met us here.[1]—I am writing at Mr. Palmer's desk, Mr. Palmer and General Kane,[2] of Pensylvania being present. The General is of our party though in a different car. Love and kisses to you all.

Yours

U. S. GRANT

ALS, DLC-USG. Written on letterhead of the Palmer House Co.

    1. On Aug. 28, [*1883*], Tuesday, USG telegraphed to William W. Smith. "My car Yellowstone leaves Erie Depot at eight Thursday you can join here or at Chicago on first of Sept" Telegram received (at 11:10 A.M.), Washington County Historical Society, Washington, Pa.

    2. Born in 1822 in Philadelphia, son of a U.S. district judge, Thomas L. Kane took an active part in the underground railroad, befriended Mormon leaders, organized the 13th Pa. Reserve ("Bucktail") regt., and rose to brig. gen. before retiring to the town he founded in northwest Pa. See *PUSG*, 19, 229; *ibid.*, 20, 167.

To Julia Dent Grant

Minnetonka Beach, Minn., Sept. 2 *1883,*

DEAR JULIA;

We arrived at this place for breakfast this morning. Minnetonka Lake is a beautiful sheet of water almost as large as Como,
in Switzerland,[1] filled with islands. The shores and some of the
islands have beautiful summer cottages upon them with occational
hotels. The one we are in is an elegant affair about twice the size
of the Kaaterskill House and apparently as well kept. To-morrow
we go back to Minneapolis[2] in the forenoon and to St Paul in the
afternoon. In the evening the banquet is to be given in this house
by the St Paul people.[3] At twelve at night we start on our journey
following the programme you have.—There are a great many people stopping at this and other houses on the lake though but few we
know. I think the trip will prove a most enjoyable one and I would
not have missed it for a greatdeal.—I will drop a line from every
point where I have an opportunity to write until we start home after which there will be no use in writing.

Love and kisses to you, Lizzie & my little pet.[4]

Yours

U. S. GRANT

ALS, Dickinson College, Carlisle, Pa. Written on letterhead of the Hotel Lafayette.

1. Actually Italy, but near the border with Switzerland.
2. On Sept. 3, 1883, during a banquet to honor Henry Villard at the Lyndale Hotel in Minneapolis, USG responded to a toast. " . . . I supposed that as a matter of
course, I should not be able to pass through St. Paul and Minneapolis without having a
word to say, and I started from New York with the expectation that I should be called
upon to say something, but unfortunately Mr. Evarts and myself have been closeted
together in the same car, and we have had abundance of time to exchange ideas, and he
has got up here in advance of me and told you every word that I intended to say. This
will teach me the lesson which I ought to have learned before, not to trust any secrets
to lawyers. However, after this exposure I do not think he will attempt the same thing
to-night. It will, probably, be well for me to say one word about Minneapolis. We have
only stopped at Chicago, St. Paul and Minneapolis since we left New York, and there
is one thing that we have discovered that is common to all these places, and that is, we
have never met a man from either of them, on the road or elsewhere, that seemed to
be ashamed of the place he had selected for his home. And I have noticed another
thing, and that is that if you enter into conversation with them with regard to some-

thing, and were not inquisitive enough to inquire of them where they were from they would manage to [*b*]ring it in some way. But Mr. Evarts and I have concluded that you have a great deal to base your pride of locality upon, and from a survey of the country about Minneapolis, I think there is room enough, land yet unimproved, not built upon, to carry out your brightest hopes in regard to the future greatness of your city. And I shall be proud to be able to visit your place after those expectations are realized." *Saint Paul and Minneapolis Pioneer Press*, Sept. 4, 1883.

3. See J. H. Hanson, *Grand Opening of the Northern Pacific Railway. Celebration at St. Paul, . . . September 3rd, 1883* (St. Paul, n. d.).

4. USG's daughter-in-law Elizabeth Chapman Grant and granddaughter Nellie Grant.

To Julia Dent Grant

St. Paul, Minn. Billings M. T., Sept. 6th *1883*

DEAR JULIA;

We have had delightful weather and much to see. The country through which we have passed is fertile and is settling up beyond all conception. From the time we struck Dacota to this point in Montana towns have sprung up all along the road varying in population from five hundred to as many thousand. The country will send out this year many million bushels of wheat and several train loads—of forty cars each—of cattle, daily from now until the close of shipping season next year. To-day, some sixty miles further west, we have the Indian war dance.[1] The programme I left you will shew where we are daily.—Love to all.

yours

U. S. GRANT

This is my third letter.

ALS, USG 3. Written on letterhead of the Northern Pacific Railroad Co.

On Sept. 4, 1883, USG spoke at Fargo, Dakota Territory. "I came out here to be impressed but I see greater evidences of enterprise in your city and prosperity in your country than I anticipated, and all promise great things for the future. Although I have crossed the United States much and visited nearly every territory as well as state, this is the first time I have ever set my foot on Dakota soil. I am glad to be on so solid and substantial a foundation. I do not like to make a speech, but I would like to shake hands with all of you but the time is too short. It is but a few years since it seemed as if I shook hands with every man, woman and child in this country. Thanking you for your kindness I beg leave to retire." *Daily Argus* (Fargo and Moorhead), Sept. 5, 1883.

On Sept. 5, USG spoke at a ceremony to lay the cornerstone of the new capitol in

Bismarck. "Ladies and gentlemen: It is with some reluctance I respond to your kind request, as you are aware from your reading, when I get to talking before a crowd I scarcely know when to quit. I am sure when I do stop to tell you of my feelings and the sights I have seen, the train would not get off on time. I never set foot in Dakota till yesterday. I had read much of your country, but I was not prepared to see what my own eyes have witnessed. With Mr. Evarts, I predict for you a prosperous future. In a few years you will rank far above the best of the states, and perhaps their representatives will see it unless congress hasten to admit you, when the next census is taken." *Ibid.*, Sept. 6, 1883.

On Sept. 7, USG responded to calls for a speech at Bozeman, Montana Territory. "Now boys, you should remember that this is not a campaign year." *Bozeman Avant-Courier*, Sept. 13, 1883, quoted in Edward W. Nolan, "'Not Without Labor and Expense:' The Villard-Northern Pacific Last Spike Excursion, 1883," *Montana: The Magazine of Western History*, 33, 3 (Summer, 1983), 5–9.

On Sept. 8, a correspondent reported USG's speech near Helena during ceremonies marking completion of the Northern Pacific Railroad. "He said he was reminded by the speeches to which had listened of the fact that he had had something to do with the great Northern Pacific enterprise. When Governor Stephens, thirty years ago, organized a surveying expedition he was lieutenant acting quartermaster commissary on the Columbia and he issued supplies for the expedition. Was he not then entitled to some of the credit which Mr. Billings had apportioned out to others? It was true while Mr. Billings contributed of his own money he paid out Uncle Sam's. This sally greatly pleased the audience, largely made up of veterans, who became perfectly wild when he said that the[s]e inter-colonial railways would have amounted to little but for the men who after the war sought the territories as fields of enterprise. They had made these railways possible and prosperous." *Daily Argus* (Fargo and Moorhead), Sept. 10, 1883. See *Harper's Weekly*, XXVII, 1396 (Sept. 22, 1883), 596, 603; *ibid.*, XXVII, 1397 (Sept. 29, 1883), 622; Katharine Villard Seckinger, ed., "The Great Railroad Celebration, 1883: A Narrative by Francis Jackson Garrison," *Montana: The Magazine of Western History*, 33, 3 (Summer, 1983), 18–23; Charles Russell, *Diary of a Visit to the United States of America in the Year 1883*, Charles George Herbermann, ed. (New York, 1910), pp. 59–61, 70–75, 108–9; Oswald Garrison Villard, *Fighting Years: Memoirs of a Liberal Editor* (New York, 1939), pp. 55–58; Robin W. Winks, *Frederick Billings: A Life* (New York, 1991), 259–60.

On Sept. 13, a correspondent reported from Portland, Ore. "Gen. Grant, Mr. Evarts, and others of the Villard party left this morning for Cascade. From there they will go directly East." *New York Times*, Sept. 14, 1883.

    1. Performed by Crow Indians.

To Thomas H. Taylor

Chicago, Sept. 19th *1883*

Gen. T. H. Taylor;
Dear General:

    I have just reached Chicago on my way East and find your letter of the 15th inst. inviting me to go by the way of Louisville to be present at the unveiling of the Statue to the old Hero, General Z. Taylor. It was my good fortune to serve under General Taylor, and very near to him, for a year before hostiliti[es] in the war with Mexico began and the first year of the war. There was no man living who I admired and respected more highly,1 and I would be glad to shew my respect for him now by witnessing the unveiling of the statue to his memory. But it will be impossible, ~~now~~. I am just winding up a long trip by rail, and my baggage is in a special train which leaves in a couple of hours with myself and party for New York.

In your letter to Mr. Palmer—to which this is an answer—I do not gather whether you received a reply to your formal invitation sent to me in New York? I received the invitation and my recollection is that I answered it to the effect that I would attend if back from the West in time. If you received no such answer please accept this as my apology.

                              Very Truly yours
                              U. S. GRANT

ALS, General Grant National Memorial, New York, N. Y. Written on stationery of the Palmer House. On June 4, 1883, a correspondent reported from Louisville. "... Yesterday Gen. Taylor, who is a near relative of President Taylor, invited Gen. Grant to attend the unveiling. The ex-President said he would be present if possible . . . ." *New York Times*, June 5, 1883. See *ibid.*, Sept. 21, 1883; *PUSG*, 30, 135.

1. In 1882, the Post Office Dept. issued a new five cent stamp honoring James A. Garfield, replacing one picturing Zachary Taylor. "... When the rates for international postage had been decided upon as 5 cents, the United States series of postage stamps had not such a value. Mr. Jewell, the Postmaster-General at the time, suggested to President Grant the propriety of having his portrait on the new stamp of the required value. Gen. Grant did not agree with his Cabinet officer. Finally, he suggested that if Mr. Jewell would insist upon consulting his wishes he (Gen. Grant) would be well pleased if the portrait of old Zach Taylor, with whom he served in the Mexican war, could be used on the new stamp . . . ." *New York Times*, April 3, 1882.

To Henry Coppée

———

                              N. Y. Sept. 26th /83

MY DEAR PROFESSOR COPPÉE

Inclosed I send you my check for my place at the Aztec dinner. I regretted not being there. But the trip over the North Pacific

road I found a compensation for all the privations and hardships of
the journey. The resources of the country along that line surpass
any thing I had imagined from all the glowing accounts I had read
or heard before starting.

Very Truly yours
U. S. GRANT

ALS (facsimile), Steven L. Hoskin, Civil War Autographs, no. 4604. The Aztec Club
held its annual dinner on Sept. 14, 1883, in New York City.

On Aug. 14, 1884, USG wrote to Henry Coppée, professor, Lehigh University,
from Long Branch, declining an invitation. "I am still very lame, and the prospects are
that I will remain so for many months yet . . . I require so much attention in dressing
and undressing I can not very well go out to remain overnight . . ." Paul C. Richards
Autographs, Catalogue No. 59 [1970], no. 23.

To Clara V. Cramer

New York City,
Sept. 27th 1883.

MY DEAR CLARA;

On my return from a trip over the North Pacific rail-road, to
the Pacific coast last Friday,[1] I found you excellent and welcome letter, with enclosures. Your Aunt was very much pleased with your
letter and poetry as well as with your essay. They all do you great
credit and I think you can well sustain yourself as a writer with
any young lady of your age in this or any other land.

My trip over the Northern route to the Pacific about completes
my personal observation of every part of our country. I was not
prepared to see so rich a country or one so rapidly developing.
Across the continent where but a few years ago the Indian held
undisputed sway there is now a continuous settlement, and every
ten ofr fifteen miles a town or city, each with spires of the school
house and the church. The soil for almost the entire distance is as
fertile as that of Illinois. I saw your Aunt Jennie[2] yesterday. She is
quite well. All my family are well and join in love to you. I think
neither your Aunt or I will ever visit Europe again. We may however change our mind But we are getting a little to old to enjoy

traveling, and then we have such pleasant homes for both Summer and Winter.

Love to your father and Mother.

yours Truly
U. S. GRANT

ALS, ICarbS. Born on Oct. 17, 1864, in Covington, Ky., Clara V. Cramer was the oldest child of USG's sister Mary. See letter to Clara V. Cramer, June 10, 1884.

1. Sept. 21, 1883.
2. USG's sister Virginia Grant Corbin.

To Ellen Grant Sartoris

New York City,
Oct. 2d 1883

DEAR DAUGHTER:

On the 21st prox. I got back from my trip to the Pacific coast, over the North Pacific road, just completed. The country through which this road passes is wonderful. I had previously been across the continent by one other road, and partially across by other routes. But little agriculture is possible along them after the foot hills are reached until well down on the other side. But by this route it is wonderfully rich all the way and is settled with little towns—some of them running up in to the thousands of population, with horse cars, streets lit with gas, daily papers, and large hotels—and big farms, making it possible to drive from one end of the road to the other with a team without camping out a single night.

Your Ma & I returned yesterday from a three days visit to Fred & Ida at Morristown, N. J. They are as happy as doves. The children are growing finely[1] and are begining to speak French. Fanny has a little son and Buck is very happy.[2] Jesse and Lizzie are still with us; but they have a flat on 26th Street ready to move into.[3] This will leave your Ma & I alone with only Bessie.[4] I do not know what your Ma would do without her. She is very smart and full of character. You see if you and Algie, with all the children,[5] come over we will have room a plenty for you.

With love to you, Algie & the children from all of us,

yours Affectionately

U. S. GRANT

P. S. Instead of sending a draft I send you my cheque which Mr. Morgan,[6] Seligman[7] or any other banker, will cash for you.

U. S. G.

ALS, ICHi.

1. Julia Grant, seven, and Ulysses S. Grant 3rd, two.
2. Chaffee Grant, born Sept. 28, 1883, joined a daughter, Miriam, recently two.
3. See letter to Ellen Grant Sartoris, Dec. 15, 1883.
4. USG's niece Elizabeth B. Sharp.
5. Algernon E., Vivien M., and Rosemary A. Sartoris, then six, four, and nearly three.
6. Junius S. Morgan.
7. J. & W. Seligman & Co. operated an office in London.

To Society of the Army of the Cumberland

NEW YORK, *October* 8, 1883.

GENTLEMEN:

I am just in receipt of your circular, inviting me to be present at the meeting of the *Society of the Army of the Cumberland,* on the 25th of October, instant. I am sorry that it will not be in my power to attend, although I should be very glad to meet the Society, and hope that I may have an opportunity on some future occasion; but, as I have accepted an invitation to attend the meeting of the *Society of the Army of the Tennessee,* on the 17th and 18th of this month,[1] I will not be able to leave home so soon after to attend your Reunion. Wishing for the Society of an army that rendered such distinguished services as the *Army of the Cumberland* did during the crisis of a civil war, a pleasant and profitable Reunion, and many returns of the same, with full ranks, I am,

Very truly,

U. S. GRANT.

Local Executive Committee
Of the Society of the Army of the Cumberland,
Cincinnati, Ohio.

Society of the Army of the Cumberland, Fifteenth Reunion, Cincinnati, Ohio, 1883 (Cincinnati, 1884), pp. 156–57. For a partial rendering of the circular, dated Oct. 5, 1883, and a facsimile invitation, see *ibid.*, pp. 14–15.

On Oct. 6, USG responded to the toast "Pro Patria" at a dinner for veterans of the 7th N. Y. Militia. " . . . We who had an active part to take in that war remember that it was the Seventh Regiment, composed of men of standing in the community, that went as a body, I believe—I was from the West, but I understand you went in a body—down to Washington when the capital was threatened, and that many who went as privates afterward finished as Generals. Many became commissioned officers—proba[*b*]ly 600 or 700 from your own single organization. I presume that it was not at all a matter of favor or because the Seventh was a crack regiment, but rather of merit. I know that many did distinguish themselves, and they made a great deal of that history which has been alluded to. Without the services of the volunteers, who practically composed the entire army, we would have had no history to speak about to-day. We have, and have had, a little band called the regular army. It was a most creditable body, and furnished men who helped you in making this history, but as an army by itself it would not be able to fight in any great war. The Government of the United States, however, has an army, and a grand army, which can meet any foe that can be brought against it. And that army is composed of the independent, intelligent, thinking, reflecting citizen, who, when he points his gun, knows not only at what he is pointing it, but why he is pointing it at his fellow human being. This is what makes the great Army of the United States. This is the organization of which the Seventh is an honorable part, forming a nucleus possessed of sufficient experience for the first onset. As wars progress these become the schoolmasters to educate others up to their standard, while they advance to a higher one. I will close by expressing the hope that you will keep up your organization, so as to be prepared to meet an enemy when he comes again: but I hope that there will never be an enemy who will have the temerity to attack us." *New York Times,* Oct. 7, 1883.

1. See letter to Mortimer D. Leggett, Oct. 13, 1883.

To Elizabeth King

New York City,
Oct. 10th 1883.

My Dear Mrs. King:

I am just in receipt of your letter of the 7th inst. Before its receipt I was not aware that Chilt. White had been a widower.[1] I have a great desire to visit Georgetown again but some how when I can get away I am called elswhere. Next week I go to Cleveland,[2] but [⸺ ⸺ ⸺] call me immediately back.—You are right in supposing that I am to busy to be punctual in my correspondence. If it was not that I keep a Stenographer to whom I can dictate answers to the great majority of letters received I could not get through.

Mrs. Cramers address is Mrs. Mary G. Cramer, Care U. S. Minister, Berne, Switzerland.

Please give my kindest regards to all my Georgetown friends.

Yours Truly
U. S. GRANT

ALS (mutilated), provided by Candace Scott, Victorville, Calif.

1. USG's childhood friend Chilton A. White joined the Ohio vols. during the Mexican War, practiced law in Georgetown, and served as Democratic U.S. Representative (1861–65). His wife died on Aug. 2, 1881. See *Memoirs*, I, 29–30; Carl N. Thompson, comp., *Historical Collections of Brown County, Ohio* (Ripley, Ohio, 1969), pp. 660–61, 696–97, 1123–24.

2. See letter to Mortimer D. Leggett, Oct. 13, 1883.

To David W. Lusk

New York City
Oct. 10th 1883.

DEAR SIR.

I have your letter of the 4th inst. with enclosures. I have no suggestions to make, or changes to ask in regard to what you say in the article which is herewith returned. I am much obliged to you for what you say though I have never felt the slightest concern for myself through all the abuse that has been heaped upon me. I was of course much annoyed that such things could happen as did while I was the Executive of the Nation. I was probably too unsuspecting.

Very Truly yours
U. S. GRANT

D. W. LUSK, ESQR
P. S. Please put me down for a copy of your book.

U. S. G.

ALS (facsimile), D. W. Lusk, *Politics and Politicians of Illinois*, . . . 2nd ed. (Springfield, 1886), between pp. 312–13. David W. Lusk, former Ill. state printer and newspaper publisher, was then preparing *Politics and Politicians: A Succinct History of the Politics of Illinois from 1856 to 1884*, . . . (Springfield, 1884). The chapter on USG (pp. 280–89) praised his Civil War exploits, castigated those who attempted to link him to the Whiskey Ring, and denounced John McDonald's *Secrets of the Great Whiskey Ring* (Chicago, 1880), as an effort to derail USG's bid for a third term. See letter to David W. Lusk, Nov. 19, 1884; *Illinois State Journal*, Oct. 28, 1889.

To Mortimer D. Leggett

New York City,
Oct. 13th 1883.

MY DEAR GENERAL LEGGETT;

I regret very much to announce to you that I will not be able to attend the re-union next week after all. I am very sorry to miss the opportunity of meeting the Veterans of my first Army command—in fact the veterans of the only Army I ever did command directly in person—but on my return from my recent trip I caught a very severe cold. I have thought nothing of it until within the last few days. It has settled into a form to make my family feel that it is necessary to do something to throw it off. In the mornings I am comparitively well; but towards evening I become so hoarse as to be scarsely able to speak. I do not think under the circumstances it would be prudent to take so long a trip by rail.

I am much obliged to you for your invitation to myself and son to be your guests on the occasion of the Army re-union, and regret that neither of us will be there to avail ourselves of your hospitality.

Very Truly yours
U. S. GRANT

ALS, University of California, Santa Barbara, Calif. On Aug. 10, 1883, USG wrote to Mortimer D. Leggett, Cleveland. "Your letter of the 1st inst inviting me to be present at the meeting of the Society of the Army of the Tennessee, on Oct 17th 18th is received, and in reply I will say that while it would afford me much pleasure to attend I will not be able to do so inasmuch as I am going to the Pacific coast about Sept. 1st and your meeting will be so early after my return that I would hardly like to go away again. Thanking you for the kind invitation . . . " LS, *ibid.* Leggett oversaw reunion arrangements. See *Report of the Proceedings of the Society of the Army of the Tennessee, at* the *Sixteenth Meeting, Held at Cleveland, Ohio, October 17th and 18th, 1883* (Cincinnati, 1885); telegram to William E. Strong, Oct. 19, 1883.

To Ivers J. Austin

———

New York, Oct 16 *1883*

I. J. AUSTIN ESQ.
NEWPORT R. I.
DEAR SIR:

Your letter of the 14th inst in relation to the services of Col Crafts J Wright at Donelson and Shiloh, is received. Col. Wright was not with me in the engagements about Forts Henry & Donelson. At least I do not remember him there, and I think I remember all field officers who were. My recollection is that he joined my command at Shiloh and served directly under Gen Sherman. I did not see much of him and cannot therefore give anything, from personal knowledge or acquaintance that would be authentic.

Truly Yours
U. S. GRANT

LS (facsimile), RWA Inc. Auction Catalog No. 39, June 2, 1996, no. 787. Ivers J. Austin, USMA 1828, soon resigned and practiced law in Boston. Austin's obituary of his USMA classmate, Crafts J. Wright, is in *Annual Reunion, United States Military Academy* (1884). For Wright, see *PUSG*, 4, 373–74, 453–55; *ibid.*, 5, 281–82.

To Edward F. Beale

———

New York City,
Oct. 17th 1883.

MY DEAR GEN. BEALE:

Mrs. Grant asks me to write inviting you, Mrs. Beale & Emily to come next Thursday—to-morrow week—and visit us. If you want to come yourself before to see the horse show come directly to our house. I do not invite Mrs. Beale and Emily before because we will have Fred & his family with us the fore part of the week. But there is always room to stick in a bachilor. If the family can not come at the time designated please fix your own time between now and January.

With best regards to all your family,

Very Truly yours
U. S. GRANT.

ALS, DLC-Decatur House Papers.

To William E. Strong

NEW-YORK, Oct. 19, 1883.

Gen. William E. Strong, Army of the Tennessee, Cleveland:

Please thank the society for the compliment of selecting me as orator for next reunion,[1] but excuse me. I should be unhappy for a whole year if I knew that such an ordeal awaited me at the next reunion. I regret exceedingly not being with you on this occasion, but I hope to be with you next year.

U. S. GRANT.

New York Times, Oct. 30, 1883 (reprinted from *Cincinnati Commercial Gazette*). Trained as a lawyer in Wis., William E. Strong served as a staff officer in the Army of the Tennessee (1863–65) and inspector gen. of the Freedmen's Bureau (1865–66) before managing a Chicago lumber co. On Wednesday, Oct. 24, 1883, Strong, Chicago, wrote to Andrew Hickenlooper, Cincinnati. " . . . After consulting with Gens. Sherman, Logan, and Leggett, it was thought best I should write to Gen. Grant upon my return to Chicago, urging him to reconsider the matter, which I did on Saturday last . . . ." *Ibid.* On Oct. 23, USG telegraphed to Strong. "Your letter received. Under all the circumstances I feel compelled to accept the responsibility put upon me by the Society of the Army of the Tennessee" Copy (quoted in Strong to Gen. William T. Sherman, Oct. 23, 1883), DLC-William T. Sherman. On Oct. 26, Sherman wrote to Strong. "Yours of the 23d is received and I congratulate you on your Eminent Success in prevailing on Gnl Grant to make an Oration next Summer at Minnetonka. It will attract a vast Crowd. I will see the General abt Novr 5–6 at his house in Nyork and will of course tell him of my own gratification &c." ALS (facsimile), Swann Galleries, Inc., Public Auction Sale 1836, Oct. 14, 1999, no. 36. See letter to Andrew Hickenlooper, July 19, 1884.

1. See *Report of the Proceedings of the Society of the Army of the Tennessee, at the Sixteenth Meeting, Held at Cleveland, Ohio, October 17th and 18th, 1883* (Cincinnati, 1885), p. 470.

To Edward F. Beale

———

New York City,
Oct. 22d 1883.

MY DEAR GENERAL BEALE:

Your letter of yesterday was received this morning. Mrs. Grant wants me to say that she wants Mrs. Beale and Emily—you too—to come up any time between this and Jan.y 1st, if Mrs. Beale is able, and she hopes she will be. We expect to visit Washington in January, and will of course, go to your house first. We may not go just at the time designated in one of your letters, but will give you timely notice.—I wish you would run up one day to see the "Horse Show." If you do, telegraph me in advance so that I may have no engagement.

Give our love to all your family, you included.

Yours Truly
U. S. GRANT

ALS, DLC-Decatur House Papers. See letter to Edward F. Beale, Oct. 17, 1883.

To George W. Childs

———

New York City,
Oct. 22d 1883.

MY DEAR MR. CHILDS:

Mrs. Grant asks me—with my hearty concurrence—to write to you and Mrs. Childs to come and visit us this Autumn,—at any time you may designate. We want Miss Peterson[1] to come with ~~with~~ you. Miss Sharp will be good company for her while we sedate old people are discussing matters that can have but little attraction for them. Of course Mrs. Grant will want to talk about fFall styles of wraps, bonnets, how this one dressed at church last Sunday &c. This could not interest the young people. Their reflections will be on more solid matter such as Cesars campaigns, Napoleons & Wellingtons battles, the next National election in our own country, the probable result to the country of a victory by either party; how the tariff is to be effected if the democrats come in, and how Worths dresses will cost if free trade prevails—Mrs. Childs and Mrs. Grant will prick up their ears at this point. Well, I give up the subject and ask you to say when you can come, and stay as long as you please. Between this and Jan.y 1st we are not expecting any other company, except Fred. & his family may come sometimes for a day or two, and General Beale and family will spend a week with us if Mrs Beales health permits, which it does not now. Tell Mr Drexel we wish, when he runs over here, he would come and stop with us. We always have room for a bachilor no matter what company we may have at the time, and of course we would only be to much pleased to have Mrs. Drexel if she comes also. We know she is not going out, but she can be as quiet as she pleases at our house.

    With kindest regards of Mrs. Grant & myself to Mrs. Childs,

Very Truly yours
U. S. GRANT

ALS, DLC-USG.

1. Probably George W. Childs' niece, Mary Peterson, then in her early twenties.

To Adam Badeau

N. Y. Oct. 25th /83

DEAR BADEAU:

    I have your letter of yesterday. I write because of your allusion to hearing a rumor that Blaine and I had formed a combination politically. You may deny the statement most peremptorily. I have not seen Blaine to speak to him since a long time before the Convention of /80. We have had no communication in writing, through other parties nor in any direct or indirect way. The republican party cannot be saved, if it is to be saved atall, by tricks and combinations of politicians. I read yesterday a circumstantial account of Blaine & I spending a week or two to-gether recently when without doubt we had fixed up matters for /84, Blaine to be President and I Senator from this state. The republican party to be saved must have a decisive declared policy. It has now no observable policy except to peddles out patronage to soreheads in order to bring them back into the foal, and avoid any positive declaration upon all leading questions.[1] I hope you may be able to get your paper before the President and Secretary of State, and that they may be induced to take strong and declared grounds on the subject it treats of.[2]

We are all well.

yours Truly

U. S. GRANT

P. S. Sheridan may be in Washington when you receive the proof sheets of your Article.[3] If so get him to review for you all of it prec[e]ding his appointment a Colonel.

U. S. G.

ALS, Munson-Williams-Proctor Institute, Utica, N. Y. In late Oct., 1883, Adam Badeau, consul gen., Havana, then on leave, stayed in New York City at the Brevoort House. *New York Times*, Oct. 29, 1883.

1. See *Badeau*, pp. 344–47; *PUSG*, 30, 126–28.
While visiting Philadelphia in late Nov., USG spoke to a reporter. "New-York is certainly Republican when the party is undivided, and I don't see anything just now to divide it. It is idle even to hazard a guess at the probable Republican candidate for President . . . . Ohio is still Republican in a Presidential year, and Pennsylvania is sure. Therefore the outlook is very promising for next year's contest . . . . There is considerable talk of [*Samuel J. Tilden*] in New-York as the one man who can carry the State, but can he? Are his friends not too sanguine?" *New York Times*, Nov. 28, 1883.
2. "The paper spoken of recommended an absolute protection by the Government of American citizens and American interests in the Island of Cuba. General Grant was strongly in favor of my views, but the Administration took a course diametrically opposite to that which I proposed. The result was the Spanish Treaty, which was so universally condemned by the country, and so ignominiously defeated in Congress in 1884." *Badeau*, pp. 551–52.
3. See Adam Badeau, "Lieut.-General Sheridan," *Century Magazine*, XXVII, 4 (Feb., 1884), 496–511. Badeau later asserted that USG "furnished some entirely new and very interesting material for the article." *Badeau*, p. 552.

To Fitz John Porter

New York, *November* 3, 1883.

Dear General: As there is some discussion as to the probable reasons for my change of mind in regard to your case, now pending before the people of the United States, I deem it proper that I should give them myself.

In the first place I never believed you to be a traitor, as many affected to believe. I thought I knew you too well to believe for one moment that you would accept the pay, rank, and command you held for the purpose of betraying the cause you were professing to serve. Then, too, your services had been too conspicuous as a staff officer at the beginning of the war and as commander of troops later, to support such a theory for a moment.

But I did believe that General Pope was so odious to some of the officers in the East that a cordial support was not given him by them. I was disposed, too, to accept the verdict of a court-martial composed as the one which tried you was. Some of the members of that court I knew personally, and had great confidence in their judgment and justice.[1] I supposed you had shared in this feeling towards Pope, and while not more guilty than others you were unfortunate in being placed in a position where specifications could be made showing this hostility.

After the close of the war, when I was requested to read your new defense, I read it with the feeling above described.[2] At the same time I read the other side as prepared—or furnished—by General Pope. This gave maps showing the positions of the two armies substantially as shown by the first of the diagrams presented by Mr. Lord, of San Francisco, from whom I copied in the article in your case,[3] and did not indicate the presence of any other force than Jackson's. Then, too, it appeared that you had actually received an order at about 5 or 5.30 in the afternoon of August 29 to attack the enemy's flank, and that, too, at a time when a fierce battle was raging in the front.

I was first shaken in my views, however, when such a man as

General Terry, who unites the lawyer with the soldier, a man of
high character and ability, and who had believed as I had, and possibly worse, after many weeks of investigation should entirely vindicate you, and be sustained too by men of the known ability of his
colleagues on the board.[4]   Until in 1881, when I re-examined for
myself,[5] my belief was that on the 29th of August, 1862, a great
battle was fought between General Pope, commanding the Union
forces, and General Jackson commanding the Confederate forces;
that you, with a corps of twelve or more thousand men, stood in
a position across the right flank of Jackson and where you could
easily get into his rear; that you received an order to do so about
5 or 5.30 o'clock, which you refused to obey because of clouds of
dust in your front, which you contended indicated an enemy in superior force to you; that you allowed Pope to get beaten while you
stood idly looking on, without raising an arm to help him. With
this understanding, and without a doubt as to the correctness of it,
I condemned you.

Now, on a full investigation of the facts, I find that the battle
was fought on the 30th of August; that your corps, commanded
directly by you in person, lost a greater percentage than any other
corps engaged; that the 4.30 order of the day before did not reach
you until night-fall; that your immediate superior[6] had cautioned
you early in the day that you were too far out to the front then; that
General Pope had cautioned you against bringing on an engagement except under such circumstances as he described, and that in
any event you must be prepared to fall back behind Bull Run that
night, where it would be necessary for you to be to receive supplies;
that from 11 o'clock of the 29th you were confronted by a force of
twice your own number, of whose presence you had positive proof,
while General Pope did not know of it.

This last fact is shown by the wording of the 4.30 order. It
directed you to attack the enemy's right and to get into his rear.
General Pope's circular of the morning of the 29th said that General Lee was advancing by way of Thoroughfare Gap. At the rate
at which he was moving he would be up the night of the 30th or
the morning of the 31st.

In his testimony before the court-martial which tried you he said, under oath, that he did not know of the arrival of Lee's command until 6 o'clock of the 29th, an hour and a half after he had dictated the order for your attack.

His circular and testimony prove conclusively that Jackson, and Jackson alone, was the enemy he intended you to attack. Your knowledge of this fact, as well as of the fact that you had another force, quite double yours, in addition in your front, would have been sufficient justification for your not attacking, even if the order had been received in time. Of course this would not apply if a battle had been raging between Jackson and Pope. At the hour you received the order all was quiet.

This very short, hastily written and incomplete summary shows why and when my mind underwent a change. I have no doubt now but the change would have taken place in 1867 if I had then made an investigation. I regret now that I did not understand your case then as I do now. Your whole life since your trial, as well as your services before, disprove the great burden of the charges then sustained by a court-martial. As long as I have a voice it shall be raised in your support without any reference to the effect upon me or others. Your restoration to the Army, simply, I would regard as a very inadequate and unjust reparation. While men—one at least—have been restored to the Army because of their gallantry and wounds, after conviction and sentence, and when there is no doubt of their guilt are given all their pay for the years they were out of the service, I can see no reason for your having less.

I hope for you a thorough vindication, not only by Congress but in the minds of your countrymen.

Faithfully yours,
U. S. GRANT.

General F. J. PORTER, *Morristown.*

HRC, 48-1-1, 3–4, 49-1-42, 3–4; SRC, 48-1-74, 32–33, 49-1-195, 33–34. On [*Nov. 3, 1883*], USG wrote to Fitz John Porter. "I have hastily to-day drafted the inclosed, and without any papers before me to correct any statement that may lack a little in accuracy, I wish you would read it over, and if you see anything requiring change suggest it to me the first time you come to the City. If the letter is all right you can retain it as it is." *General Grant's Unpublished Correspondence in the Case of Gen. Fitz-John Porter* (n. p., n. d.), p. 17. On Nov. 10, Porter, Morristown, N. J., wrote to Henry J. Hunt, retired art. col. " . . . Grant was prompted by the desire to benefit me in writing that letter. I suppose after he commenced it, he saw Lord's criticism & availed of the chance to counteract it. Grant is true of heart when he knows he is right . . . ." ALS, Gilder Lehrman Collection, NHi. On Dec. 4, U.S. Representative Henry W. Slocum of N. Y. introduced USG's letter in the House of Representatives where it was referred to the Committee on Military Affairs. *CR*, 48-1, 31. See letter to Fitz John Porter, March 27, 1884.

1. See *O.R.*, I, xii, part 2 (Supplement).
2. See *PUSG*, 16, 550–51; *ibid.*, 17, 327–40.
3. See Theodore A. Lord, *A Summary of the Case of General Fitz-John Porter* (San Francisco, 1883), p. 62; *PUSG*, 30, 421–37.
4. Maj. Gen. John M. Schofield and Col. George W. Getty reviewed Porter's case with Brig. Gen. Alfred H. Terry (1878–79). See *SED*, 46-1-37.
5. See *PUSG*, 30, 268–71.
6. Maj. Gen. Irvin McDowell.

To Alphonso Taft

Sir;

I beg to present to you the bearer of this letter Le Chevalier Oscar Von Stahl[1] who is the representative in Vienna of the Equitable Life Assurance Society of the United States, of which Company I am a Director.

The interest I take in the progress of the European Agencies of the Equitable must be my apology for writing to you, and soliciting your influence in behalf of the Society.

The Equitable Life Assurance Society of the United States, is one of the most powerful and influential organizations in the world. Its business is transacted on the Purely Mutual Plan, and each policyholder, whether a resident of the United States or of some foreign country, becomes directly interested in its prosperity and success, and shares in the profits of the business.

The Society has for a number of years transacted a larger insurance business than any other company. Its business of last year was the largest ever transacted in a single year, and it expects to write no less a sum than seventy five million of dollars in 1883, a large increase over the preceding year.

The financial report of the Society showing the details of its property and business and all other necessary information can be furnished by Mr Von Stahl.

If you can render any service, or at any time have the opportunity of saying a word in behalf of the Society, it will be highly appreciated by me.

Yours truly
U. S. Grant

New York Nov 13th 1883
To Hon Alphonso Taft
Envoy Extraordinary and Minister Plenipotentiary of the United States of America
To Austria Hungary Vienna.

LS, DLC-William H. Taft. Henry B. Hyde, who founded the Equitable Life Assurance Society of the United States in 1859, appointed USG as a director in 1882. On Nov. 23 and Dec. 1, 1882, Hyde wrote to USG for help in establishing the society's business in Brazil and Guatemala. R. Carlyle Buley, *The Equitable Life Assurance Society of the United States 1859–1964* (New York, 1967), I, 291. On Nov. 24, USG wrote to Thomas A. Osborn, U.S. minister, Rio de Janeiro, asking that he promote the society to Emperor Pedro II of Brazil. *Ibid.*, pp. 462–63. On Feb. 15, 1883, Hyde wrote to USG requesting assistance with operations in Spain. *Ibid.*, p. 289. On June 19, 1884, Hyde wrote to USG. "It is with very great regret that I have to acknowledge the receipt of your resignation as Director of this Society. I beg to assure you the Society will always remember the uniform interest you have taken in its affairs and the aid you have given in advancing its interest whenever called upon to do so." *Ibid.*, p. 263.

1. See *ibid.*, pp. 418–19, 442–45.

To Patrick H. Winston, Jr.

New York City,
Nov. 15th 1883.

Patrick H. Winston, Jr. Esq.
My Dear Sir:

I am in receipt of your letter of the 12th inst, and also of the Winston Union Republican, containing your Address to the people of North Carolina—of the south in fack. I am much obliged to you for what you are pleased to say in your letter, but cannot say that I entirely agree with you. But I can speak more freely as to the address. I agree with every word in it. As it stands it would make a good platform for any party, North & South, with only additions touching some important National matters, such as building up our Merchant Marine; adopting a more positive foreign policy; repealing the compulsory coinage clause in the "Silver Bill;" and, as I thoroughly believe, a very much more stringent naturalization law. I believe that foreigners who come to our country to make it their home—and the home of their children,—should be put through such a course as to make them feel the value and importance of the boon conferred. The length of residence before acquiring full citizenship should be materially lengthened; the ailen becoming a citizen should be able to show good character, visable means of support and should be able to speak, read and write the English language. But protection to home industries, which you put so strongly, I regard as the most important plank in any platform after "The Union must and shall be preserved."

As you say in your letter you are an entire stranger to me. But both your letter and address are of such character that I feel no hesitation in thus writing to you.

Very Truly yours
U. S. GRANT

ALS, Museum of the Confederacy, Richmond, Va. Born in 1847, Patrick H. Winston, Jr., served in the C.S. Army, graduated from the University of North Carolina (1867), practiced law in Baltimore (1868–70), and returned to N. C. (1873). In 1883, he announced his switch from the Democrats to the Republicans in *"To the People of North Carolina,"* an extended condemnation of the Democratic party. " . . . There is no hope for the South under the sway of Democracy. It has ruined once and it will ruin again. It always aims to rule or ruin . . . ." *The North State* (Greensboro), Sept. 6, 1883. An editorial commending Winston, Jr., is *ibid.* See letter to Patrick H. Winston, Jr., Dec. 24, 1883; Samuel A. Ashe, ed., *Biographical History of North Carolina: From Colonial Times to the Present* (Greensboro, 1905–17), II, 450–59.

To Maj. Joseph R. Smith

New York City,
Nov. 23d 1883.

MY DEAR COL. SMITH:

I have your letter of the 17th inst. asking my endorsement for the Surgeon Generalcy. I am estopped from recommending any one for that position by a letter which I wrote to the Secretary of War soon after the death of General Crane. My endorsement had been solicited by several aspirants. I wrote to the Secretary saying so and suggested that if I had the appointment to make I should take the highest officer on the register who was qualified for the place. On the list of officers of high rank I did not consider Baxter because I his place was obtained by special legislation

Very Truly yours
U. S. GRANT

ALS, Ralph G. Newman, Chicago, Ill. For Maj. Joseph R. Smith, see *PUSG*, 7, 413–14; *ibid.*, 17, 249; *New York Times*, Feb. 12, 1911. After Surgeon Gen. Charles H. Crane died on Oct. 10, 1883, Col. Robert Murray was chosen to fill the vacancy. See *PUSG*, 30, 364–65.

To Philip C. Garrett

NEW-YORK CITY, Nov. 24, 1883.

DEAR SIR: I will not be able to accept your invitation to be present at the opening of the Peace Convention at 10:30 on Tuesday next[1] in Philadelphia. I will be in Philadelphia at the time. But as I go to attend a wedding in West Philadelphia at noon, I will not have the time.[2] As I must return to this City in the evening, I will not be able to attend the subsequent meetings. My views on the subject of peace arbi[t]ration in the settlement of international differences have not changed. But my hope of its speedy accomplishment has diminished. It is only be keeping the subject alive, however, that it can be accomplished.

Very truly yours.
U. S. GRANT.

PHILIP C. GARRETT, ESQ.

New York Times, Nov. 30, 1883. See *ibid.*, Nov. 28, 1883. Philip C. Garrett was a Philadelphia reformer and philanthropist.

1. Nov. 27, 1883.
2. See following letter.

To Ellen Grant Sartoris

New York City,
Nov. 24th 1883.

MY DEAR DAUGHTER:

I do not know when your Ma wrote to you, but knowing that a letter from home is always pleasant I write you now without having any thing special to say.

On ~~m~~Monday—day after to-morrow—there will be a mammoth celebration, it being the centennial of the evacuation of this city by *you* Britishers. All the vessels in the harbor will be decorated, and most of them will move in procession on the water. All the city organizations, Military, temperance, historical, and the thousand and one others, will move in procession in the streets. In the evening there will be dinner parties, and other gatherings, at which it will be told in glowing language *how we did it.* I will not be at this latter. Your Ma and I go on Monday afternoon to Philadelphia to be present at the wedding of Mae Drexel who is to be married at noon the following day.[1] In Jan.y we go to Washington for a few weeks, the first at Gen. Beales, the second at W. McLean's, and, if we stay longer, the balance of the time at the hotel. In February your Ma, Bessie[2] and I will go either to Nassau or Bermuda, thence to Havana and back by way of Florida, to remain absent until the wether gets pleasant the latter part of April. You, Algie and the children must come over then to make us a long visit. We will either remain quiet at Long Branch or will make an extended visit over the Northern Pacific R. R. thence down to San Francisco, back by one of the other roads, stopping in Colorado to see the places of interest there. We will have a good time anyway if we all have our health. You must not leave any of the children at home. We want to see all of them.

We are all well. Your brothers are all doing well and are happy. As a family we are much better off than ever we were before. The necessity for strict economy does not exist, or is not so pressing, as it has heretofore been.

Yours Affectionately,

U. S. GRANT

ALS, ICHi.

1. Mae E. Drexel married Charles Stewart. See *New York Times*, Nov. 24, 28, 1883; Karal Ann Marling, *George Washington Slept Here: Colonial Revivals and American Culture 1876–1986* (Cambridge, Mass., 1988), pp. 97–101.

On Nov. 22, 1883, USG wrote to Jacob D. Vermilye *et al.* "Yours of the 19th inst, kindly inviting me to be present at the seventy ninth Anniversary celebration of the New York Historical Society on Tuesday Evening Nov. 27th is received, and in reply I shall be much pleased to accept your kind invitation." LS, NHi. The Drexel wedding explained USG's failure to keep this promise.

2. USG's niece Elizabeth B. Sharp.

To Chester A. Arthur

―――――

New York City,
Nov. 28th 1883.

THE PRESIDENT:

I take the liberty of introducing Mrs. Mary Orr Earle, of Washington City. Mrs. Earle is the daughter of the Hon. Jas. L. Orr, of South Carolina whos public services you are familial with and who, you will probably remember, died while representing this country at the Court of St. Petersburg.[1] Mr Earle, the husband, was Asst. Dist. Atty. in South Carolina at the time I left the Executive office, and is, I believe a Southern native republican. I write this introduction to place Mr. Earle in the list of worthy applicants for the position of District Attorney, for the District of Columbia.

Very respectfully
your obt. svt.
U. S. GRANT

ALS, Gary Erickson, Wauwatosa, Wis. A report on the failure to appoint a U.S. attorney, D. C., stated that "the President has been directed to the subject several times during the last month, but he has hesitated to decide what to do . . . . Mr. William E. Earle, at one time in the Government service in South Carolina, who is spoken of with great respect as a lawyer of high character and legal attainments, has been recommended by some of the District lawyers. Mr. A. S. Worthington, formerly the partner of Edwin M. Stanton, is also urged for the place, . . ." *New York Times,* Jan. 15, 1884. On Jan. 21, 1884, President Chester A. Arthur nominated Augustus S. Worthington. See William E. Earle to Benjamin Harrison, Jan. 11, 1889, Earle to Elijah W. Halford, March 22, 1889, DLC-Benjamin Harrison.

1. See *PUSG,* 24, 108.

To Alfred R. Conkling

New York City,
Dec. 3d 1883.

DEAR SIR:

I have read over the advance sheets of your excellent Guide-book to Mexico, with great pleasure. It supplies a want now for the first time being felt. Mexico with all her resou[r]ces of soil climate and mines has not attracted much of the attention of people of other lands until within the last three or four years. Now with the rapid strides she is making—and is destined to make—towards a Commercial prosperity rarely equaled by any nation in the past, travel to that country will increase many fold, and your book will give the traveler the information he wants. Information is wonderfully condensed in it and I wonder at its completeness in so little space.

Very Truly yours
U. S. GRANT

ALFRED R. CONKLING ESQ.

ALS (facsimile), Alfred R. Conkling, *Appletons' Guide to Mexico* (New York, 1884). In a preface dated Nov. 1, 1883, New York City, Alfred R. Conkling, geologist, lawyer, and nephew of Roscoe Conkling, acknowledged the assistance of USG and several others. *Ibid.,* pp. iv–v. See letter to Daniel E. Sickles, Oct. 9, 1884; *New York Times,* Sept. 19, 1917.

To John A. Logan

New York City, *December* 4, 1883.

Dear Senator: I send you inclosed the petition of Col. James Belger, United States Army, retired, for restoration of pay and rank claimed to be unjustly, if not illegally, withheld from him.

May I ask that you will give the petitioner a hearing and such action as your judgment will approve of after due consideration. One fact stands out clear, that Colonel-Belger was tried by court-martial and acquitted honorably; that the findings of the court were not approved by the Secretary of War—I say the Secretary, because I do not believe he presented the case to the President—who then dismissed the prisoner by order. It seems his accounts were settled promptly, thus affording some evidence of the injustice of the dismissal.

Very truly yours,

U. S. Grant.

Hon. John Logan, *United States Senate.*

SRC, 48-1-661, 7, 49-1-1248, 7, 50-1-2136, 8, 51-1-330, 8, 52-1-716, 4, 52-2-1253, 9; HRC, 52-1-962, 9, 52-1-1786, 5. James Belger joined the army in 1832 and had risen from private to col., additional aide-de-camp, when dismissed as of Nov. 30, 1863, after a court-martial had acquitted him on thirteen specifications of improper supply and transportation procurement. Nominated by USG as maj., q. m., on March 3, 1871, Belger was retired in 1879. Appeals to Congress to raise his retirement rank from maj. to col. led to a law in 1893 to pay his widow the difference between the retirement pay of a maj. and a lt. col. See *New York Times*, Dec. 5, 1863; HED, 41-2-72; HRC, 41-2-109; CR, 49-1, 6818-19, 50-2, 1968-73; Fannie N. Belger to James A. Garfield, June 22, 1879, Jan. 28, 1880, DLC-James A. Garfield; *U.S. Statutes at Large*, XXVII, 825.

On Jan. 7, 1868, Judge Advocate Gen. Joseph Holt had written to USG, secretary of war *ad interim*, concerning Belger's case. LS, DNA, RG 94, ACP, B2273 CB 1867. The endorsement of Bvt. Brig. Gen. John C. Kelton is *ibid.* On Jan. 8, USG wrote to Attorney Gen. Henry Stanbery. "I have the honor to enclose a copy of General Order No 90, dated Head Quarters of the Army, Washington, November 11th 1867. revoking the order dismissing Major Belger, Quartermaster's Department U. S. Army, and to request your opinion if, under this order, Major Belger is now in service and may be assigned to duty. Major Belger, Quartermaster U. S. Army, and holding the appointment of Colonel and additional Aide-de-Camp under the act of August 5th 1861 was dismissed in 1863. Section 13th act of July 28th 1866 provides 'that as vacancies may occur in the grades of Major and Captain no appointment to fill the same shall be made until the number of Majors shall be reduced to twelve' &c &c There are now fifteen Quartermasters, with the rank of Major in service as authorized by the Section of the act quoted." LS, *ibid.*, RG 60, Letters Received, War Dept. On Jan. 15, Asst. AG

Edward D. Townsend wrote to Bvt. Maj. Gen. John A. Rawlins "that a legal question has been raised as to whether Colonel Belger is an officer of the Army by virtue of the order re-revoking his dismissal, which has not, as yet, been finally settled. The Judge Advocate General has expressed the opinion that Col. Belger cannot be considered as an officer of the Army, the order revoking his dismissal operating only in removing the stigma attaching to the same. The opinion of the Attorney General has been called for but has not, as yet, been received. No action has therefore been taken upon Colonel Belger's application for assignment to duty." LS, *ibid.*, RG 108, Letters Received. See Belger to John M. Schofield, June 8, 1868, *ibid.*, RG 94, ACP, B2273 CB 1867.

On April 2, 1870, Brig. Gen. Oliver O. Howard, Washington, D. C., wrote to USG. "You will remember the case of Col. James Belger. The Committee of Congress took up his case, and I learn declined to act on the ground of not interfering with the appointing power of the President. The order discharging Col. Belger was revoked & if the simple act of reappointment was needed to carry out the intention of the revocation ought it not to have been made? I know you will do what is *right* in the case. Mrs. Belger a christian wife & mother has the whole case at heart & I hope you may find time to see her." ALS, Cooke Collection, MiU-C; press, MeB. On the same day, Frederick T. Dent endorsed this letter for USG. "respectfully refered to the QM General for his opinion whether or not Col Belger should be renominated" AES, Cooke Collection, MiU-C. Also on April 2, Q. M. Gen. Montgomery C. Meigs endorsed this letter. " . . . I think not—" AES, *ibid.*

On April 20, Belger, Washington, D. C., wrote to USG at length. " . . . I devoted more than three years after my dismissal to the service of the government in settling my accounts as Quartermaster, services required, as the accounting officers of the Treasury certify, for which I have received no compensation. This great injustice I lay before you and appeal to your powers as Chief Magistrate and to your sense of what is due to me as a faithful officer, of the army, that I may no longer suffer under such grievous wrongs. As my case now stands, innocence is no shield and judicial and executive action in my behalf, no protection; for I was honorably acquitted and dishonorbly dismissed in the same case." Copy, DNA, RG 94, ACP, B2273 CB 1867. On April 21, Brig. Gen. Edward R. S. Canby, Washington, D. C., wrote to USG supporting Belger. Copy, *ibid.* On April 22, U.S. Representative Benjamin F. Butler of Mass. wrote to USG on the same subject. Copy, *ibid.* On June 21, Col. Thomas G. Pitcher, superintendent, USMA, wrote to USG. "During some one of your pleasant visits to West Point, since I have been stationed here, we had, I think, a discussion on Belgers case, and I believe I mentioned to you that I found he had in his employ at Baltimore in 1862 a man by the name of McFarland, who was a notorious rascal, whom he had with him in Texas before the War. I do not know that I should have ever thought of the matter again, had not Genl. Schenk called my attention to it, and stated that I stood in the way of Belger's restoration to the army. I told the Genl. that I was right, and should have sworn to it, to my dying day, had not Jo Minter, my brother-in-law, whom you may recollect as an officer of the 2nd Cavalry before the War, and who happened to be on a visit to us, set me right—After my interview with Genl: S. I came home, and mentioned the fact to Minter, who said at once, that I was mistaken, that the man I was thinking of was named Hovey, and it flashed across my mind at once, that in this respect I had done Belger great injustice. In short that I had confounded McFarland with Hovey, who had been a forage master and Storekeeper under Belger at San Antonio, and who had after defrauding the Government, disappeared between two days.—I feel that I have done Belger injustice in this matter, and now desire to set him right. I have written substantially, to this effect to Belger, through Genl Schenk." LS, *ibid.*

On July 1, Orville E. Babcock wrote to U.S. Representative Robert C. Schenck of Ohio. "The President directs me to return these papers in the case of Col. Belger, and to inform you that he had directed the Secretary of War to send in the name of Col. Belger, for confirmation if existing laws would permit. The President supposed an act had passed both houses of congress authorizing this, but is informed by the Secretary of War that such is not the case, and that Col. Belger cannot be restored under existing laws. The President directs me to inform you that if Congress will pass an act authorizing the restoration of Col. Belger he will most cheerfully, since the satisfactory investigation, send in his name for restoration." Copy, *ibid.* On July 16, U.S. Senator Henry Wilson of Mass. and three others wrote to USG. "The bill for the restoration of Major James Belger to the Army, having failed, for want of time, to receive the action of the Military Committee of the Senate, we, the undersigned, being fully satisfied of the strict integrity of Major Belger, request that your Excellency will give him some employment, or recommend him for some employment under the Government. The Major is entirely without means to support his family, not having sought employment because he was confident, after your letter of July 1st inst. addressed to General Schenck, that Congress would do him justice at once. As his case was unavoidably crowded out, we hope this request will meet with your favorable consideration" Copy, *ibid.* For legislation authorizing Belger's restoration to the army, see *CG*, 41–3, 1787, 1856–57; *U.S. Statutes at Large*, XVI, 584.

On Feb. 12, 1875, William S. Harney, Baton Rouge Barracks, La., wrote to USG. "*Personal* . . . I arrived here a few days since on business in relation to my brothers estate; and was met by Col. Belger, who kindly invited me to make his house my home, which I was glad to do. In conversation with him last evening I broached the subject of his position in the Qr. Mr. Department. The Col. replied that he would like to show me all the letters &c. in his possession relating to the matter. Now General, you know, I am sure, how averse I am to troubling you on any business matter; but upon my word, I think in this case you will feel deeply interested. I have carefully looked over all the letters and documents in relation to his (Col. Belgers) trial and Honorable acquittal &c. &c. The whole proceedings in his case, are the most remarkable that I have ever heard of in all my service of about fifty six years. I know there was a prejudice against him at one time, and I myself shared in it in some degree, but was soon fully satisfied that I and others were entirely wrong, and I went immediately to see Col. Stanton on the subject, and he said to me, after a long explanation, that, 'If I could I would restore Col. Belger to his position at once.' He was not able to go to see the President. I asked him if he could write to him he said he could not write, and had not been able to do so for some time, and asked me to go and say to the President what he (I) had said to me, (you) and I did so. Mr. Stanton also stated that 'from subsequent developments, he was convinced that he had done Col. Belger great wrong, and consequently wished him restored to his proper position.' From what I know of this case myself, and from letters received by Col. Belger, from gentlemen of the highest distinction, both civil and military, and one from yourself from Long Branch, of 25th of July '70, stating that Col. Belger 'was unjustly dismissed the service', I must say that I consider he has been most cruelly and shamefully treated in this whole matter, and I hope he may be restored to proper rank and all his rights, the same as if he had not been thus treated. Col. Belger has had a very hard time since he was so unjustly left out of the army. He has a large and very interesting family, and the expense of supporting them, and the paying of counsel have embarrassed him exceedingly, and I beg that you will do all you can to restore him to his rights. I called upon Judge Long, a day or two before I left, and he informed me that you would visit Saint Louis in April, &c. Now General, I have had my house fitted up better than it was when you were last in the city, and we will all be *most happy* to see you and your family, and Genl. Babcock and Mrs. Babcock, and I think we can accommodate one or two others very comfortably. Please make my kindest regards to Mrs. Grant, . . . P. S.—I have this moment been informed by Col. Belger, that Miss Nelly and her husband had arrived and *of course* they must come with you by all means, and we will make it as *home like* and as comfortable as possible." Copy, DNA, RG 94, ACP, B2273 CB 1867.

To Estelle M. Carnochan

New York City,
Dec. 11th 1883.

MRS. CARNOCHAN;
DEAR MADAM:

Last evening I found your card at my house expressing a wish to see me concerning your brother, Major Morris. I am very sorry I was out when you called. I have an office at 2 Wall street where I go usually as soon as breakfast is over, but am generally back by four in the afternoon. I have no doubt but I will be found at the house at the hour above named every day this week, and will be happy to see you there at any time it may suit you to call while I am in.

Very Truly yours
U. S. GRANT

ALS (facsimile), Heritage Auction Galleries, Auction No. 658 (April, 2007), lot no. 25155. Born in 1838, daughter of William W. Morris (USMA 1820), Estelle Morris married John M. Carnochan, a New York City physician, in 1856. Her brother, William G. Morris, served as marshal, Calif., under USG. See *PUSG*, 19, 336–37; *ibid.*, 24, 449; *New York Times*, Feb. 19, 1884.

To Ellen Grant Sartoris

New York City,
Dec. 15th 1883.

DEAR DAUGHTER:

Your Ma is intending to write to you to-day, but I do not know whether she will do so or not. Mr. & Mrs. Childs, with Miss Pe-

terson, are to arrive this noon, to spend some days with us.[1] They
coming may prevent her writing. We are all very well, and the
family are enjoying as much prosperity as we ought to expect.
Fred & Ida are as happy as clams, at high tide, in their home in
Morristown, N. J. They live very beautifully, see a great deal of
company and, as near as I can judge, are very popular. Morristown
is entirely a country residence place within an hour of the city. It is
on high ground, is very healthy, and the society is very good. Buck
and Fanny are in flats thinking to make their farm their principle
home. But I rather think they will buy a house either here or in
Washington. Mr. Chaffee will probably be the next Senator from
Colorado.[2] This may determine them to go there. Jesse is in the
Bella.[3] This leaves us alone with only Bessie.[4]—Buck has traded
off the Casey farm[5] for some houses in the city. The latter he will
sell as fast as he can.[6] I had paid $10.000 00 on the farm and con-
sequently have that much interest in the houses. I directed him,
when my money was coming, to put $2.500 00 in bonds for each
Julia, his little daughter, Vivian and Jesse's little girl. This is my
Christmas give to those four grand-daughters.[7]

I hope you and Algie will come over in the spring and spend
the summer with us. I wrote you this before; but I want to keep
you in mind of it.

Yours Affectionately

U. S. Grant

P. S. I am writing from my office down town and do not remember
your City address. I have therefore to address to Wars-ash.

U. S. G.

ALS, ICHi.

1. See letter to George W. Childs, Oct. 22, 1883.
2. Jerome B. Chaffee, father-in-law of Ulysses S. Grant, Jr., was not elected
senator.
3. An apartment building at 48 East 26th Street.
4. USG's niece Elizabeth B. Sharp. See letter to Ellen Grant Sartoris, Oct. 2,
1883.
5. James F. Casey sold his farm at Deer Park, N. Y., which included a potentially
valuable mineral spring, to his nephew Ulysses S. Grant, Jr., in 1882. See *New York
Times*, Dec. 14, 1881, May 28, 1882.
6. Grant, Jr., completed purchases of New York City property on Feb. 23

($165,000) and May 5 ($27,500), 1884; he sold property on May 6 ($27,500) and 8 ($300,000). See recorded real estate transfers in *ibid.*, Feb. 25, May 6–7, 9, 1884.

7. Julia Grant, Miriam Grant, Vivien M. Sartoris, and Nellie Grant.

Speech

[*Dec. 22, 1883*]

MR. PRESIDENT AND GENTLEMEN OF THE NEW-ENGLAND SOCI-ETY: I might very well say that this call is a surprise to me. I came here flattering myself that I should not have to make a single remark. Your vice-president notified me to-day that he wanted me to respond to a certain sentiment. I replied to him that I would not. I came here and found that notwithstanding what I had said, he had not entirely believed me, but said that he would be very much lost if he did not have an opportunity to make a speech, and he supposed that other people were like himself. I was called upon to my surprise. I came here this evening in fear and trembling lest I should be called upon, until I looked over this programme and found that I was omitted. So I have been sitting here and having a most enjoyable dinner, without fear of being called upon to speak; yet here I am the first to be called upon. I do not know whether General Woodford is responsible for this or not. If he is, and acknowledges that he promoted it, I shall have to hold him responsible; and I will settle with him outside. I attended the dinner of the New-England Society in Brooklyn, which started yesterday and ended to-day. I was called upon there to speak; and it is not to be supposed that a person is going to say much upon the same subject twice in the same day.

I did learn some facts in regard to the Pilgrims and the Puritans at the dinner last night and this morning, which if not entirely new to me, revived back memories. I learned from Colonel Beecher, of the 13th New-York National Guard, the difference between the Pilgrim and the Puritan.[1] He was sometimes a little confused in the course of his address, and sometimes used the word Pilgrim when he means Puritan, and Puritan when he meant Pilgrim; but still I was in such a condition that I knew perfectly well what he meant. It took the Colonel some fifteen minutes, I should think, to define the difference between the Puritan and the Pilgrim; but I gathered from all he said that the difference is about this: that a Pilgrim is a Puritan evolved. The Puritan came first; and we are improving as we go along. Anything which is evolved is better than that which preceded; and the Pilgrim is therefore better than the Puritan.

I was going to give the few notes that I had prepared for this occasion to Mr. Depew, who, as I discovered, was coming last in the speeches; but now I shall defer that, and will not give them to him. I was going to say to him that, inasmuch as he comes last, he might say whatever he pleased about those who had spoken before him; and that however roughshod he might tread upon them I did not care, for I did not suppose that I was to be one of those to speak before he did. In the note which I had written to him, but which I will not now send to him, I told him that I never felt badly when other people were abused, and not always when I was abused my-self. This being Saturday night, and there being some good speakers here, and all of them wanting to speak before Sunday morning, and some of whom would hardly survive over Christmas if they did not have an opportunity to get off their speeches, I will close by saying to this New-England Society of New-York that if you will invite me again the invitation will be accepted only on condition that I am not to be called upon to make a speech.

New York Tribune, Dec. 23, 1883. USG addressed a banquet at Delmonico's.

1. Born in 1813 in Conn., Henry Ward Beecher was the nation's foremost clergy-man, head of Brooklyn's Plymouth Church since 1847, and chaplain, 13th N. Y. Militia. On Dec. 21, 1883, Beecher told the Brooklyn New England Society that the Pilgrim and the Puritan were as "leaves and blossoms of the same plant. The Pilgrim, his-torically considered, and philosophically so, is nothing but a Puritan gone to bloom. They were at the root the same thing. One was a little more advanced than the other. The Pilgrim was a Puritan plus the Pilgrim, and the Pilgrim was a Puritan also." *Brooklyn Eagle*, Dec. 22, 1883. Earlier, Benjamin D. Silliman, society president, had addressed the hardiness of the Puritans, who "would recoil from the enervating luxury and wild extravagance which have taken the place of their homely living." *Ibid.* USG also spoke. "Mr. President and Gentlemen of the New England Society—You

would have saved me a great deal of nervousness and uneasiness if you had left me to appreciate without the toast the fact that I have always been cordially welcomed by the New England Society of Brooklyn. I have had proof before not only from the New England Society but from other citizens that on public occasions I have been made quite welcome, and while I thank you all for it, it would have been a great deal easier for me to have accepted your welcomes without having had to thank you. The fact is, I am so surrounded here by good speakers that I would like very much now to throw off on one of them—and I think I will allot my time to Major Beecher, one of the gentlemen who is fortunate in not having been born a hundred years earlier, as we have just learned from your president his present occupation as chaplain of a regiment would have rendered his life probably miserable. Gentlemen, I thank you, and will leave the balance of my time to Mr. Beecher to add to his." *Ibid.*

To Edwards Pierrepont

New York City,
Dec. 23d 1883.

DEAR JUDGE,

I return you Mr. Whitney's[1] letters. In one of them—the one I received yesterday—Mr. W. speaks of being in this city Friday or Saturday—yesterday or to-day. I did not know but you ~~and~~ would bring him to see me. I would like to talk to you about the matters referred in these letters. I should not like myself to send cablegrams to China in regard to sales of Arms. So far as Mexico is concerned I have always assured the authorities there that I was always ready to serve them in any way I could consistently, and without personal advantage to my self. This related more particularly to aid in funding their debt, but may well relate to all financial matters in which they are interested. If therefore I should say anything to Mr. Romero—or to any Mexican—about the sale of arms I should say that if a sale ~~was~~ is effected no doubt I would receive a handsome commission. Whatever that commission might be the Mexican Government should have the full benefit of. I will be glad to see you at my office any day you feel like calling, between 11 & 12 o'clock. Monday I may have business to take me out at the hour named, but I think not until after twelve.

Very Truly yours
U. S. GRANT

ALS, ICarbS. On Dec. 8, 1883, USG wrote to Edwards Pierrepont. "I am not interested in, nor do I know of, any other company making efforts to sell arms in foreign
countries . . . My desire has been to secure all the trade possible to our country with
these peoples. I am now about to ship two revolving guns, one to the Micado of Japan,
the other to Li Hung Chang, of China, purchased by me to send them as a present. I
have no contingent interest in the gun further than the two above mentioned." Charles
Hamilton Auction, No. 5, Oct. 8, 1964, p. 21; Carnegie Book Shop, Catalogue No. 286
[n. d.], no. 196. On Nov. 14, a correspondent had reported from Hartford. "Two machine guns have just been completed at Pratt & Whitney's works in this city for Gen.
Grant as presents to the Viceroy of China and the Mikado of Japan . . . ." *New York*
Times, Nov. 15, 1883. On Feb. 28, 1882, USG had praised a Pratt & Whitney weapon.
"I have examined, and seen tried the Pratt Whitney machine gun, of which Earl Dun-
more is the agent for Europe, and deem the best gun of the kind yet invented. It is
simple in its construction, less likely to get out of order and free from accidents, such
as premature explosions of its charge, getting cloged by cartridge cases etc. than any
other like gun . . ." ADS Autographs, May, 1989, no. 60.

On Jan. 26, 1884, John Russell Young, U.S. minister, Peking, wrote to USG.
"Yours of the 26th of November came in the latest mail,—only sixty-five days on the
way. I will, of course, be most delighted to bring the Whitney Arms people, or any one
you recommend to the attention of the Chinese government. Most of the purchases for
arms, are made, I learn, by the Viceroys at Canton, Nanking and Tientsin.—I know
that the Krupp people, who make the German artillery, have an agent in Tientsin, who
resides there, and who, represents, I think some small arms American interest too.
He is a German, who fought in Wauls army, and is said to have made a good deal of
money. I am told that he deals with the Tartars, and subordinates under the Viceroy,
and I presume there are arrangements within arrangements, by which it is possible for
the Chinese to pay money enough for an inferior arm, to allow a fair business profit all
around,—and perhaps more.—It might be well, I would suggest to the Whitney people,
or others having large interests they would care to develope in China, to have business
relations with some of the creditable houses here, or to deal through their own agents.
To be effective an agent should have some knowledge of the Chinese character, and
their ways of doing business. In Peking can practically be done, for the reason, which
I have mentioned, that all material preparations for war, are made by the Viceroys, and
the money is raised by them from local sources of revenue, opium, salt 'squeezes' and
so on.—I shall do all in my power to serve your friends, and any recommendation of
yours, will go far with the Chinese. I shall make special inquries of Li, as to what the
Chinese are really doing about arms, and whether there is such an out[l]ook as would
justify taking any steps towards seeking business with them.—Your letter only came
last evening, and I answer at once.—There seems to be a pause in affairs here. When
the French reinforcements are all out,—say in two months, you may expect any news
from China, the most peaceful or the most warlike.—Commend me to Mrs. Grant and
all at home, . . . " ALS, USG 3. On Sept. 10, Viceroy Li Hung-chang of Chihli, Tientsin, wrote to Young. "I had been expecting to see you at Tientsin, and for that reason have delayed speaking of the Pratt and Whitney machine Gun which I received
through you two months ago as a present from General Grant. Will you be so good as
to express to the General my sincere thanks for this handsome present. It is a beautiful specimen of accurate and skilful workmanship; the mechanism is extremely simple
and effective, and I have no doubt that the gun will be found equal in firing capacity to
any machine gun now in use and superior in many respects to some. I may have occasion later on to refer to this gun again.—Meanwhile I would beg the General to accept

my thanks for his kind remembrance of me—though I would assure him that the mere mention of his name arouses pleasant recollections of our friendship. My thanks are also due to you for your courtesy in connection with this present.—With assurances of my high regard . . . ." Copy, *ibid.*

On April 7, Prime Minister Itō Hirobumi of Japan had written to USG. "It is my pleasant duty to address you and to obey the commands of His Imperial Majesty the Emperor, who has bidden me to assure you of the great pleasure he has in accepting the gun you ordered expressly for presentation to him and that arrived here quite lately in perfect order. I am to say to you that this gun shall be preserved with the greatest care so that this sovenir of the distinguished donor, who once paid us a welcome visit and who has shown such an active and friendly interest in the prosperity of His Majesty, of his Empire and people, shall last forever. In conveying to you His Majesty's sentiments and acknowledgements, I am to further express to you his sincere wishes for the health and happiness of yourself and of your family. I take this opportunity of tendering to you the assurance of my highest consideration" LS, *ibid.* A letter of transmittal to USG, dated May 6, is *ibid.*

1. Mechanical engineers Amos Whitney and Francis A. Pratt formed Pratt & Whitney, a firm that became a leader in the manufacture of machine tools, weapons, and sewing machines. See *Accuracy for Seventy Years 1860–1930* (Hartford, 1930).

To Adam Badeau

New York City.
Dec. 24th 1883.

DEAR GENERAL:

I am in receipt—and have been several days—of your letter inclosing draft for $600 00.[1] I allso received your sketch of the battles in which The Army of the Tennessee participated. I am much obliged to you for it. If I conclude to write an address for the meeting of the Society next year, of the nature I spoke of, it will aid me greatly. In my indolence I may postpone the consideration of the subject until too late, and may then be compelled to say what I do say, extemporaneously.[2] But even in this case I would have the memorandum to refer to. I am afraid now that I will be deprived of the visit I had promised myself this Winter. You know we have a good corps of servants, carriages and three teams of horses and we do not like to leave the house and all these things to run themselves. We had expected Fred and his family to come and enjoy these things. But he says now that he cannot leave his own luxuries of the same sort. Unless Jesse will move into our house we will have to stay and watch them.

There is nothing new here since you left. It is now understood that there is no concealment of Arthur's candidacy. At this time no other person looms up so that unless there is a change within the next sixty days he will be re-nominated without much opposition. I feel however that he will not get the nomination although it is impossible to predict who may.—My family are all well and doing well.

Very Truly yours

U. S. GRANT

ALS, Munson-Williams-Proctor Institute, Utica, N. Y.

On Dec. 24, 1883, USG slipped on ice near his doorstep and injured his left leg. See *New York Times* and *New York Tribune*, Dec. 28, 1883. On Dec. 27, USG telegraphed to Adam Badeau, consul gen., Havana. "Painful but not dangerous." *Badeau*, p. 554. On the same day, Julia Dent Grant telegraphed to Edward F. Beale, Washington, D. C. "The General rested quietly last night. He is perfectly well except it hurts him to move his leg. The doctors have not yet said whether the leg is broken." Telegram received, DLC-Decatur House Papers. On Dec. 28, surgeons B. Fordyce Barker and Lewis A. Stimson examined USG, "and both agreed that there was no fracture ..." *New York Times*, Dec. 29, 1883.

On Feb. 11, 1884, Julia Grant wrote to William R. Rowley. "Yesterday, on returning from the theater (I mention this as I would not have been there had the Genl been ill), I received your very interesting letter, and hasten to answer it and assure you that, although, the General has met with a very serious accident which confines him to his room, we dont think of such as thing as his being an invalid, and surely expect him soon to be out. He walks from one end of the house to another on his crutches and receives visitors until ten and eleven o'clock at night. He has not yet been down stairs as his limb is still very sensative to any motion.—In regard to the newspaper clipping you sent, the author sent a note to the Genl: saying that he was going to Mexico. The General sent him word that he *would not* see him, not that he *could not*, but he had left the note & gone (which was the previous arrangement he alluded to). In a day or two, he returned and sent his card again to see Genl Grant, who again sent word he would not see him, the same message he always sends when a Chicago Tribune reporter calls. That is the only foundation for very untrue report he made. I should be so glad if you and Mrs Rowley would pay us a visit . . . . P. S. Tell Mr. McClellen we were so sorry not to have had him dine with us, or that he did not leave his address when he called." ALS, IHi. The offending column, datelined New York City, Jan. 24, appeared in the *Chicago Tribune*, Jan. 27, 1884. See also *ibid.*, Feb. 6, 1884.

On March 25, Yoshida Kiyonari, vice minister of the Foreign Office, Tokyo, wrote to USG. "Some time ago I noticed in the papers that you had met with an accident. The items I saw did not lead me to think that you were likely to suffer any serious consequences from the fall, but I was exceedingly sorry to learn by the last mail that the injury was more extensive than had at first been apprehended. In tendering to you my sincere condolence and expressing the earnest hope that you may be speedily restored to your accustomed health, I am as well conveying to you messages from Their Excellencies Saigo, Inouye and Ito and all your other warm friends in Japan. Please accept kindest regards to yourself and Mrs. Grant in which Mrs. Yoshida heartily joins . . . P. S. Pray remember me very warmly to Col. Fred. Grant and his wife. I trust his little ones are doing well and happy. Your name's sake U. S. Grant Yoshida is growing very strong; he remembers you well by your photograph. Yanada returned to Japan by last mail . . . ." LS (incomplete), USG 3.

1. Badeau repaid money borrowed from USG. *Badeau*, p. 553.
2. See telegram to William E. Strong, Oct. 19, 1883; letter to Andrew Hickenlooper, July 19, 1884.

To Patrick H. Winston, Jr.

New York City,
Dec. 24th 1883.

P. H. WINSTON, JR.
DEAR SIR:

I was very much pleased to receive your letter of a few days since in which you withdrew your request of the 17th of this month. I did not want to withhold the publication of my first letter, and at the same time I did not wish to see it in print. I know how such letters are misinterpreted. It was written without any other thought than a hearty approval of your address. No pains were taken either in the composition or the innumeration of important subjects that ought to be embraced in the platform of a political party. I am not conscious of even having read it over after it was written. If published it might justly be sensured for its omissions, and for aught I know, its commissions. It certainly would be taken as a bid for the nomination of the republican party at their next convention. There was nothing further from my thoughts. I never was a candidate for a nomination nor did I ever want it but once. That was in 1872 after having held the office for four years. Having given up a life position of great honor for the first election I natural desired the endorsement of the people a second time. I am now happy and contented, feeling however a deep interest in our country. Nothing is so important, in my view, as the breaking down of sectional lines. Any candidate who can best do that I am in favor of. In your addrss you have shewn that the only principle actuat[ing] the so called democratic party in the South is "Controll." In the North the party has been equally ~~incontent~~ inconsistent.

Very Truly yours.

U. S. Grant

P. S. I understand your address was published in the Tribune. I did not see it. But in the daily there was an editorial speaking well of it, an[d] saying they had published it in full.[1]

U. S. G.

ALS, Patrick Dunn & Associates, Olympia, Wash. See letter to Patrick H. Winston, Jr., Nov. 15, 1883.

1. See *New York Tribune*, Dec. 15, 1883.

To Edward F. Beale

———

Newyork City Jany. 20. 84

My Dear Gen. Beale:

Your kind letter to Mrs Grant was received here on Friday morning[1] and ought to have been answered sooner. It is very kind of you and Mrs Beale to offer to prepare your billiard room for my occupancy while in Washington, but I beg you to make no change whatever. At present I am, as I was when you were here, entirely unable to leave my room, or to dress myself, and it will probably be some considerable time before I can leave; and when I do it will be just as convenient for me to go to the third floor as elsewhere. I shall not want to go to Washington at all until I am able to dress myself and to get out of the house pretty well, and of course then there will be no object in my having a room on the ground floor.

Mrs Grant and Miss Sharpe[2] join me in kindest regards to Mrs Beale and Miss Beale and think it will be quite a number of weeks before we will be able to go to Washington. In the meantime, however, we hope to have a visit from you and would be very glad to have you at our house whenever You can come.

very truly Yours

U. S. GRANT.

L (dictated to Frank F. Wood), DLC-Decatur House Papers. On Jan. 24, 1884, Thursday, USG telegraphed to Edward F. Beale, Washington, D. C. "Wrote you Sunday. Why dont you Come, am Expecting you" Telegram received, *ibid.*

1. Jan. 18.
2. Elizabeth B. Sharp.

To Adam Badeau

New York City
Jany 21. 84

DEAR GENERAL BADEAU:

I have had your several letters, all received on due time, but as I have to dictate, I will not now undertake to answer them. I am still a great sufferer, confined to my room, and have not had my clothes on since Christmas Eve, when I received my injury. It is barely possible that Mrs Grant and I may get down to Bermuda and Havana this winter, if I should recover sufficiently to travel in time to make our visit. I will say, however, that I have no idea of undertaking the task of writing any of the articles the Century requests.[1]

With kind regards to the family

Very truly Yours

U. S. GRANT

L (dictated to Frank F. Wood), Munson-Williams-Proctor Institute, Utica, N. Y.

1. In Nov., 1884, *Century Magazine* began "Battles and Leaders of the Civil War"—a series of articles that achieved great popularity. USG eventually became a contributor. See *Century Magazine*, XXVIII, 6 (Oct., 1884), 943–44; Arthur John, *The Best Years of the* Century: *Richard Watson Gilder, Scribner's Monthly, and the Century Magazine, 1870–1909* (Urbana, 1981), pp. 125–29.

To John Russell Young

―――――

NewYork City Jan 21. 1884―

Hon. John Russell Young,
Dear Sir:―

I have your letters of Nov. 13th, 29th and also one I do not remember the date of, which I have mislaid, all received about the same time.

I note particularly what you say about H— and his claims,[1] and I shall be on guard if he should appear in New York. I have no doubt that you have heard through the newspapers of an injury I received from a fall at my own door-steps on Christmas Eve. I was very much hurt, worse than I expected myself at the time. I have not been able to leave my room since, nor to dress myself, and there are no indications that I shall be out very soon, although I hope a week or two more will enable me to get out of doors, when I will write you myself. The writing I do now, as you see by this letter, is done by dictation, and there are matters contained in your letters which I cannot very well answer in that way, as they are more or less confidential.

I hope a war will be averted between France and China, but from this standpoint I cannot see how it is to be averted. It also seems to me that in this matter, not much of the sympathy is on the side of France. But notwithstanding the appearance of things, I hope that wise judgments will prevail, and that peaceful negotiations may take the place of war.[2]

Mrs. Grant and all my boys and their families are very well, and if they knew I ~~was~~ were writing, would join me in their kindest regards.

Very truly yours,
U. S. Grant

Typescript, DLC-John Russell Young.

1. For Charles E. Hill, see *PUSG*, 29, 148; letters to John Russell Young, May 18, Aug. 25, 1883.

2. The French and Chinese disputed control over Annam, modern Vietnam. Hostilities escalated before the two countries reached a settlement in April, 1885.

To Editor, Washington Evening Star

———

Newyork City Jany 22. [1884]

To the Editor of the Washington Evening Star:

In your issue of Saturday, headed "The Mexican Treaty—The Senate declines to ratify it at present—" I find the following paragraph:

"Why some Senators voted against it.—A member of Congress said to a Star reporter today: 'There were some votes, several of them at least, cast against the Mexican treaty in the Senate, for this reason: You see Grant and Romero were partners in Mexico, and they obtained some large concessions from that government in relation to railroad and steamboat lines. Now Grant is the United States commissioner and Romero the Mexican Commissioner, and both of them were exceedingly anxious to have the treaty ratified. It was suspected—and really I can't say it was more than a suspicion—that these two men, part[ners] in business, had big private int[erests] in that treaty, that it would aid them in developing the monopolies they want, and as no real good could be discovered in the t[rea]ty, nothing pat[ent] enough to outweigh this suspicion, why several Senators whom I know of concluded that the safest plan would be to vote against it"[1]

The statement that "Grant and Romero were partners in Mexico, and they obtained some large concessions from that government in relation to railroad and steamboat lines," is wholly without foundation. Mr Romero and myself never had in our lives any pecuniary transactions or business transactions of any kind. Since the close of our rebellion and the expulsion of Maximilian from Mexico there has been a warm sympathy between Mr Romero and myself, our views being coincident as to the relations that ought to exist between Mexico and the United States. We have both devoted much time to bringing about more intimate relations between the two republics, and entirely gratuitously on our own part. I myself have no pecuniary interest in any of the improvements which are taking place in Mexico with American capital, but feel a great interest in their success.[2]

In the paragraph quoted above you say: "It was suspected—and really I can't say it was more than a suspicion—that these two men, partners in business, had big private interests in that treaty; that it would aid them in developing the monopolies they want," &cc. As stated above, Mr. Romero and myself are not partners in anything. We have, neither of us—I certainly have not—any more interest in the ratification of that treaty than any other private citizen of my country. I believe its ratification would be a great step towards establishing those relations between two contiguous republics which ought to exist, and which would be of mutual advantage.[3]

I might say here that in some of the arguments which I have read in the periodicals of the time, I have seen urged against a treaty, the fact that Cuba was so near to Mexico that it would be an easy matter to ship their sugar to that country and reship it from there, thus evading the duties. Of course, stringent laws would be passed to make such acts dangerous: but aside from any law, there are two answers to that objection to the treaty, either of which is in itself conclusive as against that objection: First, Mexico has a higher tariff upon sugar than the United States has, and they have no provision in their laws for rebate of duties where imported articles are re-exported. The Second conclusive answer is that it is only crude sugar which is admitted free under the treaty, and the difference between the Cuban raw sugar and the Mexican raw sugar is so great that it would not even require an expert to tell the difference between them by the "feel" alone, if he was blindfolded.

I write this from a sick room, and by dictation, and therefore will not go into details, as I would if I was able to sit up and write myself. I might add, however, that while I have spent thousands of dollars of my own money and a great deal of time, to advance the development of Mexico by United States capital and by American influence, I have not one dollar's interest in all that has been done, and no pecuniary interest whatever in the Country, except that I am one of the Subscribers to a railroad which lies wholly to the south of the City of Mexico, and the success of which is very doubtful in these times when it is so difficult to raise capital for any such enterprises. There is no steamboat charter or other monopoly in which I have the slightest pecuniary interest. My whole interest is in developing those relations which I believe ought to exist between contiguous countries, and particularly those of like institutions, and in the case of Mexico I think it more important because of her great undeveloped resources which must make her soon a commercial state of very great importance.

Very truly Yours

U. S. GRANT

L (dictated to Frank F. Wood), DLC-USG; press, USG 3. On Jan. 22 and 26, 1884, USG wrote to Matías Romero, Mexican minister. "I send herewith my reply to the article just received this morning, with the request that you will hand it to the Editor of the Star, and request its publication. If he will not publish it, then it can be given to some other paper" "In your esteemed letter to me, enclosing a copy of my letter to the Evening Star, you mentioned you though[t] soon of coming to New York. If so, & you come by the day train I will be happy to have you & Mrs Romero dine will us the day you arrive, or if you come by the night train to have you dine with us the next day. If Mrs Romero will not be with you, I will be happy to see you." L (facsimile; dictated to Frank F. Wood) and LS (facsimile), DLC-Matías Romero. Asked on Jan. 23 to comment on USG's letter, Romero replied. "I know that Gen. Grant has not now, and has not had, any personal interest in Mexico which might be served with the ratification of the reciprocity treaty. Gen. Grant has always been a warm, sincere and disinterested friend of Mexico, and with a view to serve that country, and not with any object of personal gain, he consented to organize a company of competent gentlemen of this country for the purpose of building a road from the City of Mexico to the Mexican frontier with Guatemala, which road has not yet been begun, and is not likely to be built for the present . . . ." *Washington Evening Star,* Jan. 23, 1884. On Jan. 27, Romero was in New York City. *New York Times,* Jan. 27, 1884. On Jan. 31, USG telegraphed to Romero, Washington, D. C.. "Do not send a reporter. I have a stenographer through whom I can give anything if needed to the press." Telegram received (at 12:38 P.M.; facsimile), DLC-Matías Romero.

On Jan. 7 and 9, Frederick Dent Grant, New York City, had written to Romero. "Your letter of yesterday received Father is much better & will be able to move around I think before the end of the month I will take your letter to him & let you know what he says about the treaty. My regards to Mrs Romero" "I saw father last night & read your letter (to me) to him. He said: 'That he hardly thinks that he will be able to visit wWashington this month but if you will let him know who is the Chairman of the committee having the treaty in charge he will dictate a letter to him that may do some good' Please let me know as a letter addressed to Father would not reach him until he is well My regards to Mrs Romero & yourself" ALS (facsimiles; the first on letterhead of Grant & Ward), *ibid.*

On Feb. 12, Henry G. Howe, "Mining Engineer and U. S. Deputy Mineral Surveyor," Tombstone, Arizona Territory, wrote to USG, Washington, D. C. "Having many times been asked about the rights of Americans in Mexico and especially in Sonora, and whether they could hold mining property there, And being unable to answer them, I take the liberty of addressing you these lines, as you are one of the Commissioners appointed by the United States upon the adjustment of international commerce &c between the United States and Mexico:—1st I understand there is a law declaring or setting apart, 20 leagues south of the boundary of the United States in which no American or Foreigner can hold title to either mining property or Real Estate? 2nd Can an American hold mining property in this so called dead line if so, what are the conditions. 3rd Can an American or company of Americans hold Real Estate, Land Grants in this neutral zone? If so what is the law and what security have they. The mining and Stock raising interests along the border are so allied to each other, and there is so much uncertainty about the law that I should like from you an explicit expose of the law, so that I can have it published, so that Capitalists here can know just what their rights are; And what security they have for the money invested, in Mines or Stock, or invested in Land Grants in this Neutral zone,—or dead line. Is it not better for the United States and Mexico that the dead line that the dead line be abolished, And the valuable grazing and mining country laying in this zone thrown open to the capital that would be placed upon it for its development? While now it is nearly deserted and is only the rendevous of Smugglers and roughs from both countries, There is no reason why this border should not be the safest place in either the United States, or Mexico, yet now it is far from it. Does not all the capital that keeps up the small towns on the border come from Arizona and New Mexico? The above are a few of the many questions that suggest themselves to me and I would like to hear from you upon them, As the tendency of mining men is to explore mexico if they have any security for their investment, Trusting that I may hear from you soon in regard to the above . . ." ALS (facsimile), *ibid.* USG supplied an undated endorsement. "Respectfully referred to Sr. Romero—" E (facsimile; dictated to Frank F. Wood), *ibid.*

1. See *Evening Star,* Jan. 19, 1884.

2. On Jan. 2, a correspondent had reported from Mexico City. "The Mexican Government has declared forfeited the concession made to Gen. Grant for a submarine cable connecting Mexico, the United States, and Central America for non-fulfillment of the terms of the concession, no work having been done within the prescribed time." *New York Times,* Jan. 3, 1884. An unidentified friend of USG clarified this report. "This concession was given to the General, not as a matter of personal interest to himself, but for the Western Union Telegraph Company. That company, having ascertained that existing contracts made it undesirable to pursue the enterprise, allowed the concession to lapse . . . ." *Ibid.,* Jan. 11, 1884.

3. On Jan. 18, the Senate narrowly voted down the commercial treaty with Mexico; on March 11, the Senate agreed to an amended version. Congress failed to pass enabling legislation. See *PUSG,* 30, 465–66; Interview, [*Jan. 22, 1883*], and Speech, [*Feb. 8, 1883*]; *New York Times,* Jan. 18, 1884; Charles I. Bevans, ed., *Treaties and Other International Agreements of the United States of America 1776–1949* (Washington, 1968–76), 9, 855–64.

To Adam Badeau

————

Dec. [*Jan.*] 25th 1883[*4*].

MY DEAR GEN. BADEAU.

Mrs. Thos B. Musgrave of this city goes to Havan[a] this Winter on a short visit. I take great pleasure in presenting her to you because I regard her husband as one of my best friends in this city. I know you will take pleasure in showing Mrs Musgrave such attention, as you can and which will facilitate her travels over the island.

This is the first note I have written since my injury a month ago last night. I am improving though slowly.

Very Truly yours
U. S. GRANT

ALS, Steven Brizek, North Haledon, N. J. See letter to Fannie E. Musgrave, July 11, 1883.

To John A. Logan

————

NEW YORK CITY, January 25, 1884.
GENERAL JOHN A. LOGAN, WASHINGTON, D. C.

My Dear General: . . . P. S. I recollect some years after the Rebellion that General Schofield asked me if I intended his supersedure by your going to relieve General Thomas, and that I told him I had not.[1] He was in command of the Army of the Ohio by assignment of the President, and General Thomas was in command of the Army of the Cumberland by a similar assignment. The two armies coming together naturally fell under Thomas, who was the senior. Whether your order, as written, would have given you command of the whole without regard to seniority, it is impossible for me to say now without seeing the order. If it did not, you would naturally have commanded the whole by reason of seniority if you were the senior, and my recollection is you were. General Schofield, I remember, was appointed a major-general before you were, but not confirmed by the Senate, and was not, if my recollection serves me right, confirmed as a major-general when I took command of the military division, but I assigned him to the command of the Army of the Ohio, and he was afterwards confirmed, but I do not know of what date.[2]

> Very truly yours,
> U. S. GRANT,
> Per F. F. WOOD.

John A. Logan, *The Volunteer Soldier of America* . . . . (Chicago, 1887), p. 67. See *ibid.*, pp. 66–70; letter to John A. Logan, Feb. 14, 1884; James Pickett Jones, *"Black Jack": John A. Logan and Southern Illinois in the Civil War Era* (Tallahassee, 1967), pp. 241–43.

1. See *PUSG*, 30, 252–56.
2. The Senate confirmed John A. Logan as maj. gen. vols. on March 11, 1863, and John M. Schofield on May 12, 1864.

To John D. Rockefeller

———

171 Broadway
NewYork January 1884

DEAR SIR; You will no doubt deplore with us the marked indifference of the Citizens of NewYork to the munificent gift of the French People to the People of the United States.—A colossal Statu[e] of Liberty Enlightening the World.[1]

It was presented on the One hundredth anniversary of our National Independence, in commemoration of the ancient alliance and present friendship of the two Republics. The Statue is artistically admirable, and will prove an ornament of the harbor of NewYork of unequalled majesty and impressiveness.

Out of $250,000 needed to erect a suitable pedestal less than half has been raised, after many and strenuous exertions.[2]

The threatened stoppage of work upon the Pedestal in consequence of this neglect would produce the most unfavorable comments upon our patriotism and public spirit, not only in our own Country, but throughout the civilized world.

It has therefore been suggested that twenty of the most prominent of our citizens could be named who would gladly contribute to avert so discreditable a result, and your name has been presented as one of the twenty.

Will you be kind enough therefore to inform us if you will agree to pay $5000 towards the object, provided the others do; any previous subscription to be counted as part of the sum, and no publication of the list to be made until it shall be completed.

We know that this is hardly a time to make an appeal for money, but the necessity is imperative.

Very truly yours

U. S. Grant

Wm M. Evarts

Jos. W Drexel

J. D. Rockefeller Esqre &C. &C. &C.

LS, Rockefeller Archive Center, North Tarrytown, N. Y. Born in 1839 in N. Y., John D. Rockefeller began his career as an asst. bookkeeper in Cleveland and became wealthy as a partner in Standard Oil Co. with large business interests in New York City. On Feb. 4, 1884, Rockefeller wrote to USG, William M. Evarts, and Joseph W. Drexel. "I am in receipt of your esteemed favor, and would gladly join in the effort to raise the $100,000 00 you refer to, for the Statue of Liberty, but I have so many pledges for educational and other works, I must ask to be excused." Copy, *ibid.* For Rockefeller's $1,000 contribution to USG's retirement fund, see *PUSG*, 30, 137–38.

USG *et al.* also solicited Hamilton Fish. LS, DLC-Hamilton Fish. On Jan. 24, Fish, New York City, wrote to Drexel. "I have to acknowledge your letter (with Genl Grant & Mr Evarts) in behalf of the Bartholdi Statue & asking whether I will contribute five thousand dollars towards its erection. I am compelled, very respectfully, to decline making such contribution." ALS (press), *ibid.* The same solicitation letter was addressed to Tiffany & Co. LS (fascsimile), R. M. Smythe, Catalogue 248, May 5, 2005, Lot 206.

1. For USG's prior interest in the Statue of Liberty, see *PUSG*, 28, 156–57, 319.
2. On Dec. 3, 1883, USG had opened an "Art Loan Exhibition in aid of the Bartholdi statue pedestal fund." "I know the people of this City well enough to believe that all the funds necessary to complete this pedestal could be raised in one day if they thought it was necessary to do so. When we reflect that the statue is the gift of a people who gave us their warm sympathy in our struggle for national independence we should not let there be a want for a fund sufficient to complete it for a single day." *New York Times*, Dec. 4, 1883. See *ibid.*, Nov. 15, 27, 1882, Jan. 4, March 20, May 20, 1884.

Addressee Unknown

NEW YORK, Feb. 2. [*1884*]

Mr. ——, Galena, Ill.:

Dear Sir—I was glad to receive your letter of the 26th ult., and regret very much th[*a*]t I am not able to answer it myself. The injury that I received I think is very much improved; but pleurisy and then rheumatism have followed, and I am still an invalid and confined to my room, and part of the time to my bed. I think, however, that I am doing pretty well, and a few weeks of good health will bring me out again. Please present my kindest regards to my Galena friends that you meet. Very truly yours.

U. S. GRANT.

Indianapolis Journal, Feb. 9, 1884.

To Editor, Toledo Blade

---

*N*EW YORK CITY, Feb. 7, 1884.

Editor Blade:

DEAR SIR:—Your favor of Jan'y [*3*]1 is at hand, and in reply to the question asked there, I will say that I never gave any order to any army that I commanded during the rebellion, to make an attack where it was disobeyed.

It is possible, but I do not remember the circumstance, that I have given an order for an attack at a certain hour, and afterwards concluded that it would be better, possibly not to make it, and have sent orders countermanding, but I do not remember any such circumstance as that took place at Cold Harbor.

Truly yours,

U. S. GRANT.

Toledo Blade, Feb. 11, 1884. David R. Locke, editor, *Toledo Blade*, and widely known for his political and social commentary as the character Petroleum V. Nasby, was then on a tour of the south and not in direct control of the newspaper. An editorial, "The Battle of Cold Harbor," introduced USG's letter. "The discussion which has been going on in the columns of the B<small>LADE</small> over the reported refusal of the Army of the Potomac to renew the charge at Cold Harbor has excited general interest all over the country. Soldiers from every division in that splendid old army having written us denying the truth of the statement contained in many histories of the war, and which was first embodied by G<small>REELEY</small> in his 'American Conflict,' in these words: . . . " *Ibid.* On Feb. 14, 1884, USG again wrote to editor, *Toledo Blade.* "In further reply to yours of the 31st ult., in relation to the battle of Cold Harbor, since writing you on the 7th inst., I have thought about it, and have a sort of indistinct recollection that I did issue orders for another attack, but came to the conclusion myself, and without consultation, that it would prove a failure, and leave no compensating results, and I simply sent word, verbally, to the Corps Commanders, before the time ordered for that attack, to suspend, and then made my arrangements for a final left flank movement north of the James." *Ibid.*, Feb. 19, 1884. On the same day, USG wrote to Charles M. Failing, Belle Plaine, Iowa. "Yours of the 9th inst, inquiring in relation to the Battle of Cold Harbor is at hand. In reply I will say that I did make an order for a final charg[e] but before the hour arrived for it, I considered that it would be a failure, with much loss to ourselves and without compensating results, and I quietly sent verbal massages to the Corps Commande[rs] to withhold." L (facsimile), PCarlA. See *PUSG*, 11, 6–9, 13–14; *Memoirs*, II, 269–73, 276–77; Ernest B. Furgurson, *Not War But Murder: Cold Harbor 1864* (New York, 2000), pp. 234–37.

To John A. J. Creswell

———

New York, Feby. 14 *1884*

H<small>ON</small> J<small>NO</small>. A. J. C<small>RESWELL</small>
T<small>HE</small> P<small>ORTLAND</small> W<small>ASHINGTON</small> D. C.
D<small>EAR</small> S<small>IR</small>:

I have your letter of the 9th inst. I presume I should have been out before this but for the wretched weather we have been having ever since the accident occurred to me. Although I am not aware of ever having had a twinge of rheumatism in my life before, some two weeks after the accident occurred the rheumatism attacked me, first in the well leg, but soon transferred itself to the injured part of the other leg. I think that all I require now to be a well man is a little good weather—or the cure of the rheumatism without it. I may possibly be a little weak on the injured leg for a time, but I have no idea that I have received any permanent injury.

With kind regards of Mrs Grant and myself to yourself and Mrs Creswell

Yours Very Truly
U. S. G<small>RANT</small>

L (dictated to Frank F. Wood), DLC-John A. J. Creswell.

On Aug. 24, 1885, John A. J. Creswell, Elkton, Md., wrote to Jesse Root Grant, Jr. " . . . Please say to your dear mother, that the thoughts of Mrs Creswell and myself have frequently turned to her since we left you all in New York, and that we would fain renew to her the Kindest assurances of our lasting sympathy and affection. We shall never forget the delightful hours we have spent in the society of The General and herself. Indeed, I recall nothing in all my life with more pride and pleasure than the fact, that my name was associated with his during the years of my official life in Washington. May God graciously grant to your mother, and each of her children, all the abundant comfort that the memory of a man, so great and noble, can inspire . . . ." ALS, USGA. For Creswell's reminiscences of USG, see *Washington Evening Star,* April 4, 1885.

To John A. Logan

New York, Feby 14 *1884*

HON JOHN A. LOGAN
U. S. SENATE
WASHINGTON D. C.
DEAR SIR:

In reply to your letter of the 11th I have to say that my response must be from memory entirely, having no data at hand to refer to; but in regard to the order for you to go to Louisville and Nashville for the purpose of relieving Gen Thomas, I never thought of the question of who should command the combined armies of the Cumberland and the Ohio. I was simply dissatisfied with the slowness of Gen. Thomas moving; and sent you out with orders to relieve him. No doubt if the order had been carried out the question would immediately have arisen as to who was entitled to the combined command, provided Gen Schofield was senior in rank to you—which I do not know that he was. I know that his confirmation as a Major General took place long after yours, but I do not know the date of his commission.[1] The question in that case, of the command of the whole would have been settled in a very few hours by the use of the telegraph between Nashville and Washington. I was in Washington when you arrived at Louisville and telegraphed me that Gen Thomas had moved, and as I remember the telegram, expressing gratification that he had done so.[2] I was then on my way to Nashville myself, and remained over a day in Washington hoping that Thomas might still move. Of course I was gratified when I learned that he had moved, because it was a very delicate and unpleasant matter to remove a man of Gen Thomas' character and standing before the country, but still I had urged him so long to move that I had come to think it a duty.[3] Of course in sending you to relieve Gen Thomas I meant no reflection whatever upon Gen Schofield who was commanding the Army of the Ohio, because I thought that he had done very excellent service in punishing the entire force under Hood a few days before, some twenty five miles south of Nashville.

Very Truly Yours

U. S. GRANT

L (dictated to Frank F. Wood), CtY. On Feb. 23, 1884, USG wrote to U.S. Senator John A. Logan of Ill. "Since I have been confined to my room I have conducted all my correspondence through a Secretary, who is a stenographer, and he takes my dictation to the office and writes the letters out there as dictated, and by my direction signs my name. I intended that the letter which I wrote to you should be brought back to me for my own signature, and I sign this myself to show my entire responsibility for the one which you have just received and which I hope was satisfactory to you." LS, *ibid.* See letter to John A. Logan, Jan. 25, 1884; John M. Schofield, *Forty-Six Years in the Army* (New York, 1897), pp. 239–41.

    1. John M. Schofield's appointment as maj. gen. vols. dated from Nov. 29, 1862, as did Logan's.
    2. See *PUSG*, 13, 127–28; *Memoirs*, II, 382–84.
    3. See *PUSG*, 15, 182–83.

To Adam Badeau

———

New York, Feby 27 *1884*

GEN A. BADEAU—
HAVANA, CUBA—
MY DEAR GENERAL.

    I am in receipt of your letter of the 21st of Feby and hasten to write to you to say that Mr George Jones had entirely over estimated my condition. I think the injury that I received from my fall has been well this last six weeks, but we have had a very horrid winter here, and it has given me what I have never had before in my life—the rheumatism and it has settled in the injured leg, but on the opposite side from the injury, and is very painful and prevents my being able to walk except with crutches, and as yet I have only written one or two notes myself but have simply confined myself to dictating such answers as I have to give to letters. I drive out every good day and have been intending to go South for warmer and dryer weather than we have had here, but I put it off from week to week and do not feel sure that I will get away at all.

Very Truly Yours

U. S. GRANT

L (dictated to Frank F. Wood), Munson-Williams-Proctor Institute, Utica, N. Y. See *Badeau*, p. 555; Henry W. Taft to Alphonso Taft, Feb. 20, 1884, DLC-William H. Taft.

Invited to the annual dinner of the Harvard Club of New York City on Feb. 21, 1884, USG replied "that he hoped to be well enough to be present." *New York Times*, Feb. 22, 1884. USG did not attend.

To Isaac H. Elliott

———

NEW YORK, Feb. 27, 1884.—*To Adj—Gen. I. H. Elliott, Spring-field, Ill.*—DEAR SIR: Your favor of the 20th inst: inviting me to be present at the dedicatory exercises upon the opening of the Memorial Hall to contain the battle flags of the volunteer troops of Illinois in the late war, is received, and in reply I must say that there is no probability that my condition will be such as to [a]dmit of my being there at that time. In fact, I hope to be able to leave here for a warmer climate than New York, and be absent all of March for the benefit of my health.

Thanking you for your kind invitation, I am very truly yours,

U. S. GRANT.

Illinois State Journal, March 28, 1884. Isaac H. Elliott, former col., 33rd Ill., became Ill. AG in 1881. See *PUSG*, 4, 130–31; Elliott and Virgil G. Way, *History of the Thirty-Third Regiment Illinois Veteran Volunteer Infantry in the Civil War* ... (Gibson City, Ill., 1902), pp. 11–12, 24–25. For the dedication of Memorial Hall in Springfield on March 26, 1884, see *Illinois State Journal*, March 26–27, 1884. See also H. B. Reed, *The Back-Bone of Illinois in Front and Rear, from 1861 to 1865, and Memorial Hall, Springfield, Illinois* (Springfield, 1886).

To Edward F. Beale

———

Newyork Mch. 2, 1884

MY DEAR GENERAL BEALE:

Mrs Grant and I are very much obliged to you and Mrs Beale for your kind invitation to stop over at your house on our way to Fortress Monroe, but I would not consent to stop in Washington while in my present condition, unable to walk. I would necessarily be confined to my room all the time where I would be accessible to callers and it would overrun the house with people seeking my assistance to procure office as well as people who would call to pay their respects and whom I should be very glad to see. After the receipt of your letter, however, I had a letter written to the President of the Pennsylvania Road[1] to secure a car to take me directly from here to Newport News, and also wrote to the Hygeia Hotel at Old Point to secure rooms.

I have received no answer yet from the Railroad, but have from the Hotel saying I can have the accommodations I want. If I get an answer in time saying that I can have a car I shall leave here on Thursday Evening[2] of this week so as to reach Washington in time to connect with the six oclock train. Mrs Grant and I are very glad that you and Mrs Beale and Miss Emily contemplate going with us, and I will telegraph you the moment I learn that I can have a car in time. If it should be later than Thursday before one can be secured I will inform you at the earliest moment on what day and train we leave here.

With kindest regards to you and all your family,

Very Truly Yours

U. S. GRANT

I expected to have answered your letters last Friday but Buck, among the numerous messages that I sent by him that morning, forgot to tell Mr Wood who writes this letter at my dictation, to come up that day, and the next day being Saturday I concluded it was just as well to wait until Sunday.—

L (dictated to Frank F. Wood), DLC-Decatur House Papers. On March 5, 1884, Secretary of the Navy William E. Chandler telegraphed to USG. "The Tallapoosa, or

Despatch, is at your service, to take you and your family from Washington to Fortress Monroe, or further South, and to remain with you as long as you desire. I trust you will accept the use of one of the vessels." Copy, DNA, RG 45, Miscellaneous Letters Sent. On the same day, USG telegraphed to Chandler. "Very much obliged for your tender of Talapoosa or Dispatch but I have already arranged for special car to take my party to Newport News without change." Telegram received (at 11:46 A.M.), *ibid.*, Miscellaneous Letters Received. See letter to Edward F. Beale, [*March 8–10, 1884*].

1. George B. Roberts. See George H. Burgess and Miles C. Kennedy, *Centennial History of The Pennsylvania Railroad Company 1846–1946* (Philadelphia, 1949), pp. 385–452.

2. March 6.

To Adam Badeau

New York, Mch 3 *1884*

MY DEAR GENERAL BADEAU:

Your despatch was duly recei[ve]d and an answer returned saying letter by mail.—Under the circumstances it is impossible for me to comply with your request. In the first place I am sure it would not have benefited you in the least. The President is now openly a candidate for the nomination in June next, and knows well that I am opposed to it. Besides that, judging from the past I doubt very much whether any appointment will be made until after the action of the Chicago convention in June is known. There are now many vacancies existing, some of which have existed for a year and over, and among them very important offices for which no nominations have yet been sent to the Senate—offices such as judges of United States Courts for the States and Territories, United State Marshals &c, which must cause great inconvenience to the public service in the states and territories where those vacancies exist. Further, I would not like to ask a favor from a President whose administration I have been free to criticise and have no doubt but what my words have been reported to him very much exaggerated. If I had been able to get out I would have tried to see some person or persons who think better of the administration than I do and asked them verbally to send a note urging your appointment, but repeat I am sure to do no good between this and the 3rd of June.

My condition is improving—in fact I believe I am as well as ever was except the rheumatism has set in in the injured part of my leg, and the weather this winter has been the worst ever known in NewYork for the rheumatism. I hope in a day or two to get off.

Very truly Yours

U. S. GRANT

L (dictated to Frank F. Wood), Munson-Williams-Proctor Institute, Utica, N. Y. Adam Badeau, consul. gen., Havana, had written to USG for advice on whether he should seek another appointment. *Badeau*, p. 556. On Feb. 28, 1884, USG telegraphed to Badeau. "Dispatch received. Letter by mail." *Ibid.* See letter to Adam Badeau, April 8, 1884.

To Edward F. Beale

Old Point Comfort Va.

[*March 8–10, 1884*]

MY DEAR GENERAL BEALE:

I have your letter of Friday asking my endorsement of Gen. Ayres for the Brig. Generalcy to be made vacant by the retirement of Gen. McKenzie. I know Gen. Ayres very favorably, but I must decline from taking part in the contest for that office. I am very loth to ask any thing from this Administration further than can be granted by the different members of the Cabinet, most of whom I regard as personal friends. Then too I regard Merritt as coming next in order of services rendered though I am not going to give him—or any one—an indorsement.[1]

We arrived here without any fatigue though the weather is as bad here as in New York barring the cold. I do not think we will remain long.

We may go back by way of Washington and stop off for a few days. If we do however we will stop at a hotel[2] because of my condition and the number of people who will be calling at my room. We will make you a visit later when I am able to get about. Then too we have a large family now—three of us and two servants. I am writing with a bad hotel pen and a trembling hand.

With kindest regards of Mrs. Grant & myself, and Miss Sharp, to you, Mrs. Beale & Miss Emily, I am

Very Truly yours

U. S. GRANT.

ALS, DLC-Decatur House Papers. Following medical advice to seek a change of air, USG left New York City during the evening of March 6, 1884, on a special train for Old Point Comfort, Va. Julia Dent Grant and a niece, Elizabeth B. Sharp, traveled with USG. At a late moment, Edward F. Beale's family decided not to join USG's party. See *New York Times*, March 5, 7–8, 1884.

On March 8, a correspondent reported from Fort Monroe, Va. "Gen. Grant held a reception in his parlor at 11 o'clock this morning. Gen. Tidball, commandant, and the officers of the garrison, and other army and navy officers at the hotel called. A national salute was fired from the fort at noon in honor of Gen. Grant's arrival." *Ibid.*, March 9, 1884.

1. Mental illness led to Brig. Gen. Ranald S. Mackenzie's retirement as of March 24. Col. Romeyn B. Ayres, 2nd Art., and Col. Wesley Merritt, superintendent, USMA, lost this opportunity for promotion to Col. David S. Stanley. See *PUSG*, 12, 198; *ibid.*, 27, 155–56; Michael D. Pierce, *The Most Promising Young Officer: A Life of Ranald Slidell Mackenzie* (Norman, 1993), pp. 222–26.

2. On March 17, 3:00 P.M., USG and party departed for Washington, D. C., and checked into the Arlington Hotel that evening.

To Jerome B. Chaffee

———

[*Fort Monroe, Va.*], March 14th 1884

MY DEAR MR. CHAFFEE.

I received last evening your letter of the 12th. I saw the purported interview [with the Times] correspondent[1] referred to in your letter. I have had no interview with a Times correspondent since I have been here. I have not been interviewed by any body. The only conversation . . . Norfolk Virginian . . . . the house he did not want to leave without paying his respects in person, and that he did not call for the purpose of an interview. During a half hours conversation, or more, a ~~good~~ much was said, and the published statement in the Times gives about correctly a part of that conversation except in one important particular. I did not say the contest laid between Blaine & Arthur. What I did say in answer to who I thought would be the candidates of the two parties was, that

I had been confine[d] to my room all winter and had not much opportunity to ~~have~~ form an opinion upon the subject, that I read the
papers of course, but as I only took three ~~papers~~ at my house, and
each of them had their own candidate, and each seemed to find comfort and support in the extracts which they furnished their readers
from journals from ... [I should judge Blaine], Arthur & Logan,
in the order named, would probably have the greatest number of
delegates at the opening of the convention, but that there were a
great number of candidates besides them who would have support
so it was impossible for me to judge who would finally receive the
nomination. I would like an extract of this to be published giving
the denial to the statement that I thought the contest would be between Blaine & Arthur.[2]

I also said to the editor that Edmunds would probably be
strongly supported in the East.

In regard to my omission of expressing my preference among
the candidates for the Presidency, it was after due deliberation. I
have said a hundred times probably, and in the hearing of a much
larger number of persons, that Logan was my first choice among
all those named. This much I supposed the Civil service reformers
would tolerate without it prejudicing [the chances of the candidate
of my choice. But if I had expressed this choice at the end of a letter
in commendation of Gen. Logan the parties referred to above would
turn all their batteries against *my Candidate*, and the cry would be;
"Any body to beat Logan." This was my deliberate judgment, and
it is so yet.[3] I should probably be] in Washington by the middle
of next week. I am mending slowly under new treatment,[4] but I
can not hope for a complete recovery under a month or two yet.

                                    Very truly yours
                                    U. S. GRANT

ALS (partial facsimile), Profiles in History, Catalog 37 [Dec., 2004], no. 35. On
March 9, 1884, a Norfolk newspaper representative, probably Michael Glennan, talked
with USG at the Hygeia Hotel, Old Point Comfort, Va. "The General said he had been
so closely confined to his room for some time past that he had had but little opportunity to look into the political situation, but from what he could gather it seemed to
him that the Republicans would nominate either Mr. Blaine or Mr. Arthur. He knew
one thing, that Gen. Grant would not be a candidate before the Convention, though he

would receive a complimentary vote." Asked about campaign issues, especially "the bloody shirt," USG replied. "Well, I suppose the 'Danville investigation' will furnish ammunition for such a war, though I think the tariff question will be the vital issue." Queried on the "political significance" of racial violence in Va., USG said. "I suppose the Democrats intended to defeat the Readjusters at all hazards; but the Copiah county trouble seems to have been worse than the Danville riot, and shows up the Democrats in a very bad light. There is no question that Mississippi, and South Carolina, too, are Republican States with a fair election . . . ." *Norfolk Virginian*, March 11, 1884. For racial violence in Danville, Va., see *SRC*, 48-1-579, and Jane Dailey, *Before Jim Crow: The Politics of Race in Postemancipation Virginia* (Chapel Hill, 2000), pp. 119–27; for unrest in Copiah County, Miss., see *SRC*, 48-1-512. After learning from a published item that USG had written to Jerome B. Chaffee to state "that he expressed no political opinions for public or private use during his stay at Fortress Monroe," the Norfolk interviewer refuted USG. " . . . General Grant was asked what news he had from the political situation at the North. He replied that he had had but little opportunity to hear from political circles except through the newspapers, but it appeared to him that either Mr. Blaine or Mr. Arthur would be nominated by the Republicans. We were surprised to hear him make this statement, especially as he had not been questioned on that point. The General then spoke voluntarily with reference to the probable nominee of the Democrats, saying he had no idea who their man would be, but he saw they were talking about the old ticket of Tilden and Hendricks. Emboldened by this, the reporter then questioned him about the character of the campaign, &c., all of which was correctly reported in this paper. All this was said to the reporter alone, and General Grant knew that he was talking to a newspaper man and that his remarks would be published. If he had intimated a request that nothing he said should be printed, the request would have been complied with. Granting that the telegram in The World is authentic, General Grant's 'denial' is remarkable." *Norfolk Virginian*, March 20, 1884. For Glennan, editor of the *Norfolk Virginian* and former C.S.A. q. m., see Lenoir Chambers and Joseph E. Shank, *Salt Water & Printer's Ink: Norfolk and Its Newspapers, 1865–1965* (Chapel Hill, 1967), pp. 26–27, 202–6.

On March 18, USG, Washington, D. C., wrote to Edward F. Beale. "Please say nothing to Blaine in regard to our conversation this am. until I see you again. I do not want to meet him." ANS, DLC-Decatur House Papers. Written on letterhead of the Arlington Hotel. On March 19, President Chester A. Arthur visited USG at the Arlington. *Washington Evening Star*, March 20, 1884.

On March 21, Theron C. Crawford asked USG if he had been interviewed at Fort Monroe. "Not with my knowledge. The editor of a Norfolk paper sent up to me a written request to pay his respects as a Virginian. He said he was the editor of a Norfolk newspaper, but he said he did not call to interview me. I talked with him generally. He printed what he could remember of this conversation. There was some truth in his report and some mistakes. For instance, I did not say that I thought the contest for the Republican nomination at Chicago had narrowed down to Blaine and Arthur. What I did say was something equivalent to this: I believed from present indications that when the first ballot at the Chicago Republican Convention should be taken, Blaine, Arthur and Logan would lead in about the order named. I said also that Edmunds had considerable strength in the East, and that other candidates would have enough votes to make the result uncertain and a sound prediction impossible. In saying this I did not indicate the slightest preference . . . . I have never made any concealment of the fact that I should prefer John Logan to all the other candidates. I have said so frequently and have never had any reason to change my views. I think Logan's chances as good as those of any of the candidates." USG called "untrue" a recent report that he had discussed presidential politics with James G. Blaine and Roscoe Conkling. "I have not seen Mr. Blaine to talk with him since the spring of 1880 . . . . I have no reason to expect to see him." Beale reportedly planned a dinner party to allow USG to meet Blaine. "I know nothing of it. It is a doubtful story. I would not go to a dinner where I would be expected to meet Mr. Blaine . . . . Five months ago I believed the Republicans were facing certain defeat; I did not think they had any chance. But the Democrats have remedied that. The Democratic party can always be relied on in the case of emergency to give the Republicans a victory. Their fight in the House over the tariff has made a doubtful election certain to the Republicans. They have been warring upon the business interests in their work in the House. The result will be that a number of Democratic business men will contribute to the defeat of their own party rather than encourage its free-trade tendencies. The Republicans will have no difficulty in electing any one they shall nominate. There are two States, however, where there would be some feeling against Arthur. In his own State there is a great coolness towards him among his old friends which would create apathy in the case of his nomination, while in Ohio the Garfield element would not heartily support him." Concerning other likely Republican candidates, USG said. "I see [George F. Edmunds] is gaining strength in the East, . . . Edmunds would make a strong candidate. He has a faultless record and is a very able man . . . . I should not like to see [John Sherman] nominated." About Democratic prospects, USG said. "I[f] they have any chance at all it will be in the nomination of some man whose name will be a guarantee to the business interests of the country that war will not be made upon them . . . . [Samuel J. Tilden] is so feeble that if he should be nominated public attention would be concentrated upon the second man on the ticket . . . . [Joseph E. McDonald] is a very clever gentleman but a Free-Trader. No Free-Trader can win . . . . [Henry B. Payne] appears to be all right upon the tariff question and, although three years older than Tilden, is well preserved, with a sound and vigorous constitution. I should think he would be a good candidate for the Democrats." *New York World*, March 22, 1884. See Crawford, "General Grant's Greatest Year," *McClure's Magazine*, II, 6 (May, 1894), 535–41; George Juergens, *Joseph Pulitzer and the New York World* (Princeton, 1966), pp. 34–35; Mark Wahlgren Summers, *Rum, Romanism & Rebellion: The Making of a President 1884* (Chapel Hill, 2000), pp. 106, 111, 144–46.

1. For the *Norfolk Virginian* interview presented as if given to their own correspondent, see *New York Times*, March 11, 1884.

2. On March 17, a correspondent reported from Washington, D. C. "Gen. Grant has written a letter to ex-Senator Chaffee in New York denying the authenticity of an interview published as coming from him at Fortress Monroe in which he was made to say that he thought the contest for the Republican nomination was between Blaine and Arthur. Gen. Grant has authorized Chaffee to make a publication of the letter. Grant says that he expressed no political opinions for public or private use during his stay at Fortress Monroe." *New York World*, March 18, 1884.

3. On Dec. 14, 1883, a correspondent had reported from Washington, D. C., that Chaffee "knows that neither Grant nor Blaine is a candidate for the Presidency or desires the nomination. He went on to say that he thinks Gen. Logan would be an available candidate and would receive the cordial and earnest support of both Blaine and Grant . . . ." *New York Times*, Dec. 15, 1883.

4. Hartvig Nissen, a recent immigrant from Norway, began physical therapy on USG's hip at the Hygeia Hotel. On March 13, 1884, USG, Fort Monroe, telegraphed to Beale, Washington, D. C. "I feel much improved by the treatment of prof Wissen. Will remain here until about middle of next week" Telegram received (at 4:00 P.M.), DLC-Decatur House Papers. On [*April 10*], USG, Washington, D. C., wrote to Nissen. "As I am about leaving the city for my home in New York, it is due to you that I should say that I feel that I have received very great benefit from your massage and Swedish movement cure. Although yet on crutches, I feel that it is largely due to the changeable and bad weather of the last five weeks, which has subjected me to constant attacks of rheumatism in the injured part of my leg. Otherwise I feel that I would have been now off my crutches and walking with but very little lameness." *Washington National Republican*, April 12, 1884. On April 11, Nissen, Washington, D. C., wrote a receipt for USG for $350 to cover "50 treatments of Massage and Swedish movements" and "traveling expences." ADS, USG 3. See *New York World*, March 22, 1884; Nissen, *Autobiography* (n. p., 1921), especially pp. 21–23, and *A Manual of Instruction for Giving Swedish Movement and Massage Treatment* (Philadelphia, 1889); *New York Times*, April 23, 1924.

To Mary Mercer Thompson Ord

———

March 16th 1884.

My Dear Mrs. Ord:

In answer to your enquiry as to the identity of the table on which the the terms of surrender of the Army of Norther Va— Confederate—was written, and signed, by Gen. Lee and myself I have to say: The occurrence was at the house of a Mr. McLean, of Appomatox C. H. Va. Gen Lee and I sat beside a small marble top table during the whole of the interview on that occasion. I wrote the terms of the surrender on that table, and both Gen. Lee & myself signed it there. I know Gen. Ord bought the table and brought it away with him.

Very Truly yours
U. S. Grant

ALS, ICHi. Born in Va., Mary Mercer Thompson "Molly" Ord married Capt. Edward O. C. Ord on Oct. 15, 1854, in San Francisco, where her father practiced law. On Jan. 26, 1887, Julia Dent Grant, New York City, certified "that Mrs General Ord is the possessor of the table which General E. O. C. Ord presented to me in 1865 as the identical one General Grant used to write and sign the articles of the Appomatox surrender upon." DS, *ibid*. Probably on the same day, Julia Grant wrote to Mary Ord. "It gives me sincere pleasure to reply thus promptly to your letter of Jany 14th. I remember

that my husband wrote you a letter in regard to this table. Hoping your daughter will
soon recover her health . . . " LS (undated), *ibid.* See following letter; Horace Porter,
Campaigning with Grant (New York, 1897), pp. 476, 480; Bernarr Cresap, *Appomattox
Commander: The Story of General E. O. C. Ord* (San Diego, 1981), pp. 34–35, 117–19,
214, 379.

To George F. Edmunds

————

Washington D. C.
March 19th /84

DEAR SENATOR,

You were kind enough to say to Mrs. Grant last evening that
if she would furnish you with the full name of Mrs. General Ord,
with a memorandum of her husbands services, you would endeavor to procure for her a pension. I am sure there has not been
a more deserving case, or one where the pension was more needed,
than this.

General Ord—Ed O. C. Ord—graduated at West Point June
1839, and served continually until his retirement by Mr. Hayes. At
the time of his retirement he was a Brigadier and Brevet Major
General in the regular army. For his services in the rebellion Congress authorized his retirement as a Major General.[1] He rendered
distinguished service as a General during the entire rebellion. He
was once badly wounded in battle.[2] The last six or eight months of
the war he commanded an Army[3] and rendered most efficient service, as such, in the closing scenes around Richmond, Petersburg
and Appomattox.

General Ord contracted the Yellow Fever at Vera Cruz late last
Summer while enroute from Mexico to the United States. The disease developed itself on shipboard and he was sent to a hospital in
Havana, Cuba, on the arrival of the ship, on which he had taken
passage, at that port. He leaves a widow with three minor Children dependent upon her,[4] without a home or support. She is now
domiciled in a Government house outside of Fort Monroe, Va

Very Truly yours
U. S. GRANT

Hon. Geo. F. Edmunds U. S. S.

ALS, PHi. A law of July 5, 1884, granted Mary Mercer Thompson Ord a $50 monthly pension. See *SRC*, 48-1-787, *HRC*, 48-1-1144, 48-1-1386; *CR*, 48-1, 4468, 6026; *U.S. Statutes at Large*, XXIII, 590–91. For the increase of Ord's pension to $75 monthly, see *SRC*, 50-1-1119; *HRC*, 50-1-2596; *CR*, 50–1, 3628, 8635, 9254, 9260–61, 9296; *U.S. Statutes at Large*, XXV, 1223.

1. See *SRC*, 46-3-740; *HRC*, 46-3-58; *CR*, 46-3, 668, 827; *U.S. Statutes at Large*, XXI, 321.

2. Edward O. C. Ord received wounds during the battle of Hatchie River, Miss., Oct. 5, 1862, and the assault on Fort Harrison near Richmond, Sept. 29, 1864. See *PUSG*, 6, 119–20, 184; *ibid.*, 12, 229–30.

3. Ord took command of the Army of the James as of Jan. 8, 1865.

4. Ord died July 22, 1883. Seven of his thirteen children lived to maturity. See Bernarr Cresap, *Appomattox Commander: The Story of General E. O. C. Ord* (San Diego, 1981), pp. 35, 341–43.

On June 23 and July 10, 1884, Secretary of War Robert T. Lincoln wrote to Julia Dent Grant, New York City. "Upon my return to the city I found your note in respect to the son of General Ord. I took the first opportunity of seeing Secretary Folger in relation to the matter. The Life Saving Service is in his charge. He said to me that he did not know what the situation was in regard to that Service, but that he would not be surprised if it was possible to appoint the young man to some proper place in it. Personally, I should be very glad if he can do so, and I so expressed myself. I beg to present my compliments to yourself, and to be remembered most kindly to the General." "I enclose to you a letter which I have just received from Secretary Folger in relation to Mr Ord. I am sorry to find that the law requires peculiar qualifications not possessed by Mr Ord." LS and ALS, Robert T. Lincoln Letterbooks, IHi. Julia Grant may have tried to assist Jules G. Ord, born in 1865. See *New York Times*, July 7, 14, 1898.

Concerning Owen N. Denny

Washington D. C. March 23 /84

I take pleasure in presenting Judge O. N. Denney to the officials and other friends of mine in Mexico. The Judge has represented the United States as Consul-General to China ably and well. During my visit to that country over four years ago I saw a great deal of the Judge, and have no hesitation in endorsing him to my friends. He visits Mexico, I believe, in the interests of some capitalists who expect to make investments in that country, or not, according to the report that he may render.

U. S. Grant

Typed copy, USGA. For Owen N. Denny, consul gen., Shanghai (1879–83), see *PUSG*, 29, 147–48; *ibid.*, 30, 305, 308; *HED*, 48-1-171.

To Horace Capron

————

Washington Mch. 27, 84

COL. HORACE CAPRON, CITY
DEAR SIR:

Your letter of 22nd of March was duly received. I congratulate you upon the honor that has been done you by the Mikado of Japan. During my very pleasant visit to that country I never heard a word in regard to your services in that country that would not be flattering to you if repeated. I also feel highly complimented that the Japanese authorities should have made the request under the circumstances indicated by the proceedings in your honor, copy of which you forwarded to me.

Very truly yours,
U. S. GRANT

LS, DLC-Horace Capron. Former Commissioner of Agriculture Horace Capron worked for the Japanese government (1871–75) and was decorated with the Second Order of the "Rising Sun" (1884). See *PUSG*, 22, 37–38, 45–46; Merritt Starr, "General Horace Capron, 1804–1885," *Journal of the Illinois State Historical Society*, XVIII, 2 (July, 1925), 259–349.

To Fitz John Porter

————

Washington D. C.
March 27th 1884.

MY DEAR GENERAL PORTER.

Before the receipt of your letter of two or three days ago I had seen General Slocum, and stated to him before I heard the object of his call, that I had thought of writing to you that I feard that the passage of your bill before the meeting of the Chicago convention[1] might embarass the President. Slocum may have written to you. I have delayed writing because about the day before your letter was written I had met the Sec. of State[2] on the street—I in a carriage— and had some conversation with him. He said that he wanted to call in a day or two and have some conversation with me. He has not yet called. When he does I will find out, if I can, the fate your bill would probably meet if left with the President. I had hoped to meet the sec. before this, and before writing to you. I will inform you, or Slocum, or both, if I get any thing definite.—I sincerely hope there can be no slip in your case this time, and although still on crutches I will give it the best attention and efforts I can.

Very Truly yours
U. S. GRANT

ALS, DLC-Fitz John Porter. On Jan. 9, 1884, U.S. Representative Henry W. Slocum of N. Y. submitted the majority report recommending a bill that would overturn a court-martial that removed Fitz John Porter from the army, restore Porter to the rank of col., and place him on the retired list. *HRC*, 48-1-1. A minority report is *ibid.*, part 2. On Feb. 1, the House of Representatives passed this bill after debate that often focused on USG's support for Porter. On March 13, the Senate passed after similar debate an amended bill that deleted a provision for Porter to receive back pay. See *CR*, 48-1, 477–515, 662–707, 799–840, 1796–1809, 1825–65; *SRC*, 48-1-74. That evening, USG telegraphed to Porter, who was staying at Slocum's residence. "I congratulate you most heartily on the result to-day in the Senate." *Washington Post*, March 14, 1884. See letter to Fitz John Porter, March 30, 1884.

1. Republicans would convene to nominate a presidential candidate on June 3.
2. Frederick T. Frelinghuysen.

To Augustus H. Garland

Washington Mch. 28 /84

HON. A. H. GARLAND
U. S. SENATE
DEAR SIR:

I am only just in receipt of your letter of the 19th inst. for- warded by Senator Allison.[1] It affords me very great pleasure to bear testimony to the ability and high character of Gen. Cadmus M. Wilcox; but you are laboring under a mistake to suppose that we were class-mates at West Point. Gen. Wilcox graduated three years after me, being but one year with me at the Academy, so that I was not particularly acquainted with his proficiency at that time. But after graduation we served for some years in the same regiment[2] and were intimate acquaintances during those years; and I feel no hesitation whatever in recommending Gen. Wilcox as qualified in every way for the position which you propose to recommend him for.

Very truly yours.

U. S. GRANT

LS, University of Arkansas, Fayetteville, Ark. Augustus H. Garland practiced law in Little Rock, served as C.S.A. representative and senator, and was Democratic governor of Ark. (1874–76) before entering the U.S. Senate (1877). For Cadmus M. Wilcox, USMA 1846 and former maj. gen., C.S. Army, see *PUSG*, 11, 217; *ibid.*, 27, 264-65; *SRC*, 48-1-212.

1. Born in 1829 in Ohio, William B. Allison settled in Dubuque (1857) and became a leading Iowa Republican, serving as U.S. Representative (1863–71) and beginning a long tenure as U.S. Senator in 1873.
2. Wilcox served with USG in the 4th Inf. from initial assignment (July 1, 1846) until transfer to the 7th Inf. (Feb. 16, 1847), but they were together throughout the Mexican War.

To Fitz John Porter

———

The Arlington
Washington D. C.
March 30th /84

DEAR GENERAL:

I received your letter, inclosing copy of one you had written to the Sec. of State, today. I had an interview with the Sec. of State yesterday, at the State Department in which I used the identical arguments you did why it would be bad policy for the President to veto your bill. I suggested however that if the President had any hesitation about signing it he might let it become a law, without signature, and annouce the fact to Congress ~~of its becoming a law~~ in a message in which he might say that no Constitutional question being involved, no hasty legislation resorted to, and the measure having received the sanction of both houses of Congress as well

as of an Army Board, of Officers two of whom ~~if they~~ were prejudiced against you, or rather believed in your guilt,[1] appointed by
the President, with the consent of Congress, he could not put his
judgement, without studying the question, and without the time to
possibly study it, against all these authorities. In fact it is a question whether the decission of the Army Board, appointed as it was,
should not have been considered binding upon Congress and the
President no matter what the views of particular members. The
Sec. seemed to accept these views. He did not intimate that he had
received a letter from you on the subject. I am not at liberty to repeat what the secretary said, and I am not able to advise you as to
the best course to pursue. I do not believe that the President would
veto your bill if it should come to him. But I do not know this with
enough certainty to advise your action. If I learn any thing further
I will let you know.

Very Truly yours
U. S. Grant

Gn. F. J. Porter.

ALS, DLC-Fitz John Porter. President Chester A. Arthur could not act on a bill to
restore Fitz John Porter to the army until the House of Representatives and Senate
resolved differences over the text on June 17, 1884. See *CR*, 48-1, 3937–44, 5251–52;
letters to Fitz John Porter, March 27, July 4, 1884; Henry Watterson, *"Marse Henry:"
An Autobiography* (New York, 1919), I, 216–18.

1. Maj. Gen. John M. Schofield, Brig. Gen. Alfred H. Terry, and Col. George W.
Getty reviewed Porter's case (1878–79). Schofield and Terry started the proceedings
biased against Porter. See *PUSG*, 30, 293–94; Schofield, *Forty-Six Years in the Army*
(New York, 1897), pp. 460–61.

To John B. Gordon

Washington April 3, 1884

Gen. J. B. Gordon
chairman Central Coms, &c.
Dear sir:

Your letter of March 31st, informing me that I had been chosen
to preside at a meeting of the different Posts of the Grand Army of

the Republic and Ex-Confederates in the city of New York on the 9th inst., was duly received. The object of the meeting is to inau- guerate under the auspices of ~~both~~ soldiers of both armies a move- ment in behalf of a fund to build a home for disabled ex-confederate soldiers. I am in hearty sympathy with the movement and would be glad to accept the position of presiding officer if I ~~were~~as able to do so. You may rely on me, however, for rendering all the aid I can in carrying out the designs of the meeting.[1] I am here under treatment for the injury I received on Christmas Eve last, and will not be able to leave here until later than the 9th inst., and I cannot tell now how soon, or when, I will probably be able to go. I have received, this morning, your despatch of last evening urging that I must be there to preside; but I have to respond that it will be im- possible for me to be there on the 9th, and I cannot now fix a day when I could certainly be present.

Hoping that your meeting will insure success, and promising my support, financially and otherwise, to the movement, I am,

Very Truly Yours.

U. S. GRANT

LS, ICHi. John B. Gordon, former maj. gen., C.S. Army, served as Democratic U.S. Senator (1873–80) from Ga. He promoted Southern industrialization, railroad devel- opment, and veterans' interests. On April 6, 1884, Arthur A. Spitzer, "adjutant R. E. Lee camp No. 1, Confederate Veterans," visited USG in Washington, D. C., "to thank him for the interest he had taken in the project of building a home for disabled Confed- erate soldiers. Gen. Grant replied that he was averse to presiding at meetings of any kind, but that the object of the Cooper institute meeting was one that so heartily met with his approval he would have overcome all aversion and accepted the invitation so earnestly pressed, but for the reasons stated in his letter to Gen. Gordon. He said his heart was enlisted in the matter and that the workers in the cause could count upon his co-operation to the extent of his ability." *Washington National Republican*, April 7, 1884. See *New York Tribune*, April 10, 1879; letter to Peyton Wise, May 7, 1884.

On [April 13], USG approved a statement. "The sale of boxes for the entertain- ment to be given at the 'Metropolitan Opera House'—Evening of 30th inst, under the auspices of Comrades of the Grand Army of the Republic, in aid of the establishment of a 'Home for Destitute Ex-Confederate Soldiers,' at Richmond, Va, will take place at St James Hotel tomorrow evening   General Grant has assured his comrades of his hearty sympathy, and support in this movement in behalf of the fund" DS (facsimile), Alexander Autographs, Inc., April 20, 1999, no. 111. The entertainment was an Ama- teur League production of *Richard III*. See *New York Tribune*, May 1, 1884.

1. USG contributed $500. *Southern Historical Society Papers*, XII, 5 (May, 1884), 238.

To Sherman Publishing Co.

———

Washington April 6 /84

The Sherman Publishing Co.

New York,

Gentlemen:

Replying to yours of 4th inst, I have to say that it would require a good deal of reference to authorities for me now to give an accurate account of the surrender of Gen. Lee, and the names of the persons who were present during the interview between us. But Badeau's History was submitted to myself and three of my staff officers, who were with me the last year of the war, and received our approval in every ~~respect~~ particular except in its conclusions about the merits of different officers. Historically it was all submitted, chapter by chapter, before its publication. His account, therefore, is the account which I would substantially give if I were to write it myself.

Yours truly

U. S. Grant

LS (facsimile), University Archives, Spring, 1995, no. 44. See Adam Badeau, *Military History of Ulysses S. Grant,* . . . (New York, 1881), III, 588–613.

On May 18, 1884, USG wrote to the Sherman Publishing Co. " . . . while the second of the two engravings was taken from a recent photograph—nearly nineteen years after the close of the rebellion—myself and family like it the best . . . " Charles Hamilton Auction, Jan. 22, 1981, no. 148. This correspondence possibly involved Ben La Bree, ed., *The Pictorial Battles of the Civil War* (New York, 1885).

To Adam Badeau

———

Washington, D. C.

Apl. 8th 1884.

Dear Badeau:

I have now been here three weeks. We go back to New York on Saturday next.[1] I am still on crutches, and will probably be on them, for a month or two yet. I have had but one opportunity to talk to the Sec. of State and then did not bring up your matter because the Sec. had said to me on the Street that he wanted to come over and see me and have a talk. This was when I first arrived. I saw him at the State Dept. a day or two after, but there was a clerk in the office, and the Asst. Sec. come in frequently. I will try to have a conversation before my departure. Of course I could not ask any thing from the President having taken decided grounds against his nomination. Then too it looks as though the appointing power was being worked for all it is worth to secure deligates to Chicago. I am satisfied that the vacant foreign missions will not be filled until after the Chicago convention.

In my telegram to you I scarcely knew what to say in the limit of a dispatch.[2] The idea I wanted to convey was that I thought it better that you should have no rupture with the department unless you wanted to leave the service. You have matters pending before the court of claims[3] that probably would be better served by quiet. The administration has seemed to me to be a sort of adinterum one endeavoring to offend no one, and to avoid positive action which would draw criticism. Probably the Administration has fewer enemies—outspo[ken] ones—than any preceding it. It has fewer positive hearty friends than any except Hayes posibly. But Arthur will probably go into the convention second in the number of supporters when he would not probably have a single vote if it was not for his Army of officials, and the vacancies he has to fill.

Very Truly yours
U. S. GRANT

ALS, Munson-Williams-Proctor Institute, Utica, N. Y. Adam Badeau, consul gen., Havana, had communicated to USG his intention to resign. *Badeau,* p. 558. For Badeau's resignation, see *New York Times,* April 12–13, 15, 1884. See also letter to Adam Badeau, March 3, 1884.

1. April 12, 1884.
2. On March 14, USG, Fort Monroe, Va., had telegraphed to Badeau. "Received your letter referred to. I advise patience until after June Convention. You understand why positive action need not be effected before that." *Badeau,* p. 557.
3. See letter to Adam Badeau, July 12, 1885, note 3.

To *Absalom H. Markland*

———

THE ARLINGTON,
April 8th, '84.

Dear Colonel:

I am sorry I was out when you called. I return Mr. _____ letter. Of course if he should call I would see him. But I go to New York on Saturday,[1] where it would be more convenient probably for him. It is well to say, however, that the Mexican road with which my name is connected is not commenced, nor is it likely to be soon. I have never been over that portion of the road along which abundance of valuable cabinet and dye woods are said to exist. The information I could give, therefore, would not justify a visit to that country for the purpose of locating timber lands, much less investing in them.

Very truly yours,
U. S. GRANT.

Col. A. H. Markland.

Washington Evening Star, Aug. 1, 1885. In late July, 1885, Absalom H. Markland spoke to a reporter. "While General Grant was last in Washington I received a letter from a friend who had some surplus money which he proposed to invest in timber lands along a proposed line of railway in Mexico, of which General Grant was President. He asked me to see the General on the subject, and if the General made a favorable report or expressed a favorable opinion of the investment he would go to the office in New York and make arrangements to invest. When I called with the letter the General and Mrs. Grant were out driving. I sat down and wrote a note to the General, stating who my correspondent was, and the desire I had that he should have accurate information, also inclosing the letter of my friend . . . ." *Ibid.*

1. April 12, 1884.

Speech

———

[Washington, D. C., April 11, 1884]

VETERANS OF THE GRAND ARMY OF THE REPUBLIC: I had flattered myself that I could get away without being called upon to say a word. I am glad to have had an opportunity to be with you this evening, as it is the first time since Christmas eve, nearly three and a half months ago, that I have been able to be out of my room in the evening. I hope before many weeks, however, to be so far recovered as to be sometimes seen upon the streets of whatever city I may happen to be in. I will say that I followed Gen. Logan in his story of the Vicksburg campaign with great interest, and I have not a single correction to make, though some of the leading incidents might have been carried a little further as to the details. The incident, for instance, of receiving orders from Washington to return back from the Mississippi and to move down the river and co-operate with Banks in the movement against Port Hudson until that place was reduced, and then having New Orleans for a base of supplies to move up the river and take Vicksburg. This order was written in quite an argumentative way and stated that the plan had the sanction of the president and the secretary of war. But when the officer who brought that order delivered it to me, I said to him Gen. Halleck has spoken a little too late.[1]

This whole thing reminded me of a traveler who stopped at a restaurant and called for a raw egg. As he swallowed it down he heard a chicken chirp, but the wayfarer had only time to say, "My friend, you spoke too late." In fact, just as the order was handed to me I heard a tremendous cheer, and saw Lawler in his shirt sleeves going in with his brigade, while the rebels were pulling the cotton out of the bales in front of them, and sticking it on the ends of their bayonets as flags of truce. Another point that Logan did not make, and perhaps he did not know of it at the time, was that I had sent Sherman off to the right to prepare for crossing—[2]

It was after I got into Vicksburg that Mr. Lincoln wrote me an autograph letter that was characteristic of the man. He said: "When you got across the Mississippi river below Vicksburg I thought you should have gone down. I see now you were right and I was wrong, and I want to offer you my apology."[3] We have had men who have occupied the position that he did who probably made more mistakes, but they never admitted them.

Washington National Republican, April 12, 1884; variant text, *Washington Post*, April 12, 1884. USG spoke at a Grand Army of the Republic camp fire held at the Masonic Temple.

On March 26, 1884, Brig. Gen. John Newton, Henry J. Hunt, and James H. Stine invited USG "to accompany them on the historical visit to Fredericksburg, Chancellorsville, and the Wilderness on May 15. The general could not accept the invitation now, but said if well enough at the time he would be glad to go." *Washington National Republican*, March 27, 1884.

On March 29, Commander Clark P. Crandall and Adjt. David F. McGowan, representing Burnside Post, No. 8, Grand Army of the Republic, presented USG with laudatory resolutions at his hotel and invited him to a reception. "The general expressed his gratification at the terms of the proposal and replied that, at the present time, he is scarcely able to promise that he can get out for an evening or endure the fatigues of an evening's handshaking, but that if the improvement of his injured leg should progress as he has reason to hope it will, he will be glad to avail himself of the opportunity . . ." *Ibid.*, March 31, 1884. On April 7, USG met veterans at the Arlington Hotel in Washington, D. C. "Gen. Grant was escorted by Mr. George M. Arnold, president of the Soldiers and Sailors National league, . . . The colored veterans filed in first and stood in a circle around the room. They were mostly members of Sumner and Morton posts, G. A. R. Mr. Arnold then advanced and said: 'General: The veterans in this city, learning of your presence here, desire to pay their respects and shake hands once more with their old commander.' Gen. Grant replied: 'I am pleased to meet my old comrades again,' and shook hands cordially with each man as he passed. After the Soldiers and Sailors league came the representatives of various Grand Army posts, members of the old Third Army corps, and a number of private citizens." *Washington Post*, April 8, 1884.

On April 2, USG had expressed thanks for his welcome at a Military Order of the Loyal Legion banquet. *Ibid.*, April 3, 1884.

1. See *PUSG*, 8, 221.
2. U.S. Senator John A. Logan of Ill., who had delivered the principal address, interrupted USG. "You ought to have told me that, general, before you made the attack." *Washington National Republican*, April 12, 1884
3. See *PUSG*, 9, 197.

To John A. Logan

Apl. 25th 1884

DEAR GENERAL:

I understand that a bill has been introduced asking—or making—Gens Hunt and Getty Major Generals on the retired list.[1] This being so may I ask you to add the name of General Z. B. Tower, Eng. Corps—retired—to be put on as a Brigadier. General

Tower really deserves this entirely independently of the others—
they are deserving also—both for his services during the war and
for an injustice done him since.   He was a Brigadier early in the
war but was unfortunate enough to be so badly wounded in ~~in~~ battle in 1862 as to take him out of the field for the balance—or nearly
so—of the war.   He was in command of two Brigades at the time
he had the end of the ~~thy~~ bone, next to the knee, shot away confin-
ing him to his room for eighteen months or more.   When Gen.
~~Meigs~~ Humphries was retired[2] General Tower was next to him in
rank in the Engineer Corps.   He and Wright, who was selected to
fill the place, were Classmates at West Point, Tower being head
and Wright second.   No one who knows Tower pretends to think
that he was in any way, professionally or otherwise, disqualified for
the position of Chief of his Corps.   On the contrary both Tower and
Wright were eminently qualified for it, and had Tower been appointed instead of Wright both would now be retired Chiefs of the
Engineer Corps, Tower being a year older than his classmate.

Very Truly yours
U. S. GRANT

HON. J. A. LOGAN, U. S. S.

ALS, DLC-John A. Logan. Horatio G. Wright retired as brig. gen., chief of engineers,
as of March 6, 1884. Zealous B. Tower remained retired as col. See *PUSG*, 30, 457–58;
New York Times, March 7, 1884.

    1. Legislation concerning Henry J. Hunt and George W. Getty, both retired cols.,
never became law. See *SRC*, 47-2-54; *HRC*, 48-1-758, 49-1-3176, 50-1-1947; *CR*, 48-1,
4447–53, 5699–700; Edward G. Longacre, *The Man Behind the Guns: A Biography of
General Henry Jackson Hunt*, . . . (South Brunswick, N. J., 1977), pp. 244–46.
    2. Andrew A. Humphreys retired as brig. gen., chief of engineers, as of June 30,
1879.

Interview

[New York City, May 6, 1884]

    Well, I suppose the country is generally prosperous outside
of Wall street.   It is true the producers are not getting very high
prices for their products, but their supplies are abundant and the

manufacturers are busy in all directions, and I think the condition of the country on the whole is quite satisfactory.

I think the population will increase right along and at the ratio of increase in the past fifteen years, the country at the end of the present century, that is sixteen years hence, ought and probably will approximate 100,000,000.

I think the changes will be all over, in all directions; they will be uniform. New York City will, of course, retain her ascendancy over all other places in the country, and I expect the people living at the end of the present century will see New York the financial center of the world. The entire Western country is being rapidly built up now. For grazing and agricultural purposes the great West is far ahead of what the people imagine. In fact, they never dream of its great fertility. The whole country along the northern borders of the United States, for 300 miles south of the British possessions, as far as the valleys stretch, is wonderfully productive.

The Southern States have developed wonderfully in the last fifteen years. I see no reason why the Southern States at the end of this century should not be the leading manufacturing section, particularly in cotton fabrics and iron in all forms. I have no doubt that the development that will take place in Mexico will be as rapid in the future, as it was on our own Pacific coast when we first acquired it, and I want to see the relations between that country and ours the most cordial of any nations in the world. If they do not do so it will be our own fault. We should do everything to secure the confidence of the people of Mexico. The more prosperous the Mexican people are the more pleased we shall be, and the more it will add to our individual interest.

St. Louis Post-Dispatch, May 7, 1884. "The Mail and Express today publishes a two-column interview with Gen. Grant on the financial and political situation. The interview was held yesterday before the news of the financial difficulties in Wall street had reached him. Gen. Grant was found at his office on the corner of Broadway and Wall street, where he makes tri-weekly visits, still using his crutch . . . ." *Ibid.* Asked about the Mormon question, USG said, "I think the surest and best remedy will be to take away from Utah the present territorial government and govern the Territory by Commissioners, as they do in the District of Columbia. Then enforce the anti-polygamy laws and such laws as Congress may prescribe." Concerning the Constitution, "there are several amendments that would be of advantage to the country if they were adopted, although I don't believe in tinkering with that instrument, and am opposed to an innovation except in cases of great necessity. There is one amendment I consider of great benefit, and that is one that would make the Presidential term one of seven years instead of four, with a provision that the President holding office seven years shall thereafter be ineligible. I would suggest another amendment, such as I recommended when I occupied the executive chair, which was to the effect that in the event of the failure of Congress to pass any regular appropriations in one year then the appropriations corresponding with those of the previous year shall be continued until such time as an appropriation may be passed. Another amendment I favor is, one also recommended during my term of office, authorizing the President to approve of a portion of any act of Congress, and withholding his approval from all portions of the act he does not approve, and return the same to the House in which the bill originated with his objections, when it shall receive two-thirds of the votes of both Houses before becoming a law." USG denied having "massed troops in the Capitol at Washington with a view to preventing any attempt to inaugurate Tilden." "There were no troops massed there at all. I intended to maintain peace and order at all hazards and I proposed to see installed in the Presidential chair the man Congress declared elected, whether Tilden or Hayes. I had no desire or power to influence the question of deciding who the people elected to the Presidency. That was a matter entirely with Congress. It is true I had directed General Sherman to have his troops in Baltimore and other points near Washington so they could be brought there on telegraphic notice in case of riot or disturbance, but this step was not in the benefit of either political parties or either candidates for the presidency. There was not a soldier in arms in Washington at the time." Asked if the U.S. would annex Canada, USG replied. "If such an event ever does occur it will be in the distant future. I think we have territory enough for all our wants. All we require is good friends on both sides of us. We certainly should not desire to annex unwilling people on either side of our borders." USG thought that immigration would not "increase in the same ratio in the future as the growth of population generally. As to immigration, I would so amend the Constitution as to change the period before which citizenship can be acquired, and I would make the ceremony of acquiring citizenship such that the privilege would be appreciated when obtained. In addition to this I would not extend the privilege to any person unable to speak and write the English language, or whose moral character is questioned at the time of becoming citizens. I think this the most important of all the amendments I would suggest, except possibly one, extending the presidential term, upon which I lay much stress, because we all know how much embarrassment is caused to the business of the country by these contests every four years, and how much the public is absorbed in them. We have under our present system only about two years of peace and quiet out of the four years a president holds office. By having the president elected every seven years the election would cause much less disturbance to business. We will always have two parties in this country. When one has fulfilled its mission it is generally followed by a shaking up, and each of the new parties then find in their ranks men who previously had been in opposite parties. But, to answer your question, I don't think the mission of the Republican party is yet fulfilled, nor will it be so long as the States lately in rebellion are solidly with one party, without regard to platform or principle . . . . If the Republicans make a wise selection they will carry the next election. I think our prospects better than they were four and eight years ago." As to President Chester A. Arthur's administration, "I prefer not to criticise it. I decidedly favor Logan. There is a great prejudice against him at the present time because of his vote on the inflation bill, but if

he is nominated I think his record on the financial question clear through from the beginning can be shown to be entirely satisfactory to those Republicans who oppose him
now. He is a man of ability and a man of courage to maintain his convictions, and one
who is not swayed about by every passing breeze." *Ibid.* See *PUSG,* 24, 274; *ibid.,* 25,
65–81; *ibid.,* 27, 130–33; James Pickett Jones, *John A. Logan: Stalwart Republican from
Illinois* (Tallahassee, 1982), pp. 71–78.

To Peyton Wise

NEW YORK, May 7, 1884.

Peyton Wise, Esq., Chairman, &c.:

DEAR SIR,—I am in receipt of the formal invitation to be present at the opening of the Fair for the home of disabled Confederate
soldiers on the 14th of this month, and your kind letter accompanying it.

If it was possible for me to do so I would accept this invitation, but, as you may know, I am still on crutches—not from injuries received in conflict with those in whose behalf the Fair is
given—and cannot hope to be in good traveling condition for some
months yet.

I hope your Fair may prove a success, and that the object contemplated may receive a support which will give to all the brave
men who need it a home and a rest from cares.

The men who faced each other in deadly conflict can well afford
to be the best of friends now, and only strive for rivalry in seeing
which can be the best citizens of the grandest country on earth.

Very truly yours,
U. S. GRANT.

Southern Historical Society Papers, XII, 5 (May, 1884), 238; dated May 11, 1884, in *Richmond Dispatch,* May 15, 1884. Peyton Wise, merchant and former lt. col, C.S. Army,
served as chairman of the R. E. Lee Camp Fair, Richmond. On May 10, 1884, a correspondent reported from Richmond on liberal northern contributions. *New York
Times,* May 11, 1884. See letter to John B. Gordon, April 3, 1884; *New York Herald,*
May 8, 1884.

To Virginia Grant Corbin

———

NEW YORK CITY, May 8, 1884.

DEAR JENNIE: I presume Fred has written to you—or will write—of the great disaster to the firm of Grant & Ward. He and I will endeavor to keep you from harm . . . . We are all well, and are trying to be happy. Do not be the slightest uneasy.[1]

Give our love to Mr. and Mrs. Cramer and dear Clara. Yours affectionately,

U. S. GRANT.

M. J. Cramer, *Ulysses S. Grant: Conversations and Unpublished Letters* (New York, 1897), p. 172 (ellipses in source). The failures of Grant & Ward and the closely allied Marine National Bank on May 6, 1884, generated legal actions against Ferdinand Ward, Grant & Ward general partner and principal business agent, and James D. Fish. Fish served as both Grant & Ward general partner and Marine National Bank president. USG and Ulysses S. Grant, Jr., Grant & Ward general partners, suffered immediate and severe financial losses, as did Frederick Dent Grant and Jesse Root Grant, Jr., heavy investors in the firm. New York City newspapers followed the story for the rest of the month. See *PUSG*, 30, 136, 400–402; Deposition, [*March 26, 1885*]; Hamlin Garland, "A Romance of Wall Street: The Grant and Ward Failure," *McClure's Magazine*, X, 6 (April, 1898), 498–505; Henry Clews, *Fifty Years in Wall Street* (New York, 1908), pp. 215–21. Ward later attempted his own exoneration. See *New York Herald*, Oct. 8–15, 1885, and *ibid.* (magazine section), Dec. 19 (pp. 1–2), 26 (pp. 1–2), 1909, Jan. 2 (pp. 9–10), 9 (p. 2), 16 (p. 2), 1910.

In testimony before a referee on Dec. 27, 1884, and Jan. 21, 1885, Ulysses Grant, Jr., recalled events. " . . . I first learned that there was trouble with the Marine Bank on the first Sunday in May. Ward came to my father's house on that day and called for me. He said to me: 'I'm afraid it's all up with us.' I asked him what he meant, and he said that the Marine Bank had been heavily drawn on and was on its reserve, and unless something was done by Monday morning it would fail, and as we had $750,000 to our credit there, the failure would be sure to hurt us. He saw father and induced him to go to Mr. Vanderbilt and borrow $150,000. Father did this, promising to repay the money by a check of Grant & Ward the next morning. I took the check to Mr. Vanderbilt the next morning, but unfortunately I did not have it certified, because Ward had told me that the bank was all right after the help that we had extended to it, and that the firm was all right too. I had no idea that we were in any trouble outside of the danger of our being unable to draw on our balance at the Marine Bank, and I supposed that this danger had been tided over." "When Ward told me the Marine Bank was in a fix and that if it failed it would tie Grant & Ward up I was startled. He afterward said it was all right, and then assured me that even if the Marine Bank did fail we would be able to keep up. He told me our balance in that bank was something over $200,000. Spencer told me it was $650,000. I cautioned Ward about the bonds of Mr. Chaffee . . . . I first thought of protecting Mr. Chaffee's interests on the Monday before the failure. I went to see Mr. Elkins and showed him a letter from Ward. I thought matters were getting tangled . . . ." *New York Times*, Dec. 28, 1884, Jan. 22, 1885. For slightly different renderings of this testimony, see *New York World*, Dec. 28, 1884, Jan. 22, 1885. On May 4, 1884, Ward, New York City, had written to Stephen B. Elkins, agent for Jerome B. Chaffee, father-in-law of Ulysses Grant, Jr. "Mr. Fish has secured $100,000. This, with the $150,000 I have, will fix us all right. I thank you a thousand times for what you have done and shall see that that institution does not get into such a fix again. I can run my own business, but I cannot take care of other people's." *New York Herald*, Dec. 17, 1884. On May 5, Ward, Brooklyn, wrote to Ulysses Grant, Jr. "I am very much afraid that the end has come and that, unless something is done to-night, everything will be over to-morrow. Now, take it coolly, old boy, don't get excited, and remember that we don't want our names to go down, and we will fight before it comes. I find that Tappan has drawn $3[0]0,000 more, and this, with the check of Mr. Vanderbilt for $150,000, will, I know, end the matter. I had hoped to get more loans on the Buffalo, New York and Philadelphia bonds, but could not[.] Mr. Randall had $100,000 government four per cent bonds with us, but he got scared and drew out to-day. This was unexpected by us. Now I have got the following securities, which can be used to-morrow, and, if in any way we can get checks to-night for $500,000, it must be done and we will pay the securities to-morrow: . . . Here is $1,323,700 worth of securities, and we must get $500,000 on them and have a check dated to-day. Now go to Mr. Vanderbilt and tell him just how we stand, and that if he will do this for us, we will send him 800,000 or 900,000 of these securities in the morning, whichever he may select of them, and if he won't do it try elsewhere. For we must not go down with all these good things on hand. I am going to start out myself and see several men and may be able to do something—so go right at it, Buck, and remember that if it is not done it will be the end of our business career. This is the last draft that Tappan will have to make; but if we don't pay this $500,000 to-night it will be our last blow. I will be down sometime during the night, for I shall go everywhere, so send me word what you succeed in doing, and if you get a check send it over by a messenger. Vanderbilt can draw on the Chemical Bank if he wants to. We must have the loan for ten days anyway, till we can get the bank straight. I am going to several bank men myself, and will be home late, so don't try to find me, but try and get all you can. This is our last hope, Buck, so do all you can." *Ibid.* Elkins later testified that Ulysses Grant, Jr., visited him that evening to discuss the safety of Chaffee's bonds. *Ibid.* Also on May 5, Ward wrote to Fish. "I have a time loan of $100,000 on 150 shares of Union Dry Dock stock and $100,000 of Chicago and Atlantic notes. If you will send me these securities I will bring down a lot of bonds in their place to-day . . . . Every little helps." *New York Times*, March 14, 1885. On the same day, Ward wrote two more letters to Fish. "I have secured a loan of $250,000 from a private investor up town, and will take the securities up to him and get a check, but may not get to the bank until late in the afternoon. I will let you have the check to-night or by 9 o'clock in the morning . . . . This, with $100,000, will make us $350,000 better." "I will get two-hundred and fifty-thousand-dollar check in to-night if possible. Am doing my best to put matters through and make bank easy. I went for Spencer, and he went to Platt to get him to deposit $50,000 extra to-day. And Spencer also got $75,000 new money from Pennsylvania Coal Company. I am not leaving a stone unturned. I think Gen. Grant will get some more money from W. H. V. to-morrow." *Ibid.*, May 17, 1884.

On May 6, "Gen. Grant was informed of the difficulties of the firm early in the day. He reached the firm's office about noon and remained in the private office until 2 o'clock, when he stepped into a carriage and was driven home. He was as calm as usual, but declined to talk about the trouble. Many offers of aid were made to the ex-President, but he said that he did not feel at liberty to accept any of them until the true position of affairs could be ascertained . . . ." *Ibid.*, May 7, 1884. On the same day, Ulysses Grant, Jr., said: "I cannot deny or corroborate the reports current. We are nearly $500,000 short. Our safes are locked and until we can find Mr. Ward I cannot say how we stand." *New York Graphic*, May 6, 1884. See Adam Badeau, "The Last Days of General Grant," *Century Magazine*, XXX, 6 (Oct., 1885), 920.

On May 7, Wednesday, USG "came to the office of Grant & Ward about noon and remained until 2:15 p. m. For some time he was closeted with ex-Senator Roscoe Conkling, who is said to be acting, if not as counsel, as a friendly adviser of the ex-President. When General Grant left the office to take his coupé Mr. Conkling followed him out, and for a few minutes held a final conversation with him through the door of the coupé." *New York Tribune*, May 8, 1884. On May 8, Thursday, a reporter elaborated. "General Grant's visit to Mr. Vanderbilt was made on Sunday and then the latter's check for $150,000 was given. It is said that at the request of General Grant the check was dated as of Saturday, and the check of Grant & Ward on the Marine Bank Mr. Vanderbilt agreed not to use for a day or two. It is not believed that the ex-President knew the state of the firm's affairs, and Mr. Ward is credited with furnishing a satisfactory explanation of the circumstances under which Mr. Vanderbilt's consent was obtained. When presented the check of Grant & Ward had been rendered worthless by the two failures. The day after the failure General Grant called on Mr. Vanderbilt at the latter's desire and it is said that assurances were given that he would be fully protected in the matter, even if great sacrifices were necessary in the direction of Mrs. Grant's property." *Ibid.*, May 9, 1884. Over Vanderbilt's objections, USG transferred "two houses in Washington, one in Philadelphia, and his farm in St. Louis. If these did not settle the debt, wrote Gen. Grant to Mr. Vanderbilt, 'then my wife's house in New-York and my place at Long Branch will also be at your disposal.'" *New York Times*, May 11, 1884. On May 21, a correspondent reported from Washington, D. C. "There was placed on record in the office of the Recorder of Deeds here yesterday afternoon, a mortgage made by U. S. Grant, of New-York, to W. H. Vanderbilt upon the property known as No. 1,509 Vermont-avenue and No. 1,213 O-street in this city, to secure the sum of $150,000, loaned by Mr. Vanderbilt to Gen. Grant on the 3d inst. The instrument bears date of May 17." *Ibid.*, May 22, 1884. A report appeared on May 22. "It has been announced upon authority that General Grant has declined to receive back the property which he turned over to Mr. William H. Vanderbilt in payment of the loan of $150,000 made just before Grant & Ward failed . . . ." *New York Herald*, May 22, 1884. See letter to William H. Vanderbilt, Jan. 3, 1885.

On May 8, Thursday, the Grant & Ward partners had assigned the firm's assets to creditors. "The deed of assignment was drawn on Tuesday, and was executed on that day by Ferdinand Ward. On the following day it was signed by Gen. Grant and his son Ulysses, and yesterday, just before the document was filed, James D. Fish attached his signature . . . ." *New York Times*, May 9, 1884. On the same day, 10:00 A.M., USG visited the Grant & Ward building, "and after passing a few minutes in the office of the firm went up stairs to the room of Roscoe Conkling, his private counsel, with whom he was closeted for a long time. The General looked weary and troubled, and declined to see anybody except the most intimate friends. He left the office shortly after 2 o'clock, and entering a carriage was driven up town." *Ibid.*

Also on May 8, Frederick Grant and Jesse Grant, Jr., assigned their assets to creditors. Among his debts, Frederick Grant owed $25,000 to Virginia Grant Corbin and $7,300 to Mary Grant Cramer. USG's sons declined to make statements, leaving the financial manager, James McNamee, to convey that the two "had very intimate relations" with Grant & Ward and "transacted most of their business through it, . . . I have not the least idea of the amount of their assets or even of their character . . . . *Ibid.*

On May 24, Fish explained his relationship with Ward to a reporter. "I have known him since he was a young man on the Produce Exchange. I became acquainted with him through Sidney Green, who was at that time cashier of the Marine Bank. Mr. Green told me that he expected the young man would become his son-in-law, that he took great interest in him and considered him to be a very bright young man. Afterward Mr. Ward married Mr. Green's daughter, Ella C. I was present at the wedding, shortly after which Mr. Green died suddenly. I received a letter from Mr. Ward soon after, saying that he hoped to get a share in my confidence, and if found worthy, to retain it. Passing over the many dealings of minor importance which I afterward had with Mr. Ward, some in connection with the Produce Exchange certificates and some relating to other matters, I come down to the time when Mr. Ward spoke to me of 'Buck' Grant, saying that he was a fine fellow, and that the proposition had been made that they should go into the stock-brokerage business together. Ward asked me to put in $100,000 against $100,000 which he would put in and $100,000 which 'Buck' Grant would put in. 'Buck' Grant is the familiar name given to U. S. Grant, jr. I expressed surprise at Mr. Ward's idea that he could command $100,000 at that time, but he assured me that he could and he subsequently did put into the concern $100,000. U. S. Grant, jr., and I put in an equal amount each, articles of copartnership were drawn up and the firm was styled 'Grant & Ward.' Later, General Grant, seeing that we were making money, which we did at a rapid rate, asked to be let in with $50,000. We allowed him to come in and to put in that amount and then we made a division of the profits by sevenths, General Grant receiving one-seventh and the rest of us, that is the other three, two-sevenths each. Afterward General Grant requested that his son, Jesse R. Grant be allowed to come in. This was agreed to, Jesse R. Grant putting in $50,000, making the total capital $400,000. It has been represented that I was very intimate with Ward and was much with him at the firm's place of business. This is not true. There have been periods when three months have elapsed between my visits there, and on an average I have not been there more than ten times a year . . . . On the morning of the failure I found that we were debtor to the Clearing House about $900,000, and that this was caused by the checks of Grant & Ward against which we held no balance. Early that morning I went to Ward's house, No. 81 Pierrepont-st., Brooklyn, and said I wanted to see Mr. Ward at once. His wife came downstairs and said that Ferdinand was very tired, that he had been up late the night before, and that he begged to be excused. I replied that I must see him, and started upstairs to go to his room. I found that while his wife had delayed me by engaging me in conversation, Ward had left his room by a back stairs, and escaped from the house by means of a basement door. He went to Stamford and remained there the rest of that day. Later, some days after the bank had closed its doors, Ward came to the bank while I was there, and we had an interview in one of the upper rooms of the bank building. It was a hot one, I can tell you. I said things to him that I would not like any man to be able to say truthfully to me . . . ." *New York Tribune*, May 26, 1884. On May 29, Fish testified before a referee examining the firm. " . . . A big book was produced which Mr. Fish said was kept 'most of the time' at the Marine Bank. It showed some of the business transactions of Grant & Ward. Most of the entries were made by Mr. Ward; some by himself. It contained a record of notes maturing and discounted for the firm. Some entries showed large profits on sales of corn, etc., to the Government. Mr. Fish had never compared the price said to have been paid by the Government with the market price . . . . Mr. Fish said that he understood that Grant & Ward did not deal directly with the Government, but 'took assignments of contracts merely that had been awarded to others.' . . . Mr. Fish said that in no instance where he was informed of the price paid for the articles supposed to be furnished the Government had he inquired what the market price was. He understood that the articles consisted mainly of staple products, such as corn, oats, etc., the market price of which was easily ascertainable at the Produce Exchange. Sometimes he knew the market price at the time. 'But,' he added, 'these were for future delivery as stated by Mr. Ward, and the Government was willing to pay a fixed price much higher than the market price at the time of the contract.' He understood the delivery was to be made at points in the West. He had never inquired as to freight rates paid for transporting the grain, etc. He believed Ward's statements concerning these matters to be correct." *Ibid.*, May 30, 1884. For Ward's reaction to Fish's testimony, see *ibid.*, *New York Herald*, and *New York World*, May 31, 1884. See also *ibid.*, July 2, 11–12, 1886; *New York Times*, March 28, April 3, 1885; Memorandum, [*May, 1884*].

On May 7, William T. Sherman, St. Louis, had written to U.S. Senator John Sherman of Ohio. " . . . Look at *Grant* now—His experience in the White House poisoned his mind, and tempted his family to yearn for that Sort of honor,—he is now bankrupt— and in the very language he used to me last winter when Speaking of Horace Porters failure, 'He had lost his fortune, and more in reputation.' So will it prove in Grants case in coming into Competition with trained & experienced dealers in money—I fear he has lost Every thing—and 'more in reputation' . . . ." ALS, DLC-William T. Sherman. See Charles W. Moulton to William T. Sherman, May 9, 1884, *ibid.*

1. For brief reports on possible losses suffered by USG's sister, Virginia Corbin, and his sister-in-law, Anna E. Dent, because of the Grant & Ward failure, see *New York Tribune*, May 18, 1884. See also *Washington Post*, March 19, 1886.

To George W. Childs

———

May 10th /84

MY DEAR MR. CHILDS,

Many thanks for your kind letter of yesterday. I can not make any statement now for publication, nor even in confidance. When you saw me on Monday[1] I supposed the firm was as solid as any in the city and Mr. Ward worth more than three million outside of his interest in it, and Mr Fish and U. S. Grant Jr also both well off.

yours Truly

U. S. GRANT

P. S. By the contract of co-partnership Mr. Ward alone had the

right to sign the firm name and he alone had the key a combination
to the vault. U. S. Jr. gave no attention to the business further than
to occasionally look over the books which shew well enough.

U. S. G.

ALS, DLC-USG. On May 10, 1884, a correspondent interviewed George W. Childs in
Philadelphia concerning the Grant & Ward failure. "Gen. Grant put into the business
for his son $50,000. I knew all about that and I think no man knows more about the
General's business than myself. I did not know that he had become a general partner
and I don't think any of his friends did, for he never told me that he had entered the
firm. Last Monday I had a long conversation with him in New York and I tell you at
that time he had no idea of the firm's failure." Asked about USG's house in Philadelphia, Childs said. "Gen. Grant held that house in his own name, and of course they
could attach it. The dwelling was presented to him shortly after the close of the war by
a number of Philadelphia gentlemen. Mr. George H. Stuart was active in making the
presentation of the house. The General also owned a house in Galena, Ill., and a farm,
all of which could be attached. He held in his name about $200,000 worth of property."
Concerning the reported assignment of Julia Dent Grant's assets, Childs remarked.
"If she has done so I think she was very foolish, for it makes but a drop in the bucket.
She held in her name the house in New York and the cottage at Long Branch, and they
could not have been attached . . . . As I told you, about $300,000 is held in trust for him
which cannot be reached. It is perfectly safe and it will yield him about $15,000 a year.
The trustees will pay him the interest . . . . The General knows nothing about business,
and his son knew but little of what was going on. The son had an office in a room in
the upper part of the building where he attended to his law business, and Ward was
left to run the banking affairs on the first floor of the building. The trouble has been
brought about through Fish and Ward . . . ." *New York World*, May 11, 1884. For the
Long Branch cottages, see *ibid.*, May 12, 1884.
    On May 9, Friday, a correspondent in New York City had reported comments
from George Jones, *New York Times* publisher. "General Grant's fund of $250,000
is absolutely safe. I don't know where his enemies find their lies. The fund is invested in Toledo and Wabash second mortgage bonds, interest payable quarterly, and
guaranteed the principal and interest by the heirs of the late Governor E. D. Morgan.
Hitherto we have paid the interest annually; the 1st of May of each year has found the
General in possession of $15,140, the interest in full on the investment. Hereafter we
shall pay him quarterly, not only because he needs the money, but because we do not
mean that anyone else shall lay hands on it. General Grant could not touch a dollar of
the principal even if he desired to do so any more than I could. He can will it, however,
at his death to his heirs. I was with General Grant on Sunday last, and he was in complete ignorance of the impending disaster. Other than this fund he doesn't possess a
dollar; and more than that, he is deeply and almost irretrievably in debt. What he did
in Wall street he did for his sons, and it seems too sad that this man, who has done so
much for his country, should be left in his old age dependent on the nation he helped
to save." *Philadelphia Public Ledger*, May 10, 1884. For the trust fund, see *PUSG*, 30,
137–38; *New York Times*, Oct. 23, 1885.
    Also on May 9, a correspondent noted a report from New York City "that the li-
abilities of Messrs. Grant & Ward will exceed $10,000,000. This amount, it is said, is
over-estimated, though the knowing men of the street do not deny that there is every

possibility that the indebtedness of the bankrupt firm will exceed $7,000,000 .... The office of the firm was crowded this morning with people seeking information as to the probable outcome of the conference known to have been had between the members of the firm last night. Mr. Ward arrived at an early hour, but immediately shut himself up in his private room away from every one save his most intimate friends. He said that he would not make any statement at present .... Col. Frederick Grant said: 'I have just turned over all my claims against the firm to Mr. McNamee, my assignee. I have done this in order to get matters settled up, so that I may do something else. I cannot say what the amount of the liabilities of the firm will be, nor do I care to say what the amount of my claim is. All I had was invested with the firm, and I am now in search of a job. I do not know whether I shall remain in Wall street or not, or what line of business I shall go into. I am looking for something to do. I cannot say whether I will go into business for myself. That will depend upon whether or not anything is saved from the wreck.'" *Philadelphia Public Ledger,* May 10, 1884. On the same day, Ulysses S. Grant, Jr., spoke to a reporter. "The Grant family has lost its entire fortune; the ruin is complete. Not only have I and my father and two brothers put every cent we possessed into the firm, but we invested large sums which we borrowed from our friends, supposing that everything was going along splendidly and that we were amassing a great fortune. I first put the $17,500 yearly income on my wife's fortune into the concern and then I put the principal in with it. My father-in-law loses $500,000 which I borrowed from him. I knew very little about the affairs of the establishment. In fact, the articles of agreement of the firm provided that Mr. Ward should draw all the checks and transact all the business. Mr. Ward insisted that the business management should be left solely to him. I had the greatest confidence in him and I consider him to be a very able man. When he first proposed the partnership to me I knew that he was making plenty of money, and I said:—'Oh, you don't want to attach yourself to a slow coach like me.' He proposed the thing a couple of times before I agreed. I did not, nor did my father or brothers have the faintest idea that anything was wrong. Up to the time of the failure I believed that I was worth $1,700,000. I held the bank's notes for upward of $1,000,000. Why, I have told my friends of our fortune within a few days, little dreaming of the real state of affairs. Then came the crash. My father came down to the office on the day of the failure, and as he walked across the floor toward me I said:—'Father, everything is bursted and we cannot get a cent out of the concern.' That was the very first intimation he had that there was the slightest trouble. My brother Fred had borrowed largely from his friends, and my brother Jesse put some borrowed money into the firm on the day previous to the failure. So confident were we all that Grant & Ward were making piles of money that we invested everything we could get. I only drew out money against my own account, but I kept putting in almost as much, and the only real funds which I retained were about sufficient for our living expenses. None of us liked to keep a dollar out of the firm that was not absolutely needed, because we thought that we were losing when we kept money that might be earning a very heavy profit. Several times recently when I went to friends and asked them for loans on the promise of enormous interest they declared that such a transaction would be usurious. I never asked for these loans again. To show you how little I knew about the affairs of the firm, I said when the Marine Bank failed that it would simply prevent us for a time from giving certified checks. No one in our family had any idea that the firm had overdrawn its account. When I secured loans upon the bonds which had been given as collateral for loans from our firm I did not know that the bonds were being rehypothecated. Of course it is quit[e] apparent that the immense profits credited to members of the firm were fictitious. I do not care to go into this any further just at present, as the whole matter will be cleared up, I suppose, in the courts . . . . I do not know whether I will be able to stay in New York when this thing is cleared up, for I may have to enter into business elsewhere." *New York Herald*, May 10, 1884. See *ibid.*, May 11, 1884; *St. Louis Globe-Democrat*, May 18–19, 1884.

On Jan. 3, 1885, Grant, Jr., testified before a referee examining the Grant & Ward failure. A reporter summarized the testimony: "He said that he had a talk with Ward the day after the failure. At that time the phenomenal financier was in a state of intense nervous excitement, weeping and wringing his hands in his distress. He admitted to Mr. Grant that he had been a wicked thief and a great rascal, robbing, cheating, and deceiving him and the other members of his family from first to last. Ward was humble and penitent[.] Mr. Grant said that he then told his crushed partner that the least he could do would be to tell the truth in the matter. Ward promised to do so . . . . Mr. Grant explained, in the course of two hours' testimony, that in all his dealings with Ward he never had any other evidence of any business professed to be transacted than Ward's personal memoranda. He knew nothing of any alleged Government contracts or of any special influence his firm was supposed to have had with the Government except it might be through other parties with whom Ward claimed to have business dealings. He said that he had no idea of the magnitude of the firm's transactions as since developed, or that so many parties were interested in them . . . . Ward was the business man of the concern, the one supreme authority in financial management. He signed all the checks, indorsed all the notes, and negotiated all business transactions. No one disputed his authority, no one questioned his judgment. Mr. Grant said that on one occasion he made a purchase of stock for the firm and Ward made strenuous objections to the interference. In less than three minutes the transaction was unloaded from the shoulders of the firm on to U. S. Grant, Jr., in person. He lost $6,000 that day by his venture, and came to the conclusion that Ward was a great deal smarter man that he had heretofore given him credit for being. After that Ward had greater swing than ever. Only once did the witness sign the firm's paper . . . . When he went into the firm he supposed that his special mission was to find business for it so far as it lay in his power to do so. He was ever on the watch for opportunities to turn over a dollar. But he soon found out that really he was doing very little for the firm except to draw his share of the supposed profits. In fact, he became a customer of his own firm. Mr. Fish seldom came near the office, and ex-President Grant's visits there were even less frequent. The witness always understood that when the first articles of copartnership, with Gen. Grant included in them, were drawn up both the General and Mr. Fish were written down as special partners, though he knew nothing about their complying with specific State statutes in that particular. When Gen. Grant put $50,0000 more into the firm his son understood that both he and Mr. Fish became general partners. Gen. Grant, so his son said, occasionally inquired how the firm was getting along, and whether he had either made or lost anything during the past month or two. Young Mr. Grant explained, furthermore, that he had been in business transactions with Ward before he joined in partnership with him, and had always supposed Ward to be a very rich man. On one occasion Ward had taken him to his drawer in the safe deposit vaults and had shown him a tin box stuffed until it seemed ready to burst with securities. Ward represented at the time that in all the securities represented $1,500,000. Mr. Grant couldn't exactly explain why, but he always believed that those were good, negotiable securities, though he never examined them . . . . When the firm was first organized Mr. Fish, Mr. Ward, and young Mr. Grant each put in $100,000. Mr. Grant put in some cash, some mining stock, which afterward sold at an advance, and some of Ward's 'flour' notes. Ward claimed to have put in $100,000 in cash, and here again the other two took his word for it. Subsequently, when young Mr. Grant discovered that Ward had really put in some worthless mining stock he raised a mild objection, but the firm appeared so prosperous and the footings of profits on the books seemed so large that he didn't like to make much fuss about it. Mr. Grant seldom examined the firm's books except to glance at the footings. Ward made monthly statements up to January, 1883, just after Mr. Grant's return from his wedding trip to Europe, when he ceased making them . . . ." *New York Times,* Jan. 4, 1885. For related testimony, see *ibid.,* Feb. 1, 1885. See also *ibid.,* Sept. 9, 18, 1885, Nov. 6, 1887; *New York World,* Jan. 4, Feb. 1, 1885; Memorandum, [*May, 1884*].

1. May 5, 1884.

To Charles Wood

3 E 66th st
New York City,
May 12th /84

DEAR SIR:

Your more than kind letter of Saturday inclosing Check for $500.00 and proposing to send like amount on my note, payable in one year, without interest, is received. The money at this time would be of exceeding use to me having not enough to pay one months servant hire, or room if I were to leave my house, and nothing coming in until the First of August. I therefore accept the Check just received and this is my acknowledgement of a debt of Five Hundred Dollars, one year from this date on the terms of your letter.

Very Truly yours
U. S. GRANT

CHAS. WOOD ESQ.
LANSINGBURGH N. Y.

ALS, Ralph W. Naylor, Hopkinton, R. I. Born in 1831 in Lansingburgh, N. Y., Charles Wood managed a brush factory begun by his father. E. & C. Wood Co. flourished during the Civil War filling army contracts. On May 10, 1884, Wood, Lansingburgh, wrote to USG. "Some twenty two years ago new paper of the U S was at a discount. I will send you one thousand dollars if you indicate you will furnish your note for same amount at 12 months without interest with your option of one renewal at same rate. I enclose check for five hundred dollars on account my share due for services ending about April 1865." ALS, Mrs. Paul E. Ruestow, Jacksonville, Fla. See letters to Charles Wood, May 19, 1884, Jan. 5, 1885; *Troy Times*, April 10, 1917.

Also on May 10, Andrew J. White, London, wrote to USG. "I have noticed with pain the amount of your losses, and I have been struck with admiration to see the efforts you are making to secure the claims for money advancd to you. Your course in these personal matters shows the same self sacrificing spirit you evinced during the war for the good of the country. Although I am unknown to you personally I feel that, as an American, I am indebted to you to a certain amount. I authorise you to draw on me at 10 days for one thousand dollars, and I would suggest that it be applied to a fund for the redemtion of Mrs. Grants house which she has so nobly placed to your disposal. It is my wish that my name shall not be made public in any manner in connction with this transaction and a compliance with this request will be all the compensation I shall require." ALS, USG 3. Julia Dent Grant endorsed this letter. "I am afraid this letter never was acknowledged even. I found it as if it had been mislaid" AE (initialed, undated), *ibid.* White graduated from Yale Medical School (1846), prospered selling wholesale drugs, and eventually invested in several businesses, particularly typewriter cos. See *New York Times*, Oct. 28, 30, 1898.

On May 12, James B. Eads, New York City, wrote to USG. "I have learned with sincere regret of the disaster which has recently befallen the firm of Grant & Ward, and of the great pecuniary loss you have sustained thereby. I know nothing of the facts but what I see in the newspapers; I however venture to tresspass upon you so far as to say that I have a small balance in bank here which will be most cheerfully placed at your disposal, and which you can repay next year or at any later time that shall suit your convenience, and without interest. If the money will be of any service to you please say so and I will send you my check for five thousand dollars at once." ALS, *ibid.* Julia Grant endorsed this letter. "I am happy to say that General did not *have* to accept the generous offer of this most noble generous man one of three that came or rather offered Genl Grant assistance Mr Romero Mr Wood & the above" AE (undated), *ibid.*

To George W. Childs

[*May 15, 1884*]

The events of the last few days are much more disastrous than I supposed when the failure first occurred. The night before the failure I supposed the firm of Grant & Ward had a surplus of about $2,400,000.00 over and above the original capital of $400,000.00, as Ward reported, and the books of Grant & Ward at the bank showed it, that we were credited at the Marine Bank with more than $660,000.00. Myself and my three sons had all that we possessed, except real estate, in the bank. We also believed that there was $1,300,000.00 of unpledged securities in the vaults. This catastrophy throws us all into a different style of living. Fred, and

I have taken a little house in Morristown, N. J., where we will live together. U. S. Jr. has also taken one there.¹ My Long Branch Cottage will therefore be for rent. If you have a friend who wants it, I will be glad to let them have it. I do not want it to go to other than a pleasant neighbor.² I could bear all the pecuniary loss if that was all, but that I could be so long deceived by a man who I had such opportunity to know is humiliating. Then too to have my name and that of my family associated with what now proves to have been nothing but a fraud for at least two years back. When you met me in the office the day before the doors were closed, I believed Ward to be worth 1,000,000.00 of Dollars himself alone. With kindest regards of Mrs. Grant and Self to Mrs. Childs.

Very truly,

U. S. GRANT.

P. S. I would be glad to see you at my house, if convenient. Please regard this as confidential for the present.

Samuel T. Freeman Catalogue, Dec. 10, 1928, no. 229. On May 28, 1884, George W. Childs published an editorial contrasting USG's judgment of men in military and civilian life. *Philadelphia Public Ledger,* May 28, 1884.

    On May 13, Frederick Dent Grant had spoken to a reporter. "Yes, I am absolutely penniless, . . . Ward has ruined us all. My brother Ulysses has just rented a little cottage in Morristown, N. J., and will immediately leave the city. I also have a little house there. Whether I shall be able to keep it or not I do not know. I scarcely know where I stand. The secret of the whole trouble is the false representations made to us by Ward and his rashness in speculation . . . . My brother was not so grossly negligent as the public have been given to understand. For the past three years, almost from the very beginning of business in fact, his domestic affairs have consumed the greater portion of his time. When the firm began business he was exceedingly attentive to all its details . . . . Neither the General, my brothers nor myself ever took a cent from the firm, excepting for actual expenses. Ward, on the contrary, has been living fast and taking all he could get. Although I was but a customer, I on Tuesday morning last considered that I was worth at least $500,000, nearly all of which was on deposit with the firm at the time of the crash. I must say that neither the General, my brothers, nor myself ever suspected that Ward was speculating so rashly as recent developments indicate . . . . As far back as two years ago we heard that he had held out inducements to investors based upon the 'secret influence which Gen. Grant had at Washington for securing profitable Government contracts.' When this report reached the ears of my father he communicated it to Ward and threatened to withdraw from the firm. Ward assured him that he had never offered such inducements to any one . . . . I think [*William H. Vanderbilt*] has shown himself to be a magnanimous man. When he ascertained that father was so seriously embarrassed through the rascality of Ward, and that father had already caused Mr. McNamee to draw up conveyances of a portion of his and mother's property to satisfy the obligation, Mr. Vanderbilt sent a note to him saying that he did not desire the property, but begged father to cancel the obligation at his will. He assured father of his profoundest sympathy and wished him to take his own time to arrange for a settlement. You can rest assured, though, that while father has a cent in the world it will be employed in cancelling his indebtedness. Aside from the property the proceeds of which will be employed to settle with Mr. Vanderbilt, father will turn the remainder of his holdings in as assets to pay the indebtedness of the firm of Grant & Ward." Asked his opinion of placing USG on the army retired list with full pay, Frederick Grant said. "I think it is no more than just and right. It ought to have been done long ago. I had not heard of the passage of the bill. Father certainly needs money if he never did before. He would readily make use of the fund of $250,000, so kindly contributed by the people, to aid in satisfying his obligations were he able to do so. It is so restricted, however, that he cannot touch a cent above the interest. I am perfectly free to say that we have all of us been fools to trust our means to Ward. The gross rascality, however, which he has exhibited calls not for sympathy but for the severest condemnation." *Ibid.* On May 7, a correspondent had reported from Washington, D. C. "Mr. Edmunds introduced a bill in the Senate to-day placing General Grant on the retired list of the Army with the full pay of a general. He accompanied the introduction with remarks, in which he expressed the hope that the committee on Military Affairs would, for obvious reasons, give the matter prompt attention. The reasons referred to, of course, were General Grant's financial losses incurred by the failure of the firm of which he was a member. The bill is the same as that introduced by Senator Logan last year and passed by the Senate. There seems to be no doubt that the Senate will pass such a bill, and it is also conceded that a Democratic House would not openly reject it. Therefore the measure seems reasonably certain of success. The bill would secure to General Grant the pay of a general, $14,500, and the emoluments attached thereto, amounting in all to some $19,000." *New York Tribune,* May 8, 1884. See letter to Edward F. Beale, June 26, 1884.

On May 14, at his first appearance before the referee examining the affairs of Grant & Ward, Ferdinand Ward explained "that he simply borrowed from Peter to pay Paul. He borrowed money at a high rate of interest to pay debts previously contracted. The other partners in the firm knew comparatively little about it. Though the transactions were carried on with Grant & Ward, they were mainly personal. He did it to avoid becoming hopelessly insolvent and to endeavor to keep the actual state of affairs from the public. Not for two years had he been able to pay his debts without raising money at a high rate of interest. The crisis which had overtaken him was not unexpected. After Mr. Ward had testified for several hours he looked as though he was likely to break down from sheer weakness. His face was deathly pale . . . ." *New York Times,* May 15, 1884.

On May 17, Saturday, a correspondent reported from Pittsburgh. "In his examination on Friday, Ferdinand Ward mentioned W. W. Smith as one of a number of men who, he said, were interested in his (Ward) swindling operations. Mr. Smith is the senior partner in the banking house of Smith & Sons, of Washington, Penn., and a first cousin of General Grant. This afternoon he said: 'I first saw Ward in New-York about two years ago. After my return home, I received letters from Grant & Ward, stating that they would, if I desired, give me an opportunity to make from $2,000 to $3,000 in thirty days on an investment of $30,000. He stated that the firm had a contract to deliver a large quantity of flour at a certain figure. This flour could be bought at that time at a price so far below the price at which it was to be sold that the profit promised could be easily made. I sent them my check for $30,000 on my New-York correspondents, Morgan, Drexel & Co., and they cashed it. In return Grant & Ward sent me a

promissory note at thirty days for the amount invested and the profits that were to ac-
crue. At the end of the thirty days the note was promptly taken up. Then they wrote
me that they had a contract to supply a number of public institutions at rates which
would insure enormous profit, and I again invested, receiving, as before, a thirty day
promissory note, which was promptly taken up when it fell due. I couldn't understand
just how they were going to continue this brilliancy of operation and I made no further
investment, but allowed them to keep the profits, which accumulated with great rapid-
ity. Each month I received a promissory note for the entire amount due, which was
very large. How much? Now, I really cannot tell, but it was large, so you see I lost
nothing, but these accumulated profits which I am glad I did not draw, as they were not
legitimate earnings, and therefore not my property; indeed, had I drawn them I should
not under the circumstances have retained the money . . . .'" *New York Tribune*, May 18,
1884. See *ibid.*, *New York Herald*, and *New York Sun*, May 17, 1884.

On May 21, a correspondent reported from Washington, D. C. "A gentleman who
saw General Grant in New York last week says he is utterly broken down by the disclo-
sures which have followed the failure of the bank in which he was interested, and that
the shock has shortened his life by ten years. He talks freely about it to his intimate
friends, but keeps himself secluded and fears that he has lost the respect and confidence
of the country. The General admits that some of his friends came to him months ago
and warned him that Ward was an adventurer and was using his name in an improper
way, but his confidence in the young man was so great that he repulsed them, and
thinks he may have treated some of them coolly. He is said to be so sensitive about the
matter that he does not read the newspapers and knows but little of the magnitude of
the failure or the extent of Ward's fraudulent operations." *New York Graphic*, May 21,
1884. Ward was arrested on May 21. On May 22, Julia Dent Grant denied that Ulysses
S. Grant, Jr., had fled to Canada to escape arrest. See *St. Louis Post-Dispatch*, May 23,
1884; *New York Herald*, May 23–24, 1884; *New York World*, May 24–26, 28–30, 1884;
Julia Grant, pp. 327–28.

1. On June 1, a correspondent reported from Morristown, N. J., on the living
arrangements of USG's sons. *New York World*, June 2, 1884. USG never moved to
Morristown.

2. USG and Childs owned nearby residences in Long Branch. The Grants eventually occupied their house during the summer. See letter to Clara V. Cramer, June 10,
1884; *New York Graphic*, June 28, Aug. 2, Sept. 6, 1884.

To Charles Wood

———

New York City
May 19th /84

Charles Wood, Esq.
My Dear Sir:

I am in receipt of your very kind letter of the 17th inst. with
two Checks for Five Hundred dollars each. You have conferred
an obligation more than I can ever repay. The money of course

I do not doubt but I can return. But being caught without a hundred dollars in my pocket, and nothing coming in until August it become a serious question what to do. You in the generosity of your heart have relieved that anxiety.—Every preparation was at once made to reduce expenses to a minimum. My house at Long Branch—Mrs. Grant's—is offered for rent, and the one we occupy here will be in the fall if prospects are no brighter than at present.

Hoping that prosperity may attend you and yours, I remain

Faithfully yours

U. S. GRANT

ALS, Ralph W. Naylor, Hopkinton, R. I. On May 17, 1884, Charles Wood, Lansingburgh, N. Y., wrote to USG. "I am in receipt of yours ~~of~~ dated the 12th and enclose two five hundred dollar checks as succor in time is advantageous. The country will rally for you but large bodies move slowly. Meantime—(though I think you are in error in supposing there is nothing coming in untill Aug 1) to avoid anxiety I shoud advise the restricting of expenses within income untill Aug 1. If no better ~~plan~~ plan is practicable I would come here even untill then where you and Mrs Grant would be welcome to board &c also a horse-carriage—saddles—small farm to ride to &c" ALS, Mrs. Paul E. Ruestow, Jacksonville, Fla. On May 19, USG, New York City, wrote to Wood. "In my letter of this am I forgot to acknow[l]edge your kind invitation for ~~your~~myself and family to visit you. I am very much obliged, but for the purpose of economising Mrs. Grant and I will live for the Summer with our eldest son, in Morristown, N. J. ~~during the Summer,~~ and through the fall and winter also if it becomes necessary to rent this house. Dividing the expenses will help both." ALS, Ralph W. Naylor, Hopkinton, R. I. See letter to George W. Childs, May 15, 1884.

On May 24, Marion S. Lake, postmaster, Fayette, Mo., wrote to USG. "Do not let this little misfortune cast one shaddow over you. if need be every true soldier will Donate. I am poor but stand ready to divide with you do not hesitate if any thing is wanting, we are ready to comply. we have no Post. they is only about 10 of us, but we stand firm, and Ready & willing to do our part." ALS, USG 3. Lake had served as capt., 14th Wis.

To Cavender & Rowse

New York City
May 21st /84

CAVENDER & ROUSE:

DEAR SIRS;

Inclosed I send you Deed of Release of lot formerly held by Jas. F. Casey and subsequently purchased by me.[1] I have no recollection of the $1.500 00 matter referred to in your letter of the 16th. Possibly John Dent may know about it.[2]

I will be very glad to sell the farm and also the Carondelet property. The latter I think contains Two Hundred & One Arpents. If it could be sold in bulk, one half cash, I would take $40.000 00 for it, the purchaser paying your commissions. If the amount of land is different from this statement it is offered for the present at $200 00 pr Arpent and commissions.

Yours &c

U. S. GRANT

ALS, ICarbS. On May 10, 1884, USG telegraphed to Cavender & Rowse, real estate agents, St. Louis. "If offer of sixty-five thousand is for my farm and Mrs. Grants of Six Hundred Forty-six acres you may close." ALS (telegram sent), Warren Reeder, Hammond, Ind. On May 22, the mortgage of USG's farm to William H. Vanderbilt was recorded in St. Louis County. *St. Louis Globe-Democrat*, May 23, 1884. St. Louis newspapers reported an unsettled market for real estate. See *ibid.*, May 27, 1884; *St. Louis Post-Dispatch*, May 30, 1884. On Aug. 18, USG, Long Branch, again wrote to Cavender & Rowse. John Heise, Catalogue No. 2458 [1929], no. 129.

1. See *PUSG*, 16, 232; *ibid.*, 17, 383.
2. See *ibid.*, 24, 16–20.

To Fitch, Fox, & Brown

New York City,
May 24th /84

FITCH, FOX & BROWN:
DEAR SIRS:

Inclosed you will find deed of Corcoran st. property to Mr. W. McLean properly conveyed. We have moved about so much since leaving Washington that we can not find any papers relating to Washington City property. The abstract of title was made out by Mr. Ward[1] who I presume you know as a lawyer having much experience in that line. The absence of these papers I presume makes no difference as the deed to Mrs. Grant is a matter of record. Please send check for payment payable to Mrs. Grants order.

Yours &

U. S. GRANT

ALS, Rochester Public Library, Rochester, N. Y. On May 27, 1884, a correspondent reported from Washington, D. C. "Mrs. U. S. Grant has sold the house at No. 336 Corcoran-street, which was in her name, to Mr. John R. McLean, of the Cincinnati *Enquirer*, for $6,500." *New York Times*, May 28, 1884. Son of USG's friend Washington McLean, John R. McLean was investing in capital property. See letter to Charles Wood, Jan. 5, 1885; *Washington Evening Star*, May 31, 1884; *Badeau*, p. 423; Kathryn Allamong Jacob, *Capital Elites: High Society in Washington, D. C., after the Civil War* (Washington, 1995), pp. 179–81.

In Nov., 1883, Fitch, Fox, & Brown, real estate agents, had paid half-year property taxes totalling $137.88 on four Grant houses in Washington, D. C. D, USG 3.

1. Probably William H. Ward, an established Washington, D. C., lawyer, or one of his sons, also lawyers.

Memorandum

[*New York City, May, 1884*]

I did not wish to say anything at this time in regard to this matter of Grant & Ward, but Mr Fish having made a statement to one of the City newspapers, to the effect that he had in his possession letters from me, as to which he says, referring to the Government contracts, "in these letters he states that all of these transactions are all right and straight, and that the profits are genuine", it seems necessary that I should make a statement in regard to the matter.

Long prior to the date referred to by Mr Fish, and on the first intimation I ever had that Government contracts were contemplated by the firm of Grant & Ward, I told Mr Ward in distinct and positive terms that, if that firm contemplated having any contracts with the Government, myself and my son must retire—that while it was honorable enough to have contracts with the Government,— the Government getting all of its supplies by contract—yet there was generally more or less distrust in regard to those who habitually obtained those contracts, and I having been President of the United States was not willing that my name should be connected at all with any such transactions. Mr Ward replied that they would not of course take a Government contract if I disapproved, as they would not do anything of which I disapproved.[1]

The only matter that I know or can recollect of now, subsequent to this statement which I made to Mr Ward, which was of the nature of a Government contract, was my finding that Mr Ward was purchasing, as he said, a large amount of Oats to be kept in warehouse in Chicago, and to be delivered on a given date to the Chief Quartermaster of that Division—He said that he had no contract with the Government at all, but that the person who had a large Government contract wanted him to make the purchase and the delivery, and would allow him a certain amount for doing so. He stated that the price of Oats at that time was much below the price contracted for two months ahead, and that he could make the purchase by paying a small margin at that time, and the price he would receive on the delivery would make quite a profit, after paying storage, insurance and interest, whereas, if the purchase was deferred, Oats might be higher even than the price which the Government was to pay.

I have no recollection whatever of ever having written Mr Fish but one letter in relation to any matter of business. That letter was in reply to a note which he sent to me on his receiving a letter from General James of the Lincoln Bank, containing something in regard to a loan wanted from that Bank. If he has any letters other than this, they have been prepared by some one else, and placed before me for my signature, with an incorrect statement of their contents. My confidence in the integrity and business qualifications of the members of the firm of Grant & Ward was such that I have not hesitated to sign my name very often to papers put before me, on a mere statement of the contents, without reading them. I am very well aware that this was not business like, but it is the fact. I have never during the existence of the firm of Grant & Ward dictated any letter to any clerk or to any person in the office to be signed by me.

I have never directly or indirectly sustained a Government contract taken by the firm of Grant & Ward.

D, USG 3. On May 24, 1884, James D. Fish spoke to a reporter concerning Grant & Ward's handling of government contracts. " . . . I have in my possession documentary evidence sufficient to fully vindicate me in every particular, and that evidence is of no less value and importance than this: It is contained in autograph letters from General

Grant to me on the subject. On July 5, 1882, I wrote a letter to General Grant, in which I asked him, among many other things, especially about these Government contracts, using that very term 'Government contracts.' In reply to that letter I received two letters from General Grant, one an autograph letter—that is, a letter written body and all solely by General Grant—and a second letter written by George E. Spencer, the cashier of the firm of Grant & Ward, and signed by General Grant himself. In these letters he states that all these transactions are all right and straight, and that the profits are genuine. When these facts, and various other facts which are in my possession, and which are in black and white, are known, my vindication will be complete . . . . I wanted General Grant's letters published some days ago, but I have been overruled by my counsel . . . ." Questioned how Ferdinand Ward enticed him "into the alleged Government contract business," Fish replied. "Ward would come to me with slips of paper on which were written, for instance, Wanted by the Government 485,000 bushels of oats, or so many bushels of wheat, or so much hay, or so much of this, that or the other, which the Government was supposed to want. Within the past year he has come to me with Indian contracts, and when I asked him through whose influence he got these contracts or bought them, he gave me to understand that Senator Chaffee, General Grant, President Arthur, and various people who had political power were assisting him. He told me directly that President Arthur was in with him on some of those contracts. I seldom went to the office of Grant & Ward; but when I did I generally found there General Grant, Senator Chaffee, and various people whom he told me assisted him about these contracts . . . ." *New York Tribune*, May 26, 1884. On May 26, a reporter questioned USG on Fish's remarks. "I think fuller developments may be expected in this matter in a few days that will probably put an entirely new aspect on the matter." Asked to authenticate the letters, USG replied. "You must excuse me from answering that question. Everything will be satisfactorily cleared up in a few days." *Brooklyn Eagle*, May 26, 1884. See *PUSG*, 30, 400–402; *New York World, New York Tribune*, May 27, 28, 1884; *New York Sun, St. Louis Post-Dispatch*, May 28, 1884; *New York Herald*, May 27, 28, June 7, 1884; *New York Times*, June 9, 1885.

On May 28, USG provided nothing "in explanation of the two published letters which he wrote in answer to James D. Fish's letter about 'government contracts.' Neither would Clarence A. Seward nor Roscoe Conkling, his two lawyers, say anything to remove the bad impression which the letters caused. General Grant is willing, so his nearest and most trusted friends say, to stand or fall by the correspondence as it has been given to the public, without adding anything in the way of interpretation. The only explanation given so far is the written statement of Mr. Conkling, made by authority of General Grant, that the letter in which the General assured Mr. Fish that he believed Grant & Ward's investments to be safe was signed without being scrutinized . . . ." *Ibid.*, May 29, 1884. An editorial defending USG is *ibid.*

On June 8, J. C. Bancroft Davis, U.S. Supreme Court reporter, Washington, D. C., wrote to Hamilton Fish. " . . . What a fate has come upon Grant. His worst enemy could wish him nothing worse—What can be worse than to have the acquisition of money the sole object of life, and the luxuries it buys necessities, and to have ~~the~~ it hopelessly gone—under circumstances which compel his friends to set up that he is a fool to parry the charge that he is a knave. I will not admit to anyone that I think he had a guilty knowledge of the nebulous character of the 'government contracts'—but how could he, with his knowledge of the way in which govt business is done—have been blind if he did not shut his eyes to what he did not want to see— . . . " ALS, DLC-Hamilton Fish.

1. On Feb. 26, 1882, Ward had written to James Fish, then vacationing in Cuba, on government orders for grain. " . . . Now, a word as to the General. You know the Senate has passed the bill to retire him on pay of General, and it is now going to the House. If some of those fellows down there who oppose this bill should get hold of our having these contracts they will use it as a tool to defeat the bill; so I am very careful, and I have cautioned Smith against saying anything. So long as we keep quiet and do this business in outside names and in a quiet way the General will stick by us . . . . We are fast gaining a foothold in Washington, and if some day we can get some of those Indian contracts I will be happy, for the profit on one of them is enough to set us all up." *New York Times*, March 28, 1885. On March 2 and 5, Ward again wrote to Fish. "The Government contract business is progressing well, but we need to keep it mum, for if we don't the papers will give us fits . . . ." "I am now working to get the contract to supply certain Government stations with oats and flour. If I do this it will be a steady thing, and also very profitable, but it will take money. There is a big order to be given soon for a large amount, probably about the 25th of this month. It may take $50,000. Now, I want to know whether you think it best for me to try for this. The returns on that big contract will be coming in on April 1 or 2, and so it will not be increasing the notes but for a few days. I will do as you say . . . . Don't worry about things here. All is well." *Ibid.* For Fish's testimony concerning this correspondence at his trial and related records, see *ibid.*, March 28, 31, April 2, 1885. See also Deposition, [*March 26, 1885*].

On May 13, 1884, Ulysses S. Grant, Jr., informed a reporter that more than two years had passed "since my father told Mr. Ward that if the firm had any dealings with the United States government he would withdraw from the partnership, and would also insist that his sons should withdraw. This was said in the most earnest and emphatic manner. My father did not consider it an honorable thing for an ex-President to derive a profit from government contracts. No matter how fair the contracts were, the relation would not look well and might result in scandal. I know that my father told several persons that the firm had no government business whatever, and he never had the slightest reason to suspect otherwise. As for myself, if I thought that we were doing anything which might in the slightest manner embarrass my father, I would have left the firm at his request. Mr. Ward did privately intimate to me that he had an interest in government contracts in one sense. He told me that he was advancing money to outside men who had secured government contracts, and that he received large profits on the loans. The only official contract which he explained the character of was one for supplying oats to the army. Mr. Ward also told me that he had contracts with private corporations, such as railways. He would give the firm's check for say $50,000 to the railway officials to carry on the work of construction, perhaps, and in return would receive a warrant upon the railway company for the amount of the loan and a heavy profit added. When I asked him for any further details about the various contracts he would say, 'Oh, now, Mr. Grant, you ought to be satisfied with your profits. I am willing to do the work. If there is any loss upon these contracts I stand ready to guarantee for the firm.' It was always understood by us that Mr. Ward got these contracts and, although he used the paper of the firm, stood behind it in person to guarantee against it. Of course there were no contracts. Mr. Ward has admitted that the contracts he spoke of were all fictitious . . . ." *New York Herald*, May 14, 1884. For editorials generally friendly toward USG, see *New York Graphic*, May 13, 28, 1884.

To Leland Stanford

———

New York City
June 2d /84

My Dear Governor Stanford.

In April, before the failure of Grant & Ward, my youngest son, J. R. Grant, sent his wife, child & nurse to California to visit his father and mother-in-law, expecting to follow this month himself, to spend a couple of months. All his ready means was in the firm so that now he has neither the means to go after his family, or to bring them home. Is it too much under these circumstances for me to ask for him a pass from this city out for him and back for himself and family. He deposited with the firm on the 2d of May $86.000.00

I am very sorry to trouble you with this matter, and if it is not convenient to grant I beg that you will say so.

With Mrs. Grants and my kindest regards to Mrs Stanford and yourself

Very Truly yours
U. S. Grant

ALS, CSt. Born in 1824 in Watervliet, N. Y., Leland Stanford prospered in Calif. as a merchant, served as governor (1861–63), and gained renown as a railroad president. His wife, Jane L., pursued philanthropies. On March 13, 1884, the Stanford's only child, Leland Stanford, Jr. (born in 1868), died at Florence, Italy, while touring. On May 4, 1884, Leland Stanford arrived in New York City from Europe, and he spent the summer primarily in the east. See letter to Leland Stanford, July 2, 1884; *New York Times*, May 5, 1884; *New York Tribune*, May 23, 1884.

To Adam Badeau

———

June 4th /84

Dear General;

I do not feel now as though I could undertake the articles asked for by the Century. Possibly when I get to the country I may feel differently. But I would not have the Editors of the Magazine delay on such an uncertainty. When you come to the City we will always be glad to see you.

Very Truly yours
U. S. GRANT

GEN. A. BADEAU

ALS, Munson-Williams-Proctor Institute, Utica, N. Y. After the failure of Grant & Ward, Robert Underwood Johnson, associate editor, *Century Magazine*, wrote to Adam Badeau. "The country looks with so much regret and sympathy upon General Grant's misfortune that it would gladly welcome the announcement and especially the publication of material relating to him or by him concerning a part of his honored career in which every one takes pride. It would be glad to have its attention diverted from his present troubles, and no doubt such diversion of his own mind would be welcome to him." Johnson remarked. "Soon after, to our surprise and joy, we received a note from General Grant from Long Branch saying that if we still desired to have him write for the series he would be glad to have us send a representative to discuss the matter." Johnson, *Remembered Yesterdays* (Boston, 1923), p. 210. See letter to Adam Badeau, Jan. 21, 1884; letter to Richard Watson Gilder, June 30, 1884.

   On May 20, 1884, USG, New York City, wrote to Badeau. "I have yours of yesterday, with enclosures. I will see you any day you may call at my house." ALS, InU. Badeau had been requested to write an article on USG's personality for *Century Magazine* and may have sought a meeting with USG to discuss the project. See *Badeau*, p. 559; letter to Adam Badeau, July 21, 1884; Badeau, "General Grant," *Century Magazine*, XXX, 1 (May, 1885), 151–63.

To Clarence A. Seward

New York City
June 7th /84

CLARENCE SEWARD
ATTY. AT LAW &c
DEAR SIR:

   Herewith I send you papers which were served upon me at 10 am to-day.

   About the middle of next week I propose to leave for Long Branch for the summer unless you and Mr. Conkling think I should remain. At L. B I will always be accessible by telegraph, and can run up to the city when wanted. Will you kindly inform me whether you think there will be objection to my going.

Very Truly yours
U. S. GRANT

ALS, USG 3. An orphan raised by his uncle, William H. Seward, Clarence A. Seward graduated from Hobart College (1848) and entered upon a distinguished legal career. He served as counsel for USG, and later, for the Grant family.

On June 6, 1884, USG, represented by Blatchford, Seward, Griswold & Da Costa, signed a court document as a defendant in a suit brought by Abraham W. Platt. DS, Museum of the City of New York, New York, N. Y. On July 1, Develin & Miller, New York City, wrote to USG. "It is our duty as Counsel for the Receiver of The Marine National Bank to bring actions against the firm of Grant & Ward upon two promissory notes for $5.000 each. Will you authorize Some Attorney in this City to appear for you in this action." L, *ibid.* On July 2, USG, Long Branch, endorsed this letter. "Respectfully referred to Hon. Roscoe Conkling to answer, and to appear either in person or by Atty. I have made no answer to this note." AES, *ibid.* On Sept. 11 and 30, USG, again represented by Blatchford, Seward, Griswold & Da Costa, signed court documents in a suit brought by Walter S. Johnston, receiver, Marine National Bank. DS, *ibid.*

To Clara V. Cramer

June 10th /84

DEAR CLARA:

Your letter, with one from your Aunt Jennie, reached me a few days since. I regret that I have not more cheerful news to write you than I have. Financially the Grant family is ruined for the present, and by the most stupenduous frauds ever perpetrated.[1] But your Aunt Jennie must not fret over it. I still have a house and as long as I live she shall enjoy it as a matter of right; at least until she recovers what she has lost. Fred. is yong active, honest and intelligent and will work with a vim to recuperate his looses. Of course his first effort will be to repay his Aunts.—We go to Long Branch this week. We expected to live with Fred this summer in Morristown, N. J. But failing to rent our cottage we will occupy it and Fred will live with us and rent his if he can.

All send love to you, your pa & ma & Aunt Jennie.

Yours Affectionately

U. S. GRANT

ALS, MH. See letter to Virginia Grant Corbin, May 8, 1884; Clara V. Cramer to Grover Cleveland, May 13, 1885, DLC-Grover Cleveland; *New York Times*, Sept. 16, 1885.

On May 24, 1884, James Speed *et al.*, Louisville, wrote to USG. "We are prompted by our great regard for you to express the sympathy we feel for yourself and your family in the troubles so unexpectedly precipitated upon you At this time we feel that it would be injustice to ourselves to withhold from you the assurance that the blow you have so wrongfully suffered has only intensified our feelings of high esteem & confidence. We desire to say further that in this assurance we reflect the sentiment most heartily and cordially expressed in this community" LS (12 signatures), USG 3.

On the same day, Elizabeth Chapman Grant, San Francisco, wrote to Jesse Root Grant, Jr. " . . . Oh Jess I never can forgive myself for allowing all this misery to fall upon your dear father—I have been so devoted to him all these years— . . . I would write to your father but feel too guilty— . . . How strange it is that the reports of G & W should differ so—Who is your lawyer W̶ The papers say Conklin Why do you hesitate to use the releases from assignment—It is *surely* better for you not to go through bankruptcy *Oh I* HOPE *you wont* You know you are morally obliged to pay every cent & if you are 30 years older when you make any money it must go to your creditors—so *where* is the benefit to be derived from bankruptcy How I wish I could telegraph you— but I dare not—Your brothers are all so engrossed with their own troubles they can not advise you—Fred having no resources & being so largely in debt must fail but you are just on the point of having a large sum paid you & you *oh* you must not fail—Do not have your name in the list of bankrupts . . . " ALS (dated "Saturday 24th"), USGA. Written on stationery of the Palace Hotel. Other family correspondence on the financial affairs of Jesse Grant, Jr., from the period of Grant & Ward's failure is *ibid.*

On June 1, [*Susan E. Wallace*], Lucerne, wrote to her sister. " . . . Grant never knew what was being done in the firm. O, No, And he didn't know his Cabinet was a den of thieves, either! . . . " ADf, InHi.

On July 5, Jehangir H. Kothari, Karachi, wrote to USG. "After a long tour round the world—I have arrived safely here a few months ago. I take this opportunity of tendering you my heartfelt thanks for all your kindness shewn to me while my short sojourn in New-york. I am again more thankful to Mrs Grant for her courtesys and also for her beautiful present of a book which I perused with very great interest; I beg you to convey convey this message to her. From the latest home papers I have with very great regret read the a/c of difficulties of your firm but I sincerely trust they may be temporary ones—and you will again resume your extensive business in a flourishing state. I heartily wish you every prosperity and happiness which you so well deserve. Kindly remember me to Col: Grant . . . . P. S. Kindly let me know if I can do anything for you up here." ALS, USG 3. See Kothari, *Impressions of a First Tour Round the World in 1883 and 1884* . . . . (London, 1889), pp. 228–29; *The Times* (London), Nov. 20, 1934.

On July 7, John A. Bingham, U.S. minister, Tokyo, wrote to Frederick Dent Grant, New York City. " . . . I have read with deep sorrow of the great financial loss which has come upon your illustrious & greatly esteemed father Genl Grant and also upon you & your brothers. It is a gratification to me as it must be to all your fathers friends in all lands to know that this calamity is not because of any fault of his or of his Sons. The London Times uttered the feeling of all true men who know any thing of Genl Grant & his high character that he has the sincere sympathy & the sincere respect as well, of many in other lands as well as in the U. S. His good name & honor are safe with his grateful fellow citizens at home & abroad" ALS, USG 3. See *The Times* (London), May 13, 1884. On Oct. 2, 1885, Frederick Grant, New York City, wrote to his attorney, William A. Purrington. "Your letter asking about a rumor that Ward has stated that he paid father $206,000 in excess of what he (father) put in the firm of Grant & Ward, and paid me $250,000 in excess of what I had deposited with or loaned to him (Ward) has been received. As to father's account, I have only to say that he put into the firm of Grant & Ward $100,000 of his own money; had on deposit there $90,000 of my mother's ($40,000 belonging to the fund raised in Philadelphia to pay for the house

No. 3 East Sixty-sixth street), $25,000 from the sale of the Long Branch cottage, built while father was President; $15,000 from the sale of the Anglo-American Bank stock that mother had owned some years and $10,000 from savings from her income and allowances that father had given her and $150,000 he had obtained from Mr. Vanderbilt. My father's expenses were about $2,000 per month, $1,000 of which he allowed my mother for maintaining their home; $500 he gave in charity and $500 he kept for his own use, but gave most of this away in presents. My father's income and profits outside of the firm of Grant & Ward (after the $250,000 fund was raised), was greater than the amount he spent. Father made no investments while in the firm except those he left with the firm, and Mr. Ward had charge of the securities. As for myself I took from the firm about $———-less than I put in. What I did take out was paid as profits to those whose money I was using, except so much as it took to support my family in a modest way. I had $57,000 when I first knew Mr. Ward. Now I owe $500,000 through his treachery. I have nearly every check I ever drew in my life, a full history of every transaction I ever entered into, and if anybody who has any right to inquire into my affairs wants to know about any or all of my transactions my books are open to him. If you see fit to make public my transactions with Ward do so. There is nothing I wish to cover up. On the contrary, I would like everything known. I have done nothing I am ashamed of except that I dealt with such men as Fish and Ward. There is nothing I am sorry for except the suffering which has befallen innocent people through my confidence in these men. I was not a member of the firm, but I believe I could have been deceived just as my father and brother were had I been one of the partners. I can truly say that I regret that I did not occupy the place my father had in this firm, for I believe his disease was brought on and his death hastened by the treachery of these men." *New York Herald*, Oct. 9, 1885. Purrington asked the reporter to suppress the sum of Frederick Grant's losses so that Ferdinand Ward, then awaiting trial, could not devise a refutation. *Ibid.* For details on Frederick Grant's personal finances, see *New York Sun*, May 28–29, 1884; *New York World*, May 28, 1884, July 16, 1886; *Harper's Weekly*, XXX, 1543 (July 17, 1886), 451.

On Sept. 13, 1884, Beverley Tucker, former C.S.A. agent, Berkeley Springs, West Va., had written to Hamilton Fish. " . . . What a sad misfortune has come to your friend Genl Grant! Few outside of his devoted personal friends, deplored it more than I—& *none* denounced more unsparingly than I, the vulgar ruffianism, that characterized a portion of the Press of the Country, in regard to his connection with it . . . ." ALS, DLC Hamilton Fish.

1. In late May, Ferdinand Ward, Ludlow Street Jail, New York City, had written in response to a reporter's questions. " . . . I don't intend to make any statement, but am at work with my lawyers and bookkeepers getting at facts that will enable me to bring a good defence at my trial. I feel that when the facts are brought to light the public will be more charitable than they now are. My time is mostly employed in working on my papers. I am well treated by my keepers, and I try to keep up my spirits as best I can under the circumstances." *New York Sun*, May 30, 1884. See *ibid.*, June 1, 4, 1884; *New York World*, June 1, 3–4, 14–15, 1884.

On Sept. 19, 1885, a correspondent in New York City reported the remarks of Jerome B. Chaffee, father-in-law of Ulysses S. Grant, Jr. " . . . You can form no idea how the General took the failure and the betrayal of his trust placed in supposed friends. No one will ever know the extent of his anguish, not even his own family, for he was the bravest in their presence I was with him after the exposure of Ward. The General would suffer for hours in his large armchair, clutching nervously with his hands at the arm-rests, driving his finger-nails into the hard wood. It was a pitiful spectacle. One day he said to me: 'Chaffee I would kill Ward, as I would a snake. I believe I should do it, too, but I do not wish to be hanged for the killing of such a wretch' It is said that Grant had but one object, which sustained life in him for months, that of finishing his book and providing for his family. I know of another; he wished to live to testify in court against Ward and bring him to justice." *Los Angeles Times*, Sept. 26, 1885.

On Oct. 22, Ward's trial for grand larceny in the Court of Oyer and Terminer began with jury selection. On Oct. 27, James D. Fish testified against his former business partner Ward. "It was three or four days after the crash that Ward came to my private apartments on the second floor of the bank building. He said that he wanted to explain about matters. He said that he could not help what he had done. He admitted that he had ruined me and my family by his deception and roguery. He had broken the bank, and he had disgraced me in a community in which I had lived as a respectable citizen for 40 years. All these things he admitted. I told him that if he wasn't the most ungrateful, contemptible, and black-hearted villain that ever lived and a miserable, dirty reptile I would kill him. When I said that I caught up a chair and raised it over him. He crouched down on the floor at my feet and held up his hands and whined like a puppy . . . . I told Ward then and there that I felt so indignant that I could kill him on the spot. He said that I had been his best friend, and he admitted everything that I charged him with—deception, hypocrisy, treachery, and ingratitude . . . . I advised him to go and commit suicide—drown himself, hang himself, or anything else. I was so angry that I used the strongest words in my répertoire." *New York Times*, Oct. 28, 1885. Ward did not testify at his trial. On Oct. 29, the jury returned a guilty verdict. On Oct. 31, Judge George C. Barrett, N. Y. Supreme Court, sentenced Ward to ten years at hard labor at Sing Sing Prison. For Barrett, see "The Trial of Ward," *Harper's Weekly*, XXIX, 1508 (Nov. 14, 1885), 739; *New York Times*, June 8, 1906.

To Alfred D. Worthington

New York City,
June 10th /84

A. D. WORTHINGTON, ESQ. PUBLISHER
DEAR SIR:

Your confidential letter of the 25th of May come duly to hand no doubt, but it has been buryed under other letters until now. I would have no objection to seeing you at any time that might be convenient to you, and talk upon the subject you write about. But I do not feel equal to the task of collecting all the data necessary to write a book upon the War, or of my travels.

Very Truly yours
U. S. GRANT

ALS, USG 3. Born in 1845, Alfred D. Worthington clerked for a sarsaparilla co., served with the 6th Mass. (1864), and subsequently published subscription books in Hartford. On Nov. 7, 1883, A. D. Worthington & Co. wrote to USG, New York City. "If you will write for us such a book as we shall propose, to consist of personal recollections & reminiscences mainly, to make a vol of say 600 to 700 pp similar to Col. Dodge's 'Our Wild Indians,' we will agree to pay you a royalty on every copy sold that will net you at least twenty five thousand dollars within two years from publication. And we will bind ourselves by ample security to pay you that sum *at least* within the time named. Or we will give you twenty thousand dollars in cash outright for the Mss of such a vol, to be paid when the book is placed in our hands b[y] you, and will give you a royalty *besides*. If you are open to entertain the above or any other proposition for a book we shall be glad to confer with you. Awaiting your reply . . . " L (press), *ibid.* On Nov. 9, USG wrote to Worthington. "I have yours of the 7th instant making propositions for a book from my pen. I feel much complimented by your proposition but I schrinck from such a task." ALS, *ibid.* See Richard Irving Dodge, *Our Wild Indians: Thirty-three Years' Personal Experience among the Red Men of the Great West* (Hartford, 1882); *Hartford Courant*, May 3, 1924.

To John G. Carlisle

SOCIETY OF THE ARMY OF THE POTOMAC,
New York, June 17, 1884.

SIR: I have the honor to transmit the following proceedings of the meeting of the Society of the Army of the Potomac, held in the city of Brooklyn, June 11 and 12, 1884:[1]

"*Resolved*, That this society earnestly recommends the passage of the bill now pending in Congress providing for the purchase by the Government and preservation in the Government archives of the extensive and comprehensive series of sketches and etchings of the battles and campaigns of the Army of the Potomac, known as 'The Forbes Historical Art Collection,' and that a copy of this resolution, duly attested by our president and secretary, be transmitted to Congress."

Respectfully, your obedient servant,
U. S. GRANT,
President Society Army of the Potomac.
HORATIO C. KING,[2]
Secretary Army of the Potomac.
To the Speaker of the House of Representatives, Wa[s]hington, D. C.

HRC, 48-2-2440, 4. John G. Carlisle, Ky. lawyer and Democrat, entered Congress in 1877 and rose to speaker of the house in 1883. An art student before the Civil War, Edwin Forbes sketched battle scenes for *Frank Leslie's Illustrated Newspaper.* On July 28, 1876, Ulysses S. Grant, Jr., wrote to Forbes, New York City. "The President directs me to acknowledge the receipt of an India proof set of engravings entitled 'Life Studies of the Great Army,' which you so kindly forwarded to him, and convey to you his sincere thanks. He wishes me to assure you of his appreciation of this valuable work of art, and of the kind sentiments expressed in your note presenting it." LS, NNP. *HRC*, 48-2-2240, 2. The effort to purchase his original sketches and drawings ended after a brief procedural debate in the House of Representatives on Jan. 30, 1885. See *CR*, 48-2, 1090; *New York Tribune*, March 7, 1895; William J. Cooper, Jr., "Edwin Forbes and the Civil War," in Forbes, *Thirty Years After: An Artist's Memoir of the Civil War* (Baton Rouge, 1993), pp. vii–xvi.

1. On June 11, 1884, USG had spoken at the Brooklyn Academy of Music. "Comrades of the Society of the Army of the Potomac—I accept the trust which you have put on me to-day. I feel highly flattered that you should have selected me—one who has never been, except as an honorary member, a member of your society. But in years back, twenty years ago, our relations were intimate and close—although I was not your direct commander at that time. But my headquarters were always with you during that period, and I had the opportunity of witnessing what the Army of the Potomac did that eventful year just as well as though I had been your immediate commander. As I followed your outgoing president just one year after he left the military academy (we were both younger then), I am glad now to follow him in just the same way in this new office. If I am restored to health, as I hope to be by the time of the next annual meeting, I will expect to devote the time, whether one or two days, to whatever exercises are to be gone through with by this society; but in consequence of my present condition, I shall not be able to stay with you to-day or be with you to-morrow, I regret not being able to listen to the able address to be delivered to-night. I know it is to be excellent, because I know the man who will deliver it. He was a member of my staff during the last two years of the war, and I assure you in advance you will be interested in it. I can't say I have read it because I do not believe it has been written." *Brooklyn Eagle*, June 12, 1884. USG succeeded Brig. Gen. John Newton as society president. Horace Porter delivered the keynote address. See *The Society of the Army of the Potomac. Report of the Fifteenth Annual Re-Union, . . .* (New York, 1884).

2. Horatio C. King graduated from Dickinson College (1858), served as q. m. (1862–65), and practiced law in N. Y.

To Matías Romero

Long Branch, N. J.
June 23d 1884.

My Dear Mr. Romero:

Inclosed I send you Mrs. Grants check for $400 00 the balance still due you on the $1000 00 you were so kind as to loan me on the failure of the firm of Grant & Ward. It was a very great favor at a time when much needed, and I shall always appreciate it. But I should have waited until we met again to have have handed you this only that I wanted to write on another matter. Mrs. Grant unites with me in asking you and Mrs. Romero to come and make us a weeks visit, either immediately or at any time during our stay at Long Branch that best suits your convenience. Only let us know a few days in advance when we may expect you.[1] With kind regards of Mrs. Grant and myself to both you and Mrs Romero, I am,

Very Truly yours
U. S. GRANT

ALS (facsimile), DLC-Matías Romero. On June 26, 1884, USG wrote to Matías Romero, Mexican minister. "I just now find on my table, blowing around loose, a check for $400 00 which I thought I had sent you yesterday." ALS (facsimile), *ibid.* On May 22, 1888, Romero, Washington, D. C., wrote a letter concerning his loan to USG in May, 1884. " . . . I had, on the 12th, an interview with General Grant at his residence, No. 3 East 66th street, in the city of New York, and he informed me that all he possessed had been lost in the broken bank; even the interest on a fund of $200,000 which several New York gentlemen had raised for the purpose of giving him an income which would permit him to live decently had been negotiated previously by Ferdinand Ward, and that six months or a year would elapse before he could rely on the interest of said fund. Mrs. Grant was in the habit, he said, of drawing from the bank, a few days after the first of each month, the necessary amount to pay the house bills for the previous month; but in May, 1884, she had not yet drawn the sum required for that purpose, before the failure of the bank. They found themselves, therefore, without the necessary means to do their own marketing (these were his own words). The only amount they had at the house was, he said, as I recollect, about $18 . . . ." *Century Magazine*, XXXVI, 5 (Sept., 1888), 795.

1. On July 29, 1884, USG, Long Branch, telegraphed to Romero, Washington, D. C. "Will be pleased to have you visit us the first August or soon after" Telegram received (facsimile), DLC-Matías Romero. On July 31, Romero telegraphed to USG. "Could not be at Long Branch before the fifth of August but will try to be on that day." ALS (telegram sent; facsimile), *ibid.* On the same day, USG telegraphed to Romero, New York City. "Come on the fifth" Telegram received (facsimile), *ibid.*

To Edward F. Beale

———

Long Branch, N. J.
June 26th /84

MY DEAR GENERAL BEALE:

Your letter of yesterday just received. It is very good of you to take so much interest in the bill for my retirement. But I can not suggest any member of Congress for you to see. All the members I know personally, except Rosecrans,[1] are in favor of the bill, and I do not know of but one other, Springer,[2] who opposes it. No doubt there are others who do, but I have not heard of them expressing any particular opposition. I have not felt that the bill would pass this session if atall. I need it very much and would feel grateful for it, particularly if it should pass the house as it did the Senate. I am not as familiar with the rules of the house as I should be. But my recollection is, that a bill cannot be taken from the Speakers table except by unanimous concent. If I am correctly informed Spring and Rosecrans will not give theirs.

We all hope that Mrs. Beale and Emily are steadily improving in health. It may be that we will run up to Deer Park for a week in August. We have now a large family here. Nellie and family, and Fred and family are here. But there is always a spare room for you if you come this way, and for Mrs. Beale and Emily if they are along. With love from Mrs. Grant to your family,

Very Truly Yours
U. S. GRANT

ALS, DLC-Decatur House Papers. On May 7, 1884, U.S. Senator George F. Edmunds of Vt. introduced a bill to place USG on the retired list of the army. *CR*, 48-1, 3910. Designated S. 2169, this bill read: "That in recognition of the eminent public services of Ulysses S. Grant, late General of the Army, the President be, and he hereby is, authorized to nominate and, by and with the advice and consent of the Senate, to appoint him a general on the retired-list of the Army, with the rank and full pay of General of the Army." *Ibid.*, 48-2, 1757. On May 12, U.S. Representative Samuel S. Cox of N. Y., a Democrat, introduced a bill to retire USG. *Ibid.*, 48-1, 4078. On May 14, U.S. Senators Francis M. Cockrell and George G. Vest of Mo., both Democrats, stated their opposition to the Senate bill in response to published reports of unanimous support. *Ibid.*, p. 4146. Petitions from two Grand Army of the Republic posts in Ohio opposed reappointment legislation. See *ibid.*, p. 4944; *New York Sun*, June 3, 1884.

On May 22, Edwards Pierrepont, New York City, wrote to USG. "You have seen the evidence of the undying pride and affection with which you are regarded by the American People—The readiness with which Congress recognises your priceless services, gratifies so large a part of the Nation that we may say that is *unanimous.* I have not heard a single man or woman speak upon the subject who does not heartily sympathise with you and rejoice that the Government hastens to your relief—you never had so many devoted friends as you have to-day— ... " ALS, USG 3.

On Dec. 29, a correspondent reported from Washington, D. C. "The knowledge of General Grant's misfortune has revived the interest heretofore displayed in the bill providing for placing him on the retired list of the army with full pay. This bill was passed by the Senate last May, and still remains in the House on the Speaker's table, behind 127 other bills .... There is good reason to believe that the bill to place General Grant on the retired list of the army would receive a vote of two-thirds of the membership of both Houses, and would become a law if the opportunity were given to bring it to a vote." *Philadelphia Public Ledger,* Dec. 30, 1884. On Jan. 28, 1885, U.S. Representative Henry W. Slocum of N. Y., a Democrat, explained that two bills were pending to retire USG. "The first, which mentions Gen. Grant by name, passed the Senate with only one dissenting vote. The second, which was so framed as to avoid the difficulty expressed in the veto of the Fitz John Porter bill, passed the Senate, . . . I will support either bill. The good feeling of the House Committee towards General Grant is shown by the fact that it instructed me to bring up the first bill before the second was ever introduced or thought of. This shows the committee to be earnestly in favor of retiring the General, and that the present muddle is no trick to defeat the measure, as many people seem to think." *Washington Post,* Jan. 29, 1885. On Feb. 16, Slocum argued unsuccessfully for passage of S. 2169 in the House. Several representatives desired substitution of the second bill to avoid a likely presidential veto. See *CR,* 48-2, 1757–61; *Badeau,* pp. 440–41

On Jan. 13, Edmunds had introduced a second bill to benefit USG, designated S. 2530. "That the President of the United States be, and he hereby is, authorized, by and with the advice and consent of the Senate, to appoint on the retired-list of the Army of the United States, from among those who have been generals commanding the armies of the United States, or generals-in-chief of said Army, one person, and the total number now allowed by law to compose said retired-list shall be, on such appointment, increased accordingly." *CR,* 48-2, 649. On Jan. 14, the Senate passed a slightly amended bill, 49-9. *Ibid.,* pp. 684–85.

On Feb. 3, President Chester A. Arthur wrote to the House of Representatives drawing attention "to the pending legislation of the Senate and House of Representatives looking to a national recognition of General Grant's eminent services by providing the means for his restoration to the Army on the retired-list. That Congress, by taking such action, will give expression to the almost universal desire of the people of this nation is evident; and I earnestly urge the passage of an act similar to Senate bill No. 2530, which, while not interfering with the constitutional prerogative of appointment, will enable the President in his discretion to nominate General Grant as General upon the retired-list." *Ibid.,* p. 1241. At the end of a session running through the night of March 3 and into the late morning of March 4, the House of Representatives passed S. 2530, 198-79. *Ibid.,* pp. 2565–66. See telegram to Brig. Gen. Richard C. Drum, March 4, 1885; *New York Tribune,* March 5, 1885.

1. USG's relations with former Brig. Gen. William S. Rosecrans had been poor since Oct., 1862. After resigning his commission (1867), Rosecrans served as minister to Mexico (1868–69), moved to Calif. (1880), and was elected as a Democrat to the House of Representatives. On Feb. 16, 1885, Rosecrans, chairman, Committee on Military Affairs, spoke against legislation to retire USG as a gen. " . . . It was the interest of a great political party of this country to make the services of General Grant appear as large and important as possible, for he was their servant and tool to secure power. He himself kept an aid-de-camp in his back office and there prepared the first two volumes of Badeau's Life of Grant, upon which the students of history have put the stamp of unworthiness to be trusted. But we are told that General Grant is now poor and the public has been told from the same source that General Rosecrans will not vote for General Grant's bill because of personal ill-will. I do not think, sir, that my colleagues on this floor will believe that I am capable of descending to the depths of being guided

in a public duty by any motive of personal dislike; and if there be any gentlemen on this floor who entertain the idea that it is possible, I simply enter my solemn protest, and say that under no consideration would private dislike prevent me from doing this or any other act that my public duty prompted. I would not oppose the passage of this bill on account of any of these things to which I have alluded, nor would I oppose it on account of those other things to which I have not yet alluded, namely, statements made officially by General Grant that were false, and which he knew to be false at the time he made them and which I have shown in my official reports to be false. I say these things do not enter into my reasons at all . . . ." *CR*, 48-2, 1758–59. See *PUSG*, 30, 81; *Los Angeles Times*, March 3, 1885; Rosecrans, "The Mistakes of Grant," *North American Review*, CXLI, cccxlix (Dec., 1885), 580–99.

2. A lifelong Democrat, William M. Springer practiced law in Springfield, Ill. (partnering for four years with John A. McClernand), and opposed the Civil War as associate editor, *Illinois State Register*. Entering the House of Representatives in 1875, he became known for his partisanship and parliamentary skills. On May 23, 1884, Springer spoke against a bill to promote Col. Henry J. Hunt to maj. gen. to increase his retirement pay. " . . . In my judgment Congress is going too fast in the matter of these numerous promotions for the sake of increasing pensions. We have now a bill upon the Speaker's table which has been passed by the Senate at this session of Congress placing General Grant on the retired-list, or rather, I should say, placing him upon the rolls of the Army as a general and then retiring him with that rank, to enable him to draw a pension for the rest of his life of some $20,000 a year, or perhaps not so much . . . . That is more than the judges of the Supreme Court or any other officer of this Government receives except the General of the Army and the President of the United States. It is alleged in behalf of that bill that General Grant has been the subject of some financial misfortunes recently which commend him particularly at this time to the consideration of Congress, and that therefore because of this fact the bill for his relief should be passed at once by this House. Mr. Chairman, while I would be glad to do honor to General Grant, because of his achievements for this country, under any ordinary circumstances, yet in my judgment this is not the time nor are these the circumstances under which the Congress of the United States should come to his relief . . . ." *CR*, 48-1, 4449.

To James Campbell

———

Long Branch, N. J.
June 26th 1884

DEAR SIR:

I have your letter of the 21st inst. offering me $75 00 pr share for my two shares of St. Louis Agricultural & Mechanical Assn Stock. I will gladly sell it to you for the price offered.[1] But I had long since forgotten that I held this stock, and now cannot find the certificates I presume however that the transfer can be effected on the books of the Association which will shew that I am the owner of two shares. Even the small sum of $150 00 is a matter of great importance to me just now when every thing has been swept from me, and I will be very glad if the transfer can be effected on the books with producing the certificates.

Very Truly yours
U. S. Grant

James Campbell Banker
St. Louis, Mo.

ALS, MoSHi. Born in 1848 in Ireland, James Campbell grew up in western Va., worked as a messenger for John C. Frémont, and trained himself to be a railroad engineer. Favorable purchases of Mo. county bonds allowed Campbell to open a brokerage office in St. Louis (1877). See *St. Louis Globe-Democrat*, *St. Louis Post-Dispatch*, and *New York Times*, June 13, 1914. On June 30, 1884, Campbell, St. Louis, wrote to USG, Long Branch. "Yours of the 26th inst. is at hand and noted. In order to secure a duplicate certificate for the Fair Grounds shares it will be necessary for you to sign and have witnessed the inclosed forms, also to name to me two responsible parties who will sign the bond for you as sureties. They must both live in St. Louis. In case you are unable to give me the names of parties who would act, I will endeavor to get them myself. As soon as you return the inclosed forms properly signed, etc., and I will have secured the duplicate certificate, I will forward you my New York draft for $150." *Chicago Tribune*, Sept. 18, 1891. See *PUSG*, 30, 302; letter to James Campbell, July 3, 1884.

1. Attempting to promote a candidate for the presidency of the St. Louis Agricultural and Mechanical Association, Campbell had sent a circular letter asking non-residents with small stock holdings to sell their shares. *Chicago Tribune*, Sept. 18, 1891.

To Henry A. Barnum

June 28th /84

Dear General:

These letters are dated the very day I moved to Long Branch. They come to me while every thing in the house was in confusion consequint to a change of residence I put them in my pocket to prevent their being mislaid, and not having had occation to go to my pocket for papers until to-day forgot all about them until now. I hope you will accept this as my apology.

Very Truly yours
U. S. Grant

GEN H. A. BARNUM.

ALS, Montana Historical Society, Helena, Mont. Trained as a lawyer, Henry A. Barnum rose to brig. gen. during the Civil War and settled in New York City where he was an active Republican. See *New York Times*, Jan. 30, 1892.

On March 14, 1869, Barnum, Washington, D. C., had written to USG. "I have the honor to ask the appointment of *Naval Officer* or *Surveyor of the Port of New York* . . . . I refer you to the N. Y. Senatorial & Congressional delegations & the records of the War Dept. and I am specially permitted by *Gen Sherman, Lieut Gen. Sheridan* and Maj Gen. *Thomas* to refer you to them. With this application, therefore, and these references, I leave the matter in your hands." ALS, DNA, RG 56, Naval Officer Applications. On March 15, Norton P. Chipman, Washington, D. C., wrote to USG recommending Barnum. " . . . I beg to add that he served a most honorable part in the war and is permanently disabled from wounds received in battle. After the war closed he became an active worker for republican principles and was prominent at the last campaign as chairman of the Soldiers & Sailors National Committee & of the Committee for the State of New York. It would be a source of great gratification to thousands of our Boys in Blue to see Genl Barnum given a prominent position in the present administration" ALS, *ibid.* No appointment followed.

To Richard Watson Gilder

Long Branch, N. J.
June 30th 1884.

DEAR SIR:

Herewith I send you an article which I have prepared on the "Battle of Shiloh." If it is satisfactory, and you so desire, I will prepare one on the Siegge and capture of Vicksburg as you request. The latter however will necessarily occupy much more space. But I will condense as much as possible. I send with this article copies of correspondence bearing upon some of my statements which you are at liberty to use or not as you may deem best. It could either be added as an Appendix, or could be divided and inserted, in proper place, ɵin the body of the article.

Very Truly yours
U. S. GRANT

THE EDITOR OF THE CENTURY

ALS, DLC-USG, IB. Born in 1844 in Bordentown, N. J., Richard Watson Gilder worked as a railroad paymaster and newspaper reporter before beginning his career as poet and magazine editor. He served as editor, *Century Magazine*, from its initial issue in Nov., 1881. See Arthur John, *The Best Years of the* Century: *Richard Watson Gilder,* Scribner's Monthly, *and the* Century Magazine, *1870–1909* (Urbana, 1981).

On July 1, 1884, Century Co., publisher of *Century Magazine*, issued a check to USG for $500, subsequently endorsed: "First money ever paid to General Grant for the articles from his pen after his financial failure." Doris Harris Autographs, Catalog No. 27 [n. d.], no. 24.

To Leland Stanford

Long Branch, N. J.
July 2d 1884

DEAR GOVERNOR:

Mrs. Grant and myself extend to you and Mrs. Stanford a hearty invitation to come down here and stay with us while you remain east. We have not had yet a single hot day here since we come. You can go to the city by either boat or rail every day if you choose. There are twenty trains a day, each way, all rail, and either seven or nine trains connecting with boat at Sandy Hook.

Of course we expect Mrs. Stanford to bring her Maid, and if you have a man servant we have room for him also.

With kind regards of Mrs. Grant and myself to both you and Mrs. Stanford, I am,

Very Truly yours
U. S. GRANT

GOVERNOR LELAND STANFORD

ALS, CSt. See letter to Leland Stanford, June 2, 1884.

On April 23, 1885, U.S. Senator Leland Stanford of Calif. visited USG at his home in New York City for two hours through the late evening and then told a reporter. "The General is cheerful and firm and will probably pass a good night. Last fall it was arranged that he should visit California this spring, going over the Northern Pacific and returning by the Southern. I told him that if his present improvement continued, the trip might still be made." *New York Tribune*, April 24, 1885.

To Adam Badeau

Long Branch, N. J.
July 3d /84

DEAR BADEAU:

Yesterday I received a letter from the Editor of the Century expressing himself much pleased with my article on Shiloh, but expressing the hope that when the proof come to me I would put in some of the incidents of the second days fight. My recollection is that McCooks division was not under fire at Shiloh atall. I am not sure about Crittendens. Did Buell have any of his Army with him the second day except Nelsons division.

I commenced on the Vicksburg campaign to-day and have made considerable progress so far as pages covered. But I have not gone far from my *base.*

I do not think I will be able to get through the *Wilderness* before you go to the Mountains. But I will take Vicksburg, and will be glad to see you here. In fact I do not want to submit my Article until you have approved it.

Yours Truly
U. S. GRANT

ALS, Munson-Williams-Proctor Institute, Utica, N. Y. See *Badeau*, p. 560; letter to Adam Badeau, July 26, 1884.

To James Campbell

LONG BRANCH, N. J., July 3, 1884.—James Campbell, Banker and Broker—Dear Sir: Herewith I send you power of attorney to transfer my two shares of St. Louis Fair stock, and bond to be filled out. The stock I have transferred to you, as well as making you attorney. If this is not right you are authorized to erase your name in the first instance and to substitute Judge John F. Long. Cavander & Rowse,[1] no doubt, will sign my bond. If only one can sign, then no doubt Judge Long or most any of my numerous friends in St. Louis will. Yours truly,

U. S. GRANT.

Chicago Tribune, Sept. 18, 1891. On July 8, 1884, James Campbell, St. Louis, wrote to USG, Long Branch. "Your favor of the 3d inst., with inclosures, is at hand. I have secured the signature of Judge Long and Mr. E. S. Rowse to the bond and have filed same with the Secretary of the association. Inclosed I hand you my check, No. 1,267. for $150 on Messrs. Kelly & Little, New York, in payment for the two shares. You will please acknowledge receipt of same . . . " *Ibid.* The signed bond, dated July 7, is in MoSHi. On July 12, USG wrote to Campbell. "Your letter of the 8th inst. inclosing check for $150 00 in payment for two shares of St. Louis Agricultural & Mechanical Fair stock, is received." ALS (facsimile), unidentified newspaper clipping. See letter to James Campbell, June 26, 1884.

1. See letter to Cavender & Rowse, April 27, 1883.

To Fitz John Porter

Long Branch, N. J.
July 4th 1884

My Dear General Porter:

You can scarsely conceive the pain it caused me to read the Veto of your bill by the President yesterday. I was not prepared for it. His message is the merest sophistry. It is no doubt a great disappointment to you and your family. But I believe it will result ultimately in doing you fuller justice. You ~~were~~was dismissed unjustly, and you are entitled to restoration. That would make you a Major General from the date of dismissal to the time of restoration. I want to see this the final decission in your case.

Be of good cheer and pray that justice may yet be done you and yours.

Faithfully yours
U. S. GRANT

ALS, DLC-Fitz John Porter. On July 2, 1884, President Chester A. Arthur vetoed a bill to relieve Fitz John Porter because it encroached upon the president's appointment power and improperly set aside the sentence of a regularly constituted court-martial. ADfS (undated), DLC-Chester A. Arthur; *CR*, 48-1, 5932–33. The House of Representatives overrode Arthur's veto, but the Senate sustained it. See *ibid.*, pp. 5933–35;

HED, 48-2-175; *General Grant's Unpublished Correspondence in the Case of Gen. Fitz-John Porter* (n. p., n. d.), pp. 1–2; Thomas C. Reeves, *Gentleman Boss: The Life of Chester Alan Arthur* (New York, 1975), pp. 382–85. A bill restoring Porter to the army as a col. became law in 1886. See *HRC*, 49-1-42; *SRC*, 49-1-195; *U.S. Statutes at Large*, XXIV, 107–8.

To Adam Badeau

Long Branch, N. J.
July 9th /84

DEAR BADEAU:

I have your letter of the 7th. I write a little daily on the Vicksburg campaign. Probably will have the draft completed by this day week. I may not commence the Wilderness article for some time after, so when you want to run down, or rather when your article[1] is ready,—after next Wednesday,[2]—I will be ready with Vicksburg, and will be glad to see you.

My family are all well, and join in kindest regards to you.

Very Truly yours
U. S. GRANT

P. S. I am glad to hear that the Sec. of the Treasury is with you in your controversy with the comptroller.[3]

U. S. G.

ALS, Munson-Williams-Proctor Institute, Utica, N. Y.

1. See letter to Adam Badeau, June 4, 1884.
2. July 16, 1884.
3. See *Badeau*, p. 561.

To A. Gordon Murray

LONG BRANCH, N. J., July 10, 1884.—*A. S. Murray, Secretary, etc.*—DEAR SIR: I have your letter of the 4th inst. inviting me to stop over at Chicago the 23d of August, on my return from Minnesota, to attend exercises by the Caledonian Society of that city, and also notifying me of my election as an honorary member of the society. I can accept the latter, however, but I cannot be present at the time specified. I am still very lame from the injury received last December, and financially embarrassed from the recent failure, so that I shall not be able to attend the army meeting at which I expected to be present next month.

Thanking the Caledonians for the cordiality of their invitation, I am very truly yours,

U. S. GRANT.

Chicago Tribune, Aug. 2, 1884.

To Richard Watson Gilder

———

Long Branch, N. J.
July 15th 1884

EDITOR CENTURY MAGAZINE;
DEAR SIR:

I have now been writing on the Vicksburg Campaign two weeks, sundays and all, averaging more than four hours a day. Only now approaching Champion Hill. I fear my Article will be longer than you want. But it embraces the movements of 1862, from Grand Junction, and La Grange, and all the various devices of the winter of /62–3 to gain a footing on the east side of the Mississippi from which Vicksburg might be besieged. It will probably be the end of the month before I can send it to you.

Will you be kind enough to inform me whether you would prefer having it confined withing a certain space in the Century; and also whether, in the Wilderness battle, you wish only from the Rapid Ann to Spotsvillevania, or whether you mean by the Wilder[ness] the whole campaign north of the James river. If the latter I fear I will have to *strike*; not for *higher wages*; but because I do not want to do so much work just now.

When the proof is returned to me I shall want to add probably as much as a page, of your journal, to Shiloh.[1]

Very Truly yours
U. S. GRANT

ALS, Dartmouth College, Hanover, N. H.

1. USG did not expand this article. See Robert Underwood Johnson, *Remembered Yesterdays* (Boston, 1923), p. 216.

To Andrew Hickenlooper

———

Long Branch N. J.
July 19th 1884

DEAR GENERAL

In response to your circular announcing the time and place of the next meeting of the Society of the Army of the Tennessee, I am very sorry to announce that I will not be able to attend. It is always with regret when, for any reason, I cannot attend the re-unions of the society of the first army I had the honor to command, and the only one I ever had the immediate command of. The reget at this time is increased from the fact that on the approaching occasion, I had accepted the call to deliver the oration.

But I am yet a great sufferer from the injury received last December, being still on crutches and unable to dress or undress myself. I know you can get some one, even with the short notice he will have—who will deliver a much better oration than I could, with any length of time for preperation, hoping for a full attendance and a pleasant time.

I am General
Very Truly Yours,
U. S. GRANT.

GEN. A. HICKENLOOPER
COR. SECTY.
SOCIETY OF THE ARMY OF THE TENNESSEE.

Copy, DLC-William T. Sherman. Andrew Hickenlooper, former chief engineer, 17th Corps, and bvt. brig. gen., served as marshal, Southern District, Ohio (1866–70), and then pursued business interests. On July 22, 1884, Hickenlooper, Cincinnati, wrote to William T. Sherman, Minnetonka, Minn. "It is with extreme regret I have to announce that Genl. Grant declines to deliver the Annual Oration for reasons given in his letter, ... I am sorry the Genl did not think to advise us sooner of his disability, but I suppose his business troubles have so occupied his mind that he forgot all about it—..." ALS, *ibid.* On July 26, Sherman wrote to U.S. Senator John Sherman of Ohio lamenting that the "meeting will have less of public interest because General Grant has notified us at this the Eleventh hour that he cannot come, though he had accepted formally the place of Orator and has left us only two weeks for the Selection of another.—We did fear this conclusion but I understood that our Corresponding Secretary had received recent assurance that he would come ...." ALS, *ibid.* On Aug. 1, William E. Strong, Chicago, wrote to William Sherman. "I saw a letter to-day from General Grant to the Officials of the St. Paul R. R. dated July 23rd in which he stated that it would be impossible for him to attend the Re-Union of our Society at Lake Minnetonka on account of his lameness. He stated further, that he had notified the Secretary of the Society. I Suppose, Dayton or Hickenlooper. We propose to keep the fact of his not coming, very quite, so that the newspapers wont get hold of it. I wrote to ask what we are to do for an orator? Can you get some one to fill General Grants place? ..." ALS, *ibid.* Cushman K. Davis, former governor of Minn., replaced USG as orator. See *Report of the Proceedings of the Society of the Army of the Tennessee, At the Seventeenth Meeting,* ... (Cincinnati, 1893), pp. 68–84. See also letter to William T. Sherman, July 31, 1884.

On July 3, USG, Long Branch, wrote to Strong. "I am much obliged for the invitation .... But I have ..." Christie's, Dec. 8, 1989, no. 30.

To Adam Badeau

Long Branch, N. J.
July 21st 1884

DEAR BADEAU:

I have worked on Vicksburg every day since you left here, from two to five hours each day. It will be finished, ready for revision, to-morrow. If you feel like a change of mountain to sea air for a while I will be glad to see you. If you are not through your article you can finish it here.

Very Truly yours
U. S. GRANT

ALS, Munson-Proctor-Williams Institute, Utica, N. Y.

To Joseph L. Cornet

Long Branch, N. J.
July 23d 1884.

J. C. CORNET, ESQ.
DEAR SIR:

Your letter of the 17th come duly to hand; but I have not seen the paper of which it informs me was sent.

When I reached Appomatox C. H. Lee had been in McCleans house for some time. All there is of the apple-tree story is this: when I received a note from Lee asking to meet me, at Appomatox, where he then was, I sent him a note saying I would be there as soon as possible. There was an old apple orchard on the hillside, opposite McCleans house, where the advance of Lee's army had halted when the white flag was exhibited. A farm road run up diagonally up the hill, through the orchard. In places, where trees were close to the wheel-tracks, on the upper side of the road, the roots had been cut off by being continuously run over. This left a low bank between the road and trees so cut. When the officer (Gen. O. E. Babcock) who bore my reply to Lee reached him he was seated one one of these embankments, with his feet in the road, and his back against the tree. He was then invited to pass through our lines, to a house, to await my arrival.

Very Truly yours
U. S. GRANT

ALS, PHi. Joseph L. Cornet served as corporal, 28th Pa. See Cornet to Benjamin Harrison, June 18, 1892, DLC-Benjamin Harrison.

On Oct. 7, 1884, Cary D. Lindsay, Toledo, wrote to USG, New York City. "At Appomattox CH, in company with Lieut Col Lewis C. Hunt, of the 67th Ohio, I rode from Gen Ords position in our line, through the town, and out to the brow of the long hill overlooking the Valley in which lay the camp of Gen Lee's Army—While we sat there on our horses, the General officers of our Army, including yourself, accompanied by their staffs & Escort, came out and rode down the hill towards the confederate camp, halting in the road about half way down, and the general officers of Lee's army similarly accompanied by their staffs, came out of their camp & rode up the hill to the same place—You rode off alone some distance to the left and there met Gen Lee, and you and he, sitting on your horses, held quite a long conversation—You then returned to your respective camps, followed by the other officers respectively—The large assembly of officers was near a tree, which may have been the famous 'apple tree', and this has ever since been my version of the apple tree story As I have never seen an account of this meeting, will you kindly say, at the bottom of this sheet (returning same to me) whether you can confirm it. I am sorry to bother you about it, but some of the boys hesitate to believe it, because none of the historians of events there, have alluded to it, and I can furnish no other witness here, Col Hunt having died some years ago—I will be greatly obliged . . ." ALS, IHi. On Oct. 10, USG endorsed this letter. " Your recollection of the meeting between Gen. Lee and myself is correct; but you describe the meeting on the 10th of Apl. the day after the surrender. The apple tree story grew out of the fact that while General Lee was waiting to hear from me, on the 9th, in answer to a note he had written proposing surrender, he took a seat on the ground, resting his back against an apple tree. That was in the orchard on the hill-side opposite where we met on the 10th. He was seated in that position when General Babcock, of my staff, rode up and handed him my reply. Gen. Lee was then conducted ~~into~~ over to Mr. McLeans house, within our lines, where we first met." AES, *ibid.*

On Oct. 16, USG wrote to John L. Smith. "General Lee was seated on the ground with his back resting against an apple-tree when General Babcock delivered to him my answer to his letter requesting an interview for the purpose of arranging terms of surrender. Lee was conducted to McLean's house, within our lines, before I got up." ANS (facsimile), *History of the Corn Exchange Regiment 118th Pennsylvania Volunteers: From their First Engagement at Antietam to Appomattox* (Philadelphia, 1888), p. 677. On Oct. 3, Smith had written to USG, Long Branch. "I have read several articles in the papers of late alleging that the surrender of General Lee, at Appomattox, was not under an apple tree. I was in the 118th P. V., Corn Exchange Regiment, and on the morning of April 9th, 1865, our regiment was lying near the hill. I was early at the spot, and secured a piece of the tree. A number of officers were there also, offering five and ten dollars to the men for chips, and one of your orderlies was there and got a branch for you at the time. From this latter a set of jewelry was made by the Messrs. Spaulding & Co., of New York, for your wife, according to a paper I saw several years ago. I enclose clipping from the *Evening Telegraph* (Philadelphia) of October 2, which quotes Captain Nathan Appleton as having secured a piece of the tree. I have my piece still in my possession, and as these denials are having a run through the papers, tending to bring my relic into disrepute, and my friends tell me that the occurrence did not take place under the tree, I ask you, General, to set the matter right. Awaiting your answer, . . ." *Philadelphia Public Ledger* (Supplement), Oct. 29, 1884. See *PUSG*, 23, 132.

To Adam Badeau

Long Branch, N. J.
July 26th 1884.

DEAR BADEAU:

If you can come down after next Wednesday[1] I will be glad to see you for at least a week. I have finished Vicksburg, but have not read it over yet. Shiloh was brought back to me by the editor, with some suggestions. I have added enough to make a page or two of the Century, and, I think, improved it.[2] The latter part of the Vicksburg paper I think better than the first, but all wanting improvement.

I mention after Wednesday next for your coming because, on that day, Nellie sails for Europe. Monday, and /til she leave here, every body will be busy with her packing.

I have written you one letter since you went to Tannersville.

yours Very Truly

U. S. GRANT

ALS, Munson-Williams-Proctor Institute, Utica, N. Y. See *Badeau*, p. 562.

1. July 30, 1884.
2. Robert Underwood Johnson, associate editor, *Century Magazine*, recalled the "dismay when, on July 1, we received from the General an article on the battle of Shiloh which was substantially a copy of his dry official report of that engagement, as printed in the 'Rebellion Records', with which we had already made ourselves familiar . . . . So, with his article in my inside pocket, I went again to see the General, and, without at first letting him know of its unsuitableness to the series, I managed to draw him into a description of the engagement . . . . During his talk, with apparent casualness I had been jotting down on the newspaper I had brought with me brief memoranda of the foregoing and other points of special interest; and when he had finished I mentioned these and told him that they were typical of what was essential in depicting the battle. He seemed astonished at this, and took a quite impersonal view of the event. I told him that what was desirable for the success of the paper was to approximate to such a talk as he would make to friends after dinner, some of whom should know all about the battle and some nothing at all, and that the public, who could easily discover the geography and the movements of the engagement,—which of course could not be omitted,—was particularly interested in his point of view, in everything that concerned him, in what he planned, thought, saw, said, and did. This was a new idea to him, and when I had told him that I was convinced that he could do what was desired if he would not try too hard, he said he would begin again. So he took back the official report, and the result was the admirable article that appeared first in the *Century* for February, 1885." Johnson, *Remembered Yesterdays* (Boston, 1923), pp. 213–15. For USG's report on the battle of Shiloh printed in the *O.R.*, see *PUSG*, 5, 32–36. See also *ibid.*, pp. 340–42.

To Albion W. Tourgee

Long Branch, N. J
July 30th 1884

A. W. TOURGÉE;
CONDUCTOR CONTINENT PUB. CO.
DEAR SIR:

As you no doubt know, I am the holder of twenty shares of the "Continent Publishing Company" stock. By the agreement which I

hold, by giving notice by the first of September following subscription, of a desire to have the amount subscribed, with interest, it
will be returned in one year from date of agreement: that is, on the
20th of October 1884. When I subscribed I thought my financial
condition such that it made but little difference whether anything
was returned or not. If the publication was a success I expected to
return the stock; ⊥if it was not, to say nothing about it. Now however, in view of recent misfortunes, a thousand dollars is a large
amount to me; and I give notice that I will be glad to return my
stock now, or at the time specified, on the terms of the agreement.

I hope the company is a great success, and that the shares may
increase in value ten for one.

Very Truly yours
U. S. GRANT

ALS, deCoppet Collection, NjP. The contract and certificate for USG's stock in Our
Continent Publishing Co., both dated Oct. 20, 1883, are *ibid.* Albion W. Tourgee fol-
lowed his popular Reconstruction novels by starting *Continent*, a weekly magazine.
This publication, begun as *Our Continent* on Feb. 15, 1882, ceased with the issue dated
Aug. 20, 1884. See *PUSG*, 29, 479; letter to Albion W. Tourgee, Oct. 16, 1884; *PUSG*,
23, 392–93; Otto H. Olsen, *Carpetbagger's Crusade: The Life of Albion Winegar Tourgée*
(Baltimore, 1965), pp. 254–64.

To William T. Sherman

Long Branch, N. J.
July 31st 1884

GEN. W. T. SHERMAN,
DEAR GENERAL:

Your letter of the 28th instant, is just received. You may say to
the Veterans of the Society of the Army of the Tennessee that I regret as much as they possibly can, my inability to be with them at
their approaching re-union, and more, the cause of my constrained
absence. I have not prepared, nor did I intend to prepar[e] any thing
to say on that occasion, except that I have collected a list of the battles in which the Army of the Tennessee participated. I was astonished at the number when the list was completed. It is true, many

of these engagements were not very hard fought battles[.] But that was the fault of the enemy. They would, like many other[s,] have been heavy engagements if the enemy had *staid* long enough[.]

I left the list referred to in the house in the city, and cannot get it without going there myself, otherwise I would send it. With this in my hand I expected to extemporise what ever I might say. On this point I am now somewhat prepared. I have been engaged now more than five weeks, on two articles for the Century Magazine,— the battle of Shiloh, and the Campaign against Vicksburg—which is a his tory of the services of the Army of the Tennessee, from early in November 1862, until the 4th of July following. It is a record any Army might be proud of, even if it had no other. But the Army of the Tennessee had a record after that, unparallelled for its long Marches through an enemys country, without base of supplies, or lines of communications with friends in rear, and brilliant victories over the enemy wherever met.

With best wishes for the members of the society, collectively and individually,

> I am General
> Very Truly yours
> U. S. GRANT

ALS, DLC-William T. Sherman. On Aug. 13, 1884, William T. Sherman spoke on USG at the annual meeting of the Society of the Army of the Tennessee, Lake Minnetonka, Minn. " . . . We all knew that in December last he had sustained a fall at his door step in New York, which was followed by intense pain, and an inability to walk without crutches; but we hoped his strong and vigorous constitution would, long ere this, have repaired the damage. Again, we all know that he had been overtaken by one of those financial hurricanes—a blizzard, a very cyclone—so common in New York— the result of a false system of finance—but no soldier ever believed that General Grant personally was in the remotest degree responsible or censurable; rather, we hoped all the more, that he would enable us, by his presence on this occasion, to manifest for him the intense love and respect which he had won on the battle field, and which will survive long after Wall street shall cease to be held as synonymous with gambling in gold and credit . . . . Every word of this letter is in his own familiar handwriting, direct to the purpose, with an occasional gleam of humor peculiar to him, which satisfies me that he is with us in spirit and faith though absent in person; that many years of useful and happy life are yet in reserve for him, and that I am sure I repeat the feelings of every surviving member of the first army he ever commanded, when I assure him that we, his comrades, hope and pray that his bodily affliction will soon pass away, and that 'the clouds which now lower o'er his house may in the deep bosom of the ocean be buried.'" *Report of the Proceedings of the Society of the Army of the Tennessee, At the Seventeenth Meeting,* . . . (Cincinnati, 1893), pp. 12, 14. On Aug. 27, Grenville M. Dodge, New York City, wrote to Sherman. " . . . Your refference to *Genl Grant* was kind, just, oppertune Although I used to see him often was Vice President of one RR Co that he was President off, I never knew he was a member of the firm of *Grant & Ward*—It was *unfortunate that is all.* You and I know how little adapted to such buisness he is and when I would inquire about the boys he was always so gratified at their success and prosperity that I never had a thought as to the Gen'l. However I have yet to meet the first person ~~yet~~ that lays any blame to the General. the most I have ever heard was that he was censeurable for his neglect of his *own interests!* And while he feels it so sensibly I think by next year he will see how the people fe~~l~~el and will have ⌈risen ab⌉ove his feelings—I know he felt greatly pleased at the reception he received at the reunion—and the attention you gave it—It was a 'cyclone' but there have been so many since that it is now off the past—" ALS, DLC-William T. Sherman.

To George H. Stuart

Long Branch, N. J.
July 31st 1884

My Dear Mr. Stuart;

I have your very kind letter of the 29th instant, inviting Mrs. Grant and myself to attend the re-union of the Christian and Sanitary commissions, at Ocean Grove, from the 1st to the 3d of August. My lameness prevents me going out yet, except to drive occasionally with Mrs. Grant, but as the distance to Ocean Grove is so short we will try to avail ourselves of your invitation for either the first or second day—the latter most likely—the weather permitting. The 3d being Sunday we cannot enter the Grove that day. At night I must stay at home because of the attendence I am obliged to have in dressing and undressing.

Very Truly yours
U. S. Grant

ALS, DLC-George H. Stuart. On Aug. 2, 1884, USG spoke at the fifth annual reunion of the Christian Commission, Sanitary Commission, and Union and C.S.A. army chaplains, Ocean Grove, N. J. "It would always be very difficult for me to address such an audience as this, but now it is specially difficult after what I have heard and seen here to-day. Were I free in speech like others here I could tell of many things done by these agencies of mercy. I had special opportunities to know of service rendered, of consolations administered by the side of deathbeds; of patient, unwavering attentions to the sick; of letters written to the mourning parents of noble sons." *Philadelphia Record*, Aug. 3, 1884. See *New York Times*, Aug. 2–3, 1884; Morris S. Daniels, *The Story of Ocean Grove Related in the Year of Its Golden Jubilee* (New York, 1919), pp. 197–207.

On July 4, 1885, noon, Elwood H. Stokes, Methodist minister, and two others, Ocean Grove, N. J., telegraphed to USG, Mount McGregor, N. Y. "The citizens of Ocean Grove, N. J., assembled on this anniversary day, wish to express to General Grant and family the assurance of their undying remembrance, deep sympathy and fervent prayers, with the hope that his life may yet be spared to the nation and that at last he may rest with God." *Ibid.*, p. 206. On the same day, USG telegraphed in reply. "Please return my thanks to the citizens of Ocean Grove." *Ibid.*

On Saturday, July 30, 1881, Stokes had telegraphed to USG, Elberon, N. J. "Can you be with us on Monday at our anniversary?" *Ibid.*, p. 282. USG replied. "I am obliged to go to New York on Monday. Beg pardon for not having informed you yesterday." *Ibid.*, p. 283.

To Return I. Holcombe

———

Long Branch, N. J., August 3, 1884.

Dear Sir: In July, 1861, I was ordered with my regiment, the Twenty-first Illinois Infantry, to North Missouri, to relieve Col. Smith of the Sixteenth, who was reported surrounded on the Hannibal and St. Joseph road. On arrival at Quincy I found that the regiment (?) had scattered and fled.[1] I then went with my regiment to the junction of the road from Quincy with the one from Hannibal, where I remained for a few days, until relieved by Col. Turchin with another Illinois regiment.[2] From here I was ordered to guard the workmen engaged in rebuilding the Salt river bridge. Col. Palmer was there with his regiment at the same time. When the work was near completion I was ordered to move against Thomas Harris, who was reported to have a regiment or battalion encamped near Florida, Mo. I marched there, some 25 miles from Salt river, but found on arrival that he left about the time I started. On my return I was ordered to Mexico, Mo., by rail.[3]

Very truly yours,
U. S. Grant.

R. I. Holcombe, Esq.

History of Monroe and Shelby Counties, Missouri, . . . (St. Louis, 1884), pp. 720–21. Born in 1845 in Ohio, Return I. Holcombe served in the Mo. vols., worked as a journalist, and contributed to local histories. See Holcombe Papers, Minnesota Historical Society, St. Paul, Minn.

 1. See *PUSG*, 2, 64–65.
 2. 19th Ill. See *ibid.*, pp. 65–66.
 3. See *ibid.*, pp. 66–67, 69–70, 72–73; *Memoirs*, I, 249–50.

To James Grant Wilson

———

Long Branch, N. J.
August 3d 1884

My Dear General Wilson:

I have your letter of yesterday. On account of my continued lameness I will not be able to attend the re-union of the Society of the Army of the Tennessee this year.[1]

I have completed two of the four Articles on the war that I promised the Century Magazine, Shiloh and Vicksburg. The Wilderness Campaign—and that is to be followed by one on the closing scenes of the war—is commenced.

Very Truly yours
U. S. Grant

ALS, Buffalo Public Library, Buffalo, N. Y.

 1. See letter to Andrew Hickenlooper, July 19, 1884.

To William R. Rowley

———

Long Branch, N. J.
August 8th /84

Dear Rowley:

As I told you I am writing a few articles fon the war of the rebellion for the Century Magazine. The "Battle of Shiloh," and "The Vicksburg Campaign" are completed. I am now engaged on "The Wilderness Campaign." I have got up to the crossing of the Rapidan, and have told the story of Swinton's evedroping. But I am afraid I have not got it entirely correct. I know he was introduced by Washburne, with the assurance that he was a gentleman, and was not a newspaper correspondent, but a literary man who proposed to write a history of the war after it was over.

Will you write me the particulars of your detecting him listening; who were with me at the time; what you said to the man, and what action was taken.

My recollection is that this occurred the first night after crossing the Rapidan—May 4th 1864—and that my Hd Qrs. were in a tent not far south of the river. Badeau's history says my Hd Qrs. were, that night, in a deserted house overlooking Germania ford.[1] Please state whether it was the first night after crossing; if I occupied a tent; if neither, when and where it was.

I do not want to quote you any further than I have already done. I state the facts as I recollect them, and name you as the staff officer who detected him.

You may rember that later—when we were at Cold Harbor I think—Burnside found Swinton within his lines, arrested him and ordered him shot before night. He had given Burnside offense by his publications, a year or two before, when B was in command. Meade reported this to me and I ordered Swinburn's release and expulsion from the lines, with a warning that he was not to be found within them again.[2] I do not ask however that you say anything about this unless your memory differs, in any respect, from mine.

The Century Magazine has employed writers on every battle of the war. They are to appear in a series, commencing next Jan.y. Shiloh therefore will not probably appear before next July, and the others much later. I intend however, now that I have commensed it, to go on and finish all my connection with the war of the rebellion whether I publish it or not. If it pleases me when completed I probably will publish it.

Very Truly yours
U. S. GRANT

ALS, IHi. See *PUSG*, 24, 168–69; *Memoirs*, II, 143–45.

1. See Adam Badeau, *Military History of Ulysses S. Grant*, . . . (New York, 1881), II, 99.
    2. See *PUSG*, 11, 160–61; William Marvel, *Burnside* (Chapel Hill, 1991), p. 381.

To Robert Underwood Johnson

Long Branch, N. J.
August 9th 1884.

R. U. Johnson,
Editor Century Magazine;
Dear Sir:

Your letter of yesterday come to me last evening. As you request, I have written to General Sherman, expressing the wish that he should write the article you ask from him.

I do not think I care to write any more articles, for publication, than I have already agreed to write for the Century. These will form as much of the complete series,—which I intend to write, whether it is published or not—as ought to go into print at this time. If however you would prefer my writing Chattanooga, instead of Lee's Surrender, I will have no objec[tion] to the change.[1]

Very Truly yours
U. S. Grant

ALS (facsimile), USGA. Robert Underwood Johnson graduated from Earlham College (1871) and began a publishing career that led to his appointment as associate editor, *Century Magazine* (1881). Clarence C. Buel, asst. editor, *Century Magazine*, added an undated endorsement, presumably to Johnson. "Isn't Lee's surrender of most importance to us? In writing to U. S. G. please ack receipt of correspondence with Halleck sent by Col Grant and the 20 photos which I sent him through Col Grant for identification He has done us a service in this particular." AE (initialed), *ibid.* See following letter; Johnson, *Remembered Yesterdays* (Boston, 1923).

1. USG substituted an article on the battle of Chattanooga.

To William T. Sherman

Long Branch, N. J.
August 9th 1884.

Dear General;

I have a letter from the editor of the Century Magazine informing me that they are writing you, asking you to write an article on the "March to the Sea," for the series they are now having prepared for their Magazine, and asking me to drop you a line to fortify their request. I am writing four articles for the series; the battle of Shiloh; the Campaign against Vicksburg; the Wilderness Campaign, and the surrender of Lee. Their letter will explain the character of the article they want you to write. I hope both you and Sheridan will contribute to the series because they are to be written and, in every instance, by persons who participated in the scenes described. It is better that it should be done by persons who had the largest opportunity of witnessing all that took place.

Shiloh and Vicksburg are completed, and I am well along with "The Wilderness"

Very Truly yours
U. S. GRANT

GEN. W. T. SHERMAN

ALS, DLC-William T. Sherman. On Aug. 15, 1884, William T. Sherman, Minnetonka Beach, Minn., wrote to USG just after the annual meeting of the Society of the Army of the Tennessee. "I now Enclose you slips, a glance over which will I trust assure you of our great disappointmt at your absence. Govr Davis your substitute made an admirable address which is given in full and will repay perusal—I now have your letter of August 9, on the matter of your intended publications in the Century Magazine, and agree with you perfectly that it is well the critical campaigns should be written up—and far better that it should be done by those who saw most, and knew most of the plans & purposes— I have been approached by the Editor of this Magazine, but have uniformly answered that in the publication of my Memoirs in 1875, I had done all I proposed to do, and will adhere to that conclusion—I am a subscriber to that Magazine, the Century—and shall value it the more as it is to be made the vehicle of publication to your four articles and trust that General Sheridan will be led to follow your Example. In the Careful preservation of Reports & data, I believe he is better prepared than Either of us. You were again Elected Orator for our next meeting in Chicago, about the middle of Sep- tember 1885. I hope you will accept and then carry out the purpose as given in your letter to me of July 31—Please notify me of your acceptance or other wise, because the Committee is not discharged—but in case you decline will have to choose another—I am going with a small party up to Devils Lake this afternoon—will be at Des Moines Iowa August 20—and back to St Louis about the 25th. Hoping that you may soon be able to throw away those crutches and again mingle with your Soldier Friends to real- ize the deep hold you have on their love & respect— ... " ALS, USG 3. On Aug. [1]8, USG, Long Branch, telegraphed to Sherman. "Your letter received. I accept the invi- tation of Army of Tennessee for next year." *Report of the Proceedings of the Society of the Army of the Tennessee, At the Seventeenth Meeting,* ... (Cincinnati, 1893), p. 98. See letter to Andrew Hickenlooper, July 19, 1884; letter to William T. Sherman, July 31, 1884.

On Aug. 15, Clarence C. Buel, asst. editor, *Century Magazine,* New York City, wrote to Sherman. " ... General Grant instead of giving us one article (we already have his manuscript of 'Shiloh') has consented to write three (or four) and is now at work upon 'Vicksburg' and 'the Wilderness'. When we showed him our list of subjects and how nearly we had succeeded in realizing our hopes in regard to securing the cooperation of the generals, he was kind enough to sympathize with us over your declination, and to express a decided hope that you might take an interest in the series, after we had shown how thoroughly in earnest we are to contribute to the history of the War a series of articles, unique in personal interest, and better illustrated than battles and battlefields have ever been, before . . . ." AL (initialed), DLC-William T. Sherman. See Buel to Sherman, March 13, 1884, Sherman to editor, *Century Magazine*, Aug. 27, 1884, *ibid.*; Robert Underwood Johnson, *Remembered Yesterdays* (Boston, 1923), pp. 192–93, 202–3; Sherman, "The Grand Strategy of the War of the Rebellion," *Century Magazine*, XXXV, 4 (Feb., 1888), 582–98.

Endorsement

———

Respectfully referred to the Secretary of War.[1] I knew General Vincent during and after the war as one of the ablest and most efficient officers in the Adjutant Generals Department. I would be very glad of course if his son could get the appointment of Cadet.

U. S. Grant

Aug. 18th 1884.

AES, Louisiana State University, Baton Rouge, La. Written on a letter of Aug. 13, 1884, from Lt. Col. Thomas M. Vincent, asst. AG, San Antonio, to USG, Long Branch. "I have made an application for the appointment of my son, Thomas Norris Vincent, as Cadet, at large, U. S. Military Academy. If you can send me a letter of recommendation in his behalf, I will, my dear general, be very grateful. I have based the application on my services,—printed brief herewith enclosed, for your personal information. Please remember me to Mrs Grant. Mrs Vincent is absent, else she would have me convey in this her warm regards to both of you." ALS, *ibid.* On Aug. 23, William T. Sherman, St. Louis, wrote to President Chester A. Arthur recommending Thomas N. Vincent. ALS, *ibid.* Vincent did not attend USMA.

1. Robert T. Lincoln.

To Clarence A. Seward

———

Long Branch, N. J.
August 18th 1884.

Clarence Seward, Esq.
Dear Sir:

Nearly four years ago the Citizens of Philadelphia raised a fund for the purpose of buying a house for Mrs. Grant.[1] The house No 3

E 66th street, New York City, was purchased. There was a mortgage of $58,000 00 on the house at the time, which did not fall due
until the first of last July. The institution holding the Mortgage
was unwilling to receive the money before it was due. There was
$40,000 00 left of the money subscribed for the purchase of the
house. This money was with Drexel, Morgan, & Co. A cheque
for it was turned over to me. I was anxious to keep this money in
tact to meet the Mortgage when due, and at the same time have
it earn the interest Mrs. Grant was paying on the Mortgage. On
the advice of Mr. Ward I purchased,—or supposed I had—twelve
thousand dollars in Coney Island rail road bonds at Seventy-five,
and thirty thousand dollars worth Tonawanda (rail road) bonds at
par. These latter were represented as having with them sixteen
and two thirds thousand dollars of stock as a bonus. I have never
seen any of these securities, and have reason to believe they were
never purchased. On my bank book however I was always credited
with the dividends as they fell due.

I find now that I have Wards receipt—signed—Grant &
Ward—for the thirty thousand dollars. Investigation now shews
that he put my check to his individual credit as soon as he got it,
and not in the Marine Bank. This money belonged to Mrs. Grant.
The question I want to ask is, whether she can not recover it, and
whether or not the money which C. K. Garrison[2] is to pay to the
Assignee of Grant and Ward, can not be garnasheed for that purpose. Mr. Garrison borrowed for the firm two hundred, or two
hundred and fifty thousand dollars, and hypothecated bonds at
eighty cents. Ward rehypothecated the same bonds, but only borrowed fifty cents on the dollar. The difference between the amount
borrowed by Grant a& Ward, on these bonds, and the amount
loaned to Garrison, will come in as assets to the firm.

I write this more to ask your advice than to ask immediate action. to save this money. If it could be saved however it might be
the means of saving our house in the city.[3]

Very Truly Yours
U. S. GRANT

P. S. I return some papers that were sent from your office a few days ago. When I acknowledged the receipt of them I did not understand their import. I had only read the letter to your firm.

I do not know whether there should be an appearance for me or not, but leave the matter to your and Mr. Conklings judgement.

U. S. G.

ALS, USG 3. See letter to Clarence A. Seward, June 7, 1884.

1. See *PUSG*, 30, 137–38.

2. Heavily involved with Grant & Ward, shipping magnate Cornelius K. Garrison declared insolvency on June 20, 1884, further complicating matters for that firm and its partners. See *New York Times*, June 20–22, Aug. 9, Oct. 14, 1884; *New York Tribune*, June 21–22, 1884, May 2, 1885.

3. The Grants retained their New York City house.

To Li Hung-chang

Long Branch, N. J.
August 20th 1884

HIS EXCELLENCY LI HUNG CHANG
MY DEAR FRIEND,

My son, Col. F. D. Grant, who you met in Tientsin, visits China for the second time. He is desirous of obtaining service under the Chinese Government. He is a graduate of our Military school, at West Point, is well read, and a man of fine business capacity, and enjoys the respect and confidence of all who know him. Our Minister to China can tell you more about him from his own personal acquaintance than I want to write.

I abstain from saying any thing about the unhappy relations now existing between China and France, further than to express my deep sorrow. I hope the trouble will soon end, without the honor of China being lowered[1]

With sincer wishes for your health and welfare, and for the prosperity of your country, I am,

Very Truly
your obedient svt
U. S. GRANT

ALS, USG 3. See following letter; *New York Times*, Aug. 31, 1896.

1. French colonial expansion provoked hostilities with China that persisted until the two nations signed a treaty in June, 1885.

To John Russell Young

Long Branch, N. J.
August 20th 1884.

My Dear Commodore,

Since the late disasters that have befallen my house, through the unprecedented rascality of two individuals,[1] neither Col. F. D. nor U. S. Grant, Jr. can do any business here. They are legally responsible for debts they did not contract nor receive benefit from. These circumstances have started Fred out to seek his fortunes elswhere. He will probably go to China. If he does he will explain fully to you what you could not get in an ordinary letter, and which the papers have not fully, or correctly, stated.

Fred has every qualification to be useful either in a business or Military capacity. He is sober, industrious, intelligent, and reliable. I hope you will give him such aid as you can by your endorsement. I am sure he will not disappoint you.

My family are all well, and send their best regards.

Very Truly yours
U. S. Grant

Hon. J. R. Young
U. S. Minister &c.

ALS, USG 3. See preceding letter.

On Nov. 23, 1884, Frederick Dent Grant, New York City, wrote to President Chester A. Arthur. "Not having seen it announced that you have appointed anyone Govenor of Montana I venture to remind you of my application for the place. I am extremely anxious for the appointment as I have been a great deal in Montana, and would like to settle there . . . ." ALS, DLC-Chester A. Arthur. No appointment followed.

On Jan. 18, 1885, Frederick Grant wrote to Secretary of War Robert T. Lincoln. "your very kind letter of the 16th inst was received by me yesterday. Allow me to thank both ~~y~~You and the President for your very kind offer to nominate me, to the position of Assistant Quarter master U. S. A. When the firm of Grant & Ward failed (although I was not a member of it) I had a large amount of money on deposit with them.

I also had large liabilities, these were to be met by the monies I had on deposit. I lost my deposits, but the liabilities remained. Now I do not deem it just to my creditors for me to accept a position, where I would be comfortable, but where I would not have a chance to make, or save any thing with which to pay them. I would have been willing to take a temporary appointment . . . ." ALS, *ibid.*

 1. Ferdinand Ward and James D. Fish.

To Adam Badeau

August 26th 1884.

DEAR BADEAU;

 I am just in receipt of your letter of the 23d. I do not remember the name or the address of the Agent for the sale of the California Champaign. I have however written to Mr. Frank Wood, 2 Wall st. to send it to you. You will probably get his letter about as soon as you do this. I gave him your address. The name of the wine is Eclipse, Ex Dry

 I will be very glad to see you when we get to our house in town. I shall hope to have "The Wilderness," "Chattanooga," and possibly the biographical part of my book ready by that time. I do not expect to be in the city, to stop, before the last of September.— Fred has not gone west yet, and may not go.

Yours Truly
U. S. GRANT

ALS, Munson-Williams-Proctor Institute, Utica, N. Y. On Aug. 26, 1884, USG, Long Branch, wrote to Frank F. Wood. "Will you be kind enough to write Gen. A. Badeau, Tannersville, Green Co. N. Y. the address ~~and name~~ of the agent for the sale of California Champaign. Also the name of the wine, the extra dry, and oblige, . . . " ALS, Connecticut Historical Society, Hartford, Conn.

To Ira J. Alder

ELBERON, LONG BRANCH, N. J., Sep. 2, 1884—Ira J. Alder. Esq.—Dear Sir: Finding your letter of the 12th of July,[1] with slip inclosed containing the opinion of Governor Kirkwood of the services of Captain Twombly at Fort Donelson in 1862, I infer that it has not been answered. Lest I may have neglected it, and not wishing to treat with silence any claims of a Union soldier, I do so now. By name I do not remember the Captain now, but the successful charge made at Fort Donelson on the 16th[2] of February, 1862, was by Tuttle's regiment of, I believe, Iowa troops. Tuttle is an Iowa man, and his regiment was composed wholly from that State. Very truly yours,

U. S. GRANT.

Chicago Inter-Ocean, Aug. 9, 1885. Born in Ohio, Ira J. Alder served in the 44th Iowa, practiced law in Iowa City, and supported Republicans. Also an active Republican after the Civil War, Voltaire P. Twombly received the Medal of Honor in 1897 for his exploits at the battle of Fort Donelson. See *O.R.*, I, vii, 229–30; Alder to Benjamin Harrison, Oct. 22, 1888, DLC-Benjamin Harrison; Twombly, *The Second Iowa Infantry at Fort Donelson* . . . (Des Moines, n. d.).

    1. Printed as "August" in both the *Chicago Tribune* and *New York Times*, Aug. 10, 1885.
    2. The 15th.

Addressee Unknown

———

Long Branch, N. J.
Sept. 2d 1884.

DEAR SIR:

The 4th U. S. Infantry, to which I belonged, left New York harbor on the 5th of July, 1852, for California, by the way of the isthmus. The cholera breaking out in the regiment while on the isthmus it was detained in Panama until the disease abated. This detained the regiment so that it did not reach San Francisco until late in August. It was sent at first to Benetia Barrack where it remained but a few weeks and was then sent to Fort Vancouver, Oregon— now Washington Territory—arriving at the latter place the latter part of September, the same year.[1] In september 1853 I went, by promotion, to Bucksport, Humboldt Bay, Cal. where I remained until the following March, when I resigned, with a four months leave of absence I do not remember the exact date of my departure from San-Francisco for the east, but think it was late in May.

I was again in California·from the 22d of September 1879 to about the 7th of October.[2]

Very Truly

U. S. Grant

ALS, ICarbS. For a similar sketch of USG's time in Calif., see *PUSG*, 29, 264. See also *ibid.*, 1, 251–53, 256–64, 315–18, 329–33; Charles G. Ellington, *The Trial of U. S. Grant: The Pacific Coast Years 1852–1854* (Glendale, Calif., 1987).

On Jan. 18, 1882, USG addressed the seventh annual dinner of the Associated Pioneers of the Territorial Days of Calif., in New York City. "I went to California, gentlemen, at a later date than you pioneers. It was in 1852 that I went there, and I have been a little astonished this evening to hear your President talk about the difficulty of getting anything to eat in that country. When I was there there was no difficulty in getting anything you wanted to eat or to drink. The only difficulty was to get anything to pay for it with, but we—Gen. Ingalls and myself—worried along as well as we could, and we never went to bed without getting something from the Commissary." *New York Times*, Jan. 19, 1882.

1. Sept. 20, 1852.

2. For a more accurate chronology of USG in Calif. after his arrival at San Francisco from Japan on Sept. 20, 1879, see *PUSG*, 29.

Will

———

I Ulysses S. Grant of the City County and State of New York, being in good bodily health and of sound and disposing mind, hereby make publish and declare this Instrument following, to be my last Will and Testament, revoking and annulling all previous Wills and testamentary writings by me made of what kind soever. I make this my last Will and Testament at this time in view of the uncertainty of human life and with the intention of providing for the decent support, so far as my remaining possessions, or any power or powers of appointment given to me, may allow, of my family and the families of my children, who have been deprived of their fortunes by the fraudulent conduct of Ferdinand Ward, the partner in my late firm of Grant and Ward, to whom was entrusted by myself and my son Ulysses S. Grant Jr the business management of said firm at his own request and in reliance upon our belief in his integrity, business ability and intimate association with James D. Fish, also a partner in said firm and for many years prominent in the business circles of New York City, the President of the Marine Bank, a Receiver appointed by the Courts for insolvent business concerns, and reported to be a man of conservative and honorable business principles and trained capacity for affairs.[1]

I make the foregoing recital of the abuse of our trust and confidence in explanation of the clause herein following in reference to the payment of my debts, for the reason that the said breach of trust has resulted not only in depriving me and my sons of all that we had at stake with said firm, being very nearly all of our entire worldly possessions, but also in creating a vast aggregate of debts, apparently owing by said firm in which I was a partner, contracted without my knowledge or approval and in greater part, as it now appears, upon fraudulent, fictitious and illegal consideration. And while it is my very earnest desire to provide for the payment of my just debts, I am instructed, at the time of the present writing, that many claims will be made against members of the said firm which, though under color of law, are unmeritorious, founded in fraud and collusion and such as cannot be provided for in this Instrument. As to all debts, therefore, other than those provided for herein, which I may be considered to owe by reason of my connection with said firm, if any such there be, I can make no provision other than requesting my sons, in whose integrity and sense of honor my trust is implicit, to take such measures in concert with honest creditors as may lead to just and honorable settlements.

I now therefore devise and bequeath all the property and estate both real and personal, wherever situate and being, of which I shall die siezed and possessed, and appoint the distributees of whatever property I may have the power to distribute, including the fund raised in trust for me,[2] if such power as to that fund be given me, in the following manner:—

1 I direct that all debts contracted by me individually on behalf of myself and family, and apart from transactions of the said firm of Grant and Ward, shall be promptly paid.—

II I devise and bequeath all of my said entire estate both real and personal to my dear wife Julia Dent Grant, and appoint her to receive all property which I may have power to distribute, and also appoint her my sole Executrix of this my last Will and Testament: All this in the event that she shall survive me, Said estate in her to be absolute of fee.

III In the event that I shall survive my wife, I devise and bequeath all of my estate real and personal aforesaid to three trustees, whom I also appoint to receive any property the distribution of which I may have power to make, said trustees to be selected by my surviving sons by instrument in writing; This devise, bequest and appointment is made upon the following trusts: (1) The said entire estate and distributive funds shall be divided, and I so hereby divide them, into four equal portions, each one of which portions shall be devoted to the support of one of my children or of his or her family in manner following to wit: (2) If my son Frederick Dent Grant shall survive me the income of the first of said portions shall be paid to him during the term of his natural life, and should he die leaving a wife him surviving the income thereof shall be paid to her during the term of her widowhood, and thereafter the principal sum thereof shall be equally divided among his surviving children and grandchildren per stirpes. In the event that my said son should not survive me, I direct the said first portion to be divided on my death and I hereby so divide it into as many equal subportions as he shall leave children, posthumus children included, him surviving. The income of each of said sub-portions shall be paid to paid to the widow of my said son during her widowhood, and, if the term of her said widowhood shall continue beyond the minority of the child to whom the same shall be allotted, then at the expiration of said term, the principal of said sub-portion shall be paid to said child; If, however, said term shall cease during the minority of said child said income of said sub-portion shall be devoted to the support and maintenance of said child until the attainment of his or her majority whereupon the principal sum shall be paid to the said child with all accumulations thereon.—(3) I make like devise bequest and disposition of the second and third portions of my said entire estate and funds to be appointed as aforesaid, in favor of my sons, Ulysses Simpson Grant Jr and Jesse Root Grant, respectively, and of their respective families—(4) I devise and bequeath the remaining and fourth portion to my said trustees on the following trusts, towit: the income therefrom shall be paid to my daughter Mrs. Ellen W. Sartoris for her sole use during the term of her natural life. Upon her death, whether before or after my own, I direct my said trustees to divide her said portion, and I hereby so divide it, into as many equal portions as she shall leave children her surviving, and direct that the income of each of such said sub-portions shall be applied so far as needful to the support and education of one of her children during his or her minority, and the principal thereof with the accumulations thereon shall be paid to said child on coming of age.—In order to carry out the provisions of this my will I empower my said Executrix and trustees to sell transfer grant convey and lease, to invest in realty or approved securities, and to change investments from time to time, and generally to exercise their discretion in the management of their trust; providing that the funds entrusted to them shall not be invested in speculative securities such as could not be invested in by a trustee appointed by the Courts.—All payments herein directed to be made of income shall be made quarterly except where in view of urgent and peculiar circumstances the trustees may see fit to anticipate a payment or payments.—IN WITNESS WHEREOF I have hereunto set my hand and seal on this fifth day of September in the year of our Lord One thousand eight hundred and eighty four, and have declared and published this Instrument, consisting of six & ½ pages of paper each initialed by my initials, as my last Will and Testament the following erasures being made before my signature was made; on the fourteenth and fifteenth lines of the fourth page, the words "widowhood" and "thereafter" are written over erasures; on the fourth line from the bottom of the same page the words "to paid" are stricken out; and in this testimonium clause the word "six & ½" on the second line from the bottom of page six is written over an erasure.

U. S. GRANT

DS, DLC-USG. On Sept. 5, 1884, Henry J. Morton, Episcopal minister, and George W. Childs, both of Philadelphia, witnessed USG's will. DS, *ibid.* On Aug. 15, 1885, Childs spoke at Long Branch. "Yes; it is a mistake to say that General Grant left no will. His cottage adjoined mine, as is generally known, and every day while he was here he was at my house or I at his. One day last August he came over with a paper in his hand that, he said, was his will, and asked Dr. Morton and myself to witness it. We affixed our signatures to the document, and the General took it away. I do not know what he did with it. Perhaps some member of the family has it. I am anxious to see it produced, so that I may prove my signature. The will was drawn up by Mr. Purrington, a New York lawyer . . . ." *Philadelphia Press*, Aug. 16, 1885. USG's will was never probated. See Herbert R. Collins and David B. Weaver, *Wills of the U. S. Presidents* (New York, 1976), p. 129.

On April 9, 1886, a correspondent reported from Washington, D. C. "Col. F. D. Grant made application in the District Probate Court to-day for letters of administration on the estate of his father, Gen. U. S. Grant, and an order of publication was made. The General owned real estate in the District, and at the time of his death there was due him 22 days' pay as a retired officer of the army, amounting to $828." *New York Times*, April 10, 1886.

1. See letter to Virginia Grant Corbin, May 8, 1884.
2. See *PUSG*, 30, 137–38.

To Vivien M. Sartoris

Long Branch, N. J.
September 7th 1884.

MY DEAR LITTLE PET VIVIAN:

I got your nice little letter a week ago. We were all so glad to hear that you are all well. But your Grand-ma scolds a good deal because your Ma does not write. She has had but one letter from her.—We are all at Long Branch yet; but in one week we go back to New York, and then we go up to your Uncle Buck's to stay a week or two in the country.—Your Grand-pa has been busy ever since you left writing his campaigns which he intends to publish in a book. It will probable be a year yet before it will be ready. You must make your ma learn you to read so that you can read it when it is printed.

Your little cousins are just as well as when you was here, and play about the same. They send a great deal of love to you, Algie and Rose. Julia[1] I think wrote to you a few days ago. If she did not I will tell her to. I know she was going to write, and as she is fond of writing, and does not have to have any one to help her, I presume she did write.

We all miss you, your ma, brother and sister, very much.[2] We will expect you all to come back again next year.

Your Grand-ma has been sick in bed for two days. But the Doctor says that it will not last long. She gets dizzy when she sets up, but feels very well when she is laying down. The Doctor says she does not take enough exercise. I think you will say so too.

Grand-ma and Grand-pa send love and kisses to you, Algie, Rosemary and your Ma.

Yours Affectionately

U. S. GRANT

ALS, ICHi. Vivien M. Sartoris turned five on April 7, 1884.

1. Frederick Dent Grant's daughter Julia, then eight, later recalled letters USG wrote to her in 1884. See Julia Grant Cantacuzène, *My Life Here and There* (New York, 1921), pp. 29–30.

2. Ellen Grant Sartoris arrived in New York City from Europe on April 18. *New York Times*, April 19, 1884. For her departure from Long Branch, see letter to Adam Badeau, July 26, 1884.

To William T. Sherman

Long Branch, N. J.

September 8th 1884.

DEAR GENERAL:

Your letter inclosing one to General Fry is received. I have read and forwarded the latter. He sent his book to me also. I read the introductory, and, of course, observed the allusion he makes to Buells army rescuing &c. ~~that~~ My article on Shiloh was already in the hands of the printer so that nothing said in it was inspired by Fry's assumption. In fact in the article I do not answer any of the charges ever made against the action of the army at the battle of Shiloh, except that of being surprised, and many men being bayonetted or captured in their beds, except ~~by~~so far as a plain story of the battle contradicts impressions created.

Although my article has been in the hands of the publisher for about two months they have not yet sent me the proof. It will probably not be published before next May[1] as a series of articles are to appear in the Magazine embracing all the battles and campaigns of the war, and they will be published in the order in which they occurred.

I glanced over considerable of Fry's defense of Buell when I first received it, and find that he throws much, or all, the blame on Halleck for his Chiefs tardiness. I can understand that, because all my dispatches from Halleck were cautionary, and hedging against any possibility of blame attaching to him in case of disaster.

I unfortunately did not bring your book with me to the Branch, so that I have not had it to refer to in preparing either my Vicksburg, Shiloh or Chattanooga articles. But I am now going on writing up all my campaigns with the view of publishing them in book form. This will take me the best part of a year yet and I will add considerably to the articles that will appear in the Century.

In my article on Shiloh I stated the fact that Nelson arrived at Savannah on the afternoon of the 5th of April, and that I visited him in his camp then, and gave him the order myself to move his division up the east bank of the river next morning at early to a point where it could be ferried either to Crumps landing, or to Pittsburg landing, as required; that he did not move until 1 O'Clock on the 6th, and not then until Buell ordered; that but three regiments—of Ammens brigade—got over the river before firing seased, and those I placed in line myself; that Buell's casualties that day were two killed and one wounded, and they all members of one regiment. In fact, if my memory serves me correctly, one ball did all this and killed a scout by the name of Carson[2] beside, and all close by me near the old house on the bank of the river at the landing. I do not state this latter however because of the possibility of error in memory. I think my article sustains all you have said about Shiloh.

Yours Truly
U. S. Grant

Gn. W. T. Sherman

ALS, DLC-William T. Sherman. On Sept. 3 and 10, 1884, William T. Sherman, St. Louis, wrote to USG, Long Branch. "I await with great interest your publication of the History of the Battle of Shiloh—certain that it will settle forever the claim which Buells friends set up that his timely arrival saved us from utter destruction. General Fry has made a recent publication under the Title of 'the operations of the Army under Buell from June 10 to Oct. 30 1862 and the Buell commission' and in the very Preface recounting the work of that army (P 8) uses the expression 'rescued Grants army at the Battle of Shiloh and converted the disaster of the first day on that memorable field into a victory on the second day.' Inasmuch as Fry himself sent me the book, I have written him plainly what I think of it, and send my letter through you that you may see how I and others regard this claim, and after perusal will be obliged if you will drop it with your mail, there being no need of hurry. I remember to have seen in the Newspapers Buell['s] letter about 1864 in which he recited that he had been offered a command under Canby and Sherman but could not accept because he ranked us, and going further in saying that the war wa[s] then being conducted with a violence to private property which he did not sanction and was not willing to share. I have not kept a copy of that letter and dont know where to find it. Although you are late in the Field I am sure you will set aright some of the mistakes into which history has drifted by the perseverance and repetitions of people who love to appear in print" "I was specially gratified to learn fby your letter of Sept 8 that you had resolved to publish in a series *all* your campaigns embracing those you have promised the Century Magazine. I am sure you appreciate my reasons for declining to join in the articles proposed for the 'Century' as in my Memoires I had already done all I intended I will defend and maintain these Memoires as long as I live because I know they contain truthfully, my special thoughts and feelings at the time.—There may be errors of fact but the facts as known to me influenced *my* actions and that is all my Memoires should and ought to contain. You will now give yours—and Sheridan should the same—These would comprise nearly all which were successful and will explain why the war resulted as it did. I did not blame Fry for making the best case he could for Buell. But Buell did not create *results*. Fry's book or pamphlet is apolojetic or falls under the old French maxim 'qui s'excuse— s'accuse' It was Whitelaw Reid who was with Lew Wallace on the 6th of Apl. 1862 who took a steamboat for Cincinnati during the battle of Shiloh and then made report that we were all 'surprised' 'slaughtered in our beds' &c. &c. abusing me, abusing you and every body who stood fast. Whitelaw Reid has married the gentle sweet daughter of my old California Friend D. O. Mills of California, and to bring about reconciliation I invited him, (Whitelaw Reid) to our Cleveland Meeting of the Army of the Tennessee (1883) pledging him a courteous reception that he might recant from his publications as 'Agate' but he was afraid to meet the men whom he had so grievously slandered.— Buell and Nelson were the men who started the story and Whitelaw Reid gave it circulation and none of them had the manliness to admit *their* mistake. April 6th. *was* the Battle of Shiloh—Apr. 7; we simply gathered in the fruits of victory" Copies, *ibid.* On Sept. 3, Sherman wrote to James B. Fry, New York City. "I have been up in Minnesota this summer and on my return last week found your recent publication 'Operations of the Army under General Buell' for which I am sure I am indebted to you. I thank you of Course, and Suppose you expect some general expression of opinion from me. The War is over, the Country has entered on a new and most prosperous career, and I intend to keep out of all controversies. I am sure that in 1861 I regarded General Buell as one of our best Soldiers of whom I expected the largest measure of Service and fame—I knew of course that Military operations would be marred by Politicians who could not afford to Surrender control to men of pure military ambition and aims, and that from the very Start the operations in and near Washington would Eclipse any at the West however brilliant & Successful. I have read your book through and find some points new to me, viz that Stanton after the ridiculous Court of Inquiry or Military Commission, had offered Service to Buell under Canby and under me, and that he had declined because he for a very short time ranked us—Canby graduated in 1839 two years before Buell, and I in 1840, both in advance of Buell, and he never outranked us save for a short time in 1862.—Then Congress gave to the President the power to assign officers to Chief Command regardless of Rank the dates of commission.—This put both Canby and me *above* him, and I am sure that I offered Buell to command the three Divisions at Memphis, Vicksburg & Natchez, the Equivalent of a Corps d'Armée in the full belief that it would give him an opportunity to regain the fame to which his Military qualities entitled him.—To give a fair history of that time your book should have contained Buell's letter to the public, printed ostentatiously in all the newspapers to the effect that he was not willing to serve under Grant and Sherman who Encouraged their men to commit trespass and pillage of private property which was a disgrace to our Country—I know that in the beginning I too had the old West Point notion that Pillage was a Capital crime and have punished it by Shooting, but the Rebels wanted us to detach a Division here, a brigade there to protect their families and property while they were fighting with Lee in Virginia. This was a one sided game of War and many of us as kind hearted, as fair just, and manly of men as Buell or any body else ceased to quarrel with our own men about such minor things, and went in to subdue the Enemy, leaving minor depredations to be charged up to the account of Rebels who had forced us into the War, and deserved all they got and *more*. Buell of all men who knew the temper of the People of the South had no right to throw this in our teeth. It was on a par with McClellans accepting a nomination for President by men who would have broken up this Union because they had not the perseverance and patience to await the Result. I know that I always had and still have the kindest feelings toward Buell, and an almost unlimited respect for his personal courage and real ability as a Soldier, but when he questioned the Motives of others his Equals if not his Superiors he transcended the limits of friendly criticism. In your Preface you assume as a fact established by History which will give you all the trouble you want for the rest of your life.—Page 8, giving a resumée of the operations of Buells Army in 1862 you assert that he—'rescued Grants Army at the Battle of Shiloh and converted the disaster of the first day into a Victory on the Second day.' There are ten thousand living witnesses today who know this is not true. We, Grants Army of the Tennessee fought the first day of Shiloh without a particle of assistance from Buell, and *you Know it*; for you and Buell came to me that night, and I told you that we had still 18000 men in Line,— that Prentiss [*Lewis Wallace's*] Division of 6000 fresh men had just come in, and that I had orders from General Grant in person to attack the Enemy at daylight by Genl Grant in person the next morning. Genl Grant believes and we all do that you were derilict in coming by the Short line from Columbia so deliberately and Slowly as to Show a purpose, whilst Sidney Johnston moved around by the longer line & made his concentration and attack on us before you arrived, and long after you Should have been there to help on the *first day.* Genl Grant now driven by adversity is taking to the pen & will I am certain give some new points on this very Battle—The Battle of Apl 6, 1862 was a real Battle, hard fought with 10,000 Slaughtered or maimed on a Side.—At night we held our ground, and the Enemy was repulsed at all points. The next day the 7th was a simple 'walk over,' not one ~~tenth~~ fifth of the Execution of the day before—we had meantime recieved the accession of 6000 fresh men (Lew Wallace's Division) and before you, Buell & his Staff rode out to where I personally was, I had received orders from Genl Grant in person to attack offensively the next Morning regardless of Buell, I had not a particle of doubt that I could do so Successfully and am not willing to Submit to your or any bodys assertion that 'our defeat of the 6th was made Glorious victory of the 7th by Buells Army.' We were of course glad to have you, but had I or any man on that field Supposed that ~~you~~ you or any man with you came to claim our honors, I would have said 'go back' and honestly Speaking I think you and comrades were not over anxious to share our danger. I remember perfectly Buells manner and even when he left me, was not sure that he would venture West of the Tennessee that night. I was in hopes this absurd Claim of having 'Saved us' would have been dropped—If renewed I think both Buell and you will regret it. Every man sees things with his own eyes and from his own Standpoint, and I like to hear each Army at its Reunions claim all & more than it merits—but when we come to publish books which may be quoted we must be Careful, I stand by my Memoirs Vol 1, Pages 244, 245 &c Vol 2, ~~2~~, 5–6 For myself I am indifferent but the old Division Comdrs—Brigade Regimental &c of the Army of the Tennessee appear more sensitive on this point today than they were in 1862—" ALS, *ibid.* Fry served as provost marshal gen. with rank of brig. gen. (1864–66), retired as col., asst. AG (1881), and wrote on military topics before and after retirement. His *Operations of the Army Under Buell from June 10th to October 30th, 1862, . . .* (New York, 1884), started an extended controversy with Sherman centering on USG. See letter to William T. Sherman, Oct. 19, 1884; Fry, "An Acquaintance with Grant," *North American Review,* CXLI, cccxlix (Dec., 1885), 540–52; Stephen D. Engle, *Don Carlos Buell: Most Promising of All* (Chapel Hill, 1999), pp. 354–58.

    1. See Article, [*Feb., 1885*].
    2. For Irving W. Carson, see *PUSG,* 4, 393–94.

To Adam Badeau

Sept. 13th 1884

DEAR BADEAU,

    I have your letter of the 9th instant. There will be time enough to make the arrangements for publication when my book is completed. Rosswell Smith has been here to see.[1] There will be no difficulty about the publication at any time if they are to be the publishers. My own opinion is that they would be the best [pu]blishers. But I will make no committal until about the time for publication. I find that firm has emancipated itself from the "General Agency" for the sale of books, and procuring advertisements which enables them to sell books and advertise, much cheaper than firs using "The Agency," and still receive the same themselves that others do. The agency demands fifty-five per cent for their services. It cost the Century ten using their own agency.

I have ju[st] finished Chattanooga. I shall go on to complete my work up to where the Wilderness campaign begins, and then go back to the begining.

When we get to Washington[2] I shall have a room for you where you will always be welcome, and I shall be specially glad to have you, as soon as we are settled, to go over with me the remaining articles for the Century. We will spend a week or ten days with Buck before we settle down in the city.

Very Truly yours
U. S. GRANT

ALS, Munson-Williams-Proctor Institute, Utica, N. Y.

1. After a prosperous legal career in Ind., Roswell Smith entered publishing in New York City and emerged as president of the Century Co., which produced *Century Magazine.* On Tuesday, Sept. 9, 1884, Smith, New York City, wrote to Richard Watson Gilder, editor, *Century Magazine.* "I will write now to tell you of our interview with General Grant on Saturday. It was in every way satisfactory and I think a good impression was made on both sides. I found him thoroughly intelligent in relation to the subscription book business, and very much disgusted with the way it is usually managed. He remarked that he did not propose to pay a scalawag canvasser $6 for selling a $12 book, not worth much more than half the money, as in some cases he quoted. His ideas agree with ours—to make a good book, manufacture it handsomely, sell it at a reasonable price, and make it so commanding that we can secure competent agents at a fair commission. The day was charming at Long Branch. We dined at Mr. Childs's, and I have to thank you and Mr. Johnson for a very memorable pleasure. When the book is ready he is to come to us with it." Rosamund Gilder, ed., *Letters of Richard Watson Gilder* (Boston, 1916), pp. 123–24. See George W. Cable, *A Memory of Roswell Smith* (n. p., n. d.); Robert Underwood Johnson, *Remembered Yesterdays* (Boston, 1923), pp. 216–17.

On Sept. 12, USG, Long Branch, wrote to Smith, probably in reference to Henry Chadwick, *The Sports and Pastimes of American Boys* . . . (New York, 1884). "Please accept my thanks for the two volumes of 'American-Sports' which you kindly sent me. Your letter, and the books, were received yesterday." ALS, Gallery of History, Las Vegas, Nev.

2. USG meant New York City.

To Robert Underwood Johnson

———

Long Branch, N. J.
Sept. 16th 1884

DEAR SIR:

Col. Grant left for the city this morning, not to return again this season. I have opened your letter to him however, and answer.—It is alltogether probable that I will use the anecdote of Mr. Lincoln's remark about Mr. Stevens[1] and his over-coat when I come to that point of my Memoirs; ~~when~~ but it will not be in either of the Articles I am writing—have written, because the four are now complete—for the Century.

I inclose for you the correct story as near as I can relate it.

Yours &c
U. S. GRANT

ROBT. U. JOHNSON

When the peace Commissionrs, Stevens, Hunter and Campbell,[2] appeared a City Point the former—whom I had never met, but always understood to be a very small man—was wearing a very large overcoat, reaching near his ancles, and made of a heavy coarse material, manufactured in the south after the breaking out of the rebellion Mr. Stevens looked, in this overcoat, like a medium sized man. But when I shewed the Commissioners to the boat on which they were to be guest of the government during their stay, Mr. S. divested himself of his overcoat, and stood forth the stalwart of ninety pounds which I had understood was about his weight when in robust health.—When notified that Mr. Lincoln was on his way from Washington to meet the Commissioners, I sent the boat on which they were guests, to Hampden Roads to await the coming of the President. After the interview Mr. Lincoln run on up to City Point. It seems that Mr. Stevens was wearing his overcoat when the President boarded the boat on which the Commissionrs were, but took it off in honor of his presence: ~~F~~for about the first thing Mr Lincoln said to me when we met, was: "did you see that over-coat of Stevens'"; yes, laughing, but; "did you see him take it off," yes again, well; "was'nt it the biggest shuck and the littlest ear ever you did see".

ALS, Aurora College, Aurora, Ill. On Sept. 2, 1884, USG wrote to Robert Underwood Johnson, associate editor, *Century Magazine.* "I will remain at Long Branch until about the 15th of this month. From here I expect to go to . . . I have finished the Wilderness campaign, but have not gone over it to correct mistakes. I will not send it in until the Chattanooga article is ready to go with it." Unidentified autograph dealer catalogue, USGA; Ben Bloomfield, List DM-7, 1957, no. 45.

  1. Alexander H. Stephens. See *Memoirs*, II, 420–23.
  2. See *PUSG*, 13, 333–35, 337, 344–45.

To Drake DeKay

New York City,
Sept. 29th 1884.

Col. Drake De Kay:
Adj. Gen.l Veterans Union:

    I have not been aware until this evening that I had been re-elected as Commander-in Chief of the Union Veteran Union—or Boys in Blue.—Had I been aware of it I should have ~~decline~~ resigned after ~~in~~the recent accident which has so disabled me, in order that some more active person might take the command. As it is I must decline to take any part at the present time; and leave all action by the organization subject to the orders of *the next in Command,* if there is such an officer. If there is not, and I am authorized to designate ~~a state Commander to~~ a Commander to act in my stead, I will disignate General E. A. Carr,[1] state Commander of New York.

Respectfully
U. S. Grant

ALS, Gallery of History, Las Vegas, Nev. Named for his poet grandfather, Joseph Rodman Drake DeKay was born in 1836 in New York City, served with distinction during the Civil War, and remained active in veterans' organizations. On Sept. 25, 1884, Stephen B. Elkins, Republican National Committee, New York City, telegraphed to U.S. Senator John A. Logan of Ill., Republican vice-presidential candidate. "Should General Grants health prevent his taking active command boys in blue would it be safe for Grant to ask Genl Sherman to take his place answer to Drake DeKay thirty nine broadway NewYork" Telegram received (at 3:45 P.M.), DLC-John A. Logan. On June 15, Elkins had written to Logan concerning the campaign. " . . . Had you not better write Grant & Conkling you expect them to help" ALS, *ibid.*

On April 10, 1873, Levi P. Luckey had written to DeKay. "The President directs me to say in reply to your favor of the 6th inst. that he has no objection to the placing of his portrait at the top of the Commissions to which you refer, since the Company desire it. He does not wish, however, to name any particular likeness but leaves that to your own selection. I enclose the autograph you wish." Copy, DLC-USG, II, 2.

On Sept. 21, 1876, DeKay, Indianapolis, telegraphed to USG. "Fifty thousand veterans in Convention wish a word from their old Commander for Chairman Noyes . . . . Forward till found" Telegram received (at 12:11 P.M.), *ibid.*, IB.

On May 1, 1877, DeKay, secretary, Union Veterans' National Committee, New York City, wrote to USG. "Major General Dix having resigned the Chairmanship of this Committee, it devolves upon me as Secretary to inform you that you have been elected chairman of the 'Union Veterans' National Committee' for the years 1877–1880, by the unanimous vote of the members—whose names are hereto appended. Their ballots were accompanied by warm expressions of esteem and of gratification at your assuming once more your old position of commander in chief." ALS, *ibid.* Unsigned *"Remarks"* taken from the ballots and a list of forty-two members supporting USG's nomination are *ibid.* On May 16, USG, Philadelphia, wrote to DeKay. "I accept with great pleasure the position of Chairman of the Union Veterans' National Committee and express the hope that in my absence from the country the association may complete its organization. On my return from abroad it will afford me great pleasure to meet the Veterans, and to express to them in person my thanks for this mark of their esteem." *New York Times*, May 19, 1877.

1. USG meant Joseph B. Carr, former brig. gen., who then served as maj. gen., N. Y. militia, and N. Y. secretary of state. See *ibid.*, Feb. 25, 1895.

To Alonzo V. Richards

New York City,
Sept. 30th 1884.

MAJ. H. V. RICHARDS:
DEAR MAJOR:

I am in receipt of your letter of the 26th instant, with the inclosed. I do not call to mind any such person F. P. Cleveland. It is possible however that I have met him, and that I would recognize him if we should meet. But it is not possible that he should have ever served on my staff, because, in that event I surely should be able to call him to mind. Two years ago I might have expressed dissatisfaction of Mr Blaine, even to a st comparitive stranger; but it is not likely that I should have corresponded with him. It is certain that I have not written any such to him, or any one else, recently in which I "intimated that he (I) had in no way changed his (my) mind regarding Blaine or his (my) intention not to support him." I do not suppose that Mr. Cleveland ever made such a statement as the writer attributes to him. It would be untrue if he did.

I am taking no part in the canvass; but it is not because of any change in sentiment. I have been a republican ever since the war began, and shall continue so as long as the states in rebellion continue to cast a solid vote for the party that supported rebellion, whether they have the numerical strength to do so, with a free ballot and fair count, or not.

I hope you may be successful in your new occupation, and I know you will be happyer now that you are out of active politics.

With kind regards to Mr Miner, and your family,

Very Truly yours

U. S. GRANT

ALS, WHi. The enclosure was an undated newspaper clipping. "Special to the Chicago Daily News. ROCKFORD, Ill., Sept. 25.—The Rev. F. P. Cleveland is one of the presiding elders at the Rock River methodist conference, now in session here. The reverend gentleman, who is from the Freeport district, is a cousin of Grover Cleveland, their fathers being brothers . . . . Mr. Cleveland was formerly on the staff of Gen. Grant, and has remained his personal friend. He said that Gen. Grant told him two years ago that he (Grant) thought the democrats would succeed in getting into power this year. Blaine he considered an unsafe man, and he did not think he could support him if a candidate, and he was sure he would be. Mr. Cleveland said further that he had received a letter from Gen. Grant only two weeks ago in which the general intimated that he had in no way changed his mind regarding Blaine or his intention not to support him." Ibid. Born in 1817 in Masonville, N. Y., Festus P. Cleveland served as chaplain, 53rd Ill. An obituary note mentions that Cleveland also served "as a secret service officer under Gen. Grant." New York Times, June 5, 1900. For a fuller obituary, without this reference, see Chicago Tribune, June 5, 1900. On Oct. 10, 1884, USG telegraphed to Alonzo V. Richards, Dubuque, presumably concerning the letter dated Sept. 30. "no objection to publication" Telegram received (at 10:20 A.M.), WHi. See PUSG, 30, 172–73; letter to Henry Villard, April 24, 1883.

In late July, a newspaper had reported that USG "regards Mr. Blaine's election as almost assured. To a recent visitor at his Long Branch cottage, the General said that Mr. Blaine ought to be elected. 'He would be president of the United States in fact as well as in name,' he continued. 'He has twenty-five years of experience in public life, and knows every feature of public business. To reject such a man in all the plenitude of his knowledge, ability and will for a man of Governor Cleveland's limited experience would be beneath the good sense of the American people.'" *Philadelphia Press*, July 29, 1884. For USG's visit with James G. Blaine in New York City on Sept. 19, see *ibid.*, Sept. 20, 1884.

On Aug. 14, a correspondent had reported from Long Branch. "Gen. Grant said to-day, referring to a report that he was willing to accept the nomination of the American Political Alliance for the Presidency, 'I never heard of Ellsworth until I received a letter from him, tendering me the Presidential nomination of the American Political Alliance. I know nothing of either the Alliance or Mr. Ellsworth, with the exception of what I have read in the newspapers. I have not answered the letter, and do not intend to answer it. No committee has waited on me to see if I would accept the nomination tendered me in Mr. Ellsworth's letter. I am a Republican, and I have no interest in the Alliance or its action.'" *New York Times*, Aug. 15, 1884. The American Political Alliance, a nativist organization, eventually ran William L. Ellsworth for president on a platform that called for stricter naturalization laws and greatly restricted immigration. See *ibid.*, Aug. 7, Sept. 18–19, 21, 28, Oct. 2, 4, 16, 1884.

To Adam Badeau

—————

New York City,
Oct. 2d 1884.

DEAR BADEAU;

We are at home now, and settled, and will be glad to see you on Monday next,[1] or any day thereafter that may suit your convenience best. I finished the Wilderness campaign about a week before leaving Long Branch and have done nothing since. I propose however going to work next Monday, and to continue busily until I am done. As I told you in a previous letter there will be a room for you all the time you want to spend with us. There is room also for you to work on your own book.[2] I have taken the front room,—the small one—at the head of the stairs, for my work, and converted the boudoir into a bedroom. Where I now am there is a table to write upon, and a large desk.

Very Truly yours
U. S. GRANT

ALS, Munson-Williams-Proctor Institute, Utica, N. Y. See letter to Adam Badeau, Oct. 8, 1884; *Badeau*, pp. 564–65.

1. Oct. 6, 1884.
2. A novel published as *Conspiracy: A Cuban Romance* (New York, 1885).

To Cornelius B. V. Ward

New York City,
Oct. 4th 1884.

CORNELIUS V. V. WARD,
SEC. MAD. AVE. CONG. CHURCH.
DEAR SIR:

I herewith resign my place as Trustee in the above church. I have given notice—and now repeat it—that I give up my pew in the church because of my inability to pay the rent.

Very Truly yours
U. S. GRANT

ALS, University of Southern California, Los Angeles, Calif. For Cornelius B. V. Ward's controversial start as asst. clerk to review pew rents at the Madison Avenue Congregational Church, New York City, see *New York Times*, Feb. 24, 1884.

On Feb. 8, 1882, USG wrote to John P. Newman. "Your note of last evening was received notifying me of my election as a trustee of your new charge . . . . I can therefore meet with the other trustees . . . Meeting probably better be held at the church though immaterial to me." J. H. Benton Sale, American Art Association, March 12, 1920, no. 355. In early Jan., after Newman had been called as pastor, Madison Avenue Congregational Church, USG rented a pew for $1,000. On Jan. 15, USG and Ulysses S. Grant, Jr., heard Newman preach his first sermon in his new church. See *New York Times*, Jan. 13, 16, 1882.

On Thursday, Jan. 17, 1884, USG *et al.* wrote to Newman. "We, the Trustees of the Madison-Avenue Congregational Church, repudiate all sympathy with the improper resolution offered at the annual meeting of the church on last Wednesday night, and on the other hand commend the good sense of the meeting in laying that resolution on the table. Your pastorate in our church has been so successful spiritually and financially, your commanding position in the community as a philanthropist, minister, pulpit orator, and your personal and official intercourse with us has been so gentlemanly and kind that we sincerely trust that you will not think for a moment of leaving us, but that you will remain our revered and beloved Pastor." *Ibid.*, Jan. 18, 1884. USG did not attend a meeting that same evening "due to his physical inability to leave his house. He was, however, unanimously re-elected President of the board. It was stated that the General was very much annoyed at the assault made upon his friend Dr. Newman at the annual meeting, and also at the reports which credited him with saying that unless the church entered the Methodist denomination he would sever his connection with it." *Ibid.* On Feb. 18, Newman's opponents wrote to the trustees requesting "an ecclesiastical council to advise the church in its present difficulties." *Ibid.*, Feb. 20, 1884. In reply, USG joined an unsuccessful protest against the request. *Ibid.*, March 11, 1884. For this inconclusive council, see *ibid.*, March 12–14, 22, 1884. In June, Newman responded to a report that USG had left the Madison Avenue Congregational Church. "Why do the newspapers print such lies? I dined last night with the General, and know there is no truth whatever in the statement. He is still President of our Board of Trustees, and will remain in that position, and I shall be much obliged if THE TIMES will deny, as forcibly as it can and on my authority, the story that he has left or contemplates leaving our church." *Ibid.*, June 9, 1884. Factions within the Madison Avenue Congregational Church disputed Newman's pastorate until he resigned in Jan., 1885. See *ibid.*, Jan. 10, 12–14, 16, 23, 1885.

Newman later shared his knowledge of USG's religious experiences and views with a reporter. "He was brought up in the Methodist Episcopal Church. His father's house was the home of Methodist preachers for over 40 years. The General's earliest recollections were associated with the clergy. He had to care for their horses. He remembered that the horses were good ones and that their owners always insisted on their having plenty of oats. Many a time he was sent out by his father to take off the saddlebags and put up the horses. Once a preacher was to move from the neighborhood in which the Grants lived. He was to take his family and furniture in a wagon for 260 miles, and wanted some one to drive for him. Applying to the General's father for a driver, the old gentleman detailed Ulysses, then a lad, for that work. Afterward the preacher reported to the boy's father that never in his life had he had such a good and silent driver. The General's father was a farmer at that time. In later years he lived at Covington, Ky. He was a churchgoer always, serving in the Methodist Church as Trustee, Steward, and class leader. Wherever he went he was a ruling spirit in church affairs. He was a man of sterling character, strong will, high purposes, and at times arbitrary. His mother was modest, intelligent, and sunny in spirit. The General inherited her nature. All of his sisters were devout Methodists. One of them, Mrs. Cramer, married a Methodist preacher, now the Minister of the Government at Berne, Switzerland. The General was thus indoctrinated in the faith of the church. He held to those great principles of Christianity all his life. Accepting the Bible as the word of God to man, he regarded Christianity as divine. But his mind tended to the sunny side of Christianity. The beneficent results of the Gospel promised to him the glory of the Messiah, the universal triumph of Christianity. I became his Pastor in 1869. I have been his guest many times. And at all times, in the White House at Washington or at his cottage in Long Branch, he always had family prayer, in which he usually requested me to lead. I called at the White House on his last Sunday there—his last night in office. Mr. Hayes was then having a reception at John Sherman's. I found the General and Mrs. Grant, with Mr. and Mrs. Sartoris, quietly sitting in the Blue Room. We talked a while. Then at the General's request we all knelt in prayer. I have been with him in private and in public and with all classes of people. Yet I never heard him utter a profane word or indulge in an improper story, nor have I ever seen him smile approvingly at an immodest story which some person present happened to have the audacity to relate. He was altogether the purest man in conversation of whom I ever had knowledge. During my pastorate of six years in Washington, which included the greater part of his Presidency, he was a regular attendant at church. Storm of no kind ever kept him away. He was the most attentive and appreciative listener I ever had. To me he was an inspiration, because of his profound attention and the indirect influence I exerted through him on others. He was President of our Board of Trustees and a liberal contributor to the church. His charities were many and unostentatious . . . . He was specially interested during his tour of the world in American missions, of which he visited a large number. The educational movements connected with these missions appealed strongly to his sympathy. I have a letter from him, written in Japan, in which he unfolds the wonderful improvements in moral and educational mission work which had taken place in that country under the management of American missions. That work made a deep and lasting impression on his mind. On his return to this country he attended my church in this city, manifesting the same deep religious nature as formerly; the same reverence for God and personal belief in Christianity. He had a wonderful faith in Divine Providence, and believed in special interpositions of Providence in the affairs of men and nations. I have heard him talk by the hour on that subject, giving illustrations drawn from his own life. Once I asked him, I remember, what he considered his most providential experience. Without hesitation he said: 'My resignation from the army in 1854. I was then a Captain. If I had staid in the army I would have been still a Captain on frontier duty at the outbreak of the war and would thus have been deprived of the right to offer my services voluntarily to the country. That opportunity shaped my future.'" *Ibid.*, July 24, 1885. For Newman's eulogy of USG, see *ibid.*, Aug. 5, 1885.

To Lewis Wallace

New York City,
October 7th 1884

GENERAL LEWIS WALLACE;
DEAR GENERAL:

Your letter of the 16th of September did not get into my hands until the early part of last week, on my return from a ten days visit to my son,[1] living on a farm in the north part of Westchester County. Being busy when I read it the letter was put aside to answer last Sunday.[2] I really forgot it when the time come, but now make amends as far as I can.

My Shiloh article was written last June, and delivered to the Editor of the Century shortly after. What I say of you at that battle is quite a modification of some of the statements that went out at the time, and contains the true history as I saw and understand it. The proof has not yet been sent to me by the printers, but it will be. I intend then to make some modifications, and additions to answer a claim set up by one of Buell's staff officers, ~~since m~~ in a book, or pamphlet, published since my article was written.[3] In my article, as it now stands, I show that Nelson was at Savannah the afternoon of the 5th, and that I gave him the order myself, in person, to march at an early hour the next morning; that he did not start until 1 p. m. and that when firing ceased on the night of the

6th he had but three regiments under fire even constructively, and they I placed in position myself. His casualties were two killed, one wounded, all from the _____⁴ regt. Ind. Vols, and had no effect whatever upon the result of the battle. Also that, without Buell, I was reinforced on the 7th by your division of veterans while the enemy was not reinforced atall, and had lost more men on the first day than we had, in killed, wounded and straglers. I was very glad to see Buell, but his coming did not change the result one iota.

I will have Fred. copy from the original manuscript what I have said concerning you, in a few days, and any modifications I may propose to make in that part.

Very Truly yours

U. S. GRANT

P. S. Since writing the four articles for the Century—completed before leaving Long Branch the 17th of last month—I have concluded to continue, and write up my entire connection with the war of the rebellion. I may or may not publish it.

U. S. G.

ALS, InHi. On Sept. 16, 1884, Lewis Wallace, minister to Turkey, Crawfordsville, Ind., wrote to USG. "The *Century Co.* people inform me that they have engaged you to write a paper for them on ~~Shiloh.~~ Pittsburg Landing. Such a contribution from your hand will be important as well as most interesting. Probably I ~~should~~ ought not to trouble you ~~with any request~~ touching the subject; still I trust you will appreciate the anxieties natural to one who has been so bitterly and continuously criticised in the connection, and pardon me a few lines of request. The letter of exoneration you gave me some years ago is not permitted to be printed in the volume of reports published by the government, though I earnestly sought the favor of the Secretary of war. The terrible reflections ~~you made in endorsing~~ found in your endorsement on my official re-report of the battle, and elsewhere, go to the world wholly unqualified. It is not possible to exaggerate the misfortune thus entailed upon me. But now you have it in power to make correction in a paper which will be read far more generally than the compilation of the department. May I hope you will do it? Since my return from Europe I have for the first time read the reports of General Rawlins and McPherson and Major Rowley touching my march the first day of the battle. I shall regret all my remaining days not previously knowing their tenor; ~~of their statements. If you will kindly take them up and re-read them, you will see that nowhere does it appear that they knew that my march as originally begun was in obedience to an mistaken incorrect order. And all the time I supposed the order correctly delivered, and that they knew its terms. Had the correctness of the order been mooted, it could have been then produced, and the sad misunderstanding laid at rest. It is not to be supposed that I would could have been indifferent to the thoughts which, as it now appears, they must have had the hours they rode with me. About a year afterwards I heard for the first time~~

~~that there was a mistake.~~ for I think I could have explained to ~~them their the satis~~ the satisfaction of those gentlemen ~~the~~ every mystery of my conduct during their ride with me the afternoon of the 6th April. They did not ~~know~~ understand that ~~I~~ there was a mistake in ~~the del~~ your order as it was delivered to me, and while with them I supposed they knew why I was ~~on the road~~ where they found me. Consequently no explanation took place between us. I see now they really supposed me ~~I had was~~ lost ~~my road~~, and ~~was~~ wandering aimlessly about. Had the correctness of the order been mooted, no doubt ~~it~~ the order itself could have been produced. I would ~~never~~ not have rested until my Adjutant General had produced it. Is it to be supposed for an instant that, knowing their thoughts of me during the hours of that ride, I could have been indifferent to them? As it is, you will observe that neither of them pretends to explain my behavior. ~~This~~ Neither ~~of~~ makes allusion to a theory of explanation. The truth is I all the time supposed the necessity for the change of direction in my movement was simply due to the bad turn of the battle after the order was dispatched to me. ~~In fact t~~The whole time I was in their company I thought myself entitled to credit for the promptness with which I was obeying your orders. It never occurred to me that there was anything to explain, and I was wholly given up to the ~~business in hand.~~ movement of the division which was urgent business in hand. With reference to Major Rowley's statement that I had no knowledge of any other road than that by the old mill, and his other statement that I retained him as a guide, the explanation is that I was speaking of a cross road to the river road. I had no knowledge of such a road. In hopes of finding one I countermarched instead of facing column to the rear. One of my captains of artillery has since gone over the entire route we took from Stoney Lonesome, the place at which I received your order ~~of~~ to march, to Pittsburg Landing, and he finds me mistaken in saying we countermarched back nearly to the initial point of movement. He not only found the cross road taken, but measured the whole march chain in hand, making it a little more than 15 miles. As soon as I am permanently re-settled at home, I shall ~~make it my a duty to~~ have ~~that section~~ the Crump's Landing Section of our operations carefully surveyed and mapped, things that have not yet been done. As to my requiring a written order from you, I repeat my *absolute* denial of the statement. The order I acted upon was *unsigned*, and it is susceptible of proof that when the young Illinois Cavalryman overtook me I was already on the march. As to the slowness referred to by McPherson, Rawlins and Rowley, please try that point by comparisons. Nelson, on the other side of the river, was the whole day making six miles. Albert Sidney Johnston required three days to get his army from Corinth, scarcely 20 miles in all. From 11:30 o'clock till just dusk my march was quite 15 miles. I refer the argument to your calm judgment. I do not wonder my movement seemed slow to ~~the three gentlemen.~~ your officers. ~~It must have been intolerable to their anxieties~~ With their anxieties quickened by what they had seen on the field, it must have seemed intolerable to them. They describe me correctly as *at the head of the column*, and I did several times dismount. ~~At such times, however, it was~~ but only to wait the closing up of the division, and ~~always the officers of my staff were down the column helping push it forward.~~ reports of my own staff officers, who were kept ~~helping~~ urging the column ~~to exterti exertion~~ through the mud and mire. ~~They sought and found me with their reports at the head of the movement.~~ There is another point your officers seem not to have understood, and that was my determination not to send the division ~~peace~~piecemeal into the battle. The *whole* division was what I supposed you wanted, and I was resolved to bring you the whole division. I paid no attention to contrary suggestions from anybody. I think you will justify this pertinacity of purpose by the fact that it was impossible to tell the moment I might be attacked *en route*. The chances of such an occurrence grew sharper as I drew nearer Pittsburg Landing ~~by on the river road~~. ~~From~~ For you must remember, General, that from the moment Major Rowley overtook me with the information, then first received, that our army had been driven from the line it occupied in the morning, and was back far towards the river, I supposed it utterly unable to help me. Then whether the enemy attacked me or I them, it was only my *division*, and not a part of it, that could have achieved your desires. And on this point I have ~~always said that~~ I believed you right in thinking it possible to win the fight without assistance from the army of the Cumberland. The *elan* of the assailants was spent by 5 o'clock afternoon. Albert Sidney Johnston was dead. There were disorganized thousands of confederates ~~wandering~~ roaming over the field and looting in our camps. A vigorous assault by my division the second morning of the contest, or in the afternoon of the first day, supported ~~by~~as it would have been by the brave men who at last stopped the rebels, would have given us the victory. So I believe now; so I have ~~always~~ believed. since becoming thoroughly informed of the conditions when night fell. It is something ~~always~~ to be remembered *that Beauregard stood repulsed before Nelson arrived on the field*. ~~Moreover the enemy would have had no~~ ground, and could look for no reinforcements to ~~compensate~~ offset ~~their line for~~ my division. At your table at City Point we one day sat listening to the comments of some officers upon the battle of Pittsburg Landing. After while you remarked to me in a low tone—'If I had known then what I know now, I would have ordered you where you were marching when stopped.' The remark was made at your table, and in a confidential manner, so that I have never felt at liberty to repeat much less publish it. But times innumerable since then I have ~~thought of it, with a~~ wished ~~from at the bottom of my heart~~ that Rowley had not overtaken me for another hour that afternoon. The enemy had used the last of his reserves. I would have taken the bluff on which Sherman had been camped in the morning, and, without opposition, ~~have~~ effected my deployment. The first of the rebels struck would have been the horde plundering ~~and drinking in~~ the sutler's ~~tents~~ and and drinking in the streets of ~~in~~ the camp ~~streets~~. Their fears would have magnified my command, and rushing to their engaged lines they would have carried the word that Buell's army was ~~upon them~~ up, and ~~taking up~~ on their lines of retreat. For your sake and my own, General, and for the cause generally it was unfortunate that Rowley had not ~~got~~ lost his way as it was said I had mine. ~~In the last place~~ Finally, general, did you ever ask yourself what motive I could have had to play you falsely that day? It couldn't have been personal malice. Only a few weeks before I had been promoted Major General on your recommendation. It couldn't have been cowardice. You had seen me under fire at Donelson, and twice the second day at Pittsburg Landing you found me with my division under fire. It couldn't have been lack of resolution. I certainly showed no failing of that kind at Monocacy Junction where ~~the circumstances~~ my situation was quite as trying as at any hour of the 6th April of which I am writing. The fact is I was the victim of a mistake. ~~In~~ Captain Baxter's omission from the order you gave him for transmission to me—the omission of the road you wanted me to take in coming up; viz., *the lower or river road to Pittsburg Landing*—was the cause of my ~~false~~ movement ~~to the battle field beginning~~ at noon. It is also the ~~true~~ key of explanation of all that followed. That I took the directest and shortest road ~~to join~~ to effect a junction with the right of the army, and marched promptly upon receipt of the order, ~~is~~ are the best evidence I could have furnished of an actual desire to do my duty, and share the fortunes of the day with you whether they were good or bad. Captain Baxter's report to you of my conduct on receipt of the order to march, that I was delighted and evinced the greatest alacrity in disposition to obey, was the truth. See RAWLINS' *Compendium of Official Reports*, Vol. X, Part 1. *page* 1866. In all the years that have followed I have been patient and uncomplaining because, as you had shown a ~~disposition~~ the will to exonerate me, I believed you would follow it up on all proper occasions. And I ~~beg to~~ submit to you if this is not one of them. For the sake of the hundreds of survivors of my old division, as well as that justice may be finally and completely done to me individually, I presume to present the matter to you in this letter." ADfS, *ibid.* On Nov. 21, Wallace, New York City, recorded in a journal USG's views on *Ben-Hur.* "General Grant told me, today, that he read it through word for word; that he began in the morning, not having read a novel in ten years before, and finished it next day at noon, after reading all night. He couldn't lay it down. He was very cordial and so was Mrs. Grant The latter gave me the address of Mrs. Sartoris in London, and insisted upon my calling on her as the woman who declares *Ben-Hur* the greatest book ever written We talked the Shiloh matter all over with Grant, and he is now making the final modifications of his article to appear in the *Century.* His remarks were not entirely satisfactory and I am anxious to see the paper" D, *ibid.* USG eventually reconsidered his criticisms of Wallace. See Article, [*Feb., 1885*]; letter to *Century Magazine*, June 22, 1885; Robert Underwood Johnson, *Remembered Yesterdays* (Boston, 1923), pp. 219–20.

On June 11, 1881, "JAYHAWKER" had reported from Washington, D. C. "Yesterday I went into the room of Assistant Secretary Hitt, at the State Department, and met General Wallace coming out. While waiting to talk with Mr. Hitt I picked up from a table the first volume of Badeau's Life of Grant. Turning over the leaves I found, on page 44, the following paragraph marked: 'The assault was renewed upon Lewis Wallace with great vigor, and he, too, was compelled to fall back, though slowly and fighting hard.' On the margin, opposite the paragraph, was this inscription in the handwriting of General Wallace: 'This is a lie. I never fell back an inch. LEW WALLACE.' Turning on to pages 80 and 81 I found the following paragraph marked: 'Lewis Wallace, one of Grant's own division commanders, was equally remiss; but he, who had been a month on the ground, excused himself by stating that he had taken the wrong road, . . . ' On the bottom of the margin of page 81 General Wallace had made the following inscription: 'There are more willful falsehoods in the foregoing paragraph than in any other of the same length in English literature. LEW WALLACE.'" *Cincinnati Enquirer*, June 16, 1881. In a June 26 interview, William R. Rowley described his mission to find Wallace on the first day at Shiloh. *Chicago Inter-Ocean*, July 1, 1881. See *PUSG*, 5, 68–70; *ibid.*, 8, 59–62; *ibid.*, 18, 191–95; Robert E. Morsberger and Katharine M. Morsberger, *Lew Wallace: Militant Romantic* (New York, 1980), pp. 109–14.

1. Ulysses S. Grant, Jr.
2. Oct. 5.
3. For James B. Fry's publication, see letter to William T. Sherman, Sept. 8, 1884.
4. 36th.

To Adam Badeau

Oct. 8th 1884

DEAR BADEAU,

Your letter just received. The articles I have to examine were completed about the 10th of Sept. Of course it will not hurt to let them rest two weeks longer. But I will be glad to see you when you are ready to come. You had better bring your with you too when you do come. There will be room for you and me both in my room. If there is not a table can be put up in your bed-room.

Yours Truly
U. S. GRANT

ALS, Munson-Williams-Proctor Institute, Utica, N. Y. See letter to Adam Badeau, Oct. 2, 1884.

To Edward F. Beale

———

Oct. 8th 1884

MY DEAR GENERAL BEALE:

Any day during the next two weeks that you will come up here I will go with you to visit Mr. Backman.[1] I have a letter from him in which he says you are entirely unreliable: that you have been promising him for several year to pay him a visit, but never have done so, but thinks I may have sufficient influence to induce you. Houston[2] will go with ~~meus~~, and probably Fred. He asks me to take any friends I choose. If there is any one you would like to take bring him along.

I think you and Mrs. Beale will be much pleased with John McLean, and the family. I class them among my most intimate and best friends. When in Cincinati I have a standing invitation to make their house my home, and generally do so.[3]

Very Truly yours
U. S. GRANT

ALS, DLC-Decatur House Papers.

1. Charles Bockman. On Oct. 13 (Monday) and 19, 1884, USG wrote to Edward F. Beale. "I have written to Mr. Backman that he may expect us, with Houston and one of my sons, by the morning train from New York, over the Erie road, on Friday next. I have said to him however that we will not go if the weather is bad, and that in any event we will telegraph him before starting." "Any day this week that suits your convenience I will go with you to Mr. Backmans. If you will telegraph me the day I will inform him so that he may expect us." ALS, DLC-Decatur House Papers. See *PUSG*, 24, 165–66.

2. Possibly James B. Houston, president, Pacific Mail Steamship Co. See *New York Times*, May 29, 1903; Gerald Thompson, *Edward F. Beale & the American West* (Albuquerque, 1983), p. 222.

3. On Oct. 7, John R. McLean had married Beale's daughter Emily. See *New York Times* and *Washington Post*, Oct. 8, 1884. For USG's friendship with the McLean family, see *PUSG*, 28, 179, 182; *ibid.*, 29, 323; letter to Fitch, Fox, and Brown, May 24, 1884.

To Daniel E. Sickles

Oct 9th /84

My Dear General Sickles

I have not a book or paper referring to Sonora that I know of in my possession, nor do I know where you would likely find anything of the kind. Young Conkling—son of Hon. Frederick Conkling— has written a "Guide to Mexico" which may give some information on the subject though I do not recollect that it does. His brother has also written a history of the country which I have not yet read, and do not know now where to lay my hands on.

Very Truly Yours
U. S. Grant

Typed copy, Delbert Wenzlick, St. Louis, Mo. In early Oct., 1884, Daniel E. Sickles visited Tex. and Mexico to investigate his mining and stock raising investments. *Philadelphia Press*, Oct. 3, 1884. Frederick A. Conkling, older brother of Roscoe Conkling and New York City banker, became an active Democrat after shifting from the Republicans to the Liberal Republicans in 1872. See *New York Times*, Sept. 19, 1891; letter to Alfred R. Conkling, Dec. 3, 1883; Howard Conkling, *Mexico and the Mexicans or, Notes of Travel in the Winter and Spring of 1883* (New York, 1883), especially pp. 278–79, 293.

Testimony

[*New York City, Oct. 9, 1884*]

General Sharpe. General Grant, what is the reason there are no American merchants doing business in the city of Mexico? We understand that substantially the business is all carried on there by Germans.

General GRANT. The reason I presume is this: The duties are
so exceedingly high in Mexico that they are prohibitory, or would
be if Mexico was a manufacturer herself, but not manufacturing
they have got to get the goods anyhow. No person will pay all the
duties, and the officials are often corrupt. So that the man who will
by practice and perjury and in other ways get rid of the greatest
amount of duties will have a monopoly of the business. Americans
generally are equal to anybody else, even in rascality, so that I wonder they do not have more of the trade. But then there is another
reason—that the Germans there give longer credits to the small
retailers who buy from them, even at twelve to eighteen months,
and there have never been, probably, Americans there who could
afford to give such long credits . . . . People who could do it are generally people who would not like to practice fraud at the custom-
houses to get the goods through. But when this treaty goes into
operation which is negotiated I have no doubt that it will build up
a large trade between this country and Mexico. There has been a
very great feeling of hostility against the United States heretofore,
and it exists to a very considerable extent yet, growing out of the
Mexican war and their loss of territory by that war. It is true we
paid for it, but then they were obliged to sell; it was not a voluntary
sale. There has been a feeling of hostility to the United States ever
since that, and a feeling of fear that we were after more of their
territory. But I think that is gradually dying out, and when this
treaty goes into effect, by proper and fair dealings we will convince
them that they ought to be our good friends instead of being suspi-
cious of us, and that ultimately a large commerce will be built up.
This treaty has been ratified by both Governments, but it cannot
go into effect until Congress passes regulations.[1] Our Congress
has to pass laws regulating how it shall be carried into effect . . . .

I think it will do a great deal of good for this Board or Commission to visit Mexico, because you will see the best people there,
and it will show them, and you can give that assurance, that the
Government of the United States is looking to the building up of
commerce and trade with them and to the cultivation of the most
friendly relations, and that we want to be warm friends and sup-

porters of each other—allies as it were. We have common institutions, and are on the same continent, and are contiguous Governments; and in that way I have no doubt a great deal of good can be done in Mexico and in Central American states by the Commission. In the Central American states there is no hostility to us, because we have never threatened them, and they want to cultivate relations with us because Great Britain has gone into one of those states[2] and established herself there, and extends her limits as she wants to and as she cuts out the valuable woods. Consequently they would like to be friends and allies of ours down there. But they have no direct communication with us except on the Pacific side. Great good can be done by this Commission going to Mexico, even without any particular object, in learning so much about what we could furnish and they want—the mere presence of the Commission. And that is particularly true as your visit occurs just at this time when the treaty is being agitated.

General SHARPE. Mr. Curtis calls my attention to the fact that there has been some misunderstanding as to what road carriages were in Mexico, and wagons . . . .

General GRANT. There is no misunderstanding at all so far as those articles are admitted free, but while they are collecting duties upon them the custom-house officers will always give the construction that will give the most revenue. But when you take off the duties there will be no question at all . . . . My recollection of it in the treaty is that it includes all vehicles that go on wheels and are pulled by animals, even down to a wheelbarrow, pushed by a man, with one or two wheels. It embraces all of them. I do not think there is any ambiguity. I think you will find that it is all wheeled vehicles, including those propelled by steam, horse, or mule power . . . .

General SHARPE. Did you ever hear any discussion down there as to the reasons why the Mexican market was filled with goods from other countries which could be supplied from the United States?

General GRANT. I have never heard any other, except this of the long credits given by the Germans, and then intimations that they probably could swear off 75 per cent. of the duties, or bribe it off, while an American's conscience would not let him go more than about 60 per cent. The German thinks if he has got to do a thing which is wrong he might as well go as far as he can; he might as well be hung for an old sheep as a lamb. I have been a good bit in Mexico—two years during the Mexican war, and then I have been back there twice, and I saw a good deal of the people and something of the country. I have also been in Nicaraugua, and I have spent some five or six weeks on the Isthmus of Panama at one time, but I do not know much about the trade of either of those states—that is, I do not know anything about it from my personal observation while there. I know what the climate is, and what it is capable of producing, and the character of the soil, and all that. The communications are most all on the side of the Pacific coast . . . .

They have a railroad from the city of Mexico to San Francisco, and that would be the most expeditious way. But you could, if you wanted to, see something more of the country by going down to Acapulco and those places. There you would have to go on mules . . . .

You can go from the city of Mexico to San Francisco quicker than from the city of Mexico to Acapulco.

General SHARPE. Do you believe the Government should aid in the building of railroads with Mexico?

General GRANT. I do not think the Government could do it very well; I do not think the Government could interest itself in building railroads . . . . We have got plenty of roads to the frontier already. But I will tell you one thing that my travels abroad and in the East have satisfied me of, and it is applicable to all territory outside of Europe, that our consular regulations are bad, and that the whole consular system ought to be abolished except in European countries. You take the Germans and the English, and the French and the Dutch—any nation in Europe, but these nations in particular—and their consular service, in fact their diplomatic service, is nothing under the sun but a system of agencies for commercial purposes, and to introduce and do everything they can to establish a market for their own particular products. Our whole

diplomatic and consular service is based upon exactly the opposite
theory; practically it is to discourage the introduction of American goods and wares, which makes it a disgrace. If you go out
here and whisper to some one that is going along that an American
consul has sold an American jews-harp, that fellow, by the time he
gets down to the car, will think that the country is disgraced; and
by the time the news gets down to the printing offices the land is
hardly big enough to hold the sound of the howl of rascality by
the thought that this fellow has disgraced the country by selling
American goods at Foo Chow. And everybody gets down a map
to see where Foo-Chow is, in which this great outrage has been
committed. Our consular service regulations are good enough for
European countries while the business between ourselves and the
European states is done between the merchants of the two countries, and you cannot influence it for the better by any change of
consular regulations. But when you leave Europe then you are
among a different sort of people, a people who are weak and can
be browbeaten, and who are not able to defend themselves so well.
And where a nation is represented by people who are equally agents
for the introduction of their goods, they have a power that would
not be felt in any of the European countries at all. So that my idea
was after my trip abroad, that outside of Europe the consular service ought to be entirely abolished over all the world outside of Europe, say South America and North America south of the United
States, and including Canada, too; and that we should substitute in
place of it the appointment by the President of commercial agents—
appointments to be made by the President, and no salaries paid by
Congress, except where they would think it would justify them to
give a salary—but let that be with Congress. Then let the President say to these boards of trade all over the United States, "Send
up the names of your agents; men you would be willing to trust to
transact business for you, and sell goods for you or buy for you, as
the case might be, and I will appoint them to these various places."
They can then go there with all the authority the consul has now; it
is an advertisement to him, and it gives him protection, and if there
is no salary attached he gets the fees allowed by law; and in that
way a great trade would be built up. Take Rangoon: The lumber

and rice business there is enormous. The lumber business there is larger than that at Chicago, I should think; and they ship there an average of two or three cargoes of rice a day, that go to other parts of India or to Europe. But an American vessel can go there and lay there eighteen months, and she cannot get a cargo as long as there is a European vessel in port. An American vessel may lay there eighteen months without being able to get a cargo, because we have no representative. There is an English merchant there, with a sign of an American eagle flapping his wings as wide as this table, and he is our consul, and the man is not interested in building up or promoting American commerce. He gave me an entertainment while I was there that cost me as much as his consular fees for ten years.[3] The biggest sign he had there was "American consul," and it was an advertisement for him, and his principal business was to see that English trade was built up. With the new regulations I think it would be changed, for all the different kinds of merchants could go there. His fees at first would be only $40, but that is a place where an immense amount of our canned goods could be sold, canned vegetables and fruits, &c.; and we might consign an immense amount of ice there, and having an American there we could get a return cargo of valuable woods. Then there could be a trade got up in our calicos, and a good deal of trade in steel tools, which we make better than anybody else, and in axes, picks, &c. A fine trade could be built up there, while we have not any trade at all now. And there is a trade not only with Lower Burmah, but with Upper Burmah. You can send as consuls our commercial agents, who are selected by the boards of trade; then they would be looking about here to see what goods would sell. I spoke about that, and interested some members of Congress very much in that when I came back, and they said they would bring up a bill, but there is always a Presidential election or something on hand, so that they can never give it attention.

General SHARPE. General, would you subsidize lines of steamers?

General GRANT. I would, most assuredly, and big; I would subsidize them, and subsidize them big enough to insure them getting them. I was always in favor of that; I was in favor of it when I was

President, and am in favor of it yet, and it is the only way we can build up the carrying trade. We could do it in the name of carrying the mail, but I would give them the subsidy outright, and require them to carry the mails . . . . Of course I would not make it a perpetual thing . . . . I would subsidize a line with any proper Central American port there may be in the Caribbean Sea, certainly with Brazil and the Argentine Confederation . . . . I do not know about the necessity of subsidizing Mexican lines; there is no necessity; it is so near by that it would not be necessary . . . .

Our commercial agents would be the same as the consuls are now in the matter of getting clearances and all that, but they could be made absolutely men of business, and would attend to credits as well as clearances. If we had lines of steamships running to the South American ports and to the Central American ports, there is an enormous amount of goods we could furnish more than we do . . . .

The charter [*of the Nicaraguan Canal*] expires on the 1st of this month. I presume there will be no difficulty about getting it renewed if there was assurance that capital would be raised to build it. I do not suppose I have been able to give you much information . . . .

There is no question that we could build up an immense trade with the East with no other change than that I speak of, sending men to act for all the merchants. And it would also help our shipping business, because the goods could go in American vessels. Vessels have been going to some places in India empty, and have always good cargoes back, except American vessels. The articles that would be sold there would be canned goods, and edge tools and large amount of ice. When you go to China and Japan there is nothing that they import which we do not make a good deal better than any of the European countries who supply them, and they would gladly buy our cotton goods. That is more than everything else put together, and our cotton goods are worth as much again as the English. They would buy them if they were permitted to, but they are not. The English have boycotted us in all matters of trade. We have got all along the coast of China and Japan—particularly China—and in India, Englishmen acting as our consuls . . . .

HED, 48-2-226, 109–15. A consular and diplomatic appropriation act, approved July 7, 1884, enabled President Chester A. Arthur to appoint George H. Sharpe (see *PUSG*, 12, 190), Thomas C. Reynolds (see *ibid.*, 26, 427–28), and Kan. attorney Solon O. Thacher as commissioners to recommend means to improve commerce with Central and South America. William E. Curtis, Chicago newspaper reporter and travel writer, served as secretary to the commission. After taking testimony in New York City, the commission visited other U.S. and foreign cities. See *New York Times*, Sept. 16–17, Oct. 3, 1884, *New York Herald*, Oct. 10, 1884; Curtis, *The Capitals of Spanish America* (New York, 1888).

    1. Congress never passed the required legislation. See letter to Editor, *Washington Evening Star*, Jan. 22, 1884.

    2. British Honduras.

    3. On March 21, 1879, John Russell Young wrote in his diary about James M. Leishman, former consul, Rangoon. DLC-John Russell Young. Congress had failed to appropriate money for a consul at Rangoon since 1876. See *PUSG*, 27, 273–74.

To Albion W. Tourgee

———

3 E 66th st. N. Y. City
October 16th 1884

JUDGE A. ~~F~~W. TOURGEE:

DEAR JUDGE

    Your letter of the 13th is received. If I had know of your misfortunes at the time I wrote to you, as I did a few days after, you would not have heard from me atall. As you are aware, my entire family have not only been robbed of all we had, but myself and one son are left responsible, legally for millions fraudulantly obtained from others. Under these circumstances I was naturally looking around to obtain a little means for present uses. Under these circumstances I wrote to you. I now beg your pardon for doing so, and my excuse is, as stated before, a lack of knowledge of the condition of affairs with The Continent Publishing Company.[1]

    I send herewith the contract and certificate of stock and beg you not to give yourself another thought about the matter so far as my interest goes.

Very Truly yours
U. S. GRANT

ALS, deCoppet Collection, NjP. On Oct. 31, 1884, Albion W. Tourgee, Mayville, N. Y., wrote to USG. "I need not attempt to express my feelings on receipt of your letter with its enclosures. I think no man has ever estimated your manhood more highly that I and I am sure that no one sympathized with your misfortunes more deeply—little thinking at that time, that in so brief a period I would be receiving so much more than I gave. I do not yet know when or how it will come about but I feel the strongest confidence that at some time I shall be able to redeem your generous relinquishment, so far as mere money is concerned, but the debt of kindly obligation which your letter placed me under can never be discharged. I take the liberty of sending you herewith the last volume I have published. I know it treats of a matter of which you have thought much. Should you feel inclined to write a word in regard to it, you may be sure that it will be appreciated. The work was almost all done upon a sick-bed as I was quite unable to hold a pen more than a few minutes at a time during its preparation. Hoping and believing that your misfortunes—terrible as they are—will not mar your happiness for long and perfectly sure that they can never for a moment obscure the fame of so glorious a manhood, . . ." ALS, USG 3. See Tourgee, *Hot Plowshares* (New York, 1883); letter to Albion W. Tourgee, July 30, 1884. For a sympathetic editorial on USG's financial plight, possibly written by Tourgee, see *Continent*, V, 121 (June 4, 1884), 728–29.

1. For the failure of Tourgee's venture, see *New York Times*, Sept. 4, 1884.

To William T. Sherman

October 19th 1884.

DEAR GENERAL;

As you probably are aware, my article on Shiloh was written last June, and sent to the Century Magazine before Fry's defense of Buell was published. Last week I sent to get it to make additions, if necessary, to refute the insinuation that "Buell saved the Army on the 6th" &c. In the article I d as sent to the Magazine I did not reply to any of the misstatements about that battle except as a fair statement of all the facts, as they appeared to me, answers them. On reading the article over however I did not find it necessary to make any changes on account of Frys claim for Buell. But I was glad I sent for it. On reading the article over so long after it was written I was able to improve some of the sentences, and also to improve the article by transpositions. Being the first article I ever wrote specially for publication I would think of occurrences of the first day while writing about the second, and put them down and sent them in the order in which written instead of in the order of occurrence. Then too in the draft I had spoken particulary of the outcry against you and me after the battle, and the desire of professed loyal people, to have us punished for our ignorant butchery of men who were fighting for their country. I stated that you were not even second in rank at that battle, and why you should be selected as a victim before your seniors I could not see: that if the success of a battle ever depended upon the life of one man other than the commanding officer that battle was the one at Shiloh, and the life was that of Sherman. I concluded before sending the article to leave out all notice of these attacks, and in doing so found, on reading the article over, that I had left out all special mention of you. This I was able to introduce without bringing in the context.

I work about four hours a day, six days in a week, on my book, and am now about one third through. My idea was that it would be a volume of from four to five hundred pages. But it looks now as if it will be two volumes of nearly that number of pages each. I may be able to compress it into a single volume.

Very Truly yours

U. S. GRANT

GN. W. T. SHERMAN.

ALS, DLC-William T. Sherman. On Oct. 22, 1884, William T. Sherman, St. Louis, wrote to USG, New York City. "I was glad as always to hear from you by your letter of the 19th & appreciate the propriety of the omission in your article on Shiloh of all matters of personal controversy. Your own statement of facts will be universally received as final & conclusive. I hope you will not condense too much the contemplated Book—you can easily arrange for two volumes, with a cheaper volume including both. Gen. Fry took exception to my assertion that Buell's approach to the Battlefield was not such as entitled him to the claim of having rescued us from distruction. He seemed desirous to draw me into a controversy for publication but this I would not. I then offered two extracts of his Book 'The Army under Buell' for discussion—viz. Page 8. 'rescued Grants Army at the Battle of Shiloh & converted the disaster of the first day on that memorable field into a victory the second day.' Page 10. 'Pressing their advantage the union Armies of the Tennessee under Grant, & of the Ohio under Buell concentrated at Pittsburg Landing on the Tennessee River where being attacked on the 6th of April they gained the victory of Shiloh'. And agreed if he accepted the challange, I would name a champion equal in rank, fame & service with himself to take up the cudgels & give him all he wanted. I made this offer Oct. 1st. & have no answer; & I doubt if Fry will accept. I am specially pleased that you are able to work four hours per day, six days in the week—& infer there from that your general health is much improved." Copy, *ibid.* See letter to William T. Sherman, Sept. 8, 1884.

Also on Oct. 22, Richard Watson Gilder, editor, *Century Magazine*, wrote to his wife. "General Grant has just been in—spent some time here and wants us to publish his book or books. It made me feel badly to see him so lame." Rosamund Gilder, ed., *Letters of Richard Watson Gilder* (Boston, 1916), p. 123.

To Thomas J. Bryant

———

3 E. 66th St. N. Y. City
October 28th 1884

CAPT. T. J. BRYANT:
DEAR CAPT.

In reply to your letter of the 17th instant I have to say I never saw any of your articles on Shiloh until you sent them to me recently. As they appeared in the Grand Army Advocate I must have received them, but as I was busily engaged they escaped my attention. I have now read them over carefully and see nothing in your statements to criticise, but, on the contrary, everything to commend. You have answered the misstatements about Shiloh more in detail than I have seen them answered before. You also give a very full and very accurate account of the battle *as I saw it.*

Very Truly yours
U. S. GRANT

ALS, MdAN. Itinerant Methodist minister Thomas J. Bryant, former capt., 14th Ill., was wounded at the battle of Shiloh and resigned as of Oct. 5, 1862. The Des Moines-based *Grand Army Advocate* began weekly publication in 1882. See Bryant, *Who is Responsible for the Advance of the Army of the Tennessee Towards Corinth?* (n. p., n. d.).

To Marcus J. Wright

———

3 E 66th St. N. Y. City
Nov. 4th 1884

GEN. MARCUS J. WRIGHT, ~~ESQ~~
DEAR SIR:—

I am much obliged to you for your letter of the 1st instant, and for your kind offer of assistance in furnishing material for my articles on the war of the rebellion, written for the Century Magazine, I say written because I finished the last of the series—four in number—before leaving Long Branch. But I am now ~~engaged in~~ writing up all that portion of the war in which I was personally engaged, or where my command extended,[1] and may want the assistance you kindly offer. If so I will call upon you without hesitation.

I do not call to mind the correspondence between General Pemberton and myself and others in January 1864 in regard to captured dispatches

Very Truly yours
U. S. GRANT

P. S. I will be pleased to hear any suggestion you have to make in regard to the work I am engaged upon.

U. S. G.

ALS, deCoppet Collection, NjP. Born in 1831, Marcus J. Wright served as brig. gen., C.S. Army, and practiced law in Memphis. Appointed War Dept. agent to collect C.S.A. archives, he secured records for publication in the *O.R.* See *New York Times,* Aug. 31, 1878; Wright, "Personal Recollections of General Grant," *Confederate Veteran,* XVII, 8 (Aug., 1909), 400–403.

1. On Nov. 7, 1884, Grenville M. Dodge, New York City, wrote to USG. "I met Fred at the Republican headquarters and he asked me about the building of the bridges on the Nashville and Decatur Road, its length &c, and I told him I would write you about it. I built the bridges Franklin to Decatur, 102 miles. A great many of them were important structures; that across Duck River, the Sulphur Trestle, which was 1400 feet long and 102 high, was built in 22 working days from timber cut in the woods; and the bridge across the Tennessee was a pontoon. There were I think, about 182 structures on the line, and I had detailed for the work, nearly 1000 mechanics (soldiers) besides two or three negro regiments. I have been sick all summer, most of the time on my back, and only got to town about two weeks ago, or I should have been to see you or should have written you before this. I am very sorry to learn that you are still lame. I had hopes that the summer's rest would put you squarely on your feet. During the summer I have been West and South, trying to get relief from my old troubles. I know that it will be gratifying to you to hear, that I have yet to meet a man that served with you, or in fact anyone, whose sympathies you did not have in your misfortune, and whose support of you was not maintained just as strongly as ever. I don't believe there is another man in the world that could have gone through what you have, and retain so fully his position in the country. It was a great relief to me for I know how susceptible people are, to forget and to misconstrue, but they know you, there is no doubt about that. I will be up to see you soon, to talk with you about Mexican affairs." TLS, USG 3. On Dec. 19, Friday, Dodge twice wrote to USG. "I was not aware until my visit to you on Sunday that you were writing a history of the 'War of

the Rebellion.' I know of the articles to be published in the Century Magazine. During my visit to you at City Point, I met with an incident that may be news or of interest to you. You will doubtless remember that while I was recovering from my wound, received at Atlanta, I visited City Point and was a guest at your headquarters a week or ten days, and saw the Army of the Potomac; was up to see the battle fought on the north side of the James, and brought news of what I thought was a defeat, but which your dispatches made a victory. When I was ready to return to my command at Atlanta, I met orders from General Sherman which stopped me at Nashville and ordered me to Vicksburg, and before I reached that command you ordered me to relieve General Rosecrans in command of the Department of the Missouri, with a view of taking my troops to Thomas at Nashville. If you remember, when I left City Point, you suggested I should return by Washington, and call upon the President, and sent me in your boat. General Rufus Ingalls, your chief quartermaster, and Major-General Cyrus Boyle, of the British army, I think at that time in command in Canada, was with me. I was a very young officer, inexperienced in meeting the world, and with a great reverence for position and authority, hence I hardly knew how to reach President Lincoln nor what to say to him when I saw him. I had only a few hours to spend in Washington, and after breakfast I went directly to the White House where, in the ante-room, I met Senator Harlan of my state, who took me to Mr. Lincoln. The President met me cordially, and asked me to wait until he had dismissed the crowd, when he took me into a room back of what I now know as the cabinet room, took down a book which, if I remember rightly, was called the 'Gospel of Peace.' It was a very funny book, and he read from it, and I laughed heartily, until he made me perfectly easy and at home. He took me down to lunch and pumped out of me everything I had seen at City Point, and what results were to be expected from the movements there. My answer to him was, briefly, I had no doubt as to their success. In detail, as I remember it, my answer was, 'You know out West we believe in General Grant. We have no doubts. Give him time and he will succeed; in what way or how, I don't know, but you may depend upon it he will succeed.' Mr. Lincoln jumped up from his chair, took both my hands in his, and said: 'I am thankful to you for saying so' I was a very much embarrassed person, but it made such an impression upon me that I never forgot it. After the war when General Rawlins was with me on the plains I related the circumstances to him, and he said that the pressure and complaints at that time at Washington was very great. My confidence as to results around Richmond came from my faith—not from what I had seen there, and from the fact that all of us who had long before driven from our minds any doubts as to the final results. I well remember how confidently and enthusiastically I told President Lincoln what I felt, but could not give him a fact upon which to prove my belief. When I arose to leave, President Lincoln thanked me for calling and said, 'If you have no objections you can take my good wishes and regards with you to your army.' That night I left Washington more annoyed than otherwise that there should be so many doubts as to your success. General Rawlins may have told you of this interview, or it may be new to you. I give it as I remember it." Grenville M. Dodge, *Personal Recollections of President Abraham Lincoln, General Ulysses S. Grant and General William T. Sherman* (Council Bluffs, Iowa, 1914), pp. 80–82. "Referring to our conversation of Sunday last, I have been looking over my letterbooks and find under date Nov 23 1863, a letter to Maj R. M. Sawyer A. A. G, the following extract which may be of interest to you. 'I have with me sick and well, 12,000 men, 9,000 in one command and th̶ 3,000 in another. This includes the 111th Illinois, (in relation to which, since my last report of its detention to you, I have received no orders) but does not include the 122[n]d Illinois

Infty that I left at Eastport. Of this number four regiments will soon be mounted, say 1800 men.' In a letter to Gen'l Sherman, dated Nov 23 I stated as follows: 'I am in receipt of your letter of Nov 18 written at Bridgeport . . . . This country is loaded with corn and wheat. Not a pound of bread or meat do I draw, but run the mills and gather the stock; and if you required I could supply your command from here, when cars run, with all the forage you need . . . . The rebel forces on the South side of the Tennessee are obliged to forage on this side, and we have now got most of their boats and several of their teams.' The following is an extract from a letter to Lieut Col Bowers, dated Feb'y 4 1864, explaining the attacks upon me at that time by Col Meizener. 'You are aware that I have had to feed 12,000 men while here, also 6,000 animals: that I have mounted three regiments of Infantry with stock taken from the country and refitted my entire trains. When I arrived I had no animals fit for service, having turned over everything I had at Corinth to the 15th Army Corps before I was ordered to move; and when the order came, I moved out with just what I had and could lay my hands on. That irregularities and depredations have been committed, I have no doubt.' You will see that I had at the time I arrived at Pulaski, 12,000 men which I took from Corinth. I raised several negro regiments here; sufficient to guard this entire country, so that I could take from it when I left all the white troops I had under me. While staying here, there were furloughed and veteranized, 3,000 ~~recruits~~soldiers. The following is an extract from a letter to Maj R. M. Sawyer A. A. G. giving a statement of a portion of the bridges I built. 'I have the honor to report the duty performed by this command in repairing the Railroad from Nashville to Decatur. The Command arrived at Pulaski Nov 11 1863 and was soon after scattered along the Railroad from Columbia to Athens, and detachments of working parties placed to work on all the bridges, every bridge on the road being out. I soon after received orders to take charge of the work North of Duck River and placed parties to work on seven bridges in that region, and also a heavy detail on Duck River Bridge . . . . At Prospect a steam saw-mill was put up and is now ready for Government use. It is a fine mill and will saw 3,000 ft of lumber per day. At each of the bridges, good substantial earth-works or stockades have been built to protect troops guarding them. The work upon them has been immense and the works are very creditable ones. The watertanks, switches, tracks &c have all been rebuilt and put in order and some 2,000 cords of wood got out and put on the road, sawed ready for use, and the entire road put in perfect running order. All the work has been done by soldiers of this command, and negroes pressed into service; and when the amount of work done is consid[e]red, and the unfavorable weather taken into consideration I think it must be looked upon as very creditable to the command. The entire command during its stay, has lived off of the country, drawing nothing except sugar coffee and salt . . . . I cannot speak too highly of the industry alacrity and interest the command has shown in taking hold of and finishing the work. No emergency could arise but what some officer or man could be found [t]o meet and master it. They all seemed to appreciate the importance of opening up the communication for the future operations of the Army, and took hold of the work with the determination that it should be done at the earliest possible moment.' I find from t[h]is letter that I was mistaken about not building mills along the line of the road. Your memory upon this point is better than mine. I find that I did build mills at both Lyndville and [P]rospect: I also built the Pontoon at Decatur crossing the Tennessee at that point. I left for Chattanooga May 1st with 12,500 men to join the movement on Atlanta, and left behind one Brigade under General Stevenson, four partially organized Regiments of colored troops, mostly recru[i]ted while wintering in Middle Tennessee, and one Regiment of Cavalry, the

9th Ohio." TLS, USG 3. See *O.R.*, I, xxxi, part 3, 234–35; *ibid.*, xxxii, part 2, 451–52; *Memoirs*, II, 46–48.

On Nov. 14, AG Richard C. Drum wrote to USG. "It gives me pleasure to send you, herewith, copies of the reports of Generals Taylor and Worth, as desired in your letter of the 10th instant. General Worth does not mention when he left Perote and I have, therefore, added copies of 'record of events' from the regimental returns of the 4th and 8th Infantry and of the 2d and 3d Artillery, from May 18, 1847, from which it appears that the troops of Worth's command left Perote and vicinity, May 9–10, 1847 and, after engaging the enemy under Santa Anna, May 14th, arrived at Puebla, May 15, 1847." LS, USG 3. The enclosures are *ibid.*

On Nov. 19, Frederick Dent Grant wrote to Madison Miller. "Genl Grant directs me to answer your letter, and say that 'his article for the Magazine, has been in the hands of the printer since last June. But that it will appear again in book form, in his book on the war. He would be glad to receive your statement of the services of Prentis 2nd Brigade, for future use.'" ALS, MoSHi. See *PUSG*, 7, 503; *ibid.*, 18, 326; Miller, "The 18th Missouri Infantry on the Battlefield of Shiloh," in Charles Sheldon Sargeant, *Personal Recollections of the 18th Missouri Infantry in the War for the Union* (Unionville, Mo., 1891).

On Dec. 10, Absalom H. Markland, Washington, D. C., wrote to USG. "Referring to the subject of mail facilities for the army, during the war of the rebellion, about which we had a short conversation when I was at your house in October last I am positively certain that the suggestion for that service first came from you. I was an officer of the Post Office Dept charged with duties in connection with its interests in that part of Kentucky not occupied by the Confederate forces and along the Ohio river to Cairo Ills. On my first trip to Cairo Ills in November 1861 I met you for the first time since we separated as school boys, at Maysville Ky, in 1840. The renewal of our acquaintance at Cairo began where it left off at Maysville, that is with the warm feeling of school fellowship. I was at home at your headquarters and very soon in fellowship with your staff It was known that I was in the service of the Post Office Dept. After spending a few days at Cairo at that time I returned to Louisville Ky, where I remained until a shorttime before your contemplated movement against Fort Henry when I went again to Cairo. Preparations were then being made for the movement. You invited me to accompany you 'if I wanted to see a fight' I remember that proviso well. I did accompany you and on the morning after we left Paducah Ky going up the Tennessee river. Your head quarters was then on the Steamboat Uncle Sam, Captain G. W. Stewart. I was sitting in the forward cabin of the boat in conversation with some of the staff officers when you came from your office which was in the after cabin and asked me if I thought it possible to keep the mails up with the army as it moved and promptly collect and forward such letters as the officers soldiers might write. I supposed the question was asked of me because I was a Post office official. I remember that you gave as a reason for desiring such 'that the troops would be more more happy and contented if they could hear frequently from home and that the relatives & friends at the rear would give a greater encouragement to the prosecution of the war.' I answered your question by saying that such service could be put in successful operation. You returned to your office and shortly after came with a paper on which you had written instructions for me to take charge of the service. That paper I have among my papers relating to the war. In a day or two the official order on the subject was issued from your Adjt Genls office. After the capture of Fort Donelson I was directed by the Hon John A. Kasson, First Asst Post Master Genl to remain with you for the purpose of looking after the

Post office Departments interests within the lines of your command. Your command finally absorbed all others and thereby I took charge of all the mail arrangements for the Army of the United States. I did not suggest the army mail service. You did that. If it was managed with reasonable credit it is due that I should say that I had the hearty cooperation of all good officers & soldiers in my efforts to make it a success. This may appear like a small matter and yet it is not a small matter. Leaving out all consideration of its benefits in the time of war it demonstrated the practicability of the distribution and delivery of the mails under the most adverse circumstances and out of that demonstration grew the present rail way mail service of the country. I do not mention this matter now for the first time. Whenever it has been brought to my attention I have uniformly stated it as I state it now. It has been stated in newspaper paragraphs more than once It has been so stated by some public speakers. Genl Thomas O. Osborne, in a speech delivered in Dayton Ohio, in the presidential campaign of 1872, and which was printed at the time, gave the true version of how the army mail service, during the war of the rebellion, came about. In a letter written by you to Benson J. Lossing, one of the historians of the war you gave me the credit of suggesting that branch of Army service. I was not entitled to that credit and I am unwilling to accept it especially when I know so well to whom it belongs." ALS, USG 3. See *PUSG*, 4, 204–5; *ibid.*, 16, 269–70; *New York Times*, Feb. 16, 1885; *Washington Evening Star*, April 4, Aug. 1, 1885.

To Marcus J. Wright

——————

3 E. 66th St. N. Y. City.
Nov 143th 1884

GEN. MARCUS J. WRIGHT,

Your letter of yesterday kindly offering to furnish me any information in your office or in your possession, for the book which I am now engaged upon, is received, and I thank you very much for it. I wrote during the summer four articles for the Century Magazine on as many battles or campaigns of the war. This gave me the idea of writing up not only all the battles in which I took part but also a brief Biographical sketch of my life up to the Rebellion.

It will be some weeks yet before I reach the beginning of our late war. When I do, and particularly after getting beyond what is published in the Rebellion Records, I will no doubt have to call upon you. In the meantime if you have anything to suggest in regard to the Vicksburg campaign, Chattanooga or the Wilderness,[1] it is not to late for me to use it. The publication of the Shiloh article is probably to near at hand to make any material change in it—

All that I have written for the magazine will, no doubt, be materially changed—for the better I hope—when it goes into the book. The articles were taken up separately, and treat of events occuring in the middle of a series, and naturally will be presented differently from what they would be if taken up at the beginning, and presented in the order of their occurrence.

I remember you very well and our meeting on the cars from Memphis to Little Rock.[2]

Very Truly Yours
U. S. GRANT.

Copy, University of North Carolina, Chapel Hill, N. C. See preceding letter.

1. See "Preparing for the Wilderness Campaign," *Century Magazine*, XXXI, 4 (Feb., 1886), 573–82, which largely follows *Memoirs*, II, 116–57, 177.

2. April 14, 1880. For Marcus J. Wright's recollections of this train trip, as well as meeting USG during the Civil War, see *National Tribune*, Sept. 18, 1890. See also *ibid.*, Oct. 2, 1890.

To Ellen Grant Sartoris

———

Nov. 18th 1884

DEAR NELLIE:

The inclosed is the bit of lace your ma told you about. She takes the opportunity of sending it by Mr. Morton, our Minister to France, who sails to-morrow and will see you in London.

I am still very lame, and otherwise suffering. I have had a sore throat now for more than four months,[1] and latterly I have been suffering from neuralgie. Last Friday[2] I had three large double teeth pulled which I hope will cure the neuralgie,[3] and the Doctor is making fair progress with the sore throat.[4] The lameness is gradually improving.

All send love to you and the children.

Yours Affectionately
U. S. GRANT

ALS, ICHi.

1. See *Julia Grant*, pp. 328–29; George W. Childs, *Recollections* (Philadelphia, 1890), pp. 111–12.

2. Nov. 14, 1884.

3. On March 28, 1885, USG's dentist Frank Abbott, "chair of operative dentistry and dental therapeutics in the New York College of Dentistry for seventeen years," discussed USG's teeth. *New York Sun*, March 29, 1885. To correct inaccurate reports and to explain his treatment of USG, Abbott also wrote "General Grant's Condition," *The Independent Practitioner*, VI, 4 (April, 1885), 218–19. A related editorial is *ibid.*, p. 210.

4. Highly regarded clinician Jacob M. Da Costa, who graduated from Jefferson Medical College in Philadelphia (1852), originally treated USG's throat. In late Oct., USG consulted B. Fordyce Barker, a Bowdoin Medical College graduate (1841), an incorporator of the New York Medical College, and noted obstetrician.

To David W. Lusk

—————

Nov. 19th 1884.

D. W. LUSK ESQ.

DEAR SIR:

I received your book on the Politics and Politicians of Ill. some time last Summer. I have not read it sufficiently to say any thing about it. I have been engaged my self ~~which~~ upon work which requires much reserch, reading of reports of the war &c. which has left me but little time for other reading. I left your book at my Cottage at Long Branch so that I probably will not read it before next Summer.

If I did not acknowledge the receipt of your work ~~at the~~ at the time, and thank you for it, I wish to do so now, and to apologize for the neglect.

Very Truly yours

U. S. GRANT

ALS (facsimile), D. W. Lusk, *Politics and Politicians of Illinois, . . .* 2nd ed. (Springfield, 1886), between pp. 314–15. USG replied to a letter written in Oct., 1884, asking whether he had received a copy of the first edition. *Ibid.*, p. 313. See letter to David W. Lusk, Oct. 10, 1883.

To George W. Childs

Nov. 23d 1884

MY DEAR MR. CHILDS:

On reexamining the Contract prepared by the Century people I see that it is all in favor of the publisher, with nothing left for the Author. I am offered very much more favorable terms by ~~the~~ Chas L. Webster & Co. Mark Twain is the Company. The house is located at 658 Broadway. I inclose you their card. If you are coming to the city any time soon I will be very glad to see you and talk this

AL (partial facsimile), Sotheby's, June 19, 2003, no. 204. On Nov. 5, 1884, Joseph G. Rosengarten, Philadelphia, wrote to George W. Childs. "I have read with care the papers in reference to the proposed Contract for the publication of Genl Grants Memoirs, and beg to state the following as my views thereon: 1st as this is a Contract to be executed in New York, it should be submitted to Counsel there and completed only upon his opinion. 2nd subject to this Proviso, I suggest that in view of possible claims of creditors, the Contract should be between Mrs. Grant and the Publishers,—the General testifying his approval by becoming a witness to it,—thus avoiding any process on the part of creditors. I assume that by the law of New York, Mrs. Grant, although a married woman, is competent to make a Contract,—and that the gift of the General to her of his Memoirs, is complete,—as unpublished Ms. it has of course no market value, and creditors could not object to it on that score, nor attack the sale by her to the publisher as her own property. 3rd The terms of the Contract should be submitted to some impartial third person, an expert publisher, able to form a sound judgment of the probable sale of the book, of the cost of its production, and of the proper percentage that ought to be paid for it. The agreement made by Mr. Blaine with his publishers ought to be a fair standard of the profit that the writer should receive. 4th Would it not be well to suggest that the copyright should be taken in Mrs. Grants name, the better to enable her to make the proposed Contract and to modify it from time to time? 5th The 7th and 8th clauses seem to me to be too much in the interest of the Century Co., which certainly ought to take the risk of any temporary dullness in the sale of the book, especially in view of General Grant's wish to deal only with them, disregarding the advantages of an open competition among publishers." ALS, USG 3. See letter to Adam Badeau, Sept. 13, 1884; Memoranda, [*Dec. 18, 1884*], [*Feb., 1885*]; Robert Underwood Johnson, *Remembered Yesterdays* (Boston, 1923), pp. 217–19; *Mark Twain's Autobiography* (New York, 1924), I, 26–27, 32–37.

On March 6, 1886, Frederick Dent Grant, New York City, wrote to James G. Blaine. " . . . I wish to thank you on my own account for the excellent picture of my father you have selected as a frontispiece. It is the one my father selected himself as the picture he wished preserved of him as President . . . . He received the first volume of your 'Twenty Years of Congress,' and directed me to acknowledge it. He was much pleased with what you wrote in transmitting the book, and directed me to send you a copy of his work." Gail Hamilton, *Biography of James G. Blaine* (Norwich, Conn., 1895), p. 636 (ellipses in source).

To Elizabeth M. King

3 E. 66th St. N. Y. City
Nov. 25th 1884

MY DEAR MRS. KING.

I have understood, but do not remember now from what source, that John Morgan in his great raid through Ohio, stopped at Georgetown and compelled the people to cook a meal for his men; also that before he left that he gathered up all the horses there were in the village except the old shetland pony belonging to Mr. Darlington J. Stewart. Am I right in this information? I have stated this fact in the manuscript for my book. But as this will not be published for a year yet there is plenty of time for any changes.[1]

I am still very lame, and fear it will be many months yet before I am entirely well.

Please present my kind regards to Georgetown friends.

Very Truly yours
U. S. GRANT

ALS, USG 3. On Dec. 1, [*1884*], Elizabeth M. King, Georgetown, Ohio, wrote to USG. "In regard to Morgans raid it is said, that Morgan was not here, it was Basellduke of Ky. I presume you want *facts* When the troops came in Town they hitched their horses along the cross street, at Stuarts corner The officer had evry thing systematicly arranged While some wear serching Stables and Sheds for horses, others were going to evry house asking for food, they each one had a basket, The Ladies gave them all they asked for, they ware all verry *polite* and bowing lifted their hats when leaveing others were robing dry goods Stores adn taking the *best*, carrying off meny pieses of silk and all they could possibly carry away, A duchman had a shoe store, they *striped* that carrying all the boots and shoes they could, The Coln asked Mrs Stuart to give him some dinner she set out all he asked for, a piece of bread and butter with a glass of Butter milk he sat down to eat his dinner and did not half finish till an Orderly come in giving him a signal of some kind, he got up in a hurry and went to the front door, and the Bugle sounded and in less than five minuts they ware all mounted and left Town. After they passed your old home, several came back and broke open the Post Office, findeing nothing there but two muskets they broke them over the rocks and left them in the street and left. one went to Phillips and Lute gave him bread, butter and colde ham, she told him, she would not give him any thing only she was affraid, for she didint believe in feeding Rebles, he smiled and left. Frank King was standing on Stuarts corner and one of the men asked him where they would finde a shirt Store Frank told him to go to Ripley they would give them shirts, the fellow understood wheat he ment, got mad pulled out his Pistol and pointed it at Frank amasing him Frank straitend himself up looking him in the face, the man said after that he caut an expression of Kings black eye and regognised him as an *olde friend* that saved his life, They only got one hors that was Dr A Ellsberrys, they gave Topsy Stuart back her Pony. They ware sadly disapointed in geting no more horses. It was Newkirks and Evans store they robed and Shanes Shoe store, It was reported and believed that Johny Walker and Edd Hannah went over during the Night and gave Morgan all information he wanted in regard to ~~the~~ to Georgetown, that all the men had left with Coln Fyffe to defend them, they did not go to Riply for Riply. Your relations are well. Lucindy Powers, buried her last daughter last week with consumption As to my self, nothing chearfull or even hopefull, May God bless you dear friend is my constant prayr The Morgans took several prisoners, prisoners but released them ... If the Linement relieves you let me know, it not only relieves stiffnes but relieves pain" ALS, *ibid.*

1. USG omitted any reference to Darlington J. Stewart. See *Memoirs*, I, 35–36. See also *ibid.*, II, 504.

To Marcus J. Wright

3 E 66th St. N. Y. City
Nov. 30th 1884.

GEN. MARCUS J. WRIGHT,
DEAR GENERAL.

Herewith I send you General Pemberton's account of the surrender of Vicksburg. As the written matter is "Copy" and supposing you have what it has been copied from I do not return it, though I will if you inform me that you want it also.

~~Some~~ A gentleman from Phila sent me the same matter I return herewith, last summer. I probably left the paper at Long Branch, but do not know certainly. All there is of importance in the matter of the surrender of Vicksburg is contained in the correspondence between General Pemberton and myself. The fact is, Gen. Pemberton being a Northern man commanding a southern Army was not at the same liberty to surrender an Army that a man of southern burth would be. In adversity or defeat he become an object of suspicion, and felt it. Bowen was a southern man all over, and knew the garrison of Vicksburg had to surrender or be captured, and knew it was best to stop further effusion of blood by surrendering. He did all he could to bring about that result.

Pemberton is mistaken in several points. It was Bowen that

proposed that he and A. J. Smith should talk over the matter of the surrender and submit their views. Neither Pemberton or I objected; but we were not willing to commit ourselves to accepting such terms as they might propose. In a short time these officers returned. Bowen acted as spokesman. What he said was substantially this: the Confederate Army was to be permitted to march out with the honors of war, carrying with them their arms, colors and field batteries. The National troops were then to march in and occupy the city, and retain the sige guns, small arms not in the hands of the men, all all public property remaining. Of course I rejected the terms at once. I did agree however, before we separated, to write Pemberton what terms I would give. The correspondence is public and speaks for itself. I held no counsil of war. Hostilities having ceased officers and men soon become acquainted with the reason why. Curiosity led officers of rank—most all the General officers—to visit my headquarters with the hope of gathering some news. I talked with them very freely about the meeting between General Pemberton and myself; our correspondence &c. But in no sense was it a Counsil of War. I was very glad to give the garrison of Vicksburg the terms I did. There was a cartel in existence at that time which required either party to exchange or parole all prisoners ~~captured~~ either at Vicksburg or at a point on the James river within ten days after capture or as soon thereafter as practicable. This would have used all the transportation we had for a month. The men had behaved so well that I did not want to humiliate them. I believed that consideration for their feelings would make them less dangerous foes during the continuance of hostilities, and better citizens after the war was over.

I am very much obliged to you General for your courtisy in sending me these papers.

Very Truly yours
U. S. GRANT

ALS, NN. See *PUSG*, 8, 455–58, 467–68; letter to Marcus J. Wright, Nov. 4, 1884.

To John Russell Young

_____

[*Nov., 1884*]

My Dear Mr. Young:

I have been requested by Mr. Frazer, of the firm of Frazer Wetmore & Co. of Shanghai and Yokohama, to write to you and Li Hung Chang, in regard to a company about forming in this country for the purpose of supplying locomotives, machinery of all kinds, passenger and freight cars &c. for China and Japan. Also to take contracts if desired, to build roads, or do any other work that may be wanted; also to finance any bonds that may be wanted placed upon the market. Mr. F. is in business in this city, though he has spent much of his time in China for the last twenty-five years, and may be known to Li Hung Chang. The United States is prepared now to compete with England in the matter of Steel rails, and in locomotives and many kinds of machinery, and in fire arms, can best the world, taking into consideration quality and price.

I have not got the data to write fully on the subject Mr. Frazer requests me to write upon, but send this now because the mail for China closes to-morrow and there will not be another opportunity of writing for three weeks. Will you be kind enough to mention this matter to Li. I am always willing to help when I can to establish trade and commerce with the East. I believe too that it is to the advantage of both China and Japan to look to the United States for any thing which they must go abroad for. We have no designs in the east inimical to the peoples of those countries, and, from our geographical position and institutions, can not have. This is not the case with the strong European powers.

Our election is over, and as you will know long before you receive this, the democratic party is to be restored to power after being out twenty-four years. It is to be seen now "what they will do with it." There has been no election since /72 when the republicans could have won so easily. Blaine has very enthusiastic supporters. But the campaign was a defensive one from the start, and many thousand republicans voted directly for the democratic candidate, and more staid at home because they would not vote for a democrat under any circumstances, and would not vote for Blaine. I myself believe he would have given us a good administration if elected, but thought on account of the antagonism to him his nomination was unwise.

I am still very lame from the injury received last December. Otherwise also I am a sufferer. But I hope to be all right again in the near future.

Please present my kindest regards to Li Hung Chang, and that of Mrs Grant and Fred. I have not been as good a correspondent as I expected to be, but I have thought of you none the less for this reason.

With kind regards of all my family.

Very Truly yours
U. S. GRANT

ALS, DLC-John Russell Young. Born in 1834 in Duxbury, Mass., Everett Frazar went to Shanghai (1858), established the mercantile firm of Frazar & Co., and became resident partner of the New York City office (1872). See *New York Times*, Jan. 4, 1901; Frazar, *Korea, and Her Relations to China, Japan, and the United States* (Orange, N. J., 1884); Everett Frazar Papers, NN.

To John I. Mitchell

NewYork
Dec 5th 1884

HON JNO. J. MITCHELL
U. S. SENATOR
DEAR SIR

I learn through the press that you have introdu[ced] a bill in the Senate placing me on the pension list of the Nation. I under stand the motive which has promp[ted] this action on your part, and appreciate it very highly. But I beg you to withdraw the bill. Under no circumstances could I accept a pension even if the bill Should pas[s] both houses, and receive the approval of the President.

If a general law should pass Congress maki[ng] provision for Ex presidents of the United States, I Should have no hesitation in accepting the benefits of such a law; if my services in the army should seem to Congress and the Nation to entitle me to be placed on the retired list, with the rank I held on quitting it, I should esteem it a great honor. But I make no request further than for the with drawel of the pension bill referred to

Yours very Truly

U. S. GRANT.

Copy (in Frederick Dent Grant's hand), Ulysses Grant Dietz, Maplewood, N. J. John I. Mitchell, former lt. and capt., 136th Pa., practiced law in Tioga County, served as Republican U.S. Representative (1877–81), and entered the Senate in 1881. On Dec. 4, 1884, Mitchell introduced a bill to grant a pension to USG. *CR*, 48-2, 51. On Dec. 8, Mitchell spoke in the Senate after reading an extract from USG's letter. "I was led to introduce the bill because a recommendation on the subject was made by President Arthur, and because it happens that I am chairman of the Committee on Pensions, and I have been frequently spoken to on the subject. I confess that it did not appear to me to be the proper thing to do in this case. I have always felt that General Grant ought to be placed where he was when he laid down the great office which he won in the late war to accept the Presidency, and that he should be compensated accordingly from the time when he left the office of the Presidency. Therefore, and in view of what General Grant desires in this matter, I ask the unanimous consent of the Senate that the Committee on Pensions be discharged from the further consideration of the bill, and that I may have leave to withdraw it from the Senate." *Ibid.*, p. 67. The Senate agreed. On Dec. 1, President Chester A. Arthur had recommended in his annual message "that, in recognition of the eminent services of Ulysses S. Grant, late General of the Armies of the United States and twice President of this nation, the Congress confer upon him a suitable pension." *Foreign Relations, 1884*, p. xxii. See letter to AG Richard C. Drum, March 4, 1885.

On Dec. 11, William R. Rowley, Galena, wrote to USG. "I was much pleased last night to see your letter declining the *Honor* of being placed upon the Pension Roll, although I was *not* surprised at your action. I *was* at the Message of the President recommending it and remarked to our friends who were discussing the matter that you would never accept it. Republics are proverbially ungrateful and your case is no exception to the rule. but I am inclined now to the opinion that they will pass a retiring bill. The result of the election was *not* a great surprise to me. Of course I supported the Republican ticket but I must admit that it was an extremely hard matter for me to 'enthuse' And had not Gen Logan been" AL (incomplete), USG 3.

To Grenville M. Dodge

———

New York, Dec. 8th, 1884.

My Dear General Dodge:

I am sorry to trouble you and would not but for the circumstances under which I am placed. Since my injury of nearly a year ago I have grown very weak. A sore throat of six months standing has given me much trouble. In addition to this I have been a sufferer from neuralgia. I think a visit to the Hot Springs of Arkansas would do me much good. Can you furnish me a special car out and back? If I go I would like to start sometime between the 15th and 20th of this month, to return soon after the beginning of the new year.

Very truly yours,

U. S. GRANT.

P. S.—Mrs. Grant will accompany me, and two servants—maid and a man servant.

Grenville M. Dodge, *Personal Recollections of President Abraham Lincoln, General Ulysses S. Grant and General William T. Sherman* (Council Bluffs, Iowa, 1914), p. 109. Grenville M. Dodge, who held interests in several railroads, brought a private car to New York City, but the Grants never made the trip. *Ibid.* See following letter.

To Edward F. Beale

———

Dec. 16th 1884.

MY DEAR GENERAL BEALE:

Mrs Grant and I are very much obliged to you and Mrs. Beale for your kind invitation to visit you; but unless I improve very materially from my present conditional I will not be able to leave home this winter. I am now a great sufferer from my throat. It is nearly impossible for me to swallow enough to sustain life, and what I do swallow is attended with great pain. It pains me even to talk. I have to see the doctor daily, and he does not encourage me to think that I will be well soon. Mrs. Grant and I would go to the Hot Springs in Arkansas; but the doctor does not deem it advisable to do so.

With kindest regards to all your family,

Very Truly yours

U. S. GRANT

ALS, DLC-Decatur House Papers. On Sunday, Dec. 28, 1884, Edward F. Beale spoke to a reporter on USG's financial distress. "He said that he received a letter from Gen.

Grant recently, in which the latter said he was in very poor health, and that on Friday last he received one from Fred Grant, in which he stated that his father was confined to his room, and that his condition was such as to alarm his family. Gen. Beale added to these statements: 'It is just like him not to let even me know that his straits are so desperate. I had no idea they were anything like this, and it is my belief that this illness which I could not account for is caused by his anxiety.'" *New York Times*, Dec. 29, 1884.

To Col. Benjamin H. Grierson

New York City,
Dec. 17th 1884.

DEAR GENERAL;

I can give you testimonials of entire fitness for promotion to the grade of brigadier general in the army, and for having richly earned the promotion by gallant and meritorious services in the field. But I have declined to give recommendations recently, for army promotions, because there are so many who earned all the promotion that could be given them, on the field of battle; officers who, like yourself, served with me and would like to have my recommendation; and because I am now, in no way, responsible for the appointments made, nor does my recommendations necessarily carry any weight. During the war of the rebellion I gave you frequent testimonials of my appreciation of your services, both in orders and in official reports.[1] These are ~~official~~ public, and of course you are authorized to use them.

Very Truly yours
U. S. GRANT

GEN. B. H. GRIERSON, U. S. ARMY

ALS, DNA, RG 94, ACP, G553 CB 1865. Col. Benjamin H. Grierson visited USG in early Dec., 1884, and received a promise of this letter. See William H. Leckie and Shirley A. Leckie, *Unlikely Warriors: General Benjamin H. Grierson and His Family* (Norman, 1984), pp. 284, 288. For Grierson's promotion to brig. gen. as of April 5, 1890, see *ibid.*, pp. 303–4.

1. See *PUSG*, 8, 506–7; *ibid.*, 9, 73–74; *ibid.*, 13, 396–98; *ibid.*, 15, 589–90.

Memorandum

[*Dec. 18, 1884*]

I can not make definite arrangements until my book is near enough completion to feel sure it can be completed even if my health should further fail.—I could not make definite arrangements without giving the Century an opportunity to make an offer. I will receive proposals however, and will accept, when the proper time comes, the one I deem most favorable for me, consulting Mr. G. W. Childs in the matter. I shall not make known the offers made by different publishers.

If I had my health and strength the two volumes could be completed by May. But I suffers so much with my throat that I feel no assurance of being through by that time, or even before next fall.

AD, MoSHi. A letter dated "Thursday," [*Dec.*] 18, [*1884*] from an unidentified correspondent to "Mr C." elaborated on USG's memorandum. "I went to see General Grant today He has a bad throat & is prohibited from talking The enclosed explains the situation I dont think Mr Childs will approve of the Cty Co for the book I said all I could for Scribners & he & Col Grant assented—Ill see Mr Childs before long & hope to be of use—You can show enclosed to Mess Scribner & return them to me ..." L (illegibly initialed), *ibid.* See Frederick Anderson, ed., *Mark Twain's Notebooks & Journals* (Berkeley, 1975–79), III, 64–65; Memorandum, [*Feb., 1885*].

To William H. Vanderbilt

New York City
January 3rd 188[5]

DEAR SIR

The comments in the papers on the subject of the check which you were kind enough to loan me for a day, in May last, and the efforts being made to partially pay it off, are becoming painful to me and must be more so to you. They are, if possible, more painful to me on account of the way in which your name is brought in.[1] You had nothing possible to gain by giving me the use of your check for a day. To stop the comments I beg that you will have the property

upon which you hold a mortgage sold for what it will bring, and
have the amount credited to what I owe you. The property outside of house-hold good[s] ought to bring one hundred an[d] fifty
thousand dollars. But th[e] stringency of the times will effect the
price materially again, property is not likely to bring as much at
a forced as at a private sale. But I will be satisfied with the result
so long as you are repaid. If you will consent to this course I can
publish a card declining to receive the subscription which I know
only through the news papers is being raised to liquidate, in part
this debt. I have not in the remotest way, been consulted in this
matter.[2]

My object is, first, to see the unjust references to you corrected,
second; to see my debt to you paid[3] third; to relieve my self and
family from the humiliating publicity given to our private affairs.

Very Sincerely Yours

U. S. GRANT.

Copy (in Frederick Dent Grant's hand), Ulysses Grant Dietz, Maplewood, N. J. Probably the nation's wealthiest individual, William H. Vanderbilt managed railroads and
became known for his art collection and public benefactions. On Nov. 29, 1884, Clarence A. Seward, New York City, wrote to USG. "I have been informed that it is the
intention of certain of the creditors of the firm of Grant & Ward to endeavor to collect
the amount of their indebtedness from any and all members of the firm, and, in so doing, to contest the right of Mr. Vanderbilt to the security which was given by you to
him shortly after the borrowing from him of the $150.000. Mr Vanderbilt has been
directly informed that this contest would be made, and desires to protect himself, and
to give effect to your intention in giving him the security which he has. His counsel,
Mr. H. H. Anderson, came to see me this morning, and stated his desire of commencing a suit to foreclose the Chattel mortgage, and also of commencing a suit to procure
a judgment on the loan, and asked me, as your attorney, to admit service of the sum-
mons and complaint in each action, and to facilitate by my pleadings the recovery of
the judgments thereunder. I requested him to put his application in writing that I
might forward it to you, and I herewith enclose it. It seems to me that it would be
wise in every way to assent to Mr Vanderbilt's request, and to allow him to take the
judgments which he seeks with as little delay and as little publicity as possible; but I
did not feel at liberty without your assent to facilitate the course indicated. Will you,
therefore, kindly advise me of your instructions in the premises?" LS, Mrs. Paul E.
Ruestow, Jacksonville, Fla.

On Dec. 19, Frederick Dent Grant wrote to Grenville M. Dodge. "I will try and
be at your office tomorrow morning. If I don't get there it will be because I will be detained with father at the doctor's. Father has been very ill, but is a little better, and we
are trying to get him well enough to go to the matinee to see Raymond run for Congress
tomorrow morning and cheer him (father) up a little. We would be glad to have you

call at any time you can, particularly in the morning between 8 and 10 o'clock." Grenville M. Dodge, *Personal Recollections of President Abraham Lincoln, General Ulysses S.
Grant and General William T. Sherman* (Council Bluffs, Iowa, 1914), p. 109. On Dec. 23,
Dodge wrote to Frederick Grant. "What you said to me the other day has impressed
me so much, I want to sit down with you and your father and talk freely about these
matters. It seems impossible to me that anyone should think of taking away from him
or his family the possessions and relics of a lifetime. I know that if the people of this
nation knew the facts, they would arise in their might and prevent it. Knowing the
General as I do, I cannot understand how anyone could do such a thing. The question arises in my mind, do not Mr. Neville and Mr. Vanderbilt understand this matter,
and do they not intend to preserve to the General and his family all he had, if his own
personal obligations are paid. I know from a trip to Europe with Mr. Vanderbilt, of
his respect, I might almost say his love for General Grant, and I believe he intends to
protect him in the possession of what in the eyes of this nation really belongs to him.
I am sorry I was hurried away the other morning by a prior engagement. If you will
indicate a day or morning when I can talk over this matter with you or your father, I
know it will do no harm and may end in good. Your father must know that there is no
old soldier living, who ever fought under him that does not know that his misfortune
does not come from any fault of his; and why should he be made to suffer? The trouble
about all this is that the facts are not known, and I don't feel at liberty to make them
known until I see you again." Typescript, USG 3. See Dodge, *Personal Recollections*,
pp. 109–12.

William T. Sherman wrote a memorandum, presumably for Edward F. Beale. "On
Monday Dec 22—1884, Genl G. M Dodge, coming from Fred Grant appealed to me to
do something for Genl Grant, as his personal effects were to be sold under a Judgmt in
favor of Mr Vanderbilt—that Mr Vanderbilt had offered to sell his Entire Judgmt for
$100.000—thus throwing off $60.000.—I saw Fred Grant afterwards and he said the
Sale of the personal effects was delayed to Jan 3. 1885, and that it was desirabl to save
this property from a Sale &c—My opinion now is that Genl Grant wants Vanderbilt
to Sell his property, thus to repay himself for his loan, because in any event, this property will surely be taken by some creditor of Grant & Ward—and to support himself
& family by the proceeds of his articles in the Century, and by sale of his book which
will be ready in May–June—Inasmuch as Genl Grant prefers that no money be raised
by his Friends we should cancel all offers, and leave him to manage his own business"
ADS, DLC-Decatur House Papers. On Dec. 23, Sherman, New York City, wrote to
U.S. Senator John Sherman of Ohio. ". . . Grant is in a bad way—not so bad physically
as I had been led to suppose but mentally. Every thing is gone but that trust fund,
$250,000—at 6 pr—but his wifes house is mortgaged for $58,000, the interest, taxes
insurance &c of which costs him $5000 a year—leaving him $10.000 for the support
of himself family and dependants—He is now writing for money.—Every article of
his house—the Presents from foreign Governmts—his very Sword is attached.—Genl
G. M. Dodge will breakfast with me tomorrow so as to have a few minutes uninter-
rupted conversation with me on this business, a thing impossibe at my Room, and I
will endeavor to find out the whole truth . . . ." ALS, DLC-William T. Sherman. See
letter to William H. Vanderbilt, Jan. 10, 1885.

1. "*JUDGMENT AGAINST GEN. GRANT.* Three days prior to the failure of
Grant & Ward last May Gen. Grant borrowed $150,000 from William H. Vanderbilt,
which sum he was to repay on demand. Mr. Vanderbilt recently demanded the money,

and it was not repaid. On the 3d inst. he began a suit for it in the Supreme Court. Five days later Gen. Grant appeared in the suit and offered to allow judgment to be taken against him for the amount of the loan, with interest from May 3, and also the costs of the suit. The offer was accepted, and yesterday judgment was entered against Gen. Grant for $155,417 20." *New York Times*, Dec. 10, 1884.

Another report appeared in late Dec. "An immense amount of gossip, some of it well based, much of it without the slightest foundation, concerning General Grant and his affairs has found easy currency in many circles—social, financial and political—within the past few days. There is no doubt that the failure of Grant & Ward very seriously embarrassed General Grant, whose name appears upon the official paper as one of the partners, and who found himself suddenly precipitated in a perfect meshwork of financial difficulty. So far as the story is current concerning Mr. Vanderbilt's action in obtaining a judgment which covers all the property, real and personal, belonging to General and Mrs. Grant, is concerned a widespread misunderstanding exists . . . . The fact of the case is that the confession of judgment was made upon the suggestion of General Grant himself, and its acceptance by Mr. Vanderbilt is simply and solely a measure of precaution and defence against other and more clamorous creditors of General Grant, . . ." *New York Herald*, Dec. 30, 1884.

2. On Dec. 28, 29, and 30, reports from Philadelphia described the efforts of W. T. Sherman, Anthony J. Drexel, and George W. Childs to relieve USG's debt to Vanderbilt and to save USG's military and travel mementoes from auction. *New York Times*, Dec. 29–31, 1884. Sherman kept memoranda that itemized USG's assets and told how the men learned from telegrams that "there had been no execution and no sale authorized, and that all the proceedings were in the nature of a friendly action to Genl Grant—It was concluded that no further action was necessary, but that Mr Childs should go to NewYork to see Genl Grant tomorrow Dec 30." AD, DLC-William T. Sherman. On Dec. 29, Sherman wrote to Lt. Gen. Philip H. Sheridan. " . . . I will do all I can in the matter of Grants business condition—I think his physical condition is not so bad as the papers make out. I made him two long visits and found him much better than Fred had described—but his business Condition is worse than I had supposed— . . . I found Grant, Fred and Badeau at work on his Book which he says has made such progress that he expects to have it ready for the Press in All May— Tomorrow I will go to Drexels again by which time the Lawyers in NewYork will have decided the only practical question, Can the chattels be bought Separate & apart from the whole debt—This will require 23.000 Cash and if any in Washington want to share they can do so—for will fall on the very parties who raised the $250.000 Trust fund, and the $90.000 for the House—Those figures sound to me very large, but are but drops to the 16 millions sunk or dissipated by the Firm Grant & Ward— . . . " ALS, DLC-Philip H. Sheridan. On the same day, Sherman received "a remittance of $100, the gift of an ex-confederate soldier, to be used in behalf of General Grant, in remembrance of his magnanimity toward the South . . . ." *New York Herald*, Dec. 30, 1884. See letter to Cyrus W. Field, Jan. 6, 1885.

On Dec. 28, a correspondent had reported from Washington, D. C. "The *Republican* reporter saw several prominent gentlemen of this city to-day with reference to the news received from New-York that all of Gen. Grant's personal property, including his swords and medals, the presents received by him while abroad; his pictures, his two farms, and his houses in this city and St. Louis, have been inventoried and are to be sold to meet the judgment held by William H. Vanderbilt. Among the gentlemen were W. W. Corcoran, Gen. Beale, and Gen. Van Vliet, all of them old friends of Gen. Grant.

Mr. Corcoran said to the reporter: 'This thing shall not be done. No man who has been President of the United States should be placed in such a position.' He said that he would not start a subscription to relieve Gen. Grant of this judgment, but would not be behind any one in preventing the sale of his personal effects. He added that he thought it would be dishonorable in the people of the United States if an ex-President and a soldier like Gen. Grant should be obliged to sacrifice the trophies of his services to the country for a few thousand dollars . . . ." *New York Times*, Dec. 29, 1884. See letter to Edward F. Beale, Dec. 16, 1884; *Washington Post*, Dec. 30, 1884.

3. On May 26, 1885, a correspondent reported from Philadelphia. "The house No. 2,009 Chestnut-street, known as 'Gen. Grant's house,' was sold at auction to-day by M. Thomas & Sons under the instructions of William H. Vanderbilt, for the sum of $22,500 . . . . The sale took place at the rooms of the auctioneers by direction of Lewis H. Redner & Co., agents for Clarence Seward, of New-York, Mr. Vanderbilt's attorney. The house was assigned by Gen. Grant and his wife to Mr. Vanderbilt in the settlement of Gen. Grant's debt to Mr. Vanderbilt. The mansion was presented to the General by a committee of patriotic citizens of this city on April 12, 1865 . . . . The price for which the property was sold to-day is said by real estate experts to be very low . . . ." *New York Times*, May 27, 1885. For an account of the auction, see *Philadelphia Press*, May 27, 1885. On Aug. 27, 1884, Lewis H. Redner & Co., Philadelphia, had sent a check ($312.74) to USG's order representing the net proceeds from six months rent. D, USG 3.

To Charles Wood

New York City,
Jan.y 5th 1885.

My Dear Mr. Wood;

I take profound pleasure in enclosing to you the check which you will find with this. I wish to state to you also how great was the relief afforded by your timely loan. At the time of the failure of Grant & Ward I had not a hundred dollars in my pocket. I had paid my bills for the previous month with checks, on the firm. mMost of these were not presented until after the failure. Your checks enabled me to meet the second call, and gave me something to go upon until another turn could be made. Mrs. Grant was fortunate enough to own a couple of small houses, in Washington, one of which she sold for the sum of $6,500 00,[1] since which we have been comfortable, in means to live upon, but with nothing to pay past debts.

I return you, with the greatest pleasure, one thousand dollars of the fifteen hundred which you so kindly, and without solicitation or claim upon you, sent me. It affords me greater pleasure from the fact that I have earned this by my own work. I hope, in the near future, to send you the other five hundred.

With my best wishes to you and yours, I am,

Very Truly

U. S. GRANT

ALS, Ralph W. Naylor, Hopkinton, R. I. On Jan. 8, 1885, Charles Wood, Lansing-burgh, N. Y., wrote to USG. "I have the honor to acknowledge the receipt from you—long before due—of One Thousand Dollars being in full for like amount sent you May 17th 1884. I would state never mind the futher remittance you refer to—I will accept instead now or at anytime—information that you are in good health—which I hope you can furnish now or speedily." ALS, USG 3. On March 23 (or 28) and April 2, 1886, Frederick Dent Grant, New York City, wrote to Wood. "Enclosed please find my Mothers check for $500. This closes up the loan you made to my father in 1884. In paying this loan, my dear Mr Wood, I want to say that the obligation on our part still remains; and that the Grant family will ever be grateful to you for your kindness to the head of their family when he was in trouble. We hope to see much of you in the future, and be assured that you will ever be welcomed at the home of the Grants' as the noble and generous friend of their family." "I hope you do not ~~feel~~ think that we feel under less [ob]ligations to you now than we did before. I assure you you are wrong if you do. The Grant family will always hold in its memory your generous assistance in the time of need. I hope to see much of you in the future, and extend to you & Mrs Wood on the part of my Mother and her family a most cordial [in]vitation to our home whenever you are in New York." ALS, Ralph W. Naylor, Hopkinton, R. I. See letters to Charles Wood, May 12, 19, 1884.

On March 24, 1885, Frederick Grant had written to Wood. "Your letter of the 16 instant and box of brushes have been received. General Grant desires me to thank you for the brushes, and will send the article requested by letter as soon as he can find something appropriate." LS, Ralph W. Naylor, Hopkinton, R. I.

1. See letter to Fitch, Fox, & Brown, May 24, 1884.

To Cyrus W. Field

New York City

January 6th 1885.

MY DEAR SIR:

Through the press, and otherwise, I learn that you, with a few other friends of mine, are engaed in raising a subscription for my benefit. I appreciate both the motive and the friendship which has dictated this course on your part, but on mature reflection I regard it as due to myself and family to decline this proffered generosity.

I regret that I did not make this known earlaier.

Very Truly yours

U. S. Grant

Cyrus W. Field, Esq.

ALS, USG 3. The financier who promoted the first transatlantic telegraph cable, Cyrus W. Field led the initiative to raise funds for President James A. Garfield's family after his assassination. On Jan. 6, 1885, Field, New York City, wrote to William T. Sherman, St. Louis. "Annexed I send you copy of a letter this moment received from General Grant, which explains itself." LS, DLC-William T. Sherman. On the same day, Field telegraphed and wrote similiarly to Edward F. Beale, Washington, D. C. Telegram received and LS, DLC-Decatur House Papers. On Jan. 7, Field telegraphed to Beale. "IF GENERAL SHERMAN IS IN WASHINGTON. PLEASE SHOW HIM MY LETTER TO YOU OF YESTERDAYS DATE." Telegram received, *ibid.* On Jan. 9, Friday, Anthony J. Drexel, Philadelphia, wrote to Sherman. "Your favor of the 7th only reached me today Mr Childs and I went to New-York on Wednesday to see Mr Field who had just received the letter from Genl Grant with a request from Fred to forward copies to you at St Louis, Genl Beale, Mr Childs and myself Mr Childs went up to see Genl Grant, who said his lips were sealed, but that in a few days everything would be explained to the satisfaction of all parties. We now think that the programme which we were told was already under way to protect the personal effects when we took the matter up, has been again commenced, and therefore there is no need for the assistance of Genl Grants friends, but this is of course only an opinion, and we are awaiting further developments, in the meantime dropping the matter. We fully understand your kind intervention was based on the representation of Genl Dodge and Fred Grant whose statements were of such a nature as to warrant the action taken by us all to thus express our warm sympathy for the General in a practical way Don't let it disturb you any more— . . ." LS, DLC-William T. Sherman. On Dec. 27, 1884, 1:40 P.M., Alfred M. Hoyt, New York City, had written to his cousin Sherman. "Have only just seen Field—He saw Vanderbilt this Am, Had a long talk with him & says Vanderbilt dont want any thing but what is fair— . . ." ALS, *ibid.* On Dec. 29, Hoyt wrote to Sherman, Philadelphia. " . . . I see the papers here have gotten hold of the talk I had with Field—but no matter. I dont know how they did it—I hope it wont raise any false hopes in Grants breast. If any one, or set of people, can help Grant, I think it will be, Hamilton Fish, Drexel & Childs—Grant has helped all these people & they should take hold & put this thing through . . . . We have done all we can & we had better keep out & let others manage it" ALS, *ibid.* Also on Dec. 29, Field spoke to a reporter. "Some of the papers, I am sorry to say, have got ahead of the facts in their anxiety to be first with the news. I have not been engaged, and do not expect to be, in raising a purse for General Grant. At the request of General Sherman, brought to me by Mr. Hoyt, I called on Mr. Vanderbilt, with whom I am on intimate terms, and he generously said that if General Grant's friends would raise $100,000 he would throw off $60,000 from the debt. I sent word of this offer to General Sherman and suggested that it would be eminently proper for Mr. Hamilton Fish, who was Grant's

Secretary of State, and who is a gentleman of wealth and leisure, to draw up a subscription paper, place against his name whatever sum he desired to give and send it around among General Grant's friends. I had no doubt the sum would easily be raised. I also suggested that General Sherman broach the subject to Messrs. Drexel and Childs in Philadelphia. Mr. Hoyt told me that General Sherman got my message just as he was starting for Philadelphia, but would probably act upon it. This is all I know about the matter. I have no doubt that Mr. Grant's friends will be glad to step forward if called upon to do so. But I am sorry the matter has got into the papers. It would be much pleasanter to have the money all raised, and then surprise the General. I presume nothing will be done until we hear from General Sherman." *New York Herald*, Dec. 30, 1884. See letters to William H. Vanderbilt, Jan. 3, 10, 1885; *New York Tribune*, Dec. 28, 30, 1884, Jan. 9, 13, 1885.

On Jan. 8, 1885, Francis G. Russell, Detroit, wrote to USG. "I salute you upon your declination of the proposed private gift. It is only what could be expected of him who said 'No terms but unconditional surrender, I propose to move immediately upon your works,' and 'I will fight it out on this line if it takes all summer.' The people of this Country, who are of any account, sympathize with you because of your recent and existing troubles—for which they find no fault with you, and will heartily aid and applaud your restoration to the position, which you gave up for the Presidency. This is written as my personal expression of gratitude to one, who should live as long as history can be made." ALS, USG 3.

To Robert T. Lincoln

New York City
Jan'y 6th 1885

Honorable Robert. T. Lincoln.
Secretary of War:
Dear Sir:

On examining volume seven of the rebellion records, published by the War department I find there are ten important despatches and letters of mine omitted, or I cannot find them. The omitted dispatches are important to me because they fully refute charges which are made by General Halleck against me, to Washington, which charges must now go down to history, by authority of the government, without the evidence, recorded at the time, of their falsity.

Fortunately I haɖve a copy of the record kept at my head quarters from the beginning to the close of the war. This same record shoul[d] be found at the head quarter[s] of the Lieutenant General.¹ The omitted dispatches were all written between the 3d and 31st of March, 1862. If the record can be corrected I respectfully ask that it be done.

Very respectfully
your obt svt
F̶ ̶D̶ ̶U̶ ̶S̶ ̶G̶R̶A̶N̶[̶T̶]̶
U. S. Grant.

Copy (in Frederick Dent Grant's hand), Ulysses Grant Dietz, Maplewood, N. J. On Feb. 7 and 12, 1885, Secretary of War Robert T. Lincoln wrote to USG. "I have this morning your note dated Jany (Feby?) 6th, 1885, stating that upon examination of Volume 7 of the Rebellion Records you find there are ten important dispatches and letters omitted or not found by you. In reply I beg to inform you that Col Scott, in charge of their publication, advises me that in the absence of any more particular description of the dispatches and letters referred to by you, he thinks that you will find them all in Volume 10, part 2. He says that he has your records books and does not suppose that any thing of importance has been omitted. Col Scott also says that it is not improbable that inasmuch as you find printed at page 683 of Volume 7, the letter of General Halleck, dated March 15th, 1862, you supposed some preliminary correspondence has not been published. He says that that letter of Gen. Halleck is printed at that place, a little out of its order in date, to show Gen. Halleck's action, after having shown certain correspondence in relation to yourself; that he was not able at that time to give all the correspondence, but he did not wish to go to other matters without showing at least the conclusion, although intermediate correspondence must be looked for in a subsequent volume. If you do not find every thing that you think should be in the Records, I beg that you will indicate to me what is missing, and it will give me pleasure to do what I can to have the matter corrected . . . . P. S. A teleg. of Mar 13. 62 will be found in Part I. Vol X. p. 16." "I have your note of yesterday. I am glad to learn that you find the dispatches and letters referred to by you in the second part of Volume 10. It would have been better, although I agree with you in thinking it not a matter of much consequence to yourself, that the correspondence before the letter of Gen. Halleck should have followed what is published in the seventh volume, or at least that there should have been attached a foot note to Gen. Halleck's letter calling attention to the fact that additional and prior correspondence would be found in a subsequent volume. I think Col Scott, in making the arrangement which he did of these dispatches and letters, acted with the best intention. He advises me that the letters and telegrams in volume 10, were regarded by him as belonging to the beginning of the operations which culminated at Shiloh, and that having arranged to so use them it left the preceeding correspondence as it now is, but in order to avoid having the seventh volume appear with this imputation undisposed of he thought it sufficient, not to put in your subsequent correspondence, but to put in, although out of its regular order, the letter of Gen. Halleck, considering in his mind that that disposed of the whole matter, not merely by suggestions of your own but by the action of then superior authority." LS (press), Robert T. Lincoln Letterbooks, IHi. See *PUSG*, 4, 317–21, 334–35, 414–16.

1. Philip H. Sheridan, commanding gen., U.S. Army.

To Clarence A. Seward

———

New York City,
Jan.y 10th 1885.

MY DEAR MR. SEWARD:

I would be very much pleased to see you and Mr. Conkling at my house to-morrow, at any hour that may suit you, day or evening. The business upon which I wish to see you is very important to me.

I do not know where Mr. Conkling now resides so I can not send a note to him. May I ask if you will communicate to him this request.

Very Truly yours
U. S. GRANT

ALS, NRU.

To William H. Vanderbilt

———

New York City,
January 10th 1885.

DEAR SIR:

Mrs. Grant asks me to answer your letter of this evening, and to say that while she appreciates your great generosity in transfering to her the mortgage given to secure my debt of $150.000 00, she cannot accept it in whole. She accepts with pleasure the trust which applies to articles enumerated in your letter to go to the government of the United States, at my death, or sooner, at her option. In this matter you have anticipated the disposition which I had contemplated making of the articles. They will be delivered to the government as soon as arrangements can be made for their reception.

Papers relating to all other property will be returned, with the request that you have it sold, and the proceeds applied to the liq-

uidation of the debt which I so justly owe you. You have stated in your letter, with the minutest accuracy the history of the transaction which brought me in your debt. I have only to add that I regard your giving me your Cheque for the amount without inquiry, as an act of marked and unusual friendship. The loan was to me personally. I got the money, as I believed, to carry the Marine National bank over a day, being assured that the bank was solvent, but owing to unusual calls, needed assistance until it could call in its loans. I was assure[d] by Ferdinand Ward that the firm of Grant and Ward had over $660,000 00 to their credit, at that time, in the Marine bank, besides $1,300,000 of unpledged securities in their own vaults.

I cannot conclude without assuring you that Mrs Grants inability to avail herself of your great kindness in no way lessens either her sense of obligation, or my own.

Yours Truly
U. S. GRANT

W. H. VANDERBILT, ESQ.

ALS, DLC-Chauncey M. Depew. On Jan. 10, 1885, William H. Vanderbilt, New York City, wrote to Julia Dent Grant. "So many misrepresentations have appeared in regard to the loan made by me to General Grant, and reflecting unjustly upon him and myself, that it seems proper to briefly recite the facts. On Sunday, the 4th of May last, General Grant called at my house and asked me to lend him One hundred and fifty thousand dollars, for one day. I gave him my check without question, not because the transaction was business-like, but simply because the request came from General Grant. The misfortunes which overwhelmed him in the next twenty four hours aroused the sympathy and regret of the whole country. You and he sent me within a few days of the time, the deeds of your joint properties to cover this obligation, and urged my acceptance, on the ground that this was the only debt of honor which the General had personally incurred, and these deeds I returned. During my absence in Europe the General delivered to my attorney, mortgages upon all his own real estate, household effects, and the swords, medals, and works of Art which were the memorials of his victories, and the presents from governments all over the World. These securities were in his judgement worth the One hundred and fifty thousand dollars. At his solicitation the necessary steps were taken by judgement, etc. to reduce these properties to possession, and the articles mentioned have been this day bought in by me, and the amounts bid applied in reduction of the debt. Now that I am at liberty to treat these things as my own, the disposition of the whole matter most in accord with my feelings, is this: I present to you as your separate estate, the debt and judgement I hold against General Grant, also the Mortgages upon his real estate and all the household furniture and ornaments, coupled only with the condition, that the swords, commissions, medals, gifts from the United States, States, Cities, and foreign governments, and all articles of historical value and interest, shall at the General's death, or if you desire it, sooner, be presented to the government at Washington, where they will remain as perpetual memorials of his fame, and of the history of his time. I enclose herewith assignments to you of the mortgages and judgements, a bill of sale of the personal property, and a deed of trust in which the articles of historical interest are enumerated. A copy of this Trust deed will, with your approval, be forwarded to the President of the United States for deposit in the proper department. Trusting that this action will meet with your acceptance and approval, and with kindest regards to your husband, . . ." LS, Mrs. Paul E. Ruestow, Jacksonville, Fla. On Jan. 11, Vanderbilt wrote to USG. "On my return home last night I found your letter in answer to mine to Mrs Grant—I appreciate fully the sentiments which actuate both Mrs Grant and yourself in declining the part of my proposition relating to the real estate. I greatly regret that she feels it her duty to make this decision, as I earnestly hoped that the spirit in which the offer was made, would overcome any scruples in accepting it—But I must insist that I shall not be defeated in a purpose to which I have given so much thought, and which I have so much at heart—I will therefore as fast as the money is received from the sales of the real estate deposit it in the Union Trust Company—With the money thus realized I will at once create with that Company a Trust with proper provisions for the income to be paid to Mrs Grant during her life, and giving the power to her to make such disposition of the Principal by her will as she may elect—" ALS, *ibid.* On the same day, USG wrote to Vanderbilt. "Your letter of this date is received, Mrs Grant and I regret that you can not accept our proposition to retain the property which was mortgaged in good faith to secure a debt of honor, But your generous determination compels us to no longer resist . . . . P. S. Mrs Grant will convey her right of dower in the mortgaged property in any way that may be necessary to perfect the title thereto." Copy (in Frederick Dent Grant's hand), Ulysses Grant Dietz, Maplewood, N. J. Also on Jan. 11, Julia Grant wrote to Vanderbilt. "Upon reading your letter of this afternoon, General Grant and myself felt that it would be ungracious to refuse your princely and generous offer. Hence his note to you. But upon reflection I find that I cannot, I will not accept your munificence in any form. I beg that you will pardon this apparent vacillation and consider this answer definite and final. With ~~the~~ greatest regard, and a sense of obligation that will always remain, . . ." ADfS (marked "Copy"), ICarbS. On the same day, Julia Grant wrote to Clarence A. Seward. "After all, I found that I could not consent to the arrangement concluded today, and have sent the following note, this evening, to Mr Vanderbilt, You must blame me, and not General Grant, if you disapprove. It was I, who was most concerned." ALS, *ibid.* See letter to William H. Vanderbilt, Jan. 3, 1885; *New York World,* Jan. 13, 1885.

On Jan. 10, Vanderbilt and Julia Grant had signed a trust deed. "WHEREAS, I, *William H. Vanderbilt,* of the City of New York, by virtue of a sale made under a judgment in a suit to foreclose a chattel mortgage in the Supreme Court of this State in which I was plaintiff and Ulysses S. Grant defendant, which judgment was entered on the sixth day of December one thousand eight hundred and eighty four, and under an execution in another suit in said Court between the same parties upon a judgment entered December 9. 1884, have become the owner of the property and the articles described in the schedule hereto annexed formerly the property of said Ulysses S. Grant *Now therefore,* to carry out a purpose formed by me, and in consideration of one dollar to me paid, I do hereby transfer and convey each and every one of the articles mentioned and itemized in the said schedule to *Julia Dent Grant, To have and to hold* the same to her, her executors and administrators, upon the trust and agreement nevertheless hereby accepted and made by her that upon the death of the said Ulysses S. Grant or previously thereto at her or their option the same shall become and be the property of the Nation and shall be taken to Washington and transferred and conveyed by her and them to the United States of America . . . ." DS, Mrs. Paul E. Ruestow, Jacksonville, Fla. The enclosure is *ibid. SED*, 48-2-60, 2–5. On the same day, Vanderbilt signed another trust deed. "WHEREAS, *I, William H. Vanderbilt* of the City of New York have to-day become the purchaser of certain property sold under judgments and execution against Ulysses S. Grant and have conveyed a portion thereof consisting of swords, pictures and other articles of value or curiosity to Julia Dent Grant by an instrument in the nature of a deed of trust, the property so conveyed being described in a Schedule thereto annexed, *Now therefore,* to carry out a purpose formed by me, and in consideration of one dollar to me paid by said Julia Dent Grant, I do hereby sell, transfer and convey to the said Julia Dent Grant all of the property so purchased by me not conveyed by or described in the said conveyance and schedule *To have and to hold* the same as her sole and separate property forever without covenant by or recourse to me nevertheless . . . ." DS, Mrs. Paul E. Ruestow, Jacksonville, Fla.

On Jan. 12, Phineas T. Barnum, Bridgeport, Conn., wrote to USG. "The whole world honors and respects you. All are anxious that you should live happy and free from care. While they admire your manliness in declining the large sum recently tendered you by friends they still desire to see you achieve financial independence in an honorable manner. Of the unique and valuable trophies with which you have been honored we have all read and all have a laudable desire to see these evidences of love and respect bestowed upon you by monarchs, princes and peoples throughout the globe. While you would confer a great and enduring favor on your fellowmen and women by permitting them to see these trophies, you could at the same time remove existing embarrassments in a most satisfactory and honorable manner. I will give you $100,000 cash, besides a proportion of the profits, assuming all risks myself, if I may be permitted to exhibit these relics to a grateful and appreciative public, and I will give satisfactory bonds of $500,000 for their safe keeping and return. These precious trophies, of which all your friends are so proud, would be placed before the eyes of your millions of admirers in a manner and style at once pleasing to yourself and satisfactory to the best elements of the entire community. Remembering that the mementoes of Washington, Wellington, Napoleon, Frederick the Great, Stephen Girard and many other distinguished men have given immense pleasure to millions who have been permitted to see them, I trust you will in the honorable manner proposed gratify the public and thus inculcate the lessons of honesty, perseverance and true patriotism so admirably illustrated in your career." *New York World,* Jan. 13, 1885. On Jan. 13, Barnum communicated with the *New York Tribune.* "I wrote General Grant yesterday offering him $100,000 and other valuable considerations for the privilege of exhibiting his trophies in a style approved by himself and the best elements of society. The General has my letter. I conversed with him to-day at his house on the subject. He says the trophies are beyond his control. I did not propose to exhibit them with my travelling show, but to take them to large cities in America and Europe. I offered a $500,000 bond for their safe keeping and return." *New York Tribune,* Jan. 13, 1885. For a critical editorial, see *New York World,* Jan. 14, 1885.

On Jan. 24, Frederick Dent Grant, New York City, wrote to President Chester A. Arthur. "Mrs U. S. Grant desires me to address you and to state that on the 10th Jan'y inst a sale of articles in this house belonging to General U. S. Grant took place to satisfy a judgement against him in favor of W. H. Vanderbilt of NewYork. At the sale Mr Vanderbilt's attorney Mr C. M. Depew bought in the articles for Mr Vanderbilt. Later on the same day Mr Vanderbilt returned a trust deed for certain of these articles of great historical value, making Mrs Grant trustee for them, during the life of General Grant and afterwards transferring them to the ꞬGovernment of the United States; or at her option she might transfer them sooner. In order that the swords, medals, commissions and other objects conferred upon her husband by his country and by representative personages abroad, and most of them associated with so many patriotic memorie[s,] should neither be sacrificed nor seem to be slighted, nor the public feeling affronted, Mrs Grant accepted the trust. She is informed that you have been already addressed on this subject by Mr Vanderbilt, And anxious to be relieved of the painful responsibility of holding in trust, what were presented to her husband as honors and rewards, She desires me to request that you appoint a proper person to receive the articles, on the part of the Government of the United States." ADfS, Ulysses Grant Dietz, Maplewood, N. J. On Jan. 27, Frederick J. Phillips, Arthur's private secretary, wrote to Frederick Grant in acknowledgement. ALS, Mrs. Paul E. Ruestow, Jacksonville, Fla. On Feb. 3, Arthur wrote to the House of Representatives. "I take especial pleasure in laying before Congress the generous offer made by Mrs. Grant to give to the Government, in perpetual trust, the swords and military (and civil) testimonials lately belonging to General Grant. A copy of the deed of trust, and of a letter addressed to me by Mr William H. Vanderbilt, which I transmit herewith, will explain the nature and motives of this offer. Appreciation of General Grant's achievements and recognition of his just fame have in part taken the shape of numerous mementoes and gifts, which, while dear to him, possess for the nation an exceptional interest. These relics, of great historical value, have passed into the hands of another whose considerate action has restored the collection to Mrs. Grant as a life-trust, on the condition that at the death of General Grant, or sooner at Mrs. Grant's option, it should become the property of the Government, as set forth in the accompanying papers. In the exercise of the option thus given her Mrs. Grant elects that the trust shall forthwith determine, and asks that the Government designate a suitable place of deposit and a responsible custodian for the collection. The nature of this gift and the value of the relics which the generosity of a private citizen, joined to the high sense of public regard which animates Mrs. Grant, have thus placed at the disposal of the Government, demand full and signal recognition on behalf of the nation at the hands of its representatives. I therefore ask Congress to take suitable action to accept the trust and to provide for its secure custody, at the same time recording the appreciative gratitude of the people of the United States to the donors . . . ." *CR*, 48-2, 1241. The enclosures are *ibid.*, pp. 1241–42. On Feb. 7, the Senate passed a joint resolution accepting Julia Grant's gift and assigning the custody of the articles to the Librarian of Congress. On March 3, the resolution failed after U.S. Representative William M. Springer of Ill. objected to consideration. See *ibid.*, pp. 1366, 2530; letter to Ainsworth R. Spofford, May 22, 1885.

To Mary Grant Cramer

New York City,
Jan'y 13th, 1885.

DEAR SISTER:

I am just in receipt of Jennie's[1] letter of the 2nd of January. I am busy on my book which Fred is copying for the press. I hope to have it ready for the press by May next. But I may fail in this on account of weakness. My mouth has been very sore, but not so bad I think as the papers have made out.[2] But it has been bad enough. The rest of the family are all well.

My advice is that Mr. Cramer does not resign until he is asked to.[3] Simpson I do not suppose will be disturbed in his position. He is very competent, and the soul of honor, both qualities wanted in the Sub-treasury.[4]

I presume Jennie will be away before this reaches you . . . .

All send love.

Yours affectionately,

U. S. GRANT.

J. G. Cramer, p. 157; M. J. Cramer, *Ulysses S. Grant: Conversations and Unpublished Letters* (New York, 1897), pp. 175–76; ellipses in source.

1. USG's teenage niece Virginia E. Grant, daughter of Orvil L. Grant.
2. For assessments of USG's health by his doctors, B. Fordyce Barker and John H. Douglas, see *New York Times* and *New York Tribune*, Jan. 12, 1885.

On Jan. 2, 1885, Brig. Gen. Oliver O. Howard wrote to USG, Long Branch. "Some articles which I have seen in the press of late concerning yourself make me feel like just saying to you a word of cheer. As you have always been kind to me even when the waves of trial rolled in upon me, so have I ever been at heart appreciative and grateful to you. I know that you are too strong to need or ask sympathy, but you know also in your rugged career how the dark hours are the best test of real friends. My own difficulties have blown over and my children are growing up around me in health & heart & bid fair to give me a helping hand when in age I shall need it. So this beginning of a New Year finds me happy, hopeful and longing for the same measure of joys for my friends. I lunched with several gentlemen in Chicago last week, Gens. Gresham & Strong, Col Jackson, Mr Pullman & others. It would have gratified you, I think, to have heard how they spoke of you in wholesome praise, & appreciation of your grand work and pure character. Be pleased to accept my hearty wishes & prayers for your highest good the coming year. Should it be possible in any way that I could serve you—or add to your comfort, I should be glad indeed. Give to Mrs Grant the sincere expression of esteem of Mrs Howard & myself. Then with a craving of God's blessing, . . . " ALS (press), Howard Papers, MeB. On April 17, Howard wrote to Robert Underwood Johnson, associate editor, *Century Magazine*, who had inquired about reminiscences of USG. " . . . I had already been invited to write some for a weekly newspaper; had complied with the request and sent an article. I have, however, put in form several other short experiences in connection with the General, which show particularly the benevolent and humorous phases of his mind and heart. Please examine them and, if accepted, publish them at your own proper valuation. I send them by to-day's mail. Should you not desire these reminiscences, after your perusal and criticism, please retain them subject to my order and notify me." LS (press), *ibid.* On May 7, Howard wrote to George H. T. Holloway. "I enclose the manuscript of the 'incidents of Genl. Grant.' Do not present this Manuscript to the 'Century': anywhere else you like . . . ." LS (press), *ibid.* See *New York Times*, Aug. 3, 1885.

3. Michael John Cramer resigned as minister to Switzerland after the inaugura-
tion of President Grover Cleveland. See *ibid.*, May 19, 1885.

4. See *ibid.*, Nov. 11, 1945; *PUSG*, 30, 326.

To T. Lyle Dickey

[New York City, Jan. 18, 1885]

I must apologize for not answering your letter of some ten days
ago before this. As you know I am very busy now, and by no means
well. The map of Shiloh that you speak of is too late for the article
which I prepared for Century Magazine. I may use it however for
the book I am now engaged upon and which is far towards completion. I am also indebted to Mrs. Wallace, your daughter, for a letter received about the same time as yours, enclosing a letter from
Mrs. Wallace to her husband, written but a few days before the
battle of Shiloh.[1] I have not answered it, and have misplaced her
letter, so that I have not the address. Will you be kind enough to
make my acknowledgments.

Sotheby's, Sale 7576, Dec. 13, 2000, no. 148.

1. On Jan. 5, 1885, Ann Dickey Wallace, Ottawa, Ill., wrote to USG. "I enclose a
copy of a letter written by Maj. Gen. Lew. Wallace on April 5th 1862. His movements
on the 6th are very often discussed & many contradictory statements made. This letter is something that doubtless tells the truth, & I send it to you hoping it may be of
use for to you & through you to the public: who wish for truth. The letter was taken
from the person of Gen. W. H. L. Wallace the morning of the 7th when he was brought
to the landing mortally wounded. I put it away with other papers then & not long
since in looking them over found it, & thought it valuable as history." ALS, USG 3.
The enclosure and a related document are *ibid.* See letter to *Century Magazine*, June 22,
1885; *PUSG*, 7, 397.

To Harry St. John Dixon

NEW YORK, Jan. 23. [1885]

*Capt. H. S. Dixon, Commanding the Fresno Camp of Blue and Gray
Veterans*:

DEAR CAPTAIN: I am in receipt of your letter of the 12th instant
inclosing resolutions passed by the camp of your command favoring

my retirement, and wish to express my appreciation of it. Coming as it does from an association composed of veterans of both armies in the great sectional contest, the compliment is greater. I hope the fraternity practised by the veterans of Fresno may be patterned after by all the citizens of our country before many years roll over.

Very truly yours,

U. S. GRANT.

Washington Post, Feb. 10, 1885. Born in 1843 in Miss., Harry St. John Dixon attended the University of Virginia (1860–61), served in the C.S. Army, moved to Calif., and was elected clerk of Fresno County (1869). See Harry St. John Dixon Papers, Southern Historical Collection, University of North Carolina, Chapel Hill, N. C. On Jan. 19, 1885, U.S. Senator John F. Miller of Calif. "presented resolutions adopted by the Blue and Grey Veterans of Fresno, Cal., urging that General U. S. Grant be placed on the retired-list of the Army with the rank of General; and stating that the ex-confederates belonging to that organization especially desire that this may be done in gratitude for his determined stand in protection of their paroles of honor; which were ordered to lie on the table." *CR*, 48-2, 823.

On Jan. 23, Raleigh E. Colston, former C.S.A. brig. gen., Washington, D. C., wrote to USG. "Permit me to enclose the accompanying letter in the Washington Post of this date which very imperfectly expresses my feelings—It was abridged by the editor to save space, I suppose. In the portion omitted, (the first part) I stated what I believe with good reason to be the fact, that it is the nearly unanimous sentiment of the Confed. Veterans, especially those of the Army of N. Va, that it is only bare equity to restore you to a position as good as that which you gave up at your country's called, and that because you served as President, it should not deprive you of the rights & privileges enjoyed by your brother officers to the end of their lives. It would have been but justice, had you been placed on the retired list immediately after the termination of your presidential term. In writing this letter, I only wished to repeat the sentiment I publicly expressed in 1866, in Baltimore in a lecture upon my former friend & colleague Stonewall Jackson, that the ex-soldiers of the C. S. A. were fully sensible of the generous treatment extended to us by yourself & Genl Sherman in the hour of our defeat & that we were grateful for it. Now that we *all* rejoice in being once more and forever, it is hoped, a united people, we can appreciate all the more the magnanimity which has shed more lustre upon the American name, than even the brightest triumphs of arms. With every sincere & fervent wish for your happiness & welfare ... " ALS, USG 3. The enclosure is a clipping with Colston's letter to the editor, dated Jan. 22. " ... Let the survivors of the confederate army urge their representatives in Congress to hasten the passage of the Senate bill as a matter of strict equity, and a relief which Gen. Grant can accept with *just pride*. I doubt not he will be gratified to know that those whom he treated generously in the day of their sorrow remember him gratefully in the time of his tribulation." *Ibid.*

On Feb. 13, USG wrote to Speaker Charles Hamlin of the Maine House of Representatives. "Your letter of the 7th instant is before me. The action taken by the house of representatives in the Maine legislature I have seen in the papers, and for your part in presenting the resolution favoring my restoration to the retired list of the army I wish now to thank you." ALS, MeB. On Feb. 16, Governor Frederick

Robie of Maine approved resolutions. "That the illustrious services of the exalted citizen-soldier, Ulysses S. Grant, should be promptly recognized by the people of this country, and his restoration as General of the Army on the retired-list, as an act of justice, should be authorized by an act of Congress without delay . . . ." *CR*, 48-2, 1828. See *ibid.* for similar legislative resolutions from N. Y. (pp. 1822, 1929), Wis. (p. 2060), and Pa. (p. 2343). On March 9, Governor Frederick A. Tritle of Arizona Territory approved a similar memorial from the legislative assembly to Congress as "in harmony with the general feeling of the country, and more particularly of the almost universal sentiment of the Pacific States and Territories." Copy, DNA, RG 94, ACP, 4754 1885.

On Feb. 20, USG had written to J. Leroy Bennett, asst. AG, Ill. Grand Army of the Republic. "Through you, allow me to thank the Illinois Encampment of the G. A. R. for its kind resolution recommending my being placed on the retired list of the army." *Proceedings of Nineteenth Annual Encampment of the Department of Illinois G. A. R . . . .* (Chicago, 1885), p. 380. For the resolution, see *Chicago Tribune*, Feb. 19, 1885. Also on Feb. 20, the Calif. encampment of the Grand Army of the Republic, San Francisco, "unanimously and enthusiastically adopted" a similar resolution. *CR*, 48-2, 2004. Other resolutions supporting legislation to benefit USG were sent to Congress from the Grand Army of the Republic in Pa. (*House Journal*, 48-2, 411, 449), New Mexico Territory (*Senate Journal*, 48-2, 411), and Ind. (*ibid.*, p. 425). See telegram to AG Richard C. Drum, March 4, 1885.

To Nicholas D. Williamson

New York City,
Jan.y 23d 1885.

REV. N. D. WILLIAMSON:
DEAR SIR;

Mrs Grant is just in receipt of your letter of the 20th instant, with its enclosure. I felt great sympathy for Mrs. Colfax and her son for the sudden loss of their husband and father. But it did not occur to me at the time to send a telegram expressing my sympathy, but I felt it none the less from that fact.[1] Indeed I was suffering myself at the time acute pain in the throat, so much ~~indeed~~ that I had to suspend work that I am much interested in, and have not yet been able to resume. My lameness from a fall more than a year ago, gives me no trouble. But for more than seven months I have suffered from a sore throat. This has been giving me special trouble for a few days, resulting from a cold probably, but is now improving.[2]

Mr. Colfax and I were warm personal friends from the day of our association on the same ticket for the two highest offices in the gift of the nation, up to his untimely and unexpected death. I was always his defender against what I believed to be most unjust charges.[3] There is no doubt but I always thought that he would have been a safe successer to me had my life been taken during my term of office. But I am glad you did not use, ~~the statement~~ in your funeral sermon, the quotation you give in your letter. My memory could not have sustained its accuracy. I do not recollect any time during my term of office when I thought myself in any particular danger of sudden death.

Mrs. Grant joins me at this late day, in expressions of our heartfelt sympathy for Mrs Colfax in her berievement, in the sudden loss of a loving, christian husband, one who commanded the respect and love of his neighbors and acquaintances in life, and who will live in their greatful memory now that he is "no more."

Very Truly yours
U. S. GRANT

ALS, In. Nicholas D. Williamson, pastor of the Reformed Church in South Bend, Ind., led funeral services for Schuyler Colfax, who had died from a heart attack while traveling through Mankato, Minn., on Jan. 13, 1885. See *Chicago Tribune*, Jan. 18, 1885; Willard H. Smith, *Schuyler Colfax: The Changing Fortunes of a Political Idol* (Indianapolis, 1952), pp. 438–41.

On July 1, 1876, Williamson had written to USG. "Two or three weeks ago while in Washington, in your abscence from the White House, I left with one of the door-keepers, a card of introduction from Hon. Schuyler Colfax, which stated my wish for a brief interview with you. The object of that desired interview was to give you my hand, as that of a man who had 'believed' in you and trusted you all through from Shiloh until now, who expects the verdict of history to confirm these impressions; and who wanted to thank you, among other things, for your peace policy with the Indians,—a policy which has been so ably vindicated of late in the Senate of the United States. The reason why I write of this now, is that I may also tell you of the fervent assent we gave in my Thursday evening prayer meeting this week, to the prayer of one of my lay Elders, when he said, 'O Lord we bless Thee for the Proclamation of the President of the United States, requesting the religious observance of the Centennial Anniversary of our National Independence. And *we pray Thee to bless him for issuing it*'! Mr. Colfax is very useful, very happy, and very busy with his lectures, meeting with ovations wherever he goes. By the power of a retributive Providence, the last of his Republican slanderers and of those who aided or winked at their efforts, have gone to their political slaughter; and unless I read that same Providence amiss, the Party which has now incorporated their oft refuted and villainous slander against him in its platform, will meet with a similar fate. It is especially true of national and political sins,—

'Vengeance is mine, I will repay saith the Lord.' Mr. C. is at the home of your successor today—lecturing in Fremont Ohio. With best wishes for your welfare and that of
your family in this world and the next, . . . " ALS, USG 3. See *PUSG*, 27, 156–57.

1. When told of Colfax's death on Jan. 13, 1885, USG expressed surprise and sorrow. See *New York Herald*, Jan. 14, 1885.
2. On Jan. 21, Frederick Dent Grant wrote to Edwards Pierrepont. "Father
thanks you for the Enclosed letters. He is a little better to day Please present my regards to Mrs Pierrepont" ALS, Keya Galleries, New York, N. Y.
3. Colfax's alleged involvement in the Crédit Mobilier scandal. See *PUSG*, 24,
68–69.

To Edward F. Beale

New York City,
January 24th 1885.

MY DEAR GENERAL BEALE:

Your letter of the 20th was duly received. I am much obliged
to Mrs. Beale for her kind expressions about my Shiloh article. It
will, I have no doubt, be severely criticised. But I have told in it the
exact truth as I saw it.

Mrs. Grant says we will accept your and Mrs. Beales kind invitation to visit you soon after the 4th of March. But I have no idea
that I will be able to go. My throat is giving me much trouble,
and I must see the doctor daily. There was about two weeks of
last month, and the first of this, when I could not speak, for the
pain it gave me. I am now having a similar turn, but not so bad.
If I should be in a condition to leave the doctors care by the 4th of
March, or at any time in the spring, I will be glad to go.

Very Truly yours
U. S. GRANT

ALS, DLC-Decatur House Papers. USG's health prevented any visit to Washington,
D. C. For Edward F. Beale's reminiscences of USG, see *New York Tribune*, April 2,
1885.
On April 2, 1885, Beale, Washington, D. C., wrote to Julia Dent Grant. "Mrs
Beale has been so seriously ill that I have scarcely left her bed side, and could not
therefore come to New York. She is to day I trust out of danger, though still a very sick
woman. Our hearts have been with you hourly, and though Mrs Beales illness was so
very critical, yet her sympathy was constantly and affectionately expressed for you. As

for our great friend who is reported as approaching the inevitable departure of all living things, our hearts have wept that it must be so. His greatness has surpassed that of all men of our time, and it must be a sweet consolation to you to know how deeply seated in the minds of his countrymen is a most reverential affection for the great Spirit which is passing away. With profoundest Respect & sympathy, and love from Mrs Beale." ALS, USG 3.

To George W. Childs

New York City,
February 1st 1885,

MY DEAR MR. CHILDS;

From what I see in the papers, or rather hear from them, I fear that I have been negligent in not answering the kind invitation of you and Mrs. Childs for Mrs Grant and I to pay you a visit about this time. I am very busy writing all the time. Besides what I write on the war, my mails are very large. Every day I write a few letters in answer to matters that require immediate attention. The balance are allowed to accumulate until the number gets quite large, when Fred, and I make one job of answering. I supposed your letter was answered. I hope you and Mrs. Childs have not been put to any inconvenience on account of my apparent neglect.

The doctor will not allow me to leave the city until the weather gets warm. I am now quite well in every way except soreness of the tongue about the root, and the same thing of the tonsil just over it. It is very difficult for me to swallow enough to maintain my strength, and nothing gives me so much pain as swallowing water. But the doctor thinks, and I think, that I am now improving. I have not smoked a cigar ~~since~~ since about the 20th of November.

Please present Mrs. Grants and my kindest regards to Mrs. Childs and Miss Lizzie.[1] Mrs. Grant is now in bed, and has been for the last three days.

Very Truly yours
U. S. GRANT

P. S. Mrs. Grant asks me to enquire if any offer has been made for the Long Branch house.[2]

U. S. G.

ALS, DLC-USG. After receiving USG's letter, George W. Childs told a correspondent in Philadelphia that USG "is no doubt a very sick man. He does not complain and bears his sufferings with the bravery and courage for which he is noted, but for all that I know he suffers a great deal." *New York Times*, Feb. 4, 1885. On Feb. 8, 1885, USG spoke to a reporter. "I am feeling quite well at present, but my physician has positively prohibited my leaving New York until the weather becomes milder. I am troubled considerably from a soreness at the root of the tongue and of the tonsil, which inconveniences me very much in talking and when I attempt to swallow any liquid. My visit to Mr. Childs was intended to be a purely social one. In view of the preparations which I understand Mr. Childs had made in the shape of invitations to dinners, breakfasts and receptions, I regret very much that I had to disappoint him." *New York Herald*, Feb. 9, 1885. Childs later visited USG in New York City. See *New York Times*, April 3, 1885.

1. Possibly Elizabeth Drexel, Anthony J. Drexel's niece, who did not marry until 1890. Childs and his wife, close friends of the Drexels, were childless. See *ibid.*, Jan. 8, 1890, Aug. 13, 1928.

2. On April 23, 1885, Childs, Philadelphia, wrote to Frederick Grant. "I am glad to learn by your telegram that you have rented the cottage. I hope you got the price you asked. We are all so rejoiced to hear of your dear Fathers continued improvement. The whole nation rejoices. We think of you all constantly, and wish we could be of some service in some way. Give our best love to your Father, and if he gets strong enough to take a little trip, we should be so delighted, to have him, and your Mother, and you, and Harrison to come to Wootton. It is lovely there now. The Pennsylvania Rail Road offers your Father a special car at any time, to take you all anywhere you wish to go. All unite in love to you all." ALS, USG 3. On May 2, a correspondent reported from Long Branch. "The Summer cottage of ex-President Grant has been leased to a New-York gentleman." *New York Times*, May 3, 1885.

To William T. Sherman

New York City,
Feb.y 1st 1885.

DEAR GENERAL:

I see in some of the papers—particularly the N. Y. Tribune— that I have been *honest enough* to correct my own statements in regard to Shiloh by adopting the government map of the battlefield. As a matter of fact I adopted no map further than to make the statement from my own memory of the position of the troops at different times, and particularly the position at the close of firing on the first day. Seeing, or rather hearing, this criticism of the Tribune[1] this morning, I examined the map in the Century and find it incorrect in the position it gives your division particulary, and slightly incorrect in regard to the positions of McClernand and Hurlbut in pushing them to far to the right. This is my memory, and I do not think I am mistaken. ~~in this.~~ I know the map is wrong in the positions assigned to Buell's army, in this, that it makes three divisions of the Army of the Ohio holding our right from the river a long ways before reaching the left of Hurlbut. On the morning of the 7th ~~the troops~~ Buells Army did advance from about the positions given to them by the map. But at the close of the battle on the 6th there was but three regiments of Nelsons division on the field. They were immediately on the bluff south of the log house. During the night—all the night—the balance of Buell's army was arriving.

I would be glad to have any critism you may have to make on my statements of fact. I want to have what I say in my book, correct, or as correct as possible. It would be impossible for any one, unless it should be a rebel, to write a history of that battle that would not be criticised by such writers as Cist.[2]

Very Truly yours

U. S. GRANT

GN. W. T. SHERMAN.

ALS, DLC-William T. Sherman. On Feb. 5, 1885, William T. Sherman, St. Louis, wrote to USG. "I have received your letter of the 1st, and have seen Cists article & most of the Criticisms on your article in the Century Magazine—I regard that article as invaluable, direct, simple and will carry conviction to all who have not formed selfish or preconceived opinions. Your map is as Correct as any extant, and will enable any honest reader to locate the principal events of a Battle which covered a large area of ground—That map, styled the 'Governmt Map' was made by Pitzman under the direction of Gen Geo Thom, who came down to Shiloh with Halleck *after* the event, indeed the Survey was mostly made after we had moved forward towards Corinth. McPherson & I had before the Battle reconnoitred the ground forwards as far as 'Monterey' (10 miles)—to the Left to Hamburg, (5 m) and to the Right at the Bridge across Snake Creek,—and we fought the Battle with 'McPhersons Sketch,' and one made by myself—My hardest fighting was with McClernand on *his* Right where you first found me right in his Camps—When the lull occurred about 2. PM. we slowly & deliberately drew back to the last position—purposely to cover the bridge by which we momen-

tarily expected Lew Wallace—I found at & near the Bridge Birge's 'Squirrel tails'—
and posted them in the log house, Stables and granaries on the high ground overlooking that bridge and the muddy & overflowed bottom of Snake River. From *that* bridge
there were *two* roads, one leading to the Corinth Road, and the other leading direct
to Pittsburg Landing. A lane with fence on either Side let to the former—We threw
the fences down, and that lane was my *last* double Line—from which we were *never*
dislodged, though repeatedly attacked, and there was where you found me at *dusk* Lew
Wallace came in *after* dark, and massed his men along the Road leading to the Landing, and I squared to the left to make room for him on my Right Buell also came to
me there.—From that position Wallace, Sherman and McClernand moved forward at
daylight of the 7th—meeting little opposition till we regained McClernands camps—
and there we waited four 4 long hours for Buells troops to get abreast. When we saw
them we pitched in and did not stop till we regained the camps originally occupied—A
magazine article is 'tentative' and will enable you in your 'Memoirs' to Suppliment
any omission. Dont modify a word, but give us your old Comrades the benefit of your
matured judgmt. The ground remains, and I am assured the 'bridge' remains, so that
I *know* what was my position in the beginning, and at night—We held our ground
all day, till reenforcemt came—which ought to have come *Sooner*—If you have it not,
please write to Col L. M. Dayton Cincinati, Ohio to send you a copy of the Proceedings
Army of the Tennessee Apl 6 & 7, 1881, and look at the two maps therein with 'Buck-
lands' letter.—I have been accused of making another map to Suit my purpose—My
map is identical with 'Thomas' the Govt map, only on it I lay down my true positions
and at the beginning and end of April 6, 1862. Whitelaw Reid was stampeded early,
and his account is that of a 'fugitive'—Sills [*Buell's*] is but the echo of men who came
grudgingly on the Field, and claimed to have rescued us from inevitable destruction.—
The map is immaterial.—The facts you state in your Century Article cover all that
History will retain, that April 6, with an inferior force, we held a Superior and vehemt
enemy at Bay, till expected reenforcemt came,—but that April 6 was the *real fight*—
and April 7, a 'Walk over.'" ALS, USG 3.

1. Concerning "the battle of Pittsburg Landing, or Shiloh," USG "maintains the
ground which he and General Sherman have always held as against the critics and the
general feeling of the public at that time, and insists that there was no serious blunder
in their management of the battle, and no surprise. At the same time the inherent honesty of the man comes out in his frankly accepting a map of the position of his forces
quite different from that which his defenders have heretofore given, and far less favorable to the defence of his dispositions which his admirers have heretofore made. The
fixedness of the General's idea is shown no less in the sharp reflections upon General
Wallace and General McCook, as well as in his resolute refusal to admit that General
Buell saved the day, which, as he insists, had been practically won before Buell arrived.
No military paper General Grant can hereafter write is likely to be challenged with a
sharper scrutiny by high authorities, or from a great number of soldiers who have been
the warmest admirers of his subsequent career." *New York Tribune*, Jan. 30, 1885. See
letter to *Century Magazine*, June 22, 1885.

2. On Jan. 26, a correspondent had reported from Cincinnati. "General Henry M.
Cist, the author of 'The Army of the Cumberland,' expressed his views on General
Grant's article on the Battle of Shiloh in *The Century* for February, at considerable
length to-day. He said that he regards it as an exceedingly valuable paper. Its approval of the official map of the battle-field, as prepared on the field after the engage-

ment, leaves General Sherman and the Army of the Tennessee Society, he said, in a bad shape with their attempted corrections of official documents. He also said: 'But our troops were outnumbered and outgeneraled on April 6. Had help from Buell not been nigh, the rebels would have made short work of Grant's army on the 7th . . . . Nothing could have been more badly managed to secure success in a hotly contested engagement than the conditions under which the Federal troops fought at Shiloh.'" *New York Tribune*, Jan. 27, 1885.

To Roswell Smith

———

New York City,
February 4th 1885.

Roswell Smith, Esq.
Pres. Century Co.

I am much obliged to you for the ten copies of the Century, containing my article on Shiloh, which you were kind enough to send me on Saturday last.¹ I am also pleased at the success of the Magazine.

For three or four weeks prior to about last Saturday I suffered so much pain that I did but little work on my book. I am now however able to devote from four to six ~~weeks~~ hours each day upon it, and, if this continues, I shall hope in the course of two or three weeks to have progressed far enough to justify me in making arrangements for ~~the~~ its publication.²

Very Truly yours
U. S. Grant

ALS, Doris Harris Autographs, Los Angeles, Calif.

1. Jan. 31, 1885.
2. See letter to Adam Badeau, Sept. 13, 1884; Memoranda, [*Dec. 18, 1884*], [*Feb. 1885*].

To Otis H. Tiffany

———

New York City, Feb. 4, 1885.

My Dear Dr. Tiffany: Your letter of the 30th of January, kindly placing a pew in your church at the service of myself or any of my family, was duly received. While I thank you I cannot accept. My physical condition will not admit of my attending church or going any place where I cannot control the temperature and draughts of air, before warm weather in the spring. Where myself and family will be after that time I do not know.

Very truly yours,
U. S. GRANT.

O. H. Tiffany, *Pulpit and Platform: Sermons and Addresses* (New York, 1893), p. 211. On July 26, 1885, Otis H. Tiffany, Madison Avenue Methodist Episcopal Church, New York City, eulogized USG. *New York Times*, July 27, 1885. See *PUSG*, 24, 59–60; letter to Cornelius B. V. Ward, Oct. 4, 1884.

Memorandum

In consideration of the fact that the book which I am now engaged upon will be in competition with Badeaus History of my Campaigns, which was written with my consent, and with the expectation that it would take the place of all I would have to say on the subject; in further consideration of the fact that I shall use maps which he had prepared with great care, and at great expense, as the bases of my maps; in further consideration of the assistan which he is to give, in the preparation of my forthcoming book, I have voluntarily stipulated as as small compensation for his various services rendered to me, proposed, and to propose and bind myself, to give him, General Badeau, Five thousand dollars (5.000) from the first twenty thousand dollars (20.000) realised from the sale of my book, and an additional five thousand dollars (5.000) from the next ten thousand dollars (10.000) so realized.

U. S. GRANT

NEW YORK CITY,
FEBRUARY 7TH 1885.

ADS (facsimile), Sotheby's, Sale No. 5759, Oct. 26, 1988, no. 82. On March 2, 1885, Adam Badeau, New York City, endorsed this memorandum. "Received of Genl US Grant $250 my share of $1000 received by him this day on account of his book." AES, *ibid.*

On Oct. 15, Badeau, New York City, wrote to Julia Dent Grant. "I beg to enclose you a copy of the agreement made with me by General Grant in August 1884, and put into writing by himself on the 7th of February last. On the 2d of May he told me in the presence of Jesse, that he had informed both you and his sons of the existence of this paper, and that it met with your approval. The only payment thus far under its provisions was made on the 2d of March last. General Grant then received $1,000, the consideration for his Agreement with his publishers, and handed me $250. of this money, saying it was 'my share,' under our agreement. My receipt was endorsed on the original paper the same day. My arrangements are such that I should be glad to know about when I may expect a further payment according to the terms. These, as you will see, allow me $5,000 out of the first $20,000 profits of the book, and $5,000 additional out of the next $10,000 profits. I will be greatly obliged by an early answer so that I may be able to make my plans accordingly. I address this letter to you, Dear Mrs Grant, in the first place, because you are the assignee of the Agreement with the publishers; but more especially out of respect to the wish General Grant repeatedly expressed to me that the matter should remain exclusively between ourselves—a wish that I am as anxious now, as I have always been—to fulfil." ALS, USG 3. The enclosure is *ibid.* On Oct. 21, Frederick Dent Grant, New York City, wrote to Badeau. "Your letter of the 15th with a copy of memorandum has been received by my mother. You may expect a further payment as soon as a sum of money is received from the sale of the book which will be sometime late in the winter or early in the Spring. To avoid misunderstanding, I beg to add on behalf of my mother, that any further payments will be of such a sum as may be proper and just in view of all the circumstances attending the case. My mother desires to do exactly what my father would do if living, and every thing points to the conclusion that it was his intention, if he had lived, to pay you a reasonable and fair compensation for your work as far as it had proceeded. What work you did can be easily ascertained. It may not be so easy for mother and yourself to agree upon its value, but she earnestly hopes, and in that hope I join, that a satisfactory adjustment can be reached when the proper time arrives. I will notify you when mother is prepared to respond to your request, at which time the value of the services rendered by you can be determined Should you desire an earlier ascertainment of the amount, kindly advise me." ALS, *ibid.* On Oct. 26, Badeau wrote to Frederick Grant. "I beg to acknowledge the receipt of your letter of October 21st inst. The date at which you state I am to receive further payments under General Grant's agreement with me is entirely satisfactory, in as much as it conforms to the stipulations of the agreement itself. But the intimation that those payments will be of a sum to be hereafter determined, and that the value of my services in connection with General Grant's memoirs is yet to be ascertained is one that I cannot for one moment accept. The value of my services was determined and bargained for by General Grant himself. I have submitted his positive and formal agreement to pay me $10,000 for them; an agreement which was neither proposed nor broken by me. Upon the fulfilment of that agreement I shall insist; and as your letter suggests that a contrary course is contemplated, I now ask an immediate declaration of an intention to carry out the stipulation mentioned. Should I not receive a favorable answer to this communication by November 1st proxo I shall be obliged to take legal steps to secure my rights." ALS, *ibid.* On Oct. 28, Frederick Grant wrote to Badeau. "In reply to your letter of the 26th I beg to say, that as your view of what was intended differs from mine I see no way but to leave you to act as you think best. Should you take legal proceedings there should then be no disatisfaction on either side at the result. My mother is willing to assume any just obligation which can be established as due to you from my father. If your attorney will notify me when the proper time arrives I will take the necessary measures to have some person provided to represent my fathers estate." ALS, *ibid.*

On June 14, 1887, Badeau's attorney Stephen G. Clarke, New York City, wrote to Frederick Grant's attorney Henry M. Alexander suggesting an arbitrator. *New York Herald*, March 17, 1888. Frederick Grant subsequently wrote to Alexander. " . . . My mother, who is apparently the person against whom General B. proposes to make his claim, declines any arbitration except that of the courts. Private arbitrators, I understand, have no power to enforce their judgments, and any agreement to abide by their determination would have to be enforced eventually at law if either party should be disposed to consider the conclusion arrived at unjust. I think General B. would consider any conclusion contrary to his view unjust, and for that reason it is better, if he thinks he has any claim, that he should resort to the courts at once rather than later. Another reason for declining arbitration is that an impression seems to have been created in several quarters—by whom it is not necessary to surmise—that General B. did original work to a considerable extent upon my father's book. This impression occasionally finds utterance. No better way of putting an end to such an absurd idea could be devised than a litigation in open court by Mr. Clarke's client of what he conceives to be his claim . . . ." *Ibid.*

On July 28, Badeau, Southampton, N. Y., wrote to Clarke refuting Frederick Grant's assertions. " . . . I have twice stated in writings, which must be in the possession of General Grant's family, that I have no desire, intention or right to claim the authorship of 'General Grant's Memoirs.' I have never asserted that I furnished original matter for it to any considerable extent. I have never sought to give such an impression in private, and have scrupulously abstained from inciting any comment whatever on the subject, or making any statement for the public, whether in print or otherwise. What I did on General Grant's book he constantly and repeatedly requested me to keep secret, even from his family, and I have scrupulously conformed to his desire. In view of Colonel Grant's remarks, however, I now propose to make a statement of my connection with the memoirs, still only for General Grant's family or such persons as it may be necessary for them or me to consult and with the hope that General Grant's desire for secrecy may even yet be complied with. In June, 1884, the editors of the *Century Magazine* renewed the request they had previously made through me, that General Grant would write for their magazine, and empowered me to offer him $1,000 for two articles on any of his battles which he might select as themes. After a while he made the attempt, and when he had written a few pages he sent for me to visit him at Long Branch and showed me his work. This I revised and showed him how to enlarge the paper, and after a good deal of labor of this sort, I changing the phraseology and construction whatever I chose, and General Grant always accepting my changes, the paper was copied by Colonel Grant and taken to the editors of the *Century*. Mr. Johnson, one of the editors, at once waited on General Grant and asked for more matter, making one or two suggestions in regard to themes or treatment. I was at General Grant's house when this visit occurred, and later I revised with him the subsequent and enlarged article. But before it was completed I had left Long Branch, and he wrote to me asking for information and making such inquiries as these:—'Was McCook's division under fire at Shiloh? also Crittenden's?' 'Did Buell have any part of his army with him the second day except Nelson's division?' After completing the article on Shiloh he began one on Vicksburg, and again invited me to his house, . . . In August, accordingly, I went again to his house. The day after my arrival he asked me to take a drive, and we went out together in a buggy, he and I alone. He then told me that it had been proposed that he should write his memoirs, and that he wanted me to help him; but as he had always assured me that he would never write such a work, he did not feel at liberty to do so without my consent. He then proposed to give me $5,000 out of the first $20,000 profits he might receive, and $5,000 more out of the next $10,000—that is, 33⅓ per cent out of the first $30,000 receipts. This was without any suggestion whatever from me; the offer had evidently been planned beforehand in his own mind, and was made before I could reply to his first remark. I had expressly told him scores of times that I would not attempt to write his history if he meant ever to write one, and he had pledged himself repeatedly to me not to do so. I had devoted the best energies of my life for seventeen years to the task, and the peculiar quality and character of my book would be destroyed if he wrote. For I was now his mouthpiece. But when he spoke himself of course my especial authority would be superseded. His proposition was a bitter disappointment to me, but he was my chief and my friend and in misfortune. The book might bring him in money, and it distracted him from his troubles. I consented. Then he asked me to keep this entire matter exclusively between him and me. I at once began helping him. I remained ten days at his house, planning the entire work and revising what he wrote, including new portions of the papers on Chattanooga and the Wilderness. After my return to my summer quarters he wrote to me again in the last days of August: . . . As he was so anxious I finally postponed the completion of my own work and went to him on the 15th of October. For months I spent four or five hours a day at his side and many hours besides in my own room at work on his book. When we were together we sat at the same table, and often as soon as he had written a page he handed it to me. I did not write the original matter, and in that sense I did not compose the book. The thoughts were General Grant's, and, in most cases, the original draft of the language; but I suggested much. I told him when to insert descriptions of scenery, where to place an account of a character, how to elaborate a picture of a battle. I recalled scenes and incidents to his memory in which I had participated or with the story of which I was familiar, and I verified his statements. I did not compile data, as Colonel Grant supposes. The data were compiled and ready in my own history, and that he always took as his authority. I read up, however, several works on the Mexican War and then went over what he had written on that subject, verifying or correcting it, and almost remaking this portion, so far as construction and style are concerned. I discussed his statements and the advisability of his expressions of opinion and often persuaded him to change the one or withhold or modify the other. And then, when the subject matter was settled, I took this rough material to my own room and made any changes I saw fit in language or style. I took out whole pages. I transferred others from one part of the book to another. I modified any expressions which I disliked or disapproved, and there was not a page in the first volume nor one in the second, down to the Wilderness campaign, which did not contain a dozen alterations or modifications entirely mine. I broke up sentences, I softened or heightened the effect, I corrected the grammar, and all with the knowledge and sanction and by the express and repeated desire of General Grant. I especially constructed the work. General Grant had a very good power of clear and forcible expression in matters with which he was familiar or in which he was interested, and passages of his were often felicitous. These I always retained, and always sought to preserve his simplicity and directness and even ruggedness of language—never to betray my own share in the work. But he never knew whether what he wrote was good English, and his slips in grammar were constant. He had, besides, no idea whatever of building up a chapter or a book, or of treating a theme so as to lead up to a point, or to make a complete picture or argument. If he struck out a good sentence at the first trial, so much the better; but he could not repair or improve it, as a rule. This was no discredit to him. Literature was not his occupation or his talent. He was a soldier, not an author. I was happy to put whatever knowledge or experience or talent I had of this sort at his service, and to do this part of his work for him and with him. There was nothing dishonorable in our relation, either to him or to me. The work was a labor of love to me, and he appreciated this, and enjoyed seeing the book take different shape and color in my hands, or, rather, seeing his own thoughts and deeds brought out more clearly and more absolutely according to his own idea. But the book could not have been made what it is without me. There was no one else who had both my peculiar knowledge of the theme and the literary quality. There was no one else whom he would have allowed to do what I did. But he knew how I loved him, and how devoted I was to his fame, and he trusted me. I did my work loyally if ever a man did, and never betrayed him. I have done nothing to precipitate this question. I would not have told what I am writing now if it had not been extorted from me by the imputations referred to by his son. General Grant once said to me:—'Badeau, I know I could not do this work without you. I think I could tell a plain story so that people would understand what I meant; but I could not write such a book as this without you. You have been invaluable and indispensable to me, not only in verification and revision, but in suggestion, and I am very grateful.' Another time I proposed to leave his house, having remained a month or six weeks, but he would not hear of it. He said I was conferring a great obligation on him and his family by remaining to help him. Those were his words. He said his family understood and appreciated the service I was doing him and them. If he could afford it, he declared, he would offer me $500 or $600 a month while I stayed, in addition to my interest in the book itself. So I consented to stay. When he became ill I asked him to put the agreement into writing. He acquiesced and wrote out the agreement the same day, while I was out of the room, without any other suggestion or word from me. When he saw me alone he handed me the paper. Some one entered and I put it into my pocket and read it afterward alone. The next time he saw me he asked if it was satisfactory and I told him it was. This was on the 7th of February, 1885. The terms of the agreement were precisely those he had offered me in August preceding at Long Branch. No suggestion or modification in regard to matter or language was made by me on either occasion. When he became very ill I asked him to tell his family of the agreement, but he refused positively. He said he wished the matter to be exclusively between him and me; that he did not mean ever to give me a check. I pleaded with him, but he was immovable. I said his family might think I acted dishonorably in not revealing the arrangement, but he said they knew that there was an agreement between us, and he promised if he got very much worse to divulge its particulars. He constantly consulted me about his arrangements with his publishers, and when they became so anxious to secure his work I asked him to insert a stipulation in his agreement with them for the publishers to pay him $10,000 for the assistance he required, so that this expense should not fall upon him; but he refused, though the publishers offered to advance him any sum that he required. But on the day when he signed the contract with his publishers he received $1,000 consideration money in a check. He had this cashed at once, and the same day he handed me, when we were alone, $250 in bills, saying it was my share of what he had been paid. Still he positively refused to tell the family of our agreement, though I again urged him. He was unwilling that any one should know the amount or character of the assistance I rendered him. For I can point out literally hundreds of passages that I changed. I can show the alterations in the MS. if it has been preserved. I can show that these passages are not as General Grant originally wrote them, but as I modified them. I can give ample proof of my assertions to convince either an arbitrator or a court—or the country. There will be no doubt whatever left in the mind of any one if this matter is dragged into publicity. But this is what I do not desire. General Grant did not wish it, and I have respected his wish as sacred. I prefer, I am anxious that the character of my relation to his book should be buried forever in oblivion. I have never raised the question. I have said not one word in print about it; I have avoided it altogether, except with my lawyers or my most confidential friends. For this reason I have borne with the delay in the fulfilment of the agreement. I have not gone into the courts, although the contract expressly states that I was to receive $5,000 out of the first $20,000 profits, and $5,000 more out of the next $10,000; and Mrs. Grant has received hundreds of thousands of dollars and not paid me a penny. Doubtless she has misapprehended the facts, or she, as a woman of honor, would never have risked the dishonor to her great husband's name, of a broken agreement; she would never have failed to keep his pledged word—a word given to procure his release from a prior pledge. I have known Mrs. Grant too many years and too intimately not to appreciate her sense of honor and her delicacy. I believe if she understood the case she would see that instead of claiming either money or reputation not my due I have concealed my part of the labor performed out of regard to her husband; I have forborne to press when I might have demanded; I have submitted to delays that amount to gross injustice, to calumnies in the press that I might at once have dissipated—all for the sake of my great chief, the love I bore him, the memory of his services to the country and his friendship for me—not without a recollection of her own many gracious words and deeds. It will not be irrelevant to recall just here what I have endured rather than drag into publicity what General Grant so earnestly desired should not be divulged. I have remained a year and a half unpaid for services rendered nearly three years ago. I have submitted to false and odious imputations at the very moment when I was engaged on a work calculated to set General Grant's political services and his personal qualities in a light in which no other could place them, because no other had the knowledge enjoyed by me—a work which has been approved by his warmest and most distinguished friends, personal, military and political. I wrote in the kindest and most careful strain of General Grant's business relations and those of his sons, so that his publishers and their lawyers thanked me for the view I had set before the world of this delicate and disputed matter. I did this at the moment when my claim was scouted by his family. And when the publishers of his book were willing and anxious to publish mine, the family again interfered and prevented the fulfilment of another written agreement after it was signed. I offered to submit my work to Mrs. Grant and to correct any inaccuracies of statement, as well as to consider any points of feeling or taste with a view to defer to her wish. I proposed to discuss points in which General Grant's fame was especially involved, and had been recently and bitterly assailed, such as his relations with Rawlins and Halleck, and to consult with Mrs. Grant about the treatment of these themes, or to avoid them altogether, as she might decide; but the only answer I received was that Mrs. Grant would have nothing to do with my book; she disapproved it, but refused to say where or how. Upon this the publishers refused to publish my work unless I stipulated blindly to strike out anything that Mrs. Grant might object to. I again asked to be made acquainted with her objections, but this was again refused, and I was forced to find another publisher. Colonel Grant declares that he is perfectly willing to discuss in a friendly spirit with me any claim I may make for services in compiling data for the Personal Memoirs, that those services are susceptible of proof and that Mrs. Grant is willing to allow for them in the most generous spirit, without insisting on their valuation from any business standpoint. Colonel Grant ignores altogether the fact that there is a written agreement, drawn as well as signed by General Grant himself, which states exactly the sum to be paid and the consideration for the payment, and describes the compensation mentioned as 'small' for the services rendered; an agreement proposed by him when in full health and delivered before he made his agreement with his publishers. What I ask of the family is to carry out this agreement, to pay me $9,750, with interest from the day when they received the first payment, amounting to $30,000. Two hundred and fifty dollars, I have already said, General Grant paid me on the day when he received $1,000, all he ever drew in person. He carried out the agreement so far as he was able. The fulfilment of this written contract is better than litigation, which must inevitably divulge to all the world the secrets that General Grant so carefully hid and which I have sacredly endeavored to withhold. But if these confidential matters are dragged into the public gaze it will not be I who expose them. It will be the family of the country's hero who lay bare the secrets which he sought to cover, and it will be seen that they do this against the wishes and efforts of his faithful friend," *Ibid.*, March 21, 1888; typed copy (dated 1887), USG 3. See *Badeau*, pp. 424–31. On March 5, Frederick Grant had written to Charles L. Webster. "I understand that for some reason you do not intend to publish Genl Badeau's book. My mother wishes to refer you to the letter written some days ago declining to criticise Genl Badeau's writings; and also to inform you positively that you must not refuse to publish the book on account of any supposed objection on her part, that she can not and does not object to your conducting your business to suit yourself and will not be made responsible for any result growing out of it" Copy (in Frederick Grant's hand), Ulysses Grant Dietz, Maplewood, N. J. S. S. Scranton & Co. published *Badeau*.

On Oct. 6, Clarke wrote to Alexander. "General Badeau is tired of waiting on Colonel Fred, and I think with some reason. He has instructed us to commence proceedings. I think it fair to advise you of this before doing so." *New York Star*, March 25, 1888. On Oct. 7, Frederick Grant wrote to Alexander. "I received last night, from Mr. Whitford, the letter of Mr. Clarke saying that General Badeau was tired of waiting on 'Colonel Fred,' meaning, I presume, myself. The inclosed letter, based in part upon my interview with you yesterday, had been already prepared, but had not been carefully considered by my mother, whose views it embodied, for the reason that she did not arrive from Philadelphia, where she was visiting, until noon to-day. It has been carefully considered by each member of our family and expresses our feelings in this matter. During my father's illness General Badeau wrote him a letter, assuming that he (Badeau) was to take such a part in completing the book as no one else, not even General Grant himself, could take. That letter is full of General Badeau's exaggerated idea of his own ability, and, expressly declaring that the book cannot be completed without his aid, demands that a 'new bargain' be made, giving him as the proper compensation for his future services $1,000 a month in advance and 10 per cent. of the profits of the work; and that, too, although the memorandum which he and his attorneys call a contract was in existence. My father immediately replied to General Badeau that, after such assertions on the latter's part, any relation of a literary character between them would be impossible . . . . General Grant was stunned and pained by the attitude of General Badeau in proposing to secretly and for money take any essential share in preparing the Memoirs, . . . We act from no feeling of ill will. We are content from past association to minister to his needs, but we will not submit to his ungrateful assaults upon the memory of one who during life, through good and evil report, befriended him and gave him his only claim to remembrance in the future . . . . It is General Badeau's false and preposterous statement that any part of his work on the memoirs is secret or essential to their form or character that makes it impossible to pay him anything except what he proves himself to have earned. He claims now to have done what in my father's lifetime he proposed to do, a proposition resulting in his immediate discharge from the latter's service. It is easier to show what he actually did than it was to prove that Bathyllus did not do the work of Virgil. We are willing and especially anxious to submit the settlement of that fact to such an arbitration as we have indicated, where all the evidence may be adduced that can in any way bear upon the entire question. It is for General Badeau to decide whether he prefers the whole truth to be known or to make a technical legal fight on the point whether he has a contract founded on adequate consideration and conforcible against the assignee. My mother wishes to express to you her appreciation of your courtesy and friendly feeling and the delicacy that prompted you to decline General Badeau's retainer, and I have only to add that you are at liberty to use this letter in any way you see fit, and that I retain for myself the same privilege except as to anything there may be in it that you prefer to have unsaid. I write to you directly, instead of to General Badeau's attorneys, because Mr. Clarke's last letter was sent to you, and therefore I beg that you will again have the goodness to forward the [i]nclosure and a copy of this letter to those gentlemen." *Ibid.* The enclosure is a letter of the same day from Frederick Grant to Stanley, Clarke & Smith. "Your letter of August the 18th, 1887, addressed to Mrs. U. S. Grant and inclosing a communication to Stephen G. Clarke, Esq., from General Adam Badeau, has been received, and after due consideration of both papers my mother directs me to make you this reply, the delay in sending which is due to the fact that not until yesterday did Mr. H. M. Alexander (through whom you began your communications, instead of addressing Mrs. Grant directly) inform me of the result of his interview with Mr. Clarke. The letter and your client's document taken together make something very like a threat, that unless General Badeau receives $10,000 out of the 'hundreds of thousands of dollars' which he says Mrs. Grant has re[c]eived from her husband's memoirs, duly assigned to her for valuable consideration, he will manifest the love, gratitude and devotion that he pretends to have had for his late chief by revealing something that he was especially charged by General Grant to 'keep secret.' In other words, $10,000 is the price of this silence, and his gratitude, being of the kind defined as a lively appreciation of favors to come, ceased with the death of his benefactor. Mrs. Grant wishes General Badeau distinctly to understand that any assertion that her late husband desired anything relating to the preparation of his book kept secret is unworthy of belief and easily disproved by his own writings and utterances before his death, and that nothing will be paid to General Badeau that can now, or at any future time, be construed into 'hush money.' And in this connection it will be well to remind General Badeau's counsel that prior to the trial of Mr. James D. Fish (also their client), it was intimated that letters injurious to General Grant would be produced, and that on the very day before the trial Mr. Clarke spoke to Mr. Purrington with the view of seeking a postponement, on the ground of General Grant's health, whereupon General Grant on that same date asked the District Attorney, through counsel, to allow no delay on his account, but, rather, to push on the trial while he was still alive to meet any charge in any way affecting him . . . ." *Ibid.* See letters to Adam Badeau, [*May 2–5, 1885*], July 12, 1885.

In Oct., Badeau filed suit against Julia Grant in the N. Y Supreme Court. D (typed), Dartmouth College, Hanover, N. H. For Julia Grant's response, see *New York Sun*, March 27, 1888. On Dec. 23, Badeau, Washington, D. C., wrote to Clarke. "I have your letter of the 22d inst with its enclosures, and I beg you to understand my position distinctly. I will in no case sign any disclaimer of the authorship of Gen. Grants book for money. My claim is not for hush-money, but for payment for services rendered and for the damage done me by Gen Grants action—both admitted by him in his written agreement. It was to a settlement of this claim that I consented—in order to prevent the publicity which he was so anxious to avoid. But the attempt to foist other stipulations dishonorable to me into the release discharges me from any obligation to complete the arrangement. I now refuse any settlement except full payment of my claim of $9,750, with interest and my lawyers' full fees: to this I shall adhere, and I desire you at once to make the fact and the reasons known to Mrs Grant's lawyers, and yourself to proceed with the suit without delay. The attempt to drag me into admissions that I could only make by denying what I have sworn to—determines me. I have twice stated in writing that I have no wish or intention ever to claim the authorship of Gen Grants book; if it Can be avoided; but I have always made this statement with qualifications, and restrictions; and I never will make the statement without the qualifications; neither will I ever make it for money, or in connection with any release of Mrs Grant or General Grant's estate from their indebtedness to me," ALS, *ibid.*

On Monday, Feb. 20, 1888, Frederick Grant wrote to Roscoe Conkling. " . . . We have never objected to paying Genl Badeau any proper amount for the settlement of just claims; but my mother felt hurt at his insinuation of the existence of a *secret* existing. This intimation was outrageous, as all of my father's family knew that he had employed Genl Badeau to assist him in the preparingation of his 'memoirs,' and all of the world knew that Badeau was staying at our house for that purpose. I knew of the compensation, which was to be given to Badeau for his work, & discussed it with father. Mr eChilds told me that father had talked over this same matter subject of compensation with him Therefore, Badeau's allusions to a *secret* make cause my mother uneasy as to anxiety in the settlement of *any one claim,* . . . In order to prevent my mother's having the distress of appearing in court, which I think would effect her seriously, I, myself, am in favor of having this matter settled, even according to the way Badeau's attorneys have presented it but I should feel that if he Badeau should insists upon keeping the wording of the paper just as it is, that Badeau he intends to cause my mother some annoyance. We leplavce this matter in your hands, however, and hope it will soon be settled according to your judgement. I regret not having seeingn you today, but must leave the city this afternoon and will not return until Thursday." ADfS, Ulysses Grant Dietz, Maplewood, N. J.

In March, newspapers publicized the controversy between Badeau and the Grants. On March 19, Frederick Grant telegraphed to George W. Childs, Philadelphia. "The question with me has been all along the wording of the receipt, not the amount of money. I will not admit a question of authorship or the existence of a secret." Copy (in Frederick Grant's hand), *ibid.* On March 20 and 21, Childs wrote to Frederick Grant. "I send you our article on Badeau. It is not strong enough, as he is beneath contempt. I never did like him . . . ." "I have been house bound for several days with a severe cold and a sore throat, but I have been well enough to take the deepest interest in the infamous Badeau matter. I send enclosed our editorial in to days 'Ledger,' and our New York, and Washington correspondents mention of the matter, so we score him pretty well for one day. The papers throughout the whole country take the proper and right view of the matter. You have right and justice with you, and all will come out satisfactorily. Give our best love to your Mother and dear Ida, . . . " ALS, DLC-USG, IB. An undated letter on the same subject from Childs to Julia Grant is *ibid.* On March 21, Anthony J. Drexel, Philadelphia, wrote to Frederick Grant. "I enclose clippings from todays 'Ledger' I dont think there will be much left of Badeau by the time we get through . . . ." ALS, *ibid.* On March 19, George S. Boutwell, Washington, D. C., had written to Frederick Grant. "I am with you in your resistance to the demands of General Badeau. The conduct of Badeau was despicable in the extreme, while the letter of your Father in reply to Badeau's proposal is lustrous with those qualities for which your Father was so eminently distinguished . . . ." ALS, *ibid.* On the same day, Alice Chenoweth Smart, New York City, wrote to Frederick Grant. "My brother—Capt. Bernard Peel Chenoweth—was on your great Father's Staff for a time during the war. Your Father afterward sent him as Consul to Canton China—where he died. I was a mere child at that time; but well remember the love and admiration with which my brother always spoke of Gen. Grant. Ofcourse, I have always felt that I knew your Father; but no act of his life ever so deeply impressed me with the breadth and greatness of the man as his letters to Gen. Adam Badeau—published in today's papers. The simplicity and charity of his nature is shown there in a degree that is sublime . . . . Few public men—few really great men—can endure the test of a publication of their private letters. It is always a dangerous experiment. In your Father's case—as in Thackeray's—it has added glory of a new kind, and must, inevitably, create a new and warmer love for the *man*—apart from the soldier, and statesman. Pardon so long a letter from a stranger—who does not feel strange to your family." ALS, *ibid.* On March 24, USG's cousin Charles C. Tompkins, Charleston, West Va., wrote to Frederick Grant. "When I first had my attention called to the disgracefull conduct upon the part of Gen'l Badeau, my indignation knew no bounds, & I felt that it would be the greatest pleasure of my life, to inflict corporeal punishment upon him. I wondered how you could restrain yourself, from *caning* him upon sight. Now, that you have so completely, & effectually caught Gen'l Badeau, in the meshes of the net, of his own weaving, my indignation has turned to pity. The worst thing that can be said of a man, is to express pity for him. He then assumes a position, *beneath contempt.* Would it not be Charity, to attribute his behaviour to,—Dementia? . . . " ALS, *ibid.* On the same day, Edwin C. Bennett, St. Louis, wrote to Frederick Grant. "I have noted with satisfaction the devotion with which you have so conclusively defended your illustrious father's memory in the Badeau controversy— . . . At the time of the capture of Camp Jackson May 10 .61—he was the guest of Mrs. B. (then Mrs Lync[h]) and her family, and with them saw the prisoners march down Lynch St to the Arsenal, his comments on the cause of the war and its probable results were clear and positive in statement, and prophetic ~~in their predictions~~ . . . " ALS, *ibid.* On April 4, Bennett wrote to Frederick Grant reiterating his support. ALS, *ibid.* See *PUSG*, 2, 30–31, 247. On March 27, William B. Moore, Buffalo, had written to Frederick Grant. "As I had the honor of serving on the staff of your father at one period of the war, and my personal relations with him were contemporaneous with Badeau (although I did not make myself so conspicuous), being frequently with him personally, up to a short time before his fatal illness developed, I think myself qualified to judge something of his estimate of Badeau and of the merits of the latters claim. I always looked upon him as an upper dependent of your fathers, with much the same privileges at the White House, that a favored 'Poor relation' possessed; he either held an office under your father or was applying for one as long as the latter had an office to give or was willing to recommend him: I saw B. (once at least) in the vicinity of the White House, so drunk, that he walked in a circle two or three time round before he straightened out and 'propped' himself for a start in the direction he wanted to go; he appeared to me to be eternally working your father for what he could get out of him while in power, since then he has appeared to me to be a 'dead beat', he has been retailing, through the country papers (for pay) the small tattle of butlers and

servants of english families, whose hospitality he enjoyed while Consul General, giving the happenings in their Kitchens. It seems to me that this attempt to make mer-
chandize of what occurred in your fathers household while he was enjoying its priv-
eleges is in keeping with Badeaus whole career Your course in the matter meets the
hearty approval of every man who served with and knew the Old Hero." ALS
(signed "W. Bowen Moore"), DLC-USG, IB. For Moore, see *PUSG*, 30, 392–93. On
March 28, USG's former secretary Maj. Culver C. Sniffen, New York City, wrote to
Frederick Grant on "Badeau's astounding presumptions. It is a shame that your family
should feel called upon to go into court to make them more plain. and Mrs Sniffen and
I feel a great sympathy for Mrs Grant because of the attitude she feels bound to assume, as a consequence of Badeaus avarice and base ingratitude, in the defence of the
Generals probity—which never was and never can be in question." ALS, DLC-USG,
IB. On March 29, Sophia C. Page, Tottenville, N. Y., wrote to Frederick Grant. "I
have read your—reply—& pronounced most devoutly the Benediction—'Well done
good & faithful servant'— . . . Cannot Genl Grant's letter to Genl. Badeau—be a supplement to future editions of the 'Personal Memoirs'?—if 'Style is the Man'—that is *all*
Grant— . . . " ALS, *ibid.* For Page, see *PUSG*, 28, 178–79. Also on March 29, Maj.
Alexander Sharp, Leavenworth, Kan., wrote to Frederick Grant. "Your Aunt Ell recd
the Copy of the N. Y. Herald sent by your Mother Containg the full ac't. of the Badeau
affair. I am very much obliged to you for it: We had only the mutilated accounts of our
western papers—or I should say more correctly, abbreviated acts. What a miserable
fellow he is turning out to be: And by the way not as smart as I have given him Credit
for being. Of course I as well as many others have known for some time that he was
not as unselfish & good asa friend of either General Grant & his family as he professed
to be: but that he should have turned out to be so *ungrateful* to the best friend he ever
had the one who made him all he is & more than he can ever be again passes my com-
prehension I can only account for his present proceedings by charitably thinking that
he must be either *crazy* or drunk—perhaps *both* . . . ." ALS, DLC-USG, IB. On
March 31, Emily (Emma) Dent Casey, Washington, D. C., wrote to Frederick Grant.
"I received the 'Star' you sent me, and we all read it, and there was but one opinion expressed by all. 'It was splendid.' We had seen only parts of your answer in other papers so enjoyed reading the entire answer—There is but one opinion expressed here of
Badeau and that is He is a contemptible Dog . . . ." ALS, *ibid.* On April 5, Ely S. Parker,
New York City, wrote to Frederick Grant. "*Personal*— . . . I have a feeling that it may
be improper for me to say any thing about Gen Badeau's recently developed, grasping
and rascally, operations, but I cannot refrain from communicating directly to you the
mortification and indignation I feel in having your noble fathers name again brought
before the public only to be scandalized, and that too by a creature whom your father
made what he is. The ingratitude and ghoulishness of Badeau is beyond comprehen-
sion. I loved your father dearly, deeply and sincerely, and nothing Badeau, or any one
else, can say can swerve my loyalty to him & his honored memory. You and your dear
mother have, in this matter, the sympathy and good wishes of all right thinking and
justice loving people. My daily prayer will be that success may perch on your banner
in maintaining your fathers acts, and crown you with deserved victory—" ALS, *ibid.*
    On March 19, Absalom H. Markland, Washington, D. C., had written to Julia
Grant. "I am astounded by the correspondence of Genl Badeau. I have no words to
properly express my views of such a proceeding on his part. You will remember that
in the latter part of October 1884 Mrs Markland and my self had an enjoyable call of
some hours at your house. During that call the General and myself talked of school,

and war, days He told me of the Century papers he had prepared and the idea he had of the Memoirs. I remember that I asked him if he were really going to write them himself. His answer was 'Yes I am going to write them myself. If I did did not they would not be mine I am going to write what I know. What the records show every body already knows' I was struck with the reply and asked him if he would not require some help to refresh his memory? His answer was 'Fred will look up dates for me' To those who are at all acquainted with the Generals style of writing the book is evidence that it was his work except when he has referred to Badeaus book as authority. The statement that Genl Badeau makes that he revised the paper on Shiloh is particularly refreshing since Genl B could have known nothing of that battle save what he learned from Genl Grant. Genl B never saw General Grant until after Vicksburg and surely was not within hundreds of miles of the battle field of Shiloh on the days the battle was fought I was with Genl Grant from Cairo to the final wind up at City Point. I was his school mate in boyhood days There are many evidences that I had his confidence. I think I knew him and knowing him I can concieve of no character of reasons why Genl Badeau, or any one else, should have written to him, or to any member of his family, such letters as are published. General Badeau could never pay by manual labor, or literary experience, the debt he owed General Grant. It is painful to think he should have forgotten the debt. The sincere regards of Mrs Markland & myself to you, . . . " ALS, *ibid.* On April 5, Markland wrote to Frederick Grant. " . . . There are very many who will be glad that Genl B lived long enough to burst the bubble of his own greatness. There were some of your fathers true friends who estimated Genl B at his full value from the start and some went to their graves in the belief that Genl B would bring sorrow to your father in return for the kindness and confidence he received. There are some statements in the memoirs which Genl B. must have placed there wholly without your fathers knowledge. He says he revised and corrected the book and the ms will show it. Suppose he did? Revision & correction is not authorship . . . ." ALS, *ibid.* The Grants also received supportive letters dated March 17 from Charles H. T. Collis, Fitz John Porter, New York City; dated March 18 from John Russell Young, New York City; dated March 19 from William C. Carroll, Baltimore, John Livingston, Campville, N. Y.; dated March 20 from Capt. Charles A. Woodruff, Vancouver Barracks, Washington Territory; dated March 20 and 23 from Abram Merritt, Nyack, N. Y; dated March 21 from James B. Fry, Aloysius J. Kane, Philadelphia, George F. Thompson, Manhattan, Kan.; dated March 22 from Henry B. Cocheu, Brooklyn, John W. Fuller, Toledo, James S. de Palos, New York City; dated March 22 and April 2 from H. T. Hartley; dated March 22 and April 4 from Wellesley Bradshaw, Philadelphia; dated March 24 from Henry W. Knight, New York City; dated March 26 from H. Krebs, Jr., San Francisco; dated March 26 and April 3 from William E. Strong, Chicago; dated March 28 from Charles S. Parker, Arlington, Mass., U.S. Representative Francis B. Spinola of N. Y., Hot Springs, Ark.; dated April 1 from Robert N. Price, Denver; dated April 2 from A. G. Myers, New York City, Jane L. Stanford, Washington, D. C.; dated April 3 from Lyman K. Bass, Cairo, Egypt, S. Mimes, New York City; dated April 6 from Walter Q. Gresham, Chicago; dated April 7 from Corydon C. Brownell, Rochester, N. Y.; dated April 9 from Darwin C. Pavey (incomplete); dated April 18 from Thomas Settle, Jacksonville, Fla.; dated April 20 from Richard C. Shannon, Florence, Italy; dated June 9 from C. W. Smith, La Crosse, Wis.; undated from Mary E. W. Sherwood, New York City. *Ibid.* On April 11, Frederick Grant wrote to Pavey acknowledging his letter. ALS, CSmH.

On March 26, Matías Romero, New York City, had written to Badeau offering to mediate his dispute with the Grants. "As I told you at our interview of this afternoon, as a friend of Gen. Grant's and a friend of Mrs. Grant and her family, I regreted very much the trouble which has occurred between them and yourself, and judging from the statements and papers published by both sides in the newspapers, I thought you were not so far apart from coming to an understanding which ~~will~~ would put and end to this trouble. ~~end litigation~~ and be honorable to both.—I thought that if you sign~~ed~~ a receipt for the money that Gen Grant promised to pay you stating that you had no further claim on his Personal Memories or his estate, and disavowing any portion of the authorsip of his book substantially in the same form that you had done before, ~~Mrs~~ I would advise Mrs. Grant to pay you that money and I suppose she would do it because it is in accordanc[e] with her views on the subject as published in Col. Grant's statements . . . ." ADf, USG 3. On the same day, Romero wrote to Frederick Grant on the same subject. ALS, *ibid.* On March 27, Romero wrote to Badeau. "Referring to my letter of yesterday about your pending suit with Mrs. Grant, I beg to inform you that in an interview I had this afternoon with Colonel Grant, he told me that he had answered my letter of yesterday's date, saying that Mrs. Grant desired that any proposal to end the suit should be made to her Attorney. I have not received yet Colonel Grant's letter to me, but having to return to Washington in a few moments and not wishing to leave this matter open, I beg of you to consider as ended my intervention in the same." Typed copy, *ibid.* On March 28 and 29, Romero, Washington, D. C., wrote to Frederick Grant on the same subject. ALS, *ibid.* On March 29, Frederick Grant communicated twice with Romero expressing appreciation for his mediation efforts. Copies (in Frederick Grant's hand), Ulysses Grant Dietz, Maplewood, N. J. On April 2 and 7, Romero wrote to Frederick Grant. ". . . I found Badeau great deal more reasonable than I expected it. What I thought Mrs. Grant wanted, was a friend who would be willing to act as mediator between herself and Badeau, and I was willing to act in that capacity. For some time I thought the object I had in view, could be accomplished, and I was willing to return to New York for that purpose. But the statement you made to me in the afternoon of the 27th, to the effect that the only way in which Mrs. Grant could consider this subject, was that Badeau should propose it to her lawyer, left me the impresion that she did not approve of my interference, and under such circumstances I had no alternative but to regret ~~t~~having undertaken something that Mrs. Grant did not like, . . . " ". . . Gen. Badeau is now in Washington and in accordance with your wishes I showed to him your letter to me of March 27th and Mr. C. A. Seward's letter to you of the 28th containing a favorable opinion to the settlement I proposed to Gen. Badeau in my letter of March 26th I did not inform Badeau that you had authorized me to show those letters to him. He asked me copies of them, and I answered him that I could not give them without your permission Please, tell me whether you see any objection in my doing so. Since Mrs. Grant, as you inform me, would to have a settlement under honorable conditions and since your lawyer Mr Seward approves of the plan I suggested, I wold be willing to continue my efforts to arrive to a satisfactory conclusion, but to do this I need to have your views about the form of the receipt I drew in New York and which I understood Gen. Badeau would not object. I enclose to you a clean copy of that receipt, for your examination and submission to your lawyer. Should the form of the receipt be satisfactory please inform me what else would you require from Gen. Badeau before paying the money to him, and whether it is inmaterial to have it signed in this city or in New York, and if in this city, and if in this city whether it should be authenticated by a single notary public or more than one. In my last conversation with Gen. Badeau on this subject in New York, he said that he would sign the receipt if besides the $9750, the interest on that amount was paid to him from the date Mrs. Grant received the first instalment from sales of the book over $30,000, to date of payment. Please give me your views on this other subject. I will be very glad to see you in Washington, and would like very much that you would come to stop with us. If necessary I will go to New York just for the purpose of attending to this matter which I think is of importance to you." ALS, USG 3. On April 9, Frederick Grant wrote twice to Romero. "Your very kind letter of the 7[*th*] is received. I will go immediately to see Mr Seward and hear what h[e] has to say. Please have nothin[g] to do with Badeau until you hear further from me . . . ." "Confidential . . . I called, as promised in todays letter, upon Mr Seward who informs me that Badeau has written to his attorneys, who have been to see him (Seward). This makes it unadvisable for you to proceed further in the matter . . . ." Copies (in Frederick Grant's hand), Ulysses Grant Dietz, Maplewood, N. J. On April 11 and May 21, Romero again wrote to Frederick Grant. " . . . In compliance with your views I shall drop this subject and will dissmiss it from my mind all together. Badeau understands very well that the part I have taken in this case is that of a common friend and entirely independent from any wish or suggestion on your part, and if should ever attempt to misrepresent my position or yours in the case, I shall come out and state the facts as they really are." "I have noticed two articles published in the New York Sun of the 18th and 20th instant stating that you offered to Badeau to pay. $10.000 and that he declined your offer. In neither of those articles is my name mentioned in any manner, and on the contrary in the second it is stated that the offer was made by your *lawyer*. Should any publication be hereafter made in which my name may appear in a manner not warranted by the truth, I would like to see it to make the necessary corrections provided that you think it is proper that I should make such corrections As I do not see all the New York papers, you will oblige me very much if you do me the favor of calling my attention to any future article of that nature." ALS, USG 3.

On April 2, William A. Purrington, New York City, had written to Clarence A. Seward. "Dictated . . . . In General Badeau's reply to Col. Grant, printed in full by the Sun of this morning, Badeau says, about midway in the third paragraph, 'but I insist again and again that I have not claimed the authorship; and there is not, there can never be the slightest evidence to the contrary.' He also reiterates the statement that Mrs. Grant or Col. Grant endeavored to compromise his claim by offering sums varying from fifteen hundred dollars to eight thousand dollars. There has never been as you know so far as the Grants were concerned any objection made to Badeau's claim merely on account of its amount. It is true that they regarded the sum he asked for as exorbitant and preposterous as a measure of his services, but they did not make that an issue. On the contrary Col. Grant distinctly said to Mr. Conkling that if the se[t]tlement were made for a less sum than ten thousand dollars he wished to send afterward the difference between the claim and the amount paid, not because it was due, but as an absolute demonstration of the sincerity of General Grant's family in taking their position of willingness to give Badeau any sum that General Grant had ever contemplated giving him, regardless of whether he had earned it, notwithstanding their unwillingness to give him a penny upon his theory that the book owes its existence in its present form in any way to General Badeau. Col. Grant now wishes to submit to your consideration the question of how far it may be desirable for you to submit to Badeau's attorneys the proposition that Badeau may even now be paid ten thousand dollars upon condition of signing a statement and receipt showing a full admission on his part that the Personal Memoirs are in nowise dependent for their present character, substance or form upon his work. In short that he has done no work upon the book that can in any sen[s]e deprive it of its value as the original composition of General Grant in the fullest sense. Of course such a receipt would have to be carefully phrased, but it seems possible to Col. Grant that a paper might be drawn which would force Badeau into the position of either refusing to disclaim joint authorship or of admitting over his own signature that he did no work at all vital to the existence of the Personal Memoirs in their present shape, and in any event making it still clearer than now, if that be possible, that the question of amount has never been a factor in this controversy so far as Mrs. Grant is concerned. Col. Grant thinks this the more worthy of suggestion for the reason that Badeau, in his letter, states what is in fact true, namely, that Col. Grant's letters to Mr. Alexander and to Messrs. Stanley, Clark and Smith, defining his mother's position, were never communicated to Badeau by Mr. Alexander who considered that he had arranged the matter without sending them. Badeau has perverted this fact so as to make it appear, to a prejudiced mind at all events, that the offer of paying him ten thousand dollars was never fairly brought to his attention. I submit these suggestions to your consideration. Will you kindly have a copy of the answer in this case sent to me?" TLS, OHi. On May 14, Frederick Grant wrote to Seward. "Mr Guthrie of your firm said to me this morning that Messers. Stanley, Clark and Smith, the attorneys of General Badeau, have expressed a desire that a letter should be written on my mother's behalf stating what she was willing to do in the action brought against her by General Badeau in case it should be discontinued. My mother's position is the same today that it was when Genl Badeau first made his claim, and as it has remained ever since. Without waiving any legal right that she has in the premises in case the action should not be discontinued, or admitting that the defences interposed to General Badeau's complaint are not sufficient, my mother is perfectly willing to admit that in a memorandum of my father's upon which this action is based he indicated a desire on his part at the time of making it to pay General Badeau $10.000. for certain considerations therein mentioned. My mother has never made any objection to paying Genl Badeau the money specified in this memorandum, which was the same sum that my father requested her to pay to me for my services, merely on account of its amount. Nor has she ever desired to raise the question, unless compelled to do so by legal proceedings, of whether the consideration of the contract, if it was a contract, has been performed. She has only declined to pay any sum not legally awarded, ~~that~~ the payment of which could be construed into an admission that the services rendered by Genl Badeau upon the book were essential to its existence in its present form and substance, and that without his aid the work would not have existed . . . ." ALS, *ibid.*

On May 15, Purrington wrote to Frederick Grant. "Badeau has discharged Stanley Clarke & Smith and retained new counsel. I had a consultation with Mr Seward to day and suggested that a reference to a good referee was much more desirable than a jury trial. A Jury must find only a verdict of amount—and any sum wd be claimed by Badeau as a victory. A Referee can write a report, and what we want is a record—not sky-rockets. Mr. Seward caught at the idea as excellent, and said he would adopt it if I 'stood by him'. The 'young men' want a jury trial, but I don't think we do—" ALS, USG 3. On May 21, Badeau wrote to his attorney Daniel P. Hays, New York City. "Personal & confidential . . . I have said again and again that I do not claim the authorship of Gen Grants Personal Memoirs. My suit is not based on that ground. The nature of the services which are the subject of the suit are fully set forth in my letter to Gen Grant of May 4. 1885, . . . By this letter I am willing to stand, whether the claim is paid or the suit is tried." ALS, *ibid.*

On May 23, Julia Grant wrote at length to Seward concerning Badeau's suit. "... I have not paid General Badeau, because he has assiduously circulated a claim to joint authorship and has intimated the existænce of some dishonorable secret, which he would keep concealed if I paid him. To give him anything under the circumstances except upon ground of legal liability or the decree of arbitration, would be to assent to his claim of joint authorship and to admit an unwillingness to have the secret exposed. I therefore decline to make him any payment except upon such disclaimers on his part as above indicated. If he will make these disclaimers, I will pay him nine thousand seven hundred and fifty dollars, which, with the sum of two hundred and fifty dollars already paid to him, will make up the amount of ten thousand dollars mentioned in the memorandum he refers to .... I wish to make this restatement of the simple facts in the case, so that they may at any future time be my authoritative enunciation of my own position towards General Badeau, and my own relation, of what services he rendered under my roof. I do this so that if necessity compels such a statement to be made, this can be published. General Grant asked General Badeau to come to Long Branch in the summer of 1884 chiefly for the reason, ~~reason~~ that he had heard that his old Military Secretary was in straightened circumstances, and depressed in spirits because of pending littigation with the Government, on account of which it was understood that the latter's pay as Captain on the retired list had been stopped. It is only justice to General Badeau to say that he was successful eventually, in this littigation. General Grant said to me that the visit to the Seashore would be cheering and servicable to General Badeau. He added that as he was contemplating writing some articles for the Century Magazine, he might make some use of General Badeau's services, and in that way make him feel that he was rendering return for hospitality received, which he thought would be agreeable to the very sensitive nature of the man he was dealing with. General Grant subsequently resolved to write his book, and thinking to make use of General Badeau's services, for the necessary work that would have to be rendered by a secretary, and expecting also, to use ~~his~~ Badeau's maps, discussed the question both with his family and with others. He did not show his memorandum because it was not necessary to do so, and I did not know of its existence until it was revealed by a casual conversation. General Badeau continued under our roof, rendering some services and attending also to his own literary work, the M. S. S. of which he was in the habit of reading aloud, just as he read the M. S. S. of General Grant's aloud for criticism and suggestion. On May 2d, 1885, he gave to General Grant the letter, which my husband felt to be the most cruel blow that he had ever received, coming as it did from the one person whom he had benefited more than any other, and upon whose fidelity he had firmly relied. Immediately thereafter General Badeau left our house. His course towards us since then has been distressingly public, and I have no desire to comment upon it. This much it is proper to say. There is not a person who rendered any service to General Grant during his last illness, whose claims to compensation have not been recognized. There have been those like yourself who with no protestations that ~~that~~ they were working for love, have rendered services of the most valuable nature at the most trying time and have declined even the suggestion of money reward. For yourself, Mr. Conkling, and others whose friendship to my husband has been so well tested, my gratitude is very great. Those who have made claim for pecuniary compensation have received their demands in full, even in instances when I have been legally advised that the claims were improper and uncollectable. General Badeau is the only person who has not been paid, and the reason for his nonpayment I have already stated. It was not because the amount was large. It was not because he cruelly deserted my dying husband in the hour of need. It was because, to have paid him privately would have been to admit his claim to joint authorship and his reiterated statement that there was a secret between himself and General Grant. If he had been paid I am convinced that he would have repeated his claim to authorship, after the witnesses now alive and capable of demonstrating what he did do, were no longer able to confute his statements . . . . I will accept any settlement within the limits indicated that you may suggest, but I desire that the issues of honor and sentiment as well as of money between General Badeau and myself, shall be made very clear and distinct to him, and I therefore beg that you ~~and~~ will communicate to his attorneys, the contents of this letter, so that he may not in any future address to the 'American People' say, as he said of the previous letters, that the contents were not made known to him." LS (in Frederick Grant's hand) and typed copy, OHi; Df (typed), USG 3. On May 24, Seward wrote to Julia Grant reporting his actions in response to her letter and outlining legal difficulties to the achievement of her wishes. LS, *ibid.*

On Sept. 29 and 30, Frederick Grant wrote to Seward. "I have repeated to my mother the substance of our conversation ~~of today~~ upon the Badeau matter . . . . If it be necessary for her to give testimoney in court, in vindication of her husbands memeroy ~~it will be her duty and pleasure to~~ she will cheerfully do so . . . ." "My mother requests me to write to you to day and say that 'Although she does not want to hamper your action in the Badeau ~~ease~~ case in her opinion it would be better to fight ~~the~~ him through the courts than to settle the matter in a private way unless Genl Badeaus gives such a receipt as the one ~~Mr. Conkling wrote out~~' here to fore demanded of him." ADf, *ibid.* On Oct. 1, Purrington wrote to Frederick Grant that Badeau's attorney sought further postponement of the trial. ALS, *ibid.* On Oct. 18, Thursday, Seward wrote to Frederick Grant. "*Badeau v. Grant* . . . . This cause was called this morning, and set down for the first Monday of November . . . ." LS, *ibid.* Other correspondence related to the suit, dated between March 24 and Oct. 26, is *ibid.*

On Oct. 30, Badeau received $11,254.97 from Julia Grant and discontinued his suit. " . . . Said action and my claim being thus settled, I have no objection to repeat what I wrote to General Grant on the 4th day of May, 1885: 'I have no desire, intention or right to claim the authorship of your book. The composition is entirely your own. What assistance I have been able to render has been in suggestion, revision or verification.'" DS, *ibid.* Related legal papers, also dated Oct. 30, are in OHi. Badeau told a reporter. "I have not receded one step from the position I took at the outset. I never claimed the authorship or joint authorship of Gen. Grant's book. No words to that effect have been spoken or written by me. Consequently I have never withdrawn them . . . . I was offered, first of all, $1,500 by Col. Grant in writing; then $5,000 by Mr. Conkling; both before the said suit was brought; next $7,500 by Mr. Conkling; then $8,000; then $10,000; then $9,750, and on Oct. 31 I was paid $11,254, being the entire amount stipulated by Gen. Grant, with interest, and which had never before been offered or admitted by Col. Grant or any of his representatives. Had this not been paid the case would have been tried this week." *New York Times,* Nov. 6, 1888.

On Oct. 31, Frederick Grant wrote to Purrington. "I want to close up my accounts arising from the Badeau controversy, which ~~w~~ has been settled by Mr Seward as you know. Although, you have told me that you have no bill beyond your retainers fees to present, mother and I, in fact all of us, would be glad to remunerate you further for your services and advice in the case; which we have fully appreciated and deemed most important. Therefore, send in any bill you consider just and proper." Copy (in Frederick Grant's hand), Ulysses Grant Dietz, Maplewood, N. J. On Nov. 1, Purrington wrote to Frederick Grant. "I have received your letter asking for my bill in this case—

My services are quite covered by the retainer and I think your mother has had to pay enough on the plaintiff's account. I have written to General Badeau asking him to let me know what I am to remit him for his counsel and advice which if the case had taken the turn we expected would have been of more value to me than all the other consultations in the matter that I have had knowledge of. I will inform you of his answer. as for myself if I were not already fully paid for what I have done, the kind expressions of yr letter wd settle the balance." ALS, USG 3.

To Hamilton Fish

New York City,
February 8th 1885,

MY DEAR GOVERNOR FISH;

In the memoirs which I am engaged upon, I give a hasty sketch of the political phase of the occupation of Texas by Americans in the first instance, of the separation, annexation &c. In giving this part I have only had my own memory and opinion to rely upon. All there will be in the book that might be regarded as political will not require more than a half hour to read. What I want to ask is if you will not review that portion of my book for me, and make such suggestions as may occur to you.

There are some changes which I shall make under any circumstances, but I will defer them until I hear from you.

Very Truly yours
U. S. GRANT

P. S. Fred. can take the papers to your house if you desire it. I would go my self, with great pleasure, but I have to be very careful of my throat this weather.[1]

U. S. G.

ALS, DLC-Hamilton Fish. Hamilton Fish answered USG's letter on February 10, 1885. AE, *ibid.* See *Memoirs*, I, 53–56.

On April 4, Robert Underwood Johnson, associate editor, *Century Magazine*, wrote to Fish, New York City, requesting an article about USG as president. ALS, DLC-Hamilton Fish. For Fish's recollections of USG, see *New York Independent*, XXXVII, 1913 (July 30, 1885), 1–2.

1. On Jan. 27 and Feb. 19 (11:45 P.M.), B. Fordyce Barker, New York City, wrote to Fish. "I write a hasty line to say that I have just seen Dr Douglas who reports that

Genl Grant is doing remarkably well. The tongue and upper part of the mouth, which were the primary seat of his disease are now nearly and give him no trouble, . . . " "I have not had a moments time to write you a line until this late hour—We had our consultation at Genl Grant's this afternoon. The General said that he felt better today thatn he had for two or three weeks before. He had written during the day what would be three pages of print besides two hours of close work, when he was not writing and that he should write two hours more before going to bed. Genl Badeau also said that he had appeared better today than he had for two weeks—The sudden development of rapid progress in the disease of his throat, was evidently due to cold and threatened inflammation of tonsils which had long been the seat of disease, but this had almost entirely subsided today. I am convinced that the constitutional depression was entirely the result of moral causes in connection with the action or rather failure of action on the part of Congress—But of course, he had given no expression to this feeling to any one and he seems to have risen above it today—The gentlemen whom I called in, Drs Markoe and Sands, are not persons who would yield their convictions to any one from policy, but they entirely coincided with Dr Douglas and myself in regard to the gravity of the case, and the impossibility of giving a positive opinion as to its character, or the intensity of its malignancy. But none of us think that there any immediate danger. At the same time we all feel that the future is probably a bad termination" ALS, *ibid.* See letter to Ellen Grant Sartoris, Feb. 16, 1885.

On March 5, Julia K. Fish wrote to Julia Dent Grant. "My husband has found during his illness that the most nourishing food he could take was Green Turtle Soup. He thinks that possibly our dear General might take some, & he sends it, by the bearer— It may require straining for the General's use after it is heated—with a great deal of love . . . " ALS, USG 3.

To Samuel J. Randall

———

[New York City, Feb. 8, 1885]

I have just learned that your committee has left out the appropriation for the pay of General Marcus J. Wright, who has been engaged for some years in furnishing Confederate reports, dispatches, returns of troops &c. &c. for the rebellion record, which is now being published by the War Department. I hope this omission may be corrected. These records furnish most of the data for future histories written about the War of the Rebellion. General Wright has no doubt furnished more of the material from the Southern side than all other persons combined, leaving out those captured by the Army, and others purchased by Congress . . . I think his services will be valuable for some years yet if he is retained.

Charles Hamilton Auction, No. 41, April 23, 1970, no. 93; The 19th Century Shop, Catalogue 6, no. 73. A prominent Pa. Democrat, Samuel J. Randall entered the U.S. House of Representatives (1863), served as speaker (1875–81), and became chairman, Committee on Appropriations (1883). Legislation for the *O.R.* included $2,000 for one agent, presumably Marcus J. Wright. See *U.S. Statutes at Large*, XXIII, 412; letter to Marcus J. Wright, Nov. 4, 1884.

To George W. Dent

New York City,
February 16th 1885.

My Dear Mr. Dent;

Your letter of the 7th instant is just this moment received. I can not help you either by asking Mr. Cleveland to retain you in your present place, nor by asking Mr. Conkling to write a letter for you. I can not ask because I have held the same office Mr. Cleveland has been elected to, by the votes of the party which opposed him. I can not ask Mr. Conkling because I know he has not ~~nor will~~ taken any part in politics since he left the senate, and will not recommend any one for office. He would probably do more for me than for any one else, and would hate to decline a request I might make. But this would be one that he would decline.

My advice to you is ~~th~~ to get such recommendations for retention as you can from democrats in the state and forward that. If you can not get such a recommendation then I would recommend that you write to the incoming Secretary of the Treasury saying how long you had held your present office; how important it is that the office should be filled by a competant person, and referring him to the merchants and business men of the City, irrespective of party, as to your performance of the duty of your office. Come to think of it, I would suggest that you get, if you can, the recommendation of the men who transact business through your office, without regard to their politics.

I have been a great sufferer for the last fourteen months, and particularly so for the last four. I have had a sore throat for eight months, and neglected it until it became almost cronic. I now have to be treated twice a day, and it has only been within the last ten days that the attending physician has been willing to say that it is yealding to treatment. The balance of the family are all well.

With the active life I have lead it would be a terrible trial for me to remain in the house month in and month out, while able to be up, if I had nothing to do. But I wrote ~~three~~ four articles last summer for the Century Magazine (but one of them has appeared yet) which ~~occupied~~ filled up my time so pleasantly, that I concluded to continue the work and write my life to the close of the rebellion. If I could have four weeks of sufficient strength to devote six hours a day to writing I could have the whole of it written, and in as much more time I could make the corrections and Fred could have it all copied. Fred is of great service to me in my present labors. He does all the copying, and saves me much time by looking up referrences.

With kind regards of all the family to you and yours, I am,

Very Truly

U. S. GRANT

ALS, Charles Murray, Rose, Calif. Thomas Beck replaced George W. Dent as appraiser of merchandise, San Francisco, and found evidence of poor management. See Beck to Grover Cleveland, July 26, 1885, DLC-Grover Cleveland. For USG's nomination of his brother-in-law in 1870, see *PUSG*, 20, 139–40.

To Matías Romero

New York City,
February 16th 1885.

MY DEAR MR. ROMERO:

I received your letter announcing your return to Washington in due time. I was very glad to hear that President Diaz had asked you to continue in Washington as the representative of your government, though I did not doubt but he would do so. I hope you will be continued there for many years.

I have been a great sufferer since we met last, and continue to be yet, though I feel now that I am at last improving. You may remember that when you was at Long Branch last summer[1] I was complaining of a sore throat? I thought nothing of it at the time, and did not consult a physician about it until about a month after my return to theis city. It had then run, without care, some four months. When the doctor was seen he decided that my sore throat resulted from my system being nichotinized. I have given up smoking entirely for the last three months and feel that I am now about free of nichotine, though not of its effect.

Mrs. Grant desires to be remembered to you and Mrs. Romero.

Very Truly yours
U. S. GRANT

ALS (facsimile), DLC-Matías Romero. On Dec. 29, 1884, Matías Romero, Mexico City, wrote to USG. "I arrived here on the 26th ultimo and had my resignation accepted by President Gonzalez on the 30th—President Diaz said to me that he desired me to go back to Washington, but I postponed my answer until the arrival of Mr. Mariscal whom as you know has been appointed Secretary of Foreign Afairs. It is possible therefore that I may return to Washington. I have seen some general letters from you, to your friends in Mexico, reccommending some Gentlemen, and I have done what I could for them. Mr Work sent to me finally the deed of sale of Anton Lizardo in my name, and I have some small difficulties to accept it. He also sent to me a mortgage deed of Anton Lizardo for $25.000, in favor of Mr. Edward Washburn. which has been registered and returned to him. With my best regards for Mrs. Grant, . . . " ALS, USG 3. On Jan. 24, 1885, a correspondent reported from Mexico City, via Galveston. "Señor Romero, who recently resigned from the Washington mission, has been reappointed and will start for his post next week." *New York Times*, Jan. 26, 1885.

On March 2 and 26, Frederick Dent Grant, New York City, wrote to Romero. "Father says he would be glad to see you at any time you come. Father is very ill. My regards to Mrs Romero" "Some two or three weeks ago I wrote to you saying that Father would be glad to see you at any time you might come. Fearing you had not received the letter I write again. This morning Father spoke of you and said he would like to see you. My family join in sending regards to you and Mrs Romero" ALS (facsimile), DLC-Matías Romero. Beginning on March 26, Romero visited USG several times. See *New York Tribune*, March 27–29, 31, April 3, 5, 1885.

On May 25, Romero, Washington, D. C., wrote to Frederick Grant. "The town at the foot of the Popocatepetl after Ameca Ameca of which the General speaks in his book is (Otzumba) Ozumba I called this morning to the Hydrographic oOffice of the War Department, and asked Commande Bartlett, to loan me a copy of the last Charte of Mexico, which I sent th to that office a few days ago, and which is the best map of Mexico, stating that I desired it for the General's use. Commander Bartlett promised me to have it send directly to the General's. I hope you will receive it in time to use it for the purposes you desire it." ALS, USG 3. On May 24, Romero had visited USG. *New York Tribune*, May 25, 1885. On May 26, Romero wrote to USG. "I enclose to you, the translation you desired of Mrs. Mata's letter to you I could not make it myself and I am afraid the English is not very good, but I hope you will be able to understand it. I think I ought to say to you that I do not think you are correct when you say in you book that we consider in Mexico that we beat the United States in the war of 1846–1848. Everybody knows in Mexico, of course that we were defeated. If you celebrate the aniversary of two of those battles of that war, Churubusco and Molino del Rey, it is because we thought that our soldiers showed courage and patriotism in both and we like to honor the memory of our fallen compatriots in those battles. I make this remark because I do like that your book should have no inaccuracies" ALS, USG 3. On May 29, Frederick Grant wrote to Romero. "Your letter received I have inserted the name of the village 'Ogumba' in its proper place. I have also change the paragraph about the celebration of the battles of Mexico so as to coresponde with the statement in your letter. Father thanks you very much for having the letter translated for him Father was weighed to day and finds that he has lost four pounds, this is bad. Please present our regards to Mrs Romero and as for yourself be assured of the love and respect of your friend" ALS (facsimile), DLC-Matías Romero.

1. On Aug. 16, 1884, a correspondent had reported from Long Branch. "George W. Childs, of the Philadelphia *Ledger*, gave a dinner at his cottage this evening to the Hon. John Welch, ex-Minister to England. Gen. U. S. Grant, Gen. Romero, the Mexican Minister, and others were present. Gen. Romero and his family are guests of Gen. Grant." *New York Times*, Aug. 17, 1884.

To Ellen Grant Sartoris

February 16th 1885.

DEAR NELLIE:

Your letter of the 2d of February, to your mother, come two or three days ago. Algy arrived a few days before and come up and stayed with us until after dinner. All the family are well except me. The sore throat which you recollect I had all the time we were at Long Branch last summer has proven to be a very serious matter. I paid no attention to it until it had run four months. I found then the doctor considered it a very serious matter. Even now I have to see him twice a day. It has troubled me so much to swallow that I have fallen off nearly thirty pounds. It has only been within the last ten days that the doctor has been willing to say that the ulcers in my throat are begining to yeald to treetment. It will be a long time yet before I can possibly recover.

It would be very hard for me to be confined to the house so long a time if it was not that I have become interested in the work which

I have undertaken. It will take several months yet to complete the history of my campaigns. The indications now are that the book will be in two volumes of about four hundred and fifty pages each. I give a condensed biography of my life up to the breaking out of the rebellion. If you ever take the time to read it you will find out what sort of a boy and man I was before you knew me. I do not know whether my book will be interesting to other people or not; but all the publishers want to get it, and I have had larger offers than have ever been made for a book before. Fred. helps me greatly in my work. He does all the copying, and looks up referrences for me.

We have all been as happy as could be expected considering our great losses and my personal suffering. Philosophers profess to believe that what is is for the best. I hope it may prove so with our family.

All join me in sending love and kisses to you and all the children.

Your affectionate Papa

AL, ICHi.

On Feb. 19, George R. Elliott, New York City, wrote to John H. Douglas. "I have the honor to submit to you the following microscopical report as a result of my examination of the small piece of tissue removed by Dr. Riley at your suggestion for diagnostic purposes, from the throat of your distinguished patient Ex President Grant in your office on the morning of Feb'y. 18, 1885 . . ." Copy, USG 3. Elliott endorsed this letter. "The following is a copy of my original report rendered to Dr. Douglas." AES (undated), *ibid.* Also on Feb. 19, physicians Douglas, B. Fordyce Barker, Henry B. Sands, and Thomas M. Markoe agreed that USG suffered from cancer. See *New York Times,* March 1, 1885; Elliott, "The Microscopical Examination of Specimens Removed from General Grant's Throat," *The Medical Record,* XXVII (March 14, 1885), 289–90.

On Feb. 28, Julia Dent Grant wrote to Anna R. Hillyer. "We were very glad to hear from you my dear Mrs Hillyer We so often think of & speak of you & the old days. Dear Willie we are so so sorry to hear of his illness—I remember perfectly his fall at The Geyosa house & how frightened you were & dear Genl Hillyer as well. I hope dear Mrs Hillyer th[at] Willie improove with the coming spring—Genl Grants health is our absorbing though[t.] Genl Grant is very very ill I cannot write how ill My tears blind me . . . remember The Genl & myself with love to your family" ALS, IHi. William S. Hillyer, Jr., died at East Orange, N. J., on March 8. See *PUSG,* 25, 204–5.

On March 1, Julia C. Conkling, Utica, N. Y., wrote to Julia Grant. "The newspapers bring such alarming accounts of the General, that I am impelled to write you tho' with the misgiving that it is hardly true friendship to intrude oneself at a time of great anxiety— . . ." ALS, USG 3. Julia Grant received similar letters dated Jan. 12 from Elizabeth D. Kane, Philadelphia; dated Jan. 13 from Harriet S. Marot, Dayton;

dated March 1 from Elizabeth Stuart Phelps, Andover, Mass., dated March 2 from R. H. Davis, Jackson, Mich., Anna E. Webb, New York City; dated March 3 from Clara Bliss Hinds, Washington, D. C.; dated March 4 from Harris C. Fahnestock, New York City; dated March 8 from Jessie Benton Frémont, New Brighton, N. Y.; dated March 10 from John McDuffie, Albany, N. Y., Wesley Prettyman, Russellville, Ind.; dated March 16 from Josephine Macfeely, Washington, D. C. *Ibid.*

Memorandum

[*Feb., 1885*]

I have made up my mind that I prefer Webster & Co. to publish my book. The insentive for writing has been money which circumstances has made so essentia[l] at this time.

I believe the above company can sell a greater number than the Century. They have no other business which this will come in competition with. The Century will have two hundred pages of my book in their series. This latter it is true will be changed somewhat from the Century articles.

Webster offers better terms. An additional advantage he offers, and a very great one to, is the opportunity afforded of placing one of my sons in business[1]

AD, Mrs. Paul E. Ruestow, Jacksonville, Fla. On Feb. 3, 1885, Charles L. Webster & Co. wrote to USG. "Mr. Gilder informs [us] that over 200,000 copies of the Century containing your article have been sold while their usual circulation is but 135,000 copies. This in a measure indicates that public interest in the history of the civil war is active, and that your forthcoming book will meet with a large sale. We had no doubt of this ourselves, but with this evidence we are additionally fortified. In view of this fact, we are justified in supplementing our last offer of $50,000.00 and a royalty with an alternative offer which you may consider as more advantageous to you. We certainly wish you to reap every advantage possible from the new book. Mr. Clemens acquaintance with you is a guarantee of this, and while we of course cannot afford to publish the book without some profit to ourselves still we are willing to give you the larger share of the profits. In view of the above, and without in any way withdrawing our former offer, we beg to submit for your consideration the following alternative proposition: I. We will furnish all the capital necessary to publish the book and put it on the market, advertising it thoroughly so as to give it the largest sale possible through general agents with customary discounts allowed upon our publications. 2nd. Out of the proceeds of the sales as above we will first pay the cost of the book, which cost shall consist of the items of drawings, plates, paper, printing, binding, advertising, insurance, packing and sample books, no charge being made against cost for clerk hire or office rent. 3rd. The remainder of the proceeds and sales after deducting the above items shall be considered the net profits. 4th. We are to pay to you at stated intervals seventy per cent (70) of the above net profits and retain thirty per cent of the same as our share. 5. Should you so desire you may through Col. Fred. Grant or other person nominated by you and acceptable to us, have a personal insight in our business by appointing such person your representative in our office where a desk will be provided for him, and upon such appointment such representative shall have every privilege of investigation which he would be entitled to were he a member of the firm." Typed copy, CU-B. On Feb. 9, Frederick Dent Grant, New York City, wrote to Charles L. Webster. "Your letter of the 3rd was received the same date. Father read it and was much pleased with your offer. The first thing he wanted to do was to have Mr. G. W. Childs of Phila., to see it. Mr. C did not come until until two or three days after & advised him on the the subject. I have been intending to call and see you ever since, but have not had an opportunity yet. I will be down to see you in a day or two . . . . P. S. I have read Mark Twain's new book at nights, and kept at it as long as long as my candle would last each night until I finished it, and like Huck Finn and Tom Sawyer. Have lost much sleep, but had more fun . . . . Please let me know when Mr. Clemens will be in town." Typed copy, *ibid.* [Webster] added an endorsement, presumably to Samuel L. Clemens, on Frederick Grant's reference to *The Adventures of Huckleberry Finn.* "I sent the General an advance copy as I thought that would help matters when he saw how nicely it was gotten up." E (undated), *ibid.* On Feb. 10, Webster wrote to Frederick Grant. "Yours of the 9th is received. I will be very happy to see you at my office at any time. As I am liable to be absent occasionally, will you not kindly intimate a few hours in advance when it will be most convenient for you to call. I am glad you are pleased with the new book. Mr. Clemens will not be here until Feb'y 21st." Typed copy, *ibid.* On Feb. 27, USG and Charles L. Webster & Co. contracted to publish the *Memoirs.* Typed copy, USGA. On March 14, USG wrote to Charles L. Webster & Co. "I hereby request you to take all proper measures for secuing the copyright in my name to my forthcoming book to be published by you and to file the title page attached to this paper with the L[i]brarian of Congress at Washington," Typed copy, *ibid.* See Frederick Anderson, ed., *Mark Twain's Notebooks & Journals* (Berkeley, 1975–79), III, 96–97, 182; *Mark Twain's Autobiography* (New York, 1924), I, 38–42.

Earlier in March, a newspaper had reported on "THE GENERAL'S LITERARY WORK . . . . Many curious and anxious eyes ran over the columns of *The Century* for March expecting to find therein another paper from the pen of General Grant. The impression had gone forth that the article on Shiloh which appeared in the February number was the first of a series that were to be published regularly every month and when the March number was issued without containing the expected paper speculation was rife as to its cause. Some attributed the omission to the General's ill health; others to the fact that he was more anxious that his more important memoirs should be first completed; but it was left for *The World* to discover the fact that there had been a 'falling out' between the publishers of *The Century* and General Grant and that it was not likely that any more of his papers would be published in the magazine. The cause of the falling-out was said to be that General Grant had taken the publication of his memoirs away from *The Century* and had entered into a contract for their publication by Charles L. Webster & Co., because *The Century* could not find a place for Jesse Grant in any of its departments. The facts are that General Grant stipulated some time ago to write for *The Century* four papers on the War, and the following subjects were selected: Shiloh, Vicksburg, Chattanooga, and the Wilderness Campaign. As soon as the terms were agreed upon the General entered upon his literary work with characteristic energy, working frequently from eight to ten hour a day; and though he was hampered by the insidious disease that is now sapping his vitality, only a comparatively short interval elapsed from the time he began his labors when the papers on Shiloh, Vicksburg and Chattanooga were completed and handed over to *The Century.* They were paid for in accordance with the agreement, and are now in the possession of *The Century.* The manuscript for 'The Wilderness Campaign' is completed and is now being revised by the General as rapidly as his health and other duties will permit. There has been no falling-out between General Grant and *The Century*, and their relations are in every way cordial and pleasant. *The Century* Publishing Company entered into competition for the publication of General Grant's books and its failure to obtain the contract was simply a business incident, the General being better satisfied with the arrangements made with Webster & Co. In the negotiation for the publication of the book the question of giving his son a position was not a matter of consideration. The contract between Webster & Co. and General Grant was signed on February 28, and it is denied at the publishers' office that taking Jesse Grant into partnership, as *The World* alleged, had anything to do with awarding them the contract, for the reason that such an arrangement has not been made. Samuel L. Clemens (Mark Twain) is a silent partner in the firm of Webster & Co., but entrusts the management of the business to his nephew, Charles L. Webster, who conducted all the negotiations with General Grant. The book is to be complete in two volumes. The manuscript for the first is completed and will be delivered to Mr. Webster, the latter part of this week. The General is working as much as possible on the materials for the seecond volume, which is also nearly finished, the principal labor now being that of revision. The book will be sold by subscription, and the price will probably be $3 50 a volume. It is expected that the two volumes will be ready for delivery in October or November." *New York Tribune,* March 10, 1885. See *New York World,* March 9, 1885; Anderson, ed., *Twain's Notebooks & Journals,* III, 101, 110, 134.

On March 2, A. D. Worthington & Co. wrote to USG. "We sincerely hope that you will not regard this letter as an unwarranted intrusion during your illness. We simply write to say that according to newspaper reports you contemplate writing, or indeed have nearly completed, a book. You will remember our former correspondence about the matter, and we would respectfully ask whether it is true that you have a book in course of preparation and if so whether its publication is provided for, and if not whether we may be permitted to see you about it at a suitable time. If we had not already corresponded with you about the matter we should not think of now addressing you during your illness. We will only say that if the book is not arranged for & you are willing to confer with us about it we can make it for your interest, we think, to place it in our hands, and we shall be glad of an opportunity to consult with you about it. With sincere wishes for your speedy restoration to perfect health, . . . " L, USG 3. On March 4, Frederick Grant wrote to A. D. Worthington & Co. "Genl Grants book will be published by Chas. L. Webster & co" ALS, *ibid.* See letter to Alfred D. Worthington, June 10, 1884.

1. On March 12, Jesse Root Grant, Jr., New York City, wrote to Clemens, Hartford. "I am anxious to see you on a little business—and would like to know of your future movements: Will you be in N. Y. in the next few days?—Are you too much interested in what you are now doing to be willing to be bored by me should I come to Hartford? . . . Answer at Union League Club." ALS (on letterhead of Charles L. Webster & Co.), CU-B. In a letter dated "Saturday," Clemens, Elmira, N. Y., wrote to Jesse Grant. "I got back

last night, & am detained here for the present, but shall reach New York Wednesday or Thursday evening to ask some questions & get some information—further information, for the satisfying of hard-headed business men—& then I shall hope to see you." ALS, Nellie C. Rothwell, La Jolla, Calif. On July 4 and 18, Jesse Grant, Mount McGregor, N. Y., wrote to Clemens. "I had intended writing you a general idea of my plan but since we will meet in New York so soon I will defer the description till then. I feel that you will enter into the Turkish Railway with the same enthusiasm that I have felt. According to your telegram I will await here farther news from you when I will join you." "I see from the papers that Sir E. Thornton is to be English minister to Constantinople—I know him well—and am glad he will be there. I saw Lew Wallace and he thinks it sensible for me to go—he says the Sultan is anxious for the road to be builts and that his cabinet are are the ones who object. I am only waiting now for Stanfords letter and will get one from father probably today or tomorrow. If father thinks well of it—I will start on Aug 1st on or there abouts. I have not seen the paper Webster was to prepare—he says he sent it to you. or rather that he wrote to you about it." ALS, CU-B. On July 2, 1884, Frederick Grant, Long Branch, had written to Lewis Wallace. "Since writing you the other day I have seen my father & mother and they told me that they would be pleased to have you spend a few days with them should you be near New York I wish to see you some time before you go back to Turkey & could you spend a few days here we could talk over this business while you were here" ALS, InHi. The business involved prospects for constructing a railroad from Constantinople to the Persian Gulf. See Anderson, ed., *Twain's Notebooks & Journals*, III, 165, 170, 202; Leland Stanford to Jesse Root Grant, Jr., March 31, 1885, CU-B.

Article

THE BATTLE OF SHILOH.[1]
[Feb., 1885]

THE battle of Shiloh, fought on Sunday and Monday, the 6th and 7th of April, 1862, is perhaps less understood, or, to state the case more accurately, more persistently misunderstood, than any other engagement between National and so-called Confederate troops during the entire rebellion. Correct reports of the battle have been published, notably by Sherman,[2] Badeau,[3] and, in a speech before a meeting of veterans, by General Prentiss;[4] but all of these appeared long subsequent to the close of the rebellion, and after public opinion had been most erroneously formed.

Events had occurred before the battle, and others subsequent to it, which determined me to make no report to my then chief, General Halleck, further than was contained in a letter, written immediately after the battle, informing him that an engagement had been fought, and announcing the result.[5] The occurrences alluded to are these: after the capture of Fort Donelson, with over fifteen thousand effective men and all their munitions of war, I believed much more could be accomplished without further sacrifice of life. Clarksville, a town between Donelson and Nashville, in the State of Tennessee, and on the east bank of the Cumberland, was garrisoned by the enemy. Nashville was also garrisoned, and was probably the best provisioned depot at the time in the Confederacy. Albert Sidney Johnston occupied Bowling Green, Kentucky, with a large force. I believed, and my information justified the belief, that these places would fall into our hands without a battle, if threatened promptly. I determined not to miss this chance. But being only a district commander, and under the immediate orders of the department commander, General Halleck, whose headquarters were at St. Louis, it was my duty to communicate to him all I proposed to do, and to get his approval, if possible. I did so communicate, and receiving no reply, acted upon my own judgment.[6] The result proved that my information was correct, and sustained my judgment. What, then, was my surprise, after so much had been accomplished by the troops under my immediate command, between the time of leaving Cairo, early in February, and the 4th of March, to receive from my chief a dispatch of the latter date, saying: "You will place Major-General C. F. Smith in command of expedition, and remain yourself at Fort Henry. Why do you not obey my orders to report strength and position of your command?" I was left virtually in arrest on board a steamer, without even a guard, for about a week, when I was released and ordered to resume my command.[7]

Again: Shortly after the battle of Shiloh had been fought, General Halleck moved his headquarters to Pittsburg Landing, and assumed command of the troops in the field. Although next to him in rank, and nominally in command of my old district and army, I was ignored as much as if I had been at the most distant point of territory within my jurisdiction; and although I was in command of all the troops engaged at Shiloh, I was not permitted to see one of the reports of General Buell or his subordinates in that battle, until they were published by the War Department, long after the event. In consequence, I never myself made a full report of this engagement.[8]

WHEN I was restored to my command, on the 13th of March, I found it on the Tennessee River, part at Savanna and part at Pittsburg Landing, nine miles above, and on the opposite or western bank. I generally spent the day at Pittsburg, and returned by boat to Savanna in the evening. I was intending to remove my headquarters to Pittsburg, where I had sent all the troops immediately on my reassuming command; but Buell, with the Army of the Ohio, had been ordered to reenforce me from Columbia, Tennessee. He was expected daily, and would come in at Savanna. I remained, therefore, a few days longer than I otherwise should have done, for the purpose of meeting him on his arrival.

General Lew Wallace, with a division, had been placed by General Smith at Crump's Landing, about five miles farther down the river than Pittsburg, and also on the west bank. His position I regarded as so well chosen that he was not moved from it until the Confederate attack in force at Shiloh.

The skirmishing in our front had been so continuous from about the 3d of April up to the determined attack, that I remained on the field each night until an hour when I felt there would be no further danger before morning. In fact, on Friday, the 4th, I was very much injured by my horse falling with me and on me while I was trying to get to the front, where firing had been heard. The night was one of impenetrable darkness, with rain pouring down in torrents; nothing was visible to the eye except as revealed by the frequent flashes of lightning. Under these circumstances I had to trust to the horse, without guidance, to keep the road. I had not gone far, however, when I met General W. H. L. Wallace and General (then Colonel) McPherson coming from the direction of the front. They said all was quiet so far as the enemy was concerned. On the way back to the boat my horse's feet slipped from under him, and he fell with my leg under his body. The extreme softness of the ground, from the excessive rains of the few preceding days, no doubt saved me from a severe injury and protracted lameness.

As it was, my ankle was very much injured; so much so, that my boot had to be cut off. During the battle, and for two or three days after, I was unable to walk except with crutches.

On the 5th General Nelson, with a division of Buell's army, arrived at Savanna, and I ordered him to move up the east bank of the river, to be in a position where he could be ferried over to Crump's Landing or Pittsburg Landing, as occasion required. I had learned that General Buell himself would be at Savanna the next day, and desired to meet me on his arrival. Affairs at Pittsburg Landing had been such for several days that I did not want to be away during the day. I determined, therefore, to take a very early breakfast and ride out to meet Buell, and thus save time. He had arrived on the evening of the 5th, but had not advised me of the fact, and I was not aware of it until some time after. While I was at breakfast, however, heavy firing was heard in the direction of Pittsburg Landing, and I hastened there, sending a hurried note to Buell, informing him of the reason why I could not meet him at Savanna.[9] On the way up the river I directed the dispatch-boat to run in close to Crump's Landing, so that I could communicate with General Lew Wallace. I found him waiting on a boat, apparently expecting to see me, and I directed him to get his troops in line ready to execute any orders he might receive. He replied that his troops were already under arms and prepared to move.

Up to that time I had felt by no means certain that Crump's Landing might not be the point of attack. On reaching the front, however, about 8 A. M., I found that the attack on Shiloh was unmistakable, and that nothing more than a small guard, to protect our transports and stores at Crump's was needed. Captain Baxter, a quartermaster on my staff, was accordingly directed to go back and order General Wallace to march immediately to Pittsburg, by the road nearest the river. Captain Baxter made a memorandum of his order. About 1 P. M., not hearing from Wallace, and being much in need of reënforcements, I sent two more of my staff, Colonel McPherson and Captain Rowley, to bring him up with his division. They reported finding him marching toward Purdy, Bethel, or some point west from the river, and farther from Pittsburg by several miles than when he started. I never could see, and do not now see, why any order was necessary further than to direct him to come to Pittsburg Landing, without specifying by what route. The road was direct, and near the river. Between the two points a bridge had been built across Snake Creek by our troops, at which Wallace's command had assisted, expressly to enable the troops at the two places to support each other in case of need. Wallace did not arrive in time to take part in the first day's fight. General Wallace has since claimed that the order delivered to him by Captain Baxter was simply to join the right of the army, and that the road over which he marched would have taken him to the road from Pittsburg to Purdy, where it crosses Owl Creek, on the right of Sherman; but this is not where I had ordered him nor where I wanted him to go. Even if he were correct as to the wording of the order, it was still a very unmilitary proceeding to join the right of the army from the flank instead of from the base. His was one of three veteran divisions that had been in battle, and its absence was severely felt. Later in the war, General Wallace would never have made the mistake that he committed on the 6th of April, 1862. I presume his idea was that by taking the route he did, he would be able to come around on the flank or rear of the enemy, and thus perform an act of heroism that would redound to the credit of his command, as well as to the benefit of his country.[10]

Shiloh was a log meeting-house, some two or three miles from Pittsburg Landing, and on the ridge which divides the waters of Snake and Lick creeks, the former emptying into the Tennessee just north of Pittsburg Landing, and the latter south. Shiloh was the key to our position, and was held by Sherman. His division was at that time wholly raw, no part of it ever having been in an engagement; but I thought this deficiency was more than made up by the superiority of the commander. McClernand was on Sherman's left, with troops that had been engaged at Forts Henry and Donelson, and were therefore veterans so far as Western troops had become such at that stage of the war. Next to McClernand came Prentiss, with a raw division, and on the extreme left, Stuart, with one brigade of Sherman's division. Hurlbut was in rear of Prentiss, massed, and in reserve at the time of the onset. The division of General C. F. Smith was on the right, and in reserve. General Smith was sick in bed at Savanna, some nine miles below, but in hearing of our guns. His services on those two eventful days would no doubt have been of inestimable value had his health permitted his presence. The command of his division devolved upon Brigadier-General W. H. L. Wallace, a most estimable and able officer,—a veteran, too, for he had served a year in the Mexican war, and had been with his command at Henry and Donelson. Wallace was mortally wounded in the first day's engagement, and with the change of commanders[11] thus necessarily effected in the heat of battle, the efficiency of his division was much weakened.

The position of our troops, as here described, made a continuous line from Lick Creek, on the left, to Owl Creek, a branch of Snake Creek, on the right, facing nearly south, and possibly a little west. The water in all these streams was very high at the time, and contributed to protect our flanks. The enemy was compelled, therefore, to attack directly in front. This he did with great vigor, inflicting heavy losses on the Federal side, but suffering much heavier on his own.

The Confederate assaults were made with such disregard of losses on their own side, that our line of tents soon fell into their hands. The ground on which the battle was fought was undulating, heavily timbered, with scattered clearings, the woods giving some protection to the troops on both sides. There was also considerable underbrush. A number of attempts were made by the enemy to turn our right flank, where Sherman was posted, but every effort was repulsed with heavy loss. But the front attack was kept up so vigorously that, to prevent the success of these attempts to get on our flanks, the Federal troops were compelled several times to take positions to the rear, nearer Pittsburg Landing. When the firing ceased at night, the Federal line was more than a mile in rear of the position it had occupied in the morning.

In one of the backward moves, on the 6th, the division commanded by General Prentiss did not fall back with the others. This left his flanks exposed, which enabled the enemy to capture him, with about 2200 of his officers and men. General Badeau gives four o'clock of the 6th as about the time this capture took place.[12] He may be right as to the time, but my recollection is that the hour was later. General Prentiss himself gave the hour as 5:30.[13] I was with him, as I was with each of the division commanders that day, several times, and my recollection is that the last time I was with him was about half-past four, when his division was standing up firmly, and the general was as cool as if he had been expecting victory. But no matter whether it was four or later, the story that he and his command were surprised and captured in their camps is without any foundation whatever. If it had been true, as currently reported at the time, and yet believed by thousands of people, that Prentiss and his division had been captured in their beds, there would not have been an all-day struggle, with the loss of thousands killed and wounded on the Confederate side.

With this single exception, for a few minutes, after the capture of Prentiss, a continuous and unbroken line was maintained all day from Snake Creek or its tributaries on the right to Lick Creek or the Tennessee on the left, above Pittsburg. There was no hour during the day when there was not heavy firing and generally hard fighting at some point on the line, but seldom at all points at the same time. It was a case of Southern dash against Northern pluck and endurance.

Three of the five divisions engaged the first day at Shiloh were entirely raw, and many of them had only received their arms on the way from their States to the field. Many of them had arrived but a day or two before, and were hardly able to load their muskets according to the manual. Their officers were equally ignorant of their duties. Under these circumstances, it is not astonishing that many of the regiments broke at the first fire. In two cases, as I now remember, the colonels led their regiments from the field on first hearing the whistle of the enemy's bullets. In these cases the colonels were constitutional cowards, unfit for any military position.[14] But not so the officers and men led out of danger by them. Better troops never went upon a battle-field than many of these officers and men afterward proved themselves to be, who fled, panic-stricken, at the first whistle of bullets and shell at Shiloh.

During the whole of the first day I was continuously engaged in passing from one part of the field to another, giving directions to division commanders. In thus moving along the line, however, I never deemed it important to stay long with Sherman. Although his troops were then under fire for the first time, their commander, by his constant presence with them, inspired a confidence in officers and men that enabled them to render services on that bloody battle-field worthy of the best of veterans. McClernand was next to Sherman, and the hardest fighting was in front of these two divisions. McClernand told me himself on that day, the 6th, that he profited much by having so able a commander supporting him. A casualty to Sherman that would have taken him from the field that day would have been a sad one for the troops engaged at Shiloh. And how near we came to this! On the 6th Sherman was shot twice, once in the hand, once in the shoulder, the ball cutting his coat and making a slight wound, and a third ball passed through his hat. In addition to this he had several horses shot during the day.[15]

The nature of this battle was such that cavalry could not be used in front; I therefore formed ours into line, in rear, to stop stragglers, of whom there were many. When there would be enough of them to make a show, and after they had recovered from their fright, they would be sent to reënforce some part of the line which needed support, without regard to their companies, regiments, or brigades.

On one occasion during the day, I rode back as far as the river and met General Buell, who had just arrived; I do not remember the hour of the day, but at that time there probably were as many as four or five thousand stragglers lying under cover of the river bluff, panic-stricken, most of whom would have been shot where they lay, without resistance, before they would have taken muskets and marched to the front to protect themselves. The meeting between General Buell and myself was on the dispatch-boat used to run between the landing and Savanna. It was but brief, and related specially to his getting his troops over the river. As we left the boat together, Buell's attention was attracted by the men lying under cover of the river bank. I saw him berating them and try-

ing to shame them into joining their regiments. He even threatened them with shells from the gun-boats near by. But it was all
to no effect. Most of these men afterward proved themselves as
gallant as any of those who saved the battle from which they had
deserted. I have no doubt that this sight impressed General Buell
with the idea that a line of retreat would be a good thing just then.
If he had come in by the front instead of through the stragglers in
the rear, he would have thought and felt differently. Could he have
come through the Confederate rear, he would have witnessed there
a scene similar to that at our own. The distant rear of an army engaged in battle is not the best place from which to judge correctly
what is going on in front. In fact, later in the war, while occupying
the country between the Tennessee and the Mississippi, I learned
that the panic in the Confederate lines had not differed much from
that within our own. Some of the country people estimated the
stragglers from Johnston's army as high as 20,000. Of course, this
was an exaggeration.

The situation at the close of the first day was as follows: Extending from the top of the bluff just south of the log-house which
stood at Pittsburg Landing, Colonel J. D. Webster, of my staff, had
arranged twenty or more pieces of artillery facing south, or up the
river. This line of artillery was on the crest of a hill overlooking a
deep ravine opening into the Tennessee. Hurlbut, with his division
intact, was on the right of this artillery, extending west and possibly a little north. McClernand came next in the general line, looking more to the west. His division was complete in its organization
and ready for any duty. Sherman came next, his right extending
to Snake Creek. His command, like the other two, was complete
in its organization and ready, like its chief, for any service it might
be called upon to render. All three divisions were, as a matter of
course, more or less shattered and depleted in numbers from the
terrible battle of the day. The division of W. H. L. Wallace, as
much from the disorder arising from changes of division and brigade commanders, under heavy fire, as from any other cause, had
lost its organization, and did not occupy a place in the line as a
division. Prentiss's command was gone as a division, many of its

members having been killed, wounded, or captured. But it had rendered valiant service before its final dispersal, and had contributed a good share to the defense of Shiloh.

There was, I have said, a deep ravine in front of our left. The Tennessee River was very high at that time, and there was water to a considerable depth in the ravine. Here the enemy made a last desperate effort to turn our flank, but were repelled. The gunboats *Tyler* and *Lexington,* Gwin and Shirk commanding, with the artillery under Webster, aided the army and effectually checked their further progress. Before any of Buell's troops had reached the west bank of the Tennessee, firing had almost entirely ceased; anything like an attempt on the part of the enemy to advance had absolutely ceased. There was some artillery firing from an unseen enemy, some of his shells passing beyond us; but I do not remember that there was the whistle of a single musket-ball heard. As Buell's troops arrived in the dusk, General Buell marched several of his regiments part way down the face of the hill, where they fired briskly for some minutes, but I do not think a single man engaged in this firing received an injury; the attack had spent its force.

General Lew Wallace arrived after firing had ceased for the day, and was placed on the right. Thus night came, Wallace came, and the advance of Nelson's division came, but none—except night—in time to be of material service to the gallant men who saved Shiloh on that first day, against large odds. Buell's loss on the first day was two men killed and one wounded, all members of the Thirty-sixth Indiana infantry. The presence of two or three regiments of his army on the west bank before firing ceased had not the slightest effect in preventing the capture of Pittsburg Landing.

So confident was I before firing had ceased on the 6th that the next day would bring victory to our arms if we could only take the initiative, that I visited each division commander in person before any reënforcements had reached the field. I directed them to throw out heavy lines of skirmishers in the morning as soon as they could see, and push them forward until they found the enemy, following with their entire divisions in supporting distance, and to engage the enemy as soon as found. To Sherman I told the story of the assault at Fort Donelson,[16] and said that the same tactics would win at Shiloh. Victory was assured when Wallace arrived with his division of five thousand effective veterans, even if there had been no other support. The enemy received no reënforcements. He had suffered heavy losses in killed, wounded, and straggling, and his commander, General Albert Sidney Johnston, was dead. I was glad, however, to see the reënforcements of Buell and credit them with doing all there was for them to do. During the night of the 6th the remainder of Nelson's division, Buell's army, crossed the river, and were ready to advance in the morning, forming the left wing. Two other divisions, Crittenden's and McCook's, came up the river from Savanna in the transports, and were on the west bank early on the 7th. Buell commanded them in person. My command was thus nearly doubled in numbers and efficiency.

During the night rain fell in torrents, and our troops were exposed to the storm without shelter. I made my headquarters under a tree a few hundred yards back from the river bank. My ankle was so much swollen from the fall of my horse the Friday night preceding, and the bruise was so painful, that I could get no rest. The drenching rain would have precluded the possibility of sleep, without this additional cause. Some time after midnight, growing restive under the storm and the continuous pain, I moved back to the log-house on the bank. This had been taken as a hospital, and all night wounded men were being brought in, their wounds dressed, a leg or an arm amputated, as the case might require, and everything being done to save life or alleviate suffering. The sight was more unendurable than encountering the rebel fire, and I returned to my tree in the rain.

The advance on the morning of the 7th developed the enemy in the camps occupied by our troops before the battle began, more than a mile back from the most advanced position of the Confederates on the day before. It is known now that the enemy had not yet become informed of the arrival of Buell's command. Possibly they fell back to get the shelter of our tents during the rain, and also to get away from the shells that were dropped upon them by the gunboats every fifteen minutes during the night.

The position of the Federal troops on the morning of the 7th was as follows: General Lew Wallace on the right, Sherman to his left; then McClernand, and then Hurlbut. Nelson, of Buell's army, was on our extreme left, next to the river; Crittenden was next in line after Nelson, and on his right; McCook followed, and formed the extreme right of Buell's command. My old command thus formed the right wing, while the troops directly under Buell constituted the left wing of the army. These relative positions were retained during the entire day, or until the enemy was driven from the field.

In a very short time the battle became general all along the line. This day everything was favorable to the Federal side. We now had become the attacking party. The enemy was driven back all day, as we had been the day before, until finally he beat a precipitate retreat. The last point held by him was near the road from the landing to Corinth, on the left of Sherman and right of McClernand. About three o'clock, being near that point, and seeing that the enemy was giving way everywhere else, I gathered up a couple of regiments, or parts of regiments, from troops near by, formed them in line of battle and marched them forward, going in front myself to prevent premature or long-range firing. At this point there was a clearing between us and the enemy favorable for charging, although exposed. I knew the enemy were ready to break, and only wanted a little encouragement from us to go quickly and join their friends who had started earlier. After marching to within musket-range, I stopped and let the troops pass. The command, *Charge*, was given, and was executed with loud cheers, and with a run, when the last of the enemy broke.

During this second day I had been moving from right to left and back, to see for myself the progress made. In the early part of the afternoon, while riding with Colonel McPherson and Major Hawkins, then my chief commissary, we got beyond the left of our troops. We were moving along the northern edge of a clearing, very leisurely, toward the river above the landing. There did not appear to be an enemy to our right, until suddenly a battery with musketry opened upon us from the edge of the woods on the other side of the clearing. The shells and balls whistled about our ears very fast for about a minute. I do not think it took us longer than that to get out of range and out of sight. In the sudden start we made, Major Hawkins lost his hat. He did not stop to pick it up. When we arrived at a perfectly safe position we halted to take an account of damages. McPherson's horse was panting as if ready to drop. On examination it was found that a ball had struck him forward of the flank just back of the saddle, and had gone entirely through. In a few minutes the poor beast dropped dead; he had given no sign of injury until we came to a stop. A ball had struck the metal scabbard of my sword, just below the hilt, and broken it nearly off; before the battle was over, it had broken off entirely. There were three of us: one had lost a horse, killed, one a hat, and one a sword-scabbard. All were thankful that it was no worse.

After the rain of the night before and the frequent and heavy rains for some days previous, the roads were almost impassable. The enemy, carrying his artillery and supply trains over them in his retreat, made them still worse for troops following. I wanted to pursue, but had not the heart to order the men who had fought desperately for two days, lying in the mud and rain whenever not fighting, and I did not feel disposed to positively order Buell, or any part of his command, to pursue. Although the senior in rank at the time, I had been so only a few weeks. Buell was, and had been for some time past, a department commander, while I only commanded a district. I did not meet Buell in person until too late to get troops ready and pursue with effect; but had I seen him at the moment of the last charge, I should have at least requested him to follow.

The enemy had hardly started in retreat from his last position, when, looking back toward the river, I saw a division of troops coming up in beautiful order, as if going on parade or review. The commander was at the head of the column, and the staff seemed to be disposed about as they would have been had they been going on parade. When the head of the column came near where I was standing, it was halted, and the commanding officer, General A. McD. McCook, rode up to where I was and appealed to me not to send his division any farther, saying that they were worn out with marching and fighting. This division had marched on the 6th from a point ten or twelve miles east of Savanna, over bad roads. The men had also lost rest during the night while crossing the Tennessee, and had been engaged in the battle of the 7th. It was not, however, the rank and file or the junior officers who asked to be excused, but the division commander.[17] I rode forward several miles the day after the battle, and found that the enemy had dropped much, if not all, of their provisions, some ammunition, and the extra wheels of their caissons, lightening their loads to enable them to get off their guns. About five miles out we found their field hospital abandoned. An immediate pursuit must have resulted in the capture of a considerable number of prisoners and probably some guns.

Shiloh was the most severe battle fought at the West during the war, and but few in the East equaled it for hard, determined fighting. I saw an open field, in our possession on the second day, over which the Confederates had made repeated charges the day before, so covered with dead that it would have been possible to walk across the clearing, in any direction, stepping on dead bodies, without a foot touching the ground. On our side Federal and Confederate were mingled together in about equal proportions; but on the remainder of the field nearly all were Confederates. On one part, which had evidently not been plowed for several years, probably because the land was poor, bushes had grown up, some to the height of eight or ten feet. There was not one of these left standing unpierced by bullets. The smaller ones were all cut down.

Contrary to all my experience up to that time, and to the experience of the army I was then commanding, we were on the defensive. We were without intrenchments or defensive advantages of any sort, and more than half the army engaged the first day was without experience or even drill as soldiers. The officers with them, except the division commanders, and possibly two or three of the brigade commanders, were equally inexperienced in war. The result was a Union victory that gave the men who achieved it great confidence in themselves ever after.

The enemy fought bravely, but they had started out to defeat and destroy an army and capture a position. They failed in both, with very heavy loss in killed and wounded, and must have gone back discouraged and convinced that the "Yankee" was not an enemy to be despised.

After the battle I gave verbal instructions to division commanders to let the regiments send out parties to bury their own dead, and to detail parties, under commissioned officers from each division, to bury the Confederate dead in their respective fronts, and to report the numbers so buried. The latter part of these instructions was not carried out by all; but they were by those sent from Sherman's division, and by some of the parties sent out by McClernand. The heaviest loss sustained by the enemy was in front of these two divisions.

The criticism has often been made that the Union troops should have been intrenched at Shiloh. But up to that time the pick and spade had been but little resorted to at the West. I had, however, taken this subject under consideration soon after reassuming command in the field. McPherson, my only military engineer, had been directed to lay out a line to intrench. He did so, but reported that it would have to be made in rear of the line of encampment as it then ran. The new line, while it would be nearer the river, was yet too far away from the Tennessee, or even from the creeks, to be easily supplied with water from them; and in case of attack, these creeks would be in the hands of the enemy. But, besides this, the troops with me, officers and men, needed discipline and drill more than they did experience with the pick, shovel, and axe. Reënforcements were arriving almost daily, composed of troops that had been hastily thrown together into companies and regiments—fragments of incomplete organizations, the men and officers strangers to each other. Under all these circumstances I concluded that drill and discipline were worth more to our men than fortifications.

General Buell was a brave, intelligent officer, with as much professional pride and ambition of a commendable sort as I ever knew. I had been two years at West Point with him, and had served with him afterward, in garrison and in the Mexican war, several years more. He was not given in early life or in mature years to forming intimate acquaintances. He was studious by habit, and commanded the confidence and respect of all who knew him. He was a strict disciplinarian, and perhaps did not distinguish sufficiently the difference between the volunteer who "enlisted for the war" and the soldier who serves in time of peace. One system embraced men who risked life for a principle, and often men of social standing, competence, or wealth, and independence of character. The other includes, as a rule, only men who could not do as well in any other occupation. General Buell became an object of harsh criticism later, some going so far as to challenge his loyalty. No one who knew him ever believed him capable of a dishonorable act, and nothing could be more dishonorable than to accept high rank and command in war and then betray his trust. When I came into command of the army, in 1864, I requested the Secretary of War to restore General Buell to duty.[18]

After the war, during the summer of 1865, I traveled considerably through the North and was everywhere met by large numbers of people. Every one had his opinion about the manner in which the war had been conducted; who among the generals had failed, how, and why. Correspondents of the press were ever on hand to hear every word dropped, and were not always disposed to report correctly what did not confirm their preconceived notions, either about the conduct of the war or the individuals concerned in it. The opportunity frequently occurred for me to defend General Buell against what I believed to be most unjust charges. On one occasion a correspondent put in my mouth the very charge I had so often refuted—of disloyalty. This brought from General Buell a very severe retort, which I saw in the New York "World" some time before I received the letter itself. I could very well understand his grievance at seeing untrue and disgraceful charges apparently sustained by an officer who, at the time, was at the head of the army. I replied to him, but not through the press. I kept no copy of my letter, nor did I ever see it in print, neither did I receive an answer.[19]

General Albert Sidney Johnston commanded the Confederate forces until disabled by a wound in the afternoon of the first day.

His wound, as I understood afterward, was not necessarily fatal, or even dangerous. But he was a man who would not abandon what he deemed an important trust in the face of danger, and consequently continued in the saddle, commanding, until so exhausted by the loss of blood that he had to be taken from his horse, and soon after died. The news was not long in reaching our side, and, I suppose, was quite an encouragement to the Federal soldiers. I had known Johnston slightly in the Mexican war, and later as an officer in the regular army. He was a man of high character and ability. His contemporaries at West Point, and officers generally who came to know him personally later, and who remained on our side, expected him to prove the most formidable man to meet, that the Confederacy would produce. Nothing occurred in his brief command of an army to prove or disprove the high estimate that had been placed upon his military ability.[20]

General Beauregard was next in rank to Johnston, and succeeded to the command, which he retained to the close of the battle and during the subsequent retreat on Corinth, as well as in the siege of that place. His tactics have been severely criticised by Confederate writers, but I do not believe his fallen chief could have done any better under the circumstances. Some of these critics claim that Shiloh was won when Johnston fell, and that if he had not fallen the army under me would have been annihilated or captured. *Ifs* defeated the Confederates at Shiloh. There is little doubt that we should have been disgracefully beaten *if* all the shells and bullets fired by us had passed harmlessly over the enemy, and *if* all of theirs had taken effect. Commanding generals are liable to be killed during engagements; and the fact that when he was shot Johnston was leading a brigade to induce it to make a charge which had been repeatedly ordered, is evidence that there was neither the universal demoralization on our side nor the unbounded confidence on theirs which has been claimed. There was, in fact, no hour during the day when I doubted the eventual defeat of the enemy, although I was disappointed that reënforcements so near at hand did not arrive at an earlier hour.

The Confederates fought with courage at Shiloh, but the particular skill claimed I could not, and still cannot, see; though there is nothing to criticise except the claims put forward for it since. But the Confederate claimants for superiority in strategy, superiority in generalship, and superiority in dash and prowess are not so unjust to the Federal troops engaged at Shiloh as are many Northern writers. The troops on both sides were American, and united they need not fear any foreign foe. It is possible that the Southern man started in with a little more dash than his Northern brother; but he was correspondingly less enduring.

The endeavor of the enemy on the first day was simply to hurl their men against ours—first at one point, then at another, sometimes at several points at once. This they did with daring and energy, until at night the rebel troops were worn out. Our effort during the same time was to be prepared to resist assaults wherever made. The object of the Confederates on the second day was to get away with as much of their army and material as possible. Ours then was to drive them from our front, and to capture or destroy as great a part as possible of their men and material. We were successful in driving them back, but not so successful in captures as if further pursuit could have been made. But as it was, we captured or recaptured on the second day about as much artillery as we lost on the first; and, leaving out the one great capture of Prentiss, we took more prisoners on Monday than the enemy gained from us on Sunday. On the 6th Sherman lost seven pieces of artillery, McClernand six, Prentiss eight, and Hurlbut two batteries. On the 7th Sherman captured seven guns, McClernand three, and the Army of the Ohio twenty.

The effective strength of the Union force on the morning of the 6th was 33,000 at Shiloh. Lew Wallace brought 5000 more after nightfall. Beauregard reported the enemy's strength at 40,955. According to the custom of enumeration in the South, this number probably excluded every man enlisted as musician, or detailed as guard or nurse, and all commissioned officers,—everybody who did not carry a musket or serve a cannon. With us everybody in the field receiving pay from the Government is counted. Excluding the troops who fled, panic-stricken, before they had fired a shot, there was not a time during the 6th when we had more than 25,000 men in line. On the 7th Buell brought 20,000 more. Of his remaining two divisions, Thomas's did not reach the field during the engagement; Wood's arrived before firing had ceased, but not in time to be of much service.

Our loss in the two-days' fight was 1754 killed, 8408 wounded, and 2885 missing. Of these, 2103 were in the army of the Ohio. Beauregard reported a total loss of 10,699, of whom 1728 were killed, 8012 wounded, and 957 missing. This estimate must be incorrect. We buried, by actual count, more of the enemy's dead in front of the divisions of McClernand and Sherman alone than here reported, and 4000 was the estimate of the burial parties for the whole field. Beauregard reports the Confederate force on the 6th at over 40,000, and their total loss during the two days at 10,699; and at the same time declares that he could put only 20,000 men in battle on the morning of the 7th.[21]

The navy gave a hearty support to the army at Shiloh, as indeed it always did, both before and subsequently, when I was in command. The nature of the ground was such, however, that on this occasion it could do nothing in aid of the troops until sundown on the first day. The country was broken and heavily timbered, cutting off all view of the battle from the river, so that friends would be as much in danger from fire from the gun-boats as the foe. But about sundown, when the Federal troops were back in their last position, the right of the enemy was near the river and exposed to the fire of the two gun-boats, which was delivered with vigor and effect. After nightfall, when firing had entirely ceased on land, the commander of the fleet informed himself, proximately, of the position of our troops, and suggested the idea of dropping a shell within the lines of the enemy every fifteen minutes during the night.[22] This was done with effect, as is proved by the Confederate reports.

Up to the battle of Shiloh, I, as well as thousands of other citizens, believed that the rebellion against the Government would collapse suddenly and soon if a decisive victory could be gained over any of its armies. Donelson and Henry were such victories. An army of more than 25,000 men was captured or destroyed. Bowling Green, Columbus, and Hickman, Kentucky, fell in consequence; Clarkesville and Nashville, Tennessee, with an immense amount of stores, also fell into our hands. The Tennessee and Cumberland rivers, from their mouths to the head of navigation, were secured. But when Confederate armies were collected which not only attempted to hold a line farther south, from Memphis to Chattanooga, and Knoxville, and on to the Atlantic, but assumed the offensive, and made such a gallant effort to regain what had been lost, then, indeed, I gave up all idea of saving the Union except by complete conquest. Up to that time it had been the policy of our army, certainly of that portion commanded by me, to protect the property of the citizens whose territory was invaded, without regard to their sentiments, whether Union or Secession. After this, however, I regarded it as humane to both sides to protect the persons of those found at their homes, but to consume everything that could be used to support or supply armies. Protection was still continued over such supplies as were within lines held by us, and which we expected to continue to hold. But such supplies within the reach of Confederate armies I regarded as much contraband as arms or ordnance stores. Their destruction was accomplished without bloodshed, and tended to the same result as the destruction of armies. I continued this policy to the close of the war. Promiscuous pillaging, however, was discouraged and punished. Instructions were always given to take provisions and forage under the direction of commissioned officers, who should give receipts to owners, if at home, and turn the property over to officers of the quartermaster or commissary departments; to be issued as if furnished from our Northern depots. But much was destroyed without receipts to owners, which could not be brought within our lines, and would otherwise have gone to the support of secession and rebellion.

This policy, I believe, exercised a material influence in hastening the end.

U. S. GRANT.

Century Magazine, XXIX, 4 (Feb., 1885), 593–613. For reviews of USG's article, see
The Nation, XL, 1022 (Jan. 29, 1885), 98; *New York Sun*, March 4, 1885. See also let-
ter to William T. Sherman, Feb. 1, 1885; P. G. T. Beauregard, "The Shiloh Campaign,"
North American Review, CXLII, CCCL (Jan., 1886), 1–24, and CCCLI (Feb., 1886), 159–84.

On Jan. 5, 1885, Rollin V. Ankeny, former capt., 46th Ill., Des Moines, wrote to
USG. "The accompanying is from the Morning Leader of this city, and I hope it is
a true extract from your expected paper on Shiloh for Feby. Your old Soldiers here-
abouts (save a few) are in full accord with this text. Especially those who served in the
4th Division and 'Stayd' on the ridge overlooking Shiloh church, where we waited and
repelled furious and prolonged and repeated charges in accord with your early morning order when you directed that our Command should occupy a better line than the
first position, that proved so disastrous to the 15th Ills and the right of the 46th. I am
clear in recollection that we never left that position until after 3½ Oclok PM, it may
have been later but was not erlier. The left of our Division had a Combat known among
the participants as the 'Battle of the Hay Bales' and certain well remembered members
of regiments, of the 2d Brigade were wounded, and left on that ground. Lieut Hood
of the 46th among them, Stated that he was carried back by the confederates, Saw
Johnston die, and heard Beauregard issuing his orders for final and last attack. his
time was fixed as late as Six PM. when left by our line. our left had been turned and
we reformed, and fired into the Enemy by the left oblique they were heading for the
landing and subsequent examination of the ground Satisfied us that it was the Column
that Johnston lead in person, and pushed Prentiss to the River. we retired on the last
line of the Evening. in a short time it was dark. neither Nelson or Wallace helped that
day materially I recall possibly one or two regiments of the formers command, standing in line South of the PO. on crown of hill above the landing but did not know they
were of Buells Army until after the next days fight. we moved to the right, about dark,
to make room for Nelson' so we understood. The few to whom I refer seem to have
a desire to get a conspicuous place in the verry fore about 2 PM. and be the center of
defence on the Canvass of the Battle picture for 'Panorama at Chicago,' and have made
several verrifying trips to the field, and secured a certain Dr who lives at Corinth, and
was a surgeon on the field for Enemy. I belive that Picture will *not* tell the fac[ts] of
history, if put on canvass as now defined, and it is to be regretted if the projectors do
not defer until your paper appears. With many hopes and prayers for your welfare and
happiness, . . . " ALS, USG 3.

On Jan. 22, Theobald Forstall, vice president, Chicago Gaslight & Coke Co., and
former private, C.S. Army, who fought at Shiloh, considered USG's "assertion that he
was not surprised the morning of the attack entirely unwarranted by the facts . . . ."
Chicago Tribune, Jan. 23, 1885. For other participants on USG's article, see *ibid.*, Jan. 22,
24, 29, Feb. 2, 1885. See also *ibid.*, Jan. 30–31, Feb. 1, 1885.

On Jan. 29, Don Carlos Buell, Airdrie, Ky., wrote to editor, *Century Magazine*,
New York City. " . . . I am strongly importuned by friends and members of the Army
which I commanded, to make a critical review of the battle of Shiloh, . . . I should be
glad to know your present disposition in regard to it. It would be desirable that the
article should follow Grant's at an early day— . . . " ADfS, TxHR. On the same day,
Buell wrote to Robert Hunter, Cincinnati. " . . . The history of the battle has virtually
been written—in the official reports, if no where else fairly, and the particulars were
pretty clearly impressed upon the public mind until Grant and Sherman undertook to
contradict them and make a different history of the affair. This calls, in the opinion of

those who hold to the original facts, for a review of the case as stated by the *revolution-ists*, and I do not see how an impersonal treatment of the subject is altogether possible: a review of their statements seems to me to be absolutely necessary, if any thing is necessary . . . . The map with Grant's article is as you say, the Editor's contribution. It is the official map prepared by Halleck's Engineer. It is correct as to the topography, and totally false as to some of the essential points in Controversy—that is as to certain positions of the troops—For that, Halleck, Grant, and Sherman—especially Sherman—are responsible. It is the first great fraud in the case, and its exposure is one of the first corrections to be applied . . . ." ADfS, *ibid.* On Feb. 4, Thomas J. Bush, New York City, wrote to Buell after reading USG's article. " . . . I met Gen'l B. H. Bristow here a few days ago and he gave me some very interesting accounts of the first day at Shiloh, which prove that Gen'l Sherman could not be made to believe, after repeated reports from subaltern officers of the fact, that the attack was in force. Gen. Bristow said to me that he had a letter which he had written to his wife, from the field, soon after the battle in which he ascribes the victory at Shiloh to you and your Army. When I asked for his consent to let it be published he seem disinclined to do so saying his relations with Gen. Grant not being friendly it might be looked upon as an effort on his part to strike a man after he is down . . . ." ALS, *ibid.* See Buell, "Shiloh Reviewed," *Century Magazine*, XXXI, 5 (March, 1886), 749–81; Stephen D. Engle, *Don Carlos Buell: Most Promising of All* (Chapel Hill, 1999), pp. 355–57.

On Feb. 5, Benjamin M. Prentiss lectured in Chicago on the battle of Shiloh and defended USG from charges of drunkenness. *Chicago Tribune*, Feb. 6, 1885. Introducing Prentiss, Augustus L. Chetlain had said. "Gen. Grant in his article in the *Century* has given a clear, fair, truthful account of the battle of Shiloh. The article has caused a great deal of comment all through the country, and Gen. Prentiss tonight will give an explanation of many points in dispute and will throw light upon many things that have never been understood or have always been persistently misunderstood." *Ibid.*

On Feb. 8, William T. Sherman, St. Louis, wrote to Thomas Speed, Louisville. " . . . I have noticed the many newspaper articles about the battle of Shiloh, a renewed interest having been created by the recent articles by Generals Grant, Johnston & Jordan in the Century Magazine, . . . Inasmuch as General Grant was in chief command, saw all that appeared along the River from Savannah to Pittsburg Landing, and thence forward to each of his Divisions engaged in battle, his sphere of observation was larger than that of any Single person on our Side and therefore his account of the Battle in the 'Century' should be and will be received by the world as the best and most Satisfactory . . . ." ALS, Dartmouth College Library, Hanover, N. H.

1. See letter to Adam Badeau, July 26, 1884.

2. See *Memoirs of Gen. W. T. Sherman* (4th ed., New York, 1891), I, 251–75.

3. See Adam Badeau, *Military History of Ulysses S. Grant, . . .* (New York, 1881), I, 66–101.

4. On Jan. 12, 1882, Prentiss had spoken to the Cincinnati Society of ex-Army and Navy Officers. See *Cincinnati Gazette*, Jan. 11–14, 1882; *Cincinnati Commercial*, Jan. 13–14, 1882.

5. See *PUSG*, 5, 19–20.

6. See *ibid.*, 4, 257–62, 278–81, 286–88.

7. See *ibid.*, pp. 317–21, 331, 334–35, 358–60.

8. For the reports of Buell and his div. commanders, see *O.R.*, I, x, part 1, 291–96,

302–6, 323–27, 354–56. For USG's reasonably detailed reports, see *PUSG*, 5, 32–36, 340–42.

9. See *ibid.*, p. 17.

10. On Feb. 14, 1885, Lewis Wallace, U.S. minister, Constantinople, wrote to his son Henry L. Wallace. " . . . Now a word as to Grant's article in the *Century*. It is just as I expected and as I would have had it, since he was determined to attack me again. The editor of the magazine has offered me space for a short open letter in reply. That I declined, and asked him to give me space for a full article on the subject. As yet I have had no answer from him. I do not think he will refuse. When I get home, my first step will be to get George Brown and Ira McConnell to go to Crump's and Pittsburg Landings, and make a complete survey of my line of march and of the line my division fought over the second day of the battle. That done I will correct General Grant's map and assertions. His fling about my seeking to do a heroic action &c. I will meet with his letter of exoneration in which testifies to my prompt obedience to orders. In other words I will meet him exactly as I ought, and settle him once for all. I cannot do this, of course, until I get home . . . ." ALS, InHi. See letter to Lewis Wallace, Oct. 7, 1884; Alphonso Taft to Horace D. Taft, Feb. 15, 1885, DLC-William H. Taft; Charles Whittlesey, "Wallace at Shiloh," *Magazine of Western History*, II, 3 (July, 1885), 213–22.

11. Col. James M. Tuttle replaced Brig. Gen. William H. L. Wallace.

12. Badeau, *Military History of Ulysses S. Grant*, I, 83.

13. See *O.R.*, I, x, part 1, 279.

14. Cols. Jesse J. Appler, 53rd Ohio, and Rodney Mason, 71st Ohio. See *PUSG*, 5, 46; Wiley Sword, *Shiloh: Bloody April* (New York, 1974), pp. 171–73, 179.

15. See letter to William T. Sherman, Oct. 19, 1884.

16. See *Memoirs*, I, 307–8.

17. On Jan. 26, Jacob D. Cox, Cincinnati, had written to Sherman. " . . . I think it is a mistake for Grant to write the series of articles for the Century. The only condition on which he could *now* profitably travel over ground others have so fully explored, would be that of *thorough* dealing with all the points of controversy which have grown out of his campaigns. To do this he must read all that has been said, and meet with exactness the case as made by others. Since Badeau's book was published he cannot do what he might have done before, i. e write his memory of his career, as you did. Badeau's work is known to have been compiled under his supervision, and as to both facts and judgments on men & affairs, is *his*. A *resumé* of this will look like mere catch-penny work. To be *more* than a resume, he must do as I have said above, collect, collate and analyse all that has been said *counter* to his view as found in Badeau & so become a thorough historical controversialist on the subject; which he is manifestly not prepared to do. I see his reference to Alex. McCook is drawing fire from several quarters. I attribute what he said to his inexperience in writing for the press. He could hardly have meant to put upon McCook the burden of the responsibility for halting on Monday night. The halt needed no apology, and McCooks good conduct during the day was so conspicuous that Grant had no reason for unfavorable criticism of what he (McC.) might then have said. I conclude therefore that he could not have meant to be as severe as his words fairly mean, and that he himself will be sorry when he sees how ungracious it looks in the print. Men will ask *what new things* of that campaign has Grant to tell, that a man of his eminence in it should undertake to tell the story again? His merely *doing* it implies that he has something important to communicate; & we dont find it. He cant afford to be exhibited for the profit of the magazine publishers . . . ."

ALS, DLC-William T. Sherman. On Feb. 3, USG spoke to a reporter. "No reflection was intended on the personal courage or zeal of General McCook or the fighting qualities of his division. On the contrary, I expressly stated that his division had marched from twelve miles east of Savannah, and had been up all night getting from Savannah to the battlefield, and as a matter of fact they had been in a heavy storm of rain during the night march. General McCook's division did as good service, perhaps, as any division in the field on Monday, the 7th; and on one occasion during that day the opportunity fell to it to do service which received special commendation in the official reports of General Sherman and two other general officers of the Army of the Tennessee. The only thing that I can see in my article that can be construed as reflecting upon General McCook, although it was not so intended by me, is the statement that the request not to be sent in pursuit did not come from the officers or men of the division, but from its commander. What General McCook said was correct; his men should not have been sent in pursuit, and I acted on his advice and did not send them. The article shows this." *New York Herald,* Feb. 4, 1885. On Feb. 9, Cox again wrote to Sherman on USG's article. "You will need no assurance from me that I have always been glad when the representatives of the fugitives from Shiloh have been soundly rapped, beginning with Gov. Stanton and taking the whole list. But in Grant's case, the criticism which I found my mind making was that he did not seem to have reviewed the matter with sufficient care to avoid hitting a little wild. I see that he has himself modified what he had said of McCook, but in doing so he has to admit, practically, that he did not mean what his words fairly meant. In short it was careless writing . . ." ALS, DLC-William T. Sherman. See letter to *Century Magazine,* June 22, 1885.

18. See *Memoirs,* II, 121; Engle, *Don Carlos Buell,* pp. 298–302, 323–40.

19. See *PUSG,* 15, 447–49.

20. See *ibid.,* 28, 427–28.

21. See *O.R.,* I, x, part 1, 391.

22. The idea actually originated with Brig. Gen. William Nelson. See *ibid.,* p. 324; *O.R.* (Navy), I, xxii, 763.

To AG Richard C. Drum

———

NewYork. March 4. 1885

General Drum Adjt Genral of the Army
Washn. D. C.

I accept the position of General of the Army on the retired list.

U. S. Grant.

Copy, DNA, RG 94, ACP, 4754 1885. On March 4, 1885, AG Richard C. Drum telegraphed to USG. "You have been nominated and confirmed as General on the retired list. Please telegraph me your acceptance" Telegrams sent, *ibid.; ibid.,* Letters Sent. See *New York Tribune,* March 5–6, 1885. On March 3, President Chester A. Arthur had written to the Senate. "*I nominate* Ulysses S. Grant, formerly General Commanding the Armies of the United States, to be General on the Retired List of the Army, with the full pay of such rank." DS, DNA, RG 46, Presidential Messages. On March 13, USG signed the oath for his appointment. DS, *ibid.*, RG 94, ACP, 4754 1885. On April 30, USG signed a form. *"In compliance with the requirements of Paragraph 107 of the Regulations, I report my post-office address for the coming month as No. 3 East 66th street* New York City New York" DS, *ibid.* See *Badeau*, pp. 443–45.

On Feb. 18, George Jones, *New York Times*, had written to USG. "I enclose a letter just received from Mr Cox in which he seems confident of yet securing the passage of the retirement bill. Mr Cox and Genl Slocum have been untiring in their efforts to end" ALS, USG 3. On March 1, U.S. Representative Samuel J. Randall of Pa. wrote to George W. Childs, Philadelphia. "I had no opportunity yesterday to call up the Grant Bill but either Gen. Slocum or I will do so at the first opportunity offered. I have this matter earnestly in mind. I regret exceedingly to hear of Gen Grant's bad health . . . ." ALS, *ibid.* See Samuel S. Cox to Jones, Feb. 17, 1884, *ibid.*; letter to Edward F. Beale, June 26, 1884.

USG received congratulatory letters dated March 4 from Edwards Pierrepont and Hamilton Fish. USG 3. On March 6, Rutherford B. Hayes, Fremont, Ohio, wrote a similar letter to Frederick Dent Grant. ADfS, OFH. On March 14, Frederick Grant, New York City, replied to Hayes. ALS, *ibid.* On March 9, Frederick Grant had responded to a congratulatory letter from D. L. Kidd (USMA); on March 13, to letters from Maj. Gen. John M. Schofield (DLC-John M. Schofield) and Admiral David D. Porter (DLC-David D. Porter).

On March 4, Sarah S. Forbes, Milton, Mass., had written to Julia Dent Grant. "I have just heard that General Grant's name has been placed on the retired list of officers—I have been hoping to hear this & both Mr Forbes & myself are much pleased—We are looking forward to the pleasure of before long, reading the book which the papers tell us he is writing—That will put the country under a new & lasting obligation to him & it already owes a deep debt of gratitude to him—If not intrusive please present my kind regards to him in which Mr Forbes warmly joins me—" ALS, USG 3. On March 6, T. Lewis Banister, Marcellus, N. Y., wrote to Julia Grant. "I am an ex-officer of the former Confederate Army, now a Priest in the Episcopal Ministry, ordained since the war. I write to beg you to offer to the General, my congratulations on the passage of the bill which places him on the retired list of the Army. I have been watching with much solicitude its fate, and should have felt deep pain if any of our old Confederate officers had opposed it . . . ." ALS, *ibid.*

USG received congratulations from Grand Army of the Republic posts dated March 6, Lowville, N. Y. (General Grant National Memorial, New York, N. Y); March 19, Brooklyn (*ibid.*); March 9, New York City (*New York Tribune*, March 10, 1885); March 11, Springfield, Ill. (DNA, RG 94, ACP, 4754 1885).

On March 7, Speaker John B. Johnson of the Kan. House of Representatives had telegraphed to USG. "I am instructed by the legislature of the state of Kansas, at its hour of adjournment, to send greetings to you as grateful recipients of your valor in the field and wisdom as a statesman, and congratulations at the recognition of the nation in your restoration to a rank you surrendered in the interests of, and at the call of, your country. May God in His wisdom spare you long to live and enjoy with us the fruits of peace restored, and a country saved." *Topeka Capital*, March 8, 1885. Similar resolutions also passed legislatures in N. J. (*New York World*, March 11, 1885), Pa. (*New York Tribune*, March 10, 1885), and Ohio (General Grant National Memorial, New York, N. Y.).

Deposition

[*New York City, March 26, 1885*]

You were a partner in the firm of Grant & Ward? A.—Yes, Sir; I am informed that I was at the time the failure took place.

Q.—You became a member of that firm on or about Nov. 1, 1880? A.—I don't remember; I suppose so if the books say so. I never knew that I was anything else than a special partner clear to the end.

Q.—At or about that time you paid in $50,000 to the firm? A.—Yes, I paid in $50,000 first, and then afterward $50,000 more. I don't remember the dates.

Q.—And the second $50,000 was shortly after the first? A.— Yes, Sir.

Q.—So that in all you actually paid in $100,000? A.—I paid in $100,000.

Q.—On the 1st of May, 1884, what did you understand you were worth; about what? A.—I supposed that I was worth well nigh to a million dollars.

Q.—When did you first become acquainted with James D. Fish? A.—Well, I don't know whether I knew him before that co-partnership or not; I have no recollection. I had no suspicion of any rascality, and therefore there was nothing to confine my mind to any such dates.

Q.—Do you remember upon whose introduction you became acquainted with him? A.—I suppose it was by my son and Mr. Ward. I suppose if you should go clear back that it was my son who got acquainted with Mr. Ferdinand Ward through Mr. Ward's brother, and that the acquaintance was led on to in that way. The man was supposed, so far as I ever knew, to be a reputable banker until after the failure, and it was not astonishing that a person should make his acquaintance.

Q.—Do you remember receiving a letter from Mr. James D. Fish on or about July 6, 1882? A.—The one that was published; the one of which photographs were published?

Q.—No, I think not; but do you remember receiving any letter on that date? A.—I had a dim recollection after the failure of
receiving a letter from Mr. Fish while I was living at Long Branch,
so it might have been about that time. I went down there about the
middle of June.

Q.—Have you that letter in your possession now? A.—No, Sir.

Q.—Do you know what became of it? A.—No, Sir, I do not. I
suppose Mr. Ward took very good pains that I should not have it. I
don't suppose that I ever saw the one that was published.

Q.—Have you any recollection in relation to it? A.—I have a
recollection of receiving the letter and sitting down and writing an
answer at once; and the substance of my answer was that I had a
good deal to do that day, and that it was doubtful when I should be
able to go to see him; that if I could I would, but that I believed the
matters that his firm were engaged in were all right. Something
like that.

Q.—Haven't you any recollection as to what has become of that
letter of Mr. Fish? A.—No, Sir, I have not; because the one that
was published I do not believe was that letter.

Q.—Well, then, to the best of your recollection and present knowledge is the letter that you received at that time in your
possession? A.—I know it is not, for I have searched everywhere
for it.

Q.—Have you been in the habit of preserving your letters.
A.—No, Sir; I have never been in the habit of preserving private
letters, and if I was to try I suppose I should make a poor record.
My business in life has been such that somebody else has always
taken care of letters that had to be saved, and the only way that I
have now of preserving a letter that I wish to preserve until I do
something with it is to put it in my side coat pocket or put it in the
drawer where I write, and then when I want to look for a letter it is
about the last one I find.

Q.—You have searched for a letter of that date, or about that
date, without being able to find it[?] A.—I have; yes, Sir; I have
gone over all the letters that I find in the desk.

Q.—State your best recollection as to whether that letter was destroyed. A.—I have no recollection about it. I was in hopes that it had not been destroyed, and therefore I have looked for it.

Q.—Is the letter now shown you in your handwriting and written by you? A. (Examining the letter)—Yes, Sir; unquestionably.

Q.—This letter which you have just identified is dated July 6, 1882, and addressed to Mr. Fish, and says: "I find your letter of yesterday with a letter from Thomas L. James," &c.; have you any recollection whether the letter from Mr. Fish, to which this letter of yours is apparently a reply and to which it refers, was shown by you to Mr. Ferdinand Ward? A.—I don't know. Mr. Ferdinand Ward transacted all the business, and I suppose he brought the other letter to me and got this answer, and probably delivered it to Mr. Fish.

Q.—But you have no present recollection as to when that was? A.—No present recollection.

Q.—Your letter which you have just identified refers to a letter of Thomas L. James, President of the Lincoln National Bank, and it says: "A copy of your"—that is, Mr. Fish's—"reply to the letter of Mr. James as inclosed in the letter" of Mr. Fish; have you in your possession either of those letters? A.—No, Sir, I have not.

Q.—Do you know what has become of them? A.—No, Sir; I presume that went back to Mr. Fish.

Q.—In this letter which you have identified you say that you have appointments, &c., "so that I may not be able to come down to see you to-day, but if I can I will see you before 3 o'clock." Do you remember whether or not you did see Mr. Fish on that day? A.—I should think I did not; my recollection is that I did not see him.

Q.—Do you remember whether on that day and subsequently to the writing of your letter which you have just identified you wrote to Mr. Fish another letter? A.—No, I don't think I did.

Q.—Your recollection is not distinct, I suppose, upon that point? A.—No. Of course I can identify any letter that I ever wrote, if it is written in my own handwriting.

Q.—I show you another letter. A.—Of the same date?

Q.—Of the same date; and I ask you if the signature to that is yours? A. (examining the letter)—Well, the letter is not mine but the signature I should rather judge was mine. (Further examining the letter) I have no idea of that thing. I notice a peculiarity about the letter "t;" I don't think any person else would make that letter "s" exactly that way; the cross of that "t" in this signature might be made by me or might not. But I don't remember the letter at all; of course I didn't write it, as anybody can see.

Q.—Have you any doubt, General, as to the signature? A.—Well, I couldn't say whether I have or not. What I might say is that that "s" looks to me as though I must have made the "s" there, and the whole of it looks like my signature. I should think it would take a pretty skillful forger to write my name as nearly correct as that is done; but the crossing of the "t" is brought around and stopped a little abruptly. I might do that almost as well as anybody else, I suppose. But I do not suppose that I ever knew the contents of the letter at all; for I was in the habit of signing, when I would be busy, very often for Mr. Ward, and also for Mr. Work in other matters. I had an office in that building as President of the Mexican Railroad. I don't think Mr. Work ever put before me anything to sign that was not proper; I have no reason to believe so; but I did sign papers for different purposes for both of those men constantly.[1]

The Witness—I might state here, although I don't know whether it would have any effect or not, that at the time I went in the firm I had a very small income, but I had some money that my son had saved for me while I was gone abroad—some money that I had left and which he had so managed that I had saved some it, and he proposed to let me have half his interest in the firm, so that I would have an income to live upon, and there was afterward an income raised for me, and after that the firm generously concluded to let me in as a half partner, and then afterward as a whole partner, special, not general—generously, as I thought at the time.

Cross-examined by counsel for the Government:

By Mr. Root: Q.—Gen. Grant, what was the hour at which you were accustomed to reach your office in the morning when you were staying at Long Branch in the Summer of 1882? A.—I generally came up on a fast train; I have forgotten the time, but I think it was 8:30, or some minutes after 8 that it left Long Branch station, or rather left West End station. Sometimes I would take a later train.

Q.—So that you would reach your office at some time after 10 o'clock? A.—By that train I would reach my office just about 10 o'clock if it was not detained. Sometimes the train in crossing the river would get in later. Ten o'clock was about my arriving time at the office.

Q.—Did you observe in the letter which you received from Mr. Fish, and to which the letter which has been identified by you and marked for identification "A," being the letter first shown you and which is entirely in your handwriting, was an answer, any reference to Government contracts? A.—No; there was not. I had told Mr. Ward when it was mentioned that there never must be any Government contracts there. There is nothing wrong in being engaged in Government contracts more than in anything else, unless made wrong by the acts of the individual, but I had been President of the United States, and I did not think it was suitable for me to have my name connected with Government contracts, and I knew that there was no large profit in them except by dishonest measures. There are some men who got Government contracts year in and year out, and whether they managed their affairs dishonestly to make a profit or not, they are sometimes supposed to, and I did not think it was any place for me.

Q.—And you did not find in that letter that you received any reference to anything of that sort? A.—I did not find anything of that sort, or I should have stopped, but as a matter of fact I may never have seen that letter. Mr. Ward may just simply have given me a statement of the contents of that letter when at his office.

Q.—What did you understand to be the relations of the firm of Grant & Ward to the Marine Bank? A.—Well, I knew that Mr. Ward was a Director there, and seemed to have a great deal to do with it, but I never suspected there being anything wrong about it.

Q.—Did you at any time know or understand that the firm of Grant & Ward had engaged in Government contracts or in furnishing money to be used in carrying out Government contracts? A.—I never knew but one contract; that is, where he said there was

a transaction of that kind, and I questioned him about it and he
said he had just been out and bought 350,000 bushels of oats, I
think it was, and that there was quite a large quantity more to be
purchased in Chicago to be delivered—he told me the date when
it was to be delivered—and that the contractor hadn't the money
to do it with, and that he was doing that for a certain amount—a
stipulated amount; but the contract was to other parties. And I
said that I did not see that there was anything the matter with that.
The man had a contract from the Government for a quantity of
oats, and oats was an article that could be purchased very easily on
the Chicago market, and I said I didn't see anything wrong in that,
as we had no contract. Then afterward I began to hear—and that
wasn't long before the failure—whispers around that he was saying
that he had Government contracts, and I questioned him about it,
and he said that he had no such thing. He said that he wouldn't do
anything that was going to injure me, or anything that I requested
him not to; and he said that he had no contracts anywhere. It had
been said that he had city contracts, and he as much as said to me
that he was very well acquainted with the city officials, and that
that made it easy for him to get contracts from the city, and I told
him that I didn't know whether there was much difference between
contracts for New-York City and those made by the Government of
the United States, so far as that is concerned; and then he told me
that he had never had a contract at all of any kind with the Government of the United States or with the city of New-York; that the
way he did was—and he gave me an instance—he says, "Now here
is a man has a section of a railroad," and I don't know what road
it was; it was a road going through Pittsburg—I think connected
with the Reading Road; he said there was a man had a section of
that road to build; and he said that that man if he could have money
furnished for his horses and his tools and his little steam engine
and everything that he needed there, he could work to very much
better advantage on his contract, and that the firm of Grant &
Ward were to let him have the money to do that contract—let him
have the money to get along with. "Well," I said, "it doesn't seem
to me that that is very good security; I shouldn't regard that as

very good security for your money and mine; a man that has taken a contract and can't pay for the horses and steam engine, and picks, and plows, and shovels, and so on, can't be very good security for our money;" "Oh, but," he says, "we keep the contract in our possession, and the money is all paid into our office;" the road he said held back 10 per cent. until the work was done and they paid the contractor for every subdivision; I don't know what length of road that was that they paid for; but they kept back 10 per cent. of the contract; and that is the way he explained it, and I supposed that he was more of a business man than I was.

Q.—Did Mr. James D. Fish ever ask you any question about Government contracts? A.—No, Sir; I am very sure he never did. I know that if he had asked me I should have repudiated them and said it could not be possible.

Q.—Did he at any time after the 5th day of July, 1882, consult with you regarding the business of the firm of Grant & Ward? A.—No. Oh, I have seen him, but I am very sure that I never did consult with him. There was one occasion, which I think must have been in 1883, when we went out to the western part of Pennsylvania in the Winter, and Mr. Fish was along and a party of gentlemen, and we had a special car. Ward was with the party, but he wasn't discussed that I know of at all.

Q.—Mr. Fish was one of the party? A.—Yes, Sir, and Col. Grant was along, and there was Mr. Fish and Ferdinand Ward and Mr. James R. Smith, Mayor Edson, and Mr. J. Nelson Tappan, the Controller of the city of New-York—I think he was what they call City Chamberlain; and there was another man who was the Treasurer of the road.

Q.—Mr. Spencer? A.—Yes, Sir.

Q.—Some time in the Winter of 1883–4 Mr. Fish and Mr. Ward and yourself and these other gentlemen whom you have mentioned were together in a special car from New-York to the West? A.—Yes.

Q.—And were how many days together? A.—I should think we were altogether four days together.[2]

Q.—During that time did Mr. Fish converse at all about the

business of Grant & Ward? A.—I don't think he ever did. I made a remark, I recollect—and that is the only time that I think Mr. Ward's name was mentioned in connection with the business—to the effect that Mr. Ward was a man of wonderful ability, wonderful business capacity, or something like that, and Mr. Fish said that he had never got anything so good in his life before.

Q.—He asked you no questions at that time about Government contracts? A.—No. He seemed satisfied, as I was.

Q.—You didn't draw from the firm of Grant & Ward the profits which you were led to suppose had been made? A.—No, I did not. I left them there with the concern, and everything that I had beside, and I haven't got it out. I had some little items, but I don't know what amount, that were purchased, some of them, for me, with the money of the firm that were profits of the firm; they never were purchased, but then they were supposed to be, and I was charged with the purchase of them.

Q.—You drew, if I understand correctly, from the firm at the rate of $2,000 a month during the year 1883? A.—Yes.

Q.—And at the rate of $3,000 a month during the early part of 1884? A.—Yes.

Q.—Up to the time of the failure? A.—Yes, Sir.

Q.—And that was the limit of your drafts upon the firm? A.—That was the limit of my drafts.

Q.—As I understand it, Gen. Grant, everything that you had was lost in the failure of that firm? A.—Everything that I had in the world went. Ward came up here on Sunday night before the failure and asked me to go down with him to see Mr. Newcomb[3] to see if he couldn't get $150,000 from him; that he had himself raised $230,000, and if he could raise $150,000 more it would carry the Marine Bank through; that we had $660,000 in the Marine Bank, besides $1,300,000 of securities in our vaults; that we should be inconvenienced very much if we couldn't carry the bank through, and he said the Marine Bank was all sound and solid if it had time to collect in or draw in a little of its time loans. And I went down there with him, and Mr. Newcomb was not at home, and he asked me if I knew William H. Vanderbilt well enough to ask him, and I, after some little hesitation, said I did, and Mr. Vanderbilt loaned it to me without hesitation at all. He said at the time he gave it to me that he was lending this to me, and that he had no recollection of ever having done such a thing before, but that he would do it for me. Well, that has taken all the remaining property that I had.

Q.—The representation of Mr. Ward to you was that your firm was in danger on account of the critical condition of the Marine Bank? A.—Yes, Sir. He said that we had $1,300,000 of unpledged securities in our vault.

Q.—He did not tell you that the firm owed the Marine Bank $1,300,000? A.—Oh! no.

Q.—Or that the firm was overdrawn in the neighborhood of a million of dollars? A.—No, Sir. He said we had in our own vaults, of our own securities, $1,300,000, and that we had $660,000 to our credit in the Marine Bank—now that I think of it, it was seven hundred and odd thousand—and then he said $150,000 more that he had got of me was that much more to help the bank, and I found his statement, when I went down to the office after the failure, was correct, so far as the books of Grant & Ward showed.

Q.—Now, did Mr. Fish at any time during the Spring of 1884 communicate to you any distrust on his part of Mr. Ward? A.— No, Sir; if he had I should have been very ready, I have no doubt, to take distrust.

Q.—Did Mr. Fish at any time communicate to you the fact that during the Spring of 1884 the accounts of the firm with the Marine Bank were overdrawn? A.—No.

Q.—And you were, of course, entirely ignorant of that? A.— Entirely ignorant of that.

Q.—Who had the active management so far as you know—the active management and control of the business of Grant & Ward? A.—Ward; and nobody else had any control; he was the only one that could sign a check.

Q.—Did you know that Mr. Fish was conducting a large part of the financial business of that firm? A.—No, I didn't know it.

Q.—Did you know that Mr. Fish was raising millions of dollars for the business of that firm upon discounts and loans? A.—No, I did not.

Q.—Did you know that there was an account kept by that firm in the Marine Bank called a "special account," separate from the general account of the firm? A.—I never heard of that until since the failure; it is a recent thing in my knowledge.

Q.—Did you ever know that the firm of Grant & Ward was borrowing money from the Marine Bank upon the pretended pledge of collaterals which were not delivered to the bank? A.—I only know of that since the trial here.

Q.—Since the failure? A.—Until since the trial.

Q.—Did you ever know that the firm of Grant & Ward was borrowing money from the Marine Bank to be used in any, or in relation to any, Government contracts without giving security to the bank? A.—No.

Redirect by defendant's counsel.

By Mr. Clarke—Did you communicate to Mr. Fish in the Spring of 1884 or at any time prior to the failure of the bank any distrust on your part in respect to Mr. Ferdinand Ward? A.—I am sorry to say I did not. I had no distrust of Mr. Ward the night before the failure; not the slightest; and I recollect that my son, U. S. Grant, after the failure, said that "Ferd would come out right yet; he had no doubt he would come out right," for he had such profound friendship for his brother, Will Ward, that he didn't believe that it was possible for him to do a dishonest act. It took me a day or two to believe it was possible that Ward had committed the act he had.

By Mr. Root—Gen. Grant, you didn't know at the time that you went at Ward's instance and obtained the check for $150,000 from Mr. Vanderbilt on the 5th of May, 1884, that a week before that time Mr. Fish had been to the office of the firm and expressed his own apprehension that Mr. Ward had run away from the city? A.—I didn't know that; I never heard of it.

By Mr. Clarke—Exactly what was it, according to your present recollection, that Mr. Ward said on the Sunday before the failure in respect to the securities of the firm in the Marine Bank? A.—He didn't say he had any securities in the Marine Bank; he spoke about our own private securities, is the way I understood it; that we had

$1,300,000 in our vault, and that we had seven hundred and odd thousand dollars of money in the Marine Bank.

Q.—Seven hundred and fifty thousand dollars of money in the Marine Bank? A.—Yes.

Q.—That was Mr. Ward's statement to you on Sunday? A.—Yes, Sir.

Q.—Did Mr. Ward make to you statements from time to time as to the business of the firm and the profits that had been realized? A.—At first he used to make statements; and then later than that he used to make statements, or show them in his office; I don't remember of any recent statements, except that he would show them and show what the profits figured up; I have looked at them later, and my recollection now is that they showed the nature of the profits.

Q.—You have none of those statements in your possession? A.—No, I have not.

Q.—Were those in the nature of monthly statements? A.—In the nature of monthly statements, yes; I never read one of those statements until after the failure.

Q.—But they were statements showing from month to month the profits of the firm? A.—Yes.

New York Times, March 28, 1885. Elihu Root, U.S. attorney, Southern District, N. Y., prosecuted James D. Fish, Marine National Bank president and Grant & Ward partner, for violating national bank laws. The U.S. Circuit Court trial began on March 11, 1885. On March 26, Root told the presiding judge that USG had sent a letter "expressing his special desire that he might have an opportunity to give his testimony in the case. He was satisfied that going up to Gen. Grant's house to take his deposition would be no intrusion on him. The physicians had been consulted in the matter. Mr. Clarke, for the defense, said that he was in receipt of similiar assurances from the same source. The visitors were agreeably surprised to find Gen. Grant looking so well and so cheerful . . . . Gen. Grant spoke very distinctly, but with an apparent effort not to overtax his voice . . . . The examination lasted about three-quarters of an hour. When it was over the party had a pleasant talk with the General, expressing deep regret at his affliction and venturing to hope that after all the further progress of disease might be stopped. 'You're certainly looking remarkably well,' remarked Lawyer Smith in the course of the conversation. 'I don't know about that,' responded the patient, with a slight shake of the head: 'I am conscious of the fact that I am a very sick man.'" *Ibid.*, March 27, 1885. Stephen G. Clarke and Edwin B. Smith, counsel for James D. Fish, deposed USG, who answered questions in the presence of his legal advisor, Clarence A. Seward. Also observing were Frederick Dent Grant and Ulysses S. Grant, Jr. See *New York Tribune*, March 27, 1885. On March 27, USG's testimony "had been copied from the notes of Stenographer Fish and a type-writer copy was taken to General Grant's house in the morning. It was read over by the General and signed by him and reached the hands of Lawyer Clarke early in the afternoon. He retained possession of it until toward the close of the session, when it was read to the jury. Mr. Fish was on the witness stand while the deposition was read and he was called on to identify four letters which were referred to in General Grant's testimony . . . ." *Ibid.*, March 28, 1885. On April 1, prosecutors cross-examined Fish "about his knowledge of red ink entries in the book set apart for 'contract' accounts. Above some entries were written 'no questions.' Mr. Fish said that this referred to a special request made by Ward that no questions should be asked about the contracts. He was averse to any investigation into the contracts because it might injure Gen. Grant . . . . Mr. Fish never once inquired where such immense quantities of grain as were specified in the contracts could be bought, who paid for it, nor where it could be stored when it was purchased. He did not bother himself with details . . . ." *New York Times*, April 2, 1885. On April 2, Root continued to probe the government contract issue. *Ibid.*, April 3, 1885. On April 7, Root concluded the initial cross-examination, asking Fish "about the large loans he made to Charles H. Armstrong, Grant & Ward's colored messenger. It was a long time before he would admit that he understood that Armstrong had personally promised to pay the loans on demand and that he considered the loans valid ones . . . ." *Ibid.*, April 8, 1885. On April 8, Fish testified further. "In the latter part of 1883 I called at the office of our firm to see Mr. Ward. I met Gen. Grant in the outside office, and, after some general conversation, I asked him how business was. He answered that it was first rate; that the success of Grant & Ward was phenomenal. 'I think we have made more money during the past year,' he said, 'than any other house in Wall-street, perhaps in the city.' He said that Ward was the ablest young business man he ever saw. I asked him whether he had ever examined the books of the firm. He said no; he had only looked over the monthly statements, which were satisfactory to him." Root then cross-examined Fish. *Ibid.*, April 9, 1885. On April 9 and 10, Smith presented the closing argument for Fish. *Ibid.*, April 10–11, 1885. On April 11, Root closed the prosecution's argument. *Ibid.*, April 12, 1885. Shortly after midnight, the jury convicted Fish, who subsequently was sentenced to ten years in prison. See *ibid.*, March 12–14, 17–21, 31, April 1, 7, 13, May 31, June 27–28, 1885; *New York Tribune*, March 12–13, 17–21, 24, 31, April 1–3, 7–14, June 27–28, 1885; letter to Virginia Grant Corbin, May 8, 1884; Philip C. Jessup, *Elihu Root* (New York, 1938), I, 140–43. For the eventual commutation of Fish's prison sentence, see Ferdinand Ward to Grover Cleveland, May 8, 1886, Feb. 6, 1889, Ward to Daniel S. Lamont, Aug. 3, 1887, John D. Fish to Cleveland, July 29, 1887, DLC-Grover Cleveland; *New York Times*, Nov. 11, 1886, Jan. 24, 1887, May 12, 1889, March 31, 1912; *New York Tribune*, Nov. 11, 1886, May 11–12, 1889; *Washington Post*, Jan. 29, 1889.

On March 31, Ferdinand Ward, New York City, had written to Thomas H. Hubbard, counsel for George C. Holt, a Grant & Ward creditor seeking to void controversial real estate transfers made by Ward to William S. Warner. "I know I have no right to ask any favors of you but I cant help expressing a wish which I know you can help me in, & ask that you will do what you can in the matter. While at your office this afternoon Mr. Butler said that he was going to examine Genl. Grant in the Warner matter, but I hope that if it is possible to avoid this they will not do it. My reason for asking this is that the public have already been so ungenerous as to attribute the Generals sickness to his troubles with Grant & Ward & when the examination was made for Mr Fish the other day, the papers said that it did much to aggravate his troubles. This is so hard for me to bear that I cant help but ask that you will do what you can to save me from any more such unjust insinuations. Genl Grants testimony in the Warner case will have little or no weight. I would not say this if I did not believe it, for there is no one more anxious to have you succeed in that case than me. Please do this if you consistently can & so oblige." ALS, NN. Outlining Warner's business career in late June, a reporter wrote that he "had been a stock broker in partnership with somebody else, had failed, had afterward become a sort of confidential clerk to ex-Judge Hilton in his management of the Stewart business, and finally had gone into the office of the Mexican Central Railroad Company, which was in the same building with the office of Grant & Ward . . . ." *New York Times*, June 27, 1885. On Sept. 1, "Mr. Ward took the stand to resume his testimony in the suit of Assignee Holt to set aside the Ward conveyances to W. S. Warner. The case was suddenly adjourned on July 23, in consequence of the death of General Grant. General Hubbard took up the subject of the $30,000,000 in checks in the stupendous transactions between Ward and Warner. Ward used for reference his own tabulated two-by-three-feet account of his 'contract' patent. Sums in tens and scores of thousands of dollars were passed fleetly over . . . ." *New York Tribune*, Sept. 2, 1885. Warner's status as Ward's preferred creditor provoked public scrutiny and legal maneuvering that ended with a civil judgement denying his claim to the disputed assets. Warner afterwards left the country with his family and lived overseas until his death. See *ibid.*, July 9, 23, Oct. 17–18, 23, 1885, Jan. 6, Feb. 14, 16, March 18–19, 1886, Feb. 27, 1890; *New York Times*, March 26, July 9, 23, Sept. 2, 4, 9, Oct. 18, 23, 25, 1885, Jan. 6, 23, Feb. 14, 16, March 18, 20–21, 1886, Feb. 26, 1890; *New York Herald*, Oct. 19, 1885.

1. See *PUSG*, 30, 400–402; Memorandum, [*May, 1884*].

2. This special train trip from New York City to Rochester, N. Y., began on Nov. 15, 1883. Besides his Grant & Ward associates, USG traveled with Mayor Franklin Edson of New York City; James R. Smith, New York City merchant; J. Nelson Tappan, New York City chamberlain; and Bird W. Spencer, Erie Railroad treasurer. For Ward's account of the trip, see *New York Herald* (magazine section), Jan. 9, 1910, p. 2. For biographical information, see *New York Times*, Sept. 6, 1884 (Tappan), Sept. 25, 1904 (Edson), July 29, 1931 (Spencer).

On Nov. 16, a correspondent reported from Bradford, Pa., where USG had shaken hands with over 1,000 people before venturing out to see the highest railroad viaduct then in existence. "Gen. Grant walked to the highest point of the bridge and leaned over the hand railing. He looked down the dizzy height and removing his cigar, exclaimed to Mayor Edson, 'Judas, priest! how high we are!' He said the bridge was the most wonderful in the world. Referring to military matters, Gen. Grant said: 'I am gratified that Lieut.-Gen. Sheridan has been made commander of the army. I hope that Congress will make him General and promote Hancock to the Lieutenant-generalship.' He expressed great faith in the future of Mexican railroads, and said that the Northern Pacific Railroad, although extravagantly built and under bad management, would in time become one of the greatest railroads in America. After viewing the bridge the party returned to the city." *Ibid.*, Nov. 17, 1883. That evening, USG's train arrived in Buffalo. See *Buffalo Evening News*, *Buffalo Courier*, and *Buffalo Commercial Advertiser*, Nov. 17, 1883.

On Nov. 17, 1:30 P.M., USG's train reached Rochester. *New York Times*, Nov. 18, 1883. On the same day, USG wrote to Hulbert H. Warner. "My time will be so occupied during my stay in Rochester that I will not be able to accept your kind invitation to visit the Warner Observatory." ALS, Rochester Public Library, Rochester, N. Y.

Written on letterhead of the Rochester Club. For Warner, patent medicine promoter and entrepreneur, see *New York Times*, Oct. 14, 1894, Jan. 28, 1923. Also on Nov. 17, USG received an invitation from Daniel W. Powers. *Rochester Union and Advertiser*, Nov. 17, 1883. That evening, USG and his traveling companions visited the Powers art gallery. See *Rochester Democrat and Chronicle*, Nov. 18, 1883; Alphonso A. Hopkins, *The Powers Fire-proof Commercial and Fine Art Buildings* (Rochester, 1883).

 3. See *PUSG*, 30, 215.

To President

—————

New York
April 3rd 1885

To the President of the United States

May I ask you to favor the appointment of Ulysses S. Grant, the son of my son Frederick Grant as a cadet, at West Point, upon his application.

 In doing so, you will gratify the wishes, of

U. S. Grant

LS, USG 3. On Feb. 1, 1887, William T. Sherman, New York City, endorsed this letter. "It seems superfluous that any addition should be necessary to the above, but I cheerfully add my name in the full belief, that the child of such parents will be most worthy the appointment solicited" AES, *ibid.* On March 30, 1898, President William McKinley endorsed this letter. "I direct the appointment to be made," AES, *ibid.* A related undated letter from Ida H. Grant to Ulysses S. Grant 3rd is *ibid.* On June 21, Frederick Dent Grant, Camp Thomas, "Near Chickamauga," Ga., wrote to McKinley. "I have the honor to express my deep appreciation of the appointment of my son, Ulysses, to the Military Academy at West Point, the notification of which appointment reached me yesterday. Believe me, my dear Mr President, that your great kindness will ever be gratefully remembered and both my son and I will endeavor to prove to you in actions the gratitude which we can not express in words. With highest regards for Mrs McKinley . . . " ALS, DLC-William McKinley. Grant 3rd graduated USMA in 1903. See *New York Times*, March 29, 1898.

To Julia Dent Grant

—————

[*April 14, 1885*]

 The doctor tells me I am better to-day. I am better. I am better than I have been for two weeks.

U. S. Grant.

New York World, April 15, 1885. On Tuesday evening, April 14, 1885, Frederick Dent Grant reported: "Father's condition showed a marked improvement to-day. Apparently he has gained strength, and he certainly seems stronger. He has walked about more than for four days past. He was so well that I submitted a business paper to him. It was so prepared that my signature would have been all that was necessary. But he examined it carefully, discussed some of the points with me and then, walking into his office, sat down at the desk and signed his name . . . . This morning he was in a playful mood. After Dr. Douglas had sent out the 6.30 o'clock bulletin father asked the servant for a pad of writing paper. He took his pencil and, without making any remark, wrote this bulletin: . . . After he had finished writing he folded up the note and addressed it to mother. She was in the adjoining room, but without disturbing her, he again called the servant to him and told him to take the bulletin to her. Father thought his improvement was due to the fact that he kept very quiet on Monday." *Ibid.* For other accounts of USG's note, see *New York Times, New York Tribune,* and *New York Sun,* April 15, 1885. On April 15, John P. Newman asked "'Well, General, how goes the battle to-day?' 'I think the enemy is on the retreat,' the General jokingly replied. Then his face assumed a serious expression and he continued in a tone of mingled hope and sadness: 'Thrice have I been down in the valley of death and now I have come up.'" *New York Tribune,* April 16, 1885. See Frederick Anderson, ed., *Mark Twain's Notebooks & Journals* (Berkeley, 1975–79), III, 136. Beginning in March, New York City newspapers reported on USG's health almost daily.

Also on April 15, Frederick Grant wrote to Frederick T. Dent. "Father has been improving some lately and is better today than he has been in two weeks. Mother received a very pretty letter from aunt Hellen yesterday All with the exception of Father are well here." ALS, Harry S. Truman Library, Independence, Mo. On the same day, Dent, Washington, D. C., wrote to his son-in-law Capt. Lafayette E. Campbell. "I received a letter from Madgie yesterday in which she says you wrote to me to New York if so I did not get the letter—it is one of some three thousand piled up in the library that we had not a chance to see who they were for—while I was there even telegram came so fast we could not answer them. Now that the General is better Jessie and Badeau are doing what they can to sort the mail and I will get all of my letters a number of which have come to me already Well about Grant he is going to die soon unless a miracle saves him—the cancer has eaten up to and partly around the artry a cough might break it and suffocation would result he knows it we all know it and know it may occur at any moment he is calm—cheerfull and prepared—owing to morphine he is free from pain but is dayly growing weaker—his mind is clear and he talked a good deal to me— . . ." ALS, Mrs. Gordon Singles, Arlington, Va. On March 30, 10:00 P.M., Frederick Grant had telegraphed to Dent. "Father is easy, but very weak." *New York Times,* March 31, 1885. Dent visited USG in early April. See *New York Tribune,* April 2–5, 1885; *New York World,* April 11, 1885. On April 18, Frederick Grant wrote to Lt. Governor John C. Smith of Ill. "General Grant has just had the resolution of the 34th General Assembly of Illinois read to him. He has been too ill to have them read before. He directs me to write and thank you and through you thank the Gener[al] Assembly for their kindness in thinking of him during his severe illness. As he entered the army from the state of Illinois he feels particular[l]y flattered by the action" ALS, IHi. A message from the Ill. General Assembly, dated March 10, is in Grant Memorial Association, New York, N. Y.

On April 17, Friday, Chester A. Arthur, New York City, had written to USG. "I am greatly rejoiced at your improvement. I have been confined to my room since Monday, but as soon as my physician permits I shall go to make my congratulations to yourself & your family" ALS, USG 3. On the same day, Arthur B. Farquhar, Pennsylvania Agricultural Works, York, wrote to USG. "It must do you good I know to feel how deeply the whole country has sympathized with you, and how we rejoice at your convalescence. It would seem that the prayers of millions will be answered. You will never again have cause to mourn over the ingratitude of the country you have so grandly served. I do not know that you will see this letter, but if you do you will pardon my freedom on account of the love and gratitude I bear you. I wanted to tell you as a businessman at the head of large operations which I have always tried to conduct in the most honorable possible manner, that there is nothing in all your public career, nothing in your connection with Grant & Ward or any one else that, if understood, could possibly reflect the slightest discredit upon you, and that the whole world now understands and believes this. I wish also to say that if you should be taken from us, that your family will never want for anything that a grateful nation can do for their comfort. I was informed that you had expressed some uneasiness about this. I wish as a responsible man, to guarantee that they shall never suffer, that your mind might be entirely relieved. But I hope and believe that you will be spared to bless them, and our country for many years yet." TLS, MiU–C. On April 20, Lt. Gen. Philip H. Sheridan, Washington, D. C., telegraphed to Frederick Grant. "With Great pleasure I send my Congratulations to the General on the improved and hopeful Condition of his health." Telegram received (misdated 1884), USG 3; copy and ADfS (telegram sent), DLC-Philip H. Sheridan. Communications dated between March 20 and April 11 from Sheridan to J. Russell Jones, Frederick Grant, Adam Badeau, and Roscoe Conkling anticipating USG's death are *ibid.* Also on April 20, Porfirio Díaz, Mexico City, telegraphed to Frederick Grant on USG's health. Telegram received (in Spanish; misdated 1884), USG 3.

On April 21, Francis E. Spinner, former U.S. Treasurer, Jacksonville, Fla., wrote to USG. "Knowing that all words of Consolation to the very sick, are not only futile and vain, but that they are ofttimes absolutely annoying, I refrained from writing to inform you of the intensity of my sympathy for you, in your suffering. But, now, when everybody believes that you will recover your wonted health, I can't help but congratulate you, and say to you how very happy the last news of your greatly improved condition has made me.—That you may yet live many, many years, to enjoy the continued love and gratitude of a grateful people, is the hope, wish and prayer of Your old and sincere friend." ALS, *ibid.* On April 22, a "Chicago gentleman" recently in London delivered a note from Prime Minister William E. Gladstone to USG. "With respectful sympathy, and best wishes for a speedy recovery and a long and useful life." *New York Sun,* April 23, 1885. Gladstone's note pleased USG, who "spoke several times of it afterward, and seemed deeply touched by it." *New York Times,* April 23, 1885. On April 26, James Houston, Soledad, Calif., wrote to USG. "Please accept my heart felt sympathy for One, Who this whole American Nation is daily praying to Him, who tempers the winds to the shoren lambs, That He will again restore you to perfect health. You have Richly earned the *Crown* of *Glory,* that this American People have bestowed upon you, and when the Most High God, Shall see fit to call you to himself—My prayer is, that He, will give you a Everlasting Crown, and a Seat at his Right Hand that will never faid away—God Bless you—and Family . . . P. S. *General,* Lawson Grant your Cousin—is My Brother in law—He married Marthy Hudson in Mason County Kentucky—I married her youngest Sister—Pensy Jane—Now Dead—" ALS, USG 3. On April 29, "A Friend," Brooklyn, wrote to USG. "I have just finish a prayer that I have been saying for some time past: it is a prayer to the Blessed Virgin beseeching her to intercede with her blessed Son for your recovery. and. as this prayer has never failed me I am sure you will get well for although cancer is said to be incurable yet nothing is impossible to God. I would not write as it is not necessary, but as I am sure you will get well through this prayer I feel as I would like to let you know what the Blessed Virgin has done for you." L, *ibid.* On May 2, Lindsay Murdoch, Marble Hill, Mo., wrote to USG. "I feel impelled to address a few line to you at this time, from a sense of justice and a sincere desire to repair any injury that may have been done to your feelings or otherwise from certain statements and utterance of mine during the excitement of the whiskey ring trials and subsequent thereto, I am now well satisfied that your whole conduct during that trying period was honorable and high minded to the last degree.—From information received from the Father of Capt Lafayette Campbell U. S. A. I am well satisfied your confidence was grossly abused, by men you had placed near your person in positions of the the highest trust, who systematically suppressed confidential information transmitted to you, and deprived you of the means of properly judging the conduct of men who had abused your confidence in positions of profit and trust in which you had placed them, and who I have not the slightest doubt you would have promptly removed as soon as their proper character became known to you Your highly honorable conduct in the financial troubles you became involved in through no fault of yours, has added new lustre to your otherwise great name, and the uncomplaining fortitude with which you have borne your lamentable physical affliction has touchd a chord of sympathy in the hearts of all, This communication is dictated with the kindest of feeling, and with the sincere hope that the improving condition of your malady may lead to a complete recovery, and to restored health and an extended lease of your valuable life . . ." ALS, *ibid.*

On May 11, Cheng Tsao Ju, Chinese minister, wrote to USG. "On my voyage from Peru to the United States, I was prostrated by a paralytic stroke in consequence of which, I was kept ignorant, on landing in New York, of the fact of your serious illness. Having returned to Washington, I now seize the first opportunity to express to you my sincere sympathy. Being informed of your recent improvement, I beg to congratulate you on this pleasing news—and hope that, by the help of a kind Providence, you may soon be restored to usual health. I regret to say that I am still unable to use my right limbs—which deprives me of the pleasure of calling upon you in person. I however have requested Mr. An Yang Ming our Consul in New York, to deliver this note to you in person—and to convey to you my warmest regards." LS, *ibid.* On May 18, Kirkor Margossian, "Late Director of the Office of foreign correspondence & translation, at the Turkish Ministry of War," Constantinople, wrote to USG. "Please your Excellency allow the undersigned to express his heartfelt participation in the universal joy which the recent renewal of your precious health has given to all present & absent, who have known your illustrious person or name equally respected and admired in your Excellency's private & public life. My feelings on this happy event might be compared to those which were inspired to me, when I have been called to the signal honor and rare luck of serving as interpreter to your beloved son, on his visit with gl Sheridan [*Sherman*], to the late Sultan Abdul Aziz at the Imperial Palace of Beylerbey, on the Bosphorus, the 11th day of April 1872. My said service lasted only about a couple of hours, but its remembrance is up to this day, and will be until the last of my life, as lively and fresh, as eleven years ago, and shall assuredly be also transmitted after me to my descendants, like *a valuable souvenir.* In the meanwhile I beg to send my best wishes to your said son, and request that your Excellency will please to accept the same as well for yourself, with the expression of my sincere sentiments of profound respect and high consideration." LS, *ibid.*

On March 12, W. S. Baker, Brooklyn, had written to Frederick Grant. "I notice by the Tribune of to-day, that Mr. Brown of No Adams Mass a cancer specialist, has been invited to examine your father's throat, which may lead to his mode of treatment for cancerous affection. I would call your attention to the fact, that my mother Mrs. Joshua Baker of Hyannis Mass. under went most excrutiating torture by his treatment of a cancer, and that he had the effrontery to pronounce her cured, and falsely had printed in his circular of testimonials, that my mother was cured, which was an egregious falsehood. My mother died Augt 6 /84 of a most genuine cancer, which was the cause of her death. I write you this to warn you of such an imposter ... I most sincerely trust your great, and noble father may recover from his serious affliction" ALS, *ibid.* On March 11, a correspondent had reported from North Adams, Mass. "Wallace Brown, a son of M. E. Brown, a local cancer specialist, has gone to New-York to see General Grant, and to make an examination of his case. Dr. Brown has been introduced to General Grant's friends through S. B. Elkins, whose father the doctor relieved of a cancer of the lips two years ago. Mr. Elkins says that he has tried for five weeks to get Dr. Fordyce Barker and Dr. Douglas to consent to let Dr. Brown see the cancer, and they have not agreed to it, ... " *New York Tribune*, March 12, 1885. On March 12, Wallace E. Brown told a reporter that Frederick Grant "said that if I would tell my remedy to him I could treat his father. I said no, but I qualified it afterward by saying that if I saw the cancer and determined that I could cure it, if I did not give relief at once I would disclose my remedies, but if I cured him they would remain a secret. The Colonel replied that he thought I was too young to take charge of such an important case, whereupon I seized my hat and hurried out of the house . . . . I don't pretend to be a regular physician or a general practitioner, but I do claim that I can cure cancers when physicians have failed. I have had eight years' experience with this disease and ought to know something about it." *Ibid.*, March 13, 1885. On the same day, John H. Douglas stated that USG's "family had satisfied their minds as to Brown's usefulness, and refused to have anything to do with him. We are through with him entirely, and he cannot see the General." *Ibid.* For Brown's account of his cancer remedy, see *ibid.*, March 14, 1885. On March 21, James Rice, Windsor, Ontario, wrote to USG. "Pardon me for informing you that under proper treatment your cure is not hopeless—But beneficial results from Erroneous treatment would be Miraculous, and in direct opposition to already Established laws of restoration—Proper treatment would consist in purifying your blood, and keeping it in a cool healing Condition—as well as Subduing the inflammatory state of the Cancer—However this can Never be done by drug remedies—as the poisonous and heating properties of the Medicines produce An Abnormal Action of the Digestive organs, which action is beyond human power to Control, and when uncontrolled results in inflammation— ... Should this fall into other hands before reaching the Suffering General—I sincerely request you not to deprive him of its perusal—as many years of practical Experience in treating the sick and suffering, fully Convinces me of its importantce— ... " ALS, Cohasco, Inc., Yonkers, N. Y. On the same day, Parlemon Pelton, Persia, Iowa, wrote to USG. "I have Read of your turable Afliction. And wish to sey one thing to you. I have Faith you can be healed by the Power of God. I have been Healed in that way and know maney others that have been healed in the same wey. I will Wright you and then my dutey is done Their are two men liveing here that if you will invite them to come and see you they will most ashuredly go to you and Administer to you in the name of the Lord Jesus Christ anoint with oil and Prey over you in the name of Jesus Christ will rebuke the disease and you will be healed, but you must have faith Enough yourself to send for them They will charge you nothing they will take nothing onely their Expenses of traveling. Their Names are David and William Chambers. they know nothing of what I have Written to you. you can Wright me to send them or send to them direct. their Address is the same as mine. Dear Sir my dutey is now done and I hope the Lord will put it into your heart to do as I hav Written" ALS, NHi. USG's physicians received "letters every day from old women, cranks and quacks giving advice and offering to cure the General within a few days." *New York Tribune*, March 11, 1885. For a fuller description of these letters, see *ibid.*, March 19, 1885.

On March 22, Frederick Grant wrote to Rutherford B. Hayes, Fremont, Ohio. "Your letter of the 220th inst was received I will call the attention of Dr Douglas to the article in the paper you so kindly forwarded to me. I am glad to say father is apparently a little better today, and joins me in respects to Mrs Hayes." ALS, OFH. On March 24, Tuesday, Horace Porter discussed USG. "I presume no man in this century has had the mental strain that was put on Gen. Grant from 1861 to 1876 . . . . The effect of it on him did not appear, however, until his physical sufferings began with his fall a year ago last December. Since then he has suffered terribly: no one knows how much, for he never complains. After that fall, when he injured his hip, pleurisy set in. It was a severe attack. Then he began to suffer from neuralgia, with intense pains in the head . . . . Then this terrible disease of the tongue appeared. It has been a steady drain upon him, reducing his flesh rapidly and weakening him beyond any former experience. But he has stood it all without a murmur, just as he has taken all the reverses and trials of his life. To see him wasting and sinking in this way is more touching and excites deeper sympathy among his friends than if he made some sign of his sufferings, as ordinary men do, by grumbling and complaint. The thing from which he has suffered most of late is insomnia. When I was with him on Sunday I said it seemed strange that he should suffer from that, as he had always been a remarkably good sleeper. I reminded him that on the field, no matter what the weather or how heavily charged he might be with responsibilities, sometimes with a battle on his hands for the next day, I had seen him drop down in the mud and rain and be sound asleep in two minutes. He meant always to get eight hours' sleep. He said it was a strange thing to him that he could not sleep, and that he regretted nothing so much . . . . In talking he tries to speak without moving the tongue. This interferes with enunciation, but it saves him pain. He could enunciate well enough if it were not for this effort to keep the tongue motionless. Of course talking is tiresome. He tries to do a good deal of it, but is discouraged by his family and the physicians. The trouble on this account makes it impracticable for him to proceed with his book by dictation . . . . He has spoken to me, as he has to others, about his great desire to finish his book . . . . Work on the book has proceeded as far as the 'Crossing of the James, in the Summer of 1864.' It is the most important period of the war, and Gen. Grant is naturally anxious to cover it as he believes it should be treated. No treatise on the war can possibly be so valuable as this, and although his notes would enable another to complete the volume, he feels that no hand can do it as he can . . . . His enormous will power sustains him like a hero, as it ever did." *New York Times*, March 25, 1885.

Very early on March 29, USG nearly died from "a secretion in the throat which he was unable to eject, and which rendered breathing extremely difficult." *Ibid.*, March 30, 1885. On April 3, USG's physician B. Fordyce Barker wrote to Hamilton Fish. " . . . I have not been able to persuade myself that the end was so near, as it has been supposed to be by many others. The great danger I felt to be from sudden heart failure, and yesterday morning about four oclock it did fail so that hypodermic injections of brandy and ammonia only brought him up. I recommended yesterday that a full dose of digitalis be given at 12 & 3 am, and milk punches through the night often—The self repressed ~~exhaustion~~ excitement and exhaustion of the central vitals powers, in connection with giving his testimony in the Grant & Ward case has been the cause of his recent failure of strength, and a corresponding progress of the local disease—I knew nothing of the proposed examination, before the time, nor am aware that the other doctors did, for I should have opposed it with great vehemence— . . . " ALS, DLC-Hamilton Fish. Answering his physician's request for information to place in a medical bulletin on April 5, USG said. "You may say that I am feeling comfortable. I wish you would also express my gratitude and appreciation of the feeling that the people have shown for me in my sickness and for the prayers that that have been offered in my behalf. I am deeply touched at the expressions that have been sent to me from and the calls of those who once looked upon me as an enemy. I wish I had strength enough to see them all, and tell them personally how greatly I regard their sympathy . . . . I desire the good will of all whether heretofore friends or not." *New York Tribune,* April 6, 1885. On April 6, USG told his physicians. "My chances, I think, of pulling through this are one in a hundred. I have no doubt, but sometimes I do feel that I shall get better. I think if I have another attack of strangling I shall go off very quickly, and if you doctors can tell how long a man can live under water when he is drowning, then I think I can form some idea of the time I shall have to live when the next strangling comes on, if it does come. If I do not have the choking, I think I will linger some time, for I feel so much better the last two days." *Ibid.,* April 7, 1885. On the same day, Badeau left USG's home with a satchel. "The General appears to be somewhat improved, but much improvement cannot be expected. The Grant & Ward affair was a shock from which he will never recover. I have given up my bed in the house to the doctors." *Ibid.*

On April 7, Frederick Grant telegraphed to Matías Romero, Washington, D. C. "Father very low doubtful if he survives the night" Telegram received (facsimile), DLC-Matías Romero. Early that morning, USG "was seized with a severe fit of coughing, which was followed by a hemorrhage of arterial blood." *New York Tribune,* April 8, 1885. On April 8, Dowager Marchioness of Ely, servant of Queen Victoria, Aix-les-Bains, France, telegraphed to Julia Dent Grant and USG. "The Queen, who feels deeply for you in you anxieties, commands me to inquire after Gen. Grant." *New York Times,* April 10, 1885. On April 9, Frederick Grant telegraphed in reply. "Mrs. Grant thanks the Queen for her sympathy, and directs me to say Gen. Grant is no better." *Ibid.*

On March 2, Elijah Horr and T. Corwin Watkins, Boston, had written to USG. "The Methodis preachers of Boston and vicinity in meeting assembled at Wesleyan Hall Boston, this Monday morning, being profoundly saddened by the intelligence brought to us by the morning papers of this date concerning your condition of health, desire to express our deep sympathy for you in your affliction. An oppressive grief rests upon our hearts and a fearful foreboding as of those who stand face to face with a great personal bereavement. 'We bow our knees to the Father of Our Lord Jesus Christ that he would grant you according to the riches of his glory, to be strengthened with might by his spirit in the inner man' and that he may mercifully regard our supplications in your behalf; restore you to health and spare you to the nation for many years. We lift up our voice to the God of Nations who gave you to us in the hour of our greatest ~~national~~ peril, and by whose help you were enabled to so grandly serve the nation, praying that in a very special manner he may be near to you and bless you in what seems to be a great crisis in your disease. With hearts moved with gratitude and love we send you our Christian greetings." LS, USG 3. On March 10, F. A. Wood, secretary, International Order of Grand Templars, Jeffersonville, Ind., wrote to USG transmitting resolutions. " . . . And when in the fulness of time your weeping country-men shall with reverent care, committ the greatest and truest of America's brave and noble sons to rest, another will have been added to the sacred places of our country where American youth may best learn the grand lessons of courage valiantness and fidelity." ALS, General Grant National Memorial, New York, N. Y. On March 13, Governor Henry B. Harrison of Conn. wrote to USG transmitting "a copy of a resolu-tion which has just been passed unanimously by the General Assembly. Assuring you that the hearts of the people of Connecticut are full of the sentiments expressed by the resolution, . . . " *New York Times*, March 14, 1885. On March 27, a correspondent reported from Hartford that Frederick Grant replied to Harrison acknowledging the resolution. *Ibid.*, March 28, 1885. On March 15, Dan Macaulay, "11th Ind.," Louisville, had written to USG. "Pardon just a line of interruption—I ask for no answer—your wastebasket is handy I trust, 'trimmed and burning.' Merely this: If you could only realize how affectionately and lovingly your every hour is regarded by all people of all conditions, but more particularly your old Soldiers, you would be a very happy man. May God bless you and keep you with us in health and Satisfaction for all the years you wish to Stay." ALS, The Filson Club, Louisville, Ky. On the same day, John M. Keat-ing, Philadelphia, wrote to Frederick Grant. "Mr Childs tells me that the newspaper reports about your father's health have indeed only too serious a foundation—& as I deem that your mother must be annoyed by many letters I send you these few lines to ask you to tell her how sincerely I feel for you all in your troubles—I earnestly hope that the disease may be checked in its progress by your fathers strong constitution the power of which I well know—If you have the time won't you drop me a line—Would it annoy your father & mother if I called during some of my occasional flying trips to New York?—I know they must be overrun with visitors—" ALS, USG 3. On April 2, Col. Wesley Merritt, superintendent, USMA, telegraphed to Frederick Grant. "The Corps of Cadets request me to convey to General Grant the heartfelt sympathy of ev-ery Cadet for the great soldier and his family." Copy, USMA. On April 6, C.S.A. veterans meeting in New Orleans unanimously adopted a resolution offered by Wil-liam Preston Johnston. "That the Association of the Army of the Tennessee hear with deep regret of the pain and peril now endured by Gen. U. S. Grant. Twenty-three years ago to-day our soldiers met him on the field of battle and found him then, as ever, a soldier without fear and without malignity. In his own suffering and the sor-row of his family we tender him and them our heartfelt sympathy and ask for them the comfort and peace which come from Him who is not only Lord of Hosts, but Father of us all." *New York Times*, April 7, 1885. On April 9, 1,500 Ohio veterans authorized a telegram to USG. "The soldiers and sailors of Northern Ohio, assembled in Cleve-land to celebrate the twentieth anniversary of the surrender of Gen. Lee, with hearts surcharged with the tenderest affection for their old commander, which the lapse of 20 years has only served to strengthen and intensify send to you their most sincere sympathy in this hour of your great physical suffering. With admiration and love for you as a soldier and as the first citizen of the Republic, which only broadens and deep-ens as time passes, we tender a soldiers' greeting and God bless you." *Ibid.*, April 10, 1885. A similar resolution from N. Y. veterans is *ibid.*, April 11, 1885. On April 13, rabbis adopted a resolution. "*Whereas*, It has pleased the Almighty to visit our illustri-ous brother citizen, Ulysses S. Grant, with a sore and distressing illness almost unto death; Therefore, be it *Resolved*, That we, the Rabbis of New-York and adjacent States, in conference assembled in Philadelphia, do hereby offer our sympathy to the stricken household, and pray to the Father of all to send strength to the sufferer to enable him to fight this great battle with the heroism worthy of so great a soldier." *New York Tribune*, April 14, 1885. USG received other sympathetic communications from the Excelsior Club, Hackensack, N. J. (March 6); from legislatures in Mich. (March 19) and N. Y. (March 31); from Republicans in Columbus, Ohio (April 1) and the 21st Assembly District, N. Y. (April 15); and from the Common Council, Rochester, N. Y. (April 7). General Grant National Memorial , New York, N. Y.

On March 26, Maria Matalina Casagrande, "Fifth Ward Industrial School of the Children's Aid Society," had written to USG. "Of course you do not know me, but Miss Satterie, who is our teacher, and we all love her dearly, but I do the most of all because I am the oldest in school, and I understand things better than the little ones do. So Miss Satterie, tells us every morning about you, and dear General, we all pray that our dear Father in Heaven, will spare you to us until you are a hundred years old. We know just how you are every day, because all of our boys in school are either news-boys or boot-blacks, and the news-boys of course read it in the paper. And all of us girls know how you are, I buy a paper every night just to see how you are. Last night, I was so glad to read that you had gone for a drive. Miss Satterie always tells us you are our Hero. Then we all of us, the big ones I mean, study History and we all know what you did for us, before we were born. I am an Italian girl, almost all of us are Italian children down here in our school, but there are other children too. Some German, some Irish, and some Colored children, but we all love you and pray for you, with all our hearts and souls. When Miss Satterie told me I might write to you, I was so happy, I jumped about and my hands trembled with joy and they tremble still. I think you would like our school we are all poor children, but we all love you. Dear General Grant may Almighty God, and our dear Saviour and his blessed Mother, soon make you well again, is the prayer of your little friend." ALS, USG 3. On March 29, Daisy Todd *et al.*, New York City, wrote to USG. "We little ones of the 'Childrens Hour' of the Sixty First [*Street*] Methodist Church New York have heard that you are sick. We are very sorry and pray to God to make you well again We know that you was once our President and we have heard our fathers tell about how wise and brave you were in the great war We shall remember you when the big people now living are dead We hope your example will help us to lead nobler lives than we would have done if we had never heard of you Please accept our hearty love, good wishes and prayers." LS, General Grant National Memorial, New York, N. Y. Early on May 16, 350 children from this church paraded past USG's house. "Gen. Grant was aware of their coming, and although he had not risen for the day, hastily threw on a dressing gown and appeared at the library window as the children went by with flags and banners merrily waving. Later in the day the General visited the children in the Park, where they spent the day. They sang several songs for him and cheered him enthusiastically when he bade them good-bye." *New York Times*, May 17, 1885. On April 10, students at Clinton Avenue Institute, Brooklyn, had written to USG. "A class of young girls that has just [fi]nished the study of the history of the 'Civil War,' wish to express to you their gratitude, for what you did for our 'Union,' and to tender their heartfelt sympathy to you, in your suffering illness. Surely your name will be loved and revered, while our country endures, and there are girls and boys to study its history." L, General Grant National Memorial, New York, N. Y. On April 17, Winnie C. Daboll, St. Johns, Mich., wrote to USG. "I am a little girl and have never been to school but do my lessons at home with mamma My reader is Harpers Young People and this morning I read such a nice story about you. I went down to the news-room to buy a copy to send to you but they were all gone so mamma said I might write and tell you and if you could not read it your self perhaps some of the kind people who are with you would read it to you. My papa was a soldier and loves you very much but he is a lawyer now and does not fight any more though mamma says he often fights his old battles over again. He is Commander of the Post and last Week Thursday the 9th they had a Camp-fire and every body made speeches about General Lee's surrender to General Grant and our minister Mr Stearns told all the people how he used to know you years ago at Sacketts Harbor and that you were so good and brave and how you jumped on a mule at Chapultepec and rode through all sorts of danger to carry an order for an officer. Mamma had an uncle at that same battle and after it he was made a Captain too. He was Captain Horace B. Field of the Third Artillery of the Regular Army. He was lost off the San Francisco in a great storm at sea many years ago when mamma herself was a little girl. She says he was a brave officer and a gentleman and she loved him very much. Perhaps you knew him yourself. I shall send you a Birthday card and it will be a truely present from me I shall buy it with my own money that I have earned. Mamma says it is not a real present if you ask papa for the money to buy it with I shall put my name on it so you will know it is from me for I suppose you will get a great many. Good bye dear General Grant. I love you very much and wish I could do something to make you well" ALS, USG 3. Daboll's mother added an undated endorsement. "Will you please accept this letter which my little daughter has written? She has labored diligently over it all the afternoon and I am sure no small degree of love went into the task. 'There, mama, it is finished,' she said, after she had signed her name; 'and I am only afraid of one thing; and that is, that it will *have to pass through the hands of some Democrat who will not give it to General Grant.'* I reassured her by telling her there was not a man, woman, or child, in the length or breadth of the land, who would wrong the grand old soldier even so little as that. Accept also, dear sir, the love and honor of Winnie's father and mother. That you may be restored to health and happiness is their fervent, constant prayer." AE, *ibid.* In April, Maggie Irving, Louisville, wrote to USG. "I am a little Louisville girl that likes you so much. My father was one of your old soldiers and he never tires of telling us of the 'bravest general in the country.' Old General Grant, please, please get well. I hop you will live to be even older than that old rebel jeff davis. He don't even deserve to have his name spellt in capitale. General Grant, I don't write to you for your autograph or anything of that sort. I only write to let you know how we all love you. I hope you won't suffer a bit. General Grant pleas accept the best wishes and love of this little Louisville girl." USG Internet message board, maintained by Candace Scott, Victorville, Calif.

Public Message

[*April 27, 1885*]

To the various army posts, societies, cities, public schools, States, corporations and individuals, North and South, who have been so kind as to send their congratulations on my sixty-third birthday, I wish to offer my grateful acknowledgment. The dispatches have been so numerous and so touching in tone that it would have been impossible to answer them if I had been in perfect health.

U. S. GRANT.

New York Tribune, April 28, 1885. On April 27, 1885, Albion W. Tourgee, Mayville, N. Y., telegraphed to USG. "A household which daily forgets its own ills in tearful sympathy with yours, sends warmest wishes to the hero who has made a nation's renewed life the endless birthday of his fame." ALS (telegram sent), Chautauqua County Historical Society, Westfield, N. Y. For similar telegrams and greetings, see *New York Times* and *New York World*, April 28, 1885.

On April 24, Governor John A. Martin of Kan. had written to USG. "I have the honor to transmit, accompanying, an engrossed copy of an Executive order, issued yesterday, directing an appropriate recognition of the sixty-third anniversary of your birthday. The population of Kansas embraces a larger proportionate number of soldiers than that of any other State. It is believed that every regiment of the Union army, and very nearly every Company, is represented in this population . . . ." ALS (frayed), USG 3. The enclosure, and other birthday greetings, are in General Grant National Memorial, New York, N. Y. On April 27, Samuel Slade, Port Washington, Ohio, wrote to USG. "On this your Sixty Third birth-day, I write you to tender you my warmest sympathy in your afflictions. The children all over this broad Land (at least *those* whose parents believe that Secession and War on the Nation was a Crime) for instance each and every day when I come home with the Daily Commercial Gazette Cin. the first word from the children is, 'Papa how is Genl Grant to day'? they are as earnest in their sympathy as any old Soldier of the Land. The press give us some hope of your recovery God grant ist, is the prayer of an Ex Soldier of the 51 vol and member of the Society of the Army of the Cumberland" ALS, USG 3.

Also on April 27, a correspondent reported from Augusta, Ga., on a resolution honoring USG adopted at a Memorial Day observance by the Confederate Survivors' Association. "Remembering him now as the generous victor who, at the ever memorable meeting at Appomattox, to our immortal Lee and to the glorious 8,000 veterans, the surviving heroes of the Army of Northern Virginia, on the Ninth day of April, 1865, conceded liberal and magnanimous terms of surrender, do we, standing by the graves of our Confederate dead, and mindful of the memories which the observance of this occasion is designed to perpetuate, respectfully tender to General Grant assurances of our sincere and profound sympathy in this season of his direful extremity." *New York Tribune*, April 28, 1885. On May 25, USG received "Col. John Mason Brown, of Louisville, whose errand was to deliver the proceedings of the Louisville meeting held on the General's birthday. The General wrote requesting him to call in person, and in very feeling terms expressed his appreciation of the resolutions and speeches. The printed proceedings contain alternate speeches by officers of the Union and Confederate armies and these appear on tints of gray and blue. The vignette exhibits, under a portrait of the General, clasped hands on the uniform sleeves of the Federal and Confederate soldiers Gen. Grant conversed freely and without much effort, and warmly thanked the Confederates for the sympathy and kindly appreciation they showed. He remarked that the Louisville proceedings exhibited that state of feeling which he had for 20 years so earnestly desired." *New York Times*, May 26, 1885.

On April 28, Frederick Dent Grant had written to Hamilton Fish. "Father was much pleased with the beautiful boquet from you and Mrs Fish, and asked me to thank you for it. He also asked me to say that the wine you have of his might be sent here by express if not too much trouble to you to have it done. I am glad to say that although yesterday was a very fatiguing day to Father the show of love and respect he received had a very good effect and he is better today than he has been since his severe illness three weeks ago. With much love from all our family for you and Mrs Fish ..." ALS, DLC-Hamilton Fish. On the same day, USG referred "to the touching messages that were sent to him on his birthday from the school-children of the country, and seemed more impressed by them than by the words of distinguished men." *New York Tribune*, April 29, 1885.

To Charles L. Webster & Co.

New York, May 2, 1885.

To Charles L. Webster & Co.

Dear Sirs: My attention has been called to a paragraph in a letter published in The World newspaper of this city of Wednesday, April 29, of which the following is a part:

"The work upon his new book, about which so much has been said, is the work of Gen. Adam Badeau. Gen. Grant, I have no doubt, has furnished all of the material and all of the ideas in the memoirs as far as they have been prepared, but Badeau has done the work of composition. The most that Gen. Grant has done upon this book has been to prepare the rough notes and memoranda for its various chapters."

I will divide this into four parts and answer each of them.

First—"The work upon his new book, about which so much has been said, is the work of Gen. Adam Badeau." This is false. The composition is entirely my own.

Second—"Gen. Grant, I have no doubt, has furnished all of the material and all of the ideas in the memoirs as far as they have been prepared." This is true.

Third—"But Badeau has done the work of composition." The composition is entirely my own.

Fourth—"The most that Gen. Grant has done upon this book has been to prepare the rough notes and memoranda for its various chapters." This is false. I have not only prepared myself whatever rough notes were made, but, as above stated, have done the entire work of composition and preparing notes, and no one but myself has ever used one of such notes in any composition.

You may take such measures as you see fit to correct this report, which places me in the attitude of claiming the authorship of a book which I did not write, and is also injurious to you who are publishing and advertising such book as my work. Yours truly,

U. S. GRANT.

New York World, May 6, 1885. Theron C. Crawford provided the story, dated April 28, 1885, that prompted USG's letter. *Ibid.*, April 29, 1885. A report on USG's writing accompanied publication of this letter. "Gen. Grant has done much towards completing his book during his period of convalescence and expects to finish it within the next few days. The first volume is written and revised. Only about one hundred pages are needed to complete the second, though only a portion of it has been revised. The story of Lee's surrender was finished on Monday and revised yesterday. The General's connection with Lincoln's assassination has been related. It is his intention to begin work to-day on a description of the grand review of the Federal armies in Washington at the close of the war. He writes little himself, but dictates to a stenographer. Not only is his mind clear, but the story as he dictates it is lucid and requires but little revision. His daily average is about thirty pages and the work apparently fatigues him little, if any. The title of the book is 'The Personal Memoirs of U. S. Grant.' It tells the story of his life from childhood down to the grand review. It is replete with interesting sketches and anecdote of Lincoln and other great men, with whom Gen. Grant came in contact in civil and military life. Each volume will contain about 500 pages with numerous illustrations and maps. Charles L. Webster & Co., of this city, are the publishers. The work will be published simultaneously by them in the United States, England, France, Germany and Canada. Mr. Webster will go abroad in July to arrange for translating and publishing it in foreign countries. The first volume will be issued Dec. 1, and the second about March 1, 1886. Already orders for over 100,000 sets of the 'Memoirs' have been received without solicitation or advertising. At least 50,000 additional orders have come in which have not yet been accepted. It is expected that the sales will be unprecedentedly large. If nothing unforeseen happens the publishers expect to have all the manuscript in hand inside of a month. It will require but a few days to finish the second volume, after which it will be leisurely revised. Nearly all of volume II. has been written since the General was confined to the house by his present illness." *Ibid.*, May 6, 1885. See Frederick Anderson, ed., *Mark Twain's Notebooks & Journals* (Berkeley, 1975–79), III, 142–43; Samuel Charles Webster, ed., *Mark Twain, Business Man* (Boston, 1946), pp. 319, 323.

On March 19, Edwards Pierrepont had spoken to a reporter after visiting USG that morning. " . . . He said he was 'getting along into the second volume.' He has not been able to work upon it for some time, and the anxiety lest he may not live to finish it tells on him. He looks upon the completion of that work as a great public duty—his last service to his countrymen. This fact is the more clear to me, and the more beautiful in its unselfish sincerity, when I recall that throughout all the years of my intimacy with him he has never alluded once to his military career, except when

I have questioned him definitely about this battle or that. One would naturally suppose that such a warrior would live largely in the memory of his conquests. But Grant never spoke of them. He feels now, however, that, being in the possession of great facts of history which must otherwise die with him, it is a pressing public duty for him to spread them all before the people. This idea is in his mind almost to the exclusion of everything else. You ought to see his library. He has about forty-five or fifty huge manuscript volumes containing all his military papers, orders, notes, references, points jotted down at the moment of occurrences, and maps made at the time, and from this huge and confusing mass of information, which nobody but himself could make head or tail of, he is preparing his book. He permitted me to look some of them over. They contain the record of every day of his military life, and enable him to discuss his battles with indisputable authority . . . . As for death, Grant looks to it with a calm serenity. He is of a deeply religious nature and entertains the orthodox views of the Methodist Church, in which he was brought up . . . . Home matters and his book are pretty much all he thinks of now, and if he can finish the latter he will die content— . . ." *New York Tribune*, March 20, 1885.

After lunch on March 19, USG "went to work upon his book with an energy that was surprising to those who had observed his condition during the previous forty-eight hours. Hour after hour he stuck at his manuscript. He did not do any writing, but went rapidly along through the pages, making corrections here and there. He stopped occasionally to rest and at times took a nap for a few minutes. As soon as he awoke he went directly to his manuscript with renewed energy. At dinner time he said he would like a piece of roast mutton, and for the first time in many days showed some pleasure in eating. He rested for a time after he had finished his meal, and then went back to his book, and continued his literary labor until the evening was quite far advanced. It was evident to all that he was trying to make up for the time that he has lost during the last week, and as if he wanted to take advantage of every moment to hasten the work that will probably be the last labor of his life. His inability to work at his book has worried him greatly, and has been one of the causes that has led to his insomnia of late. When Dr. Douglas called in the evening, shortly before 10 p. m., he found the General up, bright and but little fatigued by the labors of the day. The amount of work done may be estimated when it is said that the General revised enough to keep his son and General Badeau busy for three days . . . ." *Ibid.* On April 30, USG "resumed work upon his book. He felt stronger than at any time since the improvement in his condition began. Before the bad attack that nearly ended his life, the General when engaged in literary work did most of the writing himself, and did a large share of the work of correcting and altering the manuscript. In order that he may not be fatigued, a stenographer is now employed and the General dictates to him. He works slowly and lays out his plans with great care. The book was kept by the General in such shape that even if he had died it would have been completed by General Badeau, who has been made his literary executor. He is now dealing with the events at Appomattox Court House. He dictated during the morning and afternoon for three hours, at one time speaking for an hour continuously. The amount dictated will cover about twenty-five pages of the book. He intends to go on at this rate or as rapidly as possible until the work is finished. So absorbed did he become in the business at hand that he voluntarily gave up his noonday drive and afternoon walk. Those who saw the General were surprised at the wonderful degree of mental vigor shown and the clearness with which every fact was stated . . . ." *Ibid.*, May 1, 1885. On May 1, USG "looked over the literary work done the day before, and examined some maps and orders in relation to settling some of the disputed points of the Appomattox campaign. He dictated in the afternoon for an hour and a half, and covered the series of events of this famous campaign so extensively that the little that remains to be done will probably be finished to-day. The General will continue laboring steadily at the second and last volume, and hopes to have it in the publisher's hands within two months. The proof sheets of the first volume will soon be ready . . . ." *Ibid.*, May 2, 1885. On May 2, Saturday, USG dictated in the afternoon after suffering much physical discomfort in the morning following a poor night's sleep. Frederick Dent Grant "said in the evening: 'The General worked on his book to-day for over two hours, and will on Monday assume the dictating, after which he will take a rest for a few days, and collect material for future work. The work is nearly done, and one more day's dictation will probably finish it, save perhaps the work of revision. Father is very precise and goes over his work time and time again in order to express his exact meaning.'" *Ibid.*, May 3, 1885. On May 4, USG had his easy chair "wheeled up to the table in the library, where a large pile of manuscript lay, and after giving a glance at the morning papers and commenting upon the war cloud that hung over Europe, he turned his attention to his manuscript and laid out the plan to be followed in dictating to the stenographer. He seemed delighted to get back to his desk again and went to work with a will, and when his lunch was brought at noon, he was deeply buried in a [*m*]ap representing the points of interest that cluster around the closing scenes of the War at Appomattox. After lunch the General took a short rest and then slowly dictated to the stenographer. He took frequent rests but with all the caution employed his throat felt the strain of talking and became irritable, causing slight attacks of coughing. The General remained in seclusion and was not disturbed in his work by seeing the few callers who came to the house. He desires to spend all the time he possibly can at his book and under favorable conditions the rough draft will be finished in a week. The revision will take some time, as the General is careful that his ideas shall be closely expressed, and he has spent more time in revising and editing the book than it has taken him to write it. He spent the evening quietly with his family and enjoyed the romping of his little grandchildren, who were playing near his chair . . . ." *Ibid.*, May 5, 1885. On May 5, USG "wished to take a ride, but it was decided that the air was too cold. After luncheon he went to work vigorously upon his book and wrote a portion of it himself, which he had not done before since he returned to his literary labor. He did this to relieve his throat, which became stiff and thick from the muscular contraction induced by talking . . . ." *Ibid.*, May 6, 1885. For additional details on USG's writing, see *New York Times*, May 1–3, 5–7, 1885.

To Adam Badeau

———

[*New York City, May 2–5, 1885*]

GENERAL:

Since pondering over the contents of your letter, and more particularly over the conclusions drawn from it, and reflections based upon what ~~I say~~ you say, and my knowledge of your temper and disposition—I understand the latter better than you do—I have

concluded that you and I must part all associatio[n] so far as the
preparation of any work goes which is to bear my signature. ~~goes.~~
In all other respects I hope our relations may conti[n]~~ueue~~ as they
have ~~done before~~ have always been. ~~as long as my life continues.~~
~~But in any literary work.~~ I shall always regard it as a pleasure to
do you a kindness if it comes in my way so long as our present relations exist. They will not be changed by any act of mine. But any
literary work in which we are mutually interested hereafter it must
be something to which [*my*] name is not to be attached; certainly
not further than my work bears relation to the work. It is not
probable however that I shall ever be so engaged again. My health
is still in a precarious condition, and I shall regard myself as having been almost under the care of a special providence if spared to
complete the work I am now engaged upon. You say "~~you have lost~~
~~seven months already from your own work to work for me, and~~
~~that~~ quote from your letter, "and ~~your letter~~ my novel remain[s]
unpublished for that cause" I disagree with the statement. But if
correct you have spent seven months in work for me and are not
near up with the manuscript which I have composed and written
with my own hand. Beside this Chattanooga ~~is in~~ was put in the
hands of the [Editor of the] Century without your seeing it ~~as I~~
~~remember~~ [according to my recollection]. I exclude here also the
manuscript—more than equal to 100 pages of the book—in the
hands ~~of the sten~~ writing of the stenographer, of which you have
~~not~~ read [but little] ~~either note or manuscript.~~ At this rate you
would not be through the book in the time my contract ~~f~~ calls for.
The loss would all fall upon my house in such event, and it would
include not only what you demand but the expenses incurred by
the publisher in various ways. ~~Your dates and facts~~ You say I said,
"I was about to use your ~~dates and facts~~ work for dates, facts &c.
This is a little overdrawn, at least in the idea it would con~~tain~~[vey].
Your first volume was prepared in my office, while you occupied
the position [of] ~~of~~ an officer on my staff, with the temporary
rank of Col. This gave you [pay three grades beyond your actual rank] access to papers and documents that other writers at the
time could not have convenient access to. You also had the assis-

tance of several very intelligent staff officers to aid you in hunting up data, relating insidents, furnishing military terms with which you were not then familia[r] &c. ~~I al~~ Your second & ~~volumne~~ and third volumnes, were prepared abroad while you were holding office under the government. A great deal of time was spent by my staff officers in furnishing you information that you called for from time to time, and in some instances in sending you books and papers from the Archives in Washington at the risk of their being lost.[1] You had possession of a copy of the records of my ~~Hd Qrs~~ headquarters,—my work really—kept for my special use, until you were through your work. ~~All this I know~~ I also read every chapter of your book before the latter appeared before the public. I knew what care had been taken to get the facts of history correct. I naturally would take your facts and figures before those of any other writer, knowing these facts, unless contradicted by proofs brought to light subsequent[ly] to the publication of your book. The facts you give cannot be excluded from ~~the~~ public [use], and ~~not~~ cirtainly [not] from me. Years ago I said in writing how these were obtained and made my self responsible for them, but, in terms, denied all responsibility ~~from~~[or] your reflections, deductions, comments and judgement. There is nothing in your book that I ever objected to [so] ~~more~~[uch] ~~than~~ [as] I did to your ~~far overdone~~ [continuous] praise of me personally. You say "I offered you $10,000 to help me." When I said this you replied that I knew what a pleasure it would be to you to serve me, and that you would take nothing, ~~but that I knew your circumstances which I understood.~~ [only for your circumstances which I knew] It was out of respect for your sensitiveness that I innumerated as I did, ~~the~~ in the paper which I long subsequently handed you so that, in case of my death, you could still get what I promised on the ful[fillment of yours part of the work.] I said I would like your assistance because I had never written a book and there was much work connected with such an undertaking that I ~~would~~ [was] not ~~know how to do~~ [familliariar with] I did not contemplate your writing anything for the book, but to help me arrange it, and to criticise my work so that I could correct. I knew how much disappointed you had been in the recep-

tion of your own work. I knew that you needed employment for
your support. I was financially ruined and was suffering ~~financial~~
greatly in body body as well as mind. The work which I wanted
you to do I did not think would take over two months of your time,
working an average of four hours a day, six days in a week. It
would not if done by an expeditious writer and as I want it. My
name goes to the book and I want it so in the fullest sense. For
the[is] work—it being understood by me as ~~I wanted it~~ above—I
proposed to give you $5.000 out of the first $20.000 00 ~~I might~~ received from its sale, and $5.000 00 out of the next $10.000. At that
time $30.000 was supposed to be a large amount ~~to~~ for an author
to receive from the sale of a book. About this time it was reported
that a publisher in this City would give $50.000 00 for the copy-
right. I was advised by a friend, a man of large ~~bus~~ and successful
business experience to accept it. If I had your share of the profits
would have been 20 pr. ct.

You say the work wanted of you calls upon you to connect the
disjointed fragments into a connecte[d] naritive, &c. drudgery you
would not do for any on[e] but me. For the compensation you ask I
could get very able work done by persons who would not regar[d]
the work as either drudgery or degrading. It woul[d] be degrading
to me to accept such work. I do not admit the disjointed matter you
spe[ak] of except after I became so ill that I could write but little at
a time, and that after [inter]vals, and when I supposed some one,
whose name would necessarily be given to the publi[c] (and that
name yours,) I ~~occasionally~~ would ~~think~~ occasionally think of some
thing in the way of incident, reflection, upon some phases of the
war, estimate of chara[c]ter of some leading officer of one or other
of the Armies, which I would deem it importa[nt] that I should
write myself. As sick as I was I wrote them. They were disjointed
[in] the particular that some of these scrap[s] will go in one part of
the book and some in another. You say the book cannot possibl[y]
be completed before 18~~7~~[8]6; If not ~~General~~ general I fear that its
completion would depend entirely upon both ~~my~~ [the] prolongla-
tion of my life until the work was done, and that I should retain
streng[th enough] to push the work. To be entirely frank, I do not

believe the work would ever be done by you, in case of my death, while the $1000 00 pr. month was coming in. Here now is where I understand you better than you do yourself. You are petul[ant,] your anger is easily arroused and you are overbearing even to me at ~~all~~ times, and always with those for whom you have done or are doing, literary work. Think of the publishers you have quarreled with. As an office~~r~~ holder you either quarreled or found great fault with those immediately over you. As soon as I was out of office you were ready to quarrel with the President. His untimely death prevented this, but you did quarrel with his successor, the Sec. ~~of State~~ and Ass. Sec. of state, your immediate ~~predecessors~~ superiors, and while still holding office commenced the preparation of a political novel in which all those were held up to ridicule.[2] I never listened to a word of your novel: But I was sure from its theme it would have ~~been~~[proven] a financial failure if it had been published, and that you would have been otherwise very much [disappointd] I did not advise with you because my advice was not asked; I know that in matters effecting yourself you are beyond contact at times, and when you have tendered advice you sometimes become so enraged ~~that you~~ if it is not followed that you think yourself much injured. You have no idea of this yourself, but it ~~frequen~~ has frequently happened with me. I have abstained from bring ~~your~~ [to your] notice ~~to~~ your action at the time, by ceasing to talk, or by half acquiescing and then doing as I though right afterwards ~~You~~ If I had died leaving the unfinished work upon my book. ~~unfinished you would have soon become so arrog~~ to you to complete, with $1000 00 a month in advance, you would have become so arrogant that there would have been a rupture between you and them before many days had rolled around. I ~~do~~ will not give any other reasons ~~why in writing~~ why advance payment[s] would ~~have~~ defeate the completion of the work. They do not reflect upon your honor

I will not notice at length any of the other statements contained in your letters. But you dwell upon the drudgery, the absence of fame; the sinking from sight of the work of your life if my work is completed; the better you do my work the deeper you sink yourself, or your work into obscurity &c. &c.—Allow me to say, this is

all bosh, and is evidently the work of a distempered mind that has
evidently been growing moody by too much reflection upon these
matters. Your book was a financial failure for three main reasons,
first; the period between the publication of the first volumne [&
the others] was so great that people generally forgot your work;
second; it is too long and to costly. It should have been in two
volumnes, of one or two hundred pages less than it n they now
contain. Much of this [reduction] could have been attained [made]
by leaving out the greater part about me, a portion of what you say
in praise of a few other officers, and it would have lef some space
to devote to the mention of other officer[s] of merit. The fact is,
if my book effe[cts] yours in any way it will be to call attention to
it. Third; [your publisher] either, from weariness in waiting for
the last of your book, or other cause, I suppose the sale of it was
not pushed. You say I am a man of affairs &c. and can tell a simple
story &c. A literary [man, must supply that some that some deficiency, is inferred and that you are the only man, who] can do it, &c.
If this is the case general I do not want a book bearing my name to
go before the world which I not only did not write to such such an
extent as to be fully entitled to the credit of authorship. I do not
want a secret between me and some [one else, which would destroy
my honor, if it was divulged. I can not] think of holding myself as
dependent upon any one person to supply a capacity which I am
lacking. I may fail, but I will not put myself in any such position.
    "I am the only
    "No one but myself can destroy my own book. If I dont help
you, it will retain its place; you have for you have neither the physical strength, &c" In answer to this I have only to say that for the
last twenty-fou[r] years I have been very much emplo[yed] in writing. As a soldier I wrote my own orders, directions and reports.
They were n[ot] edited nor assistance rendered. As President [I]
wrote every official document, I believe, bearing my name. (Messages of course contained abstracts from report of heads of departments, made out and sent to me before the reports themselves were
compiled. The I assume no President ever wrote out him self.) All
these have been published and widely circulated. The public have

has become accustomed to them and ~~no~~ [know] my style of writing. They know that it is not even an attempt to imitate either a literary ~~style nor~~ [or clasical style] and that it is just what it is pure and simple and nothing else. If I succeed in telling my story so that others can see, as I do, what I attempt to shew, I will be satisfied. The reader must [also be satisfied] be for he knew from the begining just what to ~~accept~~ [expect].

~~General I have written this after three day reflection and You give other reasons why I do not think that you ought to help me on any work to which is to bear my signature.~~ [your letter affords abundan[ce] of other reasons why you should not help me in any work which is to bear my name] But these are sufficient, adding only ~~that~~ what is necessary to make a part of what has been already said plain if this letter should ever be read by others than yourself. You ask for a new contract, and demand $1000 00 pr. month in advance until the work is completed, an ten pr. ct. of the entire profits arising from the sale of the work after it is put upon the market. This would make you a patner with my family as long as the book found a sale. ~~It is~~ [this is] preposterous ~~in amount~~. Not for one moment has it been entertained. This with the statements innumerated in this letter, and others contained in yours, makes it impossible ~~that we~~ for us to be associated in a work which is to bear my name. It would be degri[a]dation for me to accept honors and profit from the work of another mans brain while declairing to the public that it was ~~my own~~ the product of my own brain and hand.

~~I write this in all frankness and sorrow. When I first read your letter it was with I was filled with pain and anguish. I thought it so It was so much unlike what I had thought~~

I write frankly because I want you to know why I could not receive your services now on any terms. I hope that it will not disturb the relations which have heretofore existed between us ~~I certainly wish~~ in all other particulars. I hope sincerely that you may be able not only to realize with your pen the five to ten thousand dollars a year which you say you can earn, but twice the larger sum. Your prosperity in life ~~will~~ will gratify me. You can always be the welcome visitor at my house that you have been heretofore.

This correspondence between us may be unknow to the world if you choose. I do not ~~ask this, but will be gratified~~ if ask secrecy, but ~~it will not be made public by my act~~ the necessity for publicity will not occur through any fault of mine. Repeating my assurances of the best wishes for your success in life, and health and happiness to the end, I subscribe my self, as ever,

Your friend and
well wisher

⌈P. S. The contract. New York In your letter you speak of a contract ~~allow me to say~~ there ~~was~~ is no contract but simply ~~a~~ a ~~paper~~ memorandum I gave to you signed by ~~one~~ me alone ~~and not witnessed~~ and was intended to let my family know what I wished done in case of my death which was then expected, and which would prevent any ~~discussion~~ disagreaeble discussion arising about what my wishes were Although this bound no one, I ~~would~~ should ~~have carried it out if I had lived and my family would in case I died provided you had performed your the part expected of you. There is now would have been nothing due you until returns begian to come in from my book and now if I owe you anything it will be settled at that time.~~ ⌈have⌉ regarded it as binding upon me⌉[3]

ADf (bracketed material not in USG's hand), Ulysses Grant Dietz, Maplewood, N. J.; copy (in Frederick Dent Grant's hand) and typed copy, both dated May 5, 1885, USG 3. Frederick Dent Grant endorsed USG's draft. "Genl Grant wrote this letter ~~in answer to Badeau's of May 2nd~~ and gave it to me to copy—It is in answer to Badeau's of May 2nd I made a copy & submitted to Genl Grant to changed the arrangement and I recopied it then a paragraph was added (on white paper) and I recopied Genl Grant had me go over this copy and made some further changes and dictated a postscript which he directed & revised I then made a clean copy & handed it to Badeau's nurse a fellow called Coster . . . . It was either the 7th or 8th of May that I delivered this to Badeau's nurse" AES (undated), Ulysses Grant Dietz, Maplewood, N. J. On May 2, 1885, Adam Badeau, New York City, wrote to USG. "I beg to lay before you a few views which I am very sure have not occurred to you, absorbed as you have been in your illness and recently in your renewed work. I present them in writing because I can thus make them clearer, and because you can more carefully consider them and detect if I am in error When you sent for me in August last you said that you had always given me to suppose that my work should be the only authorized expression of your views on the war; but that you were now about to write your memoirs, and to make use of my work for your facts and dates whenever necessary, saving yourself all the labor of research; and that in consideration of these circumstances and of my assistance in preparing your own book, you offered me $10,000 out of the profits, if they should amount to $30,000. The labor I was expected to perform was such as enabled me to revise with you both the Shiloh and the Vicksburg campaigns, 250 pages—in a little more than a fortnight; for both these chapters were sent to the Century while I was at Long Branch in August. In October, I came to you in NewYork, before I was ready, giving up my own work for yours, and have since devoted myself to your service, happy and proud to aid you. Your illness first protracted and then interrupted the work, and ~~has~~ I have been detained ~~me~~ from all other avocations for seven months. I tried once or twice to write for myself, but gave this up as impossible while I was doing such work as your book demands, for I put my whole soul and ability into it. My novel is unpublished today solely for this cause. Now, that you are happily in some degree restored, and able to dictate—an entirely new state of affairs arises. Your book is about half done; the work still to be executed on Vol I, and the original composition on Vol II make necessary eight or ten months more of labor. You propose to dictate and I am to piece and prepare and connect the disjointed fragments into a connected narrative. This work is the merest literary drudgery—*such as I would never consent to do for any one but you*; five times as laborious as original composition, with none of the interest; five times as difficult under the circumstances as what I have hitherto done with you. It cannot possibly be completed as you want it, and as I should do it—before 1886. I am to have no pay until the profits of your book come in—at the earliest in March next. In the nature of things I can have no reputation or consideration from my connection with the book. I must efface myself, and yet work intensely hard without ~~further~~ increased pay, or any at all until a year and a half from the beginning of my labors. Let me say just here—I have no possible desire for the reputation or name of writing the book. The preposterous assertions in the newspapers will refute themselves. I desire the fame of my own book, not of yours. Yours is not, and will not be, the work of a literary man, but the simple story of a man of affairs and of a great general; proper for you, but not such as would add to my credit at all. With your concurrence I have striven to make it such. But your book has assumed an importance which neither you nor I anticipated last summer. It is to have a circulation of hundreds of thousands, and the larger its circulation, the greater its importance, the more completely it will supplant and stamp out mine. The better I help you to make it, the more effectually I destroy what I have spent my life in building up—my reputation as your historian. And this nobody but me can do. No literary man has the military knowledge; no military man has the literary experience; no literary or military man living—not one of your old staff even—has one tithe of my knowledge and experience on this subject—the result of twenty years study and devotion and labor. Besides which no man alive,—but your own sons, loves you so well. No one but myself can destroy my own book. If I dont help you, it will retain its place; for you have neither the physical strength nor the habits of mind yourself to make the researches to verify or correct your own memory. If you cannot yourself finish the work, nobody can do it fitly but me. Dear General, I say this frankly to show you what is expected of me—to give up a year of my life, at the age of 53, to get no shadow of reputation or consideration, to trample on my own fame, to receive no pay at present, and none at all proportionate to my position or claims—for I could easily earn five or ten thousand dollars a year, with importance and consideration besides. ~~I have~~ There is only one inducement in the world—and that is to serve you. But I have already written your military history, and I can still write your political history, and earn more, and serve your fame quite as well: while if, by any chance, your work should be unfinished or ill finished, my own would retain its place. Your name sells your work, your deeds are its theme; your own story told by yourself is what the people want; all this is indisputable; but the drudgery is all mine, and the drudgery is as indispensable as your name or as the publisher's part. Under these circumstances, considering the immense sale assured, ~~is it unfair for me to~~ the unexpected work put on me, the unanticipated damage done to my life's labor—is it unfair for me to ask that a new bargain be made. I am willing to agree to complete the work from your dictation, in the first person, with all the supervision you may be able to give, but in any event to complete it, if I am alive and well—within the present year; to claim of course, no credit whatever for the composition, but to declare, as I have always done, that you write it absolutely. For this labor I ask a thousand dollars a month, to be paid in advance, until the work is done, and afterwards ten per cent of the entire profits. The publishers—Fred told me long ago—have offered to advance any sums you desire, so that you would not be inconvenienced by the earlier payments; and unless you receive enormous gains, my share would still be small. I would engage to help you build such a monument as no man ever yet put up to his own fame, and no name would ever appear in connection with it but your own." ALS, USG 3. Frederick Grant endorsed this letter. "This letter was handed to Genl Grant on the morning of May 2nd 1885 by Badeau and in the the presence of Mrs Grant. Badeau first blushed and then ~~ob~~ turned pale. Recovering himself Badeau assumed a tragic air walking up to the sick General and saying: 'Will you read this General'. General Grant then said: 'Who is it from Badeau' and was answered by ~~the~~ Badeau: 'It is from me General will you read it at your leisure.' Badeau then left the house and did not return until May 4th. I was not in at the time this letter was delivered but was told the above immediately after I returned home about noon of the same day. Upon my return Genl Grant was much worse & was walking the floor of his room. When he saw me he turned & went to his beareau unlocked the top draw and took this letter out handed it to me saying: 'Read this & tell me what you think of it.'" AES (undated), *ibid.* On May 4, Badeau wrote to USG. "As I stated to you in my letter of Saturday I have no desire, intention or right to claim the authorship of your book. The composition is entirely your own. What assistance I have been able to render has been in suggestion, revision, or verification." ALS, *ibid.* Frederick Grant endorsed this letter. "May 4th ~~Genl~~ Badeau returned to No 3 East 66th st and on entering ~~my~~ Genl Grants office where I was sitting Badeau ~~asked me~~ enquired if 'Genl Grant had said anything to me about a letter he had handed him' I ~~told Genl~~ said to Badeau 'yes, I am making a copy of his reply now. But before giving it to you father asked me to say that he would like you to give me a letter telling just what you consider you have done upon his book' ~~Genl~~Badeau then went to his room and soon returned with this letter which he handed to me. he then went into Genl Grants room & I followed him immediately & heard Genl Grant saying 'As sick as I am Badeau you wrote it' of course meaning the letter of May 2d" AES (undated), *ibid.* Probably on May 5, USG wrote to Frederick Grant. "Get Badeau to see my letter to Webster, also to write his to me before Webster gets here this am. I want to deliver to Webster one, or both of my letters and I want Badeau's to shew him at the same time . . . . P. S. Webster is to be here at 10 30" AN (initialed, undated), Ulysses Grant Dietz, Maplewood, N. J. See preceding letter; Frederick Anderson, ed., *Mark Twain's Notebooks & Journals* (Berkeley, 1975–79), III, 205.

On May 9, Badeau wrote to USG. "I have received your letter of May 5, and shall make no attempt to change your views. I laid my own before you and they have not been accepted. You do not recognize the services which I supposed I had rendered, and you reject the idea of increased and peculiar remuneration for what I thought increased and peculiar work. You look upon my assistance as that of an ordinary clerk or literary hack: I thought I was aiding you as no one else could in doing a great work. I took it for granted that if your answer was unfavorable my connection with your book would cease, but I left it for you to sever the connection. I still however intend to write on the theme which has engaged so much of my life. I have not changed the views or feelings of twenty years because it seems to me that in one instance you are unjust, and though it is hard to believe that I am the one, of all others, selected to receive injustice at your hands—I cannot and I would not recall or unsay my past—much less yours. Since I am not to help you build up the monument on which I have already done some labor, I will attempt another, and strive to make you and your family—for whom as well as for yourself I have cherished so deep an affection—appreciate the effort. As the occasion for my remaining at your house is at an end, I will send for my trunks and boxes as soon as I have secured lodgings, and pay my respects to yourself and family when I return to town." ALS, USG 3. See letter to Adam Badeau, July 12, 1885.

1. USG wrote another version of this passage on a separate sheet. "Your remaining Volumes were written abroad while you were holding office under the government. I was President at the time, and had controll of all the executive departments. You were furnished material ~~constantly by under the~~ which you called for from time to time until your book was completed, compiled under the supervision of ~~the~~ my Secretaries, ~~the same~~ officers who had ~~served on my staff~~ [assisted you before]" ADf (bracketed material not in USG's hand), Ulysses Grant Dietz, Maplewood, N. J.

2. See Badeau, *Conspiracy: A Cuban Romance* (New York, 1885); *New York Times*, Feb. 7, 1886.

3. On March 20, 1888, Badeau, New York City, wrote *"To the American People"* to explain how this letter arose from his work with USG on *Memoirs*. " . . . After I had been a short while at his house, Gen. Grant became, as was plain, mortally ill, and late one night Col. Grant came into my room and said his father evidently would be unable to finish the work, and that I seemed the only person who could complete it. I replied that I seemed to be the most suitable. The Colonel then declared that he wished me to write the remainder of the book and let him put his name to it. I was not at liberty to discuss the matter with Col. Grant, because of Gen. Grant's injunctions, but I endeavored to show by my manner that the proposition was unacceptable. Soon after this Gen. Grant himself broached the subject in the presence of the Colonel, and said he thought 'Fred' and I would have to finish his book, but I simply replied that I hoped he would be able to do it himself. As soon as I saw the General alone I told him of the proposition of the Colonel, and said I would never consent to do for another man what I was doing for him. I would finish loyally and as well as I knew how every word that he had touched, but I would not write half a volume of original composition and let the Colonel or any one else put his name to it. The General said this was the first he had ever heard of the matter. Several times afterward, however, he said he wished I would come to some arrangement with 'Fred,' and the Colonel also told me that his father desired us to finish the work together. I had, however, at no time any desire or intention to enter into collaboration with Col. Grant. After a while Gen. Grant revived, and he then proposed to send for a stenographer and dictate to him what he could remember, and give me the matter to make over. At this time (May 1) Gen. Grant informed me that he had just notified his family of his agreement with me. He said this in the presence of his son Jesse. A mass of matter dictated by him was then handed to me, full of important mistakes, jumbling up two interviews with Mr. Lincoln that were six weeks apart, omitting one battle, and leaving out altogether an important conversation with Sheridan which led to the battle of Five Forks. It was just such matter as a man on the brink of the grave might have been expected to dictate. At the same time a statement appeared in a prominent New York newspaper that I was the real author of

Gen. Grant's book. This excited the publishers, who at once sent a lawyer to ask me to deny that I had written a line of the memoir. Such a declaration would have been absolutely false, though the statement had probably been made to them. I had scrupulously concealed the nature of my connection with the work on account of Gen. Grant's anxiety. I was willing to be silent for his sake, but I was not willing to declare what was false. I refused the application of the lawyer. The next day Col. Grant handed me a letter which I was expected to sign or verify, stating that no one except Gen. Grant had done any but clerical work on his memoirs. I refused to say that this declaration was true, and had high words on the subject with Col. Grant. This was at about 11 o'clock at night, and when I left the Colonel I went to my bedroom. Before I was undressed Gen. Grant sent a servant to ask me to go to his room. I did so, and he told me he had overheard my conversation with the Colonel, and could not sleep until he had seen me and told me that he disapproved of the Colonel's demand. He said he had told the Colonel I would object to the word clerical, and that it should not be used. He said I could trust him, and that he would do nothing to affect me without informing me in advance. I offered then to finish the work for him in the first person if he would dictate to me. He replied that he thought he could do it without me, but if not he would accept my offer. Next morning I was again in Gen. Grant's room, and two new letters were read to me by the Colonel. They were to be signed by Gen. Grant, and stated that no one but himself had written a line of his book and that I had not written a word of it, or something equivalent to this and equally strong. I declared that the assertion was positively untrue, and I appealed to Gen. Grant to confirm me. He said that the letters were not strictly correct and that the expressions had better be changed, and they were stricken out altogether. Then I was urged to verify his letter. I declared that I thought it extremely injudicious to take so much notice of a flying report: . . . It was after the arrangement for a stenographer, and while these demands for verification from me were proceeding, that I wrote the letter of May 2, which Col. Grant has published. The circumstances of the original contract had entirely changed. I had spent seven months at Gen. Grant's house instead of two or three, and his book was still incomplete; the book that we had supposed might bring in $30,000, or at the most $50,000, was to yield at least $400,000. The damage done to my own history was proportionately increased. I was expected to perform an entirely different task from that I had originally contemplated—one far more difficult. I therefore asked Gen. Grant if he did not think a different arrangement would now be fair. I did not say or suggest that I insisted on a new contract; I left it to his justice and friendship to decide. I assured him that I had no desire to claim the literary merit, which I now saw that he so much regarded, but as the enterprise had become so different from what we both had anticipated, it seemed to me proper that I should profit by the increased results which I was to do so much to secure, and be paid for the increased labor I was to perform. Had Gen. Grant been well, I have no dout that he would have consented to my proposition, or more probably would have himself proposed arrangements more advantageous and fairer to me than the original bargain. This proposition of mine, it has been said, was made when Gen. Grant was dying, and that it aggravated his last sufferings. But it was the efforts of his son to extort from me a false statement that agitated Gen. Grant; it was the machinations of that son to obtain profit and reputation out of my labors to which he was not entitled that caused this additional suffering to his great father. For if Gen. Grant was able to dictate half a volume, he was able also to consider the remuneration of the man who was to put that volume into shape. I talked with him myself more than once about my proposition, and he was entirely calm. He said nothing about breaking off our relations, but he told me that he had never mentioned the letter even to Mrs. Grant, in fact to no one but to Col. Grant; and in a few days Col. Grant handed me the letter of May 5, covering eleven foolscap pages, written in his own hand, but signed by Gen. Grant. This letter, I do not hesitate to assert, could never have received Gen. Grant's sanction had he been well in body and mind; but drugged, diseased, and under the influence of his son, he put his name to a paper unworthy of his fame, full of petty spite and vulgar malice, such as he never displayed, and, worse yet, of positive and palpable falsehood. For the letter states that the compensation he had originally offered me both he and I had at the time considered 'large;' yet the agreement itself declares, in his own hand, that the compensation was 'small.' Of course he is not responsible for the falsehood, but there it stands under his own signature. The letter is also too stupid for Gen. Grant to have written had he maintained the view it was supposed to uphold. It states positively that he had originally offered me 20 per cent. of the profits which he expected, and yet expresses indignation because I asked for 10 per cent. It admits that the work was expected to last only two or three months, and yet objects to paying for what had already required seven, and would require still more. It gives me the lie, on whose veracity his own history depends. It doubts in words the pecuniary claims of the man who had been his intimate friend for half a lifetime, and yet invites that man to be his guest and intimate companion. Gen. Grant himself declared, under recent and well-known circumstances, that he had once unwittingly put his name to an important and damaging document of the contents of which he was ignorant, when it was placed before him by a designing and unprincipled man. This is all I have to say about my letter and that signed with his name. My own, I maintain, was fair, manly, respectful, consistent with all our relations and with my regard for my chief. The other was not the letter of the Grant I had known, who had taken Vicksburg and displayed such grandeur of soul at Appomattox . . . ." *New York Sun*, March 21, 1888. On the evening of the same day, a reporter interviewed Frederick Grant and saw the original draft of USG's letter. *New York Herald*, March 21, 1888. In a long written response to Badeau, Frederick Grant described how USG wrote the letter despite "being so weak that he could not write more than a few lines without stopping." *Brooklyn Eagle*, March 25, 1888. On March 29, Badeau, New York City, wrote *"Once more to the American People"* to again question USG's authorship of this letter. *Ibid.*, April 1, 1888. See Memorandum, Feb. 7, 1885; Badeau to Daniel S. Lamont, April 3, 1888, DLC-Grover Cleveland.

To Horatio C. King

NEW YORK, May 6, 1885.

General HORATIO C. KING,

Carrollton Hotel, Baltimore:

Please thank the members of the Society of the Army of the Potomac for their partiality in electing me a second time their President.[1] I wish my health promised the probability of my being at the next meeting. I would regard it as providential should I be able to attend, but I accept the honor, though without the hope of performing the duties of the office. Wishing all members many happy re-unions,

I remain,

U. S. GRANT.

The Society of the Army of the Potomac. Report of the Sixteenth Annual Re-Union, . . . (New York, 1885), p. 16. During the business meeting held in Baltimore on May 7, 1885, USG was nominated and elected for another term as president of the Society of the Army of the Potomac. *Ibid.*, pp. 7–8. At the opening of this session, Horatio C. King, recording secretary, said. "A few days ago I had an interview with General Grant, and he said he expected to be at the meeting, but under imperative orders of his physicians he was not able to attend. He commissioned me to say to you that the words spoken to you a year ago in Brooklyn were sincere and heartfelt, and it is a great disappointment to him not to be able to be present to-day to preside over your meeting. His sympathy and his heart are with us. I think I can give you some encouragement for the hope that he may be with us another year. In the absence of General Grant, General Hunt, the Senior Vice-President, will preside." *Ibid.*, p. 6. On April 30, King, Francis P. Stevens, and Abner Doubleday had visited USG's home in New York City and spoken with Frederick Dent Grant, who commented on his father's health. "He is much better to-day, and for the first time since the severe spell has been at work upon his book. He has dictated to-day enough to make about twenty-five pages of printed matter, and he has not been out on that account. As to his going to Baltimore, I can only say he is anxious to be with you and is saving up his strength and doing all he can to be able to do so. I think it is possible, but I cannot say it is probable. If he can come I shall be with him, . . ." *New York World*, May 1, 1885. On May 9, USG "went through a large accumulation of correspondence that on account of his close attention to his book had not been attended to. Many of the letters were from his old comrads in arms and congratulated him on his re-election to the presidency of the Society of the Army of the Potomac." *New York Tribune*, May 10, 1885. On the same day, USG wrote to Edward R. Humphreys, Boston. "I Thank you sincerely for your kind letter of the 8th instant." Robert F. Batchelder, Catalog 32 [1981], no. 61. For Humphreys, see *New York Times*, March 22, 1893.

While president of the Society of the Army of the Potomac, USG signed a membership certificate for John N. Coyne, bvt. lt. col. for service with the 70th N. Y. DS (facsimile), Joseph Rubinfine, List 73, no. 30, and List 82, no. 39. On April 18, 1888, Coyne received the Medal of Honor for gallantry during the battle of Williamsburg, Va., on May 5, 1862.

1. See letter to John G. Carlisle, June 17, 1884.

Message

[*May 14, 1885*]

Tell the boys that they probably will never look into my face again, nor hear my voic[e], but they are en[g]raved on my heart, and I love them as my children. What the good Lord has spared me [*f*]or is more than I can tell, bu[t] it is perhaps to finish up my book, which I shall leave to the Boys in Blue, and in which they cannot only see me but follow me in the ac[t]s in which they helped me.

New York World, May 17, 1885. USG dictated this message for the Grand Army of the Republic annual encampment at Portland, Maine. On June 24, 1885, Frederick Dent Grant, Mount McGregor, N. Y., telegraphed to John S. Kountz. "General Grant directs me, in reply to your dispatch, to tender through you, to each one of the three hundred thousand veterans, his comrades, now represented at Portland, his thanks for their interest in his health and welfare. General Grant wishes to take this occasion to also thank them for their splendid services which have resulted in giving freedom to a race, peace to a continent, and a haven to the oppressed of the world." Robert B. Beath, *History of the Grand Army of the Republic* (New York, 1889), pp. 296–97. On the same day, veterans had adopted a resolution. "*Resolved*, by the Nineteenth National Encampment of the Grand Army of the Republic, assembled in the city of Portland, Maine, representing 300,000 soldiers and sailors in the United States, that in this, the first hour of our assembly, we tender to the distinguished comrade, soldier and statesman, General ULYSSES S. GRANT, our profound sympathy in his continued illness, and extend a soldier's greeting to our beloved Commander and Comrade, who has for months endured unspeakable agony with that characteristic fortitude that has challenged the admiration of the world." *Ibid.*, p. 296.

On March 2, William H. Barrett, Grand Army of the Republic, Post No. 160, Philadelphia, had written to USG transmitting a resolution "that the great Commander above may shortly relieve our comrade of his sufferings and spare him to receive the homage and love of his comrades of the Grand Army of the Republic and of the people of the country he has so well and so honorably served." ALS, General Grant National Memorial, New York, N. Y. On March 3, William A. McKellip, Grand Army of the Republic, Post No. 13, Westminster, Md., telegraphed to USG. "The members of this Post many of whom served under you tender their warmest most heartfelt sympathy in this your hour of grevious affliction they hope & pray that relief will speedily come that you may be restored to health & strength & remain with us [—] very many years a living interested witness of the growth & prosperity of a nation which to you more than to anyone else belongs the honor & credit of having saved from destruction" Telegram received, *ibid.* On March 17, George M. Arnold, Washington, D. C., wrote to Frederick Dent Grant. "I am glad to know that it is not now or nevr will be necessary to let Gen Grant know how the Colored people of this county feel towards him, how they love honir and pray for him, He you, and the Nation fitly understand this, I will esteem it a very great favor to us as colored men and (G. A. R.) comrades, however if you will see to it that the subject matter of the enclosed letter is made known to your father," ALS, *ibid.* Similar communications for USG came from Grand Army of the Republic posts or encampments at Brooklyn (March 11), Utah Territory (March 12), New York City (March 14 and April 10), Chicago (March 24), Fair Haven, N. Y. (April 18), and Kankakee, Ill. (April 24). *Ibid.* Expressions of concern from veterans to USG also came from the Military Order of the Loyal Legion, Mass. Commandery (March 4, *ibid.*) and N. Y. Commandery (April 1, *New York Tribune*, April 2, 1885), Old Guard Association, Dayton (March 18, General Grant National Memorial, New York, N. Y),

1st Div., 2nd Corps, Survivors Association, Philadelphia (April 4, *ibid.*), and James Hall Camp No. 29, Sons of Veterans, Jamestown, N. Y. (April 24, *ibid.*).

On April 10, "Ira E. Hicks, junior vice-commander-in-chief G. A. R., called just after noon to assure the General of the continued sympathy of the Grand Army men. Mrs. Grant seated herself by the window in her husband's room in a rocking chair and talked with him for an hour . . . . At 5 o'clock Austin Curtin, commanding Department Pennsylvania G. A. R., called and brought resolutions from the Grand Army in his State . . . ." *New York Tribune*, April 11, 1885. On the same day, a correspondent reported from Philadelphia that Post No. 51 "sent a despatch to Gen. Grant sympathizing with him in his hour of affliction, and saying that 'we learn with sincere sorrow that one whom we love and who never suffered defeat lies so near to the point of death and may succumb to that fell destroyer, and that, although he may be called to answer the long roll but a short time before us, we earnestly pray that we may all meet at the reassembling of the Grand Army of the Republic above.'" *New York World*, April 11, 1885. On April 21, a correspondent reported a telegram to USG from Jacksonville, Fla. "The Department of Florida, Grand Army of the Republic, in annual encampment here, desires to express its heartfelt pleasure in your convalescence and tender you and yours its congratulations." *New York Times*, April 22, 1885. On April 29, USG wrote to Bartholomew Stoneham, Grand Army of the Republic, Post No. 13, Jersey City. "The resolutions of sympathy of your post are received. Now that I am better I wish to acknowledge the same and to express my appreciation of the action." University Archives, Spring 1995, no. 45. The document from this post, dated April 10, is in Grant Memorial Association, New York, N. Y. Also on April 29, Frederick Grant wrote to "Comrades." "General Grant wishes me to return thanks for the greetings of the Walton Dwight and Waltrous Posts." ALS, DLC-Joseph Dade Schnell. These thanks went to posts in Lestershire (Walton Dwight) and Binghamton (Marvin Watrous), N. Y.

On May 30, Memorial Day, Grand Army of the Republic members paraded past USG's house. "After the 400 men had passed out of sight the old warrior stood at his post in the window, like a statue, looking toward the Park. Some one came up from behind and touched him, and he moved slowly away. The 7th Regiment also passed in review before the General, and he was pleased with their marching. The sight of the old soldiers, many of whom had been with the General in the Wilderness, touched him deeply, and he sat thinking in his chair for a long time after the sound of the music had died away in the distance." *New York Tribune*, May 31, 1885.

On July 21, David N. Foster and three others, Fort Wayne, wrote to USG. "The representatives of [the] Grand Army of the Republic of the State of [Indian]a, assembled at Island Park, Rome City, [India]na with one heart and voice delight to [exp]ress thus anew, their affection for their old time commander, General Ulysses S. Grant, and to assure him of their prayers that his life may be spared so long as it can seem to a wise Providence best, and their hope that his closing days may be made delightful by the ministries of kindness and by freedom from pain" LS, General Grant National Memorial, New York, N. Y. Other sympathetic communications for USG came from Grand Army of the Republic posts or encampments at New York City (May 11), Methuen, Mass. (June 30), and Round Lake, N. Y. (July 10). *Ibid.* A special Grand Army of the Republic committee conveyed a similar message to USG, dated July 13, Mount McGregor, N. Y. *Ibid.*

To Ainsworth R. Spofford

New York May 22. 1885

A. R. SPOFFORD
CONGRESSIONAL LIBRARIAN
WASHINGTON D. C.
DEAR SIR:

During the early part of the Winter Mr. Wm H. Vanderbilt purchased the medal voted to me by Congress, and other trophies of the war and of my trip around the world, with the understanding that they were to be deposited with the gGovernment of the United States, to whom they were presented by him. Some correspondence took place between Mr. Vanderbilt and the Secretary of State who referred the matter to Congress. I was so very ill at that time that I was not able to watch the progress of the action of Congress upon that or any other matter and do not know who it was finally decided should have the custody of this property, but the bill as it was introduced in Congress mentioned you as the custodian. Will you be Kind enough, therefore, to inform me if you are authorized to receive the property and, if you are not, whether you can receive it for safe keeping until such time as Congress may make proper disposition of it? I will soon be leaving the city and will be very glad to have it out of the house during the absence of myself and family.

Very truly yours.
U. S. GRANT
Gen. U. S. A. Retired.

LS, DLC-Ainsworth R. Spofford. After working as a book dealer and newspaper editor in Cincinnati, Ainsworth R. Spofford joined the Library of Congress as chief asst. (1861) and rose to librarian (1864). See letter to William H. Vanderbilt, Jan. 10, 1885.

On June 9, 1885, Secretary of War William C. Endicott wrote to Frederick Dent Grant, New York City. "I am in receipt of your letter of the 30th ultimo requesting that an officer of this Department be sent to New York to receive from Mrs. Grant the property now in her possession, consisting of swords, medals and tokens of honor, presents made to her distinguished husband, with a view to their removal for safe keeping to Washington, to be placed in the custody of the Secretary of War. I have accordingly directed Lieutenant Colonel Richard N. Batchelder of the Army to repair to NewYork with instructions to confer with Mrs. Grant on the subject and to receive and bring the articles named to Washington, where they will be held by this Department to await the further action of Congress." LS, Mrs. Paul E. Ruestow, Jacksonville, Fla. On June 12, Lt. Col. Richard N. Batchelder wrote a receipt for "the Swords, Medals, Paintings, Bronzes, Uniform, and other articles of value and art used by *General Ulysses S. Grant*, or presented to him by various Governments, Cities, &c., &c., in the World, specified on the within Schedule, as amended." DS, *ibid.* See *New York World* and *New York Tribune*, June 12, 1885. On July 31, Endicott wrote to Frederick Grant, Mount McGregor, N. Y. "*Personal* . . . I see in the newspapers that some misapprehension exists in regard to the nature of the custody by this Department of your honored father's swords, medals and tokens of honor. It appears to be thought that they have been transferred and given to the Government, and that your mother has no control over them, even if a sword were desired for use at his funeral. And in recurring to the correspondence that passed between us upon the subject I noticed that you speak of them as the property of the United States. Upon this question there should be no misunderstanding. By deed of trust, Mr. Vanderbilt and your mother conveyed them to the United States on January 10, 1885. In February following the Senate passed a joint resolution accepting this generous and valuable gift, and providing that it should be placed in the custody of the Librarian of Congress, and that the Secretary of War should receive the same for safe keeping, until the Librarian can place it in a suitable building to be provided for the use of the Library. This resolution was not considered or passed by the House of Representatives. I believe it was not reached during the session which expired March 4th. The gift not having been duly accepted by the United States, the property still belongs to Mrs. Grant and Mr. Vanderbilt; and at your request in behalf of your mother I took charge of it, to hold it in safe keeping for her to await the further action of Congress, which will doubtless be had early in the next session. Everything thus in my charge is still within her control. My custody is for her until Congress accepts the trust, and if any article or articles be desired now or at any time by her, it will be my duty as well as my pleasure to respond at once to her wishes. Please convey my respects to your mother, and trusting you may all have health and strength to pass through your great trial, . . . " LS, Ulysses Grant Dietz, Maplewood, N. J.

On Feb. 3, 1886, Samuel L. Clemens, Hartford, wrote to Julia Grant. "I expected to report to you in person, but failed of the chance. So I told Webster to tell you that I visited the houses of General & Colonel Sheridan, but both were gone to Philadelphia; so I then went to General Logan's, where I learned that the Trophies are all right: they are boxed, sealed, & under lock & key in the Treasury & in the distinct custody of the Secretary of the Treasury, there to remain in perfect safety until Congress shall determine their permanent disposition. An able critic told me the other day that the Memoirs are so noble a literary masterpiece that they will long outlast any other monument that can be erected to the memory of General Grant . . . ." ALS, USG 3. A joint resolution accepting Julia Grant's gift became law later in 1886. See *CR*, 49-1, 1592, 2025, 7943–44, 8036; *U.S. Statutes at Large*, XXIV, 348.

Memorandum

Disposition I want made of the proceeds of my book, if sales amount to more than $100.000 00

First—No check to be drawn in favor of my own business This
is a precaution against ~~malit~~ malicious creditors of Grant and Ward
garnasheeing it and thus keeping it in banks until a long suit deter-
mines to whom it shall be paid

I want a check from the publishers, payable to the holders of
a deed of trust on Mrs. Grant's house, 3 E. 66th street, New York
for the amount of the principle and interest, say $59.000 00—
Mr. Purrington[1] is to attend to this and see that all liens are can-
celed For this, and others services alread[y] rendered, up to this
date, he is to be paid not less than $500 00. Col. F. D. Grant is
to have $10.000[2] for *his services as my Secretary*, and *his labors* in
helping me *prepare my book*! For similar services U. S. Grant Jr.
and Jes. R. Grant are to have $2.500 each. After this my three
sons are to have divided equally among them all the remaining
proceeds until the amount reaches $15.000 00 for each. Checks
for these last amounts will be paid to Oliver Hoyt,[3] A. J. Drexel
and Geo. W. Childs, to invest in such securities as they may deem
best. These securities I want transferred to my daughters-in-law,
with the *understanding* that the *income belongs* to *their husbands*, and
the bonds or *stocks* are to be *transferred* to *them* when their affairs
are settled so they can hold property. The next $15.000 I want
checks payable to the same parties for the purpose of purchasing
securities in like manner, in the name of my wife, the income to
go to my daughter, and finally the principal to her or her children
in like manner. All sums received after these are paid are to go,
~~to~~ one half to the purchase of Govt. 4½ pr. ct. ~~pr~~ registered bonds
for the free and full use of Mrs. U. S. Grant, my wife, the other
half to go to my sisters, Mrs. Jinnie Corbin, and Mary G. Cramer, and to the family of my deceased brother, O. L. Grant, until
Mrs. Cramer and the family of O. L. Grant are paid in full what is
due them from the failure of Grant & Ward, without interest, and
until Mrs Corbin has been paid 5,000 After this all proceeds to be
invested in 4½ pr. ct. Govt bonds, to be the exclusive property of
Mrs. Grant.

I leave my wife apparently out of the first benefits of these donations, for the reason that the first item increases her income $3480 00 pr. annum by stoping that much interest.

U. S. GRANT

MAY 29TH 1885,

ADS, USG 3. For modifications to these directions, see letter to Julia Dent Grant, July 8, 1885.

On April 14, 1885, USG wrote to Clarence A. Seward. "The understanding was that the printing of the Shiloh and [t]he other articles in the Century Magazine should in no way bar the use of them in the Personal Memoirs of U. S. Grant." Typed copy, USGA.

On May 25, a correspondent reported from New York City that Stephen B. Elkins had visited the Grant family and had seen "some hundred pages or more" of galleys. *Philadelphia Press*, May 26, 1885. On June 10, U.S. Senator John A. Logan of Ill. visited USG for two hours and read some of the galleys. *New York Tribune*, June 11, 1885. For Logan's eulogistic note on USG, see *New York Independent*, XXXVII, 1913 (July 30, 1885). For an interview with publisher Charles L. Webster, see *Washington Post*, June 14, 1885; reprinted from *New York Sun*. See also Frederick Anderson, ed., *Mark Twain's Notebooks & Journals* (Berkeley, 1975–79), III, 141–42.

On June 22, Edward E. Henry, subscription agent, Fremont, Ohio, wrote to USG. "The people are moving en masse upon your memoirs. Ex-president Hayes subscribed for two sets: one for himself and one for the Birchard Library. Old soldiers wish to read the prospectus through. We all hope you will gain strength to live long in the land that your courage saved from destruction." ALS, USG 3.

1. William A. Purrington, who handled many legal matters for the Grant family, graduated from Harvard University (1873) and received law degrees from Columbian University (1878) and New York University (1880). See *PUSG*, 25, 329.

2. USG double-underlined this sum.

3. See *ibid.*, 26, 282–83, 361. On June 18, 1885, Frederick Dent Grant, Mount McGregor, N. Y., wrote to Oliver Hoyt. "I received from you this afternoon three letters, one forwarded to me from New York one telling me you had writen to me in N. Y. and one containing a check for $1500 00/100 drawn to Fathers order. I asked father what to write you but he is unable to speak so I think the best way out of the difficulty will be to send the check for the $10.000 or what part of it you have to his order let me have it cashed and pay the Doctors what we owe them and do what he (Father) might indicate from time to time or else place the amount to Mothers Credit at the Lincoln National Bank although the latter would mix it up with her account & I dont believe I gcould get it straightened out. Will you thank Mr Work for his kindness and say that Father would express his gratitude if he was able to do so. I enclose you Fathers receipt for the $1500 00 to return to Mr Work and will write to him" ALS (facsimile), USGA.

On Oct. 22, subscribers who had raised $250,000 for the benefit of USG in 1880–81 met at Hoyt's office in New York City to "determine what future disposition should be made of the fund. Mr. Hoyt and Mr. Jones, the two surviving Trustees, desired to submit a report of their stewardship and be relieved of further responsibility . . . ." *New York Times*, Oct. 23, 1885. A resolution adopted at this meeting shifted trusteeship from Hoyt and George Jones to the United States Trust Co.

To Harrison Terrell

New York City, June 2, 1885.

Harrison Terrell:

I give you this letter now, not knowing what the near future may bring to a person in my condition of health. This is an acknowledgment of your faithful services to me during my sickness up to this time, and which I expect will continue to the end. This is also to state further that for about four years you have lived with me, coming first at [as] butler, in which capacity you served until my illness became so serious as to require the constant attentions of a nurse, and that in both capacities I have had abundant reason to be satisfied with your attention, integrity and efficiency. I hope you may never want for a place.

Yours,

U. S. Grant.

Undated newspaper clipping (brackets in original), Grant Family Scrapbook, USGA. Born a slave in 1840 in Orange County, Va., Harrison Terrell's kindness as his master's personal servant earned him freedom in 1850. Terrell worked as a servant for professional gamblers who joined the C.S. Army, served several years as butler for George W. Riggs, and started with USG after Riggs died in 1881. On Aug. 12, 1885, Frederick Dent Grant, Mount McGregor, N. Y., wrote to Terrell. "I write to express the regrets of my Mother and family at your leaving us. You were always very attentive and faithful to my Father during his sickness and you may rely upon his family to do you whatever good we can in the future, which we hope will be both happy and successful." ALS, William J. Kaland, New York, N. Y. See *PUSG*, 30, 382; letter to Roland Worthington, July 3, 1883.

On Oct. 10, 1886, Terrell, "Valet to late Gen. Grant," Washington, D. C., wrote to Daniel S. Lamont. "When I called to see you a few days ago, you asked me whether there was a vacancy in the War Department which I could fill. At the time I knew of none. But since then, a man by the name John Ross Davis, who, I think, was a day-watchman or messenger in the Paymaster General's office, has died suddenly. If you have not yet made other arrangements for me I take the liberty of calling your attention to this place." ALS, DLC-Grover Cleveland. On Oct. 16, a correspondent reported from Washington, D. C., that Terrell had been "appointed a laborer in the Paymaster-General's office, . . . This appointment was made very promptly upon the presentation to the President and the Secretary of War of a letter of recommendation, written by Gen. Grant, . . ." *New York Times*, Oct. 17, 1886. As of July 1, 1889, Terrell worked as asst. messenger, War Dept., for $720 annually. On Dec. 18, 1902, a correspondent reported from Washington, D. C., that Terrell was "dangerously ill at his home in this city." *New York Times*, Dec. 19, 1902.

To Grover Cleveland

New York, June 13, 1885

THE PRESIDENT:

During the war Gen. Terry of the Volunteer service, a civilian and lawyer from the State of Connecticut, was selected by me to command the troops sent to capture Ft. Fisher, North Carolina. An attempt to capture the place had been made a few weeks before, when the garrison was much weaker and not so well prepared to resist, but it failed. Gen. Terry succeeded. For this success, and the ability he always showed during the rebellion as a commander of troops, I recommended him for promotion to a brigadier-generalcy in the regular army.[1] He was so promoted, but necessarily went to the foot of the list of officers of the same rank in the army.

While I was President, and before he had reached more than half way up the list of Brigadier Generals, I regarded him as the fittest man to command of any of the officers of the same grade down to him, and expressed at the time the idea that I should appoint him over the heads of his seniors, but refrained from doing so because it was in time of peace and if his ~~claims~~ seniors had been oversloughed then with the doctrine of chances they would have been retired with the rank only of Brigadier General. Gen. Terry being junior in years would still have the opportunity of reaching the major-generalcy before he reached years of compulsory retirement. For these reasons he was not made a Major General then. He is now about the head of the list of Brigadier Generals in the army and I think it would be a peculiar hardship if he should be superseded by a junior.

Hoping, Mr. President, that you will excuse me for this suggestion, I am, very truly,

Your Obedient Servant.

U. S. GRANT

General, Retired.

LS, DNA, RG 94, ACP, 567 1876. On June 16, 1885, Daniel S. Lamont wrote to USG. "The President is in receipt of your letter of the 13th. instant presenting certain con-

siderations in behalf of the advancement of Genl. Terry and directs me to say that
when the contemplated promotion is to be made, it will give him pleasure to carefully
consider your wishes in the matter, which, in the meantime, will be brought to the
attention of the Secretary of War" LS (press), DLC-Grover Cleveland. On May 25,
Brig. Gen. Alfred H. Terry, Fort Snelling, had written to Frederick Dent Grant, New
York City. *"Private* & *confidential* . . . I write to you with a good deal of hesitation
upon a subject that is of great importance to me: but which important to me as it is, I
would not desire to have brought to your attention and perhaps through you to your
father's attention unless it might be at some time when the condition of his health will
fully warrant such action. I, in common with every man in the nation, have watched
with the deepest interest the daily news of your father's condition and I rejoice to know
of the diminution of his suffering and of his brighter prospects for the future. I trust
that he may long be spared to his family and to the nation—long be spared to enjoy the
honor in which the whole world holds him. I would not for any consideration add to
the burden which he bears; but if at any time, in your judgement, the matter of which I
shall speak can be brought to his attention without fatigueing him and without annoying him even in the slightest degree, I shall be under great obligations to you, if you
will present it to him. A few days after General McDowells promotion to the grade of
Major General in 1872, General Sherman told me that in the consultation which ended
in the determination to appoint McDowell to the vacancy caused by General Meades
death, your father said 'If we were at war we should have to promote Terry; but as we
are at peace, to save all trouble, we will go by seniority and promote McDowell.' And
recently, General Sherman has said in writing that after General Meade's death your
father intended to pass over McDowell and the other brigadiers whose names were
above mine on the army register & to promote me; but that McDowell and his friends
appealed to him, Sherman, and he 'interfered' with the President in McDowell's behalf,
and may have been partly the cause of the change in your father's purpose. The facts
that until dissuaded by others, it was your father's purpose to promote me; that he
beleived me to be the best fitted of all the brigadiers for the higher place; that one of
the great commanders of all time held my services and my capacity in such estimation
are *most* gratify to me, and if I could have proof of them from himself that proof would
be of the highest importance to me. If General Sherman's recollection's are correct
and if your father's condition of health at any time should permit him to give me that
proof, I should value it beyond expression. I reiterate what I have said in respect to
~~who~~ my desire to lay no additional burden on your father; but when the proper time
comes, as I trust it will come, will you not do me the great favor of bringing the matter to his mind? Perhaps the best way of presenting it to him will be to read to him
this letter. If your father should give me the proof which I desire, perhaps it would
be most valuable to me in the form of a letter to President Cleveland, or in such other
form as would enable me to use it to defend my position in the army against those
of my juniors who are seeking already, already laying their plans, to pass over me.
Pray give to both your father and your mother my best respects and most hearty good
wishes . . ." ALS, USG 3. On April 8, William T. Sherman, St. Louis, had written to
Cleveland. "It is with feelings of great delicacy that I venture to approach you even on
paper in a matter of Professional interest, but I believe I am the only living witness of
certain transactions of the Past of great moment to a most accomplished Army officer
and Gentleman who has a right to my testimony. On the 6th of November 1872 Major
General George. G. Meade died at Philadelphia creating a vacancy among the Major
Generals of the Regular Army. General Grant was then President and I was the General in Chief. The President was at full liberty to nominate any officer to the vacancy,

and I know of my own knowledge that he seriously meant to pass over the names of Brigadiers McDowell Cooke, Pope and Howard to reach the name of Brigadier Genl A. H. Terry. General Terry's name came upon the Roster of the Regular Army on the 15th of January 1865, by reason of his brilliant capture of Fort Fisher N C. He was a gentleman of Classical Education and a lawyer in Practice when in 1861, his Country called him to her Service. He was a splendid example of the American Volunteer who about the close of the War felt that West Point had garnered all the honors. General McDowells name was at the head of the list, and to pass him over at that instant of time would have Seriously damaged his fair fame. He and his friends appealed to me, and as I had witnessed McDowells most Zealous and patriotic conduct in the very beginning I did interpose with President Grant and may have been partly the cause of his adhering to the Old Seniority rule, in promoting the Senior. This same rule will in the next vacancy promote General O. O. Howard who in like manner has personal War Claims to my respect and gratitude, for he was brave, conscientious and true to me in the final Campaign from Chattanooga to Savanah, Raleigh and Richmond. Still as I may have been partially instrumental in depriving General Terry of his just promotion in 1872, I now record my judgmt of his manliness, inteligence and great ability which Should be at once recognised if the opportunity happend" ALS, DNA, RG 94, ACP, 567 1876. On Nov. 7, 1872, Benjamin H. Bristow, Louisville, had telegraphed to USG. "While we lament the loss of Meade we rejoice that there is so good a man as Terry for the place, The army officers and your friends here are unanimously for Terry," Telegram received, *ibid.*

On Feb. 5, 1877, Terry wrote to USG. "On the 10th of January last I made application to the War Department for the correction of the Army Register in respect to the position given to my own name therein. I had discovered that I was nominated to my present grade confirmed by the Senate, commissioned and sworn before Brigadier General Howard was even nominated to the Senate and I asked for a decision that under these circumstances I am and always have been General Howard senior . . . . I have now received a letter from the Adjutant General of the Army informing me that the Honorable Secretary of War has declined to submit the question to the Attorney General, on the ground that it is one which more properly belongs to the War Department for decision and that the Secretary without giving me an opportunity to present my argument has decided the question himself—decided it adversely to me. Under these circumstances I beg permission to make an appeal to you and to your authority . . . . I have always felt that a grievous injustice was done to me by the attempt to appoint General Howard over me after I was fully commissioned. I find now that the law and the justice of the case, as I regard them, are in harmony and I therefore most earnestly ask that you will direct that the question that I raise be submitted to the Attorney General and that both General Howard and myself may be notified of the reference in order that he as well as I may be heard." LS, *ibid.* USG endorsed this letter to Attorney Gen. Alphonso Taft. AE (undated), *ibid.* On Feb. 21, 1st Lt. Francis V. Greene endorsed these papers. "The President wishes this case to go to the attorney General, and the Secretary requests the Adjutant General to draw up the 'case'" AES, *ibid.*

On March 3, 1886, President Grover Cleveland nominated Terry as maj. gen. to replace Winfield S. Hancock, who had died on Feb. 9; on March 19, Cleveland nominated Oliver O. Howard as maj. gen. to replace John Pope, retired as of March 16. See *PUSG,* 23, 280–81; Terry to Sherman, May 6, 1885, DLC-William T. Sherman; John A. Carpenter, *Sword and Olive Branch: Oliver Otis Howard* (Pittsburgh, 1964), p. 279.

1.   See *PUSG,* 13, 219–20, 227–33, 270.

To Frederick Dent Grant

———

I still think that should any thing happen to me that after you and Buck have done all you can you should get Greene to come in and help you, paying him liberally for his work. I write this now in fear that I may not be able to do any more work, and may forget the subject.

U. S. GRANT

JUNE 15TH 1885.

ANS, NN. Francis V. Greene wrote that he never assisted in preparing the *Memoirs.* AE (undated), *ibid.* See *PUSG*, 30, 415–16; *New York Times*, May 16, 1921.
     On May 5, 1885, AG Richard C. Drum had written to Frederick Grant, New York City. "In response to your note of the 2nd instant asking for the number of prisoners parolled at Appomatox and the number of cannon and muskets captured, I beg to inform you that the number of prisoners paroled of General Lee's army was as follows, viz: Commissioned Officers 2.862. Enlisted men 25.494 AGGREGATE 28.356 . . . ." LS, USG 3. On May 15, Lt. Col. Chauncey McKeever, asst. AG, wrote to Frederick Grant. "Referring to your note of the 7th inst to General Drum, asking to be informed of the number of prisoners captured and parolled from March 29th to April 9th 1865, not including those at Appomattox, I beg to inform you that the number of prisoners captured in the several battles of the army of the Potomac, army of the James and the cavalry command under General Sheridan between the 29th March 1865 and the 9th April 1865—*not including those parolled at Appomattox*—amounted to 19.132. The number parolled at Appomattox as already stated was 28.356." LS, *ibid.* On May 27, Drum wrote to Frederick Grant. "Agreeably to your request of the 17th inst. it affords me pleasure to transmit herewith certain battle reports of Generals Burnside and Meade. There are no reports of General Butler's on file covering the operations of his army in front of Richmond after June 15, 1864. General Thomas' report of the Nashville Campaign is printed on page 359, Vol. XI, of Moore's Rebellion Record, a copy of which I presume can be found in the principal public libraries of New York. Should you, however, fail to secure it there, I shall be pleased to have a copy prepared here." LS, *ibid.*

To John H. Douglas

———

[*Mount McGregor, N. Y., June 17, 1885*]

DR. Since coming to this beautiful climate and getting a complete rest for about ten hours, I have watched my pains and compared them with those of the past few weeks. I can feel plainly that my system is preparing for dissolution in three ways; one by hemhorages, one by strangulation and the third by exaustion. The first and second are liable to come at any moment to relieve me of my early sufferings; the time for the arrival of the third can be computed with almost mathematical certainty. With an increase of daily food I have fallen off in weight and strength very rapidly for the last two weeks. There can not be a hope of going far beyond this time. All any physician, or any number of them do for me now is to make my burden of pain as light as possible. I do not want any physician but yourself but I tell you so that if you are unwilling to have me go without consultation with other professional men, you can send for them. I dread them however, knowing that it means another desperate effort to save me, and more suffering.

Typed copy, DLC-USG, IC. John H. Douglas graduated from Williams College (1843), earned a medical degree from the University of Pennsylvania (1847), and became a throat specialist in New York City. See *New York Times*, May 8, 1890, Oct. 3, 1892; Brandon G. Bentz *et al.*, "The Magnanimous Professional Life and Tragic Demise of J. H. Douglas, MD," *The Laryngoscope*, 115, 8 (Aug., 2005), 1499–1504. On June 17, 1885, a correspondent reported from Mount McGregor, N. Y. "When General Grant reached his cottage after his walk to the brow of the mountain this afternoon, he was much exhausted and sank into a chair in the parlor of the cottage. Soon he indicated by signs that he wanted some writing materials, which were provided for him, and then he wrote for nearly half an hour. The result was two letters or papers. One was headed 'Memoranda for My Family.' In it the General had written that he thought he was failing, and for certain instructions that he desired carried out he referred his family to other and more definite memoranda prepared by him a little while before leaving New-York. The other note he folded and addressed to Dr. Douglas. He handed both papers to Colonel Fred Grant . . . ." *New York Tribune*, June 18, 1885. For the reaction of USG's family to the memoranda and the decision of Douglas to send for Henry B. Sands, see *ibid.* and *New York World*, June 19, 1885; *New York Times*, June 18, 1885. See also *New York World*, June 21, 1885. On June 13, USG had taken "a walk around the room after his breakfast, and jokingly remarked that he was getting himself in condition for long tramps through the woods after he got in the country. He read a number of proof sheets of his book after lunch and dictated answers to many letters that have accumulated on his hands during the last few days . . . ." *New York Tribune*, June 14, 1885. On June 14, New York City heat and USG's deteriorating condition prompted his doctors to advise a move "to Mt. McGregor near Saratoga, as soon as possible, and the time was fixed for to-morrow, instead of a week later, as was previously agreed upon. This change in the time pleased the General greatly." *Ibid.*, June 15, 1885. When asked on June 15 if the trip should be postponed because of his poor health, USG said: "Now or never!" *Ibid.*, June 16, 1885. For accounts of USG's trip to Mount McGregor on June 16, see *ibid.*, *New York Times*, and *New York World*, June 17, 1885; Thomas W. Pitkin, *The Captain Departs: Ulysses S. Grant's Last Campaign* (Carbondale, Ill., 1973), pp. 57–65.

On June 7, Silas Reed, Park City, Utah Territory, had written to USG. "It is a great pleasure to be able to read in these distant mountains, daily N. Y. telegrams of the condition of your health. And I beg permission to congratulate you upon your decision to seek, very soon, a *higher* & *drier* altitude for the Summer—I feel that the damp, Sea-level air of N. Y, has been a great drawback, if not positive injury to your health the past Spring—While I am much older than yourself, I do not forget that you have been like a Father to me, as well as to the *Great Nation* you so nobly fought to preserve. Hence you will not wonder at my intense anxiety to see your valuable life prolonged—You ought to breathe none but high & dry air, with a proper degree of warm air at all times within doors. And above all, or in unity with all, bolsterster up your physical strengths to the better guard against any encroachments upon *vital* organs—none of which are yet affected—I pray daily that God may give you Strength to complete, according to your wish, your great History of the War," ALS, CtY.

On June 17, a correspondent reported from Boston that a telegram was sent upon the suggestion of Charles Devens to USG. "*Resolved,* That the members of the Bunker Hill Monument Association assembled this day at the anniversary meeting have heard with deep emotion of the serious illness of Gen. Grant, whose name is at the head of the roll of honorary members; that they avail themselves of this occasion to renew to him the assurance of the high regard in which they hold his lofty patriotism, his pure and noble fame, and his splendid achievements, and that they earnestly trust he will yet long be spared to the country he has so greatly and so faithfully served." *New York Times,* June 18, 1885.

On June 30, A. M. Arnold, Rockbridge Baths, Va., wrote to USG. "I hope you will allow one who, when but a boy, laid down his arms at Appomattox and gave in his allegience to the Union, to express his warmest sympathy for you in this your hour of affliction. Dear General, I have watched your movements from the hour you gave me my horse and sword and told me to go home and 'assist in making a crop'—I have been proud to see the nation do you honor—And now, dear Genl in this the hour of your tribulation I weep that so brave, so magnanimous a soul must suffer as you do—My prayer to God daily is that you dear General, may be restored to perfect health. And be assured that I am not the only ex-confederate who sends his prayers daily to the throne of Grace for the restoration of the GRANDEST, the NOBLEST the BRAVEST SOLDIER and the Purest Statesman whoever graced the annals of history. May the God who overlooked you in battle and who has brought you thus far give you grace to meet whatever He has in store for you And may He Restore you to health & friends is the fervent prayer of one who at 15 years of age entered the lists against you and accepted the magnanimous terms you accorded us at Appomattox." ALS, USG 3. On July 2, a correspondent reported from Mount McGregor that this letter pleased USG. *New York Tribune,* July 3, 1885. On July 3, another correspondent reported from Mount McGregor that USG began to write a reply. *New York Times,* July 4, 1885.

To John P. Newman

———

[*Mount McGregor, N. Y., June 18, 1885*]

It is just a week to-day since I have spoken. My suffering continuous. The doctors however—Sands[1] and Douglas—say that my ailment is improving. I do not feel so.

AN, USMA. On June 20, 1885, John P. Newman told a reporter in Philadelphia that he had suppressed the final sentence when speaking to correspondents because of USG's depressed spirits. "In this original, you see, these words are blacker than the others, as though the General bore upon the pencil to make them emphatic . . . . To cheer the General up, I said: 'General, no great man ever went up on a mountain to die. You are not going to die here. None of the great characters of sacred history went upon the mountains to die . . . . I think, General, that you came, like all those great men, to see the glory of God, not to die here.'" *Philadelphia Press*, June 22, 1885. On June 18, 3:30 P.M., Newman had arrived at Mount McGregor, N. Y. See *New York Tribune*, June 19, 1885. On the same day, USG wrote to Julia Dent Grant. "Ask the Dr. to hold prayers. I want to retire early." AN (facsimile, undated), *Philadelphia Press*, June 22, 1885. USG wrote another undated note to Newman. "I am sure I am right *for me* Another might feel differantly I have no desire to live. But I do not want you to let my family know this. It would not do to be known because the papers would get it and then the family" AN, USMA.

Also on June 18, a correspondent reported from Mount McGregor. "Photographer W. H. Baker, from Saratoga, came up with a big camera in the afternoon, and succeeded in getting four good views of the family group of nine as they sat on the piazza. The plates are 22x28 inches, a very large size for the style of work. The General sat through it all unweariedly, and seemed interested in the work." *New York World*, June 19, 1885. On June 25, a correspondent reported that USG was again photographed that afternoon. *Ibid.*, June 26, 1885.

1. Henry B. Sands graduated from the College of Physicians and Surgeons in New York City (1854) and eventually earned a worldwide reputation as a surgeon. See *New York Times*, Nov. 19–20, 1888.

To John P. Gray

———

DR. Your shadow has grown no less since I met you in Utica— Mine has reduced materially

U. S. GRANT

JUNE 20TH 1885.

ANS, deCoppet Collection, NjP. John P. Gray, an authority on mental illness, had served as medical superintendent of the state asylum at Utica since 1854. For his visit with USG on June 19, 1885, see *New York Tribune* and *New York Times*, June 20, 1885. See also *ibid.*, June 23, 26, 1885.

To Century Magazine

———

SINCE the publication in THE CENTURY of my article on "The Battle of Shiloh" I have received from Mrs. W. H. L. Wallace, widow of the gallant general who was killed in the first day's fight at that battle,[1] a letter from General Lew Wallace to him, dated the morning of the 5th.[2] At the date of this letter it was well known that the Confederates had troops out along the Mobile & Ohio railroad west of Crump's landing and Pittsburg landing, and were also collecting near Shiloh. This letter shows that at that time General Lew Wallace was making preparations for the emergency that might happen for the passing of reënforcements between Shiloh and his position, extending from Crump's landing westward; and he sends the letter over the road running from Adamsville to the Pittsburg landing and Purdy road. These two roads intersect nearly a mile west of the crossing of the latter over Owl creek, where our right rested. In this letter General Lew Wallace advises General W. H. L. Wallace that he will send "to-morrow" (and his letter also says "April 5th," which is the same day the letter was dated and which, therefore, must have been written on the 4th) some cavalry to report to him at his headquarters, and suggesting the propriety of General W. H. L. Wallace's sending a company back with them for the purpose of having the cavalry at the two landings familiarize themselves with the road, so that they could "act promptly in case of emergency as guides to and from the different camps."

This modifies very materially what I have said, and what has been said by others, of the conduct of General Lew Wallace at the battle of Shiloh. It shows that he naturally, with no more experience than he had at the time in the profession of arms, would take the particular road that he did start upon in the absence of orders to move by a different road.

The mistake he made, and which probably caused his apparent dilatoriness, was that of having advanced some distance after he had found that the firing, which would be at first directly to his front and then off to the left, had fallen back until it had got very much in rear of the position of his advance. This falling back had taken place before I sent General Wallace orders to move up to Pittsburg landing, and, naturally, my order was to follow the road nearest the river. But my order was verbal, and to a staff-officer[3] who was to deliver it to General Wallace, so that I am not competent to say just what order the general actually received.

General Wallace's division was stationed, the First brigade at Crump's landing, the Second out two miles, and the Third two and a half miles out. Hearing the sounds of battle, General Wallace early ordered his First and Third brigades to concentrate on the Second. If the position of our front had not changed, the road which Wallace took would have been somewhat shorter to our right than the River road.

In this article I state that General McCook, who commanded a division of Buell's army, expressed some unwillingness to pursue the enemy on Monday, April 7th, because of the condition of his troops. General Badeau, in his history, also makes the same statement, on my authority.[4] Out of justice to General McCook and his command, I must say that they left a point twenty-two miles east of Savannah on the morning of the 6th. From the heavy rains of a few days previous and the passage of trains and artillery, the roads were necessarily deep in mud, which made marching slow. The division had not only marched through this mud the day before, but it had been in the rain all night without rest. It was engaged in the battle of the second day, and did as good service as its position allowed. In fact an opportunity occurred for it to perform a conspicuous act of gallantry which elicited the highest commendation from division commanders in the army of the Tennessee. General Sherman in both his memoirs and reports makes mention of this fact.[5] General McCook himself belongs to a family which furnished many volunteers to the army. I refer to these circumstances with minuteness because I did General McCook injustice in the article, though not to the extent one would suppose from the public press.[6] I am not willing to do any one an injustice, and if convinced that I have done one, I am always willing to make the fullest admission.

U. S. Grant.

Mount McGregor, N. Y., June 22, 1885.

Century Magazine, XXX, 5 (Sept., 1885), 776. See letter to Lewis Wallace, Oct. 7, 1884; *Memoirs,* I, 351–52, 354–55.

1. Wounded on April 6, 1862, Brig. Gen. William H. L. Wallace died on April 10.

2. On April 5, Maj. Gen. Lewis Wallace, Adamsville, Tenn., had written to W. H. L. Wallace. "Yours recd. Glad to hear from you. My cavelry from this point has been to and from your post frequently. As my 3d Brigade is here, five miles from Crump's Landing, my 2nd two & a half miles from it, I thought it would be better to open communication with you from Adamsville. I will tomorrow order Maj. Hays of the 5th Ohio Cavy to report to you at your quarters; and, if you are so disposed, proba- bly, you had better send a company to return with him, that they may familiarize them- selves with the road, to act, in case of emergency, as guides to and from our camps." ALS (facsimile), Isabel Wallace, *Life & Letters of General W. H. L. Wallace* (Chicago, 1909), opposite p. 189. See letter to T. Lyle Dickey, [*Jan. 18, 1885*].

3. Capt. Algernon S. Baxter.

4. See Adam Badeau, *Military History of Ulysses S. Grant,* . . . (New York, 1881), I, 90.

5. Brig. Gen. Alexander M. McCook's div. carried a position that had repulsed an earlier assault. See Brig. Gen. William T. Sherman's report, dated April 10, 1862, in *Memoirs of Gen. W. T. Sherman* (4th ed., New York, 1891), I, 267–68, or *O.R.*, I, x, part 1, 251–52.

6. "A dispatch published yesterday from Salt Lake City conveying news of the injured dignity of Gen. A. McD. McCook, now in command at Fort Douglas, over al- leged strictures upon his conduct in Gen. Grant's article on the battle of Shiloh, in the February *Century*, naturally attracted notice and comment among military men yesterday . . . . At Gen. Grant's house little importance was attached to the McCook dispatch. Col. Grant, who had assisted his father in preparing the manuscript, said: 'I doubt if Gen. McCook has read the *Century* article as carefully as he will before prepar- ing his reply. He did his duty at Shiloh. There has never been any intimation to the contrary. His troops made a long and hard march during the first day's battle, and on the second day they fought. Considering that the battle was very fierce and that the army was worn out, the appearance of an entire division marching up at the close "as if going on parade" was naturally a striking sight. It was probably the only appearanc[e] of order on the field. What the article stated was the truth. It was inspired by no other motive. So far as it refers to Gen. McCook, it seems to me that the allusion was com- plimentary. A man who could bring up his division "as if going on parade," after a hard day's march and another day of fighting, did what few commanders would try to do. It was an extraordinary thing, and struck my father as such and as worthy of mention. As to father's having pursued Gen. McCook for 20 years, he has never had occasion to mention him before in any of his writings, nor in any of his dispatches, nor in any military council. Their relations extended over about five days. McCook belonged to Buell's command. He came under father on the second day at Shiloh, and about four days afterward was ordered off with Buell toward Chickamauga.'" *New York Times*, Jan. 26, 1885.

To George F. Shrady

For a few night back, indeed ever since we have been here the Dr. has given me five minims on retiring and as much more an hour or two later. Last night however he reduced the 2d dose to [three] and I slept well.

I have only dictated about twenty pages since we have been here, and written out with my own hand about as much more. I have no connected account now to write. Occasionally I see something that suggest a few remarks.

I do not suppose I will ever have my voice back again at [all] strong.

Mt. McGregor, June 24, 1885

AN (date not in USG's hand), NjP. George F. Shrady graduated from the College of Physicians and Surgeons of New York (1858) and edited the *Medical Record*, where he published regular reports on USG's condition. See *New York Times*, Dec. 1, 1907; Shrady, "General Grant's Last Days," *Century Magazine*, LXXVI, 1–3 (May–July, 1908), 102–13, 275–85, 411–29. On June 24, 1885, USG wrote to Shrady. "I am having a pretty tough time Dr, though I do not suffer so much actual [pain]" "My trouble is in getting my breath" "Pretty well, though rarely more than one hour at a time" "I am growing lighter every day althoug[h] I have increased the amount of food. I have however gained a little in strength since we come up here. I cannot at this minuet get a breath through my nostrils." "I said, if you want any thing larger in the way of a spachula—is that what you call it—I saw a man behind the house here a few days ago filling a ditch with a hoe. It was larger and I think it can be borrowed." AN, NjP.

Reportedly on June 25, USG wrote to either Shrady or John H. Douglas. "I am taking more food the last two weeks than before. I have added two eggs pr day, one glass of milk and the last four or five days, about fifty pr. ct. to the beef." "I take now eight or nine eggs, seven glasses of milk and the increased quanty of beef, daily. For the last few days I have been troubled with heart-burn after meals. I think less to-day however than yesterday or the day before—" AN (undated), DLC-John H. Douglas. See *New York Tribune* and *New York World*, June 26, 1885. Probably on June 25 or 26, USG again wrote to Shrady. "Dr. Douglas has not been in to-day I wonder if it would not be a good thing for me to go down and return immediately sometimes. It is the only means of geting out I have. I set up all the way from New York City that last day, when we come up, without feeling any special fatigue. Some times, but not now. A gentleman has proposed to take me driving in his bugg[y] but he has to come [so] far that I do no[t] know that I will accept There probably will be carriages here to hire when the guests arrive My days are long and miserable except when I am employed. An hour reading or writing also tires me. Ever since the ~~spasm~~ spasm last night I have quite a tendency that way. I think however that the disposition is now abating." AN (undated), NjP.

During Shrady's visit to Mount McGregor, N. Y., in June, or a few weeks later, USG wrote other undated notes. "My feeling now is entirely different from what it was last night. Then I was restless. Now I am sleepy. At times it taxes my brain to work. Now it would not. If I had a chapter to write in my book it would give me pleasure to write it. Then I felt fresh, but it would have pained me to work. I am thankfull however that the work is done and I can not add to it." "But what I say is, I suffer pain all the time except when asleep. It is not intense at night after morphine is administered;

but after all it is pain. From the location of the disease this must continue, and even increase. My digestion is perfect, and without any artificial means to stimulate it. It shows that the morphine I take is necessary for my condition." "I was very weak when I retire[d] yesterday. I do not feel so now." "The people are very considerate. But to pass my time plasantly I woud like to be able to talk to them. I have such a horror of becoming adicted to it that I suppose that serves as a protection I do not know one tune from another. One time in traveling, when there were brass bands everywhere, and all played, is seems, the same tune, [']Hail to the Chief,' on the arrival of the train, or of my party in a re[cep]tion till I remarked at last, wi[th gr]eatest innocence, that I [th]ought I had heard that tu[ne be]fore" "In consequence of the atmosphere I have had rheumaism of the scalp all afternoon. It has been relied with a sedative a number of time which relieves it for a while and this soft cap helps it out It happens frequently." "I come in and got over an hour sleep. Since that I have had breakfast and coffee. Have been quit sick and have vomited. I propos[e] to rest a while and then resume my place on the porch" "Mr. Norton is a Texan but before he went to Texas, in 1844, he was a great admirer of Mr. Clay. In the contest of /44 between Clay and Polk, he took a vow never to cut his hair until Mr. Clay was elected President. He made up his mind long ago never to cut his hair again" "The Dr. has to pass Sing-sing to get here. He keeps his head shaved so that if they should stop him off at that point he will be prepared to stop." "The times has been killing me off for a year and a half. If it does not change it will get right in time. The Bulliten does not even pretend to decency, the Times does; It is the work of the correspondent with the Times" AN, *ibid.* USG wrote other undated notes to Shrady. "I feel that I shall have a restless sleepless night. I suffer no great amount of pain, but I do not feel satisfied in any one position. I do not think I have closed my eyes in sleep since about eight" "I have thirteen fearful hours before me before I can expect relief. I have had nearly two hours with scarsely animation enough to draw my breath." "It is postponing the final event. A great number of my acquaintances, who were well when the papers commenced announcing that I was dying are now in their graves. They were neithe[r] old nor infirm people either. I am ready now to go at any time. I know there is nothing but suffering for me while I do live" AN (facsimiles), Shrady, "General Grant's Last Days," pp. 417–19. USG wrote other undated notes, possibly to Shrady. "The papers, some of them at least, have been trying the experiment of seeing whether they can kill a man in time by publishing daily bullitins giving account of the progress of his disease; his gradually but surely sinking &c. If they keep it up long enough they will be able to point out with pride that they forecast my case with accuracy in matter what the doctors said." AN, ViHi. "I have just had an other spasm I think it was just about as bad: But Drs will disagree. Would you not advise my remaining up until near nine?" ANS (facsimile), Remember When Auctions, Inc., Catalog No. 45 [1999], no. 1641.

On June 26, a correspondent reported from Mount McGregor that evening conversation "turned upon memorable utterances that have come with spontaneity. The General was present. Dr. Newman said: 'You have seen that recent bit of unwritten history that tells of the General's first letter of acceptance, and in which it is stated that the letter had been written but not signed, when Gen. Rawlins took it from the table, read and approved it, and then Gen. Grant added the words, "Let us have peace," and signed his name.' Gen. Grant arose from his chair, entered the cottage and wrote the following, which he handed to Mr. Newman: '"Let us have peace" was not thought of up to the minute when it was written. It came naturally as a fitting close to what had been written before.'" *New York World*, June 27, 1885. See *PUSG*, 18, 263–65.

To John H. Douglas

6/26 [*1885*] "P"

~~Glasses were never of much use to me in the field.~~ ~~Always carried them.~~ [— — —] ~~highest point of M[c] Gregor is it not.~~ ~~More I should think.~~ ~~Turn around and take me back to the shade.~~ ~~It was very clear the day I walked up~~[1]

The very money I shall give you this evening is ~~a che~~ the proceed of a check sent to me by a broker saying that two friends of his had left the money with him to send to me, to help in part pay Drs. bills. They did not want their names known hence took that [— — —] it. There is five hundred more of it which I will hand you next week.

AN (portion clipped; date not in USG's hand), DLC-John H. Douglas. On June 26, 1885, a correspondent reported from Mount McGregor, N. Y., on USG's first use of a "Bath chair." "Between 11 o'clock and noon Gen. Grant entered the chair. Harrison then seized the lever and took a course up the slope towards the hotel on the bluff. It was hard tugging and the General was amused . . . . When Harrison made a facetious reference to his having become a draught horse, the General smiled, and drawing forth his pencil wrote the following: 'For a man who has been accustomed to drive fast horses this is a considerable come down in point of speed.' Reply was made that though there was less speed there was more safety. Whereupon the General glanced at Harrison and then wrote in response: 'My horse will not run away up-hill.' The General joined audibly in the laugh . . . ." *New York World*, June 27, 1885.

On June 23, 4:30 P.M., USG had written to John H. Douglas. "I said I had been adding to my book and to my coffin. I presume every strain of the mind or body is one more nail in the coffin." AN, DLC-John H. Douglas. On the same day, 5:30 P.M., USG wrote to Douglas. "I have now worked off all that I had notes of, and which often kept me thinking at night. I will not push to make more notes for the present." AN, *ibid.* A notation, presumably by Douglas, was written on a card of Charles F. Fish, Saratoga Springs, N. Y. "June 23, 5.30 p. m. After a day of comparative ease, with several hours devoted to dictating in a whisper and writing." N, *ibid.* Also on June 23, 5:30 P.M., USG again wrote to Douglas. "Several more pages since, a portion of which I wrote out," AN, *ibid.* On the same day, a correspondent reported from Mount McGregor, that USG "dictated enough to add nearly ten printed pages to his history. He had not done so much work for two weeks before leaving New-York . . . . Dr. Douglas asked General Grant after he had finished his work if he could talk in a louder key and he replied that he could, but that he spoke low to economize his strength . . . ." *New York Tribune*, June 24, 1885. For additional details, see *New York Times*, June 24, 1885.

1. See note John H. Douglas, [*June 17, 1885*].

To John H. Douglas

———

I feel worse this am on the whole than I have for some time. My mouth hurts me and Cocoane[1] ceses to give the relief it did. If its use can be curtailed however I hope it will soon have its effect again. I shall endeavor to rest again if I feel it possible.

JUNE 27 [*1885*]

AN (date not in USG's hand), DLC-John H. Douglas. Possibly on June 27, 1885, USG wrote to John H. Douglas. "I coughed very much, with a tendency to these spasms—Has Dr. Scrady gone?" "I have managed to keep quiet without doing any thing for my mouth. I presume I will be obliged to have my mouth washed out when I come to ~~use~~ take some dinner. Between Harrison during the day, and Henry at night, they keep me up to the full amount." "I used the crooked point as well as the strait one, had no trouble in getting it down. Have eaten dinner since however, but gargled after dinner. It cleared my mouth and troat very much It may be well however for you to look." "If this goes on I do not know but it will be best for me to take my first injection early. Three days ago I would scarsely have been able to endure the pain of to-day" AN (undated), *ibid.*

1. Probably in late June, USG wrote to Douglas. "I can see very plainly that it is better to have you apply the cocin when convenient than to do it myself. You can see and direct to the right spot. I must go by sensation. I can apply it all the time without regard to special necessity. Your making the application fixes a sort of limitation to the use of the medecine." "[I] see no effect whatever from the gas as yet. Mine is a different case from ordinary suffering." "If it was fixed it would remain good until used. I would not be obliged to use it at once. For instance: if it was mixed now and not used until to-morrow it would stil be good" AN (undated), *ibid.* USG wrote another undated note, presumably to Douglas or George F. Shrady. "The cocain has got to be very disagreeable. It has paralized and swollen my tongue intil my ~~moth~~ mouth will scarsely hold it. I take no more morphine in the twenty-four hours because I take three minums (drops) in the day time. That is simply left off of what I take at night. It has not been taken but once. It will only be taken when I am a great sufferer. It will be a good thing if I can keep my bed until I have recovered my stren[g]th partially." AN, ICHi. The use of cocaine as a topical pain reliever was based on recent medical research. See Joseph F. Spillane, *Cocaine: From Medical Marvel to Modern Menace in the United States, 1884–1920* (Baltimore, 2000), pp. 7–24.

To John H. Douglas

———

I have had the best night, particularly since the second injection, that I have had for many weeks. Up to 5 o'cock I was scarsely awake, and when I was required nothing to relieve pain. After that they gave me food or something every time I got awake

JUNE 28 [*1885*] SUNDAY 10.30 A. M.

AN (date not in USG's hand), DLC-John H. Douglas. On June 28, 1885, USG wrote to John H. Douglas. "The morning is so bad that I might as well lay here the way I am as to get up? For two days the passages have been very small and very hard. Not larger than a walnut friday, and even smaller yesterday" "I had then to commence taking the brush, though in a more limited manner. This ~~con~~ comfort continued until half past ten when the ulcer in the corner of the mouth commenced paining me. I infer that the effects of the morphine had lasted to that time" AN, *ibid.* On the same day, 5:00 P.M., USG twice wrote to Douglas. "It does not seem to make much diffirence about what time I prepare for bed. The secretions in my mouth commence about the same hour every day." "By retiring earlier I get more relief. I prefer taking the first when I retire. The disturbance in preparing to go to bed just as we are taking the 2d wakes me up so that I might not get to sleep" AN, *ibid.* At 5:30 P.M., USG wrote to Douglas. "Is there not danger of that mucus coming up and floping over into the windpip some day," AN, *ibid.* Possibly on June 28, USG wrote other undated notes to Douglas. "I had but little to spit up until five o'clock. I then had quite a severe spasm, and after that expectorated a great deal. When it was stopped I cleared my throat with warm water, salt and the red mixture, usin the syringe. Since that I have had comparitive comfort, but my mouth is begining to fill up again" "Cant you bring in more air. It is hot, Had you not better I took it just before dressing." AN, *ibid.* Undated notations, presumably by Douglas, are written on the latter card. "T. room 72 after coughing." "referring to coca" N, *ibid.*

To John H. Douglas

———

I do not talk Dr. because my mouth is easy now and I want to keep it so as long as possible If I should get up now I would probably go to work preparing something for writing up.

I have attended one of those re-unions of Bowens at Wood-stock.[1] They are immense affairs

JUNE 29. [*1885*] 10 A. M.

AN (date not in USG's hand), DLC-John H. Douglas. On June 29, 1885, 10:00 A.M., USG wrote to John H. Douglas. "I have had a fair passage, but no part of it seemed to be the effect of medecine. I thought I would lay here and await the action of the latter. It is sure to come now." AN, *ibid.* On the same day, 3:00 P.M., USG wrote to Douglas. "I have had a very restful day. I hope however we will have a pleasant day out side to-morrow. I gargled my throat becaus in coughing two pieces of phlen pealed of my throat and lodged before they got out. The other washing was ~~of~~ quite local." AN, *ibid.* At 4:00 P.M., USG twice wrote to Douglas. "Something you are reading you do not want me to hear," "This is always the trouble. No matter how well I get along the balance of the 24 hours, when the middl of the afternoon comes I begin to feel stuffy; stopped up and generally uncomfortable." AN, *ibid*. A notation, presumably by Douglas, is written on the first card. "refering to a letter Mrs G was having read to me—" N, *ibid*. USG wrote an undated note to Douglas. "I am about as I every day at this hour. Papers are all read. I am drowsy without being able to sleep, and time passes heavily. No worse however only that my mouth has not been washed out to-day and the Cocaine does not seem to relieve the pain" AN, *ibid*.

    1. Henry C. Bowen, publisher, *New York Independent*, sponsored Fourth of July celebrations in his native Woodstock, Conn. USG attended in 1870 and helped to plant a tree. See *PUSG*, 20, 143, 186–87; *New York Times*, July 5, 1870.

To John H. Douglas

I do not feel the slightest desire to take morphine now. In fact when I do take it it is not from a craving, but merely from a knowledge of the relief it gives. If I should go without all night I would become restless I know, partly from the loss of it and partly from the continuous pain I would have to endure.

JUNE 29. [*1885*] 4 P. M

AN (date not in USG's hand), DLC-John H. Douglas. On June 29, 1885, P.M., USG wrote to John H. Douglas. "Did I interrupt your game? I wrote four pages. I tore it off and have it. I must read up before I can write properly." "I do not think any laudnum gets down my throat. None comes into my mouth except when I draw it in. I then immediately begin to expectorate so that if any gets to the mouth the bulk of it must be throw[n] out with the mucus." AN, *ibid*. That evening, USG wrote another note to Douglas. "I used it quite a number of times yesterday. What I said was; I think twice a day and once or twice a night will be enough to use it in the future. If that does not answer, then give it up to all together." AN, *ibid*. On the same day, 10:00 P.M., USG twice wrote to Douglas. "I was going to say you always catch me at it when you go out and come in again. I have been asleep three tim[es] since you went out, and once made noise enough to propel a Hudson river boat. The last time I got awake my mouth felt stuffy. I called for Red spring water, warm, to gargle with. The first attm attempt a drop seemed to run down my throat and started me to cough. I thought it better then to use the crooked stem and wash my throat slightly." "Do as you please. But do you not think it will be better to postpone for an hour say and then do all together. I will not take Cocoane now" AN, *ibid*.

    In late June or early July, USG wrote to Douglas. "I think I will have to mosten my mouth before going to sleep. It is stiff and and sore the way it is. I have found out what the gritty matter is that settles on my face at times. The salts of the sedative that I use on my head come out below the hair and have at times a very gritty feeling to my sensative touch." AN (undated), *ibid*.

To Julia Dent Grant

————

Mt McGregor, Saratoga Co. N. Y.
June 29th 1885.

MY DEAR WIFE:

There are some matters about which I would like to talk but about which I cannot. The subject would be painful to you and the children, and, by reflex, painful to me also. When I see you and them depressed I join in the feeling.[1]

I have known for a long time that my end was approaching with certainty. How far away I could not venture to guess. I had an idea however that I would live until fall or the early part of winter. I see now, however, that the time is approaching much more rapidly. I am constantly loosing flesh and strength. The difficulty of swallowing is increasing daily. The tendency to spasms is constant. From three or four in the afternoon until relieved by Morphine I find it difficult to get breath enough to sustain me. Under these circumstances the end is not far off.

~~One~~ We are comparitive strangers in New York City; that is, we made it our home late in life. We have rarely if ever had serious sickness in the family, therefore have made no preparation for a place of buryal. This matter will necessarily come up at my death, and may cause you some embarassment to decide. I should myself select West Point above all other places but for the fact that in case West Point should be selected you would, when the time comes, I hope far in the future, be excluded from the same grounds. I therefore leave you free to select what you think the most appropriate place for depositing my earthly remains.

My will disposes of my property[2] I have left with Fred. a memorandum giving some details of how the ~~money~~ proceeds from my book are to be drawn ~~by~~ from the publisher, and how disposed of.[3]

Look after our dear children and direct them in the paths of rectitude. It would distress me far more to think that one of them could depart from an honorable, upright and virtuous life than it would to know they were prostrated on a bed of sickness from which they were never to arise alive. They have never given us any cause of alarm on their account. I earnestly pray they never will.

With these few injunctions, and the knowledge I have of your love and affections, and of the dutiful affections of all our children, I bid you a final farewell until we meet in another, and I trust ~~bet~~ better, world.

U. S. GRANT

P. S. This will be found in my coat after my demise.

U. S. G.

ALS, USG 3. See Memorandum, [*July 9–12, 1885*].
   On March 17, 1885, William T. Sherman, St. Louis, wrote to Frederick Dent Grant, New York City. "The news-papers keep us all in a nervous state about your Father, only this morning the report of his death was announced and contradicted almost in the same paragraph—I wrote to Colonel Tourtelotte, formerly of my staff who is at the Grand Hotel of New York City, to call and assure you of our great sympathy and concern. He answers that he has, and he saw your wife, who confirmed the general report of General Grant's dangerous condition. I know that your Father has all the care and attention which man and woman too can give, and that messages of sympathy only swell his pain: but I want you and the family to feel that I and mine are anxious to do anything and everything possible to manifest the love and respect we feel for him. Therefore should the General inquire, say to him that you know such to be the case. Death to us all sooner or later is inevitable, and we should prepare for it in advance, because after the event there is no time for deliberation. The family must decide the question where shall the body of General Grant be buried? West Point, New York, Washington and St Louis will contend for the honor. I somewhat believe that Mrs Grant will conclude on Bellefontaine, St. Louis. In this event if I survive General Grant, I will await the arrival of the cortege here, but, should the family select West Point, New York or Washington I will come at your bidding. I am older than your Father, and of a shorter lived race than he, therefore never dreamed of outliving him. Still if so ordained I wish to be present when he is entombed, and to be a willing witness to the great qualities which made him the conspicious figure of our eventful Epoch. Keep these facts in your memory, and act on them when the time comes, but meantime as long as there is life I have hope. With love to all the household ..." Copy, DLC-William T. Sherman. On March 22, Frederick Grant wrote to Sherman. "your letter, and it was a sad one to me, was received. When you were here last December father got so much better that I was in hopes that he was going to get well, but I have long since given up all hopes of his recovery. When it becomes his time to join the great majority I will call upon you his greatest as well as his best friend to assist him in his last battle" ALS, *ibid.* On April 1, W. T. Sherman wrote to U.S. Senator John Sherman of Ohio. "... I may at any momt be Summoned to Grants funeral, unless his family Select St Louis, where one of his Children is buried ...." ALS, *ibid.* On April 15, John Sherman wrote to W. T. Sherman. "... Gen Grant still lingers & is now hopeful not of recovery but of weeks & months. There is a profound sympathy for him which in case of his Death will be expressed by an imposing funeral. I am told that Soldiers

Home is to be his burial place . . . ." ALS, *ibid.* No evidence exists that the Grants
buried a child in St. Louis. In Aug., 1870, USG had considered purchasing a lot at
Bellefontaine Cemetery. See *PUSG*, 20, 224–25.

On June 26 and July 10, 1885, Lt. Gen. Philip H. Sheridan, Washington, D. C.,
wrote to Frederick Grant. " . . . I read every morning with great solicitude the accounts given of General Grant whom I so much love and respect. I feel so tenderly
about him that I hate to go to see him. in fact I do not believe I have nerve enough to
hold myself, and the interview would be embarrassing to both and all concerned The
General and Mrs Grant and family and you and your wife are very near to my heart.
Give my love to the General and tell him he is very near and dear to me." Copy,
DLC-Philip H. Sheridan. "While the General was so sick at one time in New York,
General Badeau & Senator Conklin wrote to me about the proper place for his burial,
and Expessing the belief that the family would like to have him buried at the Soldiers
Home in this city. I consulted with the Board of Commissioners & an invitation was
Extended which is now in my hands. A beautiful Site has been selected overlooking
the city. I do not suppose for a moment that the Genl is going to die but we are all get-
ting nearer the End and when our time comes we ourselves & our friends may not be
indifferent to the spot where we should be buried With my best & undiminished love
for the General. and warm love for his family— . . . " ALS, *ibid.* On July 23, Sheridan,
Fort Reno, Indian Territory, telegraphed to Frederick Grant, Mount McGregor, N. Y.
"Will you please express to Mrs Grant my grief at the loss of my dearest friend and
Comrade and my sincere Sympathy and Condelence with her in this hour of her great
distress" Copy (telegram sent), *ibid.* On July 23 and 24, Brig. Gen. Robert Macfeely,
commissary gen., Washington, D. C., telegraphed to Frederick Grant. "The Board
of Commissioners of the U. S. Soldiers' Home are unanimous in their desire that the
remains of General Grant may be buried within the grounds of that Institution. The
Commissioners have selected subject to approval of the family an appropriate and Commanding eminence, overlooking the City and surrounding country as an appropriate
place of Sepulture. Letter by mail." "The invitation made yesterday by telegraph and
mail that the site for burial of the General's remains in the Soldier's Home grounds
be accepted is intended to cover every wish of the deceased or family concerning any
future use of the Site." Copies, DNA, RG 192, Letters Sent.

On July 24, Henry Probasco, president, Spring Grove Cemetery, Cincinnati, telegraphed to Frederick Grant. "The Directors of the Cemetery of Spring Grove desire
from personal friendship to express their profound sympathy for your family in the loss
which they have sustained. They remember, in common with every citizen of Ohio,
that General Grant was born near to Sherman and Sheridan, his life-long friends, not
distant from this city, where today the universal sentiment demands that you should
consent that his remains may rest beside his father, mother and sister, who were laid
in this cemetery a few years since. We have, therefore, already appropriated a beautiful situation as the family lot in fee simple forever, which will be worthy to contain his
remains—a spot consecrated forever to the memory of Ohio's worthiest citizen and
immortal in the history of our country." *Cincinnati Enquirer*, July 25, 1885. On July 25,
Frederick Grant telegraphed to Probasco. "Thanks, but it was General Grant's wish
to be buried in New York or Washington." *Ibid.*, July 26, 1885.

1. On June 29, USG wrote a note, presumably for his family. "Do as I do. I
take it quietly. I give myself not the least concern. If I knew that the end was to be
to-morrow I would try and get rest in the meantime. As long as there's no progress

there's hope." *New York Tribune*, June 30, 1885. For variant text, see *New York Times*, June 30, 1885.

    2. See Will, Sept. 5, 1884.

    3. See Memorandum, May 29, 1885.

To Samuel L. Clemens

———

                      [Mount McGregor, N. Y., June 29–30, 1885]

    There is nothing binding in the understanding between the Century Magazine and me beyond what is already delivered and paid for. I should be very glad to furnish to them the Wildernes Campaign if I was not publishing a book myself on the same subject. I think they ought to let me off voluntarily under the circumstances. You can do however what you think best.

AN, CU-B. Probably on June 29 or 30, 1885, USG wrote to Samuel L. Clemens. "I have accepted pay for three articles which I suppose settles the matter. They have been delivered which further settles it." "I do not think there is any obligation under the circumstances to deliver the Wilderness Article" AN (undated), *ibid.* USG also wrote an undated note to Clemens with calculations. " . . . $9,170.00 pr article at 2 or 3 pr. word so that they would back out." AN, *ibid.* Between June 29 and July 1, Clemens visited USG at Mount McGregor, N. Y. See letter to Richard Watson Gilder, July 15, 1885; Frederick Anderson, ed., *Mark Twain's Notebooks & Journals* (Berkeley, 1975–79), III, 164–65.

    On June 21, Frederick Dent Grant, Mount McGregor, had written to Clemens. "Your very kind letter was received. aAs I agree with what you say there is no chance of an argument on the matter contained in it. My poor dear Father is worse again today. I would like (to try) to write you as nice a letter as you have me; but on account of his feeling so badly I am unable to do so. Please present my compliments to the Madam" ALS, CU-B.

To Samuel L. Clemens

———

                      [Mount McGregor, N. Y., June 29–30, 1885]

There is much more that I could do if I was a well man. I do not write quite as clearly as I could if well. If I could read it over myself many little matters of anecdote and incident would suggest themselves ~~into~~ to me.

AN, Victor Jacobs, Dayton, Ohio. Probably on June 29 or 30, 1885, USG wrote to
Samuel L. Clemens. "Have you seen any portion of the 2d Vol.—It is up to the end,
or nearly so. As much more work as I have done to-day will finish it. I have worked
faster than if I ~~had~~ did ~~when well~~ had been well. I have used my three boys and a
stenographer." "What part of the book is Fred. now on? Will the second volume be
satisfactory. If I could have two weeks of strength I could improve it very much. As I
am, however, it will have to go about as it is, with verifications and corrections by the
boys, and by suggestions which will enable me to make a point clear here and there."
"~~Meade, Burnside, Hancock, S Hooker Sed Foster, sedgewick, Hancock, Terry Griffin~~ While you have been gabing I have written a short chapter, a very short one. Have
you any thing to say you would like to have me hear. If so come in." AN, CU-B.

To John H. Douglas

———

I see the ~~t~~Times man keeps up the character of his dispatches to
the ~~times~~ paper. They are quite as untrue as they would be if he
described me as getting better from day to day. I think he might
spare my family at least from reading such stuff.

JUNE 30. [1885] P. M

AN (date not in USG's hand), DLC-John H. Douglas. In late June or early July, 1885,
USG wrote to John H. Douglas. "There was a week or such matter when I had but
little acute pain. The newspapers gave that as a sure indication that I was declining
rapidly" AN (undated), ibid. USG wrote another undated note. "Get me the N. Y.
Sun" AN, ICHi.
     On June 30, 8:00 A.M., USG twice wrote to Douglas. "I was frightened this morning because I felt so sleepy. I forgot that I had had nothing like the rest a well man
requires. My feeling this am was what we want to produce? one that enables me to
rest. But I was not quite conscious enough to reason correctly about what produced
[it.]" "If you are not in a hurry suppose you let me get up to the chamber and then
was[h] out my throat, spray my mouth and do what there is to do.—When I come
to think of it when I apply laudnum to the nose it at once looses matter that sets me
to coughing, and most any of the medecine coming to the mouth must be thrown
out with the mucus." AN (undated), DLC-John H. Douglas; typed copies (dated),
DLC-USG, IC.

To John H. Douglas

———

It will probably take several days to see the effect of discontinuing
the use of Cocoane? It might then be used once a day might it not?

say when I am retiring for the night. It is no trouble however to quit outright for the present.

JUNE 30. [*1885*] P. M

AN (date not in USG's hand), DLC-John H. Douglas. On June 30, 1885, USG wrote a note in response to a medical assessment by John H. Douglas. "The atmosphere here enables me to live in comparative comfort while I am being treated, or while nature is taking its course with my disease. I have no idea that I should have been able to come here now if I remained in the city. It is doubtful, indeed, whether I would have been alive. Now, I would be much better able to move back than to come at the time I did." *New York Tribune*, July 1, 1885. See also *New York Times*, July 1, 1885. USG twice wrote to Douglas. "It is a little hard giving up the use of Cocoane when it gives so much relief. But I suppose that it may be used two or three time a day, without injury, and possibly with benefit, when the overuse of it has been Counteracted." "12 05 I will try to observe the effect of the last injection. Pain has cesased and slight drowsynes set in. Nothing however to indicate heavyness, or the use of to much morphine.—At this hour, or a few minuets later, was given three minums of morphine Went to sleep almost immediately. Awoke at 3 30 feeling no effect of the injection." AN (undated), DLC-John H. Douglas.

On June 30, 3:00 P.M., USG wrote to Douglas. "I think I will lay down and have my mouth cleaned. I have had a long nap the pm however, I ~~wi~~ am always glad to see Mr. Drexel. But not being able to talk it is not worth while for him to give himself trouble." AN (undated), *ibid.*; typed copy (dated), DLC-USG, IC. Presumably on the same day, USG wrote an undated note, possibly to Frederick Dent Grant. "Say to Mr Drexel that I will always be pleased to see him. But it is not worth while for him to give himself any trouble to come up here expressly for that. I have such difficulty in speaking that I am no Company." AN, Grant Cottage, Wilton, N. Y. Probably in July, USG wrote an undated note, presumably to Joseph W. Drexel, owner of the cottage at Mount McGregor, N. Y. "I am glad to see you and wish I could report better progress. I am doing as well as could be expected however and have held out longer.—I hope Mrs. Drexel and the family are well." AN, *ibid.*

To Frederick Dent Grant

———

[*Mount McGregor, N. Y., June 30, 1885*]
You ought to feel happy under any circumstances. My ~~supposed~~ expected death called forth expressions of the sincerest kindness from all the people of all sections of the country. The Confederate soldier vied with the Union soldier in sounding my praise. The protestant, the Catholic and the Jew appointed days for universal prayer in my behalf. All societies passed resolutions of sympathy for me and petitions that I might recover. It looks as if my sickness

had had something to do to bring about harmony between the sections. The attention of the public has been called to your children
and they have been found to pass muster. ~~I~~ Apparently I have accomplished more while apparently dying than it falls to the lot of
most men to be able to do.

AN, USG 3. See *Memoirs,* II, *553;* note to Frederick Dent Grant, [*July 1, 1885*].
      In late June or early July, 1885, USG wrote to Frederick Dent Grant. "I was
going to get up at eleven But I had something that I wanted to write and can do that
better in bed with my table before me. I went to sleep and now forget what it is that I
want to write about. I will be able to think of it to-day." "Since seven I have only ben
dosey. I feel weak and unlike doing much. The weather must be bad." AN (undated),
USG 3.
      USG wrote other undated notes, probably at Mount McGregor. "When you go
up [to din]ner quietly whisper to Dr Douglas that I am ready and anxious to retire. I
have staid up nearly all day." "Tell Jesse to come down in fifteen or twenty minuets
and play cards with me" "Will hand you an other hundred next week." AN, Chapman
Grant, Escondido, Calif.

To John H. Douglas

————

[*Mount McGregor, N. Y., June–July, 1885*]
Mrs. Grant heard a story of a boy at College who had just got a
new coat. A classmate passing by when he was trying it on remarked that his coat was too short. Mrs. Grant in repeating
this as a good piece of wit, told it that the student with the new
coat replied that it would be a good while before he would get
another coat

AN, DLC-John H. Douglas. In an undated note, probably to Julia Dent Grant, USG
wrote: "It seems to me that it has been always since Nellie was born. If you bother me
I will leave the room. I have writing enough to do without doing it for the amusement
of other people" AN, ICHi.
      In late June or early July, 1885, USG wrote other notes to John H. Douglas. "I will
have to be careful about my writing. I see ever person I give a piece of paper to puts it
in his pocket. Some day they will be coming up against my English" "I found this am
what was the matter with my watch when you had it last night. You got the ~~split hand~~
two parts of the split hand apart and did nok know how to get them together again.
Look and I will shew you." "Henry and I will look out for the food and wake you up if
you wish, or if I would like to have your help." "It is time for me to eat something." "I
should think it would discharge itself." "I come in to have my mouth dressed and to eat
my food. The latter however I feel as though I can hardly take. I will have to ask you

Dr. to leave me my room for a few minuets. I have staved off going to the stool until this time." "It seems to me that when I take food I want to go to the stool. Just the thought of it now makes me feel like it. Do you think it best to take it. I have taken a good supply to day." "I seem to have the connection made now and breath quite freely and with but little pain. I feel however that to-night would not be a good time to commence the work of reducing the amount of morphine. Abstaining from food stopped the threatened ~~passage~~ discharge from the bowels. I think now then I can take some food with impunity and if thought desirable when I do take it the quantity might be increased one egg and a spoonful or two of beef. But I think this should be just as we are preparing for retirement." "Gerard told me that one of his little boys that I knew died. I think it was about six years ago" AN (undated), DLC-John H. Douglas.

In July, USG wrote to Douglas. "I have just come in from the other room since half past seven" AN, *ibid.*

To Frederick Dent Grant

[*Mount McGregor, N. Y., June–July, 1885*]

The Dr. was more pleased with my condition last night than at any time before since we come up here. He says that a change has taken place, for the better, that he cannot account for. Once before a change took place, unaccounted for by the profession, and now this is the second of the same kind. Read this before you give it to your Ma.

AN, USG 3.

Presumably in July, 1885, USG wrote to Frederick Dent Grant. "I am undoubtedly sinking gradually. I feel that I am growing weaker all the time. Three of the sore places I immagine I can feel roting out. I may last this month of July, but doubt it. Any hour may prove my last" AN (undated), *ibid.*

Endorsement

[*Mount McGregor, N. Y., June–July, 1885*]

Mr. Stanton was not in female apparel. He was in a dressing gown, without coat or vest. His dress was more suited to the bed chamber than in the parlor; But no part of his garb was that worn by women. I have no recollection of testimony of Mr Davis' garb except in comparing that of Mr. Stanton's to his[1]

I may touch upon Mr. Ds garb, which I understand was a gen-
tlemans morning gown. But even of this I am not sure, nor do I
any where speak ~~possibite~~ positively

AE, USG 3. Written on a letter of June 15, 1885, from Bishop William M. Green,
Sewanee, Tenn., to USG. "Though I have not the pleasure of knowing you personally,
I am not ignorant of the high and justly-honored name which you bear. My home and
field of labor lie South of Mason and Dickson's line, but I feel sure that you will, none
the less, excuse my thus addressing you, even if it should please you to refuse the request which I now, beg, respectfully to make. There have appeared lately, in one of the
Periodicals of the day some extracts from your forthcoming History of our late war,—
all of which I read with great pleasure, except one sentence, in which, speaking of the
capture of Mr Jefferson Davis, you state that he was endeavoring to make his escape
in female apparel. This slanderous story was gotten up, and published in 'Harper's
Weekly', at a time of high political excitement, when groundless rumors and disparag-
ing statements were too freely credited on both sides of the then contending parties.
From time to time, the thing has been repeated by the vulgar and the ignorant, and
the friends of Mr Davis have been willing to let it pass, as undeserving of ~~any~~ attention. But, when it appears that your noble and generous spirit is about to record your
belief in that false and foolish story, and your honored hand is prepared to pass it down
along the line of authentic History, every admirer of your name, throughout our widespread South, as well as every friend of Mr Davis would unite in most respectfully and
earnestly begging you to withold your hand. There lies before me, at this moment, a
confidential letter from Mr Davis, giving me, at my request, a circumstantial account
of his capture, and denying, most positively, that he, either made any attempt to get
away from his captors, or disguised himself in Women's clothing. A similar denial
was, I believe, subsequently, published by Mr Harrison, his Private Secretary, and by
Messrs Reagan and Lubbock, who were in company with him Let me hope then, dear
sir, that with your usual magnanimity, you will scorn to strike thus at a fallen foe; and
wound the feelings of thousands and tens of thousands of your fellow-citizens, who
since the asperities of our unhappy war have passed away, have come to regard you
with pride, and to take pleasure in your fame. We are neither ignorant of, nor ungrateful for your noble refusal to consent to the ignominious trial of Mr Davis and others,
after the surrender of the Confederate army; and we would rejoice, with your dearest
friends, to see a like course of action mark the closing scenes of your life. Permit me
to assure you, General, that the sympathies of our whole South are deeply interested in
the daily accounts of your present suffering; and that the prayers of many are offered
in your behalf. That it may please God to send you relief, and long spare you to our
now united country is the sincere and fervent prayer of . . . " ALS, *ibid.* Born in 1798
in Wilmington, N. C., Green graduated from the University of North Carolina (1818),
became the first Episcopal bishop of Miss. (1849), and was a founder of the University
of the South, Sewanee. See *Memoirs,* II, 524; Dunbar Rowland, ed., *Jefferson Davis Constitutionalist: His Letters, Papers and Speeches* (Jackson, Miss., 1923), VII, 441–45; Francis R. Lubbock to William T. Walthall, Aug. 2, 1877, in Walthall, "The True Story of
the Capture of Jefferson Davis," *Southern Historical Society Papers,* V, 3 (March, 1878),
122–24; Burton N. Harrison, "The Capture of Jefferson Davis," *Century Magazine,*
XXVII, 1 (Nov., 1883), 130–45; Chester D. Bradley, "Was Jefferson Davis Disguised
as a Woman When Captured?," *Journal of Mississippi History,* XXXVI, 3 (Aug., 1974),
243–68.

1. On Oct. 19, 1863, USG had seen Secretary of War Edwin M. Stanton in sleeping garb at the Galt House in Louisville. The incident occurred late in the evening after Stanton urgently sought USG to issue orders for Union forces to remain in Chattanooga. See *PUSG*, 9, 302; *Memoirs*, II, 19, 26; Benjamin P. Thomas and Harold M. Hyman, *Stanton: The Life and Times of Lincoln's Secretary of War* (New York, 1962), p. 291.

Draft Article Revision

[*June–July, 1885*]

Vicksburgh was important to the enemy on account of its railroad connections: the Vicksburgh & Jackson railroad connecting it with all the Southern confederacy East of the Mississippi river and the Vicksburgh & Shreveport railroad connecting it with all their country West of that great stream. It was important to the North on account of its commanding the river itself, ~~which was the~~ it being the natural outlet to the sea of all the commerce of the Northwestern ~~states~~. The Mississippi flows through a low alluvial valley many miles in width, and is very tortuous in its course, running to all points of the compass, sometimes within a few miles. This valley is bounded on the East side by a range of high lands rising in some places more than two hundred feet above the general level of the valley. Running from side to side of the valley the river occasionally washes the base of the high land, or even cuts into it forming ~~high~~ elevated and ~~almost perpendicular~~ precipitous bluffs. On the first of these south of Memphis, and some four hundred miles distant by the windings of the river from that city stands the city of Vicksburgh.

On account of its importance to both North and South ~~it~~ Vicksburg became the objective point of the Army of the Tennessee in the fall of 1862. It is generally regarded as an ~~maximom~~ in war that all great armies in an enemy's country should start from a base of supplies which should be fortified and guarded and to which the army should fall back in case of disaster. The first movement looking to Vicksburgh as an objective point was begun early in November 1862, and conformed to this ~~maximom~~. It followed the line of the ~~Missippi~~ Mississippi ~~va~~Central railroad, with Columbus, Kentucky, as a base; and soon after it started, a cooperating column was moved down the Miss. river in transports with Memphis as its base. Both of these movements failing, the entire aArmy of the Tennessee was transferred to the neighborhood of Vicksburg and landed on the opposite side of the river from that city at Milliken's bBend.

Here, after spending about three months trying to get upon the high land and also waiting for the waters of the Mississippi, to which were very high this winter, to go down recede, I determined to march below Vicksburg, take Grand Gulf, hold it and cooperate with the aid of Banks' army against Port Hudson, using New Orleans as my base of supplies. Then return against Vicksburg with the combined army keeping New Orleans as our base

In pursuance of this determination the army was marched to Hard Times a point below Vicksburg on the Louisiania side and the batteries of Vicksburg were run by the fleet and some of the transports. on the 29th of April.

The troops were at Hard Times, and the fleet under Admiral Porter made an attack upon Grand Gulf while I reconnoitered the position of the enemy on a tug to see if it was possible to make a landing. Finding that place too strong I moved the army below Grand Gulf, to De Schroomn's, running the batteries here as we had done at Vicksburg, and stopping with the transports at lLearning here from an old negro that there was a good road from Bruinsburg up to Port Gibson, I determined to cross and move upon Grand Gulf from the rear.

April 30th was spent in transporting troops across to Bruinsburg. These troops were moved out towards Port Gibson as fast as they were landed. On the 1st of May the advance met the enemy under Bowen, about two miles West of Port Gibson, where quite a severe battle was fought, resulting in the defeat of the enemy, who was were driven back on Port Gibson from the field. On May 2nd our troops moved into Port Gibson, and, finding that the bridges on over Bayou Pierre were destroyed, spent the balance of the day in rebuilding them and and crossing them, and marching to the nNorth fFork, where they encamped for the night. During the night they rebuilt the bridge across the North Fork which had also been destroyed and the next day (the 3rd) ~~after they~~ pushed on and, after considerable skirmishing, reached the Big Black near Hankinson's ferry & the Miss ~~near~~ at G. G.

~~I here came up with the advance~~ On the 3rd I went into Grand Gulf and spent the afternoon and until late that night in writing letters to Washington and orders for the next movement of the Army. Here I also received a letter from Banks stating that he could not be at Port Hudson for some days, and then with an army of only fifteen thousand men.[1] As I did not regard this force of as much value as the time which would be lost in waiting for it I determined to move on to Vicksburgh.

The 4th, 5th and 6th of May were spent in reconnoitering towards Vicksburg, and also in crossing Sherman's troops over to Grand Gulf. On the 7th, Sherman ~~was up and~~ having ~~arrived~~ joined the main body of the army, the troops across the Big Black were withdrawn and ~~I~~ the movement was commenced ~~the movement~~ to get in position on the Vicksburg & Jackson railroad so as to attack Vicksburg from the rear. This occupied the army from the 7th to the 12th, when ~~the~~ our position ~~of the army~~ was near Fourteen Mile creek, Raymond being ~~on~~ our right flank with our left resting on the Big Black. To obtain this position we fought the battle of Raymond, where Logan's and Crocker's divisions of McPherson's corps defeated the ~~army~~ Confederates under Gen. Gregg, driving him back on, Jackson; Sherman and McClernand having some skirmishing where they crossed Fourteen Mile creek ~~and McPherson McClernand also having heavy skirmishing in crossing that stream~~.

~~I now found that~~ As the army under Pemberton was on my left flank and that under Johnston on my ~~lef~~ right at Jackson, I ~~therefore~~ determined to move my army rapidly on Jackson, capturing and destroying that place as a military depot; then turn west and destroy the army under Pemberton or drive it back into Vicksburg. The 13th was spent in making these moves. On the 14th ~~we~~ Jackson was attacked with Sherman's and McPherson's corps. The place was taken and all ~~stores and s sup~~ supplies that could be of service to the enemy destroyed; as well as the railroad bridge.

On the 15th the troops were faced to the West and marched towards Pemberton, who was near Edward's station. The next day, the 16th, we met the enemy's ~~forces~~ at Champion's ~~H~~hill and after a hard fought battle defeated and drove him back towards Vicksburg, capturing nearly 3000 prisoners and 18 guns. This ~~battle~~ was the hardest fought battle of the campaign.

On the 17th we reached the Big Black, where we found the enemy intrenched. After a battle of two or three hours' ~~fight~~ duration we succeeded in carrying their works by storm, making a large capture of artillery and about twelve hundred men.

In their flight the enemy destroyed the bridge across the Big Black so that the balance of the day and night ~~were~~as spent in building bridges across that stream. We ~~got~~ acrossed ~~on~~ the morning ~~of~~ of the 18th and the outworks of Vicksburg were reached before night ~~the army taking position in front of them~~. On the 19th there was continuous skirmishing with the enemy while we were getting into better position.

The enemy's troops had been much demoralized by their defeats at Champion's ~~H~~hills and ~~other places~~ the Big Black, and I believed ~~they~~ he would not make much of an effort to hold Vicksburg. ~~and, therefore, on the night of the 19th~~ ~~a~~Accordingly, at 2 oclock I ordered an assault. It resulted in ~~obtaining~~ securing more advanced positions for all our troops, where they were fully covered from the fire of the enemy, and the siege of Vicksburg began.

Df, USG 3. After this opening, the remaining text of "The Siege of Vicksburg," *Century Magazine*, XXX, 5 (Sept., 1885), 752–65, largely matches *Memoirs*, I, 529–74. See letter to Richard Watson Gilder, July 15, 1885.

1. See *PUSG*, 8, 93.

To John H. Douglas

JULY. 1. [*1885*] 8. A. M

I feel weak from my exertions last night in throwing up. Then since that I can not help repeating two advertisements of the B & O rail road when I am half awake. The houses on their place at Deer Park are advertised as a sure cure for Malaria, or the place is, signed Robt Garrett. Pres. The other is that the water—I think— is a sure cure for catarrh. signed same. There may be no such advertisement, but I keep dreaming them all the same. It strikes me as a very sharp dodge for a gentleman to advertise his own wares in such a way. When you consider Garrett owns the water and buildings at the park; is Pres. of the road over which invalids must pass to get to the place, and is a very large owner in the stock of the road it strikes me as another instance of what a man will do for money.

JULY 1 8, A. M

AN (dates not in USG's hand), DLC-John H. Douglas. Robert Garrett became president of the Baltimore and Ohio Railroad and manager of other family interests after the death of his father, John W., in 1884. USG last visited Deer Park, Md., in Aug., 1883. On July 1, 1885, 10:00 A.M., USG wrote twice to John H. Douglas. "I have not taken any wine in six days. So far as I have tried I do not think alcoholic drinks agree with me. They seem to heat me up and have no other effect." "I can smell the Carbolic in the urine I pass. I do not think I overslept last night! I have been wide awake since nine, and feel very free from pain There is just a little pain down in the corner of my mouth, and on the tongue adjoining, with a slight sensation runing to the ear." AN, *ibid.* On the same day, USG wrote to Douglas. "I talked a goodeal with my pencil. The wine I did take was not Madeira but Tokay, and since leaving N. Y. three small wine glasses of old port. ~~About same of~~ I do not need or want either. Mrs. Grant and Fred. thought they would help me" AN, *ibid.* At 10:30 A.M. and 11:00 A.M., USG wrote to Douglas. "I have found nothing that has come so near sealing me up entirely as the vasealene,—" "I did not call for this now. I am in no hurry. The day is before me and I can not spend more than an hour in this way very well. Will you ask one of the me men to hand me my pen knife. I think too I will have to free my head a little befor commensing work." AN, *ibid.* USG wrote to Douglas. "I got all ready hoping to avoid a passag and also vomiting. I did not escape the former and do not know now that I will the latter The passage felt hurt—probably sour." AN (undated), *ibid.*

To John H. Douglas

———

I should have had that milk at eleven.

I think it was two days this morning since Cocoain was used. Do you remember?

I was surprised to see the time of day when you come in. I

thought it was but a little after twelve. I have not felt drowsey since nine.

July 1. [*1885*] 2. p. m

AN (date not in USG's hand), DLC-John H. Douglas. On July 1, 1885, 2:00 p.m., USG wrote to John H. Douglas. "I have just sent for my dinner. I feel the necessity for the Cocain more now than I have done in the two days since we have used any. The pain is not accute nor is it severe. It seems to be in the Cavity at the root of the tongue and to extend down to the lump under the chin—not the *pimple*." USG wrote other notes to Douglas. "Possibly stronger but not so well rested. Two or three times I found my self laying awak, and keeping so, supposing that I was waiting for something." "It gives less pain because I give way less. Formerly when I would get awake even after a half hours sleep I would feel accute pain requiring the use of Cocain. When I quit giving way to the use of it the pain would partialy subside and I would not feel it so much when it was used as before" "I hope I will be able to hold out without Coain. But a few times to-day my mouth wanted it very much. Had you not better go to bed soon after tea and not get up unless I wake you." AN (undated), *ibid.*

To Frederick Dent Grant

————

[*Mount McGregor, N. Y., July 1, 1885*]

If you will give me one of the papers containing notes I can write my estimate of the qualities of two or three of the generals, without notes. I want what I wrote yesterday for chapter "In conclusion" about "change of feeling between north and south having started in the expression of sympathy by all classes and sections of people for me".[1] Some one who has not the partiality of the family should be consulted.

AN, USG 3. Probably in early July, 1885, USG wrote to Frederick Dent Grant. "Send me my notes." "Do you think now that you read my pad. I did not ask you who I had written about, but, ~~w~~ did you think of any others whom I should mention." "What part are you reading up and verifying? Will you be sending any thing to the printer ~~to-night~~ this week?—first vol. of course When Buck comes I think he will stay until you are through. It will be a good thing to get the second vol. finished as soon as possible. The edition is so large that it will be impossble to get the book out at the time expected. If the plates were ready now it would be a difficult job." AN (undated), *ibid.*

1. See note to Frederick Dent Grant, [*June 30, 1885*].

To John P. Newman

I do not know that there is any special weakness.—Alcoholic stimulents are not good for me. I can feel it, or did, the few times I took Port wine. It simply heats me and then leaves me weak for a time.

I worked a good four hours to-day, and wrote a short chapter for my book.[1]

U. S. GRANT

JULY 1ST 1885

In writing this I have had no rest for my arm.

ANS, USMA. On July 1, 1885, John P. Newman visited USG at Mount McGregor, N. Y., and asked whether "he felt a steadily increasing weakness." *New York Tribune,* July 2, 1885. On the same day, USG wrote to Newman. "I rarely ever use my cane in going about the ~~roo~~ my room. Often when I go out I have to look about for it to find it." AN, USMA.

Possibly in early July, USG shared with Newman a letter "from an old Quaker" that an acquaintance later recalled from memory. "FRIEND GRANT: I am a stranger to thee. I would not intrude upon thy suffering, but I am anxious for thy soul. Trust in Jesus. He will not fail thee." *New York Times,* Aug. 11, 1885.

1. On July 1, Newman told a correspondent that USG "remembered omitting to say anything of four Generals, and what he wrote to-day was his estimate of them." *Ibid.,* July 2, 1885.

To John H. Douglas

DR. I ask you not to show this to any one, unless physicians you consult with, until the end. Particularly, I want it kept from my family. If known to one man the papers will get it and they will get it. It would only distress them almost beyond endurance to know it, and, by reflex, would distress me.

I have not changed my mind materially since I wrote you before in the same strain.[1] (Now however I know that I gain in strength some days, but when I do go back it is beyond when I started to improve.) I think the chances are very decidedly in favor of your being able to keep me alive until the change of weather towards the winter. Of course there are contingencies that might arise at any time that would carry me off very suddenly. The most probable of these are choking. Under these circumstances life is not worth living. I am very thankful[2] to have been spared this long because it has enabled me to practically complete the work in which I take so much interest. I can not stir up strength enough to review it and make additions and subtractions that would suggest themselves to me and are not likely to to any one else.

Under the above circumstances I will be the happiest the most pain I can avoid. If there is to be an extraordinary cure, such as some people believe there is to be, it will develope itself. I would say therefore to you and your collegues to make me as comfortable as you can. If it is within Gods providence that I should go now I am ready to obey His call without a murmur. I should prefer going now to enduring my present suffering for a single day without hope of recovery. As I have stated I am thankful for the providential extension of my time to enable me to continue my work. I am further thankful, and in a much greater degree thankful, because it has enabled me to see for myself the happy harmony which has so suddenly sprung up between those engaged but a few short years ago in deadly conflict. It has been an inestimable blessing to me to hear the kind expression towards me in person from all parts of our country; from people of all nationalities of all religons, and of no religion, of Confederate and National troops alike; of soldiers organizations; of mechanical, scientific religious and all other societies, embracing almost every citizen in the land. They have brought joy to my heart if they have not effected a cure. To you and your collegues I acknowledge my indebtedness for having brought me through the "valley of the shadow of death" to enable me to witness thiese thing.

U. S. Grant

Mt McGregor N. Y. July 2d 1885.

ALS (partial facsimile, final five sentences and closing), MH; typed copy, DLC-USG, IC.

On July 2, 1885, 11:00 A.M., USG wrote to John H. Douglas. "I am afraid my bowels will have to be started either by senna or the enema. When I take eoan cocain again it will be more to ascertain the effect of leaving it off than to alleviate pain, from present appearances. It looks now as though its use had become a habit, and that I would want it almost on the minuet even if asleep at the time" AN, DLC-John H. Douglas. On the same day, A.M., USG twice wrote to Douglas. "I have had no rest since you left here though I feel more like work than any morning since I have been here. I will try to rest a little however.—I have had a tremendious movement of the bowels. First there was a little liquid, tho to hard to pass until Henry inserted a pipe and a little warm water. This broke up a great mass of hard stuff which was followed by liquid. I was still left with a feeling that all ~~was not~~ had not passed that should. The pipe was reniewed with the same result. After the effect of this was apparently had fully I had a copious and natural passage. I feel much better for it all." "I do not care about the doors being closed. I thought after coming down you might want to set with me a while. I have worked ~~a~~ g and feel a little weak from it, but I can not sleek—since seven this am I have dosed off a few times, but not a half hour in the aggregate." AN, *ibid.* Also on July 2, P.M., USG wrote to Douglas. "Cocain is a failure in my case now. It hurts very much to apply it, and I do not feel that it does me much good. I do not see why it should have afforded so much relief heretofor and now stopped" AN, *ibid.*

1. See letter to John H. Douglas, [*June 17, 1885*].
2. A reporter noted that "glad was written, but scratched out and thankful substituted." *New York Times*, July 26, 1885.

To John H. Douglas

I have been writing up my views of some of our generals, and of the character of Lincoln & Stanton. I do not place Stanton as high as some people do. Mr. Lincoln cannot be extolled to ~~much~~ highly.

JULY 2. [*1885*] P. M.

AN (date not in USG's hand), DLC-John H. Douglas. See *Memoirs*, II, 536–37. See also *PUSG*, 20, 77–80; *ibid.*, 25, 258–60.

USG wrote an undated note to John H. Douglas. "This is the first of the 'jim-cracks' that has seemed to have real merit. I found it easy to ~~w~~ day to write upon for an hour, without stoping. It also makes a good invalid table ~~fo~~ to get ones meals off of." AN, DLC-John H. Douglas.

To John H. Douglas

This is the only way in which I can get my breath. If I lean forward or back much I choke directly. I shall be obliged to sleep in this position until there is a change.

JULY 3. [*1885*] 11 A.M

AN (date not in USG's hand), DLC-John H. Douglas. On July 3, 1885, USG wrote a note, presumably to John H. Douglas. "I have not slept thirty minuets at one time since yesterday noon. I am so fatigued that I scarsely know what to do with myself. I do not feel howevr that I am worse only suffering the inconveniense of not being able to sleep long in an inclining positin. I can retain my breath standing up but not reclining. If I keep getting better as I did most night there will be very little use for further improvement. But I am better this after-noon in the particular that gave me so much trouble." AN (undated), ICHi. For this note's date and context, see *New York Times*, July 4, 1885. USG also wrote to Douglas. "I did not get much rest this morning until now. I am just the reverse of yesterday. I can not hold my breathing while seated, but extended I can though at the expense of coughing every ten to fifteen minuets" "It gives considerable rest to fall asleep laying down, but I do not suppose this condition will last long. I was also awake a great many times when you were not in. I took food three time and cleansed my mouth after each. Last night too I suffered much acute pain in the mouth—old places—and had to apply coacain. I have taken none however since about nine." AN (undated), DLC-John H. Douglas.

On July 3, A.M., USG wrote to Douglas. "I do not see that there is any thing to do unless it is to spray me. It is not a great while since I cleaned my mouth and got sleep after taking food. It seems to me that I am taking food oftener than usual, about ~~seven or eight times~~ eight or nine times in twenty-four hours" AN, *ibid.* On the same day, 11:00 A.M., USG twice wrote to Douglas. "It seems to me I took food just before Henry went away, and drank nearly the tumbler ~~fooull~~ without stopping" "I have had two operations of the bowels this morning, and feel as if I should have to take an other. They were both constipated and came not many minuets apart. Nothing was done to produce them; they were natural" AN, *ibid.* At 2:00 P.M. and 3:00 P.M., USG wrote to Douglas. "It will be six hours yet before I can expect to have any relief. That would distribute it along so that I would not have full relief at any time. I prefer waiting." "~~I think my bowels are going to act again~~. The more I think about this paroxism of the throat the more I think it possible that it may take me off suddenly some day. There are times when I could not recover if lef to myself" AN (undated), *ibid.*; typed copies (dated), DLC-USG, IC. Probably on the same day, USG wrote to [*Douglas*]. "What is to be my fate to-night doctor? Will I have to lay awake again? making it a study how to get a breath? It is about as much as I could stand to go through another nite." AN (facsimile), PictureHistory.com.

USG wrote undated notes to Douglas. "I laid down on the cot and got a good rest." "I have found so much difficulty in getting my breath this evening that I tried laudanum a few minuets ago, but with the same result as for some time past. The injection has not yet had any effect. The douch has not acted well for some time. Do you think it worth the experiment of trying. I immagine I feel the morphine commencing to act." "I think laudanum is loosing its effect in the way of clearing my head now. In fact every time I have used it for a week back it appeared to me to increase the embarassment. I will not take it therefore if you do not ask it." AN, DLC-John H. Douglas.

To John H. Douglas

———

That is just pleasant without wraps.

Would you take the injection as son as my temperature is right for it. Harrison wraps me to much and if it does get cold in the night I must either get the cover off in places or keep awake to look after them. If allowed to make myself comfortable I naturally pull clothing over cold spots.

JULY 4 ⌈*1885*⌉

In health I like a cold room to sleep in. Even if water freezes in the room I sleep well. Mrs. Grant also sleeps with a window open the coldest nights

AN (date not in USG's hand), DLC-John H. Douglas. On July 4, 1885, USG wrote to John H. Douglas. "If Henry can get me in bed when it is warm he has me just where he wants me. He can then get me in a perspiration and claim, very properly, that it will not do to cool of to rapidly. The temprature was 72 when I retird. I went to sleep at once and woke up twenty minuets or so after covered with perspiration. I have done nothing since in the way of sleeping to rest me. I feel comparitively easy however. The two places in my mouth continue to give some pain and where the right hand nostril enters the mouth it is always painful." AN, *ibid.*

Also on July 4, 1:00 P.M., USG wrote to Douglas. "There is a growing weakness however. I am intensely sleepy to day but I canot hold it long. at a time.—I thought I would take a drive in my coach to-day. But I should have to expectorate so much, and would be dosing to so that I will not go." AN, *ibid.* At 7:00 P.M., USG wrote to Douglas. "~~I feel very weak this evening~~. I have been getting on very well to day. I think I would prefer waiting to the usual time." AN, *ibid.* USG also wrote to Douglas. "In coughing a while ago much blood come up—Has Dr. Sands gone—He takes a much more hopeful view of my case than I do—How old is he—I had to use the cocoan several time in quick succession this morning. I have not had to use it since. You used it once in the mean time, but that was more to let Dr. Sands see than for any thing els. I did not need it." AN (undated), *ibid.* On July 4, Henry B. Sands, then forty-five, consulted with Douglas. See *New York Tribune* and *New York Times*, July 5, 1885.

Also on July 4, Cyrus W. Field, Buckingham Palace Hotel, London, telegraphed to Herman L. Waterbury, manager, Western Union Telegraph Co., Saratoga, N. Y. "Please tell Gen Grant that Mr Phelps, the American Minister, Senator Edmunds, the Duke of Argyl, Mr John Bright and other mutual friends are to dine with me this evening and that we shall drink his health and that I do most earnestly pray that his health may improve, and that he may live for years, a blessing to his family, his country, and the world. Give my kindest regards to Mrs Grant and all of her Children and telegraph me here at once exactly how General Grant is." Telegram received, USG 3.

To Charles L. Webster & Co.

Mt McGregor
July 4th 1885

CHAS. L. WEBSTER, & CO.

DEAR SIRS:

Your letter with reference to imitations of the title page of my "Personal Memoirs" is received. It seems incredible to me that anyone would be unprincipled enough to attempt to obtain subscriptions to a book of the character you name, by leading the public to believe that it is the one which I have written. But if it has or does occurs, such is the case, however, I think your wisest course is simply to let the public know that this wrong is being done.

Yours Truly,

Df (in Frederick Dent Grant's hand), USG 3. On Aug. 18, 1885, Charles L. Webster & Co., New York City, wrote *"To the Public:* Since it was announced that General Grant was writing a book for publication great interest has been manifested by the public in it. While our relations to it have been of a strictly business character, we have recognized the fact that this was not a sufficient answer to the numerous inquiries that have been made. The circumstances under which the 'Memoirs' were written, the main purpose for which they were written, and the situation and character of the writer, gave it a dramatic interest which made it in some measure the property of the public. From time to time statements have appeared in the public journals, some grounded upon interviews, some evidently statements of parties who knew nothing of the facts in regard to the contract, the condition of the manuscript, or the time of publication. The publication of these statements having been invariably succeeded by a shower of letters inquiring as to their truth, most of them from persons who as intending purchasers have a right to the information sought, we have by private letters given such information as we thought pertinent, but in many cases we are advised by friends who desire that the book shall have as large a sale as possible that the inaccurate statements published in some of the leading newspapers of the country are calculated to mislead the public and injure the sale of the book. The contradiction of such misstatements, however strongly such errors may be contradicted, cannot keep abreast of the false rumors put in circulation. As the inaccurate reports are liable to be from time to time repeated, we have determined after some hesitation to make the following statement, and respectfuly request that the newspapers of the country will not hereafter publish anything, either in the form of interviews or otherwise, which is not in accordance with it: On the 1st of March last we entered into a contract with General Grant for the publication of his personal 'Memoirs.' The first volume was at that time completed. The second volume had been blocked out, and some work done upon it. It was in such condition that with Gen. Grant's notes it could probably have been completed by another hand. After the contract was signed he continued to work upon the second volume until prevented by the illness which is familiar to all. At such times as the disease seemed to give him temporary relief it was thought advisable that certain historical events should be treated by him, if possible, and among them the particulars of the surrender of General Lee. A trusted employe of ours, who was also a shorthand writer, attended from day to day at General Grant's house, and the work commenced. From one event he went to another, until he had written several hundred pages, and the work was subsequently completed here and at Mount McGregor by the aid of another shorthand writer and by the General's own hand. The first volume is in type. The manuscript of the second volume is all written and completed as originally intended, and will in due course be published as prepared by General Grant himself. It comes down to the close of the civil war. By the terms of our contract Mrs. Grant will receive nearly three-fourths of the profits arising from the sale of the book, and upon some sales even more. So far the book has had an unprecedented success, and unless its sale is injured by misrepresentation it will accomplish what General Grant earnestly hoped and expected. The first volume of the 'Memoirs' will be published about Dec. 1, the second volume about the 1st of March next, or as soon thereafter as is possible. Numerous cheap imitations of the book are now hawked about the country. General Grant was greatly troubled in the last days of his life that attempts should be made by others to reap the benefits of labor done by him under circumstances of almost unprecedented suffering, and the best and only comment which need be made is that which he has himself written in his letter to us as follows; . . ." *New York Times*, Aug. 20, 1885. See *ibid.*, Oct. 13, Dec. 3, 1885, Feb. 28, Oct. 14, 1886; Memorandum, [*Feb., 1885*]; Frederick Anderson, ed., *Mark Twain's Notebooks & Journals* (Berkeley, 1975–79), III, 116, 152, 155, 168, 183–84.

On Aug. 9, a reporter had asked Frederick Dent Grant about his father's book. "I think it will appear before long. We do not yet know exactly what or how much manuscript there is. The last pages my father wrote have not been looked over, and there is a large amount of matter not in form for publication. On my return to Mount McGregor I shall devote the next four weeks to looking over the manuscripts. I shall make copies of all his papers and preserve the originals. I am not yet sure whether or not there will be enough matter for two volumes, but what there is will be published with as little revising as possible. The story will be brought down to my father's death, and when this has been done whatever there is will be printed." *New York World*, Aug. 10, 1885. Frederick Grant later wrote to Charles L. Webster & Co. "In answer to your note of the 11th calling my attention to an interview published in the New-York *World* of Aug. 10, I beg to say that that portion of the interview which relates to the Personal Memoirs is entirely incorrect and calculated to mislead. As stated in your circular *the book is finished*, the two volumes together making between 1,200 and 1,300 pages, and the manuscript has been delivered to you." *New York Times*, Aug. 26, 1885.

To John H. Douglas

———

[*Mount McGregor, N. Y., July 5, 1885*]

I feel much relieved this morning. I had begun to feel that the work of getting my book to-gether was making but slow progress.

I find it about completed, and the work now to be done is mostly after it gets back in gallies. It can be sent to the printer faster than he is ready for it. There from one hundred and fifty to two hundred pages more of it than I intended. Will not cut out any thing of interest. It is possible we may find a little repetition. The whole of that however is not likely to amount to many pages. Then too there is more likelyhood of omissions.

AN, DLC-John H. Douglas. For the date and context of this note, see *New York Tribune*, July 6, 1885.

On July 5, 1885, 10:30 A.M., USG wrote to John H. Douglas. "I think I am not as weak as I was this time yesterday. Really my extreme weakness yesterday was the cause of my feeling as bad as I did. Will you remain at the house until I want that done—throat cleaned." AN, DLC-John H. Douglas. USG wrote to Douglas. "About an hour ago I coughed up a pice of stringy matter about the size of a small lizard. Not so bad to-day as yesterday. I should take about five minums now." "How much may a man reduce in weight who ought to reach 180 pounds, but who has gone up to 195. I am down now to about 130 It was 140½ seven weeks ago." AN (undated), *ibid.*

To John H. Douglas

I think quite well doctor. When I got awake over half an hour ago I did not feel in the slightes degree sleepy. I feared very much that my sleep for the night was over. But I was asleep in a minuet or two, and now feel that I can hardly keep awake long enough to get my food.

Do you not know that colored people have no regular time for sleeping? They are social and visit other servants when the families are asleep and catch their rest during the day every moment when they are not at work.

I will venture that you will ever find a colored person in their beds.

JULY 6. [*1885*]

AN (date not in USG's hand), DLC-John H. Douglas. On July 6, 1885, USG wrote to John H. Douglas. "I feel very much stronger than yesterday, and yesterday was stronger than the day befor strength aids one in enduring pain wonderfully." AN, *ibid.* USG also wrote to Douglas. "I know that what you are doing will be as likely to cure me as any think els. Nature is given a good ~~oppot~~ oportunity to act and if a cure is possible it will develope itself. All the medical scill in America, including Dr. Bron, could not find a cure" AN (undated), *ibid.* USG may refer to self-proclaimed cancer specialist Wallace E. Brown. See note to Julia Dent Grant, [*April 14, 1885*].

On July 6, 2:00 P.M., USG wrote to Douglas. "I had a very good mornings rest. Unfortunately after taking my coffee, betwen nine and ten, my mouth hurt me and I used the Cocoan. It did not give full relief all over and I touched the place still hurting again. The medicine went to the very spot and left me for a half hour or more entirely free of pain for the first time in a long while. It hurt again and unfortunately I tried the Cocoan again without benefit." AN, DLC-John H. Douglas. On the same day, 5:00 P.M., USG twice wrote to Douglas. "I am sorry you took the trouble to walk. You could have waited for the next train as well as not," "The injection worked very well, and I hope at not to great a cost. The pain left me entirely so that it was an enjoyment lay awake. I did get asleep however from the mear absence from pain, and woke up a short time before four. I then took my food, washed out my mouth and put in a little cocane which went to the right spot the first time. I have felt no pain until within the last few minuets. I had not ben out of my chair much over five minuets when I saw you coming up the hill. How is Mr. Drexel?" AN, *ibid.* Also on July 6, 9:00 P.M., USG wrote to Douglas. "I did not know you had arrived—was playing to pass time until you arrivd How much did you give me this pm? Would you then give three more now and six later at night or six now and three if I am obliged to have it in the course of the night" AN, *ibid.*

To Frederick Dent Grant

[*Mount McGregor, N. Y., July 6, 1885*]

It is a great deal better that it should be dedicated as it is. I made what reputation I have as a soldier. The troops engaged on both sides are yet living. As it is the dedication is to those we fought against as well as those we fought with. It may serve a purpose in restoring harmony. If it does it is of more importance than to simply gratify a little vanity. You will die. It is hoped the book will live. After you and the soldiers who fought are all gone the dedication will have more value than now.

AN, USG 3. On July 6, 1885, Frederick Dent Grant endorsed this note. "I said I wished you had left the dedication of your book as you at first brought to me—he re-plyed" AE, *ibid.* On May 23, USG, New York City, had written. "These volumes are dedicated to the American soldier and sailor." ANS (facsimile), *Memoirs,* I.

In late June or early July, USG wrote to Frederick Grant. "If I should dyie here make arrangemnts for embalming my body and retaining it for buryel until pleasant weather in the fall. In that case you can continue your work and insure its being ready as fast as the printers can take it. This is now my great interest in life, to see my work done There is nothing in my condition that I know of, except presentiment, on account of weakness to indicate that I may not as well live for the next three months as for the last five. Do *not* let the memory of me interfere with the progress of the book." ANS (undated), USG 3. On Aug. 16, Frederick Grant, Mount McGregor, N. Y., wrote to Felix A. Sullivan. "Accept the thanks of our family for your services in the sad duty of Embalming my Father." ALS (facsimile), Edward C. Johnson, "Life and Times of Felix Sullivan, Noted Embalmer: Part II—The Middle Years," *Casket & Sunnyside*, 104, 7 (July, 1974), 21. For elaboration, see *ibid.*, p. 20.

Probably in early July, USG wrote to Frederick Grant. "It seemed to me that I got the campaign about Petersburg, and the move to Appomattox pretty good on the last attempt. How many pages will there be besides appendix. That in 2 Vol. Have you compared much of the 2d Vol. with other writers—Lave out the incident of Mrs. Tyler after Spottsylvania I should change Spotts if I was able, and could improve Col. N. Ana and Cold Harbor" AN (undated), USG 3. For the "Mrs. Tyler" anecdote, see *Memoirs*, II, 250–51.

USG wrote other undated notes to Frederick Grant. "That is too much. Then too there is matter that I should like put in an appendix. I then We will consider whether not to leave out the appendix. It will not add much more than a cent to the Vol. Put it in" "Sketch me off the substance of the paragraph which you want me to write. I do not take hold quite as freely as I would if I had been reading the manuscript." "What are you engaged at now?" "Does what I have written fit the case." "Are you reviewing or copying? Chattanooga does not want much of either." "I think I am a little mixed in my statement about Wilson and Dana going to Knoxville. I am not sure that they did not go to where Sherman was only, with instructions to get a letter to Burnside, and a copy of it to Longstreet. The latter got his I know." "If more pages are wanted for second volume an account can be given of the siege of Knoxville of a chapter." "What are you doing now? No writing then during that time. Do you look up what other authors say? Have I left out many points. Is that entitled 'preface' or 'introduction'? Leave that to Webster & Co At that time though it was very much shorter than it is now." "D Tell Mr. Dawson to punctuate." AN, USG 3.

On July 6 and 22, Frederick Grant wrote to William R. Rowley. "Mother requests me to acknowledge the receipt of a check for $162.32 you sent her from the house & balance in bank, and thank you for attending to the matter. We were very much distressed when we heard of Mrs Rowley's death. Father sent a despatch to Louis I hope you got it. Father has improved, I think, a little since we got here and would be very glad to see you should you come. Give my love to all your family" "Your letter received. aAt present Father is too ill to bring the matter about the soldiers home up to him but when he is better I will read your letter to him and let you know what he sayes. My regards to all your family" ALS, IHi. Elizabeth Rowley had died on May 25. On May 26, William Rowley received a telegram from USG "expressing to his former staff officer the sympathy of himself and wife in this hour of his deep affliction." *Galena Gazette*, May 27, 1885. An obituary is *ibid.*, May 25, 1885.

To John H. Douglas

I do not know what it is I had you called for. But something was said, probably yesterday, about Huber A. Thomsons method of busines (in fact I do not remember exactly what was said) and I was asked to observe. I ~~no~~ know that he has been the subject of attack from the Tribune, but do not know anything about the merits of his case. Have you any recollectio[n] of what it was that was asked of me? Were you present? it seems to me you were

JULY 7, [*1885*] 6.30: A. M.

AN (date not in USG's hand), DLC–John H. Douglas. New York County Democratic leader Hubert O. Thompson was then prominent in local newspapers for his efforts to secure federal patronage in New York City. For Thompson's contentious political career, see *New York Times*, July 27, 1886.

On July 7, 1885, 2:30 A.M., USG twice wrote to John H. Douglas. "Eating is begining to grow very distasteful to me. I think I am taking to much now and there is danger of giving out. I can feel my strength increasing while the drain upon me is diminishing." "Will it be better to touch the core place in my mouth with a brush and opium? I did not feel it at the time. It may have soothed. The cocane you feel because it hurts until the part touched becomes deadened. ~~The effect~~" AN, *ibid.*

To John H. Douglas

———

I have had a pleasant morning. When my throat commences to hurt it begins with a cough. I then clear it out either coughing up the flem, garggling out or the use of the syringe. It is then the cocane would come in. I feel the want of it very much. But by keeping quiet the pain diminishes and finally disappears entirely so long as the effect of the hyperdermic remains

JULY 7. [*1885*] 11. A. M

AN (date not in USG's hand), DLC–John H. Douglas. On July 7, 1885, 1:30 P.M., USG twice wrote to John H. Douglas. "I have been reading ever since you went out and have just finished the paper through. My mouth hurts me but not so severely as it does some days." "I am sorry to say that I had a second operations of the bowels, and feel I will have to have another. If I do not I shall have to force it off. You have not had your lunch yet! Yes my voice has broken above a whisper two or three times this am" AN, *ibid.* USG wrote to Douglas. "Have you Steamed my ear to–day? If you will be here I will retire before eight o'clock to–night, taking a little food before starting." AN (undated), *ibid.* On July 7, 7:30 P.M., USG wrote to Douglas. "I have had an easy day. For the last half hour my mouth has troubled me and I have not cleansed it. Indeed it feels very free from mucus." AN, *ibid.*

To John H. Douglas

I think it does.[1] But you know for two days I have taken an injection just at the time I suffer most from stuffiness and have thereby escaped it the worst days we have had.

These have been two of the days when I have used no cocain and when I have felt the need of it more than usual. There has hardly been a time when felt it would give greater relief than just now. I think it better not to take it however because the injury done by it will be fed and kept up.[2] The benefit is but for a short time and less[3] repeated does only temporary good—very temporary.

July 7. [1885] 8. p. m

AN (date not in USG's hand), DLC-John H. Douglas. On July 7, 1885, 8:00 p.m., USG wrote to John H. Douglas. "Could not the morphine be injected elswhere than in the arms and thies? Inserting the instrument two or three times a day soon marks all the ground on such arms and legs as I now possess. It is only a few that feel sore, but when the instrument touches an old channel, one not more than a week old, it is very painful and makes a more protracted sore. I feel very full and it is difficult to get down. I was thinking before you come in whether a glass of milk sweetened might not be good to take once or twice during the day. Sugar is very nutricious and would be a change." AN, *ibid.* USG wrote to Douglas. "I feel my mouth begining to pain me as though the effect of the morphine had passed away. If it was administered now I think it would obviate the necessity of clearing the troad and mouth, and of using cocain." "I feel very badly probably because of a cross fire betwen opium and Laudanum. If relived of that I half hope to feel better. I feel as if I cannot endure it any longer. The alcoholocic stimulants must absolutely be give it" AN (undated), *ibid.* Probably in early July, USG wrote to Douglas. "I have been thinking for two weeks or more of trying to fix up a spoonful or two of alcoholic stimulant—brandy—and see if I can not disguise it so as to swallow it" AN (undated), *ibid.*

On July 7, 11:00 p.m., USG thrice wrote to Douglas. "A bad evening for the last two hours. I did not get even drowsey My mouth pained for want of Coain. I think to-morrow we will try the thing differently. When I take an injection, whether at four or not until eight, I will take half the amount. The next time will take the balance when it is wanted." "I had cesased to rest about half past ten so at about a quarter of eleven I had Henry bring me my food. I washed my mouth, took my food and then cleared up with the syringe. Got through not five minuets before you come. There is nothing to do now but to put fresh cotton in the ear and administer the injection. Is the hotel pretty full now?" "I may have to take the cocain yet. If I do I will take the liberty of waking you up to administer it. My dread is; if I do take it I will have to do so in the course of a half hour, and probably frequently between that and morning. I will then be set back to where wer were when I stopped taking it." AN, *ibid.* USG also wrote to Douglas. "Do you intend to go back to the hotel to-night whether I want an injection or not? I think then you had better runn now. But we will see better in a few minuets. The probabilities are that I shall feel no more inclination to sleep for the next hour in any event, injection or no injection. I think my tongue ~~has com~~ has commenced to diminish." "You did not give me a third injection last night did you? My recollection is that I took the second very late, the first having made me sleep so well." AN (undated), *ibid.*

 1. Douglas had asked. "Does this foggy, close weather stop up your throat?" *New York Tribune*, July 8, 1885.
 2. USG referred to how cocaine impaired his voice. *Ibid.*
 3. USG presumably meant unless.

To Edmund Didier

————

[*Mount McGregor, N. Y., July 8, 1885*]

Yes, I know; and I feel very grateful to the Christian people of the land for their prayers on my behalf. There is no sect or religion, as shown in the Old or the New Testament, to which this does not apply. Catholics, Protestants, and Jews, and all the good people of the Nation, of all politics as well as religion, and all nationalities seem to have united in wishing or praying for my improvement. I am a great sufferer all the time, but the facts I have related are compensation for much of it. All that I can do is to pray that the prayers of all those good people may be answered so far as to have us all meet in another and a better world. I cannot speak even in a whisper.

New York Times, July 9, 1885. USG wrote in reply to Edmund Didier, Catholic priest and pastor, St. Vincent's Church, Baltimore, who said: "You will have the prayers of all the people." *Ibid.* For another account, see *New York Tribune*, July 9, 1885. See also *New York Times*, May 19, 1903.

To John H. Douglas

————

If I live long enough I will become a sort of specialist in the use of certain medecines if not in the treatment of disease. It seems that one mans destiny in this world is quite as much a mystery as it is likely to be in the next. I never thought of acquiring rank in the

profession I was educated for; yet it came with two grades higher
prefixed to the rank of General officers for me. I certainly never
had either ambition or taste for a political life; yet I was twice president of the United States. ~~I am~~ If any one had suggested the idea
of my becoming an author, as they frequently did I was not sure
whether they were making sport of me or not. I have now written
a book which is in the hands of the manufacturers. I ask that you
keep these notes very private lest I become authority on the treatment of diseases. I have already to many trades to be proficent in
any. Of course I feel very much better from your application of
Cocain, the first in three days, or I should never have thought of
saying what I have said above.

JULY 8 [1885] 4 A. M.

AN (date not in USG's hand), DLC-John H. Douglas. On July 8, 1885, 11:00 A.M.,
USG twice wrote to John H. Douglas. "I feel pretty well but get sleepy sitting in the
air. Took a half hours nap. Do you want me to go in the house. I am as bright and
well now, for a time at least, as I ever will be. Will you tell Harrison to bring me
the larger ~~pads~~ pad I have been using in my room." "I believe I will go in for a short
time. Put an egg in also if you want." AN, *ibid.* USG also wrote to Douglas. "I have
just finished my granan; cleaned out my mouth and touched my throat. I think for a
change the food we have tried to-day makes a very good change of diet. The Japanese
food makes others taken with it palatable and easy to swollow. I supposed the granan
was very nutricious." AN (undated), *ibid.* Imperial Granum was a brand of cereal with
medicinal uses.

On July 8, 8:00 P.M., USG wrote to Douglas. "It is singular that I do not feel the
slightest move of morphine either in quelling pain or in any other way. It is now a full
hour since it was taken." AN (undated), *ibid.*; typed copy (dated), DLC-USG, IC.

To Julia Dent Grant

Mt McGregor, N. Y.
July 8th 1885

MY DEAREST WIFE

In memorandums which will be found with Fred. or on my person will be found a number of little bequest which I have expressed
a wish might be paid out of the proceeds of my book should the
proceeds be sufficient without curtailing the amounts my children

to much. In ~~that~~ I one of those mems. I have provided for the payment in part to the members of my family what was due them by
Fred. I now withdraw what I said about Mrs. Corbin and substitute the following: pay ~~her~~ to Mrs. Jennie Grant Corbin Twenty
five thousand dollars as fast as the receipts will justify.[1] So long as
you keep house I suggest, and strongly recommend that you have
Jennie with you as much as possible. She will be great help and
comfort to you and no trouble. I advise at the same time that you
do not keep house for the purpose of having a house when you can
make some one els a home. Only keep house because you will feel
more comfortable in doing so.

Besides the little behests I have made I feel that I would like to
give your brother Fred. $500.00.[2] and ~~advised~~ that you help Emma
in a limited way.

For the last few days although my suffering has not been as
intens as heretofore, that my end is approaching rapidly ~~I earnestly
pray and desire~~ I am sure I never will leave Mt McGregor alive.
I pray God however that it may be ~~prolonged~~ spared to complete
the necessisary work upon my book.[3] Should I dye there will be a
funeral and a breakup here. The revew of the book for the printers
will be suspended until fall. The subscriptions are so large that it
can not be got out at the stipulated time even if there is no detention. But for these considerations I would welcome the arrival of
the "Messenger of Peace," the earlyer the better.

Should my career be closed at an earlyer day I would be very
glad if the boys would make arrangements to retain quarters here
and go on with their work.

Your loving and affectionate husband,

U. S. GRANT

ALS, USG 3. On July 8, 1885, a correspondent reported from Mount McGregor,
N. Y. "The warm, clear weather tempted General Grant to go out of doors this morning, and he spent nearly an hour sitting with Mrs. Grant on the veranda. Between 1
and 2 o'clock he again took a seat on the piazza. A board was placed across the arms
of the willow chair in which he sat, and, using this as a desk, the sick man wrote for a
considerable time . . . ." *New York Tribune*, July 9, 1885.

    1. See Memorandum, May 29, 1885.
    2. On March 23, 1886, Frederick Dent Grant, New York City, wrote to Frederick T.

Dent. "Just before my beloved father died he gave some instructions about what he would like done. Among these wishes was one about you. He said he wanted to send you a little present in memory of old and happy days. That he had been very fond of you, and that if mother could spare it he would like her to send you $500 which I now enclose to you with her love. Mother says if you and Aunt Hellen can come she would like you to pay her a visit. All join in love to you and yours" ALS, ICarbS.

3. On July 2, 1885, a correspondent had reported from Mount McGregor. " . . . Writing occupied the General less to-day than yesterday. The nature of the work was similar. He treated of persons in civil life, giving his estimate of them in paragraphs, as he had of military men yesterday. It is intended to make a new chapter of military men and civilians with whom he was brought in contact during the war. He held himself closer to his work to-day than yesterday, and out of three hours' application got an hour's work. He worked yesterday for four hours to turn out an hour of work. To-day's manuscript amounted to about two-thirds as much as yesterday's . . . ." *New York Times*, July 3, 1885. On July 5, Sunday, another correspondent reported from Mount McGregor that "last week's work on the book had so ended that the General to-day felt much relieved as to its progress. He had begun to think the work of gathering the different portions of his book together was making slow headway; but he found on Saturday evening that the book was nearly completed and what still remained to be done would be finished after the matter had returned in galley proofs. General Grant expressed himself substantially in the above terms when referring to the matter this afternoon . . . ." *New York Tribune*, July 6, 1885.

To Mexican Delegation

[*Mount McGregor, N. Y., July 8, 1885*]

My great interest in Mexico dates back to the war between the United States and that country. My interest was increased when four European monarchies attempted to set up their institutions on this continent, selecting Mexico as their territory. It was an outrage on human rights for a foreign nation to attempt to transfer her institutions and her rulers to the territory of a civilized people without their consent. They were fearfully punished for their crime.[1] I hope Mexico may soon begin an upward and prosperous departure. She has all the conditions; she has the people; she has the soil; she has the climate; and she has the minerals. The conquest of Mexico will not be an easy task in the future.

New York Tribune, July 9, 1885. USG wrote in response to a statement from a committee of Mexican journalists. *Ibid.* For additional details, see *New York Times*, July 9, 1885. On July 8, 1885, 7:00 P.M., USG twice wrote to John H. Douglas. "All that fatigued me very much. I will take dinner and get to bed while you are at your dinner."

"I must avoid such afternoons as this. We had company since five and I was writing all the time." AN, DLC-John H. Douglas.

1. See *PUSG*, 15, 156–58, 316–17; *ibid.*, 17, 209–10.

To John H. Douglas

I have had a very fine rest to-day without so much sleep as to interfere with a good night sleep from now on. I may not get it but hope I will.

My swallowing is growing more difficult.

JULY 9. ⌈*1885*⌉ 11 P. M

AN (date not in USG's hand), DLC-John H. Douglas. On July 9, 1885, noon, USG wrote to John H. Douglas. "I expected to sleep well without deriving rest. But I did get a very considerable amount of rest. That last cocain did me a power of good. The water I wanted very much and it gave me an hours relief with free breathing and perfect rest." AN (undated), *ibid.*; typed copy (dated), DLC-USG, IC. At 1:00 P.M. and 3:15 P.M., USG wrote to Douglas. "I have been sitting up ever since about nine until just now. I have not been drowsey in that time. I have just taken Cocon. Excep to goggle my mouth every time I eat anything nothing has been done to it until less than an hour ago I then cleared it out pretty thoroughly. I feel very well, better than for sometime. I walked about this am with eas and pleasure" "I have rested finely and slept a little since you were here. Now is the time however when my mouth begins to fill up and I do not have it quite so pleasant It had commenced just as you come in or a few minuets before" AN, DLC-John H. Douglas. On the same day, 3:30 P.M., USG wrote to Douglas. "I touched with cocain several times, but did not use up what there was in the little bottle. For about three times to-day after I would use the coain I would lay back in a delightful absence from pain and even slept some." AN (undated), *ibid.*; typed copy (dated), DLC-USG, IC. USG also wrote to Douglas. "I had got a few days ago so that I could move my tongue about at the lower cavity without pain, and the upper one was much relieved. I suppose the disease was working elswhere. It was since resuming We do not use so much cocain now as we did and it has not the injurious effect. I put very little on the brush at a time and deposite it on the place that gives pain. Before we sloshed around, with a full brush, all over the mouth. Where there is nothing the matter it absorbs the cocain; draws up the well part, and numbs it. It does not ~~numbb~~benumb coar places." AN (undated), DLC-John H. Douglas. On July 9, 8:00 P.M., USG wrote to Douglas. "Henry will give me a bad night It is very warm and he keeps me wrapped up. On the pretext of my being wan—it will not do to expose me. If I could be left to regulate the covers I could add here or take off there as occasion requires." AN, *ibid.*

To Charles Wood

Mt McGregor N Y July 9 /85

I am very sorry that I am unable to converse even in a whisper. I am remaining in bed as long as it rests me this morning because yesterday I ha[d] a very trying day. My worst hours—most painful ones—are from four to seven in the afternoon. Yesterday we had a number of particular friends call and stay through these hours I had to converse incessantly with my pencil. About the close the Mexican editors called in a body and delivered a speech in Spanish—that had to be translated [a]nd spoken in English—I replied [&] my speech was made in English then translated and spoken in Spanish. Then there was a second speech and reply. By this time I was nearly exhausted. I am badly off this minute because the ~~doctr~~ Dr has been dressing my mouth and this is always painful. I feel very thankful to you for the kindness you did me last summer. I am glad to say that while there is much unblushing wickedness in this world yet there is a compensating generosity and grandeur of soul. In my case I have not found that Republics are ungrateful nor are the people.

Copy (facsimile; in Charles Wood's hand), USGA; *New York Times*, Aug. 5, 1892. On July 9, 1885, only Charles Wood and Robert Underwood Johnson, associate editor, *Century Magazine*, visited USG. See *ibid.* and *New York Tribune*, July 10, 1885; Johnson, *Remembered Yesterdays* (Boston, 1923), pp. 223–24. On July 3 and 15, Frederick Dent Grant, Mount McGregor, N. Y., wrote to Wood. "The 'Goddess of Liberty' you sent to Father has been received by him He has enquired of me several times if you had come He would like very much to see you If you do come please let me know" "I am unable to tell what Father was trying to say when you left but be assured that only expressions of gratitude will ever be expressed by the Grant family towards one who in the time of their trouble came forward so generously and so nobly as you did" ALS, Ralph W. Naylor, Hopkinton, R. I. See letters to Charles Wood, May 12, 19, 1884, Jan. 5, 1885.

On May 24, 1886, Frederick Grant, New York City, wrote to Wood extending an invitation for Decoration Day. ALS, Ralph W. Naylor, Hopkinton, R. I. On Oct. 13, 1889, Frederick Grant, U.S. minister, Vienna, wrote to Wood explaining his inability to lobby for higher duties on brushes. ALS, *ibid.* On April 20, 1897, Frederick Grant, police commissioner, New York City, wrote to Wood, Lansingburgh, N. Y., concerning a ticket to the dedication of USG's tomb. TLS, *ibid.* On May 15, 1905, Brig. Gen. Frederick Grant, Governor's Island, N. Y., wrote to Wood promising a military escort for the funeral of Hiram Cronk, last War of 1812 veteran. ALS, *ibid.*

Memorandum

———

[*Mount McGregor, N. Y., July 9–12, 1885*]

I am satisfied now that I will never have my voice again so as to converse, though I see no reason now, more than I have for the last thre[e] months, of immediate danger. But persons in [my] condition never know when they may be call[ed] and there are some things which should be arranged in advance. I believe I have left with you memoranda which, with my will,[1] cover all points except one. The public may be somewhat interested in the place of my bury[al.] I should designate West Point beyond all other and fix that as the place where my remains we[re] to rest but for the reason that my wife could no[t] rest in the same burying ground though ~~she~~ they can at the same place. If she objects to this then I hav[e] no choise between the vicinity of new york city and the state of Ill. I owe much to both states—Ill. gave me my first commission in the army,[2] to the citizens of N. Y. I am indebted for the means to enable me to spend my latter days without feeling pr[ivation *or*] want

AD, USG 3. Probably in early 1886, Frederick Dent Grant wrote to U.S. Representative Abraham Dowdney of N. Y. "In compliance with your request of last evening I send you the following memorandum. Riverside Park was selected as the burial place of my father, by my mother and myself, because; we believed it came nearer being the choice of my father than any other place, and that if the tomb was locate[d] where it is more people would be abl[e] to visit it than could possibly do so if it was in any other ~~place~~ city. We were lead to believe that Ne[w] York was the spot my father wished most for his last resting place by the following circumstance. About the 9th or 12th of July (1885) my father came to me at Mt McGregor and gave me two ~~letters~~ sheets of paper on which were written directions as to what he wished done in case of his death. He first spoke of New York as the place of his burial and gave these reasons, first that he liked New York and had selecte[d] it as his home: Secondly that he would be near his family (wife and children) and; Thirdly that it was through the generousity of the people of New York, principally, that he was enabled to pass his last days without suffering from actual want. After reading these papers I said to him that if I had anything to say in the matter I should select the Soldiers Home, Washington D. C[.] He then wrote in reply, that in case his funeral became a public or national affair he ~~would~~ wished me to make one condition, namely that whatever spot was selected a place should be reserved by his side for my mother. Thus believing New York to be his first choise and the city authorities here having guaranteed to me a place for my mother ~~and~~ beside him, I took the liberty of advising my mother, and decided, to accept the generous offer of the cosmopolitan city of America. We are thankful that we are thus enabled to be near my father's tomb, and that thousa[nds] of strangers who so desire can easily visit his last resting place." ADfS (undated), Ulysses Grant Dietz, Maplewood, N. J. On Jan. 5, a correspondent reported from Washington, D. C., that Dowdney introduced "a bill to aid in the erection of the Grant Monument in New-York City. The bill appropriates $200,000 for the purpose, the money to be expended under the direction of the Secretary of War by a commission to be appointed by the President, provided that none of the money shall be expended until the sum of $250,000 shall have been raised by subscription." *New York Times*, Jan. 6, 1886. Dowdney's death on Dec. 10 ended efforts to secure the bill's passage. See *ibid.*, Jan. 28, 1886; *HRC*, 49-1-181; letter to Julia Dent Grant, June 29, 1885.

Reportedly on June 24, 1885, USG had written a memorandum. "There are three places from which I wish a choice of burial place to be made: *West Point.*—I would prefer this above others but for the fact that my wife could not be placed beside me there. *Galena, or some place in Illinois.*—Because from *that* State I received my first General's commission. *New-York.*—Because the people of that city befriended me in my need." *New York Times*, July 24, 1885. On July 23, a reporter interviewed George W. Childs. " . . . Some years ago, in conversation with me, he remarked that he thought that when he died his body should be buried at West Point. He deemed that the proper place. I think he should be buried at the Soldiers' Home, near Washington. He belonged to the nation, and the people, in going to Washington, could always see the tomb of the great soldier. He desired that his wife should rest beside him. The officers of the army, I know, desire that he should be buried at West Point." *Philadelphia Press*, July 24, 1885.

Also on July 23, AG Richard C. Drum, Washington, D. C., telegraphed to Frederick Grant. "I think the general feeling here favors the interment of your Father at Arlington, as being the most proper resting place, and where the Government will take care of his grave." Copy, DNA, RG 94, ACP, Letters Sent. On the same day, Mayor William R. Grace of New York City telegraphed to Julia Dent Grant. "In advance of official action I am instructed to tender to yourself and family the deep sympathy of the Common Council and the municipal authorities of the city of New-York in your sad bereavement. I am also authorized by informal action of the authorities, which will be made official to-morrow, to tender to you a last resting place for the remains of Gen. Grant in any one of the parks of this city which you may select. I am also authorized to offer the Governor's Room at the City Hall for the purpose of allowing the body to lie in state." *New York Times*, July 24, 1885. In a letter of the same date, Grace recommended Riverside Park. *Ibid.*, July 26, 1885. John P. Newman, Mount McGregor, N. Y., wrote in his journal for July 24. "Many came. Mrs Newman is with Mrs Grant, It is decided to have the funeral on the 4th here & on the 8th in New York, & to bury him in the Central Park." AD, USMA. On July 25, Lt. Col. Chauncey McKeever, asst. AG, telegraphed to Lt. Gen. Philip H. Sheridan, Fort Reno, Indian Territory. "General Drum telegraphs from Mount McGregor, New York, that the family of General Grant have decided to have a military funeral and wish it to be under the authority and control of the National Government. New York City has been agreed upon as the place of interment. The funeral services at Mount McGregor will take place on Tuesday, the fourth of August. The remains will then be taken to Albany where they will lie in state for one day; thence to New York City and lie in state at City Hall until Saturday the Eighth of August, the date fixed for the military funeral. General Hancock has been designated to take charge of the remains at Mount McGregor, to see that they are properly conducted to New York, and to take charge of the ceremonies connected with the funeral and command the escort." Copy, DNA, RG 94, ACP, Letters Sent.

On July 28, William T. Sherman, New York City, wrote to Rutherford B. Hayes,

Fremont, Ohio. "I have just received your letter of July 24, and will gladly contribute my mite in case the Grand Army of the Republic should resolve to Erect a monumt to General Grant either over his grave or Elsewhere—I had yesterday a long and most confidential talk with Colonel Fred Grant who had been with the Mayor and Committee of the Council for this City to reconnoitre 'Central Park' and also 'Riverside Park'—The former you know—the latter is a narrow Strip along the Steep bank of the Hudson River, beginning about 76th Street, and Extending up about 3 miles, with sites of Extraordinary beauty—Col Grant was most favorably impressed with this new Park, and the Evening papers announce that Mrs Grant has formally ratified his Choice of location. There was a growing opposition to Central Park—but this new location will command almost universal approval—I understand that there will not be the least difficulty in raising the funds necessary for a beautiful & appropriate monument—I think the Grand Army of the Republic might well Endorse, and in case of failure to Secure the needful by voluntary contribution, that we vote an universal tax of $1. which would make $250,000 quite as much as any monument Should Cost—I believe however the City of New York will Erect the Monument, and might resent any offer of help from Even Genl Grants 'Army Comrades'—" ALS, OFH. See Hayes to Sherman, July 24, 1885, DLC-William T. Sherman. Also on July 28, Andrew Hickenlooper, Cincinnati, telegraphed to Sherman, New York City. "Public sentiment revolts at the idea of Genl Grants interment in Central Park All favor Soldier's Home Washington" Telegram received, *ibid.* On July 29, Sherman wrote to Hickenlooper. "Your despatch of the 28, reached me promptly—I did not answer because I could not with delicacy interfere—The family had chosen NewYork before I was consulted—but the exact spot was not fixed on till Fred Grant had personally examined, and consulted his mother— . . ." ALS, Cincinnati Historical Society, Cincinnati, Ohio. For Sherman's eulogy of USG, see *Report of the Proceedings of the Society of the Army of the Tennessee, at the Eighteenth Meeting,* . . . (Cincinnati, 1893), pp. 207–16. See also *ibid.,* pp. 178–79, 193–95, 216–43, 249–56; Allen Thorndike Rice to Sherman, March 11, 1885, Robert Underwood Johnson to Sherman, March 31, Aug. 10, 1885, DLC-William T. Sherman; Sherman to Henry C. Bowen, April 3, 1885, ICU.

Also on July 29, William S. Chapman, San Francisco, wrote to his son-in-law Jesse Root Grant, Jr. "I am glad you and Col Fred changed the sight of interment from Central Park—The spot selected is a most lovely o[ne.] . . . " AL (initialed), Keya Gallery, New York, N. Y. For the choice of Riverside Park, see *New York Herald,* July 28–29, 1885.

On July 24, Grace had written to Hamilton Fish. "In order that the City of New York, which is to be the last resting place of General Grant, should initiate a movement to provide for the erection of a National Monument to the memory of the great soldier, and that she should do well and thoroughly her part, I respectfully request you to act as one of a Committee to consider ways and means for raising the quota to be subscribed by the citizens of New York City for this object, and beg that you will attend a meeting to be held at the Mayor's Office on Tuesday next, 28th inst., at three o'clock." D, DLC-Hamilton Fish. A similar invitation, dated July 30, appointing Charles Scribner to this committee, is in NjP. On Aug. 5, Drexel, Morgan & Co., New York City, wrote to Fish. "We are in receipt of your favor of the 4th inst enclosing your check for $2.500. as a contribution to the Grant Monument Fund, for which, in behalf of the Monument Association, we beg to thank you We enclose herewith a formal receipt" L, DLC-Hamilton Fish.

On Oct. 16, Grace wrote to Julia Grant. "The Executive Committee of the Grant

Monument Association, to whom was intrusted the honored and patriotic task of soliciting funds for a suitable national memorial to the memory of your distinguished
husband, finds itself seriously hampered in its work, and to a great extent embarrassed,
by utterances which appear from time to time in the daily press, often purporting to
come from your family. Our committee is much concerned in the reports quite indus-
triously spread abroad and persistently reiterated, that on the assembling of Congress
a preconcerted effort, with the consent and approval of your family, would be begun to
have the body of General Grant removed to Washington for final sepulture. Our fund
has already reached a generous sum (nearly $90,000, and it will be $100,000 soon), but
it must be obvious that any doubt which the public may have as to the desire of the family in regard to the Riverside Park as a permanent tomb and the site of the proposed
national monument, acts as a deterrent to those who would otherwise freely give.
May I ask from you and your family a clear and emphatic expression of your wish and
preference—may I add determination—for the use of our Executive Committee?" *New
York Herald*, Oct. 30, 1885. On Oct. 29, Julia Grant, New York City, wrote to Grace.
"Your letter of the 16th came during my absence, and was received on my return from
Long Branch. Riverside was selected by myself and my family as the burial place of
my husband, General Grant. *First*—Because I believed New York was his preference.
Second—It is near the residence that I hope to occupy as long as I live, and where I will
be able to visit his resting place often. *Third*—I have believed, and am now convinced,
that the tomb will be visited by as many of his countrymen here as it would be at any
other place; and *Fourth*—The offer of a park in New York was the first which observed
and unreservedly assented to the only condition imposed by General Grant himself,
namely, that I should have a place by his side." *Ibid.* See Thomas W. Pitkin, *The Captain Departs: Ulysses S. Grant's Last Campaign* (Carbondale, Ill., 1973), pp. 95–96.

1. See Will, Sept., 5, 1884.
2. See *PUSG*, 2, 42–46.

To Simon B. Buckner

[*Mount McGregor, N. Y., July 10, 1885*]

I have witnessed since my sickness just what I have wished to see
ever since the war; harmony and good feeling between the sections.
I have always contended that if there had been no body left but the
soldiers we would have had peace in a year. Jubel Early[1] and Hill[2]
are the only two that I know of who do not seem to be satisfied
on the southern side. We have some on ours who failed to accomplish as much as they wished, or who did not get warmed up to the
fight until it was all over, who have not had quite full satisfaction.
The great Majority too of those who did not go into the war have
long since grown tired of the long controversy. We may now well

look forward to a perpetual peace at home, and a national strength strength that will secure us against any foreign complication. I believe my self that the war was worth all it cost us, fearful as that was.—Since it was over I have visited every state in Europe and a number in the East. I know, as I did not before, the value of our inheritance.

AN (facsimile), John R. Procter, "A Blue and Gray Friendship. Grant and Buckner," *Century Magazine,* LIII, 6 (April, 1897), 946–48. On July 10, 1885, a correspondent reported from Mount McGregor, N. Y. "Gen. Grant's condition seemed so easy this morning that Col. Grant, with his wife and Mrs. Sartoris, went to Round Lake to spend the day at the Grand Army reunion. They met Gen. Buckner at Saratoga, and on their report he came up at noon and saw the General . . . ." *New York Times,* July 11, 1885. On the same day, 11:30 A.M., USG wrote to John H. Douglas. "Gen. Buckner—Fort Donelson—will be here on the next train. He is coming up specially to pay his respects." AN, DLC-John H. Douglas. See *New York Times* and *Philadelphia Press,* July 16, 1885; Arndt M. Stickles, *Simon Bolivar Buckner: Borderland Knight* (Chapel Hill, 1940), pp. 324–30.

USG wrote several other notes during his meeting with Buckner. "I appreciate your calling very highly." "You look very natural, except that your hair has whitened, and you have grown stouter." "I remember Walker's condition well. He was, as I remember, many months unable to help himself. In my case I have not been confined to bed a single day; but there cannot well be a cure in my case." "I am very glad to see you indeed; and allow me to congratulate you. I still read the papers, and saw a full account of your recent marriage." "Is Mrs. Buckner here at the house with you?" "I would be very glad to see Mrs. Buckner, if she can come in and see me as I am now. Where you see me has been my bed for more than four months." "I knew your husband long before you did. We were at West Point together, and served together in the Mexican war. I was with him on a visit to the top of Popocatepetl, the highest mountain in North America. Your husband wrote an account of that trip for publication at the time. I have just written my account, which will be published in my forthcoming book." Procter, "A Blue and Gray Friendship," pp. 946, 948–49. For Buckner's marriage, his second, to Delia Claiborne, see Stickles, p. 323–24. For USG on Popocatepetl, see *Memoirs,* I, 180–84.

1. Unable to accept defeat in the Civil War, Jubal A. Early, former C.S.A. lt. gen., fled the U.S. and lived abroad until 1869. As president of the Southern Historical Society, Early published accounts of Confederate valor and aspirations that became known collectively as the "Lost Cause" interpretation. See Gary W. Gallagher, "Jubal A. Early, the Lost Cause, and Civil War History: A Persistent Legacy," in Gallagher and Alan T. Nolan, eds., *The Myth of the Lost Cause and Civil War History* (Bloomington, Ind., 2000), 35–59.

2. On April 6, 1885, Daniel H. Hill, USMA 1842 and former C.S.A. lt. gen., Macon, Ga., declined an invitation to a meeting of C.S.A. veterans at New Orleans. " . . . I expect to live and die a Confederate; heart, soul, and spirit, the right of secession has been settled by the sword, but the eternal truths of local government and resistance to centralized despotism will not die, and are essential to the preservation of the Constitution of our fathers." *New York Times,* April 15, 1885. See *PUSG,* 25, 340; Hal Bridges, *Lee's Maverick General: Daniel Harvey Hill* (New York, 1961), p. 273–75.

To John H. Douglas

———

DR. I am glad to see you. I did not know that you had come in.

I do not see how I am to avoid the use of Cocain. It would relieve me ~~just now~~ very much just now. I had better take food first
however.

JULY 10. [1885] 4.15

AN (date not in USG's hand), DLC-John H. Douglas. On July 10, 1885, 4:00 A.M.,
USG wrote to John H. Douglas. "You must have been dreaming. I heard no rain fall
and I was here all the time." AN (undated), *ibid.*; typed copy (dated), DLC-USG, IC.
At 11:40 A.M. and 4:00 P.M., USG wrote to Douglas. "I feel very much as if I had got to
the point where I must reduce my food very materially in order to be able to eat anything much longer. It is getting hard to swallow anything after the first half tumbler."
"Like yesterday I have been awake so much to-day that it should not interfere with
my sleeping to-night. Being undress I will probably retire early." AN, DLC-John H.
Douglas. USG also wrote to Douglas. "I do not feel a greatdeal of pain, but more
than through the day & ~~still free from pain~~ though it is Not much pain but enough
to be unpleasant. It is confined principally to the side of the tongue which cocan does
not help, and to the place about where the right nostril enters the mouth. I must try
to get some soft pencils. I could then write plainer and more rapidly" AN (undated),
ibid.

To John H. Douglas

———

Buck has brought up the last of first vol. in print.[1] In two weeks
if they work hard they can have the second vol. copied ready to go
to the printer. I will then feel that my work is done.

JULY 10 [1885] 11:30 A.M.

AN (facsimile; date not in USG's hand), DLC-USG; typed copy, DLC-John H. Douglas. See next text.

On July 13 and 17, 1885, a correspondent reported from Mount McGregor, N. Y.
"General Grant has not been out of doors to-day nor has he been dressed, but the
day has been one of remarkable ease. This morning he said to his physician that he
felt well; that he felt stronger, and felt like going to work. The doctor was inclined
to dissent, but in the forenoon the General wrote for nearly an hour. All his communication with Dr. Douglas to-day has been oral, his voice being distinct. Two days
ago the application of cocaine was omitted and the presence of pain was a frequent
reminder of the disease, while to-day, though still without the use of the sedative, he
has been comparatively free from pain . . . ." "The thermometer at the cottage has
registered more than 80° to-day, but General Grant has not been weakened by the
heat . . . . The quiet enjoined upon General this week has benefitted him physically,

but it is thought that he would be happier and more contented with some occupation for his mind. The sick man has been told that should he at any time desire to do any literary work, he may gratify himself in that respect." *New York Tribune*, July 14, 18, 1885.

1. On July 5, Sunday, Ulysses S. Grant, Jr., Salem Center, N. Y., had written to Charles L. Webster. "Necessary fa[m]ily arrangements prevent my getting of for Mt. McGregor before the Thursday nnight boat. I will therefore call on you on Thursday and I hope if I do not find you in I will at least find quantities of material for correction ready to be forwarded to the Colonel. I am anxious to have as much work to do as possible during my next visit to my parents and thus thus assist you to an early departure for Europe." Typescript, USGA. On July 18, a correspondent reported from Mount McGregor. "Mr. Webster, the publisher, came up to-day, bringing with him the last proof-sheets of the first volume of the General's memoirs." *New York Tribune*, July 19, 1885.

Probably in July, USG wrote to Frederick Dent Grant. "Did a letter come from the paymaster general to-day. I wanted to give Buck $300 00. If it has not come suppose you give Buck the money and I will return it as soon as the other comes." AN (undated), USG 3.

To Frederick Dent Grant

———

This is by no means a gloomy view to take of the question, but a prudent one. I had the hardest day yesterday I have had for three months, and have not rested better than I have since ten last night since we have been at Mt McGregor. I intend however to avoid any more such labor, and will rest all I can to-day. But I feel my rest already had very much relieved me.

U. S. G.

JULY 10TH 1885

AN, USG 3.

Probably before July 10, 1885, USG wrote to Frederick Dent Grant. "Where are you in the review now? When is Buck coming up again? I begin to feel anxious about the review of the second volume. There may more difficulty in placing all the parts than we think. It has been written in a very detached way." "I know that. But if it is all copied it can be delivered very fast when wanted. The point I was enquiring about is when is the middl of next week? Next Thursday or not for a week from then Any of it. We do not want a" AN (undated; second incomplete), USG 3. Probably after July 10, USG again wrote to Frederick Grant. "I was not writing on the book to-day. That is finished, so far as I am concerned. The first Vol. is in print, and the second can be furnished as fast as the printer is ready to take it." "When you come to copying manuscript for the printer will one or two or you do it? You might divide it so as to have

Buck and Mr. Dawson both copy, and you too, as much as you can. In that way it can
be got up fast." "We would necessarily be showing it and every effort would be made to
hire someone to steal it." AN (undated), *ibid.*

On July 11, Frederick Grant, Mount McGregor, N. Y. wrote to William T. Sherman asking to borrow a map that USG had used to plan the 1864 campaigns. " . . .
Father is too ill to ask him to do anything now . . . . When you see Fathers book you
will see what he thinks of you, and if you have any respect for his opinion you will conclude that ~~you~~ W. T. Sherman ~~are~~ is, and was, a very great and good man" ALS, DLC-
William T. Sherman. On July 13, William T. Sherman, St. Louis, wrote to Frederick
Grant that the map was missing. " . . . We watch the Morning papers for the bulletins
of your Fathers condition and I am rejoiced that he seems much better. I have always
been among the Sanguine to believe he would ultimately recover— . . . In common
with the whole world I await with interest the publication of your Fathers Memoirs. I
am sure he will do me. and all his old faithful co-workers full justice. I never had the
least concern on this score, where he gave the matter his personal attention, and was
only apprehensive when his time and mind were so fully occupied with public matter,
that he had to devolve much on some ~~who was~~ near him, who desired to Sow dissension
between us. I feel the Same affection & respect for him and his as of old, and will Ever
rejoice at Every thing which gives him and you increased health and happiness—I find
reasonable occupation in little things, and am seemingly as well as twenty years ago—
Present me Kindly to your Father, mother and all the family . . . " ALS, USG 3. On
July 16, Sherman again wrote to Frederick Grant about the map. ALS, *ibid.* On July 20,
Frederick Grant wrote to Sherman. " . . . Fathers II volume is done, and he gives you
credit for conceiving—planning—and executing—the march to the sea. and, I do not
think you will be displeased with anything he sayes about you. I have never heard my
father speak of you but in the kindest way. I have heard others say what, you said (or
rather they said sherman said so & so) and father answer them by saying 'I dont believe
it;' or Sherman wrote me so & so; or Oh! well Sherman was mad and did'nt mean it. If
he has ever felt hurt at you, you~~r~~ are the only one that knows of it for I can assure you
his family have never heard him speak of you except in one way—always as his friend.
I will acknowledge that all the rest of the family have at times been as mad as fire at
what we have heard that you said and all of us have shot off our mouths quite often
and when we did it in fathers presence we got reproved for it too. Dear General all
this has been called out by one sentence in your letter and I hope you will excuse me
me for writing you so much. I have often heard people speak of Washington, Lincoln
and Grant but I have always beleived that the three men this country has produced
was Grant, Sherman and Sheridan and without any one of the three the United States
would to day be thirty eight petty nations fighting among themselves." ALS, DLC-
William T. Sherman.

To John H. Douglas

7 45 AM, JULY 11TH [*1885*] woke up by biting my tongue, feeling
perfectly fresh however as if I had had a good nights natural sleep.
My breething is less obstructed than usual at the same time of day,

and the head less filled up. In fact my breathing is not obstructed
in the least. Have used no cocain during the night nor do I require
any yet.

AN, DLC-John H. Douglas. On July 11, 1885, 1:00 A.M., USG wrote to John H. Douglas. "Not sleeping does not disturb me because I have had so much sleep. And then
too I have been comparitively free from pain. I know a sick person can not feel just as
he would like all the time; but I think it a duty to let the physician know from time to
time just my feelings. It may benefit some other fellow sufferer hereafter. Wake the
Dr. up and advise with him whether anything should be done. I cleared my mouth and
throat very well just before twelve. I feel very well but have nearly a constant hicup.
Whether this indicates any thing or not I do not know; but it is inconvenient. I have
not felt a desire or need of cocain since taking it to-day." AN, *ibid.* USG presumably
wrote part of this note initially for his attendant. USG wrote undated notes to Douglas. "Cant you take a brush and get out of the mouth some mucus at the base of the left
nostril." "Since you dressed my mouth I have had no feeling of necessity for the cocain.
Now one spot requires it very much.—Did you read the leaf I handed you when you
come in?" "Rest free from pain is worth so much more than rest with it, or from weakness or exhaustion." "I should judge from the way I feel that the temperature is about
right now for a person in my condition, say 69 or thereabout." "They have been having
a fire every in the parlor a good part of the day." AN, *ibid.*

On July 11, 7:00 P.M. and 10:00 P.M., USG wrote to Douglas. "I t had that newspaper article, and a reply to write, to worry me. Mrs. Grant was very much excited on
reading the article" "I have not slept probably two hours since four yesterday. But I
get sleep enough when I rest without pain. Laying down, as I do, all the time I get all
the sleep necessary in the aggregate." AN, *ibid.* USG also wrote to Douglas. "I had
better try to eat something now. Do you not want to take the paper that had the article
in. If you do not take it now you may never see it again." AN (undated), *ibid.*

To John H. Douglas

[*Mount McGregor, N. Y., July 11, 1885*]

Fred and Mrs Grant have told me about it, but not so fully or so
well as the Dr. can. I want to see the Dr. for a few mineuets, but
I think the fatigue would be to great to hear a full account of the
meeting yesterday.—Is the Dr. at the house?

AN, DLC-John H. Douglas. On July 10, 1885, Frederick Dent Grant and his wife attended a Grand Army of the Republic reunion at Round Lake, N. Y., where they met
John P. Newman. *New York Times,* July 11, 1885. On July 11, a correspondent reported from Mount McGregor, N. Y. "The Rev. Dr. Newman, who is to preach here
to-morrow, sat for a time with Gen. Grant this afternoon. There talk was chiefly of
religious matters. Dr. Newman spoke also of the Grand Army reception to Col. Grant

at Round Lake yesterday, where the Colonel was welcomed in his father's name and made his maiden speech. The General's pride and interest were roused, and he wanted the story in detail." *Ibid.*, July 12, 1885.

To John P. Newman

[*Mount McGregor, N. Y., July 11, 1885*]

I have my book off my mind now. That relives me of a tax upon my strength which I could not avoid.

Have the papers any account of Gen. Buckner's visit here yesterday?

AN, USMA. See note to Simon B. Buckner, July 10, 1885.

Possibly on July 3, 1885, USG wrote to John P. Newman. "I had a very bad night last night though I did not suffer extra pain. My trouble was not being able to breath easily. I have not slept thirty consecutive minuets since this time yesterday." AN (date not in USG's hand), USMA. In response to Newman's request that he receive communion on Sunday, July 12, USG wrote. "I would only be too happy to do so if I felt myself fully worthy. I have a feeling in regard to taking the sacriment that no worse sin can be committed than to take it unworthily. I would prefer therefore not to take it, but to have the funeral services performed when I am gone." AN (undated), *ibid.* For the special service that Newman conducted at Mount McGregor, N. Y., on July 12, see *New York Tribune* and *New York Times*, July 13, 1885. Probably on July 13, USG wrote to Newman. "You had quite a time down at your place ~~yestrday~~ yesterday Fred tells me." AN (undated), USMA.

To Adam Badeau

Mt McGregor
July 12th 1885.

Dear General:

Since last night paticularly, and for several days before that considerably, I have thought very much about you and your affairs. It is not possible now that I can be of further assistance to you. My health and other circumstances prohibits it.

I say since yesterday particularly, &c. My first vol. is now all in print. The last of it was corrected up to be broken in pages yes-

terday. Fred says that that portion which you had gone over and
arranged gave more trouble than all the balance. He changed it
entire[ly.] He found also many inaccuracies in it when he came to
correct it by the records.

Before yesterday I was thinking of your helpless condition
without some one with means or influence to help you, and what I
really had done for you for the last twenty years and could not do
again if I would. To be frank with you you are helpless, and filled
with a false pride. With $1.500 00 pr. year you speak of my doctor,
my shoemaker, my lawyer &c. &c. as if you owned them and they
were beneath you. You grew indignant at the idea of your name
being used in a letter where "clerkship["] was mentioned so that it
might be inferred that you were the clerk. The letter had not been
used but was rejected before your outburst of indignation. Now
General I had been a clerk in a Hardware and leather store, and
supported myself and family off of the salary. I felt proud of it too.
You, a literary man, cannot sharpen a led pencil, open a box or
pack up your books. You keep a secretary, an extravigance I have
never felt myself able to indulge in.

Now for what I have done I never felt that public offices were the
perquisites of those who had the bestowal of them. On the contrary
they are themselves officials upon whom this duty has fallen, and it
is their place to see that they are worthily bestowe[d.] Through me
you got an appointment on my staff, which was a personal appointment,[1] and from there you got in the regular army which gives you
now the little income you still have. As a staff officer you did not
do me credit while in Washington. You exposed yourself disgracefully on several occasions which I knew of and whi[ch] were generally known. People remonstrated against your retention in public
place. I resisted these and retained you. I then sent you as sec.
of Legation, and then Consul General, to England. You did the
same thing there on numerous occasions that were reported to me
or to the state Department On one occasion you were sent from
London to Madrid with very important dispatches, got overcome
with liquor and switched off by the wayside and did not turn up in
Madrid for some days after you should have been there. When I
left the presidency I asked my successor—as the only request I had

to make unless I included Mr. Cramer in it—to retain you during his term He made the promise and kept his word agains[t] great pressure for your discharge, and on grounds that would have entirely exhonerated him of ~~acting in bad faith if he had done so~~. the charge of acting in bad faith had he done so[2] You have managed so as to get in a broil with every official and every unofficial with whom you have had dealings since Mr. Hayes went out of office so far as I know. Wit[h] publisher you have had disputes. With the departments of government it is the same thing. You are now in two or three suits against the government which, if you win the lawyers will get the bulk of; if you loose they have your ready cash alread[y] and you will probably loose the $1.500 00 which you are still receiving.[3]

My advice to you now General is that you look upon yourself for a while as you have heretofore looked upon others. Take up you pen and go to work earnestly Regard yourself as belonging to the publisher who pays you for your work, for the time being, and not upon him as being "My publisher." You make the offensi[ve] ownership apply to the othe[r] man always.

This advice is intended in the best of spirit, and with the hope that you may, either by following my advice, or otherwise, realize your highest expectation.

In concluding it is due to myself to say tha[t] the more I have thought of what took place just before you left my house the more strongly convinced I become that your nature is not of that unselfish kind I had supposed. I am also satisfied that my book would never have been finished as "my book" if you had been permitted to continue in the capacity you now seem disposed to think you were in. I however never regarded you in any such capacity.

Yours Truly
U. S. Grant

General A. Badeau. U. S. A. retired.

ALS, Ulysses Grant Dietz, Maplewood, N. J. Probably on July 12, 1885, USG wrote: "Note. I do not want this mailed but at your leisure copied and retained so that if thought advisable it can be sent." Typed copy (undated), USG 3. See letter to Adam Badeau, [*May 2–5, 1885*]; *New York Times*, July 24, 1885.

On June 24, Frederick Dent Grant, Mount McGregor, N. Y., had written to Samuel L. Clemens. "I enclose you a letter from Judge A. W. Tougee to Genl Badeau who forwarded it to me I wrote to Judge T. the following letter which will explain the whole matter: DEAR JUDGE: your letter to General Adam Badeau has been forwarded by him to me. I will submit it to Mr Clemens & Webster for their consideration, and if they think well of the plan I will let you know. I do think, however, that it can be carried out, as we are more or less bound up with contracts. Mr Clemens and Webster have made a very generous contract with Father & He is more than satisfied with what they have done and are doing. Thanking you for your kind interest in this matter I remain Truly yours F. D. GRANT. I did not copy thise last part of the letter in order to give *you* and *Webster soft soap* but so you would see exactly what I said in considering this matter." ALS, CU-B. The enclosure is a letter of June 10 from Albion W. Tourgee, Mayville, N. Y., to Adam Badeau. "If it was known that by sending the price of Gen. Grant's book say to yourself or Col. Fred Grant, or any one else who might be named, the book would be sent expressage paid to any address and the profit of such sale paid over to Mrs. Grant, there is no doubt that many thousands would take that method of testifying their esteem. There is no doubt that if such an agency were made public hundreds of thousands of dollars might thus be legitimately and delicately contributed to the family of Gen. Grant by those who would delight to know that they had thus helped to dispel the anxiety of his last days. I can see no objection to such a course. Of course an agent has the sole right to *canvas* in his territory but no merely formal pretext should be allowed to stand in the way of such a noble testimonial as might thus be offered to the woman whose letter to Vanderbilt matches even her husband's most heroic acts. Should this seem advisable I would like to have the privilege of first announcing or intimating the fact through the public press and urging the general's myriad of sympathizing friends to take this method of helping to brighten his last days. Unless positive objection exists I think very strongly of proposing this movement say, in the Chicago Inter-Ocean. This plan would do very much towards remedying the losses which have swept away his hardly won competence. I would apologize for writing of such a subject if the motive were not in itself a sufficient excuse" ALS, *ibid.* Clemens wrote an undated endorsement. "Col. Fred Grant—enclosing Judges Tourgée's foolish letter to General Badeau." AE, *ibid.*

On June 29, Badeau, Tannersville, N. Y., confidentially wrote to Frederick Grant. "In looking over my papers I find the enclosed, which will be better in your keeping now than mine. I trust it may be very long before you have occasion to use it, or think of it. With my best wishes for the health and happiness of your father—which means the happiness of you all—" ALS, USG 3. The enclosure is a letter of April 2 from Robert Underwood Johnson, associate editor, *Century Magazine,* to Badeau recommending that Augustus St. Gaudens make a death mask of USG. ALS, *ibid.* On March 20, Karl Gerhardt had sculpted a bust of USG "from life at the private residence of the General," which Goodwin Brothers, Elmwood, Conn., produced in replica and offered for sale. L (dated May 5), CU-B. On April 25, Frederick Grant, New York City, wrote to Gerhardt. "Allow me to acknowledge the receipt of the 'Terre Cotta' busts of my father you so kindly sent me. As they were modelled from life, and are also an excellent likeness, I thank you for them." ALS, *ibid.* Clemens supported Gerhardt. See Samuel Charles Webster, ed., *Mark Twain, Business Man* (Boston, 1946), p. 319; Frederick Anderson, ed., *Mark Twain's Notebooks & Journals* (Berkeley, 1975–79), III, 106–7, 110, 139–40. On April 4, Gerhardt, New York City, had written to Goodwin Brothers. "This afternoon Col. Fred Grant gave me personal permissin to take mask of his fathers face after death—So I shall have to remain here until his death which may occur any day ..." ALS, Connecticut Historical Society, Hartford, Conn. On Dec. 16, Frederick Grant wrote to Gerhardt. "Having written to you twice about my fathers mask, I formally demand of you its possession." Copy (in Frederick Grant's hand), Ulysses Grant Dietz, Maplewood, N. J. For the controversy surrounding USG's death mask, see Anderson, ed., *Twain's Notebooks & Journals*, III, 127–28; *New York Times*, Oct. 25, 1885; Barbara Schmidt, "Mark Twain & Karl Gerhardt," www.twainquotes.com.

On Aug. 7, Badeau had written to William T. Sherman. "I presume either Fred or Porter has told you that I am lame and ill and utterly unable to get to NewYork. I need not tell you how great a sorrow this is to me. Perhaps it was that I was destined never to see my chief succumb. After all the weary watching and wailing of the winter I did not witness his surrender to Death, and now I am not to be present when he who was never in life subdued is imprisoned in his tomb. In the confusion of the occasion the cause of my absence may not be announced. I have not seen it stated in the newspapers, but I should not wish by any chance to seem to any one lacking in respect or feeling. Will you please explain this whenever there seems occasion, and say that I applied to be appointed honorary aide to Gen.l Hancock, as soon as I knew I could not attend in person as a mourner. I am extremely anxious that Mrs Grant should herself receive the enclosed letter, which she is not of course likely to do, if I send it by ordinary means Will it be asking too great a favor if I request you to read it and hand it to her. Of course it is supererogatory, but I still am anxious to say to her at this juncture what I feel" ALS, DLC-William T. Sherman. On Aug. 9, Sherman, New York City, wrote to Julia Dent Grant. "General Badeau Enclosed the within letter through me on the Supposition that you would be here in person, and that I could hand it you—You will read and hear so much of the Funeral of yesterday that I know you will be pleased that I avoid all details and State that Such a Funeral never before occurred in America, and never will again—The happiness & well being of Every member of your family have been and ever will be the prayer of Mrs S, myself and all our household—May you continue for many years to receive tokens of love and affection and then rest at that Majestic spot on the Banks of the Hudson, made Sacred by the presence of the Mortal part of the Great and Good General, to whom you were as true as the needle to the Pole, in poverty as in wealth, in adversity as well as in Exaltation." ALS, USG 3.

1. See *PUSG*, 10, 159–61.

2. See *ibid.*, 28, 190, 313.

3. For suits related to Badeau's army status and his fees while consul gen., London, see *ibid.*, pp. 284–85, 395–96; letter to Adam Badeau, June 21, 1883; *New York Times*, Nov. 4, 19, 1886, April 17, 1887, Aug. 9, 1890; *New York Tribune*, April 16, 1889.

To John H. Douglas

For the last twenty-four hours I have suffered less pain on the whole than usual. I have felt more weakness than was real because I have not been able to go out. Just now I feel quite strong. Waiting until I get drowsey I would probably feel weak if I had to make any great exertion.

JULY 12. [*1885*] 4 A. M

AN (date not in USG's hand), DLC–John H. Douglas. On July 12, 1885, 4:00 A.M., USG thrice wrote to John H. Douglas. "It is a question of avoiding nervousness and restlessness. These I have been very free from. The trouble has been more, pain and an accumulation of mucus in the mouth and throat." "I have not looked in a glass for more than a week to see whether I look like a bloat or a ghost. I do not think I am passing urine enough. For a few days back I do not think it amounts to a pint in twenty-four hours.—I just tell you these things. They may be important and me not know it." "How is food given by injectio[n] I see Mrs. Baird has not been able to take food in any other way for some time." AN, *ibid.* For chronically ill Mary C. Baird, see E. F. Rivinus and E. M. Youssef, *Spencer Baird of the Smithsonian* (Washington, 1992), pp. 46–52.

On July 12, 4:00 A.M., USG again wrote to Douglas. "I notice that your little girls and Julia get along very happily to-gether. With their swing, their lawn tennis and nice shade they seem very happy" AN (undated), DLC–John H. Douglas; typed copy (dated), DLC–USG, IC. At 8:00 A.M., USG wrote to Douglas. "My not eating so much has help me very much. As you say the difficulty about articulation comes from the sore place inside of the cheek. It would seem that the application of cocain there would help it. But it does not." AN, DLC–John H. Douglas.

To John Eaton, Jr.

————

[*Mount McGregor, N. Y., July 12, 1885*]

I am very glad to see you, and wish I could have some conversation with you. I should like to have see you something about our use of, and utilizing the negroes down about Grand Junction, Tenn. In writing on that subject for my book I had to rely on memory.[1] No doubt there will be some mistakes though they would not be so bad as errors in the military part. I intended submitting that part to you, but I was so ill while writing it, and so inxious to get through, that I did not have the time. The first Vol. is now in print.

AN, Gilder Lehrman Collection, NHi. John Eaton, Jr., commented on this note. "Written & handed, to me, by Genl Grant on the piazza of the cottage at Mt McGregor N. Y. after the sermon by Dr. Newman, The pure in heart shall see God, 2 OC. P. M. July 12th 1885." ANS, *ibid.* See *PUSG*, 6, 315–17; Eaton, *Grant, Lincoln and the Freedmen* (New York, 1907), pp. 295–97.

On July 12, 1885, a correspondent reported from Mount McGregor that Governor David B. Hill of N. Y., Joseph W. Drexel, and William J. Arkell spent about ten minutes with USG, who "remarked with pencil that he did not feel so much an invalid as his appearance would indicate while sitting at ease in his chair." *New York Tribune,*

July 13, 1885. See Arkell, *Old Friends and Some Acquaintances* (Los Angeles, 1927), pp. 11–19, 48–51.

1. See *Memoirs*, I, 424–26.

To John H. Douglas

—————

[*Mount McGregor, N. Y., July 14, 1885*]

Last night I understood that you intended to reduce the morphine, but thought it was to come in two doses. I did not strive to get to sleep therefore ‡until I had take the second dose. When I sent for the Dr.[1] about half past ten he said he wanted me to sleep on what I had. I did so, and slept very well until about half past five. From that on I had no sleep except frequent little naps of from three to ten minuets. The Dr. told me this morning you had given me six minums. I supposed but four.

AN, DLC-John H. Douglas. On July 14, 1885, a correspondent reported from Mount McGregor, N. Y. "Dr. Douglas and Dr. Shrady were present when General Grant went to bed this evening, and his condition was reported about the same as last evening, no cocaine having been used to-day and no unusual pain having been experienced, except such of a rheumatic character as had been induced by the stormy weather. The indications are for a quiet night." *New York Tribune*, July 15, 1885.

1. Probably on July 12, USG had written a note, presumably to John H. Douglas. "The Times says Dr. Schrady is coming up to relieve you a few days. I took food about two hours ago—at 12 30" AN (undated), USG 3. On July 13, George F. Shrady returned to Mount McGregor. *New York Tribune*, July 14, 1885. See note to George F. Shrady, June 24, 1885.

To Richard Watson Gilder

—————

Mt McGregor
July 15th 1885

Editor Century Magazine
Dear Sir:

My illness having prevented me from elaborating for my "Memoirs" the articles I have sent you on the campaigns and siege of Vicksburg, and the battles about Chattanooga, I will be obliged if you will consent to the omission from those articles, First: the detailed account of the campaign of Vicksburg,[1] and Second: that part of the Chattanooga article which my son, Colonel Grant, will show you (and which has no special bearing upon the battles of Chattanooga), substituting in their places the resumé preceding the siege of Vicksburg that I have sent you,[2] and what I will send you, in place of the omitted part of the Chattanooga battles.[3] This need not interfere with your publication in the collected volumes of your War series of the entire Articles

Very Sincerely Yrs.

U. S. GRANT

LS, Abraham Lincoln Book Shop, Chicago, Ill.

In July, 1885, Frederick Dent Grant wrote to Robert Underwood Johnson, associate editor, *Century Magazine.* "I enclose you a receipt sent by Mr. Smith in a letter with a check for $1500. Will you say to Mr. Smith that Father was much affected by the letter which brought the check. Father's connection with the *Century Magazine* has been pleasant, and he feels gratified in having done business with men who have always acted the part of gentlemen. You have been generous, and if in the future I am able to do anything for your interest you will find me acting with you." Johnson, *Remembered Yesterdays* (Boston, 1923), p. 219. This check, dated July 13, with USG's signature, is held by Ulysses Grant Deitz, Maplewood, N. J.

1. Corrected proof of the Vicksburg article is in USG 3.

2. *Century Magazine* editors acceded to USG's request so that his fuller version of the Vicksburg campaign first appeared in *Memoirs.* See *Century Magazine*, XXX, 5, 805; Draft Article Revision, [*June–July, 1885*].

3. USG probably supplied the first four and a half paragraphs and the last two and a half paragraphs of original text for the *Century* article. *Century Magazine*, XXXI, 1 (Nov., 1885), 128–45. The remainder largely matches *Memoirs*, II, 17–88.

On May 25, Thomas J. Wood, Dayton, had written to USG. "Yours of the 22d inst., with inclosure, is just received, and I hasten to reply to it. 1st The statement in regard to the delay in Genl Hooker's movement, caused by obstructions in his line of march, is in accordance with the facts. 2nd Genl Sherman's position, on our left was very critical in the afternoon of Novr 25, 1863. 3d The divisions of Genl Sheridan and myself were held in readiness from an h early hour of the 25 Novr, 1863, for any movement to be ordered—4th I have no knowledge of your orders to Genl Thomas except as learned from you. Undoubtedly you know what they were. 5th The statement that I promptly moved my division to the charge of Miss the center of Missionary Ridge,—*so soon as I received the order,* is correct. 6th I can not recall that there was any unwonted severity in your manner or tone when you asked me why I had not moved as you had ordered—I, therefore, request that the clause about the unusual severity be omitted— To have used severity of manner toward me, before knowing whether I had been guilty of delay, would, I most respectfully suggest, have been equally unjust to yourself and myself. It is true what follows shows I was not only ready to obey your order, but did do it promptly. 7th I did accompany my division to the summit of Missionary Ridge on horse-back, and was, of course, much exposed; but I was not wounded in the assault. On the contrary, I accompanied my division into East Tennessee with the expedition for the relief of Genl Burnside. Trusting I have given you all the information you desire, . . . " ALS, USG 3.

To John H. Douglas

After all that however the disease is still there and must be fatal in the end. My life is precious of course to my family and would be to me if I could recover entirely. There never was one more willing to go than I am. I know most ~~of~~ people have first one and then another little thing to fix up, and never get quite through. This was partially my case. I first wanted so many days to work on my book so the Authorship would be clearly mine. It was graciously granted to me, after being apparently much lower than since, and with a capacity to do more work than I ever did in the same time. My work had been done so hastily that much was left out and I did all of it over from the crossing of the James river in June /64, to Appomattox in /65. Since that I have added as much as fifty pages to the book I should think. There is nothing more I should do to it now, and therefore I am not likely to be more ready to go than at this moment.

JULY 16. [*1885*] P. M

AN (date not in USG's hand), DLC-John H. Douglas. On July 16, 1885, P.M., USG wrote to John H. Douglas. "I feel sorry at the prospect of living through the summer and fall in the condition I am in. I do not think I can, but I may. Except that I do not gather strength I feel quite as well from day to day as I have done heretofore. But I am satisfied that I am loo~~k~~sing strength. I feel it more in the inability to move about than in any other way, or rather in the lack of desire to try to move." AN, *ibid.*

On July 18, a correspondent reported from Mount McGregor that Shrady recommended that USG "read 'The Autocrat of the Breakfast Table,' which Mrs. Grant promptly ordered. His mind needs nourishment as much as his body, the doctor thinks, and as the idea of writing has not developed beyond yesterday's suggestion the remedy of reading will be applied as soon as the book comes." *Ibid.*, July 19, 1885. On July 19, Douglas said that *Century Magazine* had invited USG to write "a short article on 'the limit for the Presidential term.'" *Ibid.*, July 20, 1885.

To John H. Douglas

I have been dressed for an hour. Have not been asleep sinc eight. I took my coffee, dressed and was ready to go out by nine. Henry informed me that I had not had my food.

JULY 17, [*1885*] 11 A. M

AN (date not in USG's hand), DLC-John H. Douglas. Probably on July 17, 1885, USG wrote to John H. Douglas. "I had my fourth movement of the bowells and fear I shall have an other. It is time for me to go and get something to eat." AN (undated), *ibid.* See *New York Tribune*, July 20, 1885.

To John H. Douglas

Hardly time for Medecine to act. I feel no effect yet.

I have been very wide awake though comparitively free from pain excep soreness of the posterior and fatigue. I was just about getting up to walk about the room. Did any one go for you? I did not send.

JULY 18. [*1885*] 10 P. M.

AN (undated), DLC-John H. Douglas; typed copy (dated), DLC-USG, IC. On July 18, 1885, 10:00 P.M., USG thrice wrote to John H. Douglas. "A thicker pillow to set on would be better." "I thought of setting bolt upright to see if I could not get sleepy. The difficulty of clearing out my head is so great because of week stomach that I thought I might try if it becomes necessary to g̶ draw laudnum through the nostril. I has to come out." "Not feeling sleepy I have been thinking of the propriety of taking food? What food do you think I should take? It makes but little difference to me in the matter of swallowing: If I could recover the tone of my stomach I think I would pick up strength." AN, DLC-John H. Douglas; the third dated from typed copy, DLC-USG, IC.

USG also wrote to Douglas. "I feel quite weak in the stomache this morning. The least effort to clear my head would make me gag or vomit, I do not know but it will be the best thing to do." "In time. I have just ordered my food. I have had a good nap and a good rest, but I am still very weak. I suppose it is better for me to rest than to take enforces exercise, particularly as we know that the weakness is partially due to two days over operation of the bowells" "I get up more because my mouth begins to hurt me than for any other reason." AN (undated), DLC-John H. Douglas.

To John H. Douglas

July 19th: [*1885*] 9.45

What time have you got doctor? I have been resting so easily that I would not have been surprised to hear it was eleven. Henry tells me that it is only a little after nine.

AN (time not in USG's hand), DLC-John H. Douglas. On July 19, 1885, 2:00 A.M., USG wrote to John H. Douglas. "I am growing feint and feel that I will be obliged to visit the stool unless something is done to stop it." AN (undated), *ibid.*; typed copy (dated), DLC-USG, IC. On the same day, USG twice wrote to Douglas. "If that is the case do you not think it advisable for me to get up and rest as the tailor does—when he is standing up." "I can however write better seated with the board before me. I do not think I should take my medecine now. I might try to go to sleep and when I want the medecine call you." AN, DLC-John H. Douglas.

USG also wrote to Douglas. "I have tried to study the question of the use of the cocain as impartially as possible considering that I am the person effected by its use. The conclusion I have come to in my case is; taken properly it gives a wonderfull amount of relief from pain. Gradually the parts near those where the medicine is applied become numb and partially paralized. The feeling is unpleasant but not painful. Without the use of it the parts not effected with diseas are pliable but of no use because their exercise moves the diseased parts and produce pain. When the medecine is being applied the tendency is to take more than there is any necessity for, and oftener. On the whole my conclusion is to take it when it seems to be so much needed as it was at times yesterday. I will try to limit its use. This latter you know how hard it is to do." AN (undated), *ibid.*

To John H. Douglas

July 19th [*1885*]

I think I am better this evening than for some time bak. Taking so much morphine last night made me feraful that I would suffer waiting for the time to-night. But that was not the case. I was not nervous but naturally wanted my medecine. I rarely rsted for thirty minuets at a time except seated and most of that time was in the open air. I feel that if my bowells could be got right and stomache strong I would feel greatly better. The sore places in my mouth give less acute pain than they did. I can not see that the disease is spreading. On the other hand I do not see that any of these are particularls on the road to recovery.

AN, DLC-John H. Douglas. On July 20, 1885, 2:00 A.M., USG wrote to John H. Douglas. "In making the summary of th̶ progress for the 19th of July I stated that all the sores of the mouth were still there: this is hardly correct. The palate is about well, and along the tongue considerably improved." AN, *ibid.*

To John H. Douglas

———

JULY 20 [*1885*]

I am satisfied that I shall have to give up coffee. It is distasteful to and is harder to take than any thing els that goes into my mouth. I feel weak and feverish after my coffee for a long time and an irresistable desire to drink in water. It has been half an hour since I took my coffee and I feel an inordinate desire for cold water yet.

AN, DLC-John H. Douglas. On July 20, 1885, 7:00 A.M., USG wrote to John H. Douglas. "During last night a movement of the bowels was suspended by the action of the medecine promptly administered. Rest for the night better than the average." AN, *ibid.*; time from typed copy, DLC-USG, IC.

Also on July 20, 4:00 P.M., USG wrote to Douglas. "What do you think of my taking the bath wagon and going down to overlook the south view?" AN, DLC-John H. Douglas. See *New York Times* and *New York Tribune*, July 21, 1885.

John P. Newman wrote in his journal for July 21. " . . . The General's ride to the Eastern outlook fatigued him & hastened his death. He was carried into the drawing room & death seemed to seize him. We gathered around him & I prayed for him. At 9. P. M. he revived & wrote three messages to his family, which surprized us. At 11. P. M. he sent us word—'There's no earthly reason for you to sit up.'" AD, USMA.

To John H. Douglas

———

JULY 22. [*1885*] I do not think I slept the last time because of the medecine which put me to sleep the first and second time so much as from a general breaking up of my loss of sleep. I think I had better try it once more.

AN, DLC-John H. Douglas.

Probably in July, 1885, USG wrote to John H. Douglas. "I do not sleep though I sometimes dose off a little. If up I am talked to and in my efforts to answer cause pain. The fact is I think I am a verb instead of a personal pronoun. A verb is any thing that signafies to be; to do; or to suffer. I signify all three." AN (undated), DLC-John H. Douglas.

To Frederick Dent Grant

FRED, If you feel the least unwell do not work until you feel like it. Your services are to important now to have you break down. I woke up a little while ago dreaming that Ida was crying and I supposed it was because you were taken suddenly ill. But this was caused by your saying before I went to sleep that you felt badly and would go and take a walk. Then too your Ma told me that you were feeling badly.

MT MCGREGOR JULY 1885

AN (date not in USG's hand), USG 3. In July, 1885, USG wrote to Frederick Dent Grant. "I did not know by [why] you were going up to the hotel I asked to have you not go without coming in to see me again." AN (bracketed word not in USG's hand), *ibid.*

On July 21, a correspondent reported from Mount McGregor, N. Y., that USG "declined alcoholic stimulants because he believed they served only to heat his system without imparting strength; he expressed himself as feeling that he could endure his condition of weakness only a short time longer, and then requested the physician to administer a hypodermic injection of morphine . . . . Dr. Douglas reported the General's condition. He said that the patient was in a critical condition and he would hazard no prediction of the future, not even of the night . . . . Colonel Grant gave orders that all manuscripts and literary effects at the cottage office should be at once packed up and made safe, as no more work on the General's memoirs would probably be done there . . . . Finally, as the hour of 10 o'clock drew near General Grant looked up and spoke to his daughter Nellie. Then he indicated a purpose to write and did so. These were instructions for his family. Handing one note to Colonel Fred the General looked up into his face with large eyes that had in them a pitiful expression. 'I have already attended to that, father,' returned the Colonel, as he bent over his parent. The General then addressed other members of the family . . . ." *New York Tribune*, July 22, 1885. John P. Newman wrote in his journal for July 22 and 23. "Pleasant day. The General is rapidly failing Yet he was anxious for us & said, 'I hope no one will be distressed on my account.' The dreaded evening hours came, & while we were at dinner, he was laid upon his bed from which he was never to rise. We hastened from dinner. All gather around him & we all knelt while I offered prayer that God would receive his departing spirit. It was a solemn moment. The night wore on. All remained up during the night." "To-

ward morning the mucus accumated in his throat & gradually filled his lungs. ~~The~~
~~d~~Death would not be denied. His hands & feet grew cold; his pulse beat 150, & his
respirations were 64 to the minute. At 8:8. he opened his eyes, took a last view of those
around him, & ~~ga~~ then closed his eyes & gave a short breath & he was gone . . . ." AD,
USMA. For other accounts of USG's final hours before his death on July 23, near 8:00
A.M., see *New York Tribune*, *New York Times*, and *Philadelphia Press*, July 23–24, 1885.
See also Julia Grant Cantacuzène, *My Life Here and There* (New York, 1921), pp. 47–56.

On July 15, Patrick Henry and Charles J. Steer, Vicksburg, had telegraphed to
USG. "It is our pleasure to present to you the following resolution, which was adopted
by a unanimous vote of the Democratic party of Warren County, in convention assembled July 14: *Resolved,* That we join in the nation's grief for the sad affliction which
has befallen Gen. U. S. Grant, America's most illustrious citizen, who is as magnanimous in peace as he was great in war." *New York World*, July 16, 1885. On July 21, a
correspondent reported from Elmira on a message from N. Y. cav. veterans to USG.
"We come to you in your far off mountain home with our heartfelt sympathy. Gladly
would we come to your aid as of old if shot and shell would dislodge the enemy so
strongly entrenched in your throat; but we can only pray that you may triumphantly
pass through your present conflict, leaning on Him who endured every human pain,
and that you may be disposed to receive the orders of the Supreme Commander either
for life or death." *New York Tribune*, July 22, 1885. Similar communications for USG
had come from the Patriotic Order of Sons of America gathered at Denver (June 18),
"colored citizens of Chicago" (June 23), and Order of United American Mechanics, San
Francisco (June 26). General Grant National Memorial, New York, N. Y.

Calendar

1883, Jan. 25.   To David Milliken, Jr., secretary, Union League Club. "Having been in Washington City since Jan.y 2d until last evening I have only just seen the invitation of the Union League Club to attend the Twentieth Anniversary of the organization of the Club, for Tuesday evening, Feb.y sixth, this am. It would have been impossible for me to have accepted had I received the invitation in time; but I would have sent my regrets promptly but for the fact stated."—ALS, University of California, Santa Barbara, Calif.

[*1883, Feb. 4–5*].   USG endorsement. "I have no expectation of being in Washington again this winter though I am liable to be called there. If so you can call on me either with or without letters."—AES, IHi. Written on a letter of Feb. 3 from Augustus C. Carey, Washington, D. C., to USG. "Do you expect to be in Washington within a few days? If so, will you please allow me a few minutes conversation at your convenience? I will bring a proper letter of introduction, and am not seeking office."—ALS, *ibid.* Carey had invented a voting machine. See *New York Times*, June 1, 1883; *SRC*, 48-1-746.

On May 30, 1873, Carey, Lynn, Mass., had written to USG. " . . . I have invented a seamless cartridge knitted from any material used in knitting, but I can make the cartridge of woolen thread or yarn and make them (by a process of my own) both water and fire proof . . . ."—ALS, DNA, RG 156, Letters Received.

1883, Feb. 5.   To Robert P. Lyon, New York City. "Your letter of Jany 29th enclosing an invitation to attend the fourth Annual Banquet of the Furniture Trade Assn, no doubt came duly to hand, but owing to my absence and the accumulation of letters while absent, it has been overlooked until this time. I should have been pleased if I had seen in time to have accepted the invitation."—LS, Herman Blum, Philadelphia, Pa.

1883, March 10.   Letter recommending DeB. Randolph Keim as chief, Bureau of Engraving and Printing, mentioned in a Keim memorandum dated March 29, 1883, acknowledging receipt of the original.—ADS, DNA, RG 56, Applications. On April 25, President Chester A. Arthur appointed Keim as chief examiner, Civil Service Commission, surprising some who saw Keim as "the warm friend and associate of men identified with machine politics."—*New York Times*, April 26, 1883. When Arthur withheld Keim's commission, supporters promised "that the President shall be made to feel the displeasure of such men as Gen. Grant, Senator Cameron, Senator Hawley, and the other prominent Republicans who are understood warmly to have espoused Keim's cause."—*Ibid.*, May 10, 1883. On May 10, Keim withdrew his name from consideration.—*Ibid.*, May 11, 1883. See *PUSG*, 20, 214–15.

[*1883*], March 27.   To Edward F. Beale, Washington, D. C. "WILL YOU FIND OUT FOR ME IF THE PRESIDENT WILL BE IN WASHINGTON TOMORROW."—Telegram received (at 12:15 P.M.), DLC-Decatur House Papers. On March 29, USG telegraphed to Beale. "I have not been able to go to Washington on account of a soar foot which prevents wearing a shoe"—Telegram received (at 1:31 P.M.), *ibid.*

1883, APRIL 10.   Secretary of War Robert T. Lincoln to USG. "I have your note of yesterday in respect to the detail of Lieut. David Price at the Military Academy. He was at the head of the list of four officers recommended to relieve Lieut Bacon whose detail will expire. No protests against his detail from his regimental officers have been received, and his name has been put in the order which is being prepared for publication."—LS, Robert T. Lincoln Letterbooks, IHi.

1883, APRIL 18.   Secretary of War Robert T. Lincoln to USG. "I have the honor to inform you that the Joint Resolution of Congress, approved December 17, 1863, thanking you and the officers and soldiers who fought under your command during the rebellion, is in the possession of this Department, my attention having been drawn thereto during the recent removal of my office into the north wing of the State, War, and Navy Departments building. As the resolution seems to belong to you, I deem it proper to ask your wishes regarding its disposal, and to remark that unless you shall otherwise request, it will be carefully preserved in the Department."—Copy, DNA, RG 107, Letters Sent, Military Affairs. On April 25, Lincoln again wrote to USG. "I have the honor to inform you that in accordance with your wishes as expressed in your communication of the 23d instant, I have this day forwarded by Express to your address, No. 3 East 66th Street New York, the Joint Resolution of Congress referred to in my letter to you of the 18th instant."—Copy, *ibid.* See *PUSG*, 9, 503–4.

1883, APRIL 25.   USG endorsement. "I know Col. Buckner well, and esteem him highly as an original & consistent Union Man, of high personal character, and one whose recommendations would go as far with me as that of any man."—AES, DNA, RG 94, ACP 1703 1883. Written on a letter of April 18, from James F. Buckner, Louisville, to USG. "The bearer of this note my young friend Jno L Sehon of Louisville desires to enter the United States Army. He is a young man of fine moral character, good education, & is in every way worthy of the position he seeks. His family are my immediate neighbors in this City; I therefore speak from intimate knowledge. He believes that you could aid him, and I have cheerfully complied with his request in addressing you this note in his behalf. I have great confidence, in his integrity, courage, & patriotism. He & his friends will appreciate any courtesy extended to him."—ALS, *ibid.* John L. Sehon was appointed 2nd lt. as of Oct. 10.

1883, APRIL 25.   Secretary of War Robert T. Lincoln to USG. "I have your letter of the 24th instant, enclosing one from Mr. Foltz, of Chambersburg, Penna, urging the admission of H. R. Hershberger to the Soldiers' Home here. I at once called for a report in the matter, and it has been made to me by the clerk of the Board of Commissioners of the Soldiers' Home, and is enclosed herewith for your information. Section 4821 of the Revised Statutes provides that certain persons described, and no others, shall be entitled to the benefits of the Home. The only classes described with which Mr. Hershberger could have any connection are these:—Soldiers of the army of the United States who have served twenty (20) years in the Same; discharged soldiers suffering by reason of disease or wounds incurred *in the Service* and in the line of their duty. It appears from this report, as also from Mr. Foltz' letter, that Mr. Hershberger served a little over six years as a soldier, and then held an appointment as Riding Master at West Point for nearly seven years. The latter position would seem to me to differ from that of a soldier in the same way as do many positions under the Quartermaster's Department, for instance, such as corral masters and others. His disability, complained of, seems to have been incurred while Riding Master; and for these reasons it has been held by the Board that he is not entitled to the benefits of the Home. I do not see how he could be admitted to it, under existing laws."—LS (press), Robert T. Lincoln Letterbooks, IHi. USG's riding instructor at USMA, H. R. Hershberger published *The Horseman: A Work on Horsemanship: . . .* (New York, 1844). See James B. Fry, "An Acquaintance With Grant," *North American Review,* CXLI, CCCXLIX (Dec., 1885), 540–41.

1883, MAY 3. To Lorenz Reich, New York City. "After apology for the delay allow me to thank you for your kind note of the 27th of April—my birthday—and also for the box of wine which accompanyied it. Both reached me on the 27th."—ALS, NHi. On Jan. 19, 1875, Levi P. Luckey had written to Reich. "The President directs me to acknowledge the receipt of your letter which has just been brought to his attention too late to reply before the ceremonies to which you so kindly invited him, though it would have been impossible for him to comply, as he cannot leave Washington at this time. He wishes your son a prosperous and happy future and that he may grow to be the pride and comfort of his parents in their declining years. He wishes me to thank you for the compliment paid him by your letter."—LS, *ibid.* A prominent hotel keeper who kept a famed wine cellar, Reich had named a son after USG. See *New York Times,* April 10, 1887, May 3, 1931.

1883, [MAY]. Circular issued by USG as president, National Rifle Association, "calling attention to the rifle match between the National Guard of this country and the Volunteer Militia of Great Britain, and soliciting subscriptions from patriotic persons to defray the expenses."—*New York Times,* May 13, 1883.

In Jan., tendered the association's presidency, USG had "replied by saying that he is fully aware of the importance of the association, looking to the possibility of future wars, and the honorable position of President of such an association, but that it would be impossible for him to attend to any of the duties of the office, and knowing from experience the amount of correspondence that would devolve upon him in answering letters that would be sent to him direct, he begged to decline the position with thanks."—*Ibid.,* Jan. 28, 1883.

On April 3, the association's board of directors elected USG as president. Chairman George W. Wingate "said that General Grant had stated that he was warmly interested in the association and appreciated the good it was accomplishing; that his engagements required him to be frequently absent from the city and he feared that he might not be able to give as much personal attention to the duties of president as ought to be given and would have to rely upon General Wingate as vice president to help him out in matters of routine, &c., but that, if the association considered his accepting the office of president would be of any help to it, he would be happy to act."—*New York Herald,* April 4, 1883.

On Jan. 8, 1884, the association held its annual meeting. "A communication was received from Gen. Grant stating that 'a recent accident' prevented him from presiding at the meeting."—*New York Times,* Jan. 9, 1884.

1883, June 1. Lt. Gen. Philip H. Sheridan, Chicago, to USG. "I take great pleasure in introducing to you by this note Captain James H. Merryman of the Life Saving Service, of which he has been for a long period the Inspector. Captain Merryman can speak for himself. He has been a close personal friend of mine for over twenty years gone bye and is a man for whom I have the very highest regard and warmest friendship."—Copy, DLC-Philip H. Sheridan.

1883, June 14. To Lawrence Mendenhall, Cincinnati Industrial Exhibition. "Your letter of June 11th is at hand, and in reply I will say that I certainly have no objections to comply with your request, but I am not aware of any ownership or control that I have over my portrait now in the Calumet Club in Chicago. If you can get the Consent of the Club of course you have mine."—LS, Doris Harris Autographs, Los Angeles, Calif. For this portrait by Thomas Le Clear, later lost in a fire, see *New York Times,* Nov. 28, 1882, Aug. 2, 1885, Jan. 18, 1893.

1883, June 26. Secretary of War Robert T. Lincoln to USG. "I have the honor to inform you that your name has been placed upon the list to receive the Official Records of the War of the Rebellion and that the volumes from No. 1 to 7 inclusive were on yesterday sent to your address. Please acknowledge receipt for the same by enclosed blank. The remaining volumes of the work will be sent to you as fast as published"—Copy, DNA, RG 107, Letters Sent, Military Affairs. On June 23, Lincoln had issued an order directing "that the names of General Ulysses S. Grant and George B. McClellan be placed upon the list to receive the Rebellion Records. General Grant's address is New York City, New York and General McClellans, Orange New Jersey."—Copy, *ibid.*

On Oct. 29, 1884, Lt. Gen. Philip H. Sheridan, act. secretary of war, wrote to USG. "Replying to your note of inquiry relative to volume eleven, part one, of the 'Official Records of the War of the Rebellion' I have the honor to state that the volume was sent to you on the 16th inst, addressed 'Gen U. S. Grant No 2 Wall St, New York City' that being the address to which the previous volumes were mailed. I would further state that this volume (eleven, part one) was sent by registered mail, and is now doubtless awaiting your disposal at the New York Post Office Will you please furnish this

Department with the address to which you wish the volumes of the Rebellion Records sent in future, if they are not now being correctly addressed to you."—Copy, *ibid.*

1883, JUNE 28. To Hamilton Fish. "Mrs. Grant and I would be pleased to have a visit from you and Mrs. Fish from Monday the 30th of July for a week. I think you would both find the seaside pleasant, and I know we would enjoy your company."—ALS, DLC-Hamilton Fish. Fish wrote to USG. "Many thanks for your very kind invitation to pay you a visit at Long Branch which Mrs Fish. I would be most happy to do ~~but~~ but for an engagement here. My wife proposes to pass the latter part of ~~Augus~~ July with Mrs Webster at Newport, & has engagements for company here in the early part of August"—ADf (undated), *ibid.*

1883, JULY 9. To Mrs. McGinnis, from Long Branch. "The Colonel left this am and Jesse and wife are to be here to spend the night with us so that I will not be able to accept your kind invitation to go over to-night."—ALS (facsimile), Benjamin Autographs [Jan. 2000], no. 4073. On July 12, a correspondent reported from Long Branch. "Secretary of War Lincoln returned from Babylon, Long Island, to-night, and is the guest of John McGinnis, Jr., at his Elberon cottage."—*New York Times,* July 13, 1883. Wall Street financier John McGinnis, Jr., had married Lydia O. Matteson, daughter of former Ill. governor Joel A. Matteson. See Johnson, *Papers,* 12, 281; Paul Fatout, *Ambrose Bierce and the Black Hills* (Norman, 1956), pp. 35–36.

1883, AUG. 28. USG endorsement. "I respectfully refer this letter to the Secretary of State, and add that if Mr. Lord can be appointed Consul to Nice—where I understand there is a vacancy—I would be much pleased."— AES, DNA, RG 59, Applications and Recommendations, Hayes-Arthur. Written on a letter of Aug. 16 from Fitz John Porter, New York City, to USG. "I have been asked by the widowed mother of Mr Walter Scott Lord, now in Nice, France, to beg you to help secure for her son, the position of Consul at that place made vacant by death. She regards your help as a certain means of success. Mr Lord is a young man of first rate ability, integrity & energy. He is a gentleman in spirit & manner—and a trusted favorite of the officials of the Del & Hudson Canal Co. He is in delicate health, on leave of absence from that Company—but is compelled to stay abroad another year or return to die.— . . . He is a nephew of Senator Harrison of Indiana who does not like to solicit office for persons outside of his State—& interfere perhaps with other Senators field . . . ."—ALS, *ibid.* Related papers are *ibid.* Walter S. Lord died Sept. 18, 1884.

1883, OCT. 8. USG endorsement. "I heartily endorse the sentiments expressed by the Comte de Paris in his letter of July 20th, and cheerfully contribute the sum of One Hundred Dollars toward the completion of the work."—Printed, DNA, RG 94, ACP, 5013 1883. On July 20, Louis Philippe Albert d'Orléans, Comte de Paris, Chateau D'Eu, wrote to Thomas S.

Townsend. "I have received your letter of the 30th ultimo, with the pamphlet concerning the work which you have undertaken. It is a work of the greatest value, but which seems to be above the strength of a single man, and the limits of a single life. I feel, therefore, the greatest admiration for your achievement, and I have instructed my bankers to subscribe a sum of One Hundred Dollars toward the expenses of its completion."—Printed, *ibid.* For Townsend's compilation of published political and military records, 1860–70, see *SRC,* 51-1-1240; *Southern Historical Society Papers,* 18 (1890), 382–85; *New York Times,* May 7, 1895.

1883, OCT. 11. USG endorsement. "Respectfully referred to the Atty. General of the United States. Having been requested by J. D. Cunningham—who has the endorsement of Gens. Longstreet & McLaws, both favorably known to me—I do not make a special recommendation of either."—AES, DNA, RG 60, Records Relating to Appointments. Written on papers including a letter of Sept. 17 from James Longstreet, U.S. marshal, Atlanta, to USG. "It gives me pleasure to ask the privilege to introduce Hon. H. D. D. Twiggs of Augusta. It is not necessary to say that Judge Twiggs is one of our most prominent men, of ofa prominent family, and of course one in whom we have pride."—ALS, *ibid.* On Sept. 16, Lafayette McLaws, postmaster, Savannah, had written to USG. "Colonel H. D. D. Twiggs of Georgia desires that I give him a letter of introduction to you, and I take the Liberty; because I have known Colonel Twiggs for a number of years and know that he is a gentleman of marked ability, and of wonderful energy and independence of character. He has since the war, been a judge of the Superior Court of his District in Georgia a Representative in the Legislature, and is a lawyer widely known through the State and elsewhere, for his ability and eloquence. He is entirely on the independent line in politics, and I believe has a very considerable following His family is one of the largest and most influential in the State, with many extensive connexions in in the North."—ALS, *ibid.* Ga. Republicans contested appointments for U.S. attorney, Northern District, and judge, Southern District. See *New York Times,* Jan. 4, 13, 17, 1884, Jan. 23, 1885; Olive Hall Shadgett, *The Republican Party in Georgia: From Reconstruction through 1900* (Athens, Ga., 1964), pp. 98–104. For Hansford D. D. Twiggs, see *HRC,* 42-2-22, part 7, pp. 1042–56.

1883, OCT. 19. To President Chester A. Arthur. "This will present Gen. T. A. McParlin, Surgeon, U. S. Army. Gen. McParlin served with distinction during the entire rebellion, and was Medical Director of the Army of the Potomac during the entire time that I served in the East, always rendering entire satisfaction in that position."—Printed copy, Gilder Lehrman Collection, NHi. See *PUSG,* 28, 509.

1883, DEC. 15. To Secretary of War Robert T. Lincoln. "I am informed that an application is to be made for the appointment of Raymond R. Stevens as 2d Lieutenant in the Army. I cordially endorse the application if made. Mr. Stevens father—a retired officer in the Navy—has spent the greater part of his life in the service of his country as did the grandfather on the mother's side."—ALS, DNA, RG 94, ACP, 5401 1884. Lincoln endorsed USG's letter to the AG. "Put this on list with a blue check mark"—AE (initialed), *ibid.* A former U.S. Naval Academy midshipman (1879–82), Raymond R. Stevens secured nomination as 2nd lt., 23rd Inf. For USG's acquaintance with Thomas H. Stevens, retired as rear admiral as of May 27, 1881, and former naval surgeon's mate Peter Christie, who died on March 5, 1853, see *PUSG,* 1, 209, 211; *ibid.,* 19, 92.

[*1883–1884*].   USG endorsement. "I concur with Gen. Lee in his estimate of the character of Gen. Longstreet."—AES (undated), Longstreet Papers, NN. Written on a letter of Oct. 21, 1868, from Robert E. Lee, Lexington, Va., to William Barclay Parsons. "Genl Longstreet I understand has closed his business in New Orleans & I do not know his present address. When I last heard of him he was in NewYork. I have always entertained a high opinion of Genl Longstreets character for uprightness integrity & honesty & should rejoice at any good that may befall him. I do not know whether the position you refer to would be agreable to him or not"—ALS, *ibid.* A later endorsement credits USG with writing his endorsement in 1883 or 1884 "in the office of Grant & Ward. at the request of Mr Parsons." Parsons, a New York City attorney, also wrote an undated note. "The reverse Autographic letter of *General Robert E. Lee,*—concurred in by *General Ulysses S. Grant*—is, in the opinion of the latter as expressed to me, the *only* paper containing *both* autographs of these celebrated military chieftains in existence except '*The Surrender at Appomattox.*'"—ANS, *ibid.* For Parsons, see *New York Times,* Jan. 1, 1888.

1884, JAN. [*5–8*].   To Samuel E. Jones, secretary, Lincoln Association, Washington, D. C. "Your letter of the 2d inst., asking my consent to the placing of my picture upon the banner of the Lincoln Association is at hand, and in reply I will say that if you are determined to have the image of any living person on your banner I can offer no objection. It would seem to be a rule, or rather suggests itself to my judgment, for such banners to take the portraits of the dead; but that is a matter for your own judgment."—*New York Times,* Jan. 12, 1884; reprinted from *Washington Evening Star,* Jan. 10, 1884. Frank F. Wood added a postcript. "The General has not yet sufficiently recovered to be able to write with ease, and therefore does not sign this note personally."—*Ibid.*

1884, MARCH 23.   To W. H. Foster, New York City, from Washington, D. C. "I do not save autographs and, consequently, do not have any of Mr. Lincoln."—LS, deCoppet Collection, NjP.

1884, JUNE 4.   To Samuel C. Wright, former sgt., 29th Mass., declining an invitation to attend a meeting of Mass. veterans. "I am still on crutches from injuries received from a fall in December last, and must expect to be for some time to come . . . ."—Paul C. Richards, Catalogue 3, April, 1962, no. 74. For

Wright's involvement in veterans' reunions, see *National Tribune*, May 29, June 26, 1884.

On Aug. 7, USG wrote to Robert S. Gordon, former corporal, 21st Ill. " . . . I . . . regret that my injuries, received more than six months ago, prevents my accepting any invitations to . . . army reunions this year."—Joseph Rubinfine, List 72 [1982], no. 24. Milton A. Ewing, corresponding secretary, later reported from Neoga, Ill. "The 10th annual Reunion of the 21st Ill., which was held at Arcola, on the 18th and 19th ult., was a very pleasant affair. We telegraphed a salutation to our old Colonel (Gen. U. S. Grant), in New York city, and received a congratulatory answer from him . . . ."— *National Tribune*, Oct. 2, 1884.

In 1884, USG telegraphed to an unknown person. "I do not go to Army meetings,"—Dr. Milton Kronovet Autographs, Catalogue 137 [1964], no. 13.

1884, JUNE 10. Testimonial. "I really can not say that I think the portraits which you send me good. I know all the Generals in the group, and would recognize most of them from the picture; but not all. It is probably an impossible task to give good pictures by the process which has to be used in taking them."—ADS, Goodspeed's Book Shop, Inc., Boston, Mass.

1884, AUG. 10. To G. Norton Cullinay, from Long Branch. "I am much obliged to the Grand Army Scout for its reply to Sir (Mr.) Garnet Wolseley's fling."—Leslie Hindman Auctioneers, Jan. 15, 1984, no. 76. On Dec. 8, 1883, Sir Garnet Joseph Wolseley, the "great English soldier," London, wrote to "*My Dear Miss S.*," identified as "an accomplished lady of Mobile, Ala., now residing in New York." "I am very grateful for your kind letter and for the valuable autographs it contains. I have long been collecting the letters of eminent people, but have had much difficulty in obtaining those of the great men on your side of the Atlantic. I have only known two heroes in my life, and General R. E. Lee is one of them, so you can well understand how I value one of his letters. I believe that when time has calmed down the angry passions of the 'North,' General Lee will be accepted in the United States as the greatest General you have ever had, and second as a patriot only to Washington himself. Stonewall Jackson, I only knew slightly, his name will live forever also in American history when that of Mr. U. S. Grant has been long forgotten, such at least is my humble opinion of these men when viewed by an outside student of military history who has no local prejudice . . . ."—*Southern Historical Society Papers*, XII, 5 (May, 1884), 232–33. For Wolseley's later assessment of USG's generalship, see James A. Rawley, ed., *The American Civil War: An English View* (Charlottesville, Va., 1964).

1884, SEPT. 13. Frederick Dent Grant, Long Branch, to John S. Griffin. "Your letter to Genl Grant was received by him in good time and put aside as he expected to get some photographs that were good & he intended sending you one. But he has not yet received any. Genl Grant directed me to answer your letter of May 3rd & thank you for your kind remarks"—ALS, MoSHi.

After resigning from the army as asst. surgeon (1854), Griffin settled in Los Angeles. See *PUSG*, 1, 284–85; *Los Angeles Times*, Aug. 24, 1898.

1885, JAN. 3. To Georgianna A. Boutwell. "Many thanks for your New Year welcome, just received. There is no family that I have ever known whos friendship I prize more highly than that of your father. I wish for him and his family many returns of new years, and that all of them may find him and his in the enjoyment of good health and peace of mind."—ALS (facsimile), George S. Boutwell, *Reminiscences of Sixty Years in Public Affairs* (New York, 1902), II, 253. On April 24, Boutwell called at USG's home for two hours in the evening.—*New York Times*, April 25, 1885. See *ibid.*, Sept. 22, 1933.

1885, JAN. 27. To U.S. Senator John Sherman of Ohio. "I regret very much that my physical condition prevents my accepting the invitation of the Commissioners appointed by Congress to provide suitable ceremonies for the Dedication of the Washington Monument, to be present to witness the same, on the 21st of February next. My throat still requires the attention of the physician, daily, though I am encouraged to believe that it is improving."—ALS (facsimile), *John Sherman's Recollections of Forty Years* ... (Chicago, 1895), II, between pp. 900–901. *SMD*, 48-2-56, 119; *SD*, 57-2-224, 287–88. USG responded to an engraved invitation. DS (facsimile), *John Sherman's Recollections*, II, between pp. 902–3. See *ibid.*, pp. 897–902; *PUSG*, 24, 86–88.

On July 19, 1875, Orville E. Babcock, Long Branch, had written to Frederick L. Harvey, Washington National Monument Society, Washington, D. C. "The President directs me to enclose you his Autograph—with permission if the Society so desire to engrave it onto the receipt. In doing this he does not endorse any plan for raising the means."—Copy, DLC-USG, II, 2. The Washington National Monument Society used USG's name in selected appeals. See *SD*, 57-2-224, 84, 87. See also *ibid.*, pp. 315–17.

1885, FEB. 5. William T. Sherman, St. Louis, to USG. "A lady for whose family I have a special friendship asks on her enclosed cards, yours and *Mrs Grants* autographs. Please send them to me as a personal favor—"—ALS, USG 3.

In late March, a newspaper reported. "Nearly every mail that is brought to the General's house contains many requests for his autograph . . . . Thus far all those who have asked for the General's autograph have received it, without any distinction as to persons, and the sick man has taken considerable pleasure in replying to these requests, even at times when he felt fatigued and unfit to do so . . . . Colonel Grant said yesterday in regard to this subject: 'It is a physical impossibility for the invalid to comply with these requests. While the making of one autograph would not require much exertion, twenty would be a day's work for him, and it would be well for the public to know that these demands cannot be met.'"—*New York Tribune*, March 22, 1885. In April, Frederick Dent Grant responded to another person seeking an autograph. "It is an impossibility . . . . I have at least five hundred pictures and

albums waiting for father's autograph. There are addressed and stamped letters bearing requests enough to fill a dry-goods box."—*Ibid.*, April 13, 1885.

1885, MARCH 3. Frederick D. Grant, New York City, to J. Rice Winchell.
"Genl Grant directs me to answer your letter of Feb 26 and say that 'He
thanks you for your kind letter but he is too ill to even answer your letter so of course he could make no engagement to lecture'"—ALS (facsimile),
Dr. Walter A. Ostromecki, Jr., Encino, Calif.

1885, MARCH 5. William A. Garden, Belmont, Wis. to USG. " . . . While
employed as Civil Engineer on the Allegheny Valley Railroad in Penna. I
was associated with Alexander Hays, who spoke of you, as a Class Mate of
his West Point. The incident referred to happened, while we were travelling
from Kittaming Pa. to Pitts. Pa.—When the Pitts. morning papers were dis-
tributed, Mr Hays, who was a large commanding looking person, was sitting
diagonally across the car from me; having glanced at his paper exclaimed in
great enthusiasm:—'Good! Grant, has been made Colonel of the Illinois Regiment'. Though many years have passed since then, still even now I recall the
thrill given, when he stood up, tremulous with emotion, the paper grasped in
his elevated right hand, with all the enthusiasms he was capable of after a
moments pause, exclaimed; 'Gentlemen, mark my words, that is the man who
will make his mark in this War.' A short time after this Mr Hays went from
Pittsburgh into the Army of the Potomac as Colonel of a Regiment of Penna:
Volunteers and was killed at the battle of 'Fair Oaks' May 30th 1862 near
Richmond Va. I never met him again in life . . . ."—ALS, USG 3.
    On June 10, David H. Williams, Allegheny, Pa., wrote to Frederick D.
Grant. "Enclosed I send a memorandum of an incident connected with the
life of your distinguished Father and of a former comrade and subsequent
lieutenant under his command, being a General at the battle of the Wilderness where his career closed. I have seen a daguerreotype with your Father
and General Hays upon one plate taken while they were in the service together as subalterns, which would indicate that they were comrades probably
class mates also at West Point. I noted not long since that some other officer
if I mistake not, General Ingalls; had fore cast a somewhat similar, the same
result, showing that the eminent subject of these predictions must have been
the possessor of abnormal qualifications, if the germ was sufficiently marked
to indicate the wonderful fruit, and serving to show that the assertions of
some, that the success of General Grant was due more to 'luck' and good
fortune than to inherent capacity and genius, is not well founded . . . ."—ALS,
ibid. The memorandum, entitled "The prediction of General Alexander Hays
at the breaking out of the Rebellion and its remarkable fulfilment," is *ibid.*

1885, MARCH 28. USG endorsement. "I concur in General Sheridan's
endorsement."—Typed copy, DNA, RG 94, ACP, 295 1891. On March 16, Lt.
Gen. Philip H. Sheridan had written an endorsement. "It gives me pleasure
to state that I have known Lieutenant Colonel George D. Ruggles for over
thirty years. I knew him before the War, during the War, and since the War.

Much of the time covered by these periods he served in my command. He has been a good, faithful officer, occupying responsible positions, in which he has acquitted himself with distinction and honor . . . ."—Typed copy (ellipsis in original), *ibid.* Lt. Col. George D. Ruggles, asst. AG, Washington, D. C., became AG, Dept. of Tex., as of June 15.

1885, MAY 11.   Frederick Dent Grant, New York City, to John L. Branch. "General Grant directs me to answer your of the 7th inst and say that it is a very pretty piece of history and he was very glad to get it. As he does not write about the beginning of the war at least only that part that he personally took part in he will not use it in his book but thanks you just the same"—ALS, Anne Branch Carter, Decatur, Ga. Trained as an engineer, Branch improved fortifications near Charleston, S. C., and served in the C.S.A. Ordnance Dept. See John Peyre Thomas, *The History of the South Carolina Military Academy* (Charleston, 1893), pp. 518–20.

1885, JUNE 12.   Frederick D. Grant, New York City, to C. F. Daniels, Macon, Ga. "Genl Grant desires me to acknowledge and thank you for the pictures (photographs) of Andersonville you so kindly sent him."—ALS (facsimile), eBay, Jan. 8, 2001.

1885, JUNE 17.   Franz Sigel, Morrisania, N. Y., to Frederick Dent Grant, Mount McGregor, N. Y. "I hope ~~you I shall be ex~~ will excuse me in addressing you the~~i~~se lines in behalf of a personal matter, which, you may well imagine, is of great importance to me. Some time ago it was my intention to write to ~~the General, your father,~~ about it, but ~~I~~ refrained from troubling him on account of the sad affliction, which has unfortunately come over him. And even now I do not wish to send this letter and enclosures directly ~~to him,~~ to your father, leaving it to your discretion to make known to him the contents at ~~su~~ a time, which you may find opportune for such a communication. ~~The As~~ ~~y~~You are probably aware, that I was relieved of the command of the Department of W. Virginia after the battle of NewMarket, in May 1864. ~~As I had~~ As I was relieved before I had an opportunity to make an official report, based on the reports of subordinate officers and having been ordered to take command of ~~the Reserve Division, camp~~ stationed at Harpers Ferry to Maryland Heights and ~~guarding~~ along the ~~Railroad~~ Baltimore Ohio R. R. from Monocacy to Parkersburg to Wheeling, ~~The following dispatch was sent from Martinsburg and reached me probably on the 11th of May at night or on the 12th. Tuesday was the 10th of May.~~ 'IRA The state of affairs before that battle, as well as the motives, which prompted me to move ~~down~~ up the Shenandoah valley ~~to W~~ from Cedar Creek to Woodstock and Mount Jackson and to engage the enemy near New Market, were never ~~fully~~ explained or, as I think, properly understood; ~~N~~nor became it publicly known, ~~what I done myself~~ how I acted personally, during that battle and why I retreated, after ~~our repulse~~ the battle, to ~~Cedar~~ Strassburg and Cedar Creek. I therefore did not find it strange, that the General said in his report of July 22 1865 page 11: 'Not regarding the operations ~~ete~~ of General Sigel as satisfac-

tory, I asked his removal from command, and Major General Hunter was appointed to supersede him.'—To be as short as possible, I shall ~~now~~ state a few
facts, relative to the plan of campaign, ~~and~~ the ~~reasons why the advance and
the~~ subsequent movements ~~to New Market~~ and the battle of New Market
itself . . . ."—ADf (incomplete), OClWHi. See *PUSG*, 10, 459–60, *ibid.*, 15,
169–70; *Memoirs*, II, 238; Stephen D. Engle, *Yankee Dutchman: The Life of
Franz Sigel* (Fayetteville, Ark., 1993), pp. 186–201.

[*1885, June–July*].   USG note. "Was that Mrs. Sherwood you were speaking of."—ANS (undated), University of California, Santa Barbara, Calif.
Mary E. W. Sherwood assessed USG in *An Epistle to Posterity: Being Ram-
bling Recollections of Many Years of My Life* (New York, 1897), pp. 105–9.

1885, July 11.   Henry Randall Waite, president, American Institute of Civics, Boston, to Frederick Dent Grant, Mount McGregor, N. Y. "I do not
suppose that your father's condition will permit him to take much interest
in the plans of the American Institute of Civics, but I am sure that it is an
institution which, were he in his usual health, would command his hearty
sympathy, . . . "—TLS, Smithsonian Institution. An honorary membership
for USG, dated July 6, is *ibid.* See Waite, "The American Institute of Civics,"
The Arena (Boston), XVIII, 92 (July, 1897), 108–15.

1885, July 20.   Frederick Dent Grant, Mount McGregor, N. Y., to Henry H.
Rood. "Your invitations to my father and myself to be present at the reunion
of the Crocker brigade has been received. Father thanks you for the invitation
to him but of course will not be able to attend. The invitation to me I will
accept, if I can possibly get away. My Father speaks so often of the gallantry
of Crocker (and his troops, especially at Raymond, Jackson and Champions
Hill,) that I am anxious to renew my acquaintance with you. (I say *renew* my
acquaintance because I was with you at both Jackson and Champions Hills.)
I believed (then) and still retain the belief that with such troops defeat was
impossible With this feeling allow me to salute Crocker's Brigade—"—ALS,
Iowa Masonic Library, Cedar Rapids, Iowa. See *Proceedings of Crocker's Iowa
Brigade, at the Third Reunion, held at Iowa City, Iowa, September 23d and 24th,
1885* (Iowa City, 1885).

[*1885, July*].   To Francis B. Gessner. "Are any of the Griffiths there yet?
The town of Batavia must now be very much dried up with all the facilities
the people have to get away. I used to take much delight in visiting there and
through Clermont. But I have made my last visit."—N, Emory University,
Atlanta, Ga. Gessner visited USG on behalf of Alphonso Taft. See Lewis
Alexander Leonard, *Life of Alphonso Taft* (New York, 1920), pp. 189–91. See
also letter to John Russell Young, May 18, 1883, note 3.

Index

BY DAVID SLAY

All letters written by USG of which the text was available for use in this volume are indexed under the names of the recipients. The dates of these letters are included in the index as an indication of the existence of text. Abbreviations used in the index are explained on pp. xxii–xxvii. Individual regts. are indexed under the names of the states in which they originated.